To Talent Alone

Gothic-style chimney piece in the Hewson Organ Room,
36 Westland Row, with inset paintings believed to be by
Angelica Kauffmann

To Talent Alone

The Royal Irish Academy of Music
1848–1998

Edited by

RICHARD PINE FRIAM

and

CHARLES ACTON FRIAM

GILL & MACMILLAN

Gill & Macmillan Ltd
Goldenbridge
Dublin 8
with associated companies throughout the world
© The Editors and Contributors 1998
0 7171 2759 1
Index compiled by Helen Litton
Print origination by
Carrigboy Typesetting Services, County Cork
Design by Peanntrónaic Teo.
Printed by ColourBooks Ltd, Dublin

This book is typeset in Ehrhardt 11pt/12pt.

1 3 5 4 2

Dedication

In 1863, in the course of a submission to the Treasury concerning the introduction of a grant to the Academy, Hercules MacDonnell argued that

> we are convinced that an institution for training teachers cannot be permanently supported, though it may properly be founded, without some aid from the State. It differs wholly from a school for amateurs, who come because they are ready and able to pay, and who are not selected for mere talent. *To talent alone* an academy should address itself, wherever found, and should seek to cultivate it without reference to cost, confident that the elevation and sound instruction of those who in turn are to teach the public are the sure and only means of spreading and raising in quality the standard of instruction.

This history of the Academy is respectfully and affectionately dedicated to the memory of all those teachers, students, administrators and governors who, during the past 150 years, by devoting their talent to the good of the Academy, have thereby created the standards by which they are to be judged, fostering, stimulating and enriching the musical life of Ireland and many other parts of the world.

Sponsors

The Director and Governors of the Royal Irish Academy of Music are grateful to the Chairman and Chief Executive of An Post for providing funding which facilitated the research and publication of this history, and to the Chairman and Director-General of Radio Telefís Éireann for making time available to Richard Pine to undertake the main research.

List of Contributors

Carol Acton
Charles Acton FRIAM
Brian Beckett
Brian Boydell FRIAM
Anna Brioscú FRIAM
Audrey Chisholm FRIAM
Derek Collins
Jeremy Dibble
Pamela Flanagan
Anthony Hughes FRIAM
Axel Klein
John F. Larchet FRIAM
Frederick May
Havelock Nelson FRIAM
John O'Conor FRIAM
Margaret O'Hea FRIAM
Annie Patterson
Richard Pine FRIAM
Philip Shields
Walter Starkie
Joan Trimble FRIAM
Marie Trimble
Valerie Walker FRIAM

Research Assistants

Derek Collins
Emilie Pine

Contents

Preface

It may seem unusual that an institution that celebrated its 'centenary' in 1956 should, only forty-two years later, be marking its sesquicentenary. But in a sense there have been three Academies: the Irish Academy of Music, which opened in 1848; the reconstituted Academy of 1856; and the statute-based Royal Irish Academy of Music of 1889, which continues to the present day. After 1856 it was usual practice for over two decades for the Academy to refer to itself as 'founded in 1848—reorganised in 1856.' From the late eighteen-sixties, however, it became ambivalent about its exact origin and by the late eighteen-seventies had 1856 as the year of its foundation—so much so that, despite authoritative statements to the contrary in various editions of Grove's *Dictionary*, the actual founding of the Academy in 1848 and its operation up to 1856 have become almost forgotten.

The Academy's story is also the story of a fourth school, the Municipal School of Music (today the DIT Conservatory of Music and Drama), the establishment of which was mooted in the eighteen-eighties as an institution complementary to the Academy and which came into existence in 1890, under the management of the RIAM, which continued to administer it during its crucial first fifteen years.

Within and beneath these stark facts are layers of experience that will be unfamiliar not only to the general reader but also to many who know the present Academy and its recent history. In his preface to *The Keeper's Recital*, Harry White speaks of aspects of music in Ireland that 'have never been disclosed' and says: 'In a climate which thrives on enquiry, which consents to the superiority of ideas over the continued recital of facts, the presence of music remains undiscovered.' We believe that this history will not only disclose the narrative facts of the Academy's day-to-day workings, and the development of its ideas for music education, but also illuminate the general history of musical activity in Ireland since the early nineteenth century—discovering its presence and importance in Irish society. Where George Moore wrote of the 'untilled field' and Daniel Corkery and Arnold Bax (in their different ways) of the 'hidden Ireland', we now see—to continue the literary analogy—something more of Heaney's 'opened ground'.

The compiling of this history has involved much digging, in the course of which we have been conscious of the fact that it is not only the history of a music academy but also a social and cultural history, spanning the most significant period in Irish experience, from the Great Famine to independence, and the enormous changes that have taken place in Ireland since accession to the European Union. Political, religious, sectarian, educational and economic storms have taken place in that time, many of which have directly involved, and have taken place within, the Academy.

We have been especially conscious of what Séamus Heaney has recently called 'the culture of commemoration'. It is not alone poetry that, in his words, 'allows people access to the depths of their heritage without bullying others into those depths.' To celebrate the anniversary of the Academy in a year that also commemorates 1798—with all its continuing emotive strength within the acoustic of republicanism, nationalism, and religious freedom—is a salutary reminder that both the 'culture' and the 'politics' of commemoration can become killing-fields.

Inevitably, an institution such as the Academy attracts, or creates, figures who become larger than life, assuming an idiosyncratic status that threatens to—or in some cases does—dominate the contemporary scene. The names of Michele Esposito, John F. Larchet, Dorothy Stokes, Dina Copeman, Rhona Marshall and Maud Aiken instantly spring to mind, to which the longer memory will add those of Joseph Robinson and Sir Robert Stewart, while the researcher immediately encounters Francis Brady and Hercules MacDonnell as immensely influential joint secretaries during the Academy's formative years. To have portrayed these and other figures, in Oliver Cromwell's terms, 'roughnesses . . . warts, and everything' would perhaps have been too revealing, as well as too flattering to their personalities. But all great men and women are at least partially clay-footed, and we have not hesitated to observe their imperfections where these impinged on the operations of the Academy.

A sequential narrative would soon have become dull and unwieldy—even unconvincing, perhaps—because the sheer extent of the facts relating to staff, students and the curriculum could not have been encompassed in a single volume. And, because there are gaps in the Academy's records and elsewhere, it would have been impossible to be comprehensive. The present work is therefore of necessity episodic, and in some places we have concentrated on certain traits or personalities, in the belief that this will create an understanding of the institution as a whole.

Also, it seemed important to us to reconstruct the earlier period, in which the Academy found its feet, and therefore more space has been given to the years 1848–1920 than to the later decades. People have had to be reclaimed from obscurity, whereas many of the figures of the past fifty years still live brightly in remembrance. Moreover, it has been necessary at all times, for reasons of space, to be selective, and it would therefore have been invidious to mention in any great detail many of those flourishing today while excluding others. And some recent students are still far too young to be assessed: we would not wish them to be embarrassed in twenty or thirty years' time by what we might say today.

A further reason for the relative brevity of chapter 7 (covering the period 1922–98) is that it is supplemented by detailed descriptions of the Academy's examinations and scholarships and the Local Centre system and by the *intermezzo* relating to the Students' Musical Union.

But we cannot agree with Rev. W. W. Cazalet, who, in his history of the Royal Academy of Music (1854), concentrated on its first decade: 'it is this portion alone that has any interest, for when all the struggles and trouble attending its establishment are at an end, the records of a mere routine of business give no interest for publication.' While 'mere routine' cannot be described without tedium for writer and reader alike, the work of establishing an academy is only part of the struggle, and the profile of the governors and staff who kept it running is a vital part of its continuing success, not least because we need to know what kind of people they were outside the Academy as much as how they behaved within its walls.

Walter Starkie called the Academy 'a vast theatre of Memory . . . inhabited by countless friends . . . in a continuous performance.' While we have observed hundreds of these friends, and given them some identity, there are many other unnamed ghosts. In addition to the greater picture there is a plurality of their smaller narratives, some of which will never be told. In fact the Academy has both a corporate existence, which, at least since 1889, has been relatively seamless, and a sum of these individual lives, large and small, which give it its day-to-day vitality.

The four main narrative chapters (chapters 3, 4, 5, and 7) describe the Academy's inception and growth. They have been culled chiefly from the RIAM Archive (now in the National Archives, Dublin) and are based on research carried out by ourselves and our research assistants. The task of assimilating this material into a cohesive narrative has been largely that of Richard Pine. In addition, we commissioned specialist contributions on specific areas of Academy activity that, in our view, merited separate treatment: on the musical context for an academy in the eighteen-forties, on education, composition, piano teaching, and performance, and on the Academy library.

We also decided that the story as a whole should be illuminated by personal insights from former students, which we have designated *intermezzi*. Some of these—by Walter Starkie, Frederick May, Marie Trimble, and John F. Larchet—are reprinted from the 'Centenary' booklet edited by T. S. C. Dagg. Others—by Joan Trimble, Brian Boydell, Carol Acton, Anna Brioscú, Valerie Walker, Audrey Chisholm, and the late Havelock Nelson—were commissioned for this book. We have also included an article written by Annie Patterson describing her own student days in the eighteen-seventies, and a lecture by Margaret O'Hea on 'The Responsibilities of a Music Teacher', which was first published in 1895. We thus find in this volume personal reminiscences of the Academy encompassing well over a century and linking today's teachers and students with the Academy's original foundations.

A further extended *intermezzo* is provided by the inclusion of correspondence to Edith Best (née Oldham) from her mother and from her mentor, Sir George Grove, during and after the period of her scholarship at the Royal College of Music in London in 1883–86, preserved by her and donated by her husband's executor to the RCM. This valuable insight into the conditions and prospects facing a young music student at that time is also a unique perspective on the early years of someone who went on to become a senior teacher in the institution—not least because few of these letters have previously been published.

Invariably, in the evolution of an institution such as the RIAM, a body of folklore builds up, like a deposit, on its staircases and in its foyers. To invoke George Moore again, Dublin is 'a city of remarkable acoustic properties,' and we have respected the reverberations of such lore when we have been confident of its authenticity. We have been conscious throughout that the Academy was one of a cadre of institutions—mainly schools and hospitals—that were born in the wake, and in the shadow, of the Famine, and that it therefore has a place in a larger acoustic to which those reverberations also pertain.

Acknowledgments

One author of an institutional history whom we consulted told us that 'poetry, however bad one is at writing it, is a relatively sane alternative.' It was a helpful reminder of the quaintness, if not the madness, of our task, not least because this history ends with the launch of the Academy's poetry anthology by Ireland's most recent Nobel laureate. We have found it a privilege to work on this project, not least because it has brought us into contact with so many experts in various fields, without whose contribution we could not have even contemplated the present work.

Our first debt is to our sponsors, which is acknowledged above. Our next is to our research assistants, Derek Collins and Emilie Pine, whose availability was entirely due to the generosity of our sponsors, and to the authors of the specialist chapters, whose insight and expert knowledge have helped to shape our own thoughts on the overall picture. Naturally we are deeply indebted to the authors of the specialist chapters and of the *intermezzi*. To Joan Trimble FRIAM, whose commitment to the project was immense and whose knowledge of the period is unrivalled, we cannot sufficiently express our gratitude for the assistance and advice she afforded us.

Several people were asked to read parts, or all, of this book and to comment on it: in particular we must mention again Joan Trimble and also Prof. Harry White, Leo Gibney, and John O'Conor.

In the course of our research we have incurred many debts of gratitude to very many people, some of them representing institutions, others having family or professional connections with past staff and students, others in a purely personal capacity.

To the staff, former staff and Governors of the RIAM itself, including the current Chairman of the Board, Leo Gibney, his predecessor, Anna Brioscú, and the Director, Dr John O'Conor; our fellow-Governors Declan McDonagh, Hylda Beckett, and Pat Cummins; to the Secretary, Dorothy Shiel, the Registrar, Anthony Madigan, and the Librarian, Philip Shields; the Director's personal assistant, Dorothy McAuley, Ciara Higgins (public relations), and the Head Porter, Billy Bebbington; to Enid Chaloner, Dr Veronica Dunne, Margaret Furlong, the late Dr Joseph Groocock, David Lee, Bernadette Marmion, Marie Moran, John O'Sullivan, Jaroslav Vaneček, and Deirdre Ward.

The librarians of the National Archives, Dublin, the Royal Academy of Music, the Royal College of Music (in particular Celia Clarke, who guided us to, and through, the correspondence of Edith Oldham, Ann Oldham, and George Grove), the Royal Scottish Academy of Music and Drama, Glasgow University, the Paris Conservatoire, the Ferenc Liszt Academy, the Sibelius Academy, and the Finnish Music Information Centre; the Gilbert Library, Pearse Street, Dublin; the National Library of Ireland; the British Library Periodicals Section at Colindale; Mary Clarke and Gráinne Doran (Dublin Corporation Archives); Bernard Meehan, Keeper of Manuscripts, Trinity College, Dublin; Des Gaffney (RTE Stills); the staff of the Italian Cultural Institute; Antoinette Doris (Secretary to the Commissioners of Charitable Donations and Bequests); the Home Office (Constitutional and Community Policy Directorate), London; the Royal Archives, Windsor Castle; the Librarian of the Royal Dublin Society; Geoff Oakley, Steinway and Sons, London; and James Yorke, Assistant Curator, Victoria and Albert Museum, London.

Without the active assistance of the staff of the *Dictionary of Irish Biography,* a project of the Royal Irish Academy, and in particular the wholehearted support of Helen Andrews, this book would have been much the poorer.

And to: Dr Angela Barone, Lady Caroline Borg, Dr Barra Boydell, Prof. Brian Boydell, Pauline Bracken, Alice Brough, Aodhagán Brioscú, Prof. Davis Coakley, Sir Alfred Cochrane, Sir Toby Coghill, Prof. Louis Cullen, Mrs May Curtin, Noel Dagg, the late Norris Davidson, Master Terry de Valera, Prof. John Dillon, Morgan Dockrell, Prof. Terence Dolan, the Marquess of Downshire, Prof. Roy Foster, John Gibson, Prof. David Greer, Frank Heneghan, William Hoffmann, Dr Roy Johnston, Deirdre Kelly, Dr Colum Kenny, Prof. James Knowlson, J. F. Levey, Dr Marie McCarthy, Máirtín McCullough, Maurice McDonough, Tom and Bernadette Marmion, Heather and Raymond Marshall, Sheila May, Fiona Murphy, Eimear Ó Broin, Vera O'Donovan, Dr John O'Grady, Dr Susan Parkes, Homan Potterton, Cmdt Joseph Ryan, Prof. Jan Smaczny, Denis Stephens, Annabel Stewart, Prof. Jeffrey Switzer, and Paul Tansey.

Terminology

Until 1883 the Academy was governed by a Committee, from 1883 to 1889 by a Council, and thereafter by a Board of Governors under the 'Blue Scheme'. To avoid tedious repetition and confusion, we have referred to the members of these various boards as 'governors' up to 1883 and as 'Governors' thereafter. The 'Scheme' inaugurated in 1889, by which the Academy is still administered, was printed on blue paper and within the Academy has always been called the 'Blue Scheme', a term we have retained. The Irish Academy of Music received the 'Royal' distinction in 1872; we have referred throughout the book to the Academy and, where appropriate, to the RIAM. In the interests of brevity this abbreviation has been employed silently where 'Royal Irish Academy of Music' occurs within quotations.

Personal postscript by Charles Acton

Personal postscript by Richard Pine

In 1994 Richard Pine pointed out at a Governors' meeting that 1998 would be the Academy's sesquicentenary. Among other things, our colleagues decided that we should be invited to edit a history of the Academy. Full of enthusiasm for the idea, but taken unawares, I accepted the invitation on condition that Richard should do all the work and that I, as an octogenarian, should do nothing. Richard in fact planned the research on which the narrative chapters were based, and wrote them. I have been mostly successful in being a sleeping partner, but I want to make clear that most of the credit for the book belongs to Richard.

In 1994 I asked Charles Acton if he would act with me as co-editor of the Academy history, to which he agreed. I understood from the start that he would be unable, on account of his advanced years, to contribute a great deal of time or energy, and, as the project unfolded, ill-health did indeed incapacitate him. However, it was for Charles's knowledge and guidance, and the clarity of his judgment, that I needed his co-operation, which he has given unstintingly. The book could not have been conceived, or written, or edited, without him.

Abbreviations

Throughout the text we have had occasion to refer to *The New Grove Dictionary of Music and Musicians,* edited in twenty volumes by Stanley Sadie (London: Macmillan 1980). This is cited as *NG.* We have referred to previous editions of Grove's *Dictionary* as follows:

Grove I: A Dictionary of Music and Musicians, AD 1450–1889, edited by Sir George Grove, 5 vols. (London: Macmillan 1879–89)

Grove II: A Dictionary of Music . . . edited by J. Fuller Maitland, 5 vols. (1904–10)

Grove III: A Dictionary of Music . . . edited by H. C. Colles, 5 vols. (1927)

Grove IV: A Dictionary of Music . . . edited by H. C. Colles, 5 vols. (1940)

Grove V: A Dictionary of Music . . . edited by Eric Blom, 9 vols. (1954)

We have also referred to the following organisations by their initials:

CCDB:	Commissioners of Charitable Donations and Bequests
DIT:	Dublin Institute of Technology
MSM:	Municipal School of Music
NGI:	National Gallery of Ireland
NICO:	New Irish Chamber Orchestra
NSO:	National Symphony Orchestra
RAM:	Royal Academy of Music

RCM: Royal College of Music
RDS: Royal Dublin Society
RÉ: Radio Éireann
RÉLO: Radio Éireann Light Orchestra
RÉSO: Radio Éireann Symphony Orchestra
RTÉ: Radio Telefis Éireann
RTÉSO: Radio Telefis Éireann Symphony Orchestra

Money equivalents

We have calculated present-day prices on items purchased by the Academy where we felt it would be helpful to do so, by reference to a logarithmic table published by the *Financial Times* on 24 July 1994. According to this, a pound at 1700 values would be worth sixty pounds today; at 1850 values it would be worth forty pounds today. The conversion of wages and salaries is much more complex, since no index exists equivalent to the median index for prices. Wages and salaries have risen faster than prices, and therefore our conversions of these must of necessity be regarded as the minimum level at which they would be contemplated today. This is especially so because at the time of the Academy's foundation, and for many decades thereafter, the profession of music teaching was not organised on anything like a unionised basis, and, since it was common for teachers to work privately in addition to their institutional work, the salaries paid by the Academy would not have been regarded as representing an adequate total income.

Contributors

The editors

Richard Pine was educated at Westminster School and Trinity College, Dublin, where he won the Vice-Chancellor's Prize for English and was president of the University Philosophical Society. In addition to a public affairs appointment at Radio Telefís Éireann, he lectures frequently in universities and research institutes in Europe and the United States, is a noted broadcaster and critic, and from 1978 to 1988 was a consultant on cultural development programmes to the Council of Europe. His books include *The Dublin Gate Theatre, 1928–1978* (1984), *Brian Friel and Ireland's Drama* (1990), *Lawrence Durrell: The Mindscape* (1994), and *The Thief of Reason: Oscar Wilde and Modern Ireland* (1995). In 1998 he edited *Music in Ireland, 1848–1998*, a series of Thomas Davis Lectures on RTÉ radio marking the sesquicentenary of the RIAM. He is a former deputy music critic of the *Irish Times*, secretary of the Irish Writers' Union, chairman of the Media Association of Ireland, and co-editor of the *Irish Literary Supplement*. He has been a governor of the RIAM since 1989 and was elected to fellowship in 1998.

Charles Acton, of a County Wicklow family, was music critic of the *Irish Times* from 1955 until his retirement in 1987. The recipient of the inaugural Seán O'Boyle Award in 1986 for his services to Irish music, he has been a governor of the RIAM since 1954, receiving fellowship in 1990 and being elected vice-president in 1998. He has contributed to many periodicals and is the author of *Irish Music and Musicians* (1978) and *Acton's Music: Reviews of Dublin's Musical Life, 1955–1985* (1996). He was invited to join the London Critics' Circle, of whose music section he has been the only critic working in Ireland.

Contributors

Carol Acton studied at the RIAM under Rhona Marshall, Nancie Lord, and Jaroslav Vaneček, subsequently teaching violin at the RIAM and piano and orchestra at the Hall School, Monkstown. She was leader of the Dublin Orchestral Players, deputy music critic of the *Irish Times*, music critic of the *Sunday Press*, and a feature writer for *Image* and *New Hibernia*. She was the administrator of the music scheme of the Cultural Relations Committee of the then Department of External Affairs and Irish contact person of the International Amateur Chamber Music Players.

Brian Beckett, who is a graduate of Trinity College, Dublin, has lectured in piano since 1973 at the Royal Irish Academy of Music, where he is also an examiner for the local centre examination system, chairing the Committee of Senior Examiners from 1986 to 1995.

Brian Boydell was educated at Rugby, in natural sciences at Cambridge and in music at the Royal College of Music and Trinity College, Dublin, and has since developed an all-round career as a musician, becoming most prominent as a composer and as professor of music at Trinity College, Dublin (where he is a fellow emeritus) from 1962 to 1982, having previously held a professorship of singing at the RIAM. He has been decorated by the Italian government and in 1990 was elected to fellowship of the RIAM. His publications include *A Dublin Musical Calendar, 1700–1760* (1988) and *Rotunda Music in Eighteenth-Century Dublin* (1992). His compositions include *Symphonic Inscapes* (1968), two string quartets (1947, 1957), *In Memoriam Mahatma Gandhi* (1948), a violin concerto (1954), *Megalithic Ritual Dances* (1956), *Masai Mara* (1988) and *Viking Lip Music* (1995). He has exhibited at the White Stag group of painters.

Anna Brioscú was educated at Loreto College (St Stephen's Green) and University College, Dublin. She was an Irish-language columnist for the *Evening Press* 1970–72 and was appointed a member of Coimisiún um Athbheochan na Gaeilge in 1958. She was a Governor of the RIAM from 1975, becoming a vice-president and chairperson of the Board in 1981, until her retirement in 1994. She was elected to fellowship in 1995 and in 1996 obtained a diploma in psychology from St Patrick's College, Maynooth.

Derek Collins graduated from Queen's University, Belfast, where he held an organ scholarship and where he is currently completing his PhD on concert activity in Dublin 1792–1842. Since moving to Dublin in 1995 he has taught at the DIT College of Music and is an examiner for the RIAM.

Jeremy Dibble is head of the Music Department at the University of Durham. He graduated from Trinity College, Cambridge, before gaining his PhD on the music of Sir Hubert Parry at the University of Southampton and holding a lectureship in music at University College, Cork. He is the author of *C. Hubert H. Parry: His Life and Music* (1992) and is at present working on a companion volume on Sir Charles Villiers Stanford as well as contributing to the *Revised New Grove Dictionary* and *Irish Musical Studies, 2*.

Pamela Flanagan MA MScEd was educated at Trinity College, Dublin, and Dublin City University. A former student of John O'Conor for piano and Aisling Drury Byrne and Jacqueline du Pré for cello, she joined the RIAM teaching staff in 1979 and was appointed professor of harmony and counterpoint in 1984. A former chairperson of the Board of Studies, she is at present head of the Musicianship Faculty and chairs many of the Academy's degree programme boards. She is also secretary of the Council of Heads of Music in Higher Education.

Anthony Hughes is professor of music emeritus at University College, Dublin, where he taught from 1958 until 1991, having previously taught piano at the RIAM from 1949 to 1958 and developed a notable career as a solo pianist. He was educated at the RIAM, UCD, and Vienna State Academy of Music. He has been chairman of the Feis Ceoil and of the RDS Music Committee, vice-president of the RDS Council, president of Dublin Grand Opera Society, chairman of the Board of Trustees of the National Library of Ireland, and a member of the Cultural Relations Committee of the Department of Foreign Affairs, and is a director of the Irish Youth Orchestra. In 1955 he won the Arnold Bax Gold Medal, in 1981 he was decorated by the Italian government, and he became a fellow of the RIAM in 1990.

Axel Klein is a musicologist specialising in Irish classical music in the twentieth century. He graduated from the universities of Hildesheim and Dublin (Trinity College) and, in addition to contributing to *Die Musik in Geschichte und Gegenwart* and *The Revised Grove Dictionary*, is the author of *Die Musik Irlands im 20. Jahrhundert* (1996).

John O'Conor is Director of the Royal Irish Academy of Music, where he has held a piano professorship since 1976. A world-renowned concert pianist, he was educated at University College, Dublin, and the Hochschule für Musik, Vienna, where he won the International Beethoven Piano Competition (1973) and the Bösendorfer Competition (1975). His many recordings include the complete sonatas and bagatelles of Beethoven and the complete nocturnes and sonatas of John Field. He is co-founder and artistic director of the Guardian Dublin International Piano Competition and serves on the juries of many international competitions, including Leeds, Vienna, Munich, Cleveland, and Washington. He has received an honorary doctorate from the National University of Ireland and a fellowship from the RIAM and has been decorated by the Italian, French and Polish governments.

Philip Shields studied music and history at Trinity College, Dublin. He worked in the Research Centre Library in Arthur Guinness and Company and the Vistar Information Service in Limerick before taking up his present position as Librarian of the RIAM in 1992.

Joan Trimble is a pianist and composer and a vice-president of the RIAM. She studied at the RIAM (of which she holds an honorary fellowship), Trinity College, Dublin, and the Royal College of Music. She also holds an honorary MA from Queen's University, Belfast. In addition to her concert schedule as a pianist—particularly her two-piano partnership with her sister Valerie—she was professor of piano at the RCM from 1959 to 1977. She has composed opera and a wide spectrum of orchestral and chamber music. She is a former member of the Northern Ireland Arts Council and the Board of Ulster Television and is at present chairperson of William Trimble Ltd, publishers of the *Impartial Reporter* (Enniskillen).

Illustrations

Within text

Between pages 168 and 169

Between pages 328 and 329

1

Introduction

RICHARD PINE

Education in nineteenth-century Ireland;
the role of a music academy; culture, politics, and nationalism;
the Academy a coalition of interests; 1848; Ireland and Britain;
Ireland and Europe; Ireland a musical nation;
survey of literature on music in Ireland.

The Irish Academy of Music, which opened its doors on 1 March 1848, was the first approach in Ireland to systematic music education based on the principles of public service. Aspects of professional training that, by default, had until then been developed along serendipitous lines were now to be addressed in a practical and policy-driven manner.

Public education in Ireland had been subject to reform since 1831, when a state system of primary schooling was instituted with the establishment of the Board of Commissioners of National Education[1] (chaired by the third Duke of Leinster).[2] Thereafter, even though similar initiatives in secondary education would not take place until the eighteen-seventies, the close association in a 'mixed economy' of government and the educational sector, serving a society that was undergoing radical transformations, would intimately concern the transmission of values and standards in music that it was the Academy's role to promote. It is the story of a sustained growth that carried the founding impetus of the Academy through the turbulence of the late nineteenth and early twentieth centuries and underpins its continuing centrality to the Irish music world.

The foundation of the Academy closely followed the establishment in Cork, Belfast and Galway of the Queen's Colleges, dubbed by their critics—first among them Daniel O'Connell—the 'godless colleges',[3] because their professors were appointed without regard to religious denomination or, indeed, nationality. (It was this, as much as the issue of violence, that split the Repeal Association and brought Young Ireland into being, a point of singular importance for the creation of the Academy.) Of Queen's College,

Cork, it was said in 1864 that 'it is the Professors who make the College . . .
The College Authorities must needs appoint men to the great trust of professorships who combine genius in the Science they teach with academic
tastes and habits—cultivated minds with high moral excellence and conscientiousness in the discharge of their duties.'[4] The Irish Academy of Music,
likewise, was conducted on non-denominational lines, its guiding principle
being the appointment of the best available teachers, whatever their origin,
and its purpose being solely to recognise and meet the needs of potential
musicians, their teachers, and their audiences. Although there were close
associations with Trinity College, Dublin, which in turn had strong links
with the two Protestant cathedrals of Dublin, the Academy differed sharply
from TCD (with its ethos distinctly allied to that of the established Church
of Ireland) and from the start adopted a flexible and cosmopolitan approach
to its work.

It might be argued that music, as a pure science or art, lent itself naturally
to a non-sectarian approach; but for two reasons this cannot be assumed in
the Irish context. Firstly, music and nationalism enjoyed a symbiosis that
informed the separatist movement in both Irish culture and politics, as
much so as that between literature and politics;[5] while, secondly, the concept of control in Irish education, however clear the original ambition may
have been that it be non-sectarian, became increasingly firmly linked to
denominational management as the nineteenth century progressed.

The core values of such educational initiatives were closely related to the
questions of Irishness and Irish identity, however ambiguous they might be
in the light of Ireland's political status, and these values shaped approaches
to the central issues: the social, economic and educational improvement of
the country, large parts of which were in the throes of famine and sickness
and subject to political unrest; the identification and development of human
and material resources; the removal of inequity and inequality; above all,
the modernisation of Irish society,[6] with all the challenges and uncertainties
that 'the modern' would bring—in the words of the *Nation*, 'self-respect,
self-rule and self-reliance,'[7] coupled with what has been called 'a generous
and comprehensive nationalism.'[8]

Thus the issues that were to be addressed and negotiated, either explicitly
or implicitly, from the very outset of the Academy, were not only those of
how music education was to be conducted in the public service but of how
such an institution would relate to the overall educational system; how it
would reflect and respond to social change; how it would play a part in
developing the role of music in Irish society; and how a sense of national
identity, and in particular a sense of musical nationalism, would inform its
proceedings.[9] The role of music in itself would provide a complex set of
issues, involving questions of pedagogy, performance, composition, and
appreciation. In the purely educational context the concept of the right to
universal education, evolving in the eighteen-forties, was embraced by the
Academy in its gradual extension of educational services and in its concept
of what constituted a musical education. All this took place within the
larger world of social, political and economic realities—many of which had

yet to be teased out—and these help to illuminate, and are illuminated by, the facts of life such as wages, conditions of employment, ideas of propriety—even the state of the drains—and the re-establishment of Dublin as a city of consequence.[10]

The question of what exactly was meant by the term 'national', by differing types of Irish people with differing ideas of self-determination and outlooks on the 'dual monarchy', must have been in the minds of the Academy's governors, both in running the Academy and in their own lives. The events of 1916–23 and the war years 1939–45 seem hardly to have affected its daily operation. But the transition from British rule in the eighteen-forties, fifties, and sixties, troubled by famine, disease, political unrest, and economic unease; the disestablishment of the Church of Ireland and the growing strength and confidence of the Catholic Church; the cultural militancy of the eighteen-nineties and early nineteen hundreds; *de facto* independence in the fledgling Free State, with its constitutional indeterminacy and political instability—all had a direct bearing on the character the Academy would assume and on its capacity to develop as a major institution. Although they seldom intersected, the life of the Academy and the events of the emergent state marched along parallel lines. With the opening of cultural vistas, the growth of arts management by the state and the development of orchestras, in particular, in the burgeoning era for the arts that opened in the nineteen-sixties, the more direct involvement for which both sides of the equation had been preparing themselves became evident.

The idea of a nation—its ethos and ideology, its social and cultural realities, its function, its physical infrastructure, its external relations—occupied Ireland throughout the nineteenth century and can be said to retain a high place on its present agenda. Like the Academy itself, Ireland was experiencing constitutional growth of an unprecedented nature, with all its attendant pains and triumphs. The hesitancy of the Academy in addressing satisfactorily all these issues at all times may be attributed to the inhibition felt by many similar institutions, including the emergent indigenous education system and the general political framework, in the face of an almost unappeasable need to take possession of a workable sense of national identity.

The fact that several of the Academy's early Council were close associates of prominent figures such as Thomas Davis, William Smith O'Brien (himself an early subscriber to the Academy),[11] and George Petrie, 'the intellectual linchpin of the Celtic Revival,'[12] was no accident: the precepts of Young Ireland and its cultural partners were present in the first endeavours of the Academy, and that combination (which we noted above) of genius, cultivation, morality and conscientiousness was their hallmark also. In John Hutchinson's words, they were 'secular intellectuals', typical of the 'liberal middle-class improver[s]' who provide the socio-political thrust of nationalism in such societies, free from religious and, largely, political divisions.[13]

The pursuit of that sense of identity that would invest Irish people of all persuasions with a satisfying self-regard and would make it possible for Ireland to become a real and autonomous political entity could be—and was—translated into specific cultural terms. With some notable exceptions (a feature common to all great institutions), the personnel of the Academy (both its governing body and its teaching staff) possessed these distinguishing characteristics. If we add to that the political inexperience that, it has been said, also attends moral earnestness,[14] the coincidence of the Academy with cognate undertakings becomes apparent. It comes as no surprise to discover that in the nineteen-twenties and thirties—even, in the case of Dorothy Stokes, the seventies—people with strong family links with Daniel O'Connell, Young Ireland and the Irish cultural renaissance continued to be deeply associated with the Academy.

Ireland was not alone in the job of building a sense of nationhood. Throughout Europe, *Völkerfrühling* (springtime of the nations) was, in Lewis Namier's words, 'the passionate creed of the intellectuals.'[15] But in Ireland the search was less tangible and the goal more elusive. While it could be maintained—indeed while it was essential to maintain—that 'an Irish nation still existed, separate, numerous and hostile,'[16] it also seemed that 'Providence never intended Ireland to be a great nation.'[17]

Namier observed that 'the English language lacks a word to describe a "nationality" distinct from, or contrasted with, the citizenship derived from territory and State.'[18] In Ireland, both before and after independence, what constituted 'Irish' or 'Irishness' was an open question, intimately concerned with the move towards citizenship and the development of a grammar, in the English language but derived from, and serving the needs of, an Irish sensibility and ultimately an Irish polity. It was a question of creating networks that had both a systemic and an organic basis, on the shoulders of which constitutional growth could take place. Never simple, the type and degree of complexity was problematic. To many, the answer was Leopold Bloom's: 'a nation is the same people living in the same place';[19] to many others it was impossible to achieve, because people who regarded each other as different lived not together but apart, in a place that they also thought of as different; Bloom, we recall, found himself qualifying his definition: 'or also living in different places.'[20] The epitomes of such attitudes were the Protestant concept of the Ascendancy, in the seventeen-eighties, constituting the nation, succeeded by that of O'Connell in 1826: 'the Catholic people of Ireland are a nation.'[21] Neither the neat equation of language and geography nor the existence of an infrastructure—both characteristic of most of Europe—was available in Ireland as a basis for building.

Richard Kearney suggests five ways of defining the nation: as a state, as a territory, as an ethnic entity, as an 'extended family', and 'nation as *culture*.'[22] Again, it is tempting to say that such distinctions and separations do not concern the subject of music, at least 'classical', 'mainstream', western European music, with its Viennese centre, were it not for the fact that Ireland's peripheral location, its dilemma in negotiating its place in that mainstream, its difficulty in coming to terms with the notions of 'state', 'territory' and nationality, its emphasis on the conjunction of nation and culture, call into question not only the teaching and appreciation of 'classical' genres but also the nature and function of pedagogy, of access to opportunity, and of creativity itself. It is equally tempting to follow Kearney's well-argued and long-argued case for the creation in the mind of a 'fifth province'[23] and to hope that music might be regarded as just such a state, free from concrete and practical realities; but the inherent function of music as an intellectual or ideological force as well as a science of sounds, and music as a presence in our daily lives—a rhythmic substratum of abstract consciousness that occasionally becomes manifest, concrete, and palpable—does not permit this: 'the long absence of music . . . from the Irish mind', as Harry White puts it, demands to be addressed.[24]

As Namier observed, 'the less there was in 1848 . . . of an existing substructure on which to build a national State, the more there was of antiquarian ferreting';[25] and nowhere was this more evident than in Ireland. Long before the partition of 1922, Ireland suffered an indefinable sense of *terra irredenta*, and this was no less evident in music and the pursuit of what 'Irish music' might be than in other political and cultural areas.[26] After the implementation of the Coulson endowment in 1889, one specific question that vexed the Governors of the Academy (in which, in the eighteen-eighties and nineties, several members of the real-life Bloom family studied and taught)[27] was: what constituted 'respectable Irish parents'?—Miss Coulson's will having limited certain applications of her endowment to the offspring of such.

The modernisation of European society coincided with this new consciousness of nationhood. As Joseph Lee has said, the distinguishing marks of rural life 'were disappearing all over western Europe as the parish ceased to form a mental boundary of the masses.'[28] They yielded their place in people's minds to images of movement and power: Ireland in 1845 had 65 miles of railways, 2,000 in 1872, and 3,500 in 1914.[29] For a country that would manifest its renaissance in primarily literary forms, it had a higher than average reading ability: despite its lack of an integrated secondary school system, 47 per cent of those over the age of five could read in 1841; by 1911 this had risen to 88 per cent.[30] In 1873 it was estimated that there was one graduate per 3,095 people in Ireland, as contrasted with 1 per 6,486 in England.[31]

Change both threatened and strengthened Irish society—an irony that would be evident a century later to Éamon de Valera in his own mental picture of the Ireland he hoped to create. Change moved people from the uniform to the individual, yet it also created masses and mass tensions. In Ireland, as Joseph Ryan has critically observed, 'an age that exhorted uniformity also required diversity, but it had to be a communal diversity, a uniform difference.'[32] This would in its turn bear directly on the creation of a school of music devoted to group as well as one-to-one tuition and to the nurturing of individual talent as much as to the transmission of traditional methods and values. It also led to dichotomies bordering on the contradictious. Only a few months before the Academy was founded, Alexis Soyer of the Reform Club had set up his soup-kitchen in Dublin; the city was pervaded by typhoid from June 1847 until the following February; trade was at a standstill.[33]

Into this situation—a crucible in which many of the vital ingredients were either missing or not yet identified—the founders of the Academy chose, for thoroughly practical reasons, to introduce an institution that offers a textbook example of the 'art of the possible'. We have emphasised the phenomenon of modernisation at this point in Irish history. It can also be characterised as a 'search for stability',[34] in which public and private bodies sometimes co-operated and sometimes clashed. It was a society in which no-one quite knew what was needed or how it was to be achieved, where no-one was in command either of the resources or of an overview of where culture and politics were going. In 1847 the Earl of Clarendon said, 'A great social revolution is now going on in Ireland, the accumulated evils of misgovernment and mismanagement are now coming to a crisis,'[35] while in the same year the *Times* forecast that 'a tremendous crash must come in which all interests and all classes will be swept away.'[36] The prospect was based only partly on the evidence of the Famine: it summed up the history of the country since the Act of Union in 1800, a period that had seen 114 commissions and 61 special committees reporting on the 'state of Ireland'.[37]

It was a statesman of Irish descent, Count Taaffe, who espoused '*immer fortwurschteln*' (always muddle along) as a way of managing the affairs of the Austro-Hungarian Empire. But a condition of masterly inactivity could no longer suit Ireland or the Irish musical situation. The pragmatism of the early Academy contrasts sharply with the disarray and search for principle of revolutionary Europe. It was perhaps fortunate that during its first twenty years the Irish Academy of Music was conducted as a private charitable institution (although very visibly) and not drawn into this web of disarray. By the time it was itself the subject of scrutiny by a commission, it had evolved its own modus operandi; if it had at times stumbled, its failings were its own, its leaps were exercises of its own faith, and by 1868 its substantial record of achievement was self-explanatory and self-made.

The most vital feature of the early Academy was the fact that its founders represented a coalition (or network) of interests and outlooks—successfully so. Within the confines of the early board-room an educational philosophy and praxis were teased out by Young Irelanders, old Ascendancy, the rising professions, Protestant, Catholic, Presbyterian and Quaker and, from 1889, with the reconfiguration of the institution on a statutory basis, a strong cohort of aldermen, councillors and other appointees of Dublin Corporation. It was, within the social constraints and realities of the middle of the nineteenth century, a classless and non-denominational body,[38] fully cognisant of the fact that the society in which it functioned was undergoing the severe transition from rural to urban life, from agriculture to industry, from pastoral to mercantile, from a stultifying vulnerability on almost every front to all that is meant by 'the shock of the new.'[39]

Ireland in 1848 was hardly monolithic, nor were its elements homogeneous. The deep historical distinctions and divisions between the Pale and the rest of the country were accentuated by the phenomenon of the Great Famine—divisions that the rise of Belfast as an economic force would shortly complicate. The chief irony of the foundation of such an academy in 1848 is that while it can be seen as part of an exponential growth in educational policy and pragmatism, it must also be seen in a political and social context that made the vast majority of Irish people singularly ill-placed to participate in this particular form of cultural development. This is due to two factors, both of which were of international significance. The first is the fact that, after a period of relative recovery from the effects of crop failures in 1847, the crops again failed in 1848, unexpectedly, four months after the opening of the Academy; this was not, however, a purely Irish phenomenon, since large parts of the Continent had been similarly affected in 1847, with concomitant typhus and cholera epidemics. The second factor is the widespread momentum towards revolution in the Europe of 1848 (the year of publication of the Communist Manifesto), which, in addition to toppling Louis-Philippe in France, brought popular but intellectually led opposition to government in most of central and western Europe, with, in effect, more sustained and significant repercussions in the cultural than the political arena.[40]

While crop failure in 1847 had been a major factor in bringing revolutionary fever to a head in many parts of Europe in 1848, nowhere else did it acquire the legendary *persona* that Ireland—and its subsequent diaspora—bestowed on the 'Great Famine', because no other country had suffered such a disaster since the Black Death. The fact that the land so precious to the smallholder and peasant failed to provide subsistence was another irony that made the subsequent attempts to resolve the dichotomy of landlord and tenant more fraught with tension and mistrust.

These ironies are compounded by the fact that whereas the Irish famine went largely uncomprehended by the governments of Europe (with the obvious exception of the British), the revolutionary thrust of figures such as Mazzini, Louis Napoléon and Kossuth extended only slightly into Ireland. The Ballingarry 'rising' of July 1848 by William Smith O'Brien, and the suppression in the same month of the *Nation*, was a peculiarly Irish occasion, which ignited no European flame and imported into Ireland none of the political acumen that made that year so significant in the evolution of national sentiment and, ultimately, self-government. As the nationalist historian P. S. O'Hegarty (father of an Academy teacher, Gráinne Yeats) said in the nineteen-fifties, 'never in all history was there an insurrection conducted so ineptly.'[41] It was the ineptitude of the revolt or, put another way, Ireland's inappropriateness for what it most needed—a separation from Britain, both culturally and politically—that marks it out as the uneasy product, and victim, of history.

Namier opens his survey of 1848, 'the revolution of the intellectuals', by reference to the funeral of Daniel O'Connell in Rome on 30 June 1847, when the aptly named Father Joachim Ventura spoke of '*la rivoluzione chi minaccia di fare il giro del globo*'[42] (the revolution that threatens to embrace the world). Elsewhere, Namier spoke of 'the numerous Irelands scattered all over Europe [in which] turmoil and strife were bound to result from the rise of the lower classes, and especially the peasantry, to political consciousness and action.'[43] Yet not even theoretically had Ireland a place among the nations of the world. Although the genius of Young Ireland had many similarities, and contacts, with the separatist movements in countries such as Hungary, Poland, and pre-unification Italy (which were extensively reported in the *Nation*),[44] Mazzini himself had discounted Ireland as a potentially viable unit of nationalism when founding the People's International League and identifying the nations of the future.[45]

Mazzini was wrong in thinking that Ireland was insufficiently different from England, but, like Cavour, he regarded the Union as a necessary evil, Cavour having postulated independence as merely 'a brilliant dream',[46] whereas reform and progress would help to eradicate difference.

The complexity of the situation increases when we reflect on the fact that, under the consequential constraints of the Act of Union, one of the aims of the Academy's founders was to establish what was consistently regarded as a national conservatoire—one that would both serve and articulate the musical essence of a nation distinct from England and English ways yet tied economically and politically to Britain. As we shall see, through personal contacts the directors of the Academy were able to maintain close links with the management of conservatoires in Paris and Italy and would have wished to keep these as their principal focus, but as a pioneering model in music education the Royal Academy of Music (founded along similar lines in London in 1822) was the point of immediate appeal and emulation—both institutions, during the crucial period of the eighteen-sixties, having the Duke of Leinster as their vice-president.

Ireland was generally considered to be an innately musical country (the 'land of song'): in 1825 an (anonymous) article on 'Music and genius of the Irish' stated that 'musical talent is indigenous to the Irish.'[47] England, on the other hand, was characterised at that time (by the German musical establishment) as *das Land ohne Musik*[48] (the land without music), and yet Ireland was subject, until 1922, to British diktats in educational development, an imperial tenet being that music, taught under such terms, was a civilising influence.[49] Ireland produced Balfe, Wallace, Sullivan, and Stanford, yet it was in England that their contribution to the revival of *English* music, and primarily opera, was made. (In 1881 Stanford would write to Sir Robert Stewart regarding the premiere of his opera *The Veiled Prophet*: 'It is an Irishman's work on an Irish poet's story, [but] there is unfortunately no opening for a prophet (even a "veiled prophet") who writes opera, in his own country, so perforce I must come to the land of north Teutons [Hannover] from which perhaps in the course of years it may cross the silver streak.')[50]

The irony continued into the nineteen-fifties, when we find Sir Arnold Bax, the holder of one of England's most *recherché* titles, 'Master of the King's Music', writing that Stanford, Charles Wood and Harty 'never penetrated to within a thousand miles of the Hidden Ireland' and that he considered himself 'a naturalized Gael'. 'I . . . love her [Ireland] better than any land "beneath the visiting moon".'[51] This is but an echo of Stanford's ambivalence as he commuted in his affections—and in his inspiration—between the land of his birth and that of his achievement, or of Sir Robert Stewart's ambiguity in preferring to look beyond England in his musical tastes, while referring (despite his Scottish ancestry) to 'we English folks'[52]—a trait copied by his student Annie Patterson, who wrote of the Union as 'our own country' without ceasing to be Irish and proud of it.[53]

The crux of the matter, which is also a musical crux, is the relationship between *sameness* and *difference*, the symbiotic captivity of coloniser and colonised, in which each needs, feeds off, offends yet attracts and stimulates the other. Perhaps nowhere more so than in the study and execution of music is the creative confluence of sameness and difference more crucial—between teacher and student, between composer and performer, between performer and audience, but above all between tradition, continuity, and change. Just as in politics, so in cultural matters, Irish identity had to be established as different from English before it could be true to itself. Even though the *transitus* has produced painful episodes, for example in the continuing discovery of what constitutes 'Irish' music, the journey—so often vividly illustrated in the transactions of the Academy—has been undertaken.

This has been so not least because the musicality of Irish people was assumed to be coaeval with their aptness for musical instruction and a flair for expression. That this may have been a factor in encouraging the founders of the Academy is suggested by the fact that contemporary accounts imply that the 'natural condition . . . [that] turned towards gaiety and happiness' observed by Walter Scott[54] helped to sustain the people through the rigours of the Famine. It was, of course, hardly the peasant class—in whom this was discerned—who would provide the raw material of the Academy, but the public spirit of the endeavour, at exactly this time, suggests to us that there was at least the glimmer of a hope that the broader achievement might see a meeting of the Anglo-Irish tradition and that of the Irish countryside—if only to continue the bridge-building that had been attempted in the patronage of Carolan and the Belfast Harp Festival, and by composers and teachers such as Giordani and Geminiani in the eighteenth century and Logier in the nineteenth.[55] It was a nice feat of one pianist performing in Dublin in 1820 to have played 'God Save the King' with one hand and 'St Patrick's Day' with the other—even though the *Dublin Magazine* stated that 'it is impossible that two airs so diametrically opposed to each other in time, style and accent should blend well.'[56]

Ironically, for a people whose innate musicality was constantly stressed as a prime distinguishing characteristic, music has taken third place to literature and the visual arts in cultural significance during the past century. Although the fusion of words and music has been a source of cultural and political strength throughout this period, the development of indigenous composition, the relationship of 'Irish' music to that of the European classical and folkloric mainstreams, musicology itself, have occupied a limbo, hardly touched by cognate but discrete studies in literature—what Joseph Ryan wryly calls 'an area largely innocent of scholarship.'[57]

General histories of Ireland have only very summarily described educational development, and the changing fortunes of music and music education have hardly been mentioned therein, the exceptions being an article by Brian Boydell in the *New History of Ireland*, volume 4, on 'Music, 1700–1850',[58] which provides a neat précis of his researches into eighteenth and early nineteenth-century music activity in Dublin,[59] and another by Aloys Fleischmann in *New History of Ireland*, volume 6, on 'Music and society,

1850–1920'.[60] Few incursions into cultural history have had more than a literary or visual focus: Terence Brown, in *Ireland: A Social and Cultural History, 1922–79*,[61] accords music a peripheral role,[62] while Jeanne Sheehy, in her otherwise pioneering study *The Rediscovery of Ireland's Past*,[63] almost completely ignores music as a cultural force.

Even at times when music was marginalised or diminished within the curriculum as a whole, the concern for music's place and role in Irish cultural development has been reflected in what might be called the literature of neglect. *Provision for the Arts* (commonly referred to as the Richards Report, 1976) was a systematic appraisal of the then arts scene that of necessity analysed the institutional condition of music but was able to reflect neither on the evolution of that condition nor on the development needs of music as a cultural force or a cultural experience.[64] Bruce Arnold contributed a chapter entitled 'Politics and the arts: the Dáil debates' to *Unequal Achievement*,[65] a survey of social, political and cultural administration in Ireland, but by definition it recited the legislative history leading to the establishment of An Chomhairle Ealaíon (the Arts Council) rather than examining any particular branch of the arts tree. Likewise Brian Kennedy, in his account of the establishment of the Arts Council and its forerunners, *Dreams and Responsibilities*,[66] necessarily advances across a broad front, in which music receives scant attention *per se*.

There has been no equivalent in musical terms of *Writing Ireland* by Cairns and Richards (1988)[67] or the more recent *Inventing Ireland* by Declan Kiberd[68] and Joep Leerssen's *Remembrance and Imagination*[69] until the publication in 1998 of *The Keeper's Recital* by Harry White, a stringent intellectual analysis of the relationship of music to culture in modern Ireland.[70] An equally relevant text, Joseph Ryan's thesis 'Nationalism and music in Ireland', remains unpublished.[71] Another survey, *Ireland and the Arts*, edited by Tim Pat Coogan, contained less than nine pages on classical music.[72]

The chief histories of Irish education, by Akenson, McElligott, and Coolahan, are studies of the evolution of an educational framework and choose not to explore the development of individual strands in the curricula.[73] The sole account of, and argument for, the role of the arts in education, by Ciarán Benson, accords no specific attention to music in primary education but devotes nine paragraphs to music in post-primary education (where drama receives three, literature two, film two, and dance one) and considers in separate sections the needs of teacher training and training for a career in music.[74] Up to now only one (brief) report has been published exclusively dealing with music education, and this was limited to the primary and post-primary schools system,[75] while a pioneering study of the history of music education in Ireland by Marie McCarthy is also unpublished.[76]

In 1996 a review group ('PIANO'), chaired by John O'Conor, reported to the Minister for Arts, Culture and the Gaeltacht on the provision for orchestras and related matters, in the course of which serious concern was expressed for the state of music education throughout the educational system—a concern also reflected in the many responses to the Green Paper on education at the same period.[77]

Scrutiny of individual Irish writers is legion, but while, after long neglect, many Irish painters have recently become the subject of important monographs, only one modern Irish composer—Seán Ó Riada—has received comparable attention.[78] Axel Klein's pioneering survey, *Die Musik Irlands im 20. Jahrhundert*, does much to rectify this lacuna, with its painstaking *catalogue raisonné* and descriptive essays.

Music in Ireland, a 'symposium' gathered by Aloys Fleischmann in 1952,[79] set up a benchmark for its time in its comprehensiveness and in the vigour with which it pursued individual topics. In a sense it represents the culmination of a period of strident commentary on the state of music in Ireland that had been prosecuted in the pages of the *Bell* from 1940 until 1954 by writers such as Charles Acton, Walter Beckett, Michael Bowles, Brian Boydell, Edgar Deale, Patrick Delany, Frederick May, Joseph O'Neill, James Plunkett, and Fleischmann himself—almost all of them practitioners in music—whose concerns continue to be relevant to this day. But, with the exception of a survey carried out in 1961 by Joseph Groocock,[80] Fleischmann's symposium has had to wait until this year for a successor,[81] while the urgings of the *Bell* have encouraged no comparable voices in later periodicals.[82] The appearance since 1990 of *Irish Musical Studies* has done much to identify and fill a lacuna in Irish musicology, in particular in relating music in Ireland to other cultural areas.

The collections of Bunting, Petrie and others in the nineteenth century represented an attempt to match cognate literary gatherings, map-making exercises intended to establish a terrain and to describe and discuss its characteristics; there has been no modern equivalent in music to emulate the *Field Day Anthology of Irish Writing*; and, although it is greatly needed, the call for an 'Encyclopaedia of Music in Ireland' is, as yet, unsupported.[83]

Despite the alleged centrality of music in the Irish character and in Irish life, there is a dearth of literature on the subject from almost every viewpoint.[84] The issues identified above as those that the new Academy would find itself addressing have yet to receive the attention they demand, not merely from a focused history such as the present study, but from a wider and more diverse number of directions. What has appeared has mostly tended to occlude cultural politics in the interests of studying political culture.

The present focus therefore attempts partially to redress that imbalance, by presenting at least the main instances in which cultural politics and political culture met and explored each other during the past century and a half, setting in train an examination of how a determined group of people, from diverse and disparate outlooks and persuasions, succeeded in answering the question that vexed Sir Robert Peel at that time: 'What thing should be done, and what time it should be done, and in what mode.'[85] It does so with the benefit of hindsight, knowing that what was needed was a national conservatoire; that in 1848 the time was *now*; and that the mode was that of the utmost expedition.

2

Music in Dublin, 1800–1848

DEREK COLLINS

Economic and social change after 1800; musical activity, 1800–31;
Roman Catholic churches; Dublin Music Festival, 1831;
visiting virtuosi; military music; promenade concerts;
new musical societies and choirs; music industry; teaching.

The founding of the Irish Academy of Music in 1848 took place at a particularly significant time in the history of music in Dublin. The circumstances of its establishment may be viewed in the context of social, economic and political developments, not only in Ireland but throughout Europe, during the eighteenth and nineteenth centuries.

For much of the eighteenth century the performance of music was confined to the great European political and religious centres, and to a large extent functioned as an entertainment that enriched the lives of a relatively small and aristocratic section of society. Composers and musicians relied almost exclusively on the patronage of wealthy individuals, to whom their work was often dedicated. Towards the end of the eighteenth century a turbulent period of wars and revolutions redefined the political and economic hierarchies in Europe. Empowered by the economic benefits of industrial-isation, and motivated to reform by the philosophies of the Enlightenment, a new and highly influential middle class quickly established itself.

The subsequent development of musical activity reflects the involvement of the new middle class on two levels: as spectators and as practitioners. As the popularity of attending musical events grew, there was a corresponding increase in the number and size of venues. Together with this, composers began to develop larger ensembles, more complex formal structures, and greater emotional impact in their scores. The desire of the new audience to be involved as practitioners was effectively catered for by the music industry. The techniques of mass production that were developed during the Industrial Revolution were successfully applied to the manufacture of instruments, particularly to the pianoforte. As the cost of instruments fell to within the means of middle-class families, music education became available to an increasing number of people through specialist schools and academies. Involvement with music became fashionable as a manifestation of prosperity; the 'piano in the parlour' came to be a desirable symbol of social standing, which accorded well with the early Victorian ethos of decorum and propriety.[1] Music publishers, in addition to their normal business, produced self-tutor books and simple arrangements of popular tunes for a wide variety of instruments and ensembles.

As the competence of amateur performers developed, numerous musical societies were established to provide opportunities for ensemble performance. The founding of the Irish Academy of Music was the direct result of a widely perceived need to educate instrumentalists for performance in the growing number of musical societies in Dublin. The extent to which these general trends in European cultural history influenced developments in Dublin is illustrated in musical activity in the period before the founding of the Academy.

While considerable scholarly attention has been directed to musical activity during the eighteenth century,[2] the subsequent period has yet to be explored in similar detail.[3] In particular, there is a need to investigate the relationships between the professional musicians associated with Christ Church and St Patrick's Cathedrals, the many amateur music clubs, such as the Hibernian Catch Club, charities, which had a traditional interest in the performance of fashionable music, and the slowly emerging new pattern of music societies. To some extent, the decline in musical activity in Dublin in the aftermath of the Act of Union was social and economic, as hospitals found it necessary to develop new sources of finance in addition to charity concerts; it was also the result of political change, as the American War of Independence, the French Revolution and the abolition of serfdom in Austria precipitated a crisis that was echoed in the 1798 rising in Ireland and subsequent legislative measures, not the least of which was the retention in Dublin Castle of a viceregal administration.[4]

These developments also encouraged a gradual shift from private to public patronage. In this period of transition, the resilience and economic needs of a small number of musicians and charities helped to establish a more secure base and a wider enthusiasm for music among a larger section of the population than previously. Many of the eighteenth-century traditions of performance were enthusiastically adopted by the audiences of the nineteenth century. Although it is tempting to draw a dividing line with the beginning of a new century, particularly when major political events such as the Act of Union coincide, the early years of the nineteenth century illustrate how aristocratic and public patronage gradually combined. As musical events became increasingly popular among the public, a new source of finance established itself, which survived the loss of private patronage.

The popularity of music among the growing middle class was encouraged by a variety of activities. In addition to the concerts organised among the resident professional musicians in Dublin, which formed a constant attraction, a number of special events featuring renowned visitors, or the spectacle of exceptionally large-scale musical forces, were particularly successful in stimulating public enthusiasm. Although performances in London frequently provided the model for similar events in Dublin, and many distinguished musicians from London left an enduring influence, Dublin developed an independent musical tradition of considerable vitality.

Perhaps the most significant musical organisation that illustrates the balance of private and public patronage during the period of transition and the influence of London performances was the Irish Musical Fund Society.[5] Founded in 1787 by a group of noblemen and musicians, which included David La Touche and Bartlett Cooke, the society gave an annual 'Commemoration of Handel' concert most years until 1820, after which only two concerts appear to have taken place, in 1828 and 1857, the latter conducted by Joseph Robinson.[6] Almost all the music presented was taken from the oratorios of Handel, principally *Messiah*; however, the growing popularity of Haydn led to performances of extracts from *The Creation*, while from 1817 Beethoven's Hallelujah Chorus from *The Mount of Olives* also appears.[7] The society performed in various Dublin churches, but after 1794 its performances were generally given in the Rotunda.[8] The choral forces frequently included the members of the Dublin Cathedral choirs and an amateur group known as the Sons of Handel, who made their first appearance at these concerts in 1795.[9] In notices placed in the Dublin newspapers after the performances, the society, in addition to thanking the leading instrumentalists and vocal soloists, was careful to acknowledge the contribution of amateurs in boosting the scale of the performance. The society also published lists of its subscribers, and in the decade around the Act of Union, 1796–1806, these show the steady support of the nobility and increasing support of the middle class in their growth from about fifty to over eighty names.[10] This would appear to contradict the view that 1800 acted as a cut-off date for aristocratic patronage. The performances of the Irish Musical Fund are particularly significant in that they initiate, with the active participation of amateur musicians, large-scale performances of oratorio.

Whereas in the eighteenth century the musical societies applied their efforts most effectively to hospital charities, in the nineteenth century educational and orphan charities were foremost in the promotion of music as a means of fund-raising. In the first quarter of the century at least twenty charities held musical events; fifteen of these were school or orphan charities.[11] Most of these charity performances took place in the Dublin churches and were accompanied by the preaching of a special 'charity sermon'.

Towards the end of the eighteenth century, performances were held both in Catholic chapels and Protestant churches. A notable performance of Giordani's *Te Deum* took place in Francis Street chapel in 1789 in celebration of George III's return to health and was attended by a congregation of about three thousand, with many Protestant noblemen among the performers and audience.[12] In the nineteenth century a number of important benefits resulted from the increasing religious toleration that, championed by Daniel O'Connell, finally led to Catholic Emancipation in 1829.[13]

In the early decades of the nineteenth century the building of a number of large chapels in Dublin introduced music to a wider section of the community. For many of the middle and lower classes, liturgical performances provided the only opportunity to experience the work of European composers. Charity sermon events became a regular feature of musical activity in Townsend Street chapel from 1800, Clarendon Street chapel from 1808, St Paul's, Arran Quay, and Bridge Street chapel from 1809, and Denmark Street chapel from 1810.[14] Occasional performances also took place in numerous other chapels and churches.

In the decades immediately before Emancipation and shortly afterwards five substantial chapels were built that became important venues for the performance of sacred music: St Michael's and St John's, Lower Exchange Street, dedicated on 21 December 1813; the Church of the Conception, Marlborough Street, dedicated on 14 November 1825; the Church of St Nicholas Without, Francis Street, dedicated on 15 February 1832; St Francis Xavier's, Upper Gardiner Street, which although unfinished was used for performances from 14 May 1833; and St Andrew's, Westland Row, dedicated on 29 January 1834.[15] Music for the weekly services was provided by the organists and choirs of each of these chapels, who performed many of the masses of Haydn and Mozart. Oratorio performances uniting the resident choir and organist with amateur and professional singers and instrumentalists became increasingly frequent and large in scale. Apart from Handel's *Messiah*, Haydn's *Creation*, and Mozart's *Requiem*, complete performances of large choral works were relatively rare. The oratorio programmes were typically miscellaneous selections from a variety of sources, though most frequently from Handel, Haydn and Mozart and, additionally, from Beethoven's oratorio *The Mount of Olives*.

As large-scale sacred concerts and oratorio performances became popular in Britain, these grand occasions attained the special status of music festivals.[16] They were perceived as celebrations of both musical achievement and regional pride and acquired great social importance. The first 'Dublin Grand Musical Festival' took place in August 1814 and was organised by the Lord Mayor and Corporation.[17] The original idea for organising a second festival in 1830–31 came from leading members of two amateur musical organisations, the Philharmonic and Anacreontic Societies. This latter group, which included the brothers William and Henry Hudson, both of whom were folk music collectors, resolved to engage 'the principal performers in the Empire,' to establish a guarantee fund by subscription, and to solicit through the office of the Lord Lieutenant the patronage of the monarchy.[18] Public enthusiasm for the festival is reflected in the fact that in less than two weeks the fund received donations of over two thousand pounds.[19] Sir George Smart was announced as conductor and authorised to engage the leading London musicians.[20]

The Festival Choral Society first appeared in a lavish concert organised by the eminent Dublin cellist Samuel Pigott in the Rotunda on 4 March 1831. Along with singers from the Anacreontic Society, the Philharmonic Society and boys of the cathedral choir they formed a large chorus that was accompanied by an orchestra, resulting in a total of 150 performers.[21]

In making plans for the festival, the committee discussed a proposal to erect a new music hall in Lower Abbey Street, capable of holding 2,200 people, at a cost of £15,000.[22] Although it was decided that such a building could not be finished in time, this illustrates a remarkable degree of anticipation—and was perhaps the earliest occasion on which the building of a public concert hall in Dublin was discussed.

The Grand Musical Festival took place from Monday 29 August to Monday 5 September 1831 and was patronised by the King and Queen and over a hundred of the English and Irish nobility.[23] The events included the first performance in Ireland or Britain of *The Triumph of Faith* by Ferdinand Ries, performances of Spohr's *The Last Judgement*, and many symphonic works. Although the chorus included singers from Irish and English cathedrals, and the orchestra contained many distinguished British and Continental players,[24] the musical and social highlight was the appearance of Paganini, who was induced to remain until mid-October, giving twenty-two performances throughout Ireland.[25]

The visit of Paganini, and the very substantial fees he commanded, illustrate the elevated status of the touring virtuoso during the nineteenth century.[26] From the eighteen-twenties a number of virtuoso performers excited considerable interest among the public in Dublin. The first piano virtuoso to visit Dublin was Frédéric Kalkbrenner, in 1824.[27] Ignaz Moscheles gave performances in 1826 of programmes that featured some of his own solo pieces and concertos, and during his stay he offered tuition at two guineas a lesson.[28] In 1828 Johann Baptist Cramer, considered by Beethoven to be the finest pianist of his time, gave two performances in the Rotunda.[29]

The German-born Henri Herz, principal pianist and composer to the court of France, visited Dublin to perform and teach in 1834 and 1836.[30] Between 29 October and 25 November 1834 he gave six concerts at the Rotunda, where he introduced much of his own music, including the Adagio and Rondo in D, Concerto in C minor, and Concerto in A. Also in these concerts he introduced, for the first time in Dublin, 'extemporaneous performances' based on themes presented by the audience. These proved highly popular and marked the beginning of a fashion for such improvised pieces. Herz continued to draw on much of his own music and improvisations for four concerts given in the Rotunda in November 1836. In the third and fourth of these, on 17 and 25 November, he was joined by some of the principal pianists and teachers of Dublin in his Grand Double Quartet for Four Pianofortes and Eight Performers. This was performed by Henri Herz with Miss Ashe, Miss Thomasine Allen, Miss Jackson, Miss Bunting, Mr Wilkinson, Mr Conran, and Mr Bussell.

In 1837 Dublin received visits from three international virtuosi: the French harpist Nicholas-Charles Bochsa,[31] the exponent of Erard's newly invented double-action harp; the Norwegian violinist Ole Bull; and the German pianist Sigismond Thalberg. Each of these engaged the services of local musicians and promoted events that occasionally involved large musical forces. Bull, soon to become the principal founder of the Norwegian National

Theatre in Bergen, gave four performances in the Theatre Royal and two concerts in the Rotunda, the second of which, on 16 February, featured an improvised duet with Bochsa.[32] Although Bull's playing was reported to be less extravagant than Paganini's, he was hailed as his only rival.[33] Among the many display pieces that excited Dublin audiences was the Quartet for Solo Violin, which exploited Bull's legendary ability to play four independent parts simultaneously. This piece, made possible by a flatter bridge and longer and heavier bow than usual, attempted to outdo Paganini's famous Duo. It would be almost a quarter of a century before Bull would pay a return visit to Dublin.

Sigismond Thalberg gave three concerts in the Rotunda in December 1837 and three performances in the Theatre Royal in January 1838.[34] He was thereafter a frequent visitor to Dublin, appearing with the Anacreontics in 1842 and the Philharmonic in 1845 and 1849.[35] Thalberg was one of the greatest pianists of his time, and considerable debate raged among such notable musicians as Fétis, Mendelssohn and Berlioz about the primacy of Thalberg or Liszt. Many of Thalberg's concert pieces took the form of fantasias on well-known themes, which was also a genre favoured by George Osborne.

The most distinguished musician to visit Ireland was Franz Liszt, who gave concerts between 21 December 1840 and 17 January 1841 in Dublin, Cork, Clonmel, Limerick, and Belfast.[36] While in Dublin, Liszt performed duets with the local cellist Pigott, accompanied other members of the touring party, extemporised on themes given by the audience, and played a number of his own solo works.[37] These included his operatic paraphrase of the finale of Donizetti's *Lucia di Lammermoor*, the Grand Galop Chromatique, and the Hexaméron Variations. The latter two works appeared in a new form of entertainment, 'piano recitals', which Liszt had introduced at the Hanover Square Rooms, London, on 9 June 1840.[38] Although the solo recital is now a fundamental part of musical activity, events that featured a single performer 'reciting' a series of solo pieces had not occurred before this date.

Although Liszt's performances in Dublin were well received, his Irish tour was marred by difficult weather conditions and poor organisation. Having travelled through the night from Cork to Clonmel, the touring party arrived to find that the concert had been forgotten. Liszt insisted that the programme be given in the hotel sitting-room to an audience of only twenty-five and endured the journey back to Dublin in a blizzard, sitting on the outside of the coach through the night. Although he had been contracted for 500 guineas a month, he received little of his fee, as the tour was a financial disaster, and Lavenu, the tour director, lost more than a thousand pounds.

While the dedication of musical amateurs to the mastery of their chosen instrument was inspired by such world virtuosi, it was also encouraged by the numerous ensembles that visited Dublin. These included the Ethiopian Harmonists in 1847 and 1849, the Rainer Family or Tyrolean Minstrels (whose *Jödel* is said to have fascinated Dublin audiences),[39] the Russian Horn Band (1831–32), the Dulang Band (1839), the Distin Brass Quintet

(1839), and the Collins Family, who presented 'classical chamber concerts' in 1840–41. In 1838 Joseph Strauss the elder brought his band to the Rotunda for concerts featuring, in addition to his own music, overtures by Auber and Rossini.[40]

In 1827 (and again in 1830) Dublin received visits from the distinguished Hermann Brothers' String Quartet (who were neither brothers nor named Hermann),[41] which included the cellist Joseph Lidel, who was to become one of the first teachers in the Irish Academy. By April 1830 the quartet had decided to disband, and Anton Popp, the second violinist, and Lidel remained in Dublin and settled at 7 Chatham Street, where Popp taught singing, the flute and German, and Lidel taught cello and guitar and accompanied ladies on the piano and harp.[42] By 1847 he was still being referred to as 'Mr Liddel Hermann' [*sic*] in a performance of *Elijah* at the Antient Concerts.[43]

Although brass and reed bands had been a feature of performance dating back to the eighteenth century, particularly in the pleasure gardens of Dublin, these ensembles became increasingly popular from the eighteen-thirties.[44] The military bands that had entertained the nobility during their summer promenades in such gardens as the Rotunda no doubt gave an impression of colour and ceremony to the lower classes as they led their regiments through the streets of Dublin. These bands were adopted as the model for similar ensembles raised among the growing trade unions of the early decades of the nineteenth century. Technical improvements in the design of wind and brass instruments, particularly the development of the key and valve systems, helped to facilitate public participation. Members of the regimental and the public bands took on a teaching role, as the popularity of these ensembles spread.

Johann Bernhard Logier was a particularly important promoter of military music. Born in Germany, he came to Ireland about 1790 with the Marquess of Abercorn's regimental band and became bandmaster of the Kilkenny Militia in 1806.[45] In 1809 he settled in Dublin, working as a pianist, bassoon player, and composer. Later he was to develop an important system for piano tuition. In July 1810 he opened a music shop at 76 Lower Sackville Street (O'Connell Street), which dealt particularly in military instruments.[46] In December 1811 his business moved to 27 Lower Sackville Street, where from February 1813 he also manufactured bugles, trumpets, horns, trombones, and drums.[47] His compositions mark the first attempt to introduce large military bands into the concert room.[48]

Large-scale military band performances continued through the middle of the nineteenth century. Two notable occasions that illustrate the level of this activity before the opening of the Academy occurred on 27 and 30 December 1847.[49] The events were promoted by Mr Mackintosh in the New Music Hall and were announced as 'Grand Military Monster Concert'.[50] The programmes featured over two hundred musicians from the bands of the 17th Lancers, 49th Regiment, and 75th Regiment.

The military band model was enthusiastically adopted on a national scale by the temperance movement, which, from its inception by Father Mathew in 1838, founded numerous bands among its members. The rapid growth of these groups is illustrated by the vast total abstinence demonstration in the Phoenix Park on St Patrick's Day 1841, in which almost every temperance society was led by its own band.[51]

During this period the regimental bands remained a popular attraction in the public gardens. The extent of their activity may be seen in the outdoor promenade performances given by the bands of the 19th, 84th and 88th Regiments, which alternated in twenty-five concerts given in the Portobello Gardens between 18 May and 16 September 1840.[52] Although bands founded to lead marches and demonstrations had—and continue to have—a social or political message, they also fulfilled an important role in bringing music to wider audiences.

In July 1840 Messrs Pigott, Wilkinson and Rudersdorff began a series of promenade concerts in the Round Room of the Rotunda, which were to prove highly successful. Samuel Pigott, whose name first appears as cellist in the Irish Musical Fund concert of 1818, was an experienced performer and promoter.[53] His benefit concerts, begun in 1822, became important annual events from the eighteen-thirties.[54] Wilkinson, who appeared mainly as a flautist from 1820, was also a pianist, conductor, and teacher.[55] Joseph Rudersdorff, who had been principal violin in the opera houses of Moscow and Hamburg, was brought to Dublin to play in Pigott's benefit concert on 19 April 1839 and to conduct an orchestra of over a hundred on 15 May 1840 for the same purpose.[56] Together they assembled an orchestra of sixty performers and planned four promenade concerts, on 22, 25, 27 and 29 July 1840.[57] Their programmes contained popular vocal and instrumental solos, dance music, and overtures. Public enthusiasm for the events led to further performances, and a remarkable series of thirty-three concerts was given by 4 June 1841. As the series progressed, Beethoven's *Fidelio* and *Egmont* overtures, a septet, the 'Battle' Symphony (op. 91) and the 'Pastoral' Symphony were introduced, as was Mendelssohn's overture *A Midsummer Night's Dream*.[58]

Pigott, Wilkinson and Rudersdorff continued to promote concerts, engaging Louis Jullien and his band for seven concerts in June 1841 at the Rotunda.[59] Jullien was a most colourful French conductor and composer (with thirty-five Christian names, including Thomas Thomas Thomas-Thomas and Julio Césare) who moved from Paris to London in 1838 and from 1840 gave numerous performances and concert tours throughout Britain with his band.[60] He and his ensemble of about fifty, which included many distinguished soloists, had just completed a series of five performances at the Theatre Royal, Hawkins Street, which formed the beginning of their first Irish tour.[61] Pigott, Wilkinson and Rudersdorff combined their promenade orchestra with Jullien's band, making an ensemble of up to 110, which was described as 'the best Orchestra ever congregated within the walls of the Rotunda.'[62]

In the following summer months Jullien and his band, increased to seventy performers with the assistance of local musicians, gave ten promenade concerts in the Portobello Gardens and Monkstown Castle Gardens.[63] In

September the principal soloists joined local musicians in four concerts at the Theatre Royal.[64] Finally, for 1841, Pigott engaged Jullien and most of his band, boosted to fifty performers once more with local help, for thirteen promenade concerts in the Rotunda between 1 and 21 December.[65]

The popularity of Jullien and his band, established by the visits of 1841, led to annual return trips, usually comprising at least six Dublin concerts. In all, Jullien and his band completed thirteen consecutive annual visits before their departure for America in 1853.[66]

The early visits of the Dulang and Jullien bands and the promotions by Pigott, Wilkinson and Rudersdorff are important in that they began a tradition of indoor promenade concerts. The fashion for orchestral promenade concerts contributed to the successful launch of an important new performing venue, which opened on 2 February 1841. The New Music Hall in Lower Abbey Street, built on the site of a former circus by Mr Classon, offered seated accommodation for 2,000 people in three areas: ground floor 800, gallery 600, side boxes and dress circle 600.[67] With the ground floor seats removed the hall could significantly increase its capacity. A separate indoor promenade area of over 100 yards in length offered space for an additional thousand people. The Music Hall opened with an extensive series of vocal and instrumental promenade concerts organised by three distinguished Dublin musicians: Joseph Robinson, W. S. Conran, and James Barton.[68] The series, which resulted in nine performances between 2 February and 26 March, was planned on a lavish scale.[69] After the opening concert, which featured an orchestra of 50 and chorus of 60, the forces were dramatically increased to an orchestra of 110 and chorus of 70. By March the chorus had grown to 86, so that the final three concerts presented a total of almost two hundred musicians. The success of the series is reflected in one report that suggests that 'since the Musical Festival there has not been in this city a chorus and orchestra of such power.'[70]

When the Music Hall reopened in November 1841 for the winter season, Mr Mackintosh, who previously alternated the job of leader with Barton, began a series of concerts with an orchestra of fifty, which featured vocal soloists rather than a chorus. By the end of the year Mackintosh had completed fourteen concerts, and the position of the Music Hall as second only to the Rotunda was established.[71]

The year 1841 is notable not only because of these visits and performances but also because it represents one of the busiest years before the founding of the Academy. In all, over 150 concert events took place, many of which illustrate the substantial musical resources now available in the city.[72]

The most important factor in the expansion of amateur performance was the establishment of a significant number of musical societies during the first half of the nineteenth century. The history of these societies is often difficult to trace, as their involvement with music for personal satisfaction, rather than financial gain, required little attention from the press.[73] In many instances such mention as there was provides the only evidence of their existence. Nevertheless it would seem that these societies increased in number from about four to at least thirteen between 1800 and 1850, with a possible nine additional groups active in this period.

The earliest and longest-running amateur society was the Hibernian Catch Club, founded in 1680 by the Vicars Choral of St Patrick's and Christ Church Cathedrals.[74] This society, which admitted lay members from 1770, is representative of several catch or glee clubs that met in the convivial atmosphere of a hotel or tavern for dinner, followed by musical entertainment. The oldest amateur society that continued to function in the nineteenth century was the Anacreontic Society, founded in 1740.[75] Although it was founded as a strictly amateur society for the promotion of instrumental music, members of the profession appear as section leaders, soloists, and conductors, in programmes that feature a wide range of instrumental and vocal music. As the majority of events in their season, usually from November to June, were private, we cannot fully assess their size or frequency; however, the society did appear in some public performances.[76] They offered their assistance in the orchestra for the Irish Musical Fund Society's 'Commemoration of Handel' in 1794 and, with the Hibernian Catch Club and Irish Harmonic Club, took part in a concert at the Rotunda on 15 January 1806 that raised £139 9s 10d towards the Nelson Monument.[77] In 1817 they assisted in three concerts of 'Sacred and Ancient Music' for the benefit of the poor.[78] Musicians involved with the society included Paul Alday, a distinguished violinist and composer, who acted as leader between 1819 and 1828 and secretary between 1824 and 1830.[79] Also involved as conductors were Sir John Stevenson, who was vice-president in 1822, Francis J. Robinson, John Barton, and William Sarsfield Conran.[80] An impression of the repertoire of the society can be gained from the more substantial works performed during the eighteen-twenties. These include unidentified symphonies and quartets by Haydn and Beethoven, Mozart's *Requiem* and 'Jupiter' Symphony, the overture to *Der Freischütz*, a piano concerto by Weber, and Alday's Violin Concerto, Quartet in C, and Symphony in C.[81]

The activities of the Sons of Handel are most closely associated with those of the Irish Musical Fund, in whose concerts they frequently appeared. It seems likely that the Sons of Handel were formed in 1790 to support the Handel commemorations, as there is little evidence in their history of other performances. Only between 1822 and 1824 do they appear to perform independently of the charity, when they held an annual concert and dinner.[82] Although it is not clear who established the group, two conductors were particularly associated with it: Jonathan Blewitt and Francis Robinson. Blewitt, musical director of Crow Street Theatre from 1813 and a pianist, received a presentation box in 1824 in recognition of his services. Francis Robinson conducted a notable concert on 31 March 1824, which included Handel's 'Occasional Overture', the finale from Mozart's *Don Giovanni*, and a selection of arias and choruses from Handel's *Messiah* with, for the first time in Ireland, additional accompaniments by Mozart. This performance also featured vocal solos from two of Robinson's sons, Francis James (tenor) and William (bass). In the last two years in which they appeared, the Sons of Handel performed choruses by Handel, Haydn and Weber and symphonies by Mozart, Haydn and Alday, who for some time was leader of the orchestra.

One of the most influential amateur orchestral societies was the Philharmonic Society, which was founded in 1826 and was active until 1866.[83] The society was founded and conducted by Henry Bussell, a violinist and pianist, and led by J. R. Mackintosh.[84] Although it is not clear just how many performances took place in their early years, from about 1845 they averaged five or six concerts in a season, usually from January to June. Few details remain of the size of the orchestra. A total of 100 or 150 appeared on special occasions, when the society was joined by other groups;[85] an average of between 50 and 60 is more likely.[86] Although the society was joined by singers who performed various solo and ensemble pieces, the majority of the repertoire was orchestral and marks the introduction of larger-scale romantic music. In addition to overtures by Beethoven, Donizetti and Weber, they gave important performances of symphonies by Beethoven (second, fifth, and sixth), Kalliwoda (second and third), and Mendelssohn (first, second, and third), and Ries's sixth.[87] The brass section of the society appears to have undertaken independent engagements as the Philharmonic Brass Band.[88]

An important group with which the Philharmonic occasionally joined forces was the Society of Antient Concerts. This was founded in 1834 and conducted by Joseph Robinson, an eminent singer, and was active until he relinquished his position in 1863.[89] After meeting in Robinson's house and in rooms now belonging to the Royal Irish Academy, the society renovated a building in Great Brunswick Street (Pearse Street), which it opened in 1843 as the Antient Concert Rooms.[90] This was an important addition to the performing venues in Dublin and attracted many societies, including the Philharmonic.[91] The building had a capacity of between nine hundred and a thousand, with an additional two hundred in the gallery of its hall and at least one small room that was used as a committee room.

The Antient Concerts Society was a particular exponent of the works of Mendelssohn and gave the first Irish performance of the oratorio *Elijah* on 9 December 1847.[92] The forces involved give an indication of the society's strength, which amounted to nine vocal soloists, a chorus of 150, and an orchestra of 38.[93] The society continued to give Irish premieres of Mendelssohn's choral works, presenting the *42nd Psalm* on 17 February 1848, the oratorio *St Paul* on 23 February 1849, and *Athalie* on 8 February 1850.[94] In the majority of concerts the orchestral section was led by R. M. Levey.[95]

Although the University of Dublin Choral Society was founded as a student rather than a public choir, it gave performances outside the university with the assistance of boy trebles from the cathedrals.[96] Founded in 1837 after informal meetings in the rooms of Hercules MacDonnell, its first conductor was Joseph Robinson. Robert Prescott Stewart, who was appointed conductor in 1847, continued Robinson's interest in reviving music when he presented on 17 December an anthem by J. S. Bach, which was reported to be 'the first vocal piece of that composer ever performed in Ireland.'[97]

During the eighteen-forties a remarkable number of public choirs make their first appearance: the Sacred Harmonic Society (1841); the Metropolitan Choral (1842), in which Bussell, Lidel, John Robinson and William Elliott Hudson were involved; the Amateur Melophonic (1844); the Dublin Madrigal Society, founded by Gustavus Geary in 1846; and the Dublin Choral Society (1847), conducted by Lidel. The Orpheus Choral Society also appears to have been founded between 1837 and 1844.

Finally, the activity of the amateur societies is illustrated by two remarkable performances given in the Rotunda on 5 and 12 February 1847 'for the relief of the Poor of the city.'[98] The performance of Handel's oratorio *Israel in Egypt*, conducted by Stewart and repeated by public demand, involved eleven amateur musical societies. These were the Hibernian Catch Club, the Philharmonic Brass Band, and the Anacreontic, Philharmonic, Antient Concerts, University Choral, Orpheus Choral, Amateur Harmonic, Amateur Melophonic, Dublin Madrigal and Ladies' Choral Societies. Although the concert notices announced 250 performers, the reviews gave a figure of at least 400. In either case the musical forces would have included the majority of the principal performers in Dublin and represent an unprecedented level of co-operation among the societies.

Public enthusiasm for private practice and participation in the ever-increasing number of musical societies and bands encouraged great activity in the music trade. The number of music printers, publishers and sellers increased from seventeen to twenty-seven between 1815 and 1820; the number of instrument-makers likewise rose from twenty-seven to forty-two in the early eighteen-twenties. In the five years from 1820 a remarkable total of sixty-one music traders operated in Dublin.[99] However, after this peak there was an equally dramatic reduction in the music trade to below the levels of 1800. Although the reasons for this are unclear and require further analysis, it may be that businesses that could offer the largest stock at the most competitive prices were in a better position than smaller firms to attract and maintain their share of the market. While the number of businesses decreased, there may have been an expansion in size to meet public demand.

Many of the music businesses of the nineteenth century were owned by musicians. The more prominent members of the profession were particularly successful, as they were in a strong position to attract business by virtue of their public image and perceived authority. In the early part of the century one of the leading businesses was established by J. Willis, a singer, flautist and composer, whose wife was a pianist. Willis took over Goulding and Company of 7 Westmoreland Street in 1815.[100] In addition to selling music he opened in 1820 the first circulating library, where an annual subscription of three pounds entitled the borrower to between seven hundred and eight hundred volumes, containing up to forty thousand pieces of music.[101] Willis's firm was in turn taken over in 1836 by Francis J. Robinson, Henry Bussell, and William Robinson, who effectively pooled their authority as leading musicians.[102]

An illustration of a firm that survived beyond 1850 by having a large stock was Marcus Moses and Company, which in the middle eighteen-thirties advertised three hundred pianos.[103] Although the piano business of M'Cullagh and M'Cullagh at 108 Grafton Street was under no direct threat from the cellist and music-seller Pigott, who moved to within a few doors (to number 112) in 1836, their eventual collaboration helped sustain business.[104]

During the first half of the nineteenth century, as public interest in music increased, there was a corresponding expansion in music education. The institutions in Dublin that had traditionally provided music education—the cathedrals and Trinity College—continued to fulfil this important role. The oldest teaching establishment, the choir school of St Patrick's Cathedral (founded in 1432 by Archbishop Richard Talbot), and the choir of Christ Church Cathedral (first recorded in 1539) provided musical education for boy choristers.[105] Although the number of choristers in each cathedral changed from time to time, the choirs were of equal strength in 1835, with twelve men and six boys in each.[106] At this time each cathedral employed both an organist and a music master to undertake the boys' education. Many of the choristers continued their professional activities as adult vicars choral, becoming important performers, composers and teachers. Among the more notable vicars choral were Sir John Stevenson, Philip Cogan, Dr John Spray, Dr John Smith, Robert Jager, David Weyman, Symeon Buggine, the four sons of Francis Robinson (Francis James, William, John, and Joseph), and Sir Robert Stewart.[107]

Although the University of Dublin awarded its first BMus to Thomas Bateson in 1612, relatively few music degrees were conferred before the middle of the nineteenth century.[108] The degree of DMus (*honoris causa*) was occasionally conferred on leading members of the profession and, like the BMus, was awarded in recognition of the merits of a submitted composition. Examinations in the broader areas of music were introduced when Sir Robert Stewart was elected to the chair in 1861.[109] The professorship created for Lord Mornington, who held the post from 1764 to 1774, was vacant for much of the early nineteenth century, until the appointment of Dr Smith in 1845.[110]

Educating singers, mostly men and boys, became more widespread with the establishment of choirs in the growing number of Catholic churches that resulted from Emancipation. Organists appointed to most of the larger chapels and a number of the smaller ones began training part-time singers for the performance of church music. Chief among the most notable chapel choirs was the choir of the Church of the Conception (now the Pro-Cathedral), Marlborough Street, under the direction from 1827 to 1848 of Haydn Corri.[111]

Corri, who had settled in Dublin from Edinburgh in 1821, teaching piano, singing, and composition, was to become an influential musician. In 1825, continuing the practice of some teachers (Miss Bennett from 1821, Mr and Mrs E. C. Allen from 1825, and others), he offered tuition to an apprentice.[112] Apprentices, who paid a fee, were usually between the ages of twelve and fourteen, were occasionally resident, and undertook some of the more rudimentary duties, acting as copyists and preparatory teachers. In return they received a range of lessons, often including performing, composing, figured bass, and analysis. Although there may not have been an entirely equal balance of benefits in all cases, this system was an important means of educating would-be professionals in a range of activities.

Tuition in performance was mostly delivered through private instrumental and vocal lessons, usually taken once (though not uncommonly twice) a week and typically lasting between half an hour and an hour. Although the division is somewhat artificial, the teachers may be viewed in three broad groups: part-time freelance teachers, full-time professional teachers, and visiting specialists. Members of the theatre orchestras and leading instrumentalists of the musical societies often supplemented their income with freelance teaching; many also sold and repaired instruments. As their public image and reputation as performers attracted pupils, relatively few resorted to advertising in the press; it is difficult, therefore, to assess the number of instrumental teachers or the extent of their activity.

Professional teachers—those for whom teaching was their main income—were in the majority of cases teachers of piano or singing, or both. Many operated 'academies', often, though not exclusively, based at their home, or travelled to pupils and schools. These included Wilkinson and Lidel and, after Lidel's retirement, Madame Morosini; Mr and Miss Dignam (4 Rathmines Road); and Señora de la Vega, 'native of Spain', who taught guitar and singing. Quite frequently whole families became involved in extensive teaching practices, for example Mr and Mrs Corri and their son Patrick, Mr and Mrs Willis and their two daughters, Mr Logier and his son Theobald, his daughter and son-in-law Mr and Mrs E. C. Allen, Mr and Mrs Ashe and their three daughters, William Wilkinson and his wife, and Francis Robinson and his four sons and probably two daughters. A number of teachers also developed and published their own teaching methods.[113]

Information about the fees charged by teachers was almost always available only by request. Although there was some variation, most teachers charged in advance for a series of six lessons, with some requiring an entrance fee of between half a guinea and one guinea (forty-two pounds in today's money). Fees published by Madame Panormo in 1835 of one guinea for six singing lessons were described as moderate, given her status, but are likely to be typical.[114] Although much of the instrumental teaching was centred in Dublin and the immediate area, a few teachers travelled beyond the city. The opening of the railway from Dublin to Kingstown (Dún Laoghaire) in 1835 greatly facilitated music teaching, first in Blackrock and Kingstown and later in other areas.[115] Subsequent advertisements offering tuition in these areas, including those of Haydn Corri, would appear to have taken advantage of the new service's reported journey time of sixteen minutes.[116]

A notable contribution to piano teaching on an international level was made by Johann Logier, who applied the discipline of his military background to developing his 'chiroplast', which he patented in 1814.[117] This mechanism, which was attached to the front of a piano, regulated the movements of the hands. Logier published detailed teaching methods and studies for simultaneous performance by groups of students. His system

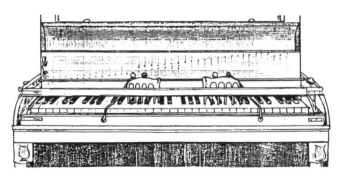

achieved much success, and public examinations of his pupils—probably the earliest pupils' concerts—were well received.[118] His methods were adopted by distinguished Dublin pianists, at least seven of whom opened 'Logerian academies': Blewitt, William Walsh, Spray and Smith jointly, Browne, W. S. Conran, and E. C. Allen.[119] By August 1816, Logerian academies were established in Edinburgh, Glasgow, Preston and Liverpool and by November 1817 in London, where the system was enthusiastically endorsed by Louis Spohr in 1824.[120] Although it is not surprising that Logier's chiroplast attracted severe criticism, he also received letters of commendation from Clementi, Cramer, Shield, Wesley, Kalkbrenner, William Warren, and J. A. Stevenson.[121] In 1822 Logier was invited to establish his method in Berlin, from where it spread throughout the Prussian states, to Germany and beyond. In 1826 he returned to Dublin, not only well rewarded for his efforts but in receipt of a gold snuff box presented by the King of Prussia.[122] Exports of the chiroplast continued to Germany and later to America, and it was still being sold in England as late as 1877.[123]

Logier's daughter, a talented pianist and teacher, married E. C. Allen in 1819 and, despite being widowed in 1833 with ten children, remained the chief exponent of his system in Dublin.[124] The Allens' academy at 56 Rutland Square (Parnell Square) was exceptionally well equipped, with fourteen pianos, many of which would have been used in their concerts, which alternated solo and simultaneous performances by as many as twelve pianists.[125] In 1830 a remarkable total of ten concerts was given by the pupils of Mr and Mrs Allen, from a wide repertoire, which included orchestral transcriptions and original piano music by Czerny, Dussek, Herz, Mozart, Rossini, and Kalkbrenner.[126]

Visiting specialists, particularly the touring virtuosi, who were generally pianists or singers, directed their tuition towards higher-level pupils or members of the profession. Their tuition helped establish new performance techniques, spread new repertoire, and provided a point of contact with the latest European trends. Visiting singers from the Continent frequently advertised tuition in 'the true art of singing' in their national style or language.

Music education was provided for a wider section of the public by the amateur bands and choral societies. Tuition on wind and brass instruments was promoted by the temperance and trade union movements. Members of the regimental bands stationed in Dublin were no doubt keen to supplement their earnings by performing and teaching, as the bands were financed entirely from the private income of the officers.[127] Band tuition tended to be group or ensemble-based and would not necessarily have provided soloists of professional standard in more than a few cases. Nevertheless, these were an important addition to the profession.

Amateur singing was most effectively catered for by the numerous choral societies in Dublin. Apart from providing a musical resource and a rare opportunity for all social classes to meet on equal terms, the societies offered singers, particularly female sopranos and altos (who were not necessarily included in church choirs and who were unable to afford private lessons), an experience of tuition and performance.

General interest in music was also stimulated by a small number of public lectures. On 21 November 1814 Logier began a series of twelve— two a week—at his house, 24 Lower Sackville Street (O'Connell Street), on harmony and composition.[128] Admission to the series was one guinea. These, the first of their kind, proved highly popular, attracting significant notice from the press and members of the profession, and were repeated by demand from 12 May 1815.[129] Logier gave a further series of twelve weekly lectures, beginning on 31 January 1829, which also dealt with the analysis of music by Haydn, Mozart, and Beethoven.[130] A Mr Philips gave two lectures on singing in January 1821 and another two on 14 and 28 January 1824 in the Freemasons' Hall, Dawson Street, in which he contrasted the English and Italian styles. Again, these attracted much attention and were reported at length in the press.[131]

Although the abolition of advertisement duty in August 1853 encouraged more music teachers to use the press, it is difficult to estimate the size of the profession at this period.[132] Street directories from the middle of the century suggest a thriving profession. While Henry Shaw's directory of 1850 overlooks some poorer areas of the city, and some teachers may not have stated their profession, it does include some forty-seven 'professors of music', no doubt teaching at various levels.[133]

By the middle eighteen-forties the traditions of performance established in the eighteenth century had survived the period of decline that surrounded the turn of the century and were enthusiastically adopted by a new audience, who made them their own. Musical events gradually increased from about ten a year in 1800 to an average of thirty around 1820 and sixty-four in the middle eighteen-forties.[134] Public participation in music had expanded the scale and frequency of performance, and music education was now available to a much greater proportion of the people.

Intermezzo

The Responsibilities of a Music Teacher

MARGARET O'HEA

Read to a meeting of the Incorporated Society of Musicians, January 1895

Although the term 'music teacher', strictly speaking, applies to all those engaged educationally in any or every branch of music, scientific, theoretic, and vocal, I am using it in its more ordinary and general acceptation, that of teaching pupils to play instruments. While my personal experiences are almost altogether derived from many years of teaching the pianoforte, I think the impressions I have received and which I purpose to relate are applicable in a great measure to other branches of the art. Music teachers should not deceive themselves with the fallacy that, the art they impart not being in these days a direct branch of general education, their duties are fulfilled by giving accurate technical instruction, however good. I will endeavour during the course of this short paper to sketch an abstract portrait of a good music teacher, without, I need hardly say, laying any personal claim to the possession of any of the perfections I try to depict.

The teacher should, early in the student's career, impress the fact that music is a language in which to express the innate sense of the beautiful which all mankind possesses, and that he is being taught so as to have the use of that language in which to speak his emotions—the technique to be regarded as its alphabet. In every way, the heart, soul and mind should be awakened to a love, reverence and enthusiasm for art in its true sense. For how many play instruments, and even with a certain brilliancy, using merely the eye, ear, and touch, without a genuine musical thought or feeling? This is also applicable, though in a slightly different way, to singers. It is this want which causes so many performances to be both uninteresting and tiresome. There are yet others who do not even realise that music has any higher aim than to be a pleasing sound or a display of what they consider a showy accomplishment.

The immediate or direct points of a pupil's performance for which the teacher is obviously responsible are accuracy, method, and style. In *accuracy* I include notes, time, fingering (according to the instrument), and the ordinary marks upon the music; in *method* a thoroughly good, well-developed technique, producing a full musical tone, together with those varieties of touch which can be mechanically acquired; in *style* correct tempo, rhythm, phrasing, and general reading of the composition.

Emotional expression, capacity for subtle changes of tone, insight to the deeper meaning and beauty of the various themes and phrases and mental grasp of a work as a whole are all natural gifts. These when possessed more or less fully soon assert themselves.

Still much can be done by the teacher to develop and foster them. Sometimes too they may be to a certain degree latent in a pupil, and here the teacher should do all possible to arouse them, pointing out the possession of them by the great artists and holding them up as leading to the highest excellence in performance, the full interpretation of the composer's ideas. Less gifted pupils also may, by having their minds directed to these artistic qualities, learn to recognise them in the playing of others and thus add immensely to their intellectual enjoyment of music throughout their lives.

The taste of the pupil has also to be carefully cultivated, even while the solid foundation of technique is being laid. This can best be done by giving from the beginning the simpler works of the great masters, together with a good series of studies to open and develop the execution. For this it is necessary to have a progressive course of music arranged for the earlier stages of instruction. Though not holding rigidly to it, particular cases requiring special consideration still up to the point when accuracy, as I have described it, is attained, a decided course may mostly be followed with the best results. It is later, when the means to express the emotions have been fairly obtained, that individual treatment in the selection of music becomes so important. Then the judgment of the teacher shows itself in giving music that will on the one hand bring out the stronger natural qualities of the pupil and on the other educate and develop as far as possible the weaker ones.

A thorough knowledge of the theory of music should be insisted upon, and the study of harmony, as also of the history of music, made to be regarded as a pleasure as well as an absolute necessity. Sometimes ambitious young performers are inclined to regard the science of music as dry and the time spent upon it more or less wasted. Here the influence of the teacher should come in to direct and instruct the youthful mind, impressing the fact that, as music combines science and art, it is impossible to be a true musician without having well mastered both.

The too much neglected study of solfeggi is a requirement not properly understood and should also be made compulsory. The capability to hear music, with the mind from a score, is what every music student ought to have, according to the degree of his general advancement.

A system of practice should be laid down so that the pupil may derive full benefit from the time given to the instrument. Desultory practice returns but poor results, and many thousands of hours every year go for naught while music students, though bodily present and seemingly engaged at their instruments, let their thoughts wander off to every trivial distraction. To make even a moderate success at any of the arts, full concentration of mind during study or practice is essential, and this cannot be too often or too seriously insisted on.

A certain portion of every day's practice should be allotted to the reading of music, so as to obtain facility in playing at sight, an acquirement the value and importance of which it would be impossible to overestimate. Then, too, students should be stimulated to learn their music by heart, as when able to play without the printed copy so much more freedom and expression can be thrown into the performance, and other obvious advantages are also gained. Teachers should open the minds of their pupils to the comprehension of what true, just expression is, making it clear that there are many forms of it. Even in musical circles there are sometimes very erroneous views current upon this fundamental point. The term 'expressive playing' usually means putting tenderness and pathos into certain phrases, as often as possible, without any deliberate consideration as to whether that kind of expression was intended by the composer, or suitable to the particular composition. I do not mean for one moment to underrate the value of these delightful emotions, as I do not forget the fact that while the Greeks considered grandeur and repose as the most sublime qualities in art, they admitted that even these could fatigue, but that pathos never failed to sway the human heart. We do not, however, want to be always in tears, and a student should learn contrast and climax.

On this latter point Mr Ruskin in his *Modern Painters* says: 'In all the noblest compositions utmost power is permitted, but only for a short time, or over a short space.' 'Music', he adds, 'must rise to its utmost loudness and fall from it, as colour must be graduated to its extreme brightness and descend from it.'

The various phases of emotion should also be explained to the student. To play passionate music with the requisite fire and depth, playful movements with appropriate lightness and sparkle, majestic ones with becoming gravity, and so on throughout the whole gamut of feeling—unless all this be realised, a musical performance becomes as artistically absurd as if an actor were to play a tragedy like a farce, or a farce like a tragedy.

In addition to the direct instruction by which the student's musical taste should be cultivated, much can be done by urging the artistic benefit to be derived from the study of the great poets, of the best prose literature, by seeing fine pictures and sculpture, and being present at high-class dramatic performances. All these tend to enlighten the mind and deepen the emotional feelings. Above all, the student should be directed never to lose an opportunity of hearing good music, well given. How much can be learned from hearing fine orchestras and choruses, as also the great artists in every branch of music, I have not now time to dwell upon, but I am sure all those present know by personal experience what light has been shed into their minds while listening to those gifted beings.

None should adopt the profession of teaching music who do not love the work and who have not a far higher and more enthusiastic interest in it than a mere monetary one. With much less skill and toil other paths of life would prove far more remunerative. Indeed, as a rule, save in very exceptional instances, the arts are not lucrative, for it is true of all of them what the celebrated philosopher Locke said: 'It is very seldom seen that anyone discovers mines of gold or silver in Parnassus. 'Tis a pleasant air, but a barren soil.'

I must now say a few words upon the moral responsibilities of a teacher. They are the gravest and most important of all, and are very often not sufficiently considered. To bear a high character, so as to command the personal respect of the students, is the first requirement. I cannot imagine anything more deteriorating to the young, both morally and artistically, than to be placed under the instruction of those in whose sterling qualities they cannot believe. Teachers deficient in such can never be really successful. 'As man is, so is his work' is a truism now very generally accepted.

How, too, can young minds dissociate the artist from the man (or woman) with whom they are brought into contact? The personal want of faith is thus liable to extend even to the teaching received. Should there unfortunately be any moral taint in the teacher's mind, how easily by some slight suggestion or innuendo it can reach that of the pupil and deprive it in a moment of the freshness which can never return! In all dealings a teacher should be thoroughly reliable and should show upright and honourable feeling. Lessons carelessly given, time unnecessarily cut short, anything deceitful, underhand or untruthful, have an influence for evil on the young which is not always understood.

Self-control, command of temper, patience and courtesy of manner come without effort to those naturally possessing the requisites of a teacher. Those less endowed should endeavour in every way to cultivate these essential qualifications. If one cannot control oneself, it is not possible to control others.

At the same time the teacher should be simple and unaffected. Any approach to priggishness, to personal glorification or to airs of superiority should be carefully avoided. Beyond all, he should endeavour to win the confidence and good will of even the humblest and least gifted pupil.

The last characteristic upon which I shall touch is enthusiasm. When happily possessed by the teacher it quickly communicates itself to the pupil, and under its inspiring influence difficulties fade away, work becomes a pleasure, and wonderful results are attained. Its power can be best described by a quotation from an eloquent fellow-countryman of ours, which in conclusion I shall give: 'What is there truly great which enthusiasm has not won for man? The glorious works of art, the immortal productions of the understanding, the incredible labours of heroes and patriots have been prompted by enthusiasm and by little else. Cold and dull were our existence here below unless the deep passions of the soul stirred by enthusiasm were sometimes summoned into action for high, noble and intellectual aims.'

Margaret O'Hea (1843–1938) was a member of a remarkable family that in many ways typified the transition from British rule to independence and from O'Connellite politics through Young Ireland to Parnellite nationalism. Her father, James O'Hea (1809–92), was a close associate of Sir Colman O'Loghlen in the service of Daniel O'Connell, who called him 'my loved friend' and whom he defended in the state trial of 1844. He became a Circuit Court judge. A pupil of Henrietta Flynn and later of Sir Robert Stewart at the Academy, which she entered in 1865, Margaret O'Hea taught at the RIAM (in succession to Mademoiselle Gayrard) for fifty-five years, from 1873 to 1928, becoming Esposito's assistant at the local centres in 1909 and a professor. She was awarded the FRIAM in 1931. Dina Copeman—whom she befriended, taught, and to some extent supported—believed that she was partly responsible for securing the Coulson Bequest to the Academy. Her sister Alice (c. 1855–1937) taught singing for forty-seven years, beginning as a student teacher in 1889 and becoming professor in 1926. Another sister, Mary, taught 'declamation' for thirty-four years, from 1902. The three sisters therefore spent an aggregate of 136 years in the service of the RIAM. A fourth sister, Ellen, who died young in 1880, had been a member of the Academy junior vocal class in 1866 and became the author of operettas, including The Rose and the Ring, *under the name Elena Norton; one of her works was staged at the Academy in 1877. Their brother, Fergus (1850–1922), has been called 'one of the finest political cartoonists of the Victorian era,' working (under the pen-name 'Spex') in support of Parnell in papers such as* Young Ireland, Irish Fireside, *and* Zozimus.

3

Foundations I
1848–1870

Prospectus; original committee; links with other organisations; influence of Young Ireland; Antient Concert Rooms; benefit concerts; half-yearly examinations; declining fortunes; 1856 reorganisation; new committee; move to 18 St Stephen's Green; performance of Maritana*; amateur opera recitals; business arrangements; office of secretary; declaration of intent by students; charity ball; increase in subscribers; marionette opera; comparison with Continental conservatoires; campaign for grant, 1864–70; purchase of 36 Westland Row.*

'A' musical people by nature, all we want is instruction,' opined the *Freeman's Journal* in 1851.[1] To satisfy that want, a detailed prospectus had been circulated in Dublin in January 1848, arguing the case for the creation of an academy. It indicated concern that Dublin, 'the second city of the Empire, a city celebrated for its musical taste,'[2] enjoyed only indifferent musical performances, which it attributed largely to the lack of an adequate resident and indigenous orchestra.

In the three following years the establishment of the Irish Academy of Music had gone so far towards meeting that need that the *Freeman's Journal* could say that 'this instruction is here offered of first-class character and on reasonable terms . . . Surely there will be no lack of subscribers to an undertaking of so national and so scientific a character.'[3]

That the institution could be regarded as national is indicative of the fact that at that time there was a growing awareness among the intelligentsia of an equally pressing need: the development of a sense of Ireland as a separate and distinct cultural and social entity—whether or not it remained within the political ambit of Britain.[4] On an ideological level—however problematic—a sense of Irishness pervaded the fledgling Academy, while on a practical level it assiduously addressed itself to the training of musicians to meet the immediate needs of a city with the thriving choral tradition discussed above by Derek Collins.

Although there was, as Collins has demonstrated, a burgeoning musical life in Dublin after the Act of Union and the consequent changes in the axis of patronage, the catalogue of choirs, teachers, publishers, instrument makers, retailers and concerts does not add up to an organic structure. Something had gone out of the life that had evolved from the old system, and, as we shall see, it would be well into the twentieth century before anything resembling an integrated musical life re-emerged. Most importantly, however, there was no educational infrastructure to underpin the largely amateur initiatives. The virgin territory on which the Academy set its plough was one requiring the inculcation of basic skills of musical literacy through recognised educational channels. The creation of the Academy could in itself be regarded as icing preceding the cake for which it was intended, similar to the provision of third-level colleges before an adequate system of secondary schooling.

The essence of the new academy was to be stability. The prospectus, published in part in *Saunders's News-Letter* on 29 January 1848, referred to the fact that Dublin's musical life was 'dependent upon the limited orchestra of the Theatre [Royal] . . . and such military bands as may happen to be quartered in our garrison.' The bands were not only undependable with regard to the length of their stay but 'are quite incompetent to perform with that delicacy essential to the concert room.' The recent successes in choral music were attributable to 'the element of *permanence*' in the performers' availability for concerted practice, 'a result utterly unattainable . . . when the materials are in a state of perpetual change.'

The following year *Saunders's News-Letter* could refer to 'the necessity of an academy' in these terms: 'Almost all the lads leaving our choirs, when the voice is undergoing change, are obliged to become teachers of an art in which they require instruction themselves: they have no academy to apply to, where competent teachers are to be had adequate to their means of payment, and where a library of the works of the great masters is kept for their use (a thing indispensable for the acquirement of any art or science).'[5] Without such an academy, Ireland would continue a provincial, dependent sub-culture, at the mercy of 'perpetual change.' With it, it had the chance of expressing its own cultural aspirations, in its own style and according to its own resources, with a degree of stability to be discovered within those resources. In 1869, during the campaign for a government grant, the *Irish Times* would sarcastically argue that 'perhaps a Chancellor of the Exchequer may yet be found so liberal minded that he will concede to us a small portion of our own revenues for the support of our own National Academy?'[6]

If Dublin was a 'deposed capital',[7] in the sense of having lost its parliament, there is, as Collins's research indicates, little evidence that its cultural life diminished significantly. While it is true that musical life in eighteenth-century Dublin surpassed 'in both quantum and quality'[8] that of the nineteenth century, it is equally true, as Joseph Ryan says, that 'there is a tendency to magnify the grandeur of the period beyond the level that can be corroborated by scholarly research.'[9] The music presented by Dublin societies in the middle of the nineteenth century often equalled that of the earlier period with regard to the music played and the artists performing (with the exception of the unique phenomenon of *Messiah*). It was in fact the withdrawal of the earlier patronage that created a space in which such middle-class entrepreneurs and philanthropists could evolve their own institutions and practices. By 1861 the *Irish Times* could say that the IAM's ambition of establishing an 'institution for musical culture analogous to that in London and similar to those which are supported by the State in all the principal continental towns' had already created 'a permanent School of Art.'[10]

There is a considerable distinction to be drawn between the Irish Academy of Music and other 'academies' of this and earlier periods. In 1757 Garret Wellesley, later the Earl of Mornington, established a 'Musical Academy' at the Fishamble Street Music Hall. It was a choral and orchestral society, exclusive of professional musicians or teachers, performing largely for charitable purposes. It continued until 1778, when it became (under statute) the Charitable Musical Society.[11] Although it was extremely limited in scope and motivation, this is probably the nearest equivalent to a public service educational initiative until the foundation of the IAM. Other self-styled academies, including Logier's, were commercial enterprises for the private gain of their proprietors. These include the establishments of Mrs Allen (Logier's daughter), the Corri family, William Wilkinson, and their many successors and competitors. The move can be seen as consonant with the emergence of a public school of art education in Dublin, promoted by the RDS from 1745, in common with establishments in, for example, Paris, Rome, St Petersburg, and Florence, as contrasted with the existence of private, commercially operated schools of art, of which there were many in Dublin at that time.[12]

The original proposal envisaged 'an Academy for the cultivation of instrumental music,' the principal requirement being the training of orchestral musicians in both wind and strings. It was argued that, in addition to serving the interests of the Dublin musical societies, this would provide a means to 'suitable and profitable employment'—the utility of which would be successfully demonstrated by the Academy within fifteen years of its foundation. It was also suggested that it would provide an opportunity for the choristers of the three Dublin cathedrals—St Patrick's, Christ Church, and the Catholic Pro-Cathedral of St Mary (which had opened in Marlborough Street in 1825)—to 'perfect and complete their musical education,' besides acquiring some instrumental proficiency. To include the Pro-Cathedral in such a prospectus, less than twenty years after Emancipation, was an act both of ecumenism and of realism.[13]

It is also possible that the incipient Academy drew on the model of the Royal Academy of Music in London, which argued that its establishment in 1822 had resulted firstly in the extension of musical knowledge, secondly in the improvement of church music, thirdly in the music of the military bands, and fourthly in the expansion of the manufacture and sale of instruments.[14]

The interested parties in such an endeavour would be precisely those musical societies described above by Collins—groups that, although largely amateur in status, included some singers of professional standard, such as

John Stanford and Hercules and Emily MacDonnell. The concert of 1847 for the relief of the poor may well have concentrated the minds of the Academy's founders on the possibilities for coalescence. ('When', asked Hercules MacDonnell, 'will eleven Dublin Musical Societies meet together again in harmony?')[15] Aware of the need to support such an undertaking by means of subscription, they called on 'the active co-operation' of the interested parties. While the fees would be substantial (from three to six guineas a year, or £120 to £240 in today's money), the institution could not survive without voluntary donations. A donor of five pounds would become a governor; ten pounds would make him or her a governor for life; while twenty pounds would secure a life governorship, with free admission for self and three others to all events. The annual subscription, however, was only five shillings (ten pounds in today's money). A subscription was not simply a subvention to enable the Academy to bridge the deficit between fees and costs: it was a form of fostering or, in the original sense of the word, sponsoring. In appealing for subscribers, the chairman of the Committee would say in 1852 that a subscription 'would enable a citizen to forward any well-deserving musical pupil,'[16] and in fact in 1866 we find Joseph Robinson emphasising to the Lord Lieutenant that 'one of the cleverest pupils in the . . . Academy would fail to obtain a proper musical education if patrons of the institution, acquainted with the circumstance, had not subscribed for the purpose.'[17]

There were to be four classes: one for violin and tenor (viola); one for cello and double bass; one for reed (woodwind); and one for brass band. 'It is in contemplation, when the funds of the Institution permit, to have other departments. A Class for the study of the Pianoforte and Organ will be the first to be added.' Examinations were to be held half-yearly, at Christmas and midsummer, 'at which latter examination Prizes will be awarded to the most deserving Pupils; and in cases of superior merit a Scholarship will be awarded in each department, entitling the holder to gratuitous instruction for two years'—although this was an ambition that remained unrealised for many years.

The certification of students was envisaged from the outset.

> On leaving the Academy the Students will receive, according to their merits, certificates as to their conduct, the studies they have been engaged in, and their general fitness to undertake the duties of the Professing of Music. All who receive the highest order of these certificates (whose services are expected where the interests of the Institution are concerned) will be registered as Associates, and entitled (under the control of the Committee) to the following privileges:—The power of recommending Candidates for admission to the Academy; admission to the general Rehearsals and Concerts; and a claim to the aid and assistance of the Institution in their professional career.

Another feature of the original conception of the Academy was the participation of student-teachers, 'those who are most capable' being appointed 'sub-Professors'.

IRISH ACADEMY OF MUSIC.

CHAIRMAN OF COMMITTEE,

Walter Berwick, Esq, Q C.

VICE CHAIRMAN,

The Rev Charles Graves, F T C D.

COMMITTEE,

Wm E Hudson, Esq	Richard J Greene, Esq
Wyndham Goold, Esq	George Schoales, Esq
Doctor Smith	S J Pigott, Esq
Henry Bussell, Esq	Francis Robinson, Esq
Walter Sweetman, Esq	John Stanford, Esq
Joseph Robinson, Esq	

TREASURER,

Wyndham Goold, Esq.

SECRETARY, PRO TEM.,

John Stanford, Esq, 3 Upper Fitzwilliam-street.

Persons desirous of becoming Pupils of the Academy are requested to make application to the Secretary or to any Member of the Committee.

The following Professors have been already engaged, and Classes are now in process of formation:—

Two Classes	...	..	Violin
One ditto	...	...	Viola
One ditto	...	...	Violoncello
One ditto	...	..	Double Bass

PROFESSOR OF VIOLIN,

Mr R M Levey

(Leader and Director of Music, Theatre Royal, and Leader of Antient-Concert Society).

VIOLONCELLO,

Mr J Lidel

(Principal Violoncello of Philharmonic and Antient Concerts).

The Committee are about concluding an engagement with an eminent Professor to superintend the Classes for Wind Instruments. Persons wishing to join these Classes are also requested to make application to the Secretary or any Member of the Committee, who will give every information as to Terms, &c. &c.

TERMS.

First Class to pay Six Guineas per Annum, and are bound to give their services gratuitously at the Concerts of the Academy so long as they continue Pupils.

Second Class to pay Three Guineas per Annum, and are bound to Give their services gratuitously at whatever Concerts the Committee of Management may please to make engagements during the first four years.

Who were the chief movers in this initiative? Many of the self-appointed committee, such as Francis Robinson and his brother Joseph, were deeply involved in Dublin musical life, yet almost all came from different backgrounds, motivations, and outlooks. The Robinsons' father (also Francis) had founded the Sons of Handel, was one of the initiators in 1826 of the Philharmonic Society, and was organist of both Christ Church and St Patrick's Cathedrals—in which he was succeeded by his third son, John (1812–44). Of his four sons, who formed a remarkable vocal quartet, the eldest, Francis (1799–1872), was Charles Villiers Stanford's first harmony teacher and had produced an edition of *Moore's Melodies*.[18]

The youngest son, Joseph (1816–98), was one of the most significant and controversial figures in the progress of the Academy during its first fifty years. As founder of the Society of Antient Concerts (in 1834, at the age of eighteen) and the Dublin Musical Society (in 1876), and as conductor of the Philharmonic concerts, Joseph Robinson was a central point of reference in Dublin musical life generally and in particular as a choral trainer and conductor. He was described by Stanford as 'both by culture and ability one of the best musicians of our time,'[19] someone who enjoyed the friendship of Thalberg, Rubinstein, and Joachim, frequent performers with the Philharmonic.[20] As a friend of Mendelssohn he was, in Stanford's words, 'in direct possession of the traditions of . . . execution' of Mendelssohn's oratorios[21] and became a remarkable interpreter of *St Paul* and *Elijah* (of which he had attended the first performance in Birmingham in 1846). Mendelssohn orchestrated 'Hear My Prayer' for Robinson, specifically for performance by the Antient Concerts Society.[22] In 1847 he conducted the first performance outside Germany of Mendelssohn's *Antigone*.[23] His first wife, Fanny Arthur (1831–79), was a talented pianist, a pupil of Thalberg and Sterndale Bennett and a member of the Academy's teaching staff.[24] He was also a prolific composer and arranger: his 'Sylvan Hours: A Pastoral Scene', like many of his works, was a setting of words by John F. Waller LLD; he also set words by Henry Hudson and—almost obligatorily—Thomas Moore, many of which were made for the Strollers. Fanny Arthur was also highly respected for her sacred cantata 'God Is Love' and a charming *mélodie pour piano*, 'Le Chant du Moulin'.

Henry Bussell (*c.* 1807–82) was in business with Francis Robinson junior and William Robinson (the second of the brothers) as a piano dealer at 7 Westmoreland Street, Dublin—the 'Harmonic Saloon' and later the 'Royal Harmonic Saloon'; their advertisements stated that their pianos were 'selected at the eminent manufactories in London by Mr. Joseph Robinson.'[25] (William Robinson also owned a foundry in Parkgate Street, Dublin, which supplied materials for the renovation of the Antient Concert Rooms, which, according to George Osborne, earned him the nickname 'the harmonious blacksmith'.)[26] Bussell was founder-secretary in 1826 of the Philharmonic, with which in 1856 he conducted the Irish premiere of Beethoven's Ninth Symphony. According to the anonymous author of the gossipy *Recollections of Dublin Castle and of Dublin Society*, Bussell was 'a name anything but suggestive of his style of conducting, which was of a torpid sort . . . the orchestra, in fact, usually conducted *him*.'[27] He was also one of the founders (with Lidel, John Robinson, W. E. Hudson, and W. S. Conran) in 1842 of the Metropolitan Choral Society.[28]

Samuel Pigott (d. 1853), the founder of a music firm at 112 Grafton Street, whose name still survives in Dublin, was a cellist, described by R. M. Levey as having 'exquisite tone, faultless execution and classic style,' ranking with Robert Lindley, then the greatest of English cellists;[29] he was also secretary of the Anacreontic Society. Bussell and Pigott provided committee rooms for their respective societies at their premises. Pigott owned a Stradivarius cello, which, after his death, was sold to Piatti and was played at concerts in Ireland in 1997 by its present owner, the Mexican Carlos Prieto.

William Elliott Hudson (1796–1853) and his brother Henry, sons of a United Irishman who was also state dentist, were folklore collectors and arrangers of folk songs; William composed music for 'The Mourning of the Dead' ('Who fears to speak of ninety-eight?') by John Kells Ingram and published the *Citizen*, a short-lived newspaper, in 1840–41. Charlotte Dolby sang his 'Your Loss Will Break My Heart' to 'rapturous applause' at a Philharmonic concert. Like John Edward Pigot (who enters the story in 1856), he was a close associate of Thomas Davis. He was also typical of this coterie in that he was a barrister, later a taxing master, and closely linked with O'Connell, who in 1835 had appointed him (and David R. Pigot) to act on his behalf in electoral matters.[30] In 1833 he had been a member of the commission presided over by Louis Perrin to inquire into abuses in the municipal corporations.[31] He founded the Irish Archaeological Society in 1840 and the Celtic Society in 1845, which amalgamated in 1853 to form the Ossianic Society. In 1825 he published an article in the *Dublin Philosophical Journal and Scientific Review* proposing a 'Universal Alphabet', not at all unlike that suggested a century later by Shaw. It is believed that shortly before his early death he became a Catholic.[32]

By contrast with these quasi-political figures, the Cambridge-born John Smith (1797–1861) had recently been appointed to the chair of music at TCD, which had been vacant for forty years since the death of the first incumbent, the Earl of Mornington. The author of *Cathedral Music* and of *A Treatise on the Theory and Practice of Music: With the Principles of Harmony and Composition and an Approved Method of Learning to Sing by Note and in Parts Intended as a Class-Book for Academies*,[33] Smith received an honorary DMus (TCD) in 1827 and held the honorary positions of Master of the Royal State Band in Ireland, Chief Composer of State Music in Ireland, and Composer of the Chapel Royal (Dublin Castle). He had published a collection of *Irish Minstrelsy* and composed an oratorio, *The Revelation*,[34] and had carried on a 'Logerian' academy since 1816 with his uncle, John Spray; he was therefore representative of the cross-section of music-makers who both taught and studied, both pursuing the 'classical' traditions and trying to approximate to the native ones.[35] His son, Richard, and his daughter-in-law were noted singers, and his grandsons, Sidney and Wellesley, were later enrolled as pupils in the Academy.[36]

The remaining 'ordinary' members of the Committee were John Schoales, a barrister and a founder of the Antient Concerts; Walter Sweetman MRIA (1797–1882), also a barrister, whose father, John Sweetman, had been involved in the 1798 rebellion (Walter was chairman of the RDS Committee of Manufactures and, with Petrie and Thomas Hutton, a member of the committee of the National Exhibition in Cork in 1852); and Richard Jonas Greene, father of the bass-baritone Harry Plunket Greene and the diplomat Sir Conyngham Greene, who was the son of a law lord and who in his turn would become involved with the Academy in 1856.

The treasurer of the Academy was to be Wyndham Goold (1814–54), a barrister, son of a master in Chancery and a brother-in-law of the Earl of Dunraven of Adare Manor and of Sir Robert Gore-Booth of Lissadell. He was MP for the safe 'family' seat of County Limerick from 1850 until his early death from apoplexy.[37] (He was succeeded as treasurer in 1850 by William George Dubedat.) Announced as secretary 'pro tem' was John Stanford, father of Charles Villiers Stanford, a lawyer and amateur cellist who would have become an opera singer but for the objections of his family. He became examiner in the Court of Chancery and one of the finest bass voices of his time, singing on occasion with the Franco-Irish Luigi Lablache[38] (father-in-law of Thalberg), his son Federico and Jenny Lind during their several visits to Dublin.[39] He was also an expert on explosives, and had an explosive temper.

These enthusiasts chose two distinguished members of the establishment to represent them as chairman and vice-chairman. The chairman was Walter Berwick QC (1800–68), a nephew of Henry Grattan, a leading lawyer 'devoted to acts of charity and philanthropy'[40] who was to become Serjeant-at-Law in 1855 and judge of the Court of Bankruptcy in 1859. He died in the Abergele train disaster of 1868. With Walter Sweetman, J. E. Pigot and his father, David, Maziere Brady, Thomas Hutton, Sir Colman O'Loghlen and J. H. Monahan—all senior figures in the history of the Academy and many of them sharing a common membership of the recently formed St Stephen's Green Club[41]—he was an organiser of the Industrial Exhibition in Dublin in 1853, which provided the impetus for the establishment of the National Gallery of Ireland.[42] His brother Edward became president of Queen's College, Galway.

The vice-chairman was Charles Graves (1812–99),[43] scion of a long-established Church of Ireland clerical family, at that time professor of mathematics at TCD and later secretary of the RIA (then vigorously collecting early manuscripts) and Bishop of Limerick, the father of Alfred Perceval Graves and grandfather of Robert Graves. He became an expert on ogham and, in addition to his scholarly and church pursuits, was a founder-member of the TCD Choral Society. His son Alfred Perceval wrote in his memoirs that their house was 'a literary and musical centre,' visited by figures such as Lord Dunraven, Sir Thomas Larcom, and the Joy, Blackburne and Stanford families.[44] In 1852 *Saunders's News-Letter*, referring to the IAM as 'a national and highly useful institute,' averred that 'when we find such men as the Chief Baron, Mr. Greene of the Chancery

Bar, Rev. Charles Graves . . . and a host of others of a high order of intellect, sustaining and promoting it, we must regard it as deserving of the support of the public generally.'[45] Almost twenty years later he would lend his stature to the founding of a 'ladies' college' and was instrumental in obtaining the agreement of the Princess of Wales to its being named after her: Alexandra College.[46]

The question must be asked whether the formation of the Irish Academy of Music was merely an attempt to bolster a sagging Ascendancy hegemony, with its adherence to European upper-class culture. Joseph Ryan observes that while 'Ireland appeared possessed of many of the ingredients necessary for a musical recrudescence,' there was little new to show either for its store of folk music or for its eighteenth-century musical energy: 'no musical infrastructure, no scheme of training, little regular employment, and no creative tradition.'[47] Was this academy therefore a regression rather than a recrudescence? Was it part of what Marie McCarthy calls 'an educational system that, in practice, sought to inculcate the cultural values of Anglo-Irish society'?[48]

On the negative side, the fact that the original committee consisted almost entirely of Protestants might suggest, *prima facie*, that exclusivity was intended or, on second inspection, that the members might adopt a patronising attitude to education. The easy connection between them (they lived mostly within a stone's throw of each other in the Merrion-Fitzwilliam axis of Dublin's residential squares) also suggests the same kind of social and cultural empathy that supported the impetus of the literary revival forty years later. As F. S. L. Lyons said of the latter phenomenon, 'this possibility of discussing and planning in private without the distraction of public meetings and committees . . . allowed the new movement to develop so fast and . . . also, it must be said, gave it from the outset a distinctly autocratic character.'[49] And it may have been too great a reliance on the self-sufficiency of too small a group of enthusiasts that brought the Academy near to closure in 1854–55 and that did indeed necessitate public meetings in later years, introducing the Academy to a wider net of potential supporters as well as critics.

By the natural laws of association of the time, the founders could legitimately be regarded as an élite or coterie; conversely, however closely knit they may have been, there is no evidence that they acted as a clique or cabal. It was stated in the prospectus that 'Candidates for admission must be recommended by a Subscriber,' and in this way the Committee was indeed exercising a form of social control; but this was normal for the time and was also a practice in the RAM that continued into the twentieth century.[50] In fact the tenor of their educational philosophy was consonant with that of the educationalist Sir Thomas Wyse MP, who, recognising the changes that had taken place and were to come, also realised that a radical re-examination of educational methods and procedures would be necessary (no doubt similar to those faced by educationalists in the light of today's technological revolution). Already in 1836 Wyse had called for a national system of music education, which would integrate music into general public education, with higher education including a properly founded and regulated conservatoire, believing that the lack of such a system, coupled with 'the jobbing system of our professors,' was responsible for the dearth of musical expression and consequently the lack of aesthetics as a 'secondary morality'.[51] And in 1835 in the House of Commons he had declared (although his remarks fell on deaf or inhospitable ears):

> We live in a new world, and with other minds than those which have preceded us . . . It is not enough to follow precedents, we must create them . . . Facility of communication renders us more sensible for every impulse—public opinion has acquired more activity, extension and energy—combination, for any given cause, is infinitely more easy.[52]

On the positive side, another interpretation of the founders' motivations is that of benevolence. If music could be regarded as a civilising element, then the process of acculturation (the transfer of a cultural view of life, and of cultural skills, from one part of society to another) might be seen as part of a 'Protestant crusade' in educational terms, parallel to the deployment of resources to make Ireland a more modern and capable place. There must be a suspicion that, in addition to furthering their own musical ends, the founders were attempting to 'elevate' those less culturally fortunate than themselves.

Furthermore, underlying the basic and immediate motivation of the Academy's founders, which would see a return to a more stable and dependable musical life, was no doubt a more ideological desire to make this national recrudescence a reality. As 'John Eglinton' (William Magee) was to write in 1902, 'the modern Irishman whether he liked it or not was the son of the *mariage de convenance* of the Union'[53] and therefore constituted 'a young nationality, with a world of new enterprise and purpose in his soul, new thought and invention in his brain, passion as yet unexpended in his heart.'[54] It was a combination of necessity and opportunity, which the Academy typified in its cultivation of the art of the possible.

The identification of resources, which Robert Kane had pioneered in material terms[55] and bodies such as the RDS had pioneered in artistic, agricultural and industrial matters,[56] was a process of mapping strengths indigenous to Ireland and therefore suitable for a policy of self-reliance.[57] The major exhibitions in Cork and Dublin in 1852–53 were a part of this, intended 'to display to the country its own resources and capabilities—to inspire confidence—to remove doubt—to banish prejudice.'[58] To the same end the Repeal Association (and, after the split with O'Connell on the issue of the Queen's Colleges, the Young Ireland Confederation) formed a quasi-parliamentary gathering—an opposition in waiting—by means of which the intelligentsia in a slow, and largely invisible, fashion applied itself to assessing the changes necessary in Ireland and the means at the disposal of whatever agencies would be responsible for initiating and managing that change. Lawyers, doctors, educationalists and the new profession of economists fed the political classes with a digest of the country's conditions, needs and resources, of which the many pamphlets assembled for the use of the Repeal Association are typical.[59]

Francis Brady, who, from his appearance on the Academy scene in 1856, was the most important figure in its entire history on the administrative side (as Esposito was on the artistic), was the author of three such pamphlets, on borough franchises, borough elections, and county franchises, of which the last, dated 29 April 1844, says that it

> contains an unanswerable vindication of the complaints of the people of Ireland, that the British parliament has not done them equal and impartial justice.[60]

Brady, like other members of the Parliamentary Committee that prepared these reports, such as Colman O'Loghlen and Henry Grattan (junior) MP (himself a subscriber to the Academy and, as proprietor of the *Freeman's Journal*, immensely important to its public relations strategy),[61] was typical of the rising generation of the intelligentsia. He came from a legal background (his father, Maziere Brady, was Lord Chancellor),[62] he was vehement in his concern for the reform of the legal profession[63] as well as the administration of his country, and he was deeply involved in the pursuit, or recovery, of the Irish heritage.[64]

Whether in the pursuit of Irish music or of European art music, these people shared what has been called a 'messianic tradition',[65] the ambition of 'restoring' Ireland to a former glory—however notional that might be; and, even though it was not directly applied to the day-to-day running of the IAM, there is ample evidence of their serious involvement in such a 'recrudescence'. Their motivation—stretching well into the later decades of the century—originated as much in the cultural dynamism of Young Ireland as in the practical needs of Dublin's musical life. Joep Leerssen's view, that 'the quest for national identity . . . was national in its trans-partisan agenda,'[66] is applicable to the striking coalition of interests present throughout the history of the Academy—a coalition in which the tapestry of the rapidly changing establishment, landed gentry, professional city Protestants, Huguenot immigrants, the rising Catholic professional and commercial classes, the families of artists, politicians, clerics, and academics, was consistently enriched by the arrival of new blood released by the ambitions and tensions of the emergent cultural, social and political realities. In 1870 the IAM would inform Gladstone that it 'has united in its favour more individuals of different ranks and opinions on all subjects than usually combine for any undertaking in Ireland.'[67]

Joseph Ryan believes that 'there is a decided contrast between the devotion of the group of which Petrie was a leading member and that to which Joseph Robinson was aligned,'[68] suggesting that whereas Petrie wished to uncover the treasures of Irish folklore, the Robinson 'coterie' turned its face away from such a 'narrow form' towards 'the whole European experience of music . . . untouched by any desire to create a divaricated national idiom.' In fact Graves, Sweetman and Bussell were members of both the first Academy of 1848 and the Society for the Preservation and Publication of the Melodies of Ireland, founded in 1851 with Petrie as its president. In addition, Thomas Beatty, F. W. Brady, Robert Callwell, J. E. Pigot, Thomas Rice Henn and W. R. (later Sir William) Wilde, all members of the 'Petrie' Society, became responsible members of, or subscribers to, the reconstituted Academy of 1856. Although William Hudson had died before the 'Petrie' Society had borne fruit, his brother and collaborator Henry was on its Council. And William Stokes, the Earl of Dunraven and Sir Alexander MacDonnell,[69] all stalwart supporters of the Academy, were also involved in the 'Petrie' initiative.[70]

Far from excluding an interest in indigenous or 'traditional' music from the Academy, these men, from a wide variety of backgrounds, brought a strong consciousness of it to their board-room and showed themselves perfectly capable of pursuing such divergence. In common they had the characteristics of an incipient intelligentsia, orienting mass sentiment towards independent thought. Even though it had little direct contact with Mazzini's Giovine Italia (1831) or La Giovine Europa (1834), the movement nicknamed Young Ireland was fired by the same certainty: that a separate entity existed with a moral claim to independence, which could be brought to national consciousness by means of a common cultural outlook. R. M. Levey, in his *Annals of the Theatre Royal*, recalled that on 3 September 1855 *Il trovatore* had been produced, and made the point that 'the music of "Young Italy" had scarcely yet been heard' and was 'a novel and startling event in Dublin,' the 'matchless genius' of Viardot's Azucena coming in for particular praise.[71]

The philosophy of Young Ireland, so close in literal terms to that of 'Irish Ireland' sixty years later yet so far from it ideologically, centred, in Davis's view, on the shaping of a sense of identity through cultural activity. It was natural, therefore, that the Petrie initiative of reclamation would concentrate on ensuring the survival of the distinctive cultural hallmark of Irish identity that famine and emigration had largely eliminated from the social landscape. Petrie in fact had adopted the motto of the *Nation* ('to create an Irish public opinion racy of the soil') as an apologia for his research on the heels of the famine devastation. 'I could not suppress a misgiving that . . . there no longer existed amongst my countrymen such sufficient amount of a racy feeling of nationality and cultivation of mind.'[72]

Davis himself had condemned the influence of European music on the Irish imagination—'paltry scented things from Italy.'[73] Like many a critic in later decades bemoaning the absence of Irish-born composition, Davis identified the lack of contemporary music in succession to that of Carolan: 'Those we have do not compose Irish-like music, nor for Ireland. Their rewards are from a foreign public . . . Balfe is very sweet and Rooke very emphatic, but not one passion or association in Ireland's heart would answer to their songs.'[74] Harry White has called the alternative songs that Davis promoted in the *Nation* 'hymns of romantic nationalism . . . [that] exemplify the function of music in a sectarian culture.'[75] By contrast, the pragmatism of the early Academy in fact led it away from sectarianism: instead it demanded of necessity that musical nationalism (as a means of transmission of cultural values) be less visible than the direct transmission of musical skills. Separation from foreign influence and independence from foreign rule were in fact different pursuits, and it was possible for each to be present or absent in the Academy's internal transactions and its dealings with educational and political agencies without regard to the other. Predominantly, however, the music studied in the Academy was non-nationalist and non-colonial. English music was studied, as were 'things from Italy'; so too was earlier music and contemporary music, in fact music across the cultural spectrum of what we would today regard as the classical repertoire.

It is what Joseph Ryan calls 'the protean character of nationalism . . . the ability to adapt to changing circumstances'[76] that informed the pragmatism of the Academy's founders ('a few gentlemen who loved music wisely and well,' as the *Freeman's Journal* would call them)[77] and enabled them to overcome their disappointments in 1854–55. Anglo-Ireland, as a hyphenated culture, cannot have had a more successful manifestation than the creation of the Academy, while, in Harry White's words, identifying 'the function of music in Ascendancy thought as a dislocated articulation of two cultures.'[78]

To illustrate this we might give examples of the music and the social connections enjoyed by such people in their everyday lives. On 16 February 1848, two weeks before the Academy opened, a musical at-home took place at 4 Upper Merrion Street, Dublin, the home of David Walker, Judge-Advocate General and neighbour of Walter Berwick, which was typical of the private entertainment enjoyed by a mixed coterie of professional and amateur musicians. From the professionals, Elizabeth Meeke (another Merrion Street neighbour and a subscriber to the Academy) and Henrietta Flynn, both of them teachers of Charles Villiers Stanford, played 'Hommage à Handel' by their teacher, Moscheles, and Miss Flynn also played four of Mendelssohn's Songs without Words, a nocturne by Chopin, and an étude by Carl Meyer. Madame Morosini (later a staff member of the RIAM, whose name is still commemorated in the Morosini-Whelan School of Dancing) sang the cavatina 'Ah, quel giorno' from Rossini's *Semiramide*; and Joseph Lidel played his own solo composition 'Robert le Diable'. On occasion, visiting celebrities, such as Mrs Sims Reeves and the harp virtuoso Charles Oberthür, would put in an appearance at such gatherings.[79]

From the amateurs, the MacDonnells (Emily 'had a superb voice, and could sing anything in the prima donna's *répertoire*'[80]), John Stanford and Robert and William Tennant[81] joined in quartets, quintets and choruses from Bellini's *La sonnambula*, Donizetti's *Lucia di Lammermoor*, and Verdi's *Ernani*. From surviving records of the period 1848–62[82] the chief participants in such at-homes, in addition to those mentioned, were Joseph Robinson, Capt. Sandes, three members of the Mayne family (Miss P., Miss A., and Miss Sarah), members of the Henn family, Anna Walker, Susan Griffith, Capt. W. Palliser, Maj. Hume, Mrs Edward Geale, James Strathearne Close (a barrister), Mr Brereton, William Stokes, and Wilhelm Elsner. Sir Jocelyn Coghill and Dr J. P. Mahaffy each took part once.[83] Of these, Coghill, Elsner, the Maynes, Henns, Geales, Stokeses, Morosinis, Sandes and Palliser would become involved in the Academy as teachers, students, governors, and subscribers.[84]

In addition there was considerable common membership of musical activities (as we have noted above in the case of the 'Petrie' Society). In 1861, for example, Francis Robinson was treasurer of the Philharmonic Society, with Henry Hudson as a member of the Committee. T. A. Jones was librarian, Henry Mecredy treasurer and John Norwood secretary of the University of Dublin Choral Society. Justice Blackburne was president of the Antient Concerts, with Lord Dunraven and Lord Monck and the Lord Chief Baron, Greene, as vice-presidents, Henry Hudson, W. G. Dubedat and T. A. Jones as trustees, John Stanford, Francis Robinson and Robert Berkeley on the Committee, Richard Smith as librarian, John Kincaid as treasurer, and Robert Exham as honorary secretary. The brothers Hudson, John and William Robinson and Bussell were all involved in the Metropolitan Choral Society (founded 1842).[85] Judges Berwick and Brady were trustees of the 'Royal Art-Union of Ireland, established 1858 under the auspices of the Committee of the Irish Institution.' All these names recur in the minutes and literature of the Irish Academy of Music.

It will be clear from this brief picture of Dublin musical organisation that there was a heavy reliance on legal and aristocratic circles to provide social respectability, and on a relatively small group of enthusiasts to actually conduct the affairs of the societies. But it also points to the high degree of musical involvement and accomplishment of all concerned in pursuing an aesthetic life that they found rewarding in addition to its social attractions.

Following the circulation and publication of its prospectus, the Committee placed advertisements in the *Freeman's Journal* on 5 February 1848, announcing that R. M. Levey, 'Leader and Director of Music, Theatre Royal and Leader of Antient Concert Society,' and Joseph Lidel, 'Principal Violoncellist of Philharmonic and Antient Concerts,' had been engaged for violin, viola, cello and double-bass classes, and that 'the Committee are about concluding an engagement with an eminent Professor to superintend the Classes for Wind Instruments.' It was stated that students 'are bound to give their services gratuitously at the Concerts of the Academy'—a regulation that persists to the present.[86] Three days later, on 8 February, though his identity was not disclosed, the engagement of the wind professor was confirmed, to teach the complete range of woodwind and brass as well as 'double drums'. Presumably, since the orchestra was required to complement the existing choral talent, vocal studies were not envisaged at this point, nor, for the same reason, was there any urgency about establishing a piano class.

Richard Michael Levey (1811–99) had been appointed leader of the Theatre Royal orchestra in 1834, a position he retained until the destruction of the theatre by fire in 1880. 'He was a rough player, but an admirable leader of an orchestra,' Charles Stanford recalled, 'and often as a conductor managed to make sows' ears resemble silk purses.'[87] The composer of over a hundred overtures for plays staged in the Theatre Royal and elsewhere, he had conducted the Irish premiere of Balfe's *The Maid of Artois* in 1840 and, like many others, published several volumes of *Dance Music of Ireland* (1858–78). He was also secretary for a time of the Dublin Madrigal Society and of the charitable Musical Fund Society, for whom Catherine Hayes sang in 1856.[88] Born O'Shaughnessy, he had dropped his surname, Stanford tells us, 'for what he considered to be a more musical one. Joachim was much amused to see a Levi, of whom he knew many in Germany, with a snub nose and a most Hibernian grin.'[89] He had been a fellow-student of Balfe's at James Barton's establishment, and they remained lifelong friends.[90] He had a large family—one source suggests twenty children by three wives[91]—one of whom, William Charles Levey (1837–94), became conductor and musical director at Drury Lane and Covent Garden, his twin, John (1837–91), being an author and comedian.[92] A Richard Levey appeared as a young solo harpist with the Madrigal Society in 1856,[93] while another son, R. M. Levey junior, adopted the stage name Paganini Redivivus. Levey was also the grandfather of a later Academy teacher, Hubert Rooney.[94]

It is curious that, though giving the secretary's address, to which enquiries were to be directed (John Stanford then lived at 3 Upper Fitzwilliam Street, shortly afterwards moving to 2 Herbert Street, where C. V. Stanford was born), the advertisement made no mention of the address at which classes would take place. The Academy in fact held its first classes at the Antient Concert Rooms, a former gasworks in Great Brunswick Street (Pearse Street), acquired and rebuilt by the Antient Concerts Society, and we must suppose that, as the focus of orchestral music at the time, the venue would have been obvious to most. Even in May 1848, when, after two months, additional classes were announced in the *Freeman's Journal*,[95] the Academy's premises would still have been a matter of conjecture for the uninitiated. This advertisement again alluded to the formation of classes for wind instruments, suggesting that the previous announcement had been premature or that enrolments had been insufficient.

On 14 June 1849 the Antient Concerts Society gave a benefit in aid of the fledgling Academy. This is notable for two reasons: firstly because fund-raising events of this kind became a vital third source of income for the next fifteen years, and secondly because the attendance of the Lord Lieutenant and his wife, the Countess of Clarendon, marked the opening of an ambivalent relationship with the British government in Ireland that was to continue up to and include the Governor-Generalship of the Irish Free State. In the same year, during the controversial visit of Queen Victoria,[96] Stanford, Joseph and Fanny Robinson and Hercules and Emily MacDonnell played and sang for her at the Viceregal Lodge (now Áras an Uachtaráin), a service that the MacDonnells and three of the Robinson brothers repeated during her visit of 1853.[97] In 1851 and 1853 the then Lord Lieutenant, the Earl of St Germans, similarly smiled on the Academy; the connection proved valuable in the eighteen-sixties when the Academy, through the good offices of the Lord Lieutenant, was pressing on the Treasury its case for a grant.

The benefit concert was extensively advertised throughout early June and supported editorially by the *Freeman's Journal*, which pointed out the valuable work of the Antient Concerts Society in raising musical con-

Antient Concert Hall.

sciousness and standards in 'our ruined city'[98] and thus 'inciting' a sense of national pride in the achievement of local talent. *Saunders's News-Letter* also exhorted 'all of those who wish to found and perpetuate useful and civilising institutions in the country' to support the concert, and asserted that music entices youth 'from idle and vicious enjoyment . . . leading them to seek in the social circles of home innocent recreation and entertainment, in companionship with those whose influence is always for good . . . The benefit of such an institution will be the means of disseminating a knowledge of music amongst the humbler classes in Ireland, thereby elevating them, making them happier and, of course, more prosperous.'[99]

The concert, attended, besides the viceregal party, by the Lord Chancellor (Sir Maziere Brady) and his daughters and the Chief Justice (Lord Blackburne), consisted chiefly of vocal numbers sung by, among others, Stanford, Francis and John Robinson, and a visiting soprano, Charlotte Dolby,[100] in madrigals, quartets, and extracts from *Macbeth*[101] and Haydn's *The Seasons*. The value of the event to the IAM may be judged from the fact that a benefit given by Jullien in aid of the Sick and Indigent Roomkeepers' Society in April 1848 raised £551, half the gross receipts of the concert.[102]

To demonstrate the standards and progress of the students, the Academy's practice of holding a 'half-yearly examination' (more accurately a public exhibition), usually in January and July of each year, was in effect a 'public practical test of its efficiency and success in promoting scientific musical culture,' as the *Irish Times* was to describe it some years later.[103] This had been the practice of the RAM since its foundation,[104] but it may also have been prompted in the incipient IAM by the fact that 'Mrs Allen's Academy' held similar students' exhibitions, and the Academy may have adopted this means of attracting pupils not least in order to counter the opposition. The repertoire at such an exhibition was fairly dependable: violin ensembles from

Spohr, a brass quintet,[105] violin solos from Rode, an 'Irish Melody and Planxty' for solo violin, and piano solos. The inclusion in the programme of overtures—Boïeldieu's *La Dame blanche*, which was to become a favourite war-horse, and Weber's *Oberon*—suggests that the Academy had already succeeded in forming an orchestra, however modest. Evidence from the newspapers tells us that a Herr Klausman had been recruited as a wind teacher, thus making a full orchestral presence more feasible.[106]

A serious blow befell the IAM only nine months after its opening. On 20 November 1848 the *Freeman's Journal* announced that protracted indisposition 'compels Mr. Liddel [*sic*] to retire from amongst us and seek in his native land that restoration to health which he has ceased to hope for here.' It was not to be until 1851 that a worthwhile successor was found, in the person of Wilhelm Elsner, recruited from Frankfurt, largely, it is suggested, through the efforts of John Stanford.[107] Elsner family tradition has it that, as a 22-year-old, he may have been actively involved in the revolution of 1848 in his native city, which he certainly witnessed at first hand, and that there may have been a family connection with Josef Elsner, the Polish teacher of Chopin.[108]

In 1851 the Antient Concerts gave another benefit for the Academy, this time consisting simply of excerpts from *Messiah*. Drawing its readers' attention to the event, the *Freeman's Journal* solicited support for 'this admirable institution', which

> supplied a desideratum long wished for by many who recognised and appreciated the musical talent richly, though wildly, exuberant amongst the youth of Ireland, and requiring only judicious cultivation for its successful development . . . The opening of the academy may be said to form an era in the history of musical art in Ireland—one from which may yet be dated the restoration of her eminence as a musical nation.[109]

Saunders's News-Letter also supported the continuing initiative, publishing extracts from the Committee's recent report that make it clear that, despite the fact that 'they have had a year of great difficulty to struggle through' (largely through a falling off in subscriptions), student numbers had greatly increased. There were now twelve in the violin class, ten in the cello, and five in the brass.[110] With these forces, the brave little orchestra was able to perform a half-yearly examination in June 1851, with Beethoven's Symphony in C (No. 1) and the overtures to Mozart's *Don Giovanni* and *The Marriage of Figaro* and Méhul's *Joseph*.[111]

It should be noted that two of the junior performers were the sons of R. M. Levey, one, William, aged twelve, playing Hummel's Piano Concerto in A minor, op. 85, 'in a manner which reminds us . . . of Osborne,'[112] the other, Richard, aged fourteen, playing a violin solo by Mendelssohn. Others were Masters Hughes (violin), Woodward (violin—a recently published Romance Sans Paroles by the young Vieuxtemps), J. Gunn (cello), and W. Raymond (horn), while Catherine Cruise sang 'Que le voce'.

However, the Academy had decided that students alone did not constitute a sufficient attraction to the public and, announcing the half-yearly examination, added:

> In order to render this examination the more interesting, and to afford the subscribers an opportunity of judging of the great progress made by the pupils in orchestral accompaniment, several leading artistes in this city, and amongst them Mr. Francis and Mr. Joseph Robinson, and Mr. Richard Smith, have most kindly offered their valuable assistance.[113]

The performance was also to be aided by two visiting artists, Madame D'Anterny (prima donna at the Paris Opéra) and the soprano Elizabeth Rainforth.[114]

'The performance', said *Saunders's News-Letter*, 'was to a great extent experimental, and the classic character of much of the music, and the manner in which it was executed, speak well for the progress of the Academy.'[115] The *Freeman's Journal* confirmed the achievements of 'this national institution' in by now familiar messianic terms:

> Give this institution but the funds . . . and many of us will yet live to see the genius of our nation, through its aid, developing its natural resources with a success which but few ever dreamt of.[116]

For the half-yearly examination on 30 January 1852, the Committee was able to announce that 'Mr. Joseph Robinson will sing a song composed expressly for the benefit of the Academy of Music by M. W. Balfe Esq.'[117] This was 'The Sun's Last Smile Is Beaming', to words by J. F. Waller. Balfe was at that time at the peak of his career, having scored an international hit with *The Bohemian Girl* in 1843 and having succeeded Costa as conductor of Her Majesty's Theatre, London, in 1846.

It was at this concert that the vice-chairman, Dr Graves, spoke publicly of the fortunes of the Academy. Having 'congratulated the society on its improved prospects', and having referred to the 'salutary and happy influences of music in elevating and humanizing social feeling,' he asserted that 'it was the duty of government to assist in developing this sublime branch of art as well as those of drawing and design.'[118] This is the first public instance of a view that must have been widely held by the Committee since the Academy's inception, and the analogy drawn between it and the schools of art and design is instructive. If we judge by the experiences of the contemporary art school operating under the aegis of the RDS (the incipient NCAD), the Academy was in part fortunate to have escaped the increasingly centralised system of art education controlled by the British government through the Department of Science and Art in South Kensington, London, and in part disadvantaged by not being drawn into the net with regard to financial support and official recognition. By 1849, when the RDS art schools came under government control through the Board of Trade and were redefined as the School of Design, the society had conducted a public service institution by private means for over a century. By 1877, when it finally surrendered responsibility to London, the Dublin Metropolitan School of Art had become enmeshed in the administrative system developed by Henry Cole, secretary of the department from 1857 to 1873, which had utilitarian and technical design as its core rather than drawing and painting in their own right.[119] Within that period, art education nevertheless developed along systematic lines, whereas music education, although burgeoning under the control of the IAM's governing body, lacked the specific focus that South Kensington put on Dublin (by defining a curriculum and a distinction between the various branches of art and their application) and of course lacked a regular assured income by way of grant. In 1849, for example, the School of Design enjoyed a grant of £1,500, subject to the sum being matched by local sub-scriptions.[120] It would be twenty years before the IAM could attract such support, and then at a much lower level.

Moreover, the absence of control meant that the idea that music could be taught for utilitarian purposes alone did not arise, but it is probably a disadvantage that the associated question of educating 'artisans' was not raised earlier than the debate in the late eighteen-eighties, which led to the creation of the Municipal School of Music under the RIAM. On the other hand, the Academy had from the outset a governing body giving detailed and direct instruction to its appointed officers, and thus evolving a modus operandi that was singularly lacking in the operations of the art college.[121]

By May 1852, however, Dr Graves's words seem to have fallen on un-responsive ears. No IAM records have survived from this period, so we can only surmise from the evidence of contemporary newspapers that the Academy had entered into more difficult times. The *Freeman's Journal* for 4 May 1852 carried the following advertisement:

VIOLIN CLASS

Mr. Levey begs to announce that at the request of several friends he is induced to form an elementary violin class; also, one for more advanced Students, on the exact system of the Conservatoire of Paris, and Musical Academy of Leipsic.

It is ironic that the conservatoires of Paris and Leipzig should be invoked at a time when the Irish academy was at a low ebb. The advertisement suggests that the Academy as a whole had failed to attract the support of either subscribers or students in sufficient numbers to make it possible to continue its current work but that there remained a demand for violin tuition at all levels.

That the Academy's fortunes rose as well as fell is further suggested by the fact that in the following February it was once again announcing a 'half-yearly concert'; but the poor attendance reported by the *Freeman's Journal* may have been only partly due to the severe weather.[122] Despite another benefit performance of *Messiah* by the Antient Concerts Society on 13 May 1853, with a band and chorus of 250, we find Levey opening the autumn season of that year with the announcement: 'ACADEMY OF MUSIC: Mr. Levey's violin class will commence on the 1st of October,' giving his private address, 193 Great Brunswick Street, as the venue,[123] at which he would be joined by Elsner's cello class.[124]

In October 1854 we again find Levey and Elsner advertising their classes at 193 Great Brunswick Street.[125] However, in June 1855 the Academy again announced its examination concert for violin and cello, with vocal music 'to be performed by eminent professors,'[126] indicating that there was a steady flow of pupils, the *Freeman's Journal* informing its readers that 'the classes are numerously filled.'[127] The concert consisted of Haydn's Symphony in D, No. 7, and the overture to *Die Zauberflöte*, played by the strings, with piano accompaniment by the young William Levey; while another junior member of the family, Haydn Levey, played a cello solo. Among other rising stars, Masters Hughes, Charles Grandison and Master Thompson (the first two would become important staff members) performed violin solos and ensembles.[128]

The fact that information on these classes was also distributed by Henry Bussell's shop indicates that this was a measure of retrenchment on the part of the Academy, rather than an independent move by Levey and Elsner. At the time of the reorganisation in 1855–56 it was stated that 'the classes continuing open are the violin class under Mr. Levey and the violoncello class under Herr Elsner,'[129] so that, in the absence of any evidence to the contrary, we must assume that from 1852 onwards there had been little interest in the wind and brass classes and, more importantly, that the funds at the disposal of the Committee had been inadequate to maintain them. The advertisement for the half-yearly examination-concert in June 1854 states that admission would be free to 'all those who *were* subscribers' (emphasis added), suggesting that the collection of subscriptions had been abandoned but that it was still hoped to attract former supporters.[130]

It is possible that this retrenchment may have been due in part to competition. In addition to those 'academies' already open for business before the inauguration of the IAM, several others opened in its wake, perhaps sensing that a rising tide would lift other boats. P. W. Gormley opened an 'Academy for Vocal and Instrumental Music' in October 1849 at 24 North Earl Street, teaching piano, organ, violin, and singing, offering positions to 'articled pupils'.[131] Gormley also engaged in instrument retailing and presented vocal and instrumental concerts in both Dublin and Kingstown (Dún Laoghaire) featuring Irish melodies and Italian operatic numbers, at one of which Moscheles's 'Recollections of Ireland', op. 69, for piano and orchestra was played.[132] In 1850, Haydn Corri reasserted himself as a teacher of singing, piano, organ and theory 'upon a principle quite original, saving the pupil much time and labour,' at his 'Private Academy of the Fine Arts' at 51 Queen Square (Pearse Square), which by 1853 also included 'dancing and kallisthenic exercises' as well as drawing and painting.[133]

In 1850 W. J. Graham, organist of St Paul's, Arran Quay, offered tuition in organ and piano at his home (Prospect, Glasnevin) or twice a week in Kingstown; by 1854 he was running his 'Musical Academy' at 13 Blackhall Place.[134] In 1852 Mr and Mrs Fallon taught piano and singing at 1 Parliament Street (the premises of Shade's music shop) and at their 'Academy' in Rathmines Road.[135] In 1854 Mrs Smith 'of the Societies' Concerts' (wife of Richard Smith and daughter-in-law of Dr John Smith) had a vocal academy at 18 Lower Baggot Street,[136] while in the same year Alban Croft (author of a *famille nombreuse* of talented performers)[137] advertised the moving of his Italian and English singing and piano classes to 38 Belvedere Place.[138]

Vocal instruction was also available from one of Balfe's daughters, Mrs Dodd, at 14 Lower Ormond Quay.[139] In 1850 Joseph Scates announced the moving of his Concertina Repository and Academy to 1 Leinster Street and in 1853 to 26 College Green, while Mrs Allen now informed her clients that her Academy was 'under the patronage of Her Excellency the Countess of Clarendon.'[140]

More significantly, perhaps, the Mechanics' Institute (later to become the home of the Abbey Theatre) advertised in 1850 for teachers of strings and wind to form classes,[141] while the previous year J. W. Glover, 'Musical Professor to the Board of Education' (he was professor at the Marlborough Street Model School, succeeded Haydn Corri as director of music at the Pro-Cathedral,[142] and later became a powerful figure in music education), had announced his 'New School of Music', teaching piano and singing at 7 North Cumberland Street—'eminent Professors in each department,'[143] terms 4 guineas per year (he was the only one to state his terms publicly). Glover later also taught piano at the Royal Irish Institution; 'his Improved System of Pianoforte Playing . . . in which the art of playing . . . is made plain to the humblest capacity and a sound practical knowledge of the instrument may be acquired in a series of fifty lessons.'[144]

In Kingstown the Misses Dockrall, at least one of whom had been a pupil of Glover,[145] had a Musical Academy at the Assembly Rooms on Mondays and Thursdays from late 1851.[146] In 1853 J. P. Lynch (editor of *Melodies of Ireland* and author of *Irish Melodies for Piano*, published by Bussell) offered lessons in piano, guitar and singing at 7 Mount Pleasant Square and also visited Dalkey twice a week, the new railway allowing him to take in Blackrock and Kingstown on the way.[147] In 1855 Mrs Alexander Eiffe announced that she 'professionally visits on the Kingstown and Dalkey line two days in the week.'[148] In 1856 we find the Dublin Athenæum in Grafton Street (president, Isaac Butt QC MP) advertising a ladies' piano class at ten shillings per quarter[149] and a Mrs Pearce ('pupil of Signors Crivelli and M. Balfe') advertising a 'Musical Academy' for Italian and English singing at 14 Hardwicke Street.[150] A son of Johann Bernhard Logier, A. R. Logier, was also teaching at 4 Peafield Terrace, Blackrock.[151]

On the other hand, few of these schools competed directly with the IAM (where neither piano nor voice tuition was yet available), and only the Mechanics' Institute and P. W. Gormley appear to have specifically offered string teaching. And the availability of the railway meant that students could find their way to the city as easily as teachers could reach the south-eastern suburbs.

A flavour of the musical fare available to concert-goers at the time of the Academy's foundation may be had from programmes given by the Philharmonic Society and Antient Concerts Society in 1848. The Philharmonic, conducted by Bussell, performed a varied programme typical of the time, including Beethoven's *Egmont* Overture, Mendelssohn's Sinfonia No. 3, the overture to Auber's *La Part du Diable*, and a large number of vocal items by Verdi, Paccini, Fosca, Bellini, Curschmann, Balfe, Palestrina, Meyerbeer,

Donizetti, and Rossini, performed by (among others) Elizabeth Rainforth and Richard Smith. Lidel played his own solo 'Concerto' and Miss Flynn a fantasia by Benedict on airs from *Don Pasquale*, which the *Freeman's Journal* considered 'most ineffective.'[152] Two weeks later the Antients, conducted by Joseph Robinson, 'to whom the society is indebted for its present exalted position,'[153] performed a tripartite concert, the first part of which consisted of excerpts from Handel's *Sampson*, the second of Mendelssohn's setting of Psalm 42, a quartet and a motet by Haydn, and Beethoven's Benedictus, and the third of selections from *Elijah* and *St Paul* and short works by Spohr and Hummel. The soloists included Francis Robinson, Gustavus Geary, Mrs Wilkinson, Mrs Smith, and John Stanford.

In 1850 and subsequent years the Mechanics' Institute became the venue for lectures and classes for working men, which included 'Grand Vocal and Instrumental Concerts' with a 'band' of thirty, including many leading instrumentalists, such as A. W. Levey and the Academy's wind teacher, Herr Klausman, on horn.[154] By 1858 it was offering classes for women in piano and classes for men in violin, piano, flute, concertina and conopean at eight shillings a quarter (two lessons a week).[155]

Meanwhile R. M. Levey—in addition to his duties at the Theatre Royal —and Wilhelm Elsner continued to provide the orchestral backbone of many concerts, such as those of the Philharmonic,[156] and also provided chamber music with the 'Dublin Quartette Concerts' (Levey father and son, Wilkinson, and Elsner), which so absorbed their audience that on one occasion the *Freeman's Journal* reported that 'it was gratifying to observe the silent attention of all present, so unusual an occurrence at an instrumental concert.'[157] These consisted not only of string quartets and quintets but also vocal items (without which one might be forgiven for thinking that the audience would not go home satisfied) and sonatas. On 20 March 1855 we find the young Theodore Logier playing the piano part of a Mendelssohn cello sonata.[158] Chamber music *per se* was a generally neglected medium, which caused the *Freeman's Journal* to comment:

> We are perfectly aware that this order of music presents many impediments to its frequent performance, such as the procuring of four competent players, willing to meet and practice together till the ideas of the composer are so clearly understood by them that they can with safety reveal them to others.[159]

The centrality of such performers as Levey and Elsner across the spectrum of music-making is therefore the more to be appreciated. A Theatre Royal benefit in 1854 saw William Levey (piano), William H. Levey (making his first professional appearance, at the age of six) and Elsner providing the instrumental core,[160] while the younger Levey capitalised on his extreme youth by appearing frequently in public thereafter, including what can best be described as 'miscellaneous' concerts at the Mechanics' Institute under the direction of his elder brother A. W.[161] Elsner also presented 'Classical Quartett Concerts' on his own initiative, 'after the manner of "Die Quartett Unterhaltungen" [conversation concerts] at Frankfort [his native city].'[162]

In 1848 a row had developed among Dublin musicians over the visits of Jullien. Invited to conduct concerts for the Anacreontic Society, of which he had been elected an honorary member in 1841, which would feature Drury Lane soloists for the benefit of some Dublin charities, Jullien found himself nearly barred by a group of musicians, including R. M. Levey, Joseph Lidel, James Barton, J. W. Glover, and William Wilkinson, who considered him unsuited to the occasion. A meeting of the 'Instrumental Musicians of the City of Dublin' resolved that

> at the present time, when the greatest exertions are making in every branch of science towards fostering and encouraging native talent, we must deplore the existence of a practice lately adopted by some of the Instrumental Musical Societies of Dublin . . . of engaging, and expending large sums of money on, Foreign Artists to the injury and discouragement of the resident professors.[163]

Jullien succeeded, however, in directing the concerts and in mounting further cycles of his large-scale celebrity concerts. The meeting gives us some indication of the ability of the musicians in question to organise a concerted objection to the threat of outside competition, which we will find raising its head only too soon in the case of the Academy.

Among distinguished visiting artists at this time we should note that in 1848 Benedict presented a morning concert featuring the considerable vocal talents of Giovanni Mario, a political exile because of his association with Mazzini, his companion, Giulia Grisi, and others, with accompaniment provided by himself (piano) and R. M. Levey.[164] Thalberg gave a matinée in 1849 with Nicola Lablache;[165] the Irish début of Ede Remenyi, the Hungarian violin wizard (who was also a political refugee at the time), was a notable event;[166] the double-bass virtuoso Bottesini, who had first played in Dublin in a Jullien concert in 1849, appeared with the Philharmonic in 1852;[167] Madame Pleyel and Charlotte Dolby appeared at the Philharmonic in 1852 (the former in Weber's Konzertstück and Liszt's Fantasia on Meyerbeer's *Le Prophète*)[168] and again in Jullien concerts in 1855;[169] while, also in 1852, Mrs Robinson presented two concerts featuring Joachim,[170] who visited the Antient Concerts in 1858 (the same year as Rubinstein) in the company of Madame Lemmens-Sherrington and again in 1859. In 1856 Clara Schumann appeared at the Philharmonic, playing the Mendelssohn concerto in addition to her husband's 'Schlummerlied'.[171]

Several visiting celebrities gave short-term tuition during their stay, the most notable being the sisters and brother of the renowned tenor John Sims Reeves, who,

> having arrived . . . to assist at the Philharmonic and other concerts and having been induced to protract their stay in this City, propose to give Instruction in Singing and the Pianoforte on the principle adopted in the Royal Academy of Music in London, where they studied under Signor [Domenico] Crivelli and the best masters—pursuing the plan followed in the great Schools of Music in Milan and Naples.[172]

Another, Madame d'Aranda, 'a pupil of Liszt, having arrived from Paris' in October 1853, advertised lessons at her residence, 5 Sallymount Avenue, Cullenswood (Ranelagh).[173]

A further feature of the domestic musical scene in the eighteen-fifties was the concern for 'national' music. At the end of 1849 William Murphy BMus, a frequent artist in a variety of concerts, gave six lectures on 'The National Music of Ireland' at the Mechanics' Institute, which appear to have been thoroughly researched and which incorporated musical illustrations provided by a number of vocalists, accompanied by the ubiquitous R. M. Levey.[174] In March 1850 the 'Irish Melodists' announced their formation 'for the practice and cultivation of our national music.'[175] In 1852, Gustavus Geary's 'National Concert' featured 'purely and exclusively Irish' music, causing the *Freeman's Journal* to declare that 'no selection of musical composition could have presented more exquisite beauty and variety.'[176] The Royal Choral Institute's concert of 8 February 1854 featured the Irish premiere of Schumann's 'Paradise and the Péri', based on Moore's poem 'Lalla Rookh', which excited national pride in the editor, and presumably the readers, of the *Freeman's Journal*.[177]

With the reorganisation of the Academy in 1856 we see a more nationally focused institution coming into existence. Thirty years previously, Thomas Crofton Croker had written:

> The virtues of patience, of prudence, and industry seldom are included in the composition of our Irishman: he projects gigantic schemes, but wants perseverance to realize any work of magnitude: his conceptions are grand and vivid, but his execution is feeble and indolent.[178]

Although the founders of the IAM had shown patience and prudence, the scheme had perhaps been too grand for the resources available. Is it possible that, like the Ballingarry 'rising' of the same year, it had failed to become sufficiently popular to secure commonplace support? And could this explain why so many associates of Young Ireland rallied in 1856 (the year that also saw the foundation of a National and Literary Society or 'Phoenix Society') to save the institution?[179] In any case, the declining fortunes of the Academy may have been part of a general drop in interest in music. In 1848 *Thom's Directory* listed 65 teachers of music; by 1856 the number had fallen to 47, although by 1860 it had increased dramatically to 70 and by 1870 to 87.

Typical of what Harry White has called the 'slender continuity of commitment' to musical development in mid-century,[180] a circular distributed by Francis Brady on 29 December 1855 stated that 'some of its pupils are now earning an independent livelihood and assisting in the support of their families, from the education they have received in the Academy.'[181] This in itself shows that, in addition to its principal purpose, the Academy had also moved towards partially achieving its second aim, of creating a corps of professional musicians.

The circular attributed the Academy's decline 'in the last two or three years' firstly to the low level of the subscription:

A far greater number of subscriptions was necessary for the support of the Academy than it was reasonable to expect it to obtain until it shall have awakened a wide and general interest and secured a hold upon the public mind.

This problem would be overcome by raising the subscription from five shillings to a pound a year (forty pounds today). Secondly, the circular identified a flaw in the Academy's modus operandi that continues to be a bugbear of all such music academies to this day:

> The parents of many of the junior pupils, from whose instruction the greatest amount of good was to be hoped, found the attendance of their children at the Academy to interfere too much with the prosecution of their studies at the schools for general instruction that they were obliged to forego the advantages of the Academy for the more essential elements of education.

To overcome this obstacle, a method of originality and vision was proposed. The new Academy would 'combine a sound General Education in English and in the modern languages with the best musical instruction so that the entire education of the pupils may be conducted within the walls of the Academy.' This too would prove a scheme more optimistic than real, although the insistence on the importance of Italian classes for the vocal students would continue well into the twentieth century. When, in 1886, during negotiations on the framing of a scheme for the future governance of the Academy, it was suggested that it should 'make some connexion with some educational institution by which pupils would get a general education also,' Francis Brady said that 'when the academy was originally started we tried to give them a general education, but it was too expensive.'[182] Nevertheless, today the 'Blue Scheme' continues to embody this ambitious possibility in clause 24: 'The Governors may also establish and maintain classes, and may provide instruction, in the Academy, in Modern Languages, and in any other subjects of general education which they may deem useful to students of music.' It is the same ambition that was written into the constitution of the RAM:

> The first object in the education of the students will consist in a strict attention to their religious and moral instruction. Next, the study of their own and the Italian language, writing and arithmetic, and their general instruction in the various branches of music, particularly in the art of singing, and in the study of pianoforte and organ, of harmony and of composition.[183]

The circular also referred to a matter that was at the core of the Academy's *raison d'être*:

> It is intended to receive as pupils none but children who manifest a decided talent for music. There is no doubt that in this country there are many instances of musical talent uncultivated from the want of opportunity, such as the Academy will afford. The expense of the

education offered by the Academy will be most moderate, and it is proposed to reward the most successful of the pupils in each year by remitting the entire, or a portion of, the fees for the ensuing year.

The need to keep the fees as low as possible, so as to make facilities available to the widest possible public, was evident, as was the desire to award scholarships. Whether this signalled an intention to deliberately seek or foster students who were financially disadvantaged was an ambiguous point that would raise its head twenty years later, when Brady was to tell the Educational Endowments Commission that, although the Academy had always wanted to aid talented pupils, 'we have never thought it desirable to give free instruction for what may be called poverty without merit.'[184]

Musical classes would continue to be available to those who pursued their general studies elsewhere. Fees for music classes were raised from the previous level of three guineas to four pounds a year, and for music together with general education were fixed at eight pounds.

A meeting was held on 4 January 1856 to consider these proposals, those attending agreeing to constitute the new Committee, with Brady and Hercules MacDonnell as honorary secretaries.[185] It was agreed to look for new premises and to wait, before reopening, for the appointment (already advertised) of a resident master *cum* secretary to teach the general class as well as keep the Academy records. 'Candidates for the Office of Master and Secretary are requested to send in their applications with copies of the testimonials . . . Persons applying must be fully competent to give the best instruction in the usual elements of an English education [*sic*]. Salary £50 per annum [£2,000 today].'[186]

The most surprising aspect of the renewed enterprise is that the two men given most power and responsibility, Brady and MacDonnell, should have been (or appear to have been) previously uninvolved; and also that at that time they were comparatively young, Brady being thirty-two and MacDonnell thirty-seven. It is clear from the fact that Brady was the author of the circular that he was at least knowledgeable about the Academy's circumstances and concerned about its future (his family had been regular attenders at its concerts). MacDonnell, as we have seen, had been deeply involved in musical affairs for some years. Like the other main movers, he was a barrister and accustomed to positions of influence and academic background; his father, Richard MacDonnell (who had married Jane Graves, the niece of Bishop Graves's grandfather), was at that time provost of TCD, having been appointed in 1852, and president of the Dublin Athenæum.[187] Hercules's elder brother, also Richard (knighted 1856), became Chief Justice of the Gambia and an explorer of the African continent and subsequently held appointments in South Australia and Nova Scotia, retiring as governor of Hong Kong in 1872.[188]

Hercules himself had a comparatively modest career. A scholar of TCD (and gold medallist) in ethics and logic, and a founder of its Choral Society —as, later, of the Strollers, of which he was secretary and later president— he was called to the bar in 1842 and retired into comparative obscurity as registrar of the Court of Bankruptcy and secretary to the Commissioners of

Charitable Donations and Bequests, and died in 1900, aged eighty-one. He edited the *Statutes and Charters* of TCD in 1844. C. V. Stanford asserted that he had been for a time music critic of the *Irish Times*, reviewing the inaugural Bayreuth festival in 1876, but although articles did appear that he may have written,[189] there were no reviews as such.[190] L. E. Steele, however, tells us that MacDonnell did write a paper on Bayreuth and another on 'Musical Acoustics'; in 1889 he published a paper on 'Eternal Rest or Motion', which excited scientific discussion.[191] He was also a modest composer: his song 'Emmeline' (words by J. F. Waller) was published by Bussell, along with songs by Balfe, the Earl of Belfast, Robert Tennant, J. F. Waller and Dr Smith, in 1853,[192] and he wrote several settings for the Strollers.[193] And we know that he and his wife, Emily (née Moylan), were enthusiastic and frequent amateur performers of oratorio and opera. Stanford records that Hercules 'had a baritone voice of great power, and possessed a dramatic temperament which gave great incisiveness to his delivery,' while Emily was 'a dramatic soprano with a voice which would have rivalled even the greatest prima donna of her day.'[194] He sang the bass solo role in the first London performance of Rossini's *Stabat Mater* in 1842 under Balfe. It is said that he retired with a meagre pension, that he was a keen yachtsman, and that 'to the end his clothes were of a nautical cut. A regular attender at the [Strollers'] practices, he had an amusing habit before he sat down of spreading a copy of the *Evening Mail* upon his chair.'[195]

Brady, whom we have already mentioned in connection with his legal and political affiliations, was a writer of verse and occasionally set others' words to music. The Academy library possesses copies of his songs 'Come Back to Erin' ('Performed before Their Majesties King Edward VII and Queen Alexandra May 4th 1904 by Pupils of the Royal Irish Academy of Music'), with melody by Claribel, arranged by T. R. G. Jozé, published by Boosey; 'The Sailor Boy's Return', 'sung with great success by Miss Agnes Treacy,' for which he wrote both words and music (published by Doremi and dedicated to the Duchess of Abercorn); and a pair of songs, also published by Doremi, 'The Song of Glaucus' (text by Lord Lytton, from the *Last Days of Pompeii*) and 'The Song of Life' (words and music by Brady). At the time of his death it was stated that he had recently collaborated with Esposito on an arrangement of 'The Coolin' and that he was the author of the song 'In My Wild Mountain Valley', which Benedict included in *The Lily of Killarney*.[196] Hercules MacDonnell states that Brady organised opera recitals, including one of *Guy Mannering*, but no record of these can be traced.[197]

Of the original Committee, Berwick, Graves, Smith, Bussell and the Robinsons remained (with the stockbroker W. G. Dubedat, who had succeeded Goold as treasurer).[198] Of the newcomers, Thomas Beatty, a distinguished doctor, and Robert Exham, a wine merchant, were to prove consistently dependable over the coming decades. Beatty was president of both the RCPI and the RCSI and secretary of the Medico-Philosophical (dining) Society, to which his friends William Wilde and Whitley Stokes belonged. Through Robert Corbet he was related to the family of W. B. Yeats.[199] The report of his funeral, in 1872, is so typical of the way in which the death of such a figure was observed by what we would today call the 'network' within which he operated that we reproduce it as an appendix to this chapter.

Another doctor and the son of a Church of Ireland clergyman, Evory Kennedy (1807–86) had become master of the Rotunda at the early age of thirty and was the founder of the Dublin Obstetrical Society and president of the College of Surgeons in 1853–54.[200] As a Home Ruler he unsuccessfully contested his native Donegal constituency in 1874. S. N. Elrington was a ballad and song writer whose words were set to music by, among others, G. W. Torrance. Cheyne Brady, presumably a relation of Maziere and of Francis Brady, was secretary of the Court of Bankruptcy, and would later write the histories of Dr Steevens's Hospital and the Royal Hospital for Incurables. B. C. Lloyd QC, a relative of Oscar Wilde's future wife, Constance Lloyd, was a neighbour of the Brady family in Upper Pembroke Street and later took over as treasurer; Edmund Digges La Touche[201] and John Norwood were also barristers, Thomas Archer was a solicitor, as were Henry Bastable, R. J. Macrory, and T. Magrath, while J. H. Macdermott traded as a druggist and chemist. It is notable that J. W. Glover was temporarily brought into the Academy as a Committee member at this time. A new tier of responsibility was introduced with the appointment of three trustees, Berwick, Brady, and MacDonnell, a feature of the Academy's need for fiscal rectitude up to the formulation of the 'Blue Scheme'.

Thomas Maxwell Hutton, with his brother Lucius Octavius, carried on the family coachbuilding business at 115–119 Summer Hill (where the Irish state coach was built in 1853) after the death in 1865 of their father, Thomas— 'honest Tom Hutton . . . a most shrewd, sensible man,' as O'Connell described him.[202] An ancestor, Henry, had been Lord Mayor of Dublin in 1803. Their sister Annie had been the *inamorata* of Thomas Davis,[203] and their uncle, Robert, had been O'Connell's running mate in their successful election for the Dublin City constituency in the 1837 general election. Although Robert was anti-Repeal, he was a federalist and therefore valuable to O'Connell: 'Though his opinions do not concur with mine I respect him much . . . He has a considerable following, especially of Dissenters. Our cause needs the support of every class and we should show them that we value their aid as well as that of other Protestants.'[204] The *Evening Post* of 29 July 1837 recorded that the coachbuilders' trade union expressed their support for his candidature. When Harriet Martineau, visiting Dublin in 1852, observed Thomas Hutton's method of doing business, she was unknowingly describing the same modus operandi that was being applied to the Academy: 'The principle is . . . to make the best possible . . . and to use their own judgement as to how this is to be done . . . Their fellow townsmen now see what a blessing it is that they have been so resolute in holding to their determination.'[205] Hutton was described at his death in 1896 as 'a Liberal of the old stamp . . . devoted largely to public enterprises,' with a 'deep interest in everything that concerned the material welfare of Ireland.'[206] He became a trustee of the Academy's endowments in 1870 and remained so during the crucial period up to 1887.

However, the most notable name from the political and cultural point of view among those attending on 4 January was that of John Edward Pigot (1822–71). His father, David Pigot, had been elected an O'Connellite MP for Clonmel in 1839, when he became Solicitor-General, and was returned in 1840 and 1841, becoming Attorney-General. He succeeded Maziere Brady as Chief Baron of the Exchequer in 1846, a post he was to retain until 1873. John Pigot was a Young Irelander, being a member of the Council 1847–49 and closely associated with John Blake Dillon, Charles Gavan Duffy, and John (later Judge) O'Hagan. In 1845 he had been joint secretary with Samuel Ferguson of the Committee to erect a memorial to Davis; the Committee also included Thomas Hutton, Robert Callwell, W. E. Hudson, and Sir Colman O'Loghlen.[207] Pigot had a penchant for Irish folk music and literature, which led him into the collecting fraternity; his collection provided 156 tunes for Joyce's *Old Irish Music and Songs* (1909), together with 255 from William Forde and Joyce's own 429. He was also treasurer of the Celtic Society and a member of the RIA and of the 'Petrie' Society and had written extensively on the art works in the Exhibition of 1853. His younger brother, David, also a barrister, became master of the Court of Exchequer.

It is as an associate of Thomas Davis that Pigot's career is most instructive.[208] It was to Pigot that Davis wrote, a propos the Repeal pamphlets, that 'these are preparations for self-rule.'[209] Jane Welsh Carlyle, meeting Pigot in London in 1845, had recorded: 'If there be . . . an insurrection in Ireland . . . Mr. Pigott [*sic*] will rise to be a Robespierre of some sort,'[210] and Pigot had been the 'hero' of M. W. Savage's satirical novel of Young Ireland, *The Falcon Family*. He became the military correspondent of the *Nation*, writing articles on guerrilla warfare, and was prevented from becoming deeply embroiled in the abortive 1848 rising only through the counsel of his father. 'This matter of nationality has been to me from childhood a sacred religion; and I mean the word in its highest sense,' he wrote to Smith O'Brien.[211]

But Pigot believed that the enthusiasm of youth was no substitute for experience, and in 1847 he had earnestly tried not to become a member of the Confederation, on grounds of inexperience of public life. He felt that one should have 'earned a position which is a reality in the country'[212]—a sentiment well attuned to the pragmatism of the ambitious young Academy. In fact letters to Pigot from Davis and O'Connell suitably frame such pragmatism: as Pigot prepared for his career as a lawyer in 1844, Davis said, 'I am glad you are working at law—'twill harden your mind,'[213] while a few months later O'Connell observed, 'If you make yourself master of the *practice* of the courts you will succeed but otherwise I think you can not'[214]—both excellent pieces of practical advice for the conduct or study of any discipline, including music. As a lawyer, Pigot had defended William Smith O'Brien and John Mitchel in 1848, before becoming disillusioned with politics. He had been devastated by Davis's early death in 1845 ('After his death I could think and speak no more of politics, because my previous plans had included him as a sort of corner stone'[215]), and in 1865 he emigrated to India, where he was highly successful at the bar. He returned to Dublin in 1871, where he met his early death. The judgment of the *Nation* at the time of his death, that he led a 'life of silent, self-denying, earnest labour' and that 'he was not a man of the platform, although its pillars were sometimes set by his hands,' is typical of the contribution made by generations of like-minded people to the growth of the Academy.[216] As the author of a memorandum that provided the basis for the formation of the National Gallery of Ireland,[217] Pigot was obviously in an excellent position to contribute to the founding of a similar cultural institution, and his early death probably deprived the IAM of practical, as well as idealistic, advice and example.

Following the meeting of 5 January a new prospectus had been distributed, announcing that 'the instruction in the Academy will be found adapted, not only for those who may intend to devote themselves to music as a profession, but also for amateurs who may not otherwise be enabled to obtain the best musical education,'[218] thus establishing another potential point of ambiguity in the distinction between professional and amateur pupils.

Prof. Smith had offered his services *gratis* and was announced as professor of vocal music and harmony, thus extending the range of tuition available, while Herr Waetzig, conductor of the Queen's Band, was appointed to teach wind instruments as well as German.[219] Professors of English, French and Italian were to be recruited; the secretary would teach English, mathematics, book-keeping, grammar, and geography.[220]

The first surviving minute of the reconstituted Academy is dated 18 April 1856 and was signed by John Edward Pigot. It recorded that in the interim S. H. Sloane—'engaged from the teachers trained by the National Board of Education'—had been appointed resident master and secretary, that premises had been taken at 18 St Stephen's Green, at an annual rent of eighty pounds, and that the new Academy had opened on 12 February. Elsner agreed to occupy the top floor of four rooms at a rent of twenty-five pounds, but at the end of the year he must have realised that he had expected too much of his new quarters; on 4 November he notified the governors of 'his intention of giving up his rooms in the Academy in consequence of the noise of pupils practising.'

Within a month of the reopening a benefit was given at the Antient Concert Rooms, which is remarkable for several reasons: firstly, because we see the renewed connection between the Academy and the establishment—the event being supported and, as far as we can tell, organised by the Marquess and Marchioness of Downshire;[221] secondly, because, in the words of the letter of thanks sent by the Academy to Lady Downshire and published in the Dublin *Daily Express* of 15 April, 'you, Madam, succeeded in uniting . . . the talent of a numerous corps of amateurs, such as never before has been here assembled' (reminiscent no doubt of the eleven-pronged effort of 1847); thirdly, because it consisted of a performance of Wallace's *Maritana* (1845), 'an opera composed by one of [Ireland's] gifted sons of genius'; and finally because, after the deduction of expenses of £122 5s 4d, the gross receipts of £596 8s 6d yielded a net balance of £474 3s 2d (say £20,000 today), which succeeded in keeping the Academy's finances buoyant for the next decade, £400 being invested immediately in government stock.[222]

Under Lady Downshire's direction a committee of 'patronesses' was established, including the Countess of Howth, Countess of Clonmel, Countess of Bective, and Countess of Milltown (the last wrote a verse prologue to the opera, which was spoken by her son, the Hon. Edward Leeson), Viscountess Massarene and Ferrard, the Countess of Cloncurry, Lady Staples, Lady Coghill, and Mrs Henry Grattan, chiefly to sell tickets at 10s each, or £1 4s for a family of three.[223] Subscriptions opened on Saturday 9 February and had sold out by the following Thursday, ten days before the performance.[224] More remarkable with regard to music is the fact that, as the *Freeman's Journal* records, the conductor, Aloys Ketenus—a violinist introduced to Dublin through his interest in the career of Miss Flynn[225]—'manifestly knew little about the direction of either band or chorus,' and the performance was held together by Lady Downshire, 'who presided at the pianoforte throughout.' Nor were the individual performances of the best: Sir Jocelyn Coghill, as the King of Spain, and Mr Gore (an aide-de-camp to the Lord Lieutenant) as Lazarillo, succeeded in 'getting through their parts fairly.'[226] Capt. Palliser as the Marquis de Montefiori seems to have fared somewhat better, and the *Freeman's Journal* also praised the *mise-en-scène* by Hercules MacDonnell.

The open letter to Lady Downshire—very similar in style to the form of 'loyal address' the Academy was to make to successive Lords Lieutenant—stated that 'this national Academy . . . seeks to diffuse a sound taste and a high order of musical knowledge amongst classes whose means do not at present permit of such attainments' and that 'it will also be the province of the Academy to single out the few endowed with more exalted talents, to teach them to deserve, and thus to win, success.' The ambiguity relating to potential pupils of limited means, and to the Academy's ambition of awarding scholarships, was thus given further expression.

Because of the close-knit nature of Dublin musical society, which at this point does not seem to have exhibited any of the divisions or personal animosities that developed a decade or so later, it was possible to rely on well-wishers to continue the concerts, from which the Academy benefited financially. For example, Hercules MacDonnell was central to the 'Mystics' dining club from 1851 to 1857, among whom he was known as 'Heinrich', other members being William Wilde, with the nickname 'Willie Wildrake', Robert Stewart, as 'Bach', John F. Waller (whose verses were frequently set to music), who had the pseudonym 'Jonathan Freke-Slingsby', and T. A. Jones (later PRHA), whose nickname is not recalled.[227]

The Strollers—still a thriving body—started meeting in 1864–65, among their founders being Sir Jocelyn Coghill, Alan Close, Viscount Southwell, Dr Thomas Nedley, and Hercules MacDonnell, who was to be secretary for many years.[228] At first—reflecting contemporary musical activity—the activities were oriented more towards drama than towards music, with 'garrison theatricals' involving a large number of temporarily resident army officers. William Bentham (IAM) was a later addition to the membership (he sang in *Guy Mannering* in 1868 and *The Brigand* in 1873), while conductors of the company included Academy figures such as T. R. G. Jozé (1887–93), Charles Marchant (1893–1920), and T. H. Weaving (1928–58). T. S. C. Dagg, vice-president of the RIAM, was president of the Strollers from 1955 to 1958. They met at the Academy's premises at 18 St Stephen's Green for several years and later at 36 Westland Row.[229] The Instrumental Music Club (also meeting in the IAM premises) was formed in 1874, almost all its founders (Francis Cruise, J. F. Elrington, John Stanford, Thomas Farrell, Henry Doyle, and H. Vivian Yeo) being on the Committee of the IAM.[230] Of the members of the Strollers whom we should note as a further indication of the overlapping membership among Dublin societies, Brady, Coghill, Alan Close, Henry Doyle, Bentham, Nedley, Vivian Yeo and John Stanford are typical.[231]

The choral scene in Dublin had livened considerably after the formation of the TCD Choral Society in 1836 (one of the principal founders being MacDonnell). In 1855 they gave a curtailed concert performance of Mozart's *Don Giovanni*, with Joseph Robinson as Don Giovanni, Richard Smith as Leporello, Gustavus Geary as Don Ottavio, Grattan Kelly as the Commendatore, Mrs Dodd as Elvira, Fanny Cruise as Zerlina, and Julia Cruise as Donna Anna. While greeting and applauding the performance from a musical point of view, the *Freeman's Journal* criticised the endeavour, since opera was 'unfit for the concert room,' especially when so much concert music lay neglected.[232]

Three years later, on 23 and 26 April 1858, a similar cast assembled for the first of many of the Academy's own self-help enterprises, with a Ladies' Committee headed by the Lady Mayoress, Lady Downshire, Lady Drogheda, and the Countess of Howth, and an Executive Committee of Sir Jocelyn Coghill, Hutton, Brady, MacDonnell, Stanford, and Robinson. Again *Don Giovanni* was performed (Joseph Robinson this time conducting), the amateur cast including Mrs Bennett, Miss A. Walker, Hercules and Emily MacDonnell, John Stanford, Maj. Hume, Alan Close, and Francis Robinson. Tickets at ten shillings each represented an expenditure in today's money of approximately fifteen pounds. The performance was described as a 'marionette opera', a form of presentation popular in the eighteenth century, of which Dublin was to see a humorous revival in 1862. On this occasion *Saunders's News-Letter* reported that puppets were employed to carry out the actions on stage, while the singers occupied the orchestra pit. 'Their mimic grief or love, the whimsical gestures and artificial emotion, in conjunction with the real feelings and animated vocalization of the singers . . . rendered the opera unique and intensely amusing.'[233]

Two years later Lady de Vere, Mrs Edward Geale, Stanford, Close and MacDonnell sang in *I puritani*, the ticket price having fallen to eight shillings. A wry insight into the attractiveness of such an amateur performance is given by the *Freeman's Journal*, which, in urging its readers to support the event, suggested that they would witness 'those who, except upon charitable occasions, are heard only in the private circles of the fashionable world.'[234] The advice was taken; 'hundreds had to be disappointed in consequence of every available space . . . having been engaged.'[235] Of Lady de Vere's performance as Elvira the *Freeman's Journal* tells us 'it was one of the most graceful and beautiful . . . musical readings which we have ever heard, and illustrated in a forcible manner the advantages which music derives from being rendered by a person of education and refined tastes.'[236] Perhaps to emphasise the point, the paper published a full list of the amateur chorus, which included Mrs F. W. Brady, Emily and Mary MacDonnell, a brace of Misses Stokes, Maj. Bagot, Robert Exham, T. A. Jones, B. W. Rooke, and J. P. Mahaffy.[237] (From a press announcement that the performance in the Antient Concert Rooms would displace Mr Gaskin's advanced singing classes we can infer that the rooms were still being used for teaching under the auspices of the Antients.)[238]

On 25 September 1860 the secretary recorded in his day book that he had written 'as directed by H. MacDonnell' to several opera singers, including Francesco Graziani, Giovanni Mario, Pauline Viardot, and Giulia Grisi, all of whom were then singing in *Orfeo* in the Italian opera season. It is possible that MacDonnell, who by virtue of his own involvement with opera would have been well acquainted with such artists,[239] hoped to persuade them to give a concert specially for the benefit of the Academy, or indeed to appear in an Academy production, but nothing came of it. MacDonnell would have had the entrée to this cosmopolitan world through his friendship with Viardot (née Garcia), who had sung Azucena in Dublin in 1858 and the two following years.[240]

On 6 February 1861 the 'Annual Amateur Opera Recital in aid of the funds of the IAM' was announced for the eleventh, at which excerpts from *Lucia di Lammermoor* and *Sonnambula* were to be performed. In *Lucia* Mrs MacDonnell appeared as Lucia, Jones as Arturo, MacDonnell as Enrico, and Stanford as Raimondo, with the role of Edgardo sung by Mrs Geale (the niece of Lady Morgan), who had studied with Nicolo Rubini. The *Irish Times* tells us that 'we should, indeed, have preferred a tenor voice in this part but since it was to be committed to a lady, it could not have been trusted to a more finished vocalist.'[241] *Sonnambula* was sung by Mrs Frederic Magennis (Amina), Miss Howley (Lisa), Silvia Hort (Teresa),[242] J. Scott (Elvino), and Capt. W. Palliser (Rodolpho), with an amateur chorus.

'The Irish Academy of Music is the only national institution for the cultivation of music in any civilised country which receives no aid from the State,' commented the *Irish Times*.[243] Two days later it felt the need to reflect on the Academy's progress since 1848, observing that

> the younger pupils receive a sound English education within the walls of the Academy but, to be admitted, they must exhibit a decided talent for music. The classes for female pupils are restricted to ladies who intend making music their profession as governesses or otherwise. All the pupils are thoroughly instructed in harmony and composition. The admirable manner in which the choruses were performed . . . is in itself sufficient proof of the efficiency of the training they receive . . . In any city on the Continent *conservatoires* are supported at the public expense.

> A grant is conceded annually to the Academy of Music in London [on
> this point the *Irish Times* was misinformed]. In this city alone is so
> useful an institution suffered to depend upon private subscriptions and
> the proceeds of concerts given by amateurs.[244]

The paper also recorded that at the Lord Lieutenant's request Mrs
Magennis encored her aria 'Ah, non giunge' ('It is only once in a generation
such an Amina appears'), while *Saunders's News-Letter* compared her voice to
that of Gassier—'pure, resonant and flexible . . . fluent, graceful and finished.'[245] The performance, which was repeated on 2 March, raised a further
£25 (£750 today). On the same occasion the *Freeman's Journal* observed a
mixed sign of patriotism that would persist in Academy concerts for several
decades: 'The young lady pupils of the academy were costumed *salon* [*sic*]
les règles in pure white dresses—the sopranos on one side wearing green
wreaths in their hair and green ribbons, the contraltos being distinguished
by wreaths of crimson flowers.'[246]

A year later, the Academy's operas were *Ernani*—with Mrs Magennis
singing Elvira, Mrs Wray Palliser as Giovanna, V. Bartolucci as Don Carlo,
Jones as Don Ricardo, and Alan Close as Silva, with Scott in the title role—
and Flotow's *Marta*, with mainly the same artists and Sir Jocelyn Coghill
as Lord Tristan. Because of a full house on 9 April the performance was
repeated on the fifteenth, attended by, among others, Viscount Gough. The
chorus (again listed in full in the press)[247] was of a similar composition to
that for *I puritani*, with the addition of some Henns, Maynes, Churchills,
Jacobs, a Col. Summerville, a Mr Yeo, and a Mrs Swanzy—its effectiveness
being attributed by the *Freeman's Journal* 'to the careful preliminary training
of Mr. John O'Rorke.'[248] Scott, regrettably, 'showed himself altogether
unequal to the "M'appari" [in *Marta*], particularly the high passage with
which this most expressive song reaches its climax'—but, the indulgent
reviewer tells us, the audience, in the tolerant fashion that persisted for too
long in Dublin, 'was generous, and relieved the singer from his natural
embarrassment by insisting on an encore.'[249]

Another performance of *Sonnambula* in 1863 elicited an outburst of
patriotic fervour from 'P.F.', writing in the *Dublin Evening Mail*, contrasting
'that grim faith of our century which grinds down all ends and angles, and
polishes all the components of society into a revolting smoothness' with
'the Celtic spirit,' which could inspire 'softness . . . modesty . . . graciousness,
and . . . tunefulness . . . happily joining us to Italian natures.'[250]

Meanwhile other benefits continued. A donation of five pounds from the
Amateur Musical Society (founded by George Lee, the lover of Shaw's
mother, soon to style himself Vandeleur Lee) was received in June 1858,[251]
and the minutes of 19 April 1859 record a further donation of twenty-five
pounds, the proceeds of a concert by the same society; and a week later
there was some suggestion of this being repeated. The society hired rooms
from the Academy (as would many other bodies in later years), for which
they paid £7 in 1858/59 and £5 15s the following year.[252]

We do not know why the Academy should have decided to move from the Antient Concert Rooms, unless it was thought that the premises would become too cramped should it succeed in expanding to the extent of the original conception. A cryptic note in the minutes of 11 April 1856 that the Committee was considering publishing its correspondence with the Antient Concerts Society suggests that some dispute may have taken place that they wished to clarify in the press; but nothing more is known of this. It is equally possible that the Committee felt that the Academy should stand on its own feet, rather than continue a 'lodging' arrangement with the Antient Concerts.

Whatever the reason, it plunged the Committee into the business not only of running a music academy but of housekeeping. Household goods had to be acquired for the resident master, and he was equipped with a mahogany table at £1 10s (£60 today), a breakfast service at £1 16s 5d, teaspoons and egg spoons at £1 3s, and chairs and a fender at £2 19s.[253] The gas supply cost £3 to connect, exclusive of fittings.[254] Music stands for the pupils cost 6s 3d each.[255] A few months later, two looking-glasses and a small clock were purchased,[256] but Mr Sloane (or, as events proved, his successor) had to wait two years for any further provision, when a brass bed, six plates, three dishes, six tumblers and a kettle were acquired.[257]

The purchase of instruments was naturally an important item of expenditure in the early days. Significantly, brass instruments to a total of £37 (£1,500 today) were bought in 1856, including a B flat bass tuba (four pistons) and an E flat tenor tuba (three pistons),[258] in 1857 two B flat clarinets at £2 each from McNeale of Capel Street,[259] and in 1858 a French horn at £2 10s (£100 today), a tenor saxophone—an unusual acquisition for the time—at £4 (£160 today), and a valve trombone.[260] In 1862 we find the Academy buying wind tutors for clarinet, oboe (by Henri Brod), cornet, horn (Louis-François Dauprat), flute (François Devienne), and bassoon (Eugene Jancourt and Bordagni or Bordogny).[261] The purchase of a Collard piano was contemplated in 1856, but fortunately Collards donated the instrument[262]—a practice they repeated in 1861[263] and that was continued by Cadby (a semi-grand) in 1862.[264] (At the time, a Broadwood grand cost £135, a semi-grand between £90 and £110, and comparable uprights £45 to £80; in 1851 Collards advertised 'semi-cottage' instruments at £33,[265] while inferior instruments, for example a six-octave square piano by Kirkman, could cost about £10.)[266]

To transact these and other pertinent matters, the Committee elected to meet each Thursday morning at half past eight and to pay ten shillings each term for their breakfasts.[267] They not only took all the decisions relating to finance and conditions of employment but also committed themselves personally to the financial wellbeing of the endeavour. On 10 September 1857 we find Walter Berwick lending fifty pounds to the Academy to ease its cash flow rather than cut into capital; it would be five months before he would be repaid. Two months later, each governor contributed five pounds by way of personal guarantee towards the costs of organising the recital of *Don Giovanni*.

Despite such commitment, it did prove necessary in 1858 and 1859 to sell a total of £250 of the stocks to meet liabilities,[268] giving us some indication of the gap between fees and subscriptions on one side of the balance sheet and salaries, premises and general running costs on the other. It was always the policy of the Academy to attract the best available teachers, if necessary by paying premium salaries, which could be further augmented by private teaching. It would be several decades before the levels of remuneration would be standardised, but a minute of 5 October 1857 records that string teachers were paid £20 per year together with £2 per pupil (although Elsner himself received £3), and this is confirmed by a minute of 1861 that shows Miss Kelly (piano) and Charles Grandison (violin) receiving £20, while Elsner earned a salary of between £7 5s and £8 5s per quarter. By contrast, it appears that teachers in the School of Art were paid much higher salaries: in the eighteen-thirties, for example, they received £80 per year, between three and four times the salaries paid in the Academy.[269]

Realising that it was essential not only to have the good will of influential subscribers but also to secure their subscriptions, the Committee employed a messenger, Mr Martin, to collect subscriptions, for which he was paid a commission of 5 per cent, and to distribute circulars at six pence per thousand. The secretary's day book for the years 1858 to 1863 makes it clear that Martin and his successors fully justified their retention. But they were not alone, since the governors, and the honorary secretaries in particular, also busied themselves in collecting subscriptions and soliciting new members, which are recorded *in extenso* in the secretary's day book: '29 March [1860] Lord Dunraven attended and paid up his own subscription plus those of Sir Robert Gore-Booth and others (total £5.10.0).'

Finance was a constant headache, and the question of how to proceed on a broad educational front while managing the day-to-day cash flow occupied the governors at every meeting. In November 1857 the French teacher, M. Blum, was told that funds did not permit the purchase of a dictionary,[270] and perhaps lack of facilities led to the French classes being discontinued in 1858;[271] while the following May the gas bill was paid only when the Gas Company threatened legal action.[272] When in January 1859 Scriber, the clockmaker, requested payment for work done—the sum amounted to 3s 6d—he was left waiting until (the secretary recorded) his 'man called and was excessively urgent about the money due . . . The clock now goes well.' Scriber was eventually paid on 11 February.[273]

On occasion the governors must have felt that the Academy could ask too much of them, and sometimes meetings were without a quorum. On 5 January 1858 the minutes tersely record that 'Mr. Hercules MacDonnell breakfasted alone,' and on 13 July the same year, 'Mr. Exham solus.' On 2 October 1861 only Berwick (now a judge), Joseph Robinson and Francis Robinson attended, and the minutes record, 'Nothing done but breakfast.' On another occasion governors, but no breakfast, appeared, causing an outburst of indignation: on 17 October 1866 the minutes recorded, 'No breakfast was ready this morning. Ordered, that there be breakfast every Wednesday, unless specifically countermanded.'

Several apparently unrelated incidents seem to have contributed between 1856 and 1858 to some dissatisfaction with the way the Academy was being run. Herr Waetzig, who had been on the staff only since the reopening in February, resigned seven months later, to be succeeded by a Mr Clements;[274] two months later J. A. L. Rungeling was appointed professor of wind,[275] but neither he nor Clements is heard of again in connection with the institution.[276] On 28 April 1857 it was resolved to advertise in the *Musical World* for a wind teacher.

In 1857 Sloane, the master and secretary, was severely chided for the slowness in payment of fees[277]—arrears of fifty-nine pounds were reported—and by January 1858 he had been dismissed, being succeeded by Mr Powell. Powell, however, tendered his resignation in June[278] and was in turn succeeded during the next term by Robert Wheeler, who was to remain in office for ten years.[279] He was succeeded by Mr Browne in 1868, at a reduced salary of thirty pounds a year but with free apartments, gas, and coal.[280] During this period we note that 'a special meeting [was] to be called to investigate charges made respecting the management of the establishment,'[281] and Brady, MacDonnell and Pigot were appointed a sub-committee 'to draw up such a Minute of Rules as may be necessary to define the duties of the Assistant Secretary and Master of the General Class and to report on the best means of regulating the general management of the Academy in future';[282] but who had made the charges or how the situation was resolved we cannot tell, in the absence of the sub-committee's report, nor do we know whether Sloane's and Powell's defects were their own or those of the system (or lack of it) imposed by the governors.

Nor is it open to us at this remove to tell whether personality clashes or inadequate conditions played any part in the turnover of teaching or administrative staff. The fact that in 1862 Mr Reilly, the then wind teacher, was dismissed for 'the discreditable performance' of his pupils at their annual concert (he was succeeded by Harry Hardy, at a salary of forty pounds a year)[283] suggests that, in that department at least, the failure to secure an adequate teacher may have been a mutual problem. So too do the admonitions (which we shall see repeated into modern times) to teachers who missed lessons without prior notice—meted out even to staff as senior as Levey and Elsner.[284] On 29 January 1862 'the secretary reports that none of the teachers (Mr. Levey, Mr. Elsner, Mr. Reilly) attended this morning. They had gone to Cork to assist at a Music Festival. Mr. Levey sent a deputy (Mr. Grandison) to his class. Neither Mr. Reilly or Mr. Elsner made any arrangements for instruction of their classes.' And a week later it was recorded that 'with reference to the absence of Mr. Elsner & Mr. Reilly last Wednesday the Secretary is directed to inform them that in future the Committee will require an efficient deputy to be provided in case of their absence.'[285]

We do know, however, that in November 1858 Wheeler was still trying to establish a system that would not only put general education in the Academy on a proper footing but would also allow him to augment his income by private teaching. He pointed out to the Committee 'that his duties as Secretary *occasionally* oblige him to leave the class-room of

General Instruction, that disorder may arise among his pupils during his absence,' and 'that *one* of his *own private pupils* might be permitted to study in the General class-room who would volunteer to act as *monitor and* to *maintain order* during the absence of the Secretary'—a point on which Brady inscribed, 'Consideration postponed.' At the same time Wheeler suggested that 'the large map of the world . . . ought to be varnished in order to preserve it' and recorded that he 'hopes to be shortly prepared with some plan (not liable to error) of keeping account of payments made by his pupils.'[286]

Nevertheless, despite these lacunae in management, the Academy was expanding. 'Mrs. Joseph Robinson, Miss Arthur' was now teaching piano, while her husband, assisted by Julia Cruise (Mrs Levey) held a vocal class. (The fees were six pounds a year, or ten pounds for piano and vocal studies combined.) Young Philip Hughes had been appointed as an assistant to Levey.[287] Evening classes had begun soon after the move to the new premises, in response to the needs of those who 'may not be able to attend during the day time'[288]—strings on Tuesday and Thursday and wind on Monday and Wednesday—while classes 'for tuition of females' (more often referred to as 'ladies' classes') began in October 1856, attracting ten applications, with singing on Monday, Wednesday and Friday and harmony on Saturday.[289]

Not all ambitions could be fulfilled, however. In early 1857 it was decided to canvass interest among the vocal and piano students in Italian classes, which were offered at 10s 6d for two hours each week; the reply was nil.[290] From 1859 we gain an insight into a perennial problem for parents whose children manifest not only an interest in music but also a rounded personality that includes other pursuits. Henry Crofton of Garville Road, Rathgar, told the secretary that he had 'some intention of placing his son in the General Class & also the piano class, but objects to the late hours for the boys' piano class—as it would cause too much confinement for a boy of tender age.' A week later he had called again and 'is inclined to place his son in the General Class and also in the piano class—wishes that instruction in the piano could be given earlier in the day or at least that some other day should be substituted for Saturday in order that a boy might have Saturday after 12 o'clock for relaxation.'[291]

By October 1856 the Academy was able to make its fullest public announcement so far, offering classes in harmony and composition, singing, strings, wind, English, French, and general education,[292] while piano classes for women were to begin the following January, under the direction of Fanny Arthur, who earlier that year had given what *Saunders's News-Letter* announced as 'the first . . . regular pianoforte recital' to be heard in Dublin —a much-disputed claim.[293] On 15 October Prof. Smith gave an inaugural lecture in which he asserted the simple need for education in harmony to supplement the Irish natural musical personality, which would then give them the same innate capacity for part-singing as the 'Hebrews' and the Germans. The lecturer went on to describe the history of notation and the evolution of scales, before making some somewhat condescending remarks about the incidence of fifths in Irish jigs and hoping 'that we would always support our national music, which we had every right to do.'[294]

The pupils' concert in June 1857 showed a marked development from that of 1851. The overture to *La Dame blanche* reappeared, in company with its sister *The Caliph of Bagdad*, together with a Mozart piano quartet, Irish airs, airs and choruses from Mendelssohn's *Athalie*, a piano trio by Mayseder, and a chorus from Meyerbeer's *Les Huguenots*. The deficiencies in the orchestral complement were made good by hiring five bandsmen at 8s 6d each and a drummer at 7s 6d. Commenting on the palpable rise in standards since the expansion of the classes, the press generally applauded the students, in particular the vocalists Bessie Herbert and Louie Perrin, the string players Grandison and Farrell (soon to become the Academy's first scholar),[295] and the pianist Miss Foster. Another student performer, a Miss Davis, was to be disciplined some time later for impropriety in the classroom: she had 'spoken . . . in such a manner as to set a bad example' and was not to be readmitted without an apology.[296]

On 27 January 1857 the Committee had taken a decision that would have serious repercussions for many years and would not be resolved until the Academy's functions were exactly defined in the 'Blue Scheme' of 1889. It was ordered that

> a Book be prepared for each of the classes for Ladies which shall contain a Declaration in the following words and that every Female Pupil before being admitted either to the Vocal or Piano Forte class shall be required to sign this Declaration in the Book as a preliminary before being permitted to take any lesson.

> DECLARATION

> I the undersigned request admission as a pupil in the Irish Academy of Music and I undertake to observe all rules which shall from time to time be prescribed by the Committee respecting the management of the Classes: and I do hereby declare that in applying for admission to the Academy it is my intention to adopt Music as my profession, either alone, or as part of the general Profession of Teaching.

The object was to ensure that the Academy would not become a subsidised school for the dilettante offspring, especially the daughters, of gentlefolk but would remain a training-ground for professionals. In the case of young women, the career opportunities as teachers (mainly in schools) and as governesses or tutors were more widely available than they were for men, whereas, conversely, there were few women orchestral players or solo performers (except singers). It could be assumed, however, that men or boys enrolling for classes had a musical profession in mind, whereas women might be sent merely in order to acquire an 'accomplishment' to grace the salon and increase their marrageability.[297]

The procedure involved a record by the secretary that, for example, 'Eliza Anne McEnery . . . proposes to enter the junior piano class . . . She has read the declaration . . . and assents to same—it being her intention to adopt music as part of the general profession of teaching,' to which the applicant added her signature and subscribed: 'This is correct.'[298] After January 1863 it was necessary simply to sign the form and be 'made to understand . . . that they declare the truth.' Three months after its introduction the first casualty of this scheme was a Mrs Dunne, whose daughters, applying to enter the piano class, had refused to sign the declaration; she was informed 'that her daughters cannot be admitted to the Academy.'[299] This resulted in many prospective pupils being turned away, and in time it was to give the governors many headaches as they grappled with the question of whether or not to admit 'amateurs'.

A further regulation that appears to have been introduced in 1859 is that relating to two-subject study. Early that year, press announcements informed intending students that 'each pupil will be required to learn a stringed or wind instrument in addition to the pianoforte, and also to attend Professor Smith's lectures on Harmony and Composition.'[300] This heralded the insistence on professional students having a second instrument and on students in most categories undertaking studies in the theory of music.

The Academy from the time of its reorganisation engaged in useful community relations. On 24 February 1857 it was decided to take in six boys from the Board of Education's Model School in Marlborough Street, and in November 1858 this figure was doubled.[301] The IAM's Finance Committee book of 1857 contains a copy of the following minute of the Commissioners of National Education:

> Read letter 853-57 from the Sec. of the I.A.M. calling attention to the opportunity which it offers for the cultivation of the art, the advantage which, it is suggested, the Commissioners should avail themselves of in the education of such of the children of the Model Schools as have a talent for music, Ordered, that Mr. Glover be requested to recommend *six boys* from amongst the pupils of the Model Schools who have evinced a decided talent for music, who are to be sent (with the sanction of their parents) to attend the classes of the Institution referred to, at such times as will not interfere with their studies in the Model N.S.— the board to defray the cost of their instruction, viz: £4 a year each.

A year later:

> Read Letter 6734-58 from R. Wheeler, Sec. to the I.A.M., stating that the Committee of that institution are desirous of receiving an increased number of pupils from the Central Model Schools, should the Commissioners deem it expedient to enlarge the class paid for by them, and which at present is limited to *six boys*. Ordered—that Mr. Wheeler be informed that the Commissioners have agreed to select six lads for admission to the Academy (in addition to the number already paid for) keeping in view their aptitude for benefiting from instruction in instrumental music, the usual fees (£4) to be paid by the Board.

P. W. Joyce[302]—who was to become a Governor of the Academy in 1871 —was headmaster of the Model School, the author of *A Handbook of*

School Management (1863), and, in association with Patrick Keenan, a major influence on educational thinking and methods. By 1865 he was actively promoting the education by the Academy of both girls and boys from the Model Schools.[303] The arrangement with the schools was to continue until 1922.[304]

Another important (but silent) aspect of the Academy's activity was the education of those who could not afford the fees—by way not of scholarship but of subvention. In 1863 we find the secretary recording that 'Miss Mary Ann Morgan left the Academy June 2nd 1863—has been affected with deafness—has been under the care of Dr. Hardy, Merrion Square—wishes to recommence in the piano class but cannot afford to pay for the time she has been absent. Her father resides at 30 Upper Erne St.—states he has eight children unprovided for—he will pay half yearly and will struggle to do so.' At the same time 'Mrs. Harrison of Manor St. has five children, her resources for their education arise from tuitions—these have declined during the summer months—as not able to keep her daughters in the Academy & hopes she will not be charged for the four months during which her daughters were absent.'[305] In 1873 Theodore Logier, grandson of the famous teacher, was admitted to the second piano class, and, although the minutes record that he was to receive free tuition, the secretary's day book for 1873 and the two following years shows that his fees were in fact paid by George Sproule, a member of the Committee.[306] Young Logier is also recorded as having played at Academy concerts in 1876 (a Scarlatti piano sonata), in 1878 (Mozart's Fantasia in D minor and Hiller's Waltz in D flat), and in 1880 (the *andante* from Hummel's Fantasia in E flat). In 1881, on the representation of Raoul de Versan, he was still having half his fees remitted, the other half being paid 'out of moneys collected from friends.'[307]

Subsidies (or quasi-scholarships) were also awarded to encourage the study of less popular instruments.

> Resolved that in order to encourage the study of the Violoncello and Double Bass the Committee will nominate to the two free places in Mr. Elsner's class for the current year the two boys whom Mr. Elsner and Mr. Robinson shall report to be the most promising students of music who shall present themselves; and that Mr. Elsner and Mr. Robinson be requested to communicate this Resolution to such professors, classes and choirs in Dublin as they may believe likely to propose promising candidates for admission to this class.[308]

In 1862 Sir Jocelyn Coghill, a subscriber since 1856, became a member of the Committee[309] and immediately offered the Academy an 'opera-extravaganza', *The Bridal of Triermain*, which had been composed by Alan Close, with a libretto by himself based on the novel by Walter Scott. The offer was accepted, and the opera, which was in fact a marionette affair, was staged in the Antient Concert Rooms in December that year. It is significant in that it repeated the puppet technique employed in 1858 in *Don Giovanni*, that it was taken from Scott (a stock source of romantic opera), and that it was written by two Irish amateurs. *Saunders's News-Letter* found the libretto 'though brisk and funny . . . a great deal too long' and, while praising the general endeavour, thought that 'if the marionettes were discarded, the libretto abridged, and the entire work adapted for a performance with stage vocalists, it might gain by the change.' The *Evening Mail*, on the other hand, thought that Coghill's burlesque (perhaps presaging his descendant Neville Coghill's version of *The Canterbury Tales*) 'would be no discredit to Mr. Burnand' (the leading satirist of the day) and went on to discourse knowledgeably on the subject of Italian marionette practice.[310] It also gave examples of Coghill's excruciatingly poor accomplishments as a punster: 'Not Jenny Lind so well the notes did handle, Nor Grisi to her hold a greasy candle.' The *Irish Times* and *Freeman's Journal* were polite, and all agreed that the singing, by Julia Cruise, Mr (presumably Evory) Kennedy, Mr Herbert, and Mr Dollard, was commendable.[311]

We should also take note of a further fund-raising initiative from this period. In April 1865 the Committee decided to take advantage of the occasion of the Dublin International Exhibition, with its impressive 'Exhibition Palace' in Earlsfort Terrace (the present National Concert Hall), to hold a charity Ball on 12 May 1865. The list of 'patronesses', headed by the wife of the Lord Lieutenant, Lady Wodehouse, included a trio of marchionesses (including Lady Downshire), a sextet of countesses, and some of the more elevated commoners, such as the Hon. Mrs King Harman, Lady Staples, Lady Coghill, and Mrs Cusack Smith. Tickets for Academy subscribers were fifteen shillings for gentlemen and ten shillings for ladies, and twice that for non-members. A special train was announced to leave Westland Row the following morning at three o'clock, calling at all stations to Kingstown and Bray. The *Freeman's Journal* estimated that three thousand people had attended, 'a scene of splendour and festivity that dazzled and delighted . . . more like a fairy scene than an earthly reality,'[312] the wonder being attributable, of course, to the international display of artefacts, especially the illuminated glass and mirrors. Dancing was to an augmented Academy band of forty, under the direction of Harry Hardy.

The Exhibition Palace was to provide the Academy with further opportunities for fund-raising. On 30 May 1867 a concert was given (including the overture to Arne's *Artaxerxes*, a number of piano duets, and a cantata, 'Sylvan Hours', by Joseph Robinson, receiving the first of many performances) as part of a 'Fancy Fair' occupying the main hall and consisting of a pot-pourri of bizarre exhibits, ranging from a Chinese umbrella 'presented to Sir Richard M'Causland by the residents of Singapore' to a watercolour depicting a 'flying column' such as had recently been engaged in the pursuit of Fenian guerrillas.[313] We have to bear in mind, however, that, for reasons of social inhibitions, such events could not attract any but the upper and middle classes and therefore served to reinforce a social reality that hindered, rather than aided, the expansion of the Academy.[314]

Despite these initiatives, finance continued to be a problem. In late 1864 the board recorded that 'in order to defray the Professors' salaries now overdue the Royal Bank be requested to grant permission to overdraw the account to the extent of fifty pounds.'[315] There would be many such occasions in subsequent years, on one of which the secretary was instructed to move to a bank that *would* accommodate the Academy's pressing needs,[316] as the governors resisted the pressure to increase fees while maintaining the ethos of the institution.

Benefit concerts and similar endeavours not only brought a large capital sum to the IAM but also attracted new subscribers, whose regular donations and social cachet were twin points of advantage. Within a few months of reopening in 1856 the Academy had enrolled Sir William Wilde, Sir Jocelyn Coghill and Lady Donoughmore and, in the following two years, William Smith O'Brien, Dr C. Benson (a founder of Baggot Street Hospital), Charles Hemphill, and Dr William Stokes. By 1863 the list of subscribers had grown from less than 40 to 224, of whom at least 10 per cent were actively involved in the management of the institution. These included Sir Vere de Vere of Curragh Chase, County Limerick, Lord and Lady Ashtown of Woodlawn, County Galway, John Esmonde MP, Benjamin Lee Guinness, Patrick Keenan, J. D. Rosenthal, and two noted members of the Cecilian movement, Bishop Nicholas Donnelly and Canon Myles MacManus. The eccentric Sir Philip Crampton, who married Victoire Balfe, daughter of M. W. Balfe, and was said to have been the richest surgeon in the country (commemorated by an equally eccentric stone pineapple in College Street, Dublin), was a member until his death in 1858. John Jameson, distiller, of Airfield House, Donnybrook, John Lentaigne, director of the prison service, Lt-Col. Thomas Larcom, initiator of the Ordnance Survey in Ireland and then Permanent Under-Secretary at Dublin Castle, Lord Gough, head of British forces in Ireland, William Dargan, pioneer of Irish railways and co-founder of the National Gallery, a Mrs Parnell with an address in Temple Street and the impecunious Robert Corbet (collateral of W. B. Yeats and castellator of 'Sandymount Castle') are typical of the people who decided that this 'useful and national' institution was worthy of their support.

The Academy's public relations strategy seems to have been effective. In 1865 the *Freeman's Journal* pointed out that 'notwithstanding all the "talk talk" there is amongst us about love of music, appreciative audiences, patronage &c., the only musical training institution in the city would long since have ceased to have an existence were it not for the zeal, energy, taste and public spirit displayed by a few ladies and gentlemen.'[317] This, as before, was by way of soliciting support for the annual concert, of which it reported particularly favourably on the début of Mary Marmion (singing 'Porgi amor'),[318] while the *Irish Times* also gave substantial credit to the Academy, drawing attention to its claim for financial support from the government on the same basis as the art schools and praising the performance of a twelve-year-old Miss Martin playing Hummel's Rondo Brilliant in A, op. 56, and Thalberg's Fantasia on Irish Airs, Elsner and his daughter in a Mendelssohn duo concertante, and Miss Jackson and Miss O'Hea in Weber's Konzertstück. 'Another concert equally successful will make the institution known as a musical academy second to none in the United Kingdom.'[319]

Of the 159 subscribers in 1863 whose occupation or affiliation we have been able to identify, sixty (over 25 per cent of the total of 224) were lawyers;

twenty-three (9 per cent) were in trade, commerce, or manufacture; twenty-one (almost 10 per cent) belonged to the gentry or nobility; fifteen (6 per cent) were doctors; eight (3 per cent) were clergy; five were academics or involved in education; five were politicians; six belonged to various other professions; and three (including Lentaigne and Larcom) were public servants. Only nine (3 per cent) were involved professionally in music, and a further one (T. A. Jones) was an artist in another discipline.

Of equal interest is the geographical spread (or lack of it) of their addresses, which are given for 218 of the total. These are heavily concentrated in Fitzwilliam Square and its environs (26), Merrion Square and Merrion Street (22), Leeson Street (10), St Stephen's Green (7), Harcourt Street (5), Upper Mount Street (5), Herbert Street and Herbert Place (5), Baggot Street (4), Mountjoy Square (4), and Rutland Square (Parnell Square) (3), while 30 lived in the suburbs—some in recent developments, such as Patrick Keenan at Victoria Terrace, Rathgar, others in mansions, such as Viscount Monck at Charleville, Enniskerry, or the Goughs at St Helen's, Booterstown. Several traders subscribed, most of them in Grafton Street or Sackville Street (O'Connell Street), of whom the most notable were Messrs Browne and Nolan, since Browne had been a close associate of O'Connell and the publisher of the Repeal pamphlets.

Probably typical of the middle-class clientele in the Academy were the Marmion sisters, Mary and Lizzie, the daughters of a well-to-do corn salesman, William Marmion, and his French wife, Herminie (née Cordier), whose family fortunes became restricted after his early death in 1878, which extinguished his very respectable annual salary of £500. The Marmions, who lived first at 57 Queen Street and later moved to 2 Blackhall Place, had six children who survived infancy, one of whom, Joseph (1858–1923), became Abbot of the Belgian Benedictine monastery of Maredsous and an influential Catholic writer.[320] In 1864 the eldest child, Mary, entered the senior piano class and, with her sister Lizzie (1849–1918), the junior vocal class.[321] Mary was commended by the newspapers for her singing of 'Porgi amor' and 'With verdure clad' at Academy concerts in 1865 and 1867 and, in the lists of successful students published in support of the application for government funding at that time, is listed as a soprano singing at the Pro-Cathedral and as a concert artist. In 1868 she is listed as a soloist with Bessie Herbert on the same programme as Piatti and Dannreuther at a Philharmonic concert.[322] It is quite likely that if she had decided to pursue music as a career she would have joined the Academy staff, in the company of near-contemporaries such as Annie Irwin and Elizabeth Scott-Fennell. Lizzie, like her younger sisters Flora (1853–92) and Rosie (d. 1930), entered the Convent of Mercy, Clonakilty, in 1870. Flora subsequently founded the Convent of Mercy, Dunmore East, where she was superior from 1883 to 1895.

Nothing in the first sixteen years of the Academy's existence can compare in significance with the first of two protracted episodes that eventually saw it gaining its real status as a charitable institution, intimately involved with the system of public education. This was the campaign to secure a government grant, which began in 1864 and concluded successfully in 1870. (The second was the availability in 1880 of the Coulson funds, described below.)

Running throughout the history of the Academy has been the question of the role, status and function of a national music education institution. Soon after its foundation, the Academy began to make analogies with the conservatoires of the Continent, most of which had come into existence in recent decades—Milan in 1807, Naples in 1810, and Leipzig (under the direction of Mendelssohn) in 1843. That in Paris (dating from 1795), for reasons of ideology and stature, must have been predominantly in the minds of Dublin, as well as the Academy of Music in London, founded in 1822 and incorporated by Royal Charter in 1830. As we shall see, a heated debate on the nature of a 'national school of music' took place in the eighteen-eighties and nineties, while in more recent times the idea of a merger of the RIAM and the College of Music to form a national conservatoire has been vigorously canvassed. Today, as John O'Conor's concluding chapter indicates, the ambition to give Ireland such an institution is no less cherished than previously.

Despite the fact that the Academy itself, and the influential press, referred to the institution as 'national' in character, it was not until its governors had successfully secured, first, the government grant in 1870 and then (and more importantly) the Coulson endowment in 1886–89, and put the latter into operation, that it could be regarded as the 'truly national institution' that it aspired to become. Joseph Ryan observes that many such institutions 'had to confront the pertinent decision as to the espousal of a national or a cosmopolitan ethos' and asks whether what he perceives as an absence of such tension in Ireland is due to the fact that music 'was simply not sufficiently crucial to occasion such a dispute' or whether national and cosmopolitan traditions in Ireland were so 'disjoint' that such an institution could not impinge on both at once.[323]

Since there was such commerce between Ireland and France in the late eighteenth century on the ideological plane, in particular in relation to the growth of republicanism, a comparison between the origins of the RIAM and of the Paris Conservatoire will prove instructive. The Paris institution originated in the immediate aftermath of the Revolution and took its inspiration from the Revolution itself. It reflected the need partly for stability, similar to (though on a much more extensive scale than) the IAM, and partly for an aesthetic complement to the revolutionary ideology.[324] It is worth contemplating the prospect of how Young Ireland or their predecessors, the United Irishmen, might have established such a conservatoire had not the 1798, 1803, 1848–49 or 1861 risings been so ineffective and had they been in a position instead to harness to the task the vision of educationalists like Thomas Wyse—to elucidate a policy and practice for music education that, as in Paris, would combine the Italian precedent for integrated procedure with a sense of national independence and identity. Music might thus have developed a much more penetrating ideological role than circumstances in fact permitted, and the debates of the eighteen-seventies and later over the function (and indeed the management) of a conservatoire or 'national school of music' would have taken place much sooner.

As Jérome Thébaux says of the Paris Conservatoire and of its absorption of the national opera school, it became 'an institution that made it possible to reshape the musical landscape and to provide France with a national music.'[325] In the case of Paris, furthermore, this had a two-pronged effect: 'This renaissance, so ardently wished for, had the twin features of transmitting knowledge and of directing emotional energy into ideas of the common good.'[326]

The same possibility existed within the Irish academy, but until much later it existed subcutaneously, and its exploration was conducted at a subliminal level. In Paris, for example, it seemed imperative to establish a canon of musical studies, in which prescribed methods and texts were not only insisted on but incorporated in the institution through its own printing press.[327] In Dublin, by contrast, there was little or no pre-ordained syllabus and, apart from the use of Dr Smith's textbook, no evidence of a policy on methods of instruction. When in fact it came to the point where the question of piano method was crucial (in order to secure the Coulson funds, which were conditional on the method of Frédéric Kalkbrenner being employed), the IAM could blithely say (in the words of Francis Brady) that 'we have a copy of it; it is a very good method, but . . . it is almost the only method, and it is very simple when you come to look at it . . . teaching you how to put your hands on the pianoforte . . . the method that has always been taught'[328]—the inference being that the method was so obvious as to be at least commonplace, if not meaningless. In place of such prescription, IAM teachers were left to devise their own methods, and the institution as a whole was probably in a better position—certainly in the later decades of the nineteenth century—to develop a cosmopolitan atmosphere than other such bodies.

Even Paris had its difficulties, at times not having a clear idea whether it was to serve the needs of the nation or to obey the pressures of the market. As we have seen in the rather different context of Ireland in the eighteen-fifties, 'the Conservatoire became the prow of a non-existent ship.'[329]

As we mentioned in chapter 1, the RAM was a natural focus of attention and enquiry for the IAM. Bernarr Rainbow has said that the RAM 'was in constant financial straits for its first 40 years,'[330] dependent on a mixture of subscriptions and donations and in danger of closing only a few years after its opening. The RAM (which opened with ten boys and ten girls, out of an application of thirty-two boys and fourteen girls) enjoyed a foundation balance of over £4,300 from initial subscriptions and donations and an annual subscription list of over £500; it gained £1,000 from a benefit concert in 1823, but by 1824 it appears that it was running at an annual loss of £1,500, even with an increase in fees to £30 or £40 and with professors agreeing to teach free of charge for three months.[331] A minute of 1853, contemplating a memorial to Prince Albert, notes that the institution was then running at a loss of £300 a year, despite generous contributions from the Queen[332] and a charity ball held annually from 1835 to 1849 that brought in a total net profit of £10,000.[333]

There is no evidence that the IAM was in contact with any other academy or conservatoire until the eighteen-sixties. But we are entitled to speculate that the founders' aspiration of creating a national institution at least mirrored that of other peoples in similar circumstances, Scotland being the nearest geographically,[334] Hungary politically, and Poland and Finland ideologically.

The institution that evolved into today's Royal Scottish Academy of Music and Drama had its origins at the same time as those of the IAM, in that a Glasgow Commercial College, established in 1845, became in 1847 the Glasgow Athenæum, teaching music, which in turn became in 1890 a corporate body, the Athenæum School of Music, on lines similar to the Guildhall School, with eight hundred students and sixty teachers.[335] Simultaneously the Scottish Vocal Music Association (founded 1856) set up an Academy of Music in 1858, which awarded diplomas in harmony and counterpoint and gave classes in singing and piano. 'Some time between 1875 and 1880,' H. G. Farmer tells us, 'efforts were made in Edinburgh to establish a Scottish Academy of Music,'[336] but in 1881 it was still stated (erroneously) that 'Scotland is the only nation in Europe that has no National School of Music.'[337]

Poland saw its first conservatory of music in Warsaw (with Jozef Elsner as director)[338] in 1821; it was closed after the 1831 rebellion and reopened in 1861, the same year as the opening of the Chopin School of Music.[339]

In Finland the Academy of Music (today's Sibelius Academy) was founded in 1882, the same year that Kajanus established the Helsinki Orchestral Society,[340] and there are striking parallels between Ireland and Finland (which, together with those relating to Scotland, Poland and Hungary, are given further consideration in an appendix to this chapter).

The first we learn of the campaign for a government grant to the IAM is a report in the *Irish Times* of 2 March 1864 of a deputation to the Lord Lieutenant, asking for his recommendation in support of an application to the Treasury for an annual parliamentary grant as a supplement to its current funding from fees and subscriptions. The Lord Lieutenant, the Earl of Carlisle, had, like his predecessors, looked favourably on the IAM and gave this request his blessing. 'A stronger proof of the estimation in which the Academy is held', said the *Irish Times*, 'could not be afforded than that found in the influential character of the deputation.' This consisted of the Lord Chancellor (Brady's father), the Lord Justice of Appeal (Francis Blackburne, a previous Lord Chancellor), the Duke of Leinster, Dr Graves (recently elevated as Dean of Clonfert and soon to become Bishop of Limerick), the Right Hon. Alexander MacDonnell (Commissioner of National Education, no relation to Hercules), who was there to support the efficacy of what would today be called the Academy's 'outreach' programme, together with Brady himself, Joseph Robinson, R. M. Levey, and two lay members of the Committee, Judge J. H. Monahan[341] and Dr Thomas Beatty. It is doubtful if any similar institution in Ireland could have fielded a more influential team of advocates to press its case.

The significance of the presence of the Duke of Leinster lies not merely in the fact that he was the premier Irish peer or that he was an enthusiastic musician (and benefactor of the Academy)[342] but that he was also closely associated with the RAM. He had been a director of the company governing its activities since 1839 and had become a vice-president in 1864.[343] During the RAM's own negotiations with the government, he had attended and presided at some of the more crucial meetings. We can assume that much of the adroit handling of the IAM's application during the years ahead was due to his advice and guidance.

The case itself was based on the fact that the RAM was to receive a grant in that year's estimates and that, as a comparable institution providing 'a superior musical education' but inhibited by lack of funds from fully carrying out its objectives, the IAM deserved parity. In support of its claim, the Academy pointed out that it had educated 350 pupils and had at present 96 students on its books—a fact that it would employ consistently in later years to emphasise that not merely *pro rata* but in absolute numbers it had more students than the RAM.

Lack of funds was attributed principally to the falling off in revenue from benefit concerts, which had previously shown 'the interest taken in the academy by the people of Ireland.' Reasserting the original reasons for founding the Academy and, by implication, the argument for government funding advanced by Graves in 1852, the Committee pointed out that a healthy musical life had always been dependent on 'the casual presence in Dublin of amateurs of distinguished ability,' which 'cannot be permanently relied on as a means of supplying adequate funds.' Specifically, the deputation mentioned harmony and composition, and elocution and modern languages, as elements lacking in the complete musical education, thus reviving the principle of general education voiced in 1856. Alexander MacDonnell's emphasis on the advantages of the Academy to the Model Schools was supplemented by the Duke of Leinster's assertion that it was hoped to extend tuition to the Masonic Orphans' School (again, he was associated with this institution).

This application failed, because the grant to the RAM was regarded as 'experimental', but a crucial point was conceded by Gladstone, who, as Chancellor of the Exchequer, agreed that, should the grant to the RAM become stable, there would be a similar entitlement in the case of Ireland.

At the end of 1866 a second deputation met the new Lord Lieutenant, the Duke of Abercorn, with, on this occasion, a renewed appeal supported by fifty (out of a total of sixty-six) Irish MPs. The accounts for 1865 and 1866 showed that whereas the Academy had profited from a benefit concert in 1865 to the extent of almost £150 (£6,000 today), the next year had seen a complete disappearance of such income (even though the balance sheet showed a net profit of £85 on the year and included an income of £200 from the ball).

On this occasion, the deputation consisted of the Duke of Leinster and Sir Colman O'Loghlen, who was to prove one of the Academy's most influential and stalwart supporters at Westminster and in Whitehall,[344] and three other MPs but was otherwise less high-powered than its predecessor, its other members being the honorary secretaries and some members of the legal and medical professions, who, however well connected socially, had not the same cachet in Viceregal circles as the chiefs of the judiciary. Nevertheless, there was no hesitation on the Academy's part in urging the Lords of the Treasury to act fairly in relation to Ireland: the experimental year in respect of the RAM 'had now elapsed, and those interested in the Irish Academy thought that the time had come round when they should call the attention of the Government to its claims for aid from the public funds.'[345] Dublin continued to compare favourably with London: the RAM had a grant of £500 and subscriptions of £300 and charged annual fees of thirty guineas (£1,850 today)—over three times the fees in the IAM. Its annual budget was £2,766. Nevertheless, on a total budget of £850, which included no grant, the IAM educated the same number of pupils, at much lower fees.

Presenting the case for the IAM, Hercules MacDonnell said that the commission investigating the question of the grant to the RAM had acknowledged that 'though such an institution could be started by voluntary efforts, it could not be well maintained. In England it failed—the subscriptions fell off, and the Irish Academy would be similarly fated but for the subscriptions of its patrons and friends.' In tandem with this, O'Loghlen reminded the Lord Lieutenant that 'Mr. Gladstone said that on principle the Irish Academy had an equal right to [such] aid' as the RAM—this, of course, being the IAM's strongest card.

Referring to the report of the RAM commission, the delegation pointed out that

> in the Commissioners' report great stress had been laid on the necessity of charging low fees, the object being that talent should be sought out amongst those who could not afford to pay the higher fees . . . In England they observed that musical talent of a higher order was often found amongst the poorer classes, and they insisted particularly upon an academy being founded in which such talent might be developed. Such a thing was simply impossible in England . . . [They] thought that His Excellency would admit that the circumstances of this country were such that it was no disgrace for them to come here and ask for Government aid.[346]

There was, however, another obstacle relating to the RAM. 'Mr. MacDonnell wished to mention that there was a difficulty in England as to whether the grant should be given to the old academy or to a new institution.'[347] In anticipation of a possible reorganisation of music education in England, the Duke of Leinster said that if the government gave the grant to the Irish Academy 'they were willing to carry out any suggestion that the Government might wish to make.'[348] It was a very sensible precaution, since the likelihood of musical education being drawn into the net of the South Kensington system was very great and, in the outcome, was to delay a decision on the matter for three more years. But it was also quite beyond the power of the IAM to influence the situation.

However, the Lord Lieutenant promised his support for a grant of £500. 'I think you are perfectly justified in asking for this support. In fact, it is a national thing.'[349] Subsequently, the delegation was interviewed by the Chief Secretary, Lord Mayo, with, apparently, equal success.[350] But only a year later the Chief Secretary informed the Academy that the Treasury regarded its other sources of revenue as 'very precarious',[351] even though it considered it necessary to provide special facilities for music education, not least in training teachers of music. To this the IAM replied in terms that give the present book its title:

> We are convinced that an institution for training teachers cannot be permanently supported, though it may properly be founded, without some aid from the State. It differs wholly from a school for amateurs, who come because they are ready and able to pay, and who are not selected for mere talent. To talent alone an academy should address itself, wherever found and should seek to cultivate it without reference to cost, confident that the elevation and sound instruction of those who in turn are to teach the public are the sure and only means of spreading and raising in quality the standard of instruction.[352]

This was in itself an ideological point as well as one of practicality and therefore applicable to all societies in which the principle of education was at work. Once the principle was accepted, the real issue therefore was one of degree or relationship. To this the IAM addressed itself as follows:

> In England the principle has been practically conceded—first, by the formation of art schools, and such institutions as that at South Kensington; and lately in music by the grant to the English Academy. In Ireland, so much less wealthy a country, State aid is infinitely more necessary. The people are thought to possess much untutored artistic capacity; but those who ask the aid of an academy, and seek to earn their living by art, are precisely those who are least able to pay sufficient fees. Indeed, this difference of the countries is so marked, that the directors of the Irish Academy find, by experience, they cannot charge at a rate of more than a third of the English scale.

There, however, the matter rested. We could be forgiven for thinking that the Treasury played cat-and-mouse with the Academy for the next few months, since the Academy's letter remained unanswered until in April 1867 the Treasury requested a copy of it and then in May blandly stated that the application had been received too late to be considered for inclusion in the estimates.

A further delegation, consisting of the Duke of Leinster 'and other influential gentlemen,' then visited George Ward Hunt, financial secretary to the Treasury and shortly to become Chancellor of the Exchequer, who 'most unequivocally stated that we had proved our case and that if a grant were given at all to maintain any institution in England it necessarily followed that a like favour should be bestowed on Ireland.' The delegation, clearly unused to such disingenuous conduct by a senior politician, 'considered that to be tantamount to a complete promise.' Yet in November 1867 Lord Mayo informed MacDonnell that the Chancellor had decided against the grant to the RAM.[353] 'That was an event they had not foreseen or expected'—or, as the *Freeman's Journal* put it, 'no kindly patronage in a practical shape was extended towards it by our rulers and those in high places beyond a profusion of promises all rendered peculiarly remarkable by none of them being fulfilled.'[354]

It is at this point that the brinkmanship began that saw the IAM manipulating public opinion in order to force politicians to fulfil the 'profusion of promises'. In a show of strength, a *conversazione* was held in the Exhibition Palace on 10 February 1868, at which the chief performers were four singing students, two of whom, Bessie Herbert and Elisabeth Scott-Fennell, would soon become members of the staff.

The next evening, building on the favourable public impression created by the *conversazione*, a meeting was held at the Mansion House, the purpose of which was 'to ascertain the feelings of subscribers on the present position of affairs.' With the support of the *Freeman's Journal*, the Academy made it clear that it had no intention of surrendering to adverse circumstances, unlike the RAM, which, in the same situation, was threatening to close. 'They were of opinion that they should not in any respect follow the example of the English institution. It was not at all impossible to continue the institution independently as at present.' The *Freeman's Journal* agreed:

> The moment the yearly grant of 500*l* was taken from the London Academy of Music, its committee . . . declare it must close its doors, and turn its pupils and its professors adrift upon the world. Here in Ireland, we manage matters in quite a different style. Unaccustomed to Government favours, we continue to get on without them and when, in reply to our petition for a share of the money that we pay ourselves, we are met with a contumelious refusal, we only nerve ourselves for fresh efforts in the cause we have at heart and make up our minds that it shall not fail.[355]

There was, however, a suggestion that closure was a possible course. 'The Committee believe the closing of the Academy of Music would be felt as a serious loss to the public education of the people of Ireland.' This brinkmanship was evident in all the Academy's dealings with the government: when the grant had been secured, the governors told the subscribers, 'Had the decision been adverse . . . they were . . . prepared to recommend the closing of the Academy.'[356] MacDonnell obviously expected reorganisation of art education, with South Kensington at its hub, and told the meeting of 11 February that 'he did not object to this institution being affiliated to that museum, but he held it to be necessary that a native and local institution should exist for the fostering and discovery of native genius,' thus neatly accommodating the ambitions of this 'national institution' and the political reality of Henry Cole's projected system. In 1864–65 Cole had been instrumental in an attempt to reform the RAM's contribution to music education, which, although unsuccessful, led eventually to the formation of a National Training School, which became the RCM. (A year later the *Irish Times*, which had pursued a policy of no taxation without education, exhorted its readers to 'atone for the niggard spirit of the State by their own liberality,' adding mischievously, 'perhaps we might hope for encouragement from England if Irish musical talent was not so pre-eminent.')[357]

But 'the committee did not wish to conceal from itself or the subscribers that its resources had been much crippled by the failure of some of its usual means of collecting funds, owing to the calamities that need only be referred to' (presumably by this MacDonnell meant the Fenian disturbances of 1866–67, which would have inhibited, to some extent, social events such as fund-raisers). As a counter-measure, Brady put forward the view that 'support of the Academy ought not to be confined to Dublin, but that the other cities of Ireland ought, and he had no doubt would, contribute to maintain in the metropolis an institution from which they derived considerable benefit'—a point to which he would return in 1870.

The meeting was told that the establishment of a special fund of £200 would tide the Academy over for two years, during which it confidently (and, as it turned out, correctly) expected to have obtained the grant. The meeting 'of the friends of our National Musical Institution,' as the *Freeman's Journal* put it, succeeded in raising immediate pledges of £100 in donations, mostly of five pounds each and mainly from the Committee, with Brady senior and Pigot senior subscribing five pounds each and the Lord Lieutenant twenty pounds.

From a letter from the Treasury to the Directors of the RAM we learn that in April 1868 the two institutions were again being considered jointly (and negatively):

> The Directors of the Irish Academy of Music have of late made repeated applications for assistance from public funds, and the Directors of the Royal Academy of Music will of course admit that the Irish institution is equally with their own entitled to the favourable consideration of Government. My Lords have accordingly reviewed the claims of both Academies and they have come to the conclusion that, in the present state of the question of musical instruction they would not be justified in asking Parliament for a vote in aid of either of them.[358]

A turning-point came in September and October 1868, when the Commission on Science and Art in Ireland (under the chairmanship of the Marquess of Kildare, son of the Duke of Leinster)[359] heard evidence in Dublin, including submissions by Brady (on 26 September) and MacDonnell (on 29 September), and visited the Academy on 1 October. It was told that the principal demand for tuition came from girls seeking a career as governesses or in private family teaching and that 166 male pupils and 206 female had studied piano since 1856, together with a further 183 female singing students. It was argued that, to obtain the best teachers, the highest salaries had to be paid but that the Academy could not continue, let alone develop, unless it could command enough funds to improve its premises and expand its curriculum. MacDonnell put forward the considerable point that a government grant would enable the Academy to establish scholarships for the free education of needy pupils, besides attracting extra voluntary support, which would enable the Academy to subvent travelling costs for pupils from the provinces.[360]

MacDonnell returned to a familiar theme by stressing that it was important to evaluate 'what the resources . . . are in music,' arguing that employing foreign artists at Irish concerts—'those luxuries which are now become part of the necessities of civilized life'—was a waste of such resources if properly trained Irish students could take their place.[361] He also vigorously asserted that if the expected centralisation of educational power resulted in a metropolitan school of music with an Irish branch in Dublin, control should nevertheless remain in Ireland. 'Let us send our accounts to any public body in London to check . . . but after that it seems to me that it is impossible to work the thing here in Ireland unless the details are carried out by a local committee . . . It would never do to carry to the other side of the water the question whether John Smith should pay 5*l* or 10*l* or whether Miss Jones should be in the first or second vocal class.'[362] Questioned (by G. A. Hamilton) on his affiliation on the national question, MacDonnell was equivocal, and therefore effective. 'Would you consider the Dublin institution a provincial one?' 'Comparatively, and I should much rather that it was so, although it ought to be of sufficient magnitude to meet the wants of the whole of Ireland, and in that sense be national.'[363]

Francis Brady, probably the most influential and authoritative speaker on behalf of the Academy, told the commission that the chief need of the institution was to enlarge the premises, to increase the courses offered for which fees would not be paid, and to give more free instruction. For this, the Academy's income would have to be increased from £550 to £1,100.[364]

It is surprising, therefore, to discover that in fact, on the eve of the making of the government grant, the Academy was more than breaking even. In 1869 receipts exceeded expenditure by £30 on a turnover of £676, and in 1870 by £130 on a turnover of £890 (including a grant of £150). Salaries in both years were more than covered by pupils' fees.

From Brady's evidence we also learn something further of the daily life of the Academy. Singing was taught on Mondays and Thursdays, piano on Tuesdays and Fridays, and strings and wind on Wednesdays and Saturdays. Girls, because they had a greater incentive in gaining the Certificate of Proficiency, paid eight pounds a year, twice the rate paid by boys, who needed encouragement to learn music. (In particular, the Academy wanted to be able to give free instruction in wind instruments.) Conversely, teachers of piano and singing were paid considerably more than those of strings; as a result, by this time Joseph and Fanny Robinson were each earning approximately £100 a year and Miss Bennett (second piano teacher) £80, whereas Levey received only £40 to £50 and Elsner £25 to £30.

Brady, like MacDonnell, was quite agreeable to ultimate control being centred in London, as far as accounts were concerned, as long as the benefits of the system accrued to the Academy, which he hoped would include scholarships to whatever new school was instituted in London. Progress from Dublin to London should be natural and based on merit: 'there should be no distinction whatever between the Irish people and the English and Scotch, except the fact of their living in the several countries which they inhabit.' He did believe, however, that if possible the private subscriptions should be maintained, and agreed that if necessary a government grant could be conditional on the subscriptions being maintained at a certain level, as in fact transpired. They represented 'a public and independent interest' that, as we shall see, was necessary to maintain the sense of an academy directed by both public and private funding, just as the governors would be private citizens disinterestedly administering that funding.

In a not unconstructive, but not necessarily friendly or indeed disinterested, submission, Sir Robert Stewart and Dr J. P. Mahaffy (Mahaffy had been elected to the Committee on 27 November 1866 but there is no evidence of his having ever participated in its affairs)[365] observed that, from want of funds, the IAM 'has degenerated to a great extent into a school for pianoforte playing and for singing,' to the neglect of the study of organ and harmony[366]— Stewart's own area of expertise. They also pointed out that none of the halls or rooms in the Exhibition building (mooted as a venue for the new schools of art), 'however spacious or elegant,' was suitable for concerts, thus reopening the question of providing an adequate concert hall for Dublin.

The most significant development came in the evidence of the powerful Henry Cole, who had previously inspected the RDS art schools in 1853 and 1854. He wanted to see a loose amalgam of public and private institutions in a purpose-built centre on Leinster Lawn. Taking the 'South Kensington' view of the English metropolis as the centre of the universe, he said, 'Perfect justice to Ireland . . . would treat Dublin like Birmingham,' but in a dramatic departure from that viewpoint—and from the concept of a centralised 'Science and Art College'—he continued: 'Great Britain owes every possible compensation to Ireland for the years of tyranny and injustice to which Ireland has been subjected.' One of the commissioners, Rev. Dr Haughton, retorted, 'Oh, that is politics,' to which Cole rejoined by quoting the recent statement by Sir Stafford Northcote, then Secretary for India and a future Chancellor of the Exchequer: 'We owe a debt to Ireland . . . because she is part of the nation towards which we pursued a policy which ought to make us blush' (referring to the penal laws). He added: 'I don't speak merely as an official but from a sentiment as a tax payer that I am defending the expenditure of public money on Ireland. I say Dublin has a right to have more spent upon her than Birmingham or Glasgow.'

'Here', the minutes tell us, 'the room was cleared in order that the Commissioners might decide whether this line of examination should proceed.'[367] On resumption, Cole also promoted the argument that he said had been shared by his former political masters, 'that Ireland was not to be treated with strict logic, and that it had claims for a different kind of treatment.'[368] Speaking specifically of the IAM, and reverting to his South Kensington mentality, Cole said:

> If at any time we have a national training school for teaching music . . .
> there should be a branch in Dublin . . . The object of a training school

is to find out those persons that have musical aptitude, who may be the poorest of the poor, and to train them for the good of the community. If you depend on the self-supporting system you are besieged by people who think they have got these gifts, and who are willing to pay money for the cultivation of them, and you cannot carry out the main object of the institution in its purity. Therefore my own opinion would be to have all the instruction at a national academy of music, given at public cost; to have it at least gratuitously; and to have admission to it absolutely upon the merit and qualifications of the students. I think there ought to be a branch of such an institution in Dublin, with an adequate grant to find out all the musical talent that may exist in Ireland, and to cultivate it as far as means would allow in Dublin . . . It would be a great mistake to attempt to establish in Dublin a small institution, calling itself a national academy. If you call it a branch of the head central place, and deal properly with it, I believe that will be the right way of administering it.[369]

Here we see the germs of a plan that the Academy had every reason to consider capable of execution: to bring music into the centralised net of art education and to provincialise its administration.

Although the institution had not been named in the commission's terms of reference, its report nevertheless included observations on the Academy, which, it considered, 'appears to be fettered from want of increased funds.'[370] It could not make recommendations, however, without exceeding its brief, and pointed out that 'pending . . . the organization of a complete system of musical education and a well-considered scheme of scholarships for supporting promising students and perfecting their education we do not feel ourselves in a position to make a specific recommendation as to how the State subsidies should be distributed.'

By March 1869 the Committee was still expecting such a development 'in connection with the Department of Science and Art,' but it is clear that they also knew that any grant to the IAM would be conditional on its continuing its own fund-raising efforts.[371] Furthermore, a special meeting of subscribers on 9 March 1869 was told that the extra funds raised a year previously would keep the Academy open until the end of the year but that 'its further progress will depend upon the Irish people for it does not seem possible that while other subjects engross the attention of the Government [presumably the disestablishment of the Church of Ireland and preparation for the first Land Act] any large plan of musical education will be brought forward.'[372] The same newspaper that had asked for 'a small portion of our own revenues' for the support of a national institution also commented that it was 'as if an evil genius always interposed between the State and an Irish object,' looked forward to 'more generous and civilizing times,' and asked well-wishers to 'atone for the niggard spirit of the State by their own liberality.'[373]

There the matter again rested for a further year, when the Treasury decided to solve the problems emanating from Dublin by offering the Academy

seventy pounds a year to enable it to send two students on scholarship to
the RAM.

> Their Lordships have come to the conclusion that, assuming the object
> of the Irish Academy to be the training of professional musicians, it will
> be best attained by facilitating the admission of some of its more
> promising pupils to the classes of the RAM in London, where advanced
> instruction is afforded by the increased number of Professors and of
> musical performances which the larger capital offers.[374]

Within a couple of days the Academy had moved behind the scenes to
contact Gladstone through the offices of O'Loghlen, who was informed:

> He is, as you know, friendly to the Institution and is prepared to deal
> with it on the same principle as the English Academy. But the grant to
> the latter was given under certain conditions, which must not be lost
> sight of in dealing with the former. In particular he considers essential
> that the character of the instruction given should be solid and wide
> enough to be of real public benefit by means of the diffusion of musical
> knowledge and the improvement of musical taste, this condition appeared
> to be on the whole satisfied in the case of the English Academy, but it
> is not so clear in regard to the Irish and in default of its establishing a
> title to direct support from public funds he does not disapprove the
> proposal made by the Treasury to encourage the scientific study of
> Music by the offer of exhibitions in connection with the Academy in
> London.[375]

In the face of this apparent reversal of Gladstone's declared intentions,
the IAM replied indignantly and at length to Gladstone himself, setting out
the full case for 'direct aid from the public funds.'[376] The Committee
realised that the Treasury's decision had been based on a London perspective of a 'provincial capital' and that they had tended to override the
matter of principle on which the claims of Dublin had been established.

These claims were now rehearsed for Gladstone's benefit. The original
founders of the Academy 'believed that such an institution was much
needed in a population of considerable artistic capacity and that it would
attract a sufficient number of pupils to permanently advance musical taste
and to promote musical knowledge in Ireland.' The numbers educated now
exceeded five hundred and the number of pupils annually on the books was
eighty-nine, 'exceeding the average of the English Academy for the five
years previous & obtaining at present . . . a very large attendance considering
the greater difficulties to be encountered in this country.' To this letter was
appended a list of sixty former pupils considered particularly noteworthy
for having taken their places in the profession.[377] In addition, the Academy
might have pointed to the fact that in 1873 the orchestra resident at the
Dublin Industrial Exhibition Palace was largely composed of Academy staff,
pupils, and former pupils.

An inescapable note of frustration is evident in the letter, which emphasises 'that the correspondence in reference to Government aid has extended

over a period of six years, has been carried on with different departments, and under three successive administrations, during which time the various details were fully discussed.' The attitude clearly suggests that the fault lay neither with Dublin Castle nor with Downing Street but in the intransigence of Whitehall. 'The result was that the Irish Government which possesses the fullest means of local enquiry and information, strongly advocated its claims on several occasions . . . The Earl of Carlisle . . . the Duke of Abercorn . . . the Earl of Mayo . . . took opportunities of ascertaining the merits of this question.'

Urging that the Academy was 'of real public benefit,' it turned to the current situation vis-à-vis the Treasury offer, which, 'however advantageous as *supplemental* aid will not assist the Committee in accomplishing the primary object of maintaining an institution in *Ireland* . . . It [is] infinitely more important that an establishment should be substantially assisted here to train the various pupils who could not possibly commence their studies in London, one which, under local management, should be fitted to discover local talent and be able to assist its early struggles.'

To the Treasury itself the IAM responded that the proposal to finance Irish students at the RAM 'will at present in no degree aid them in their main object' and asked that if it was too late to obtain a supplementary grant that year, the seventy pounds on offer should be paid directly to the IAM. Significantly, the letter also stated that the Academy would have no objection 'to the grant being conditional on the Academy maintaining its income from fees and subscriptions.'[378]

In reply, the Treasury repeated its view that 'the best means of improving musical instruction in Ireland is to begin by affording the Irish students the best means of learning their profession.'[379] It is possible that if, instead of 'Stewart, Bennett, Kelly,' and so on, the Academy staff list had included (as it soon would) a handful of Simonettis, Caracciolos and Rudersdorffs, London might have taken a more respectful view of the teaching standards and abilities of Dublin. At that date the RAM had among its staff no-one more exotic than Otto Goldschmidt (the husband of Jenny Lind), as vice-principal, and was in any case in the throes of temporary closure. It is difficult to see on what other basis the superiority of London over Dublin was assumed, and it becomes, conversely, easy to understand the increasing frustration of the IAM.

Brady and MacDonnell retorted that the Treasury clearly could not have read their letter to Gladstone and bluntly suggested that they should do so. They added the pertinent observation that the cost of supporting any Irish students in London would in fact exceed the value of the scholarships on offer.[380] They appended the text of a resolution adopted at a public meeting in the Mansion House on 11 July, the Lord Mayor of Dublin presiding, that 'an Academy for public instruction in music is much needed in Dublin and ought to be encouraged by State aid,'[381] and reiterated the uselessness and self-defeating nature of the current proposal. The text was also sent (as before) to all Irish MPs, urging that they raise the matter in the House of Commons at the next opportunity.

Almost by return of post the Treasury conceded, making an experimental grant of £150 directly to the IAM, conditional on satisfactory progress being made.[382] Rather than tugging the forelock at a concession that must have come as a surprise, the Academy calmly stuck to its guns, accepting the grant but pointing out that 'a considerable amount of success has attended the working of the Academy hitherto and every effort will be made to render it more efficient, but it can scarcely be expected that any very largely increased results can be attained for the sum granted.'[383]

The refusal of the Academy to regard the new vista with anything but realism is typical of its continued efforts to increase the basis of its financial, political and moral support. The idea of attracting that support from outside the metropolis having already been mooted, a circular dated October 1870 stated that 'the institution has been maintained . . . principally if not exclusively [by] persons in or near to Dublin . . . The Committee feel . . . that to meet the requirements of the enlarged operations they contemplate, they may fairly expect an increased number of subscribers and may look for them from the provinces as well as the metropolis.'[384] The argument put forward to the local authorities was that

> the benefits of the Academy are not confined to Dublin, but affect the progress of musical education and taste throughout Ireland. Pupils from various parts of the country come to it for instruction, and numerous teachers trained by it are settled throughout Ireland. Public musical performances in the provinces are largely aided by artists trained in the Academy.

The current total of eighty-nine students 'will be largely increased if subscriptions be formed in different counties to send up from each locality, for instruction, any who may be found to possess peculiar talent.'

Immediately in prospect was removal to a more suitable premises, for which an initial sum of £1,000 was required.

> By this means, the Academy will secure permanent accommodation suitable to its more extended and National character. They [the Committee] think the whole of Ireland should participate in this work, as it will in the advantages to be derived from it; and they therefore propose that a

collection should be made, and a sum of not less than £32 should be contributed by each of the 32 counties . . . The Committee therefore confidently hope for your co-operation in their efforts to establish upon a firm basis this most useful and thoroughly National institution.

The result was a deafening provincial silence. Given that libraries would not be empowered to make funds available for such projects until the enactment of the Local Government (Ireland) Act (1898), and that an Arts Act specifically empowering local authorities to contribute to arts projects was not placed on the statute book until 1973, it was perhaps too soon to expect county authorities to rise to such bait.

But the premises in question, the Academy's present home at 36 Westland Row, a house occupied for business by the somewhat testy lawyer Henry de Burgh LLD of Belcamp, Raheny (c. 1819–76),[385] was acquired for £2,000, of which half was paid immediately and half was mortgaged to de Burgh and repaid shortly after his death. The two basement rooms, the stables, the back drawing-room and one room on the third floor were already let, which suited the Academy ideally, as it was able to recover these as its needs expanded. 'You are to keep matting or carpet on the front stairs, and not let servants with family or children occupy any of the upper portion of the house,' de Burgh admonished his mortgagors, later insisting that 'my carpet is not the newest yet if the *canaille* are to be admitted it might be as well to superadd some matting.'[386] On these terms, the Academy removed from St Stephen's Green on 29 October 1870.

Appendix 1

Report of the Funeral of Dr Thomas Edward Beatty

The remains of this much-respected and distinguished physician were removed from his late residence, 62 Lower Mount-street, for interment in St. Ann's Church, at nine o'clock yesterday morning. They were followed by a large number of carriages belonging to the most respectable section of the citizens, to whom the deceased had much endeared himself. The body was enclosed in a suite of coffins, the outer one being of polished oak, with rich brass mountings. The breastplate bore the following inscription:—

THOMAS EDWARD BEATTY,
Born 1st January, 1800
Died 3rd May, 1872.

The order of procession observed on the occasion was as follows:—

Students.
Representatives of the Irish Academy of Music.
Office Bearers of Royal Irish Academy.

The Mace.
The President of Royal Irish Academy.
Representatives of the Order of Friendly Brothers of St. Patrick.

The Representatives of the Free and Accepted Masons of Ireland were:—

The R. W. the Deputy Grand Master, R. W. Shekleton, Esq.; the R. W. the Grand Secretary, Major General the Right Honorable F. P. Dunne, as Representatives of the Grand Lodge; the Vice President of the Grand Chapter of Prince Masons, the Hon. Judge Townsend; the Grand Treasurer of the Grand Chapter of Prince Masons, Charles T. Waimsley, Esq; the President of the College of Philosophical Masons, E. William Maunsell, Esq.; the Secretary of the College of Philosophical Masons, Lucius H. Deering, Esq.; the President of the 32nd and 31st Degrees, George Chatterton, Esq.; the Secretary of the 31st Degree, Theophilus E. St. George, Esq.; the Secretary of the Knights of the Sun, W. Allen, Esq.; the Secretary of the Masonic Female Orphan School, E. R. D. La Touche, Esq.; the Assistant Secretary of the Female Orphan School, Samuel B. Oldham, Esq.
Governor and Court of Apothecaries' Hall of Ireland.
Office Bearers of the Royal College of Surgeons.
The Mace.
President of the Royal College of Surgeons.
Office Bearers of the King's and Queen's College of Physicians.
The Mace.
President of the College of Physicians.
The body.
Chief Mourners.
Medical Attendants upon the Deceased.
Carriage of the Deceased.
Carriage of the Lord Mayor of Dublin.
Carriages of the Fellows of the College of Physicians, attending in their Robes.
Carriages of the Fellows of the College of Surgeons, attending in their Robes.
Carriages of Friends, and all attending in other than Corporate capacities.

The chief mourners were:—

Mr. Calcott Beatty, Rev. John Beatty, Mr. W. Beatty, Mr. Frederick Beatty, Mr. Brooke Wolseley, Dr. Guinness Beatty, Mr. Edward Beatty, Mr. Robert Beatty, Mr. E. J. Mayne, Mr. Ellis Mayne, Mr. Pelham J. M. Mayne, Dr. Stokes, Dr. Butcher, Dr. Rawdon Macnamara, and Dr. Tufnell.

Amongst those who attended or sent their carriages were:—

> The Right Hon. the Lord Mayor, Sir Arthur Guinness, Bart;
> Sir Francis Brady, Bart; Sir Dominic Corrigan, Bart, M.P.; Sir
> William Wilde, Sir John Marcus Stewart, Bart; the Vice
> Chancellor, Sir John Barrington, D.L.; Major General Dunne,
> Master Brooke, Master Coles, the Very Rev. the Dean of Ferns,
> Colonel Acton, Major Bowdler, Colonel Hilliard, the Ven.
> Archdeacon Wolsley, Captain Huband, Croker Barrington, Rev.
> Dr. Salmon, Dr. Todd, Q.C.; Dr. Bigger, Rev. T. J. Gray, Dr.
> Cruise, Dr. Gordon, V.P., College of Physicians; Humphrey
> Minchin, M. B.; Echlin Molyneux, President of the Dublin Knot
> of Friendly Brothers; Dr. Lyons, E. Gibson, E. Bewley, R. W.
> Boyle, William Jameson, Dr. F. Battersby, Vokes Mackey, J.P.;
> Dr. Wheeler, Dr. Lucus, Dr. Ireland, Dr. Banks, E. F. Beatty,
> Rev. Mr. Fuller, George C. Garnett, James Wilson, Rev. C. F.
> Lucas, Mr. W. Corrigan, Dr. Owens, J.P.

Appendix 2

A note on music education in Scotland, Poland, Finland and Hungary in the nineteenth century

An indication has been given in this chapter of the origins of the present-day Scottish Academy of Music and Drama, which was conceived in 1847 as the 'Glasgow Athenæum'. Fortuitously, the key dates in the history of the RIAM and the Scottish academy almost coincide, although there was less continuity of either purpose or method in the Glasgow endeavour than in that of Dublin. In 1890, after over forty years of experiment and a year after the RIAM was reconstituted, the Glasgow Athenæum took the step of forming a School of Music on the lines of a Continental conservatoire, with Allan Macbeth, a graduate of Leipzig, as principal. Art classes continued to be a feature of the extra-musical curriculum, as were those in elocution and dramatic art, which provided the nucleus of the dual structure of today's Academy.[387]

There appears, from both Farmer's *History of Music in Scotland* and James Lauder's golden jubilee account of the Glasgow Athenæum, no evidence of nationalist motives in establishing a school of music; and even though it was referred to by 1897 as a 'public School of Music' there was no perceived need to refer to it as a 'national institution', in the same way as the Irish academy was recognised and welcomed by the press.

Music education in Poland developed in the nineteenth century from the existing music societies in Lvov, Cracow, Warsaw, and Vilnius. Although Poland as an independent state did not come into existence until 1918 (its territory being governed variously by Austria, Prussia, and Russia), music education had a national character. Textbooks and other musicological literature were written in Polish, and the Institute of Music in Warsaw (today the Frederick Chopin Academy of Music) was the only school under Russian occupation where lectures were conducted in Polish.[388]

Harry White draws attention to the parallels between Polish and Irish cultural nationalism, which saw Thomas Moore's poetry exciting the 'national poet' of Poland, Adam Mickiewicz. In 1842 Charles Gavan Duffy was underlining the fact that Moore's *Melodies* 'not only have appeared in every European language but they supplied the Poles with their most revolutionary songs'[389]—Gavan Duffy's point that the songs 'bear translation' being a supreme irony, not least because he is here on the verge of suggesting that Moore was a cultural icon appreciated everywhere more than in his own country.

The foundation in 1882 of the present-day Sibelius Academy in Finland belongs to a period of emergent cultural nationalism not at all unlike that in Ireland in the same period, which revolved around a language question (Finnish and Swedish) and the status of indigenous folk music and folklore, as well as that of political self-determination, which, as in Ireland, led to a civil war immediately following independence, which continues to be divisive.

As the Anglo-Irish poet Samuel Ferguson attempted (but, it is generally agreed, failed) to be the midwife to a rebirth of Irish folk memory through poetry, and thus to unite coloniser and colonised in a common sense of identity, so in Finland—with remarkable success, which to this day reverberates within Finnish cultural expression—the Kalevala (1835), a composite work of Finnish mythology by the Swedish Finn Elias Lonnröt, gave Finns a literature of iconic, even totemic, significance, which has linguistic and musical dimensions present in the work of Sibelius, his predecessors, contemporaries, and successors. Sibelius's *Kullervo Symphony* (1892), for example, was preceded by Fillip von Schantz's *Kullervo Overture* (1860) and Kajanus's *Kullervon Kuolema* (Death of Kullervo) and followed as recently as 1992 by Aulis Sallinen's opera *Kullervo*. Over 330 works based on themes in the *Kalevala* had been composed by 1985.[389] As in Ireland with Petrie and his collaborators and followers, so in mid-nineteenth-century Finland collectors of folk music started to assemble a corpus of work that began to be digested in parallel with the development of an interest in mainstream Continental (predominantly Viennese) music, which had been present in the Swedish-oriented society first of Abö (Turku) and later of Helsingfors (Helsinki) since the end of the eighteenth century.

It is significant that in Finland also, text-based music was of importance to cultural nationalism, as was the participation of the Swedish section of the population, for example the composer Crusell (1775–1838) and the professor Fredrik Pacius (1809–91). Lack of space prevents us from giving more than a brief mention of the fact that language played a crucial role in the development of a consciousness of Finnishness in music-making, which reached its first milestone in 1882, when, in the words of Toivo Haapanen, 'Finland . . . entered its musical maturity' with the foundation of an academy and a municipal orchestra in Helsinki, the former under the directorship of

Martin Wegelius (1846–1906), the latter under Robert Kajanus (1856–1933), who correspond in a sense to Joseph Robinson and Michele Esposito of the IAM. Henceforth, Finnish musical development was to be inclusive and exploratory, employing the services of romantic nationalists such as Johan Svendsen, who inspired Kajanus to write works based on the *Kalevala*, such as his Suomalainen Rapsodia (Finnish Rhapsodies),[390] works that, if circumstances had developed along similar lines, might have found an Irish parallel by a Dublin-based Stanford or Harty, employing texts generated by Ferguson and associates.

Where Sibelius provided Finland with a musical literature that mirrored and extended the *Kalevala*, Ireland in the outcome found no such pioneer. After Stanford and Harty, Larchet was a poor and inhibited local artist striving for some sense of equilibrium. Greater strides may be said to have been made by outsiders trying to be insiders, such as Bax and Moeran, the former having no Anglo-Irish connections except those in his imagination. In particular, Sibelius provided Finnish composers with an example of how to transcend the claims of folk music, or to employ them in a cosmopolitan way, without being hidebound by their emotional effects or musical limitations—a feature almost completely lacking in Irish composition to this day.

Stanford had detected a similarity between Irish and Hungarian folk song—a similarity that nevertheless finds Ireland still awaiting its Bartók and Kodály.[391] With Bartók, the motivation for his research was less a sense of national awakening than 'a taste for wild flowers'.[392] But the conditions for their recovery were strikingly similar, along the lines we have noted for the beginnings of cultural nationalism, with an intelligentsia trying to imagine a way of ensuring their survival in the mainstream of western music.

In Hungary, a Conservatory of the Pest-Buda Society of Musicians had opened in 1840, coinciding with the first attempts at the collection of folk music and with the opening of the National Theatre, which promoted the consciously nationalist operas of Ferenc Erkel. It was succeeded, firstly, in 1867 by a National Music School and then in 1875 by the Budapest Academy of Music, on lines envisaged by Liszt and partly financed by proceeds from his concerts,[393] with the full title National Hungarian Royal Academy of Music, thus nicely indicating the ambivalence of the 'dual monarchy'. At first it was a piano academy, with five teachers (including Liszt) and thirty-eight students; voice and organ were added in 1883, violin in 1884, and cello in 1886. But, in Bartók's retrospective view, Liszt was in fact damaging rather than enhancing the chances of folk survival, since 'he started from an international standpoint and developed towards national aims'[394]—a criticism that could perhaps be levelled at Stanford. Nevertheless, the 'divergence of folk music and composed music' was avoided in the work of both Bartók and Kodály, as it was in that of Sibelius.

Thus we have differing examples of the way in which countries experiencing the exodus from an imperial culture and the entrée to an indigenous, locally centred cultural life dealt with the options available to them in practising and articulating their ideas of identity and its expression.

Intermezzo

The Academy's Premises, 1848–1998

The Academy itself has occupied three buildings since its foundation, and the Municipal School of Music a fourth, at the City Assembly House in South William Street. Of these the present building in Westland Row is the most important, architecturally speaking, but each of the others (one of which has been demolished) has its points of interest.

The Antient Concert Rooms in Great Brunswick Street (Pearse Street) were originally the premises of the Dublin Oil Gas Light Company and were acquired by the Antient Concerts Society in 1843, nine years after its foundation. The building was substantially modified and on 20 April 1843 opened as Dublin's newest concert hall. The *Dublin Evening Mail* reported the next day that

> the principal room . . . is in the Ionic style, and beautifully proportioned, being nearly a double cube of 43 feet, or 86 feet long, exclusive of the recess for the organ at the back of the orchestra, and it is calculated to accommodate between 900 and 1000 persons. At the extremity of the hall and facing the orchestra, supported on metal pillars, is a light-looking elliptical gallery, capable of holding two hundred persons . . . The room, besides being lofty, is well ventilated by admitting warmed or cold air diffusedly round the bottom of the room, and carrying off the foul air through ornamental openings in the ceiling and thence, by inverted funnels in the roof, out of the building. The seats are supported on light-looking cast iron framing with scroll arms, and backed with mahogany, affording altogether a degree of comfort that was not known in any music-room in Dublin before. We may safely say that when the seats are cushioned, a new organ put up, and the painting and decorations completed, it will display an appearance representing architectural beauty, combined with comfort, such as no other hall in this country possesses.

The organ was installed by Telford in 1846. The front section of the building contained offices and the rooms in which the Academy's teaching took place. Although the Antient Concerts Society came to an end in 1864, the hall was to remain a leading venue for concerts well into the twentieth century. Esposito gave the Sunday afternoon concerts here from 1905 to 1914, and after moving its teaching rooms elsewhere the Academy frequently returned to the main hall for students' concerts. The 'double cube' dimensions it shared with what is now the National Concert Hall, the Metropolitan Hall in Abbey Street (now demolished), the Musikvereinsaal in Vienna, the

Concertgebouw in Amsterdam, and the Boston Symphony Hall. Later it became a cinema, at one time named the Academy (although the choice of name is more likely to have been made as a suggestion of the famous London cinema of the same name than for any desire to recall its days as a centre of music education). It is now unoccupied and almost derelict.

The move in 1856, on foot of the Academy's reorganisation, brought it to a handsome if unexceptional house, 18 St Stephen's Green, which was built in 1798 on the site of an earlier house. It was a three-bay two-storey house at the end of a terrace of four, which was demolished and replaced in 1971 by the Stephen Court offices, separated from its imposing neighbour, the University Club in number 17, by a narrow access lane. Originally occupied by a William Luby, by 1850 it had become a commercial premises, occupied by Nicholas Walsh, an upholsterer, and Peter Walsh, a piano maker, who had added an extra storey. It became vacant in 1852 and in 1854 was taken over by Patrick Carroll, an ironmonger, and Richard Barnett, a dentist. In 1856 the Academy rented it from Carroll at eighty pounds a year, with, as we have seen, Wilhelm Elsner occupying the top floor for a brief time. After the Academy moved to Westland Row the building had a variety of uses, until its eventual demise.

The chief building in the RIAM's present complex is a house of outstanding architectural features and significance. Its origins can be traced to 29 June 1772 (not, as generally supposed, 1771), when William Phillips of Phillips Green, County Wicklow, conveyed to Nicholas Tench of Fassaroe, County Wicklow, and the city of Dublin, land in Westland Brickfields formerly in the possession of William Clements, the vice-provost of TCD. The tenure was a renewable leasehold of fifty-eight pounds a year, subsequently converted in 1857 into a fee farm grant. The parcel of land consisted of a frontage of 140 feet in Westland Row and stretched 212 feet from front to back. The street itself had previously been named simply Westland's, after William Westland, who had owned part of that area.

Under the terms of the deed Tench was to erect 'four good and substantial dwelling houses.' The Academy's house, today number 36, was numbered 4, the other three houses (of which numbers 34 and 35—originally 2 and 3—remain) having similar architectural features on their façades. These houses occupied the portion of the street up to the junction with Park Street, East (today Lincoln Place and Fenian Street).

The subsequent ownership of the house saw it passing in 1775 to Stephen Ram and in 1790 to Richard Waddy and after his death to his son, the splendidly named Cadwallader Waddy of Kilmacow, County Kilkenny, who sold it in 1824 to Thomas Disney for £1,200. In 1848 Disney sold his interest to John Aylmer of Courtown, County Wexford, for £1,400, giving rise ever since to the erroneous belief that it had been the home of Sir George Aylmer, to whom John was related. When John Aylmer died in 1857 it was inherited by his son Michael, who sold it to William Tyndall, a bootmaker of Grafton Street, for £1,630. Tyndall sold it to Henry de Burgh in 1860 for £1,200, and in 1870, as we have seen, it was acquired by the Academy for £2,000.

Under the terms of the original lease it was incumbent on the occupier not to use the premises as a shop, alehouse or tavern or to carry on the trade of 'soap boiler, chandler, baker, butcher, distiller, sugar boiler, brewer, druggist, tanner, skinner, lime burner, hatter, silversmith, coppersmith, pewterer, blacksmith or any other noisy or offensive trade.' This was partly in order to ensure that the street would develop as a couth residential and professional area, free from trade, and partly to keep it safe from the health hazards associated with the occupations listed. In later years the Academy was itself to be affected by the fact that such pursuits were taking place in neighbouring premises: in 1931, for example, these included an abattoir, a chromium-plating company, and a forge.

Tench, who also erected houses in Ely Place, clearly set out to create a fine house, with smaller and less grand editions in the neighbouring houses—a feature of row-building common in nearby Merrion Square and Merrion Street. A four-bay house of four storeys and basement, it has a handsome granite façade at ground-floor level and red brick above, with granite quoins on both corners, the tall windows of the first floor having surrounds of Portland stone. Many original features remain, including the lamps on the front steps, the brass-bound lock and drop-handle on the front door, the mahogany doors (those on the first floor inlaid), some marble chimney-pieces, the chair-rails, skirting-boards, and stone staircase. In 1873 the governors irresponsibly sold the original fireplaces from the first-floor rooms, and they were threatened with legal action by an irate de Burgh, who, as mortgagor, still had an interest in the property, unless the pieces were reinstated. The minutes of 22 and 29 January note acceptance of the offer of £60 (£1,800 in today's money) together with the replacement pieces, which are in place today.

The plasterwork on the barrel-vaulted staircase ceiling, in the chief reception rooms and on the relief plaques on the walls of the entrance hall is believed to be that of Michael Stapleton, one of the chief stuccodores of the time, as it closely matches similar work in Clonmell House, Harcourt Street. The painted murals in the present board-room (the chief ground-floor room) and the ceiling paintings in the smaller first-floor room are probably by Peter de Grée, a Dutch artist living in London who worked extensively in Ireland from 1785 to 1789. The opinion has also been expressed that they may be the work of Angelica Kauffmann or François Boucher, but as the latter died in 1770 this is unlikely, unless they were brought to the house at a later date. De Grée himself would obviously have undertaken the work, which is very reminiscent of other examples by him in 52 St Stephen's Green, after the house was built.

In 1877 Sir Thomas Jones PRHA told his fellow-governors that when the whitewash at that time covering the drawing-room ceiling had been removed it had been discovered 'that the ceiling was of very beautiful workmanship and had been painted in oil colours,' and it was decided to restore it. In Jones's opinion 'the paintings on the ceiling are believed to be the work of Boucher,' and one of the smaller paintings was sent to London for inspection, although there is no subsequent record of this.

A most unusual feature of the rooms on the first floor is the pewter decoration on skirting-boards, chair-rail, doorcases and windowcases, the only other house in Dublin known to have this being the University Club at 17 St Stephen's Green.

Apart from remedial work carried out between the nineteen-fifties and seventies, very little has changed in the house, the main alterations being the removal in 1871 of the wall (referred to in the minutes as a partition) between the front and rear rooms on the first floor, at a cost of £17 10s (today £525) to create a large concert room, where later the organ was to be installed, and the replacement of the original windows on the rear wall by Gothic-style windowcases (installed at a cost of £2 14s each), complemented by a most unusual Gothic-style chimneypiece, the paintings on which it has also been suggested are the work of Kauffmann. Henry de Burgh gave permission for the entrance hall to be partitioned to form a secretary's office, and this continued until some time in the twentieth century. At some point before 1850 an ironwork balcony had been added to the first floor, but, as an anachronism, this was removed during renovations in 1960. The façade also received an addition in 1932 when, in preparation for the Eucharistic Congress, three flagpoles were installed to carry the national, papal and Eucharistic Congress flags.

At the rear of the premises was a considerable yard with stables, over which at various times new buildings were constructed. The Governors had among them the distinguished architect Sir Thomas Drew RHA, who oversaw much of the extension, which included the original band room and additional teaching rooms, at a cost of £310 in 1890. This expansion was undertaken under heavy pressure of numbers on existing accommodation and as a practical alternative to the prospect of being able to secure premises elsewhere. A sign of changing times was the installation of a bicycle run from the street to the basement area in 1899, while an indication of a perennial concern was the insertion of glass panels in the doors of the teaching rooms. It has long been part of Academy lore that this was necessary to discourage the sexual harassment of pupils by Joseph Robinson, whose reputation as a womaniser was legendary, but as this work was undertaken a few months after his death the blame cannot be laid directly at his door.

Other signs of modernisation were (after some debate on the subject) the subscription to a telephone line in 1904, at £6 a year (£200 today)— although the installing of the equipment in the back hall rather than the secretary's office, where one might expect to find it, suggests that little importance was attached to it as a tool of business—and in 1914 the installation of electricity, which had been deferred when first suggested in 1893 and again in 1909.

Numbers 37 and 38 Westland Row were acquired in 1915 as part of the Academy's urgent need for expansion, which had already seen the rear yard covered with an amalgam of built-on short-term solutions to a long-term problem, and the ensuing decades were to see a similar extension into the gardens of these new acquisitions, right up to the conversion in 1992 of a surviving stable into what is today the Esposito Hall. Previously, in fact from 1891 until the acquisition of the houses on the other side, sporadic attempts were made to purchase number 35 (in 1897 for £800) from the owners, the Dublin and Kingstown Railway Company, and interest in the premises was still being expressed in the nineteen-eighties.

Numbers 37 and 38, which were bought for £250, are architecturally negligible, and it came as a complete shock to the Governors in 1976 to be informed by Dublin City Council that they were listed for preservation— an error that they were relieved to find corrected a month later. These houses date from the middle of the nineteenth century and were owned mostly by tradesmen. By coincidence, number 37 was sold in 1868 by Sir Francis Cruise (later to become a Governor of the Academy) to a fellow-doctor, James Byrne, who sold it in 1882 to a victualler, Edmond Long, who had acquired its neighbour in 1870 and who, after a series of profitable sub-leases (including letting number 37 in 1903 to the Dublin Diocese), sold both houses to the Academy in 1915. Number 38 was for many years surplus to requirements and from 1935 to 1945 was a private hotel managed by a Miss O'Hanlon, from whom the Academy bought back, at a cost of £3,800, the remaining eleven years of her 21-year interest in the lease, which she had purchased for £1,000.

The rediscovery of the ceiling paintings in 1877 was followed almost a century later by that of the granite frontage, which at some time after 1850 had been covered with cement. New roofs had been put on numbers 36 and 37 at a cost of £370 in 1926 (today £5,550), but in 1960 the need for total renovation of the fabric of number 36 revealed extensive faults throughout the three houses. An initial estimate of £13,000 shot up to £23,000 (today £230,000) as dry rot and other problems were detected, reinstatement and renovation of much of the façade accounting for £3,000 of the total. Generous support was received from the Hospitals Trust (£1,000), Arthur

Guinness and Company (£500), Radio Éireann (£200), and many personal and business subscriptions, which amounted to over £3,000. Later, in 1985, further work became inevitable, and at this stage the cost of over £250,000 was almost entirely met by Government grant.

Returning to premises of a finer quality, we conclude this intermezzo with a brief account of the Assembly House in South William Street, which was the premises of the Municipal School of Music from 1890 until 1908, for almost all of that period under the direction of the Academy. Coincidentally built at almost the same time as 36 Westland Row (1765–71), it also has a frontage of granite surmounted by brick and has artistic associations, in that it was built (at a cost of approximately £2,500) to house the annual exhibitions and art school of the Society of Artists. At first it consisted of a shell building, within which the exhibition hall, known as the Octagon Room, was situated. Later, as government support was obtained, the frontage was added, in which the school, or 'academy', was to be established.

The society, however, came to an end in 1780. The building subsequently gave a home to the outlawed College Historical Society, and to the City Assembly, which became Dublin Corporation and occupied the premises formally from 1809 to 1852. The Court of Conscience, a curiosity of the Irish legal system, before which the RIAM would find itself during negotiations on conditions at the Municipal School of Music, sat in the house from 1811 until it became defunct in 1924. The house has been the meeting place of the Old Dublin Society since 1934 and the Civic Museum since 1953. Although the very fine accommodation includes the Octagon Room, the facilities afforded to the Municipal School of Music were in the basement—ill-lit, cramped, draughty, and insanitary.

4

Foundations II
1871–1889

Cultural chauvinism; royal approval; the Albert Scholarships; the
Vandeleur bequest; RCM scholarships; Sir Robert Stewart; choral classes;
Joseph Robinson; Italian professors; the Elsner family; staff and
conditions; the Coulson bequest; negotiations with two Boards
of Commissioners; the Blue Scheme.

hree days after the Academy had moved into its new home,
Henry de Burgh received a letter from his sub-tenants, the
engineers Cotton and Flemyng, who occupied the rear drawing-
room of the still-partitioned first floor.

> It is simply impossible for us to do any business with the noise going on
> in the next room and we must at once move. This of course you must
> have foreseen yet we think we should have had some notice of it, being
> extremely inconvenient to us to shift now with Parliamentary work on
> hands. We trust you may prevail on the musical people to mitigate the
> nuisance during office hours for a week by which time we shall have
> found other rooms we hope.[1]

If a musician such as Wilhelm Elsner could not tolerate the 'nuisance'
made by 'musical people', it was unlikely that a firm of engineers would
find it at all congenial. It was a small sign of the fact that the period from
1870 to 1889 saw a steady if controversial expansion in the work of the
Academy, in its financial fortunes and in its personnel.

For the first time in twenty-two years the Academy had achieved not
only state recognition but also a house of outstanding beauty that it could
regard as its home. Within another two years it would obtain the prefix
'Royal' and in another five would attract funds to establish the 'Albert
Scholarships'. Ten years after moving to Westland Row it would receive a
significant bequest from Richard Ormsby Vandeleur and also would
become aware of the legacy of Elizabeth Coulson, which, after almost a

further decade of wrangling and political persuasion, would give it the financial security it needed to safeguard its future.

The areas of controversy were partly related to staff and partly caused by external perception of the Academy's administration. They demonstrate the ability of figures such as Brady to handle difficult situations and to remain obdurate in the face of unacceptable pressures. In fact, during this period Brady emerges by force of circumstance as a figure of extraordinary circumspection and ability, whereas Hercules MacDonnell becomes unnoticeable, resigning as honorary secretary in 1876[2] (in which post he was succeeded by Henry Doyle[3]) and eventually, and inexplicably, resigning from the Board in 1878. What can have caused this is unknown: MacDonnell even refused the invitation to become one of the founder vice-presidents of the Academy in 1888–89, but there is no evidence of any ill-feeling between himself and any other party.

The protracted negotiations relating to the Coulson bequest were a watershed, in the course of which the old Academy was, in effect, dismantled and a new institution set in its place. Brady's part in this cannot be exaggerated, and although his authority did not go unchallenged he continued as a powerful presence in the Academy up to his death in 1909— over half a century since he had become involved in its restructuring.

The period that saw the extraordinary growth in the Academy's fortunes began with a row, typical of the cultural nationalism of a society in the early stages of a transformation from dependence to independence, which is characterised by vigorous chauvinistic journalism.[4] In the events of 1871 we witness a resurgence of the protectionism that had sought to exclude Jullien from Dublin (and Irish) music-making.

The expansion of the Academy's activities necessitated an extra appointment in the piano faculty, to which it was intended to elect a Mademoiselle Gayrard. The Council minutes of 12 May 1871 record:

> The Council having been informed that the hostile and inaccurate articles on the IAM in the Freeman's Journal of the 10th, 11th 12th inst. were founded on the statements and suggestions supplied by a member of the Council, [resolved] That (assuming this information to be correct) such conduct on the part of a member of this body appears to the Council to be deserving of the greatest censure, as tending to destroy the mutual confidence which should exist among them; especially considering the perfect freedom of discussion always allowed at the meetings of the Council.[5]

The articles in question had argued chauvinistically that an Irish academy should support Irish teachers.

> It is creditable to the wise foresight of the managing council in securing the highest order of teaching ability, and is a proof that our educated musical public is satisfied with the system and style adopted by the present professors of the Academy. We trust now that an opportunity of doing so has presented itself, that the Council of the Academy will recognise the value and the proficiency of its own instruction and its

own pupils by appointing one of the very many who have distinguished themselves in its classes . . . It would be a monstrous injustice to ignore their claims, it would be an offensive insult to its present professional staff, and a condemnation out of their own mouths of the Academy—a public acknowledgement that it was little better than a sham and a swindle, by the very members of that council, who have been hitherto so energetic in asking for it funds, friends and privilege.[6]

We do not know with any certainty who the candidate or candidates in the mind of the writer may have been, but the article may well have been written on behalf of Margaret O'Hea, the next recruit to the piano faculty, who had become a senior piano student in 1865 and was to feature largely in the future of the Academy.[7]

We have heard some whisperings that a friendly scheme of an exotic importation is under consideration but we are unwilling to believe it. It would be certain to be disasterous [*sic*] to the Academy; it would alienate its truest and most unselfish supporters; it would be disheartening to its pupils, and be attended with all the disgraceful and ruinous consequences of cliquism and jobbery. We purposely abstain from any appeal to the subscribers of the Academy funds to step in and protect it from such a catastrophe, and we do so because we believe that the council would not entertain such a proposal, or if they would, that they could not carry it. We are much mistaken in our estimation of the council, if they be the men to echo the bitter taunt that, even in their own country, 'No Irish need apply.'

The 'exotic importation', Mademoiselle Gayrard, became the object of abuse in subsequent columns.

The following day an anonymous letter to the *Freeman's Journal* attempted to put both sides of the argument.

The trenchant article . . . referring to the IAM came upon many of your readers as a surprise; especially upon those who believe that second-rate pupils trained in the Academy play better than the 'exotic' probably referred to. But it may be said that 'an inferior player may be a good teacher.' That is quite possible, and such mediocrity may suit private families for home instruction. Surely no just grounds can be assigned for seeking it out, and placing it in the front of a national institution established ostensibly to realise the highest professional talent. We in Ireland will not attempt to debar any native of a foreign country, especially one of a nation dear to Ireland. But we are not called upon to exercise our generosity by inflicting a gross injustice upon native talent. No conservatoire on the Continent would select an Irish or English professor inferior to their own second-rate pupils and insult their best pupils by placing such a person over them . . . Very many of the pupils have contributed from thirty pounds to sixty pounds [in annual fees] to sustain this institution. They now find their just expectations of some recognition of their industry and ability defeated by the machinations of a clique.[8]

The choice between an Irish and a non-Irish candidate may well have been one the Board had to make, but the notion of advancing pupils to the ranks of the staff was a new one, which, however meritorious, would in itself have required some self-examination on their part.

The *Freeman's Journal* returned to the fray next day with further vituperation.

> Irish talent has been spurned—Irish industry has been discouraged, and the reasonable hopes of young Irish ladies of undoubted ability have been offensively and unfeelingly blasted . . . For this painful and nation-ally humiliating result the council will have themselves to blame, and the reproach of a discreditable failure will attach for ever to the actors in the recent blunder. We do not intend to say a disparaging word of the lady who has been 'imported' . . . save to protest, as we most emphat-ically do, against the claim set up for her of superior qualifications. We do not admit the claim, nor do we think the verdict of the public will approve it. It is a hard thing for a parent who has spent in fees to the Academy some forty or fifty pounds for 'finishing' lessons for their daughter, to be told that the style she has acquired from the previous and present teachers on its staff is a bad one, and that she is not fitted to give lessons to those who are to succeed her in its classes. And this is all the harder to bear when it is remembered that the teaching of the Academy was and is specially designed for young ladies who are to make their livelihood by the profession . . . We have heard it alleged in justification of the unfortunate selection, that foreign artists will draw better than those who have grown up amongst ourselves. Well, then, if so, let the council be consistent; let them sweep away Mr. Levey, Miss Fennell, Mr. Robinson, Miss Herbert, and others of the professional staff ('the Curse of Swift' is on them and they are only Irish) and fill their places with 'exotics' from the conservatories at Milan, at Vienna, at Munich, at Paris or Timbuctoo. Away with them, and then heigh for the 'Irish' Academy.[9]

The popularity of the alternative candidate, whose identity must have been known to at least some of the *Freeman's* readers, must at this stage have become an embarrassment to her, although it is difficult not to suspect that some element of media manipulation had been at work on her behalf and with her consent. Clearly the *Freeman's Journal*, previously so eloquent in support of the Academy, had been persuaded from some quarter that its recruitment policy went against Irish interests, legitimate or not. The editorial continued:

> The people of Dublin are always content with their own, and in the instance in question now would have hailed with delight a recognition of native worth and industry, unless it were to be ignored by some outside element of superior attractiveness and superior attainments . . . We scout with indignation an insinuation we have heard urged that the Academy classes are unable to finish a pupil capable of undertaking the duties of professor. This is not true, and, if we thought it were, we

should pronounce it to be a flagrant piece of dishonesty to be asking private support and public money for an incompetent and incapable institution that, after fifteen or sixteen [*sic*] years' tinkering at 'finishing off' could not furnish a single lady fit to teach the elements of piano playing . . . If the council could not find sufficient ability to profess amongst its own pupils, it had only to search amongst the many professionals of our city, and be sure to find a teacher suited even to their ambitious and excruciatingly exacting requirements. Heaven knows that the opportunities for the reward of Irish talent and Irish industry—for the reimbursing of much expenditure at the cost of much stinting and many self-denials in the little circle of home—are rare enough, and, when one of such does occur, it is galling to be told that in its distribution the stranger must have the preference.

Fear of 'the stranger', and the idea that 'the people of Dublin are always content with their own', are not entirely comfortable bedfellows. The former, when applied to English musicians, however understandable from a nationalist viewpoint, would not have held water, since many of the existing staff were English or came from English stock. When applied to people from continental Europe it becomes even less tenable. But in the self-satisfied expression of local enthusiasm the writer was clearly abandoning any pretence at impartiality, standards, or indeed nationalism.

The furore seems to have been not so much anti-Gayrard as pro-O'Hea, and in the outcome proved to have been ill-judged. Who Mademoiselle Gayrard was we cannot establish. But the governors were adamant that they would not be deflected from their intention of appointing her. The *Freeman's Journal* of 18 May announced the confirmation of the appointment and the declaration that, 'while the council have always selected teachers from among the pupils of the academy, when as well qualified as other candidates, they have not rejected, and will not reject, foreign talent whenever to do so would not be for the advantage of the pupils of the academy.'

At the annual general meeting of the Academy, held in November that year, the members were told that in some classes

> it has been necessary to appoint additional teachers. In the pianoforte class for young ladies this has been especially the case, and the council have much pleasure in noticing the appointment of Madlle. Gayrard as teacher. They do not wish to revive the collection of unfounded attacks made upon the council at the time of this appointment. A statement was prepared and printed on the subject by the council. The result hitherto in the great attention of Mdlle. Gayrard, and the progress of the pupils under her, has fully justified the course adopted by the council in carrying out the rule, on which they have always acted, of appointing the best teachers they could secure in Dublin.[10]

In view of subsequent appointments to the vocal faculty in the eighteen-seventies and eighties and to the strings faculty in later decades, the action of the Board was decisive and essential if the rich and variegated texture of the teaching staff were to be preserved and developed. By the time the Board reported to the members in 1873 it was in a position to state that 'as a proof of the solid instruction given in the Academy . . . its former pupils are now among the leading vocalists in public concerts in Ireland, and . . . when recently it was found necessary to appoint additional teachers to the Academy, the best qualified for the position were found among those who had received their education within its walls.'[11] The Academy was therefore able, by adhering to its policy of appointing none but the best, to answer the criticism of two years previously and to demonstrate that that policy succeeded in developing an internal momentum that could eventually sustain itself. Nevertheless the mixture of native and foreign staff (and today among the student body too) continues to be a necessity, for a variety of cultural and social reasons as well as satisfying a basic musical need for a variety of styles and temperaments.

It was also at this time that the IAM became 'Royal'. The Duke of Edinburgh, Queen Victoria's second son, had attended an Academy concert at the Exhibition Palace on 5 June 1872, which the governors manipulated to the maximum in achieving publicity that would drive home the present status and future claims of the institution. The usually laudatory press plaudits were on this occasion taken up with furthering the achievements of staff and students.

> The annual concert of the pupils of the Irish Academy of Music, which had been announced under the distinguished patronage of his Royal Highness the Duke of Edinburgh, took place last evening, before one of the most brilliant audiences ever assembled within the walls of the Exhibition Palace. Independently of the intrinsic merit of the programme and of the attraction afforded by the visit of a Royal Duke, there were many reasons why the concert should have proved a success. The Irish Academy of Music, guided as it is by some of the first professors of the divine art in Ireland, has done much since its foundation, in 1848, to foster and develop a taste for pure music. The result of its labours has been the attainment of a degree of proficiency on the part of the pupils, both in vocal and instrumental music, which has largely tended to revive the somewhat faded repute of Dublin as a centre for the cultivation of musical talent.[12]

The only blemish on the evening was the inconvenience caused to the audience and performers by the duke arriving three-quarters of an hour late, some attributing this to an over-run in the day's engagements, others to the fact that, whereas he had intended to be present for only the second part of the concert, the organisers had delayed the start on the assumption that he would arrive in time for the beginning. However, the duke was not merely politely impressed but genuinely and enthusiastically so, with the result that through his good offices the Academy petitioned the Queen to become its patron and to recognise its status as equal to that of the RAM in London. The IAM thus became the Royal Irish Academy of Music by royal command.[13]

Further extensions of the Academy's status and interests took place in the eighteen-seventies in the form of donations and bequests, from the Begley, McGuckin and Vandeleur families, and from the fund established to commemorate Prince Albert, husband of Queen Victoria, who had died in 1861. The Begley Prize was founded by Dr W. C. Begley in 1876 in memory of his sister, Maria Begley; and the way in which it was inaugurated is indicative of the problems, as well as the advantages, that can accrue to the beneficiary of such a gift. Dr Begley's solicitor had written to Brady:

> He wishes that a Premium or Prize should be found to be called the 'Maria Begley' Prize to consist of at least £5 that is of 5 newly minted or fresh gold sovereigns from the Bank which have not undergone circulation in an envelope or purse with the words Maria Begley Prize for distinguished Merit 1877—or whatever year the Examination takes place in and the award is made. This award shall be for general and particular merit to the most merititious young lady *herself*, to *be made use of as she likes and quite irrespective of any scholarship or payment of fees* and shall be made at the principal Annual Examination of the year. And the Chairman or President of the day shall remark to the Recipient that Miss Maria Begley was enabled by the exertion of her talents and accomplishments not only to maintain herself in a good position in society with every respect & comfort but to assist her family & friends or some such *truthful* & encouraging remarks as you and I can both verify.[14]

Brady's reply warmly accepted the gift of £125 intended to finance the annual £5 prize but commented that

> the Conditions mentioned by Dr. Begley we see no difficulty in complying with, although as a rule it is not wise to attach conditions to gifts, which, in progress of time, it may be difficult or inexpedient to carry out. It would be an additional favor were Dr. Begley to give the Academy of Music any particulars of his sister's life which would be of interest in connexion with the gift and of advantage to the students of the Academy. I believe she was a pupil & intimate friend of the celebrated Madame Catalani.[15]

Begley himself wrote that he

> wished the amount to be expended in the purchase of an annuity of £5 at least in perpetuity and that that sum should be given annually to a student of the Academy for proficiency in the theory and practice of Music *not a medal* nor *books* not *certificate* of merit, but *five pounds in money* of the current coin of the realm, I look upon this condition as most important, one not to be departed from on any account whatever.[16]

His letter had crossed in the post with Brady's, and he immediately saw the point.

> Seeing the readiness with which Sir Francis Brady has assented to the wish I ventured to express in accordance with your suggestion that the interest of my sister's £125 should be given annually in money and not

otherwise I think it would be unbecoming in me to stipulate further in the matter I spoke of, proficiency in the theory and practice of music, but if she whose little means I am endeavouring to distribute to the best of my ability were amongst us I feel confident that she would laugh & be surprised at my presuming to offer any suggestion in such a matter for my knowledge of music is extremely small, just sufficient to enable me to distinguish God Save the Queen from Rule Britannia and Patrick's Day from both.[17]

Someone who *could* tell the difference was Barton McGuckin (1852–1917),[18] then nearing the height of his powers as a singer and determined to have his own way. He wrote to Brady:

> My intentions relative to the Prize which I propose to give every year to the Pupils of the Royal Academy are these; that it should take the form of a gold medal of the value of five pounds. I have carefully considered your suggestion that the Prize should be in the form of money but I am afraid that however useful the money might be in certain cases, yet that when once spent the Winner would have nothing left as a memento of her success while a Pupil in the Academy as it is my desire she should. My second suggestion is, that the competitors should sing an English Ballad and a solo from some Oratorio which I shall choose and forward the names of immediately also at the time of examination I shall send a song to test the abilities of the Pupils in sightsinging. I would further suggest that the examination should take place in the month of December in each year. I also desire that the choice of judges should remain with me of course with the approval of your Committee. A lover of music myself, I wish to use my utmost endeavours to promote the Art in my native Country and although my efforts to attain a high position in my Profession have been construed by many into a desire to desert and forget my Country, I can sincerely say that no man in it or out of it is prouder of his native land or more desirous of seeing it happy and prosperous than I am. Having just heard that you are giving a Pupils Concert on next Tuesday, and as I intend if possible, being in Dublin on that day I hope to see you and have a further talk with you on the subject.[19]

Brady replied: 'I may say that both the Prize fund given by Dr. Begley and Lord O'Hagan and the Prince Consort Prize Fund have been given absolutely to the discretion of the Council as to the mode of competition, experience shewing that the fewer are the conditions attached to such gifts, the better. Circumstances often make the most carefully considered conditions very difficult, and sometimes impossible of fulfilment.'[20] And McGuckin eventually acceded to this point: 'I . . . hope they will sing one Oratorio song and one English ballad. This is the only thing I wish for.'[21]

An index of Brady's social and political competence, which we shall see demonstrated to the full in the Coulson negotiations, is his ability to write to the RIAM the following letter in his capacity as secretary of the Prince Consort Memorial Committee:

Gentlemen—I have the honour to acquaint you that the Committee of the Prince Consort Memorial Fund have allocated to the Royal Irish Academy of Music the sum of £940.13.10 Government new three per cent stock portion of the surplus fund remaining in the hands of the Trustees on completion of the Memorial. This Fund is to be called 'Prince Albert Prize Fund' it is to be invested by the Trustees of the Academy and the annual interest is to be applied in prizes to the Students of the Academy according to the judgment of the governing body of the Academy for the time being. An equal sum has been given to the Royal Hibernian Academy of Arts. The Committee considered this mode of applying the fund, as the fittest manner of perpetuating the memory of the Prince Consort who was a distinguished and accomplished Patron of the Arts of Painting & Music. This distribution of the Fund has received the sanction of Her Majesty the Queen who has directed the Committee to be informed that she fully approves of the plan which seems to Her Majesty a very good one.[22]

The method of employing this fund was somewhat confusing. The sum was actually used to pay off the remaining £1,000 of the mortgage on 36 Westland Row, and the prize fund was thereafter financed as an assignment of the mortgage, so that the 5 per cent currently being paid on the mortgage could be reassigned out of the annual income of the Academy to paying the annual costs of awarding the scholarships. The exact financing of this was to be worked out when the first scholars were elected. At the end of 1878 the Academy announced the first competition for the scholarships, which would shortly satisfy that want complained of in the choral concerts of recent years.

The Council of the Royal Irish Academy of Music, with the object of encouraging the development of musical talent, will hold an Examination for Voices, *Open to all Ireland*, and if, among the competitors, there are found voices of sufficient merit, the Council will select so many of the candidates as they may think deserving, and give them the advantage of free instruction in the Academy for one year. If sufficient progress be made, and diligence shown, the Council will extend the period of instruction for a further term.

The Examination will be held on Friday, the 8th November.[23]

In the matter of the Vandeleur bequest the Academy is to this day almost as embarrassed by its ignorance of the benefactor as it is in the case of Elizabeth Coulson. We know that Richard John Ormsby Vandeleur was the son of Gen. Sir Ormsby Vandeleur (1763–1849), who commanded the 4th Cavalry Brigade at Waterloo; yet no record of his own achievements or way of life has reached us. *Burke's Landed Gentry of Ireland* records not even his date of birth, merely the fact that he died unmarried, and the newspapers of the time record his death on 27 May 1879 without comment. By his will, dated 26 January 1878, he bequeathed to the RIAM

my musical instruments etc. etc. consisting of a Grand Piano, two violins, and a tenor [i.e. viola], to be given by them as prizes in such manner as they shall think fit to the most efficient students.

And I bequeath the following legacies to the RIAM—the sum of £1,000 . . . I direct that the said Richard S. Reeves and Robert Reeves or the survivor of them [or] the executors or administrators of such survivor shall invest the sum of £4,000 in the purchase of Government new £3 per cent stock or Government £3 per cent consolidated Bank Annuities, and transfer the same to the Commissioners of Charitable Donations and Bequests in Ireland upon the Trusts hereinafter declared concerning the same that is to say upon trust that the said Commissioners shall from time to time apply the dividends of the said stock to the Trustees or Trustee or the Council for the time being of the said Academy (without being bound to see to the application thereof and without requiring any scheme to be settled for the application of the said dividends) upon trust that the said trustees or Trustee or the said Council of the said Academy shall apply the said dividends for the purpose of endowing scholarships for the pupils of the said Academy who shall show the greatest proficiency in vocal and instrumental music such scholarships to be for five years and to be called the 'Vandeleur Scholarships' the election to each such scholarship to be by examination but the details as to the number and endowment of the said scholarships and the mode and time of examination to be decided by the Council for the time being of the said Academy but subject to this restriction, that not less than one third of the said dividend be employed in endowing such scholarships for encouraging proficiency in instrumental music (other than the pianoforte and organ).

The Council thus had £1,000 unconditionally, £4,000 tied to scholarships, two violins and a viola at its disposal—the largest donation it had received up to that time, the money alone being worth over £170,000 today. In addition, and with hindsight perhaps more significantly, the violins would be almost priceless on today's market. On 13 May 1880 Brady made the forward-looking suggestion that some of the Vandeleur Scholarship fund might be used 'towards the maintenance and education of students at some of the foreign Conservatoires whenever there are pupils in the Academy of sufficient merit,' but as nothing further came of this it seems that even if he had been able to persuade his fellow-governors of its wisdom it may have been rejected by the Commissioners as being outside the terms of the bequest.

There is some confusion about exactly what occurred between the making of Vandeleur's will and its execution after his death. The Council resolved on 12 November 'that the violins bequeathed by Mr. Vandeleur be denominated the "Vandeleur Prize Violins" and be kept in the Academy to be played on by Pupils in competing for prizes and performing in public, as the Council may from time to time direct.' In time, one of the Academy's prize pupils, Madeleine Moore (later Madeleine Larchet) would frequently receive permission to play the Stradivarius at feiseanna and at Academy prize-winners' concerts.[24] It appears, however, that Vandeleur's collection consisted of not two but three violins, since on 12 August 1880 three—the Stradivari, a Maggini and a Guarneri—were played by Gilbert Betjemann to test which would be surrendered and which retained. The expert judges included R. M. Levey, Carl Rosa, Albert Randegger, and, from among the governors, Exham, Yeo, Brady, Nedley, and Jones. They considered the Maggini to be best, the Stradivari second, and the Guarneri third, and the last (which may have been the 'tenor') was therefore sent back.

The Stradivari, dated 1683, remained in the Academy until 1912, when it was sent to Hills in London, who valued it at £600 (equivalent to £18,000 today, far below its current market value), and it was sold by them the next year for £500.[25] 'The money is badly needed by the Academy to effect greatly needed improvements,' including an extension to the band room, the *Freeman's Journal* told its readers after a timely intervention by the secretary to win over the reporter, who had set out to write a piece highly critical of the Academy's decision. 'The violin may leave the country, but the result will be that the students at the institution will benefit by the increased accommodation.' (As we have seen, part of the money was used to purchase the adjoining houses, numbers 37 and 38.)

The practice is for Strads to acquire a nickname by which they are known in the trade and by connoisseurs. This instrument became known as the 'Irish Academy' and subsequently as the 'Headley'. The definitive *Iconography* records that it was subsequently owned by Jay and later by Kramer.[26]

A new dimension was added to the life and international significance of the RIAM by the award in 1883 to three of its students of scholarships at the newly opened Royal College of Music in London. In the life and career of one of them, Edith Oldham, this was to be a momentous step, bringing her into contact with Sir George Grove (a relationship that is described in the *intermezzo* that follows this chapter).

The project of founding the RCM, which developed out of the National Training School (of which Arthur Sullivan had been principal), had been canvassed by Grove throughout Britain in the preceding fourteen months, with the active encouragement of the Prince of Wales. His purpose was not only to solicit the support of municipalities for the £110,000 that this had succeeded in raising but also to draw attention to the fifty scholarships that would be available. The staff recruited included Ernst Pauer (a pupil of F. X. W. Mozart), Franklin Taylor (who had studied with Moscheles) and Arabella Goddard (a pupil of Kalkbrenner) in the piano faculty, Henry Holmes and Richard Gompertz for strings, Walter Parratt for organ, Frederick Bridge, Stanford and Parry for composition, and Henry Lazarus, among others, for wind. Jenny Lind-Goldschmidt had been coaxed out of retirement to teach voice.[27]

The competition for the scholarships had seen an entry of 1,588, of whom 480 were auditioned. In Dublin, where the examinations were held in the Royal University, Sir Robert Stewart had been nominated by the vice-chancellor of the University of Dublin as one of the examiners, and Dublin Corporation appointed Joseph Smith and Luigi Caracciolo, as 'two of the most competent professional musicians obtainable,' to represent the municipality as honorary examiners.[28] Of the fifty places (fifteen of them carrying maintenance awards), seventeen were awarded for piano, thirteen for singing, eight for violin, six for composition, two for cello, and one each for organ, clarinet, flute, and harp. A further forty-two students enrolled as fee-paying pupils. Six scholarships went to Ireland, two to Scotland, and one to Wales, with the remainder distributed throughout England. At the opening (which was also the occasion for announcing that knighthoods were to be bestowed on Macfarren, Sullivan, and Grove), Grove made the point that 'the occupations of the scholars are as various as the places from which they come. I find that a mill-girl, the daughter of a brickmaker, and the son of a blacksmith take high places in singing, and the son of a labourer in violin playing.'[29]

Of the six Irish, three were RIAM students: Francis Bulkley (clarinet) and Louisa (Louie) Kellett and Edith Oldham (piano, both of whom received maintenance grants). Grove wrote to the Lord Mayor:

> Dublin has come out well in the examinations . . . The scholarships provide for their musical education . . . Mr. Bulkley does not claim maintenance, but the other two are evidently in such circumstances that if they are not maintained they must give up the aid to which their capacity and promise strongly entitle them. At the same time the funds at the disposal of the Prince of Wales for this purpose are so limited that I fear we cannot maintain the young ladies. Under these circumstances can anything be done by the Corporation of Dublin or by individuals to meet the case? Maintenance will cost from £55 to £60 a year each. Dublin has not yet contributed at all to the College, and the present opportunity seems to me one which your Lordship will probably be glad to embrace for getting some contribution towards this great object.[30]

It might be a feather in Dublin's cap to have three of its students chosen in such a way, but it was quite another matter to be sending out of the country funds badly needed to support institutions at home. The letter was noted, but there appears to have been no response.

Nevertheless Kellett and Oldham, two of the most outstanding students of recent years and potentially serious rivals,[31] were maintained. Oldham had just lost her father, a well-known Dublin merchant, and Kellett was soon to lose hers, the registrar of the Dental Hospital in Beresford Place. Of the other Irish students, one, Anna Russell, a voice student, came from Limerick, and another (to achieve considerable distinction) was Charles Wood, from Armagh;[32] we do not know the identity of the sixth.

It is clear from a letter of 5 February 1886 that Grove felt strongly for both Edith and Louie: 'My heart would break if anything were to happen to either of my two dear friends.' It was to Edith and Louie jointly that Grove wrote to describe the final stages of his daughter Millie's illness at the end of 1886.[33] Meanwhile, on 7 April 1884 he wrote to Louie's father: 'Dear Mr. Kellett, I have promised Louie to write a word to you about her, and indeed I am glad to do so for she is so good and hard working and satisfactory a girl that I am glad of the opportunity of saying so to you.

Always ready with her work, always anxious to do what her master wants—what more can you or I want, my dear Mr. Kellett?'[34] On 7 May he wrote to Brady: 'Dear Sir Francis, Thank you for your pleasant note and the gratifying enclosure [a cheque for five pounds] which shall be duly applied to the benefit of your protégée . . . I am very glad to hear your good opinion of the girls. There is a great deal still to be done but I have little doubt they will come well through it.'[35] In July 1886 the *Irish Times* wrote that in the report of the RCM 'an Irish scholar, Miss Louisa Kellett, receives the distinction of having her name placed at the head of the list of pianoforte students who "passed with honours".'[36]

Louie Kellett's illness, tuberculosis, was reported by Grove to Edith in a series of increasingly harrowing letters. In July 1887 she 'is very bad, with her mother & sister on the road to starvation—how can she help it?' (The Kelletts were afflicted with poverty after the death of Louie's father, although the younger sister, Josephine, was able to complete her education and obtain a teaching post at the Girls' High School, Brighton. 'Poor Joe [Josephine]! to be bound to that carcase of a mother,' Grove would later write to Edith.)[37] By August, Grove, who was so devoted to his students that his entire life seems to have been put at their disposal, was managing the Kelletts' money matters;[38] by September Louie 'has been overdoing it terribly and neglecting herself in every way. I hope it is taken in time but in the meanwhile it has given us all a bad fright'; by November 'Louie . . . is evidently so weak that she can't even speak.' Three weeks later, 'I hardly dare to hope for her future.' In January 1888, in hospital in Ventnor, Isle of Wight, 'she can't move a step or speak above a whisper and has virtually been in bed for 6 or 8 weeks past.' On 2 March, Grove told Edith: 'Poor Louie has made another step downwards her legs are swelling which is always a sign of the end approaching. I am glad that she does not know of it—for in talking of her birthday March 10 she asks for a "nice *lasting* present".' On the thirteenth 'I paid L 2 visits oh she is so bad; just fluttering on the edge of the grave . . . so thin and shrunk you never saw its equal.' On St Patrick's Day he wrote that Louie had died two days earlier. 'That simplicity was the chief thing that attracted me to her . . . her reticence and reserve were quite remarkable. I hardly ever met a person so *unable* to utter her feelings (which were very strong) except perhaps her sister, who is absolutely dumb . . . You are right too, I fancy, about her life at Dublin. It must have been *wretched*—her father was the one exception & she *adored* him, and it was his death which killed her.'[39]

Francis David Bulkley, with an address at 3 Northbrook Avenue, Dublin, was sixteen at the time of his election to the scholarship. In addition to clarinet, which he studied with the legendary Henry Lazarus,[40] he took violin as his second instrument, studying with Richard Gompertz. His father, David, whose profession is listed in the RCM scholars' register as 'comedian', was also dead, and he stayed with his guardian in Hounslow, Middlesex. In his first term Lazarus reported that he was 'very persevering and improved but not a good timist,' but thereafter he made considerable progress; in violin he appeared to Gompertz at the start to be 'industrious and anxious to do his best,' but despite his diligence he made little significant progress. He seems to have satisfied his examiners in harmony (A. J. Caldicott and Stephen Kemp) and was considered by Holmes to be an excellent member of the orchestra. He graduated in 1886 in the second class. Although his scholarship was renewed for a further year, he vanishes from our sight and is heard of no more.

Louisa Kellett (marked in the register as 'Ill from September 1887, deceased') also took violin as her second instrument. In piano, Taylor at first considered she had 'bad habits of inaccuracy beginning to shew marked improvement, very painstaking,' and her progress in the next two years was marked. Gompertz thought she had 'decided talent' and would 'make her second study successful,' while in harmony Eaton Faning found her 'intelligent, painstaking and promising.' Despite her reputation for wildness, her report for general conduct found her 'exemplary, excellent in every way.'

Edith Oldham, who, as we shall see, began piano with Pauer but transferred to Taylor, was considered 'very talented & industrious but sometimes wanting earnest perseverance,' and in her second term—perhaps as a result of the transfer—was making 'very uneven progress.' Her second subject was singing, which she studied with Gertrude Mayfield and Eliza Mazzucato (daughter of the director of the Milan Conservatory and later a distinguished composer in America). Mayfield was very ill (she died a year later), and Edith had no tuition in her first term; in her second term she showed herself to be 'anxious to improve' and in her third to have 'a small voice but true.' Bridge found her to be reasonably good at harmony and counterpoint. In general attendance, several absences were noted because of illness, but as far as general conduct was concerned, Grove marked: 'Excellent, all that I could wish.' By the following year Taylor found her to be 'not all reliable,' but there was marked progress throughout the year, as there was in singing, and in 1887 she graduated ARCM.

Anna Russell, from 6 Broad Street, Limerick, also suffered from the fact that her father (a baker) was dead, and it may have been her early insecurity in London that caused Mrs Goldschmidt to think in her first term that her 'voice [was] not worth tuition—might make a good teacher.' In the second, her 'organisation [was] very inartistic,' but by the third 'the flexibility of her voice [had] much improved,' and thereafter she made good progress, gaining the ARCM in 1888.[41]

Three years after the first intake, Grove wrote again to Dublin Corporation that 'it is much to be hoped that Dublin, and indeed Ireland generally, may give us as good scholars this time as you did before. It is no exaggeration to say that the Irish contingent are in every way a credit and satisfaction to the College. The scholarships of Miss Kellett, Miss Oldham, Mr. Bulkley and Mr. Charles Wood have all been extended by the Council owing to their promise and industry . . . Whatever the political differences of England and Ireland, in Music they will, at any rate, be of one mind.'[42] This was the year in which another RIAM pianist, Ethel Sharpe (known affectionately to Grove as E♯), won a scholarship to the RCM (she had started in the Academy in 1870). And a year later Bridge, writing to Brady in connection with his work as an extern examiner at the RIAM, said, 'The Irish pupils at our Royal College are about our best! If you get Home Rule you will have to keep them I suppose. We should be sorry.'[43]

We have seen that Sir Robert Stewart and J. P. Mahaffy had commented adversely on the IAM's failure to teach harmony. The Academy's response to this was to attempt, in March 1869, to accommodate Stewart's criticism by offering him the professorship of harmony and composition, which had been vacant since the death of Dr Smith.[44] By way of explanation and rapprochement, Brady wrote to Stewart on 6 March:

> The Committee have . . . reason to think, that the Academy will prob-ably be aided by a grant from the public funds, and that the amount may depend upon the efforts used by the Committee to afford the best musical instruction. With that view they have determined to appoint a Professor of Harmony and Composition, in the expectation of increased support from the subscribers to defray the requisite expenses. It is a class for which the Pupils will not pay and therefore the entire cost falls upon the Institution. The Committee think it right to explain to you the reason why they have hitherto been unable to fill up so important a Professorship, and they hope your interest in promoting the art of Music in Ireland will secure to the Academy the advantage of your teaching. The terms I am instructed to offer you are at the rate of £40 yearly to the end of the present year. The future arrangements to depend on the progress of the Academy.

Stewart's reply of 9 March is to some extent disingenuous, since it becomes clear that he was extremely sensitive on the subject of fees.

> I am sorry my answer is not in accordance with the kind wishes expressed both by you and your Co Secretary my friend MacDonnell but, I never wish to undertake what I do not carry out thoroughly, and I am far too much overworked to undertake more engagements. I have again and again refused pupils during this season (who would have paid me at a rate in accordance with enclosed could I have devoted the time to them. I mention this for your own private information, for I don't wish to advertise my terms which I need not say I have never done). Will you express my best acknowledgements to your brother-Committee.

However, the Academy was anxious to have Stewart within the fold and six months later resolved to offer him £100 a year as a second piano professor, in tandem with Fanny Arthur, with the additional inducement of a weekly lecture in harmony at half a guinea.[45] Once on the staff, Stewart rapidly became a central figure in its affairs, immediately becoming a member of the Board, which he chaired only a week after joining the staff, and becoming a vice-president in 1889. He thus cemented his commanding place in Irish music, which already embraced the position of organist at both Protestant cathedrals, the Chapel Royal (Dublin Castle), and TCD Chapel, as well as the chair of music at TCD, distinctions that earned him a knighthood in 1872.

Although largely self-taught as a musician, Stewart was responsible for raising teaching standards to what he regarded as an acceptable European level. He instituted a written examination as a qualification for the BMus in TCD, a practice adopted fifteen years later at Oxford and Cambridge. An undistinguished composer himself (apart from his highly respected output for church use), his composition was confined largely to the production of occasional music, such as his 'Installation March', the Tercentenary Ode for TCD in 1892, and the fantasia composed for the Boston Peace Festival of 1872, which combined the melodies of 'Let Erin Remember' and 'Yankee Doodle'. But believing, as Hercules MacDonnell recalled, that 'a horse that keeps going round in a mill will never be fit for a Derby,'[46] he pioneered the appreciation of Verdi, Liszt, and Wagner, whose music he had set out to discover at first hand by visits to Bayreuth, in the company of Stanford, MacDonnell, and Raoul de Versan.

By nature, however, Stewart, although genial, was also what we would today call 'pushy', and even 'grasping', as far as advancement and his earning capacity were concerned—most probably from a deep-seated anxiety about money. It has been suggested that it was his second wife's social ambitions that caused him to overwork,[47] but these anxieties were evident well before the death of his first wife. His object, as his biographer, Olinthus Vignoles, put it, was 'to lay by everything he could spare from his professional earnings for the benefit of his wife and daughters . . . His economies were the very reverse of stinginess.'[48] It is most likely, however, that, like Esposito, he was constitutionally incapable of sitting at rest but must be always actively engaging in what he professed. J. C. Culwick, in many ways his disciple, said he was 'a constant and indefatigable worker. Activity was his natural state.'[49]

By 1878, Stewart had become concerned that his income was falling. It is significant that he appears to have been less than enthusiastic about his harmony lessons, and it is also clear that he considered himself to be much more than an ordinary professor in the institution.

> Holyrood, Bray
>
> My dear Sir Francis, I am not satisfied with my position at 36 W.R; from £98 to £91 per term, I have come down to £32 or £36, and even this wretched sum is made up by adding £8 or £10 earned in Harmony lectures. You remember that I always objected to teach harmony unless you all saw that I had a good piano class, not two or 3, as I have had all this term on one day & 5 or 6 on the other. In this week I have but 9 pupils! (you know what the rest have per diem) I don't care for the barren hours of figuring in advertisements & prospectuses of heading classes & signing certificates only: I wish to get a fair share of pupils. When you had no grant and only depended on pupils' fees I had £50 the first term and it has constantly been up to £75 & £60: you must only make some arrangement for me by which I shall not be utterly sacrificed as I have been. I suggest that you shall ask the Council to allot me 3 hours Monday and 3 hours on Thursday: 6 in all: . . . I trust you will agree to this very feasible, & very moderate amount. It is not worth

fighting for indeed, but it is better than the 2 or 3 lonely girls I have had all this term on one of my days. It could never be supposed a man in my position could be contented with a pittance like this. If one had the barren honour of 'Principal of RAM' like my friend Prof. Macfarren, it might console one for poor pay; but I am in no better position than the very humblest of your staff . . . since therefore I serve as a mere teacher, let me at least have something worthwhile by doing so.

P.S. I shall be glad to make way for Robinson if you think he would return & don't see your way to grant this moderate request.[50]

The postscript is double-edged. Robinson, as we shall see, had resigned from the Academy in a show of temper, but it was Stewart who had ousted Robinson as conductor of the Philharmonic. (Their rivalry as young men must have been quite intense: Stewart, for example, at the age of twenty-one had conducted the combined Famine concert of *Israel in Egypt* in 1847 to which we have alluded.)

The Council resolved to try to increase the number of Stewart's pupils by advancing some from junior to senior level,[51] and Brady wrote to him pointing out that he had received £134 from the Academy in 1874, £121 in 1875, £129 in 1876, and £128 in 1877, paying at Stewart's rate for private tuition. 'I believe there will be a large class for you this term, but you cannot expect the Council to lose money by giving you pupils who cannot pay the fees or who can hardly play their notes. Try and induce pupils of talent to come to the Academy & you will soon find your class increase.'[52] To this Stewart replied:

> I have your letter of 14 March. If I was assured that I got my share of pupils, I don't want to grasp at more: no one can accuse me of illiberality but my two or three pupils on Mondays . . . contrast very forcibly with the numbers of 8, 9, 10 & more regularly with others . . . There are pupils with us who are used to be knocked about (Sydney Smith said the children of the poor are not *brought up* but *dragged* up) these creatures are used to it but there are others who are used to feather treatment & if any of our governing body hurt or insult or mortify them, a dislike of the institution gets hold of them: this is no fancy of mine & I tell it to you as you feel most interest in the place, but I don't want you to speak publicly of it. I think we 'dragoon' the girls too much.
>
> P.S. . . . I am constantly the means of sending you pupils, & not always for myself—rightly or wrongly I am looked on as a sort of Principal or head of the place, both in England & in the provinces. Of course those in Dublin know I have perhaps *less* influence *within* [the] Academy than even your pupil teachers . . . I really *have* some little character (in spite of Robinson's snarling).

The result was that Stewart's fears were allayed and his class increased, perhaps at the expense of another teacher, Alexandre Billet, who in the same year found the number of his pupils dwindling. By the end of 1879, with the new organ installed, Stewart (assisted by T. R. G. Jozé and Charles Marchant) was able to add a professorship of organ to his other tenures. By

1887 he was receiving £100 a year for eight hours' teaching per week of harmony, counterpoint, and composition (which from 1884 also included a class for 'writing and copying music'),[53] and at the reconstitution of the Academy in 1889 he was paid this salary together with £173 in respect of hourly rates for piano—a total of £273 (about £9,000 in today's money), together with his professorial salary from TCD and his two cathedral stipends.

It seems that Stewart too was capable of 'snarling'. George Grove wrote to Edith Oldham: 'I think him one of the cleverest, most musical people in the Academy—but Lord what a common person he is—how full of jibes and intrigues—and wrath if you don't fall in with them!'[54] Among the pupils who revered him were Culwick, Annie Patterson, C. V. Stanford, and J. M. Synge. Culwick credited him with having 'done much to recall music in Ireland back from a degradation to which it had sunk' and called him 'our champion before the world,'[55] while Synge, when he heard of Stewart's death in 1894, called him 'my beloved harmony teacher . . . the cleverest Irish musician and one of the kindest of men.'[56] Annie Patterson followed Stewart's lead in lecturing publicly on Irish music, as did Culwick, who, remarkably, referred to the complementarity of English and Irish music as that between 'the strength of the masculine and the sweetness of the feminine.'[57] His influence on these four cannot be underestimated, since they, among others, fuelled the cultural revival of the eighteen-nineties and later.

Stewart was also the teacher of Dr George Sinclair (1863–1917), who became organist of Hereford Cathedral (where he was responsible for the conduct of the Three Choirs Festival) and the model for the eleventh of Elgar's Enigma Variations. Born in England, Sinclair had spent his youth in Dublin before becoming assistant organist at Gloucester at the age of sixteen. He was to return to Dublin many times as a recitalist and examiner.

Stewart's remarks about his status inside and outside the Academy were borne out when he died in 1894, when the Academy received a letter of condolence from the then principal of the RAM, Alexander Mackenzie.

> I . . . write in the name of my Directors and the Committee of Management expressing our deep and sincere regret at the news of the unexpected and sudden death of your honoured principal [*sic*] Sir Robert Stewart. Believe me, we are truly sensible of the great loss which your national institution, as well as the musical world at large, has sustained: and I, having had the honour of his genial acquaintance, am personally in complete sympathy with you all in this distress.[58]

The effect of Stewart's sudden death was not unlike that of Robinson's departure from the Academy in 1875, in that it required three people to replace him, Robinson returning as senior professor of piano, Jozé and Marchant as 'colleagues and Professors of the organ' at 7s 6d per hour, and Jozé (nominated by Brady and W. R. Molloy) elected professor of harmony (in preference to Culwick, who was sponsored by Cree and Esposito, and Joseph Smith, who was supported by Robinson) at a salary of £100. Jozé relinquished his secretaryship of the Academy and was succeeded by C. Grahame Harvey.[59]

Stewart's chief focus had been the cathedral, and his attachment to song-writing was a natural extension of cathedral life, since it was in the glee clubs and similar fraternities that that life found its social aspect. He was so adept at the organ that it is said he could play with one hand while writing a letter with the other, and his capacity for improvisation was legendary. Culwick observes that a cantata that developed the theme of 'Eileen Aroon' was 'an intellectual *tour de force*,'[60] and it was this technical mastery, coupled with inventiveness, that made him such a fine teacher of counterpoint.

Synge recorded Stewart's lectures in his notebook and conducted his studies with Stewart in counterpoint and analysis in parallel with a close reading of Frederick Gore Ouseley's *Treatise on Musical Form*.[61] On 18 November 1889 he attended Stewart's lecture in the RIAM, which we reproduce as he recorded it, to demonstrate the type of lecture to which a serious music student of the time would be exposed.

> The early history of music is veiled in much obscurity. The music of the first Christians was vocal and antiphonal. The council of Laodicea in 367 A.D. first inaugurated trained choirs. Ambrose Bishop of Milan (300) on the other hand upheld congregational singing. He is said to have made the first collection of tunes. A school of singing was founded at Rome by Hillary. The Christian [. . .] are [. . .] proved to be related by similarity of the terms they used. Gregory used the first fifteen letters of the Greek alphabet so much altered as to be scarcely recognisable to designate from d in bas clef to d in high clef which was about the extent of their music. Gerart thinks Gregory taught orally only. Some of the first attempts at musical notation were neuma, that is, little lines and marks placed over the words of a hymn. Two men of note at time were Hucbald Elmonensi a monk of St Amand 930 A.D.[62] and Guido early part of the 11th century H— first taught harmony which consisted of the canto fermo with the 4th above and the 5th beneath. The Greek music forbid the 9 and 6th This was called organum, of which, there were two species, one admitting other intervals between the consonants. Descant came into use in the 13th century, it consisted of two or more parts with a Cantus fermus. These parts were sometimes improvised, the accidentals were often not written but put in by the singer this was called musica ficta. This lead [*sic*] to measured music and the line table which was unnecessary while the parts moved note against note. The ears of musicians now grew weary of the rude organism, the singers were ahead of the theorists.[63]

While the subject of another Stewart lecture, 'Ancient Irish Music: The Clarseach,' might seem worlds apart from this, the general tenor of the discussion follows a similar pattern: the retrieval of valued information and the spirit and aesthetic value it conveyed.

To the ordinary listener all harps are alike, and a harp but a harp, yet all the same, there are harps and harps, and between the ancient Irish harp and the modern Erard at 120 guineas, with its perfected scale, its enharmonic changes, and its new powers of modulation, the difference is very great. Perhaps one of the most beautiful effects of the modern harp with catgut strings is its faultless pianissimo, which, aroused by the soft touch of a woman's hand, leaves nothing to be desired; and yet it must be confessed that in some respects the ancient wire strung harp of Ireland affects us more deeply. A sweet tone of complaint is peculiar to it, which cannot be produced by any strings of catgut. It was doubtless these sad tones, clearly mingling their vibrations, to which Giraldus referred when he alluded to 'the tinkling of the small strings sporting with freedom under the deep notes of the bass,' an effect which was, of course, intensified by the peculiar manner in which harpers of the very old Irish school (such players as Denis a Hempsy) were accustomed to catch the wires, viz., between the fleshy finger tips and the nails, the latter being suffered to grow long for this purpose. It has always struck the writer of these few remarks as an instance of those apparent contradictions which abound in Irish affairs, that so few Irish girls can be induced to study the national instrument, an instrument which, apart from its musical charm, is so peculiarly graceful to behold. Formerly the Council of the Irish Academy of Music made many efforts to remedy this. They during the last two years went so far as to engage one of the first English harpists to visit Dublin, offering instruction from her gratis, to any girls willing to accept it. We are, however, in great hopes that in the near future another harp class will be set on foot under the auspices of the new governing body of the Academy, a school musically led and guided by the talented daughter of the late lamented Alexander M. Sullivan, the niece of our recent chief magistrate, the Right Hon. T. D. Sullivan; and surely, if there be any force in heredity, the young lady to whom we allude cannot but be both talented and good.[64]

Stewart's knowledge is all the more remarkable since wire-strung harps had disappeared after 1830 and were not to reappear until demonstrated by Mary Rowland in 1961 and then pioneered by Gráinne Yeats.

Although Stewart's own imagination was 'enclosed' by TCD and the cathedrals, further exploration reveals that his sense of responsibility brought him further afield, like a traveller in his own land. He may have suspended his unsuccessful professorial lectures at TCD, but in 1873 we find that he delivered a series entitled 'Musica Hibernica', which shows him to have been—or at least to have considered himself—in the company of Bunting, Moore, Stevenson, and Hudson, an aspect of his career not mentioned in his official biography.

Later, Stewart was engaged in a projected work of 'Irish musical biography', of which his contribution to *Grove I*—articles on 'Irish music,' Moore, and O'Carolan—was the stimulus. Researching the life of James Augustine Wade (1801–45) for *Grove* (his significance was sufficient to ensure his survival into the pages of *New Grove*), he found himself fulminating over the neglect into which such figures sank within years of their death.

> It is wonderful how soon the Irish people forget their talented countrymen . . . I found the same unaccountably dull forgetfulness about the memory of Stevenson, Rooke, and Balfe. A silly bias towards politics, an appreciation of religious asperity, seems alone to animate our people; they never forget the leaders of religious or political party, but about a Carolan, a Hogan, a Rooke, a Barry, or an Augustine Wade they never seem to trouble their heads.[65]

We may infer from this that Stewart was anxious to include Irish composers as a generic type, rather than to differentiate them one from another. We should not lose sight of the fact that this most Protestant of men on one occasion reviewed a performance of Haller's Requiem in the Church of the Three Patrons, Rathgar, for *Lyra Ecclesiastica*, the journal of the Cecilian movement.[66]

While it is undoubtedly accurate to view Stewart as, in Harry White's words, 'a mouthpiece for Establishment understanding of music' who saw 'musical composition [as] necessarily an outgrowth of [an imperial] conception of Ireland,'[67] it is also valid to see his interest in the 'classical' aspects of Irish music as a desire to accommodate the essence of Ireland in his teaching. Like his pupil Stanford after him, Stewart included 'stylized indigenous material in his compositions [as] a matter of exotic colour rather than distinctive identity, musical or otherwise.' Even if, as White suggests, 'the ethnic tradition was effectively irrelevant to his understanding of art music, as the greater population of Ireland was to his own explicit establishment view,' he was 'a force in Irish music as one wholly conversant with that tradition and prepared to impart it to others . . . As an educator . . . his range of influence was profound.'[68]

In some ways, in fact, Stewart was a bridge in the Irish revival between the early pioneers and the discussion of authenticity in relation to Irish music (which will occupy us in chapter 5). His approach was to combine an 'archaeological' attitude, such as Petrie's, with an associative critical faculty, making broad connections between Ireland and Phoenicia, which he argued was the origin of both the curach and the caoineadh, examples of which he demonstrated by means of the College Chapel choir, discussing the harp and the bagpipes in similar fashion.[69]

Stewart's achievements should not allow us to overlook those of a Dubliner of Spanish origin, Thomas Richard Gonsalvez Jozé (1853–1924), who, although a minor figure, deserves to be recognised for having made an important contribution to the work of the Academy—as teacher of piano, organ and theory and conductor of the orchestra, as well as secretary during the crucial years before and after the implementation of the Blue Scheme—and to the cathedrals and the social life that revolved around them, including the Strollers and the Catch Club, for whom he wrote much music. As a composer and arranger he collaborated with Stewart and others, besides writing a comic opera, *Les Amourettes* (1885), and a cantata, *The Prophecy of Capys*, to words by Macaulay, for which he was awarded his doctorate.

We have deferred a consideration of the choral scene in Dublin until this point, as the Academy did not open a choral class until 1871. This in itself is surprising, since Joseph Robinson, as one of the chief choral conductors of the time, would presumably have wanted to put such activity on a professional basis—not least in his mind being the original ambition of the IAM to bring together singers and orchestra in a more effective manner.

It may of course be that the existence of organisations such as the Royal Choral Institute, founded in 1851 'for the public performance of the highest class of choral music both sacred and secular,'[70] with Glover and Keenan at its helm, went so far towards fulfilling the functions of a vocal academy that Robinson and his colleagues saw no need to compete. Certainly the underlying intention of the institute—'to establish in this country a large body of choristers, composed chiefly of the working classes, capable of performing the best classical works, the performance of which is at present exclusively confined to private societies'—would have acted as a deterrent rather than a provocation to those, such as Robinson, whose activities were essentially private and tended to exclude the lower orders.

About 1853 the Royal Choral Institute seems to have merged its interests with the Royal Irish Institution, where Glover was actively promoting the Wilhem method of music education. On this the *Freeman's Journal* commented:

> It would be difficult to over-rate the advantage likely to arise from a more widespread musical knowledge, and in the gratifying progress so lately evinced in this important branch of education we are mainly indebted to this popular system. Where is the parent who would deprive his children of so charming an accomplishment as that of vocal music, which is now brought within the reach of the community at large, and not as hitherto the privilege of the few?[71]

In addition to the Institute was the 'Dublin Mercantile Choral Union', which also seemed to have a bias in favour of 'the less wealthy classes.'[72] Little, however, seems to have been achieved on any sustained basis by any of these societies to widen the audience or the list of performers for choral music. The educational system itself did not help, and social movement between classes had not yet reached the level where, in the period of cultural nationalism, a rich amateur and a poor professional could sit side by side. Dublin society was far too stratified for that.

So, despite the astonishing proliferation of choral societies in the previous thirty years (twenty-two music societies had been formed between 1841 and 1867, of which most were choral),[73] the aspirations of the IAM had been frustrated, not least by the collapse in 1864 of Robinson's own Antient Concerts Society. The decision, therefore, by the Academy in 1871 to instigate a choral class was a late development and one whose fortunes demonstrate the difficulty of attracting more than a core of enthusiasts in pursuit of lost glory and future enlightenment.

On 22 March 1871 MacDonnell proposed a mixed evening class of a hundred, each paying a pound a year, under the direction of Robinson, assisted by William Power O'Donoghue, to start in October. It gave its first performance on 16 May at the Antient Concert Rooms, the programme consisting of a Mozart motet, miscellaneous part-songs, and the sacred cantata 'God is Love' by Mrs Robinson (Fanny Arthur), which was to become a mainstay of the Academy repertoire for many years to come. The *Freeman's Journal* obligingly reported:

> Some time since the Committeee of the Academy wisely determined on supplying a great musical want by establishing a choral class, in which the pupils would be taught to sing effectively together, and learn how to give due interpretation and effect to choral compositions . . . It is with sincere pleasure we have to speak of it generally most approvingly.[74]

The *Irish Times* was less congratulatory and rather more perceptive. Remarking that a Dublin chorus was a difficult entity to conjure up, it did commend the performance of 'God is Love' but asked 'why the solo parts for male voices were entrusted to gentlemen not pupils of the Academy'— an omission that would shortly be remedied by the creation of vocal scholarships. But the report continued:

> Dr. W. P. O'Donoghue was, ostensibly, the conductor, and we believe the baton could not be in more efficient hands, but we witnessed some supplementary display in this particular, which we trust for the credit of all parties concerned will not be again repeated at any future concerts. Such demonstrations tend not only to weaken the collective efficiency of the performers but also tend to impress the audience with the idea that there is no one individual in the Academy competent to discharge the important functions incidental to this position.[75]

This observation was clearly directed against Robinson, who—we can assume—asserted himself during the performance by providing 'supplementary' conducting, thus subverting the authority of the appointed conductor. From the tone taken by the *Irish Times*, few readers can have been left in doubt about the nature of the 'demonstration', and it underlines a problem that became acute at this time, namely the egomania of Robinson in relation to his colleagues, which came near to ruining the Academy within the next three years.

Within a further year the Academy had acquired the library of the defunct Antient Concerts Society, thus increasing its capacity for large choral performances by having at its fingertips the scores used in most of the essential choral events of the past thirty years. At that time it was announced that the choral class would increase from one hundred to two hundred, the level at which the costs would become viable, but this was an ambition it would find impossible to realise. Both the practices and the performances, it was pointedly stated, would be under the conductorship of Robinson. In addition, a preparatory class, under Joseph Mullen, would be formed. The

Evening Mail greeted this development by commenting that 'the subscription to it will be amazingly small, when the advantage of being taught by so distinguished a musician is remembered—one who is too true a genius and too fine a master of his art to permit of any bad work passing from under his hands.'[76]

Six months later the fruit of their labours was evident in a performance on 15 May 1874 at the Exhibition Palace of Haydn's Imperial Mass, Mendelssohn's setting of Psalm 42, and Beethoven's Choral Fantasy. The soloists were Bessie Herbert, Miss Sherlock (an Academy scholar), Barton McGuckin (of whom the Academy would hear a great deal in future), and Grattan Kelly. A further six months passed, and the class contemplated the performance of Beethoven's Mass in C and Mendelssohn's *Laudate Sion.*

The thinly veiled criticism by the *Irish Times*, and the undoubtedly deserved accolade from the *Evening Mail*, serve to encapsulate Robinson's strengths and weaknesses. Given the friendship between his father and Robinson, C. V. Stanford has left us probably the fairest summary of his character:

> His personality was unique. He had strong likes and dislikes. His heroes were 'giants,' and his enemies 'impostors' . . . He had, like Costa, the grip of a field-marshal. He never brooked contradiction in his own business, and he was a martinet, though a kindly one. As a conductor of choral and orchestral works he was certainly in the front rank, and if he had lived in England would undoubtedly have held any important post as a matter of course, and held it admirably, for he possessed both the temperament and electricity necessary to a conductor.[77]

In his private life he was also a man of mixed principles. By popular legend he was a philanderer, showing little fidelity to his wife, which may or may not have exacerbated the nervous illness that eventually caused her suicide (in 1879 she jumped from the roof of their house at 3 Lower Fitzwilliam Street, today the United Arts Club). John O'Donovan believed that their marriage was unconsummated and that her suicide may have been provoked by his affair with the wife of a senior fellow of TCD named Shaw.[78] Shortly afterwards Robinson married again, and, like his first wife, his second, Mary Ellen (by whom he had a son), joined the Academy piano staff, from which she resigned in ill-health in 1907, aged fifty-four.[79]

There have been several periods in the history of the RIAM when Continental musicians of distinction—chiefly Italians and Germans—have formed the core of the teaching staff, and, of course, for most of its history (from Joseph Lidel at the very beginning up to the present day) individual figures from throughout the world (western and eastern Europe, America and Australasia) have contributed their special skills and character to the general mélange. But one period in particular, from 1875 to 1882, stands out because of the humour and pathos of its transactions, and the fact that it brought to the Academy the major figure of Michele Esposito.

We have already seen that Joseph Robinson could be 'difficult'—that he was a maestro who demanded *uno duce, una voce.* In 1875 it is clear that

Robinson was not getting everything his own way, and he signalled his (and his wife's) intention 'to retire from the Academy at the end of the term.'[80] This the Council made strenuous efforts to resist, urging Robinson to reconsider the matter, but without success. No doubt they were anxious to avoid any public dispute about the running of the Academy that Robinson, as a much-respected figure and a founder of the institution, might stir up, besides the inconvenience of losing an undeniably good teacher and con- ductor and finding replacements for both him and Fanny Arthur. As they acknowledged in their letter (penned, as usual, by Brady),

> this is a step of very serious consequence in the opinion of the Council as well to the Academy as to the progress of musical education in Ireland. You are quite aware that in order to fill the positions now held by Mrs. Robinson and you it would most likely be necessary to endeavour to induce teachers of eminence to settle in Dublin from England or the Continent. The funds at the disposal of the Council are very inadequate for this purpose. Therefore in all probability the present high standard of instruction in the Academy must be lowered. You also are well aware of the many Pupils who, but for the education given them in the Academy by Mrs. Robinson & you would not have been able to acquire the instruction which has placed them in very high positions in their art as public performers & teachers. To Pupils of this class your resignation will prove a very serious loss indeed. You do not assign any reason for your wish & the Council are altogether unaware of any adequate cause. The only motive they can ascribe for Mrs. Robinson's & your resignation is to be found in letters recently written by you & verbal commu- nications, to the same effect, in which you claim an absolute right to control some of the most important arrangements for the education of the Pupils in the Academy independently of the Council. Now we think that on consideration you cannot seriously insist on this power being vested in you. Practically your wishes have been almost invariably carried out. Not only have the Council at all times been most anxious to defer to your judgement and to show the high respect they entertain for the experience and great abilities of Mrs. Robinson & yourself but as you know the Council consist almost entirely of your own personal friends, it has been a pleasure to them to act in every way in their power so as to meet your wishes. The Council have however a very responsible duty to discharge to the public and they are also accountable to Parliament & the Government for the expenditure of the public funds entrusted to their administration. You must assuredly see that it is impossible for them to give the control of the education of the Pupils to any one Professor, although they would naturally as they have invariably done attach the greatest weight in the opinion of teachers so eminent as Mrs. Robinson & you. To act otherwise would be distinctly to abandon the trust which the Government has thought fit to confide to them & would imperil the continuance of the aid from the public funds which they at present receive. We have thought it right & due to you to put these considerations before you & we trust that you & Mrs. Robinson will feel

their importance & not deprive the Academy of your services as Professors & put the Council to the pain of severing a connexion which has endured for so many years.[81]

But the Robinsons were as unwavering in their determination as they were silent in their reasons.

The immediate effect of the Robinsons' resignation was two-fold: the appointment of Alexandre Billet as a piano teacher, and the closure of the choral class. Billet gave an inaugural recital on 2 October 1875, playing Beethoven (Sonata in G), Handel (Allegro and Fugue in F, 'Harmonious Blacksmith'), Moscheles (La leggerezza), Field (Rondo 'Midi'), Bach (Prelude and Fugue in A minor), Raff (Minuet in E), Chopin (Étude in G flat), Mendelssohn (Étude in F minor), Brahms (Hungarian Dances Nos. 6 and 7), and Rubinstein (Valse Impromptu), of which the writer of the 'Music and Drama' gossip column of the *Irish Times* wrote: 'Not having had the plea-sure of being present, I am unable to speak from personal knowledge . . . but I am assured on highly competent authority that his performance created a most favourable impression . . . He exhibited great facility and exquisite taste . . . and proved himself fully worthy of the high reputation which he has earned.'[82]

Billet was one of the most highly regarded piano teachers of his day,[83] having worked with Liszt and having held professorships at the con-servatoire of Geneva. However, he may not have been particularly adroit at selling himself, as later circumstances were to show.

While the Robinsons' decision still seemed to be hanging in the balance, Hercules MacDonnell had moved on 30 June 1875 that, because of the increasing expense and administrative work required for the concerts of the choral class, it should be terminated but that the Academy should 'afford every encouragement in its power to the formation of a Choral Society having for its object the like promotion of high class performances,' includ-ing the use of its rooms and library 'as well as their hearty sympathy and co-operation.'[84] Doubtless this step was taken to ensure that in the event of Robinson carrying out his threat there should be no grounds on his part for accusing the Academy of ill-will. When Robinson indeed left the Academy, the closure of the class was confirmed on 10 November 1875 and the reason for both its formation and its closure stated clearly:

> When it was formed . . . there was no public organisation in Dublin for the study of choral music . . . Very considerable progress in chorus and part singing was made by the class and the Council were enabled from time to time to produce with much success . . . several works of the Great Masters [but in view of the financial costs] the Council could not continue to sustain so serious a demand on its resources . . . The Council had not come to a final decision as to what course was best to recommend . . . in order to continue the progress of the study of choral music which they had thus originated, but were in hopes that some plan independent of them might be suggested to which they would be able to give their support and encouragement. They are gratified to learn that

such a plan has been formed. The Council have not had any official notification of the details proposed, but . . . they have reason to believe that a society is in process of formation which will . . . steadily pursue the course suggested by them.[85]

This society was the Dublin Musical Society, which, after several transformations, ultimately evolved into the Culwick Choral Society. Its first concert took place on 6 April 1876, and the society went a long way, under the direction first of Robinson and later of Joseph Smith, to consolidate and amalgamate the choral forces in Dublin.

To replace Robinson was no easy matter. The annual report for 1875 noted that 'some changes have taken place in the staff,' without mentioning Robinson by name—an omission of some seriousness if we reflect on his enormous contribution as a founder, governor and teacher for the previous twenty-seven years. The report, dated February 1876, stated:

> In the department of the vocal classes the engagement of an additional professor who shall devote himself more particularly to the cultivation of Dramatic and Italian singing, has, for a considerable period, occupied the attention of the Council; and they expect shortly to appoint a teacher worthy of filling so responsible a position.

It went on to note the foundation of the Dublin Musical Society and to offer it the good will previously promised:

> They will be ready to assist, so far as they can, the newly-formed Society, and feel that the expense incurred by them, and the time and attention they devoted to the subject, have not been without useful result, if they have tended to the establishing of a Society more exclusively devoted to the study and performance of the works of the great masters.

Predictably, the Dublin Musical Society had many supporters in common with the Academy and other music initiatives. Valentine Blake Dillon (a future Lord Mayor of Dublin and soon to enter our story in his capacity as an alderman), James Drury, Dr D. B. Dunne, W. Purser Geoghegan, William Martin Murphy MP and Dr Richard Littledale were all members of its Committee.

At this point MacDonnell's connection with the international singing community once again proved useful. He consulted Carl Rosa, Madame Balfe, Pauline Viardot and Giovanni Mario in search of candidates. The names suggested included Eugénie Garcia (no doubt sponsored by her sister-in-law, Viardot). On 28 December he wrote to the director of the Royal College of Music in Naples asking for a recommendation, to which Paolo Serrao responded:

> Illustrious Sir: I reply, with some delay . . . having been occupied in looking for a professor such as you desire. In Naples there are very many professors of singing who on account of family ties are unwilling to leave their country; however, I have succeeded in finding Signor

Luigi Caracciolo, a pupil of our Conservatorio, who besides being an excellent singing master is also an excellent accompanist & composer and has already written an opera which has attained a great success. He is a man of 27 years of age and of high education. I am proud to propose him and am sure that the Irish Institute will gain a great advantage . . . Signor Caracciolo accepts the post with a stipend . . . of £150 [£4,500 today] for 5 hours of lessons twice a week and 12% for every hour's lessons which he may have to give in addition. The vacation to be 10 weeks . . . I have to inform you that Signor C. only speaks Italian and French but would learn English quickly, having great talent.[86]

On 25 March 1876 Caracciolo began a three-month trial period, and the appointment was confirmed on 4 July. During this period MacDonnell wrote to Michael Costa and Pauline Viardot regarding the correct methods to be adopted at the Academy and was encouraged not to restrict the teaching to any particular regimen. It appears that MacDonnell's letter contained details of a teaching method whose efficacy was the subject of his enquiry. Since it elicited a negative response, we might be forgiven for thinking that the method could not have been Caracciolo's, since the response should have put paid to his chances of being kept on, but in the light of subsequent developments it does appear that it was indeed his schema that was being tested. Costa wrote: 'Every teaching master has his own peculiar way to instruct, and provided the pupils improve he must not be restricted in his manner of teaching.'[87] Pauline Viardot replied:

> I think that when a good teacher has a pupil whom he wishes to lead far off and make a first rate singer of, the longer he keeps her singing exercises the better it is, but I do not think he need do that more than six months at the longest. It is very difficult to determine before hand, because the way of teaching differs according to the voice, capacities and intelligence of the pupil. But in any case six months of exercise ought to be sufficient for any pupil unless it is an idiot. After three months, songs are generally introduced in the teaching. The development of the voice requires it; I think it renders the pupil's ear more musical, and the pupil herself takes more interest in her studies, there being more variety. Yes, decidedly, quiet classical songs ought to be studied as soon as the pupil's voice is even in all the registers. Pupils must not be disgusted with their lessons . . . For the pupils you bring up in your Conservatoire who are mostly destined to become governesses, the singing business ought to be made easy. The thing a singing master ought to attend to with the greatest severity is the intonation. To form the *ear* as well as the voice, that is the most important thing, especially in England [*sic*].[88]

It seems extraordinary that at this stage MacDonnell should not only have consulted Joseph Robinson on the matter but also shown him Costa's and Viardot's letters. Although we might well think that his 'retirement' at the age of sixty was natural, it does not explain how he still had the energy to transfer his work to the formation of the new society and, eventually, to return to the Academy staff in 1887 (at the age of seventy-one), where he remained almost until his death in 1898. Yet his letter to MacDonnell is constructive and friendly:

> My Dear Heck:
>
> I have read your correspondence with Costa and Viardot and I quite agree with the ideas which seem to be common to all the writers.
>
> The first principle I would insist on is, that it is absurd to lay down an iron rule to be applied to all classes alike, more especially where you cannot secure a Pupil's remaining a sufficient number of years. To subject *every* Pupil to a probation of twelve months' *Solfeggi*, without relief, would be, I fear, to deter nearly every one from beginning, and spoil many who had the courage to make the experiment. In an Academy, as in general teaching, there must always be a great majority who can only hope, without being great singers, to become respectable vocalists, and earn money by giving or superintending tuition. For exceptional cases, where we find a promise of great voice and talent, exceptional teaching may be possible or proper; but, for the general average (with which we have to deal when large numbers are concerned), it is different; we must adopt an average system. In any case, I doubt if more than three months could be usefully employed in Vocalises alone. It would not only discourage, but fail to develop the taste of most Pupils. You should, along with the mechanism of the voice, teach also the ear and taste; this can only be done by teaching songs as well—songs of a good, not a vulgar class. The young Pupil cannot sing them effectively, nor is it meant she should, but learns much in the effort—in fact the production of the tone, the singing of the scales, &c., *might* all be taught through the medium of songs. A *good* master will make a lesson out of any material; with a bad it is of little consequence what means he uses. The songs used should be varied according to the peculiarities of the Pupil; indeed, it is often good to give those which the Pupil is least suited to do well, but which may serve to correct defects.
>
> The various songs I have taught my Pupils (who are now teachers) have been chosen so as to give the requisite variety. I have endeavoured to make the most of them either of a classical or a high character, but only those who know the special nature of each Pupil can say precisely what should or should not be given to each. I may instance such a songs as Schubert's 'Ave Maria,' which requires a first-class Artist to give full expression to; but, as the study of a few simple notes in the best style, none can be better to teach the production of sustained tone and pure 'Cantabile' singing, while it has the advantage of drawing out any power of expression the pupil may have.
>
> In conclusion, I think it decidedly wrong to try such a system as is stated in your letter to be suggested, and that it would be like prescribing a quack pill to cure every disease. It requires a skilled Doctor to prescribe according to each patient's constitution.[89]

But although Robinson had clearly not fallen out with either Brady or MacDonnell, he bore a considerable grudge against the institution and therefore was capable of distinguishing between his friends and their corporate allegiances. In 1880 he wrote to Thomas Mayne: 'Although the number of soprani in the DMS is complete, I shall be happy to add your daughter's name to the list provided she is a private pupil of Miss Barnewell. I will not admit any pupil belonging to the RIA of Music.' Appended to the letter, now in the Academy archives, is a note in Brady's hand: 'The original of the above is in my possession.'[90]

By January 1878, Caracciolo was being referred to as 'Head of the Vocal Department',[91] and the Council had adopted his recommendation that 'one Professor only should be responsible for the methods of teaching singing in all the classes. It should be his function to propose the arrangements respecting authors and books to be adopted . . . and to explain to the other Professors how these arrangements are to be carried out.'[92] Presumably, up to this point the governors had tried to avoid giving full rein to another dictator, but from this date Caracciolo's centrality to, and pre-eminence in, the Academy was assured.

He seems to have thrown himself into his work, the first fruits of which were the election of six Albert scholars, after examining 195 women on 8 November 1878 and 121 men the next day. Lizzie Connell, Mary Fallon, Mary Broe, D. Reginald Christian, Albert Christian and Daniel Purcell were the successful candidates.[93] At this point the governors

> proceeded to consider how many of the above the resources of the Academy would enable them to elect as free pupils. It appears that each pupil receiving two lessons from Signor Caracciolo would cost the Academy £14 a year. Towards meeting this cost the Council agreed to set apart the Prince Albert Prize fund, the interest on which amounts to £44 yearly. Signor Caracciolo recommended that if possible one of each quality of voice should be selected. This would entail an expenditure of £84 yearly for six pupils, in order to meet the financial resources of the Academy. Signor Caracciolo offered to accept the sum of £44 for the six pupils, but the Council thought this reduction too much to accept. Finally it was agreed that he should be paid £60 yearly for the six free pupils.

In April 1879 Caracciolo complained that there had been some interference with his students 'by persons not connected with the Academy' (which suggests the haunting presence of Robinson), causing the governors to 'express their undiminished confidence in Signor Caracciolo as the Professor of Singing and their sense of the marked improvement in the progress of the singing class under his direction.'[94] They should, however, have seen that trouble was on the way. A month later, Caracciolo submitted a memorandum.

> Gentlemen
>   In compliance with your request, I have the honour of submitting to you that it is not possible for me to establish and secure one uniform system in the singing classes as long as my position as Director of the

Vocal Department is not thoroughly recognized and acquiesced by the teachers who should be subordinate to me, and so long as the Council does not place at my disposal means which shall be sufficiently efficacious for securing that my system shall be carried out in conformity with my own ideas. I have therefore the honour of submitting for your consideration the measures which I believe to be necessary in order to obtain the desired effect.

I   It should be officially notified to all the teachers who are to be subordinate to me that they are required to teach according to my system, and that I am at liberty to decline all connection with such teachers as openly disregard my authority.

II   That each pupil of all the classes under my direction should be obliged to take one lesson from me every month; and, if necessary, the respective teacher should be required to be present during the lesson, in order to receive from me personal instruction in the manner of teaching their pupils.

III   That I may have the right of transferring pupils from one class to another according to their progress and abilities, and in order to avoid any difficulties on this head I request that the fees for admission to all the vocal classes, higher and lower alike, shall be reduced to the same identical amount.

IV   That I shall be authorized to assemble all the vocal classes on the same days and the same hours in order that I may be able to be always at the service of the teachers and the pupils for all requisite explanations and illustrations with reference to the teaching or to the method of study.

V   That in consideration of my new office of Vocal Director the Council will have the goodness to review my former contract and to determine how my new duties shall be remunerated.[95]

—with much of which the Council acquiesced.

In December, Caracciolo achieved the establishment of a choral class.[96] A year later he proposed its enlargement, and with it the recruitment from Milan of Cavaliere Giuseppe Bozzelli, at £100 a year.[97] In this case, it was Caracciolo who was unaware of the trouble he was storing up for himself. The governors having acceded to Caracciolo's request, Bozzelli arrived in Dublin on 13 February 1881[98] and clearly made good progress, as he was elected to the Council twelve months later. That year he and the choir received permission to give a concert (on 6 May) in aid of the victims of the earthquake at Casamicciola, near Naples, at which they performed Sterndale Bennett's 'The May Queen' and Rossini's *Stabat Mater*, raising ten pounds.

On 23 November the governors granted Caracciolo three months' leave 'on account of depressed health,' but he had clearly returned to Dublin the following February, when Michael Quarry's abrupt resignation created a vacancy in the piano school. On 4 February 1882 Brady had written to Quarry:

> The Council . . . regret to find that the present arrangement of the boys' pianoforte classes is not satisfactory to you . . . The Council think it their duty in the interest of the Academy to make arrangements which will relieve you from the responsibility of superintending the classes. It is with much regret I make this communication to you, but the Council of the Academy as trustees of public funds are sometimes obliged to act contrary to their personal inclination.

To which Quarry replied:

> Dear Sir Francis Brady—I resign my class at the Academy. Had I been told when the post was offered to me that I was only to teach such boys as the Council thought fit to send me, I should not have accepted the appointment.[99]

Caracciolo immediately communicated with his friend Michele Esposito, then living in Paris, who applied for, and was offered, the position.

> A letter was read from Sig. Esposito from Paris in answer to the advertisement for a Professor of the Pianoforte to take charge of the boys' classes. It was resolved to offer him a temporary engagement on the following terms: that he would give eight hours a week (if required) at such hours and as the Council shall appoint at the rate of £100 per annum, the first engagement to be for 6 months only.[100]

A week later, Brady explained the nature of the appointment:

> No member of Council having attended except Sig. Caracciolo with me, I was in a difficult position as to what to do respecting Sig. Esposito, he having declined the proposal agreed to in last meeting. But considering the great importance of securing a thoroughly competent head of the male pianoforte class, & the extremely high recommendation by Sig. Caracciolo of Sig. Esposito, I authorized Sig. Caracciolo to propose the following arrangement for three months: Sig. Esposito to be paid £40 for three months for six hours a week and £5 travelling expenses from Paris. If the engagement continue beyond three months the payment to be at the rate of £100 a year for six hours a week, and 10/– for extra hours.[101]

The appointment of Esposito was therefore due, firstly, to Quarry's departure but, secondly, and more importantly, to the lucky accident of Caracciolo having returned in time to alert him. It also clarifies a common misconception (perpetuated, for example, by John F. Larchet in the Academy's 'centenary' history) that Esposito had succeeded Caracciolo as professor of piano, which of course Caracciolo never had been.

Equally, the rise to prominence of Bozzelli was due to Caracciolo's absence, since on 3 May 1882 the governors recorded:

> Resolved under the circumstances of Sig. Bozzelli having had the entire training of the Choir Class during the absence of Sig. Caracciolo from Nov. 23rd 1881 to January 24th 1882 and from the time of his return to the present and having prepared the music for the next concert, that Sig. Bozzelli do conduct the concert.

Both Caracciolo and Bozzelli had attended this meeting (the other participants being Jones, in the chair, Kirwan, Farrell, and Brady), and although there is no record of his having dissented, Caracciolo immediately thereafter wrote to Brady: 'As I am firmly convinced that you have wronged me with your resolution of this afternoon and as I cannot acknowledge that you had the right of doing so, I cannot do otherwise than tender my resignation and disconnect myself with the RIAM,'[102] to which the Council, having met on the fifth (Jones, Kirwan, Billet, Jozé, Bentham, Stewart and Brady attending), replied: 'At a special meeting of the Council held this afternoon we were directed to acknowledge the receipt of your letter of the 3rd inst., and to express the regret of the Council that you have tendered your resignation. We enclose a copy of the resolution to which you refer, which appears to the Council to afford a very inadequate reason for the determination you have arrived at.'

There followed a protracted correspondence between Brady and Caracciolo.

Dear Signor Caracciolo—If things remain as they are will you suggest what you think will be the best arrangement to make and I know the Council will consider it most anxiously so as to meet your views. You know exactly what the difficulties are and how far you and Bozzelli can work together. Of course the Council must look to what they consider rightly or wrongly to be the interest of the Academy and I know they would wish both you and Bozzelli to come to some settlement between yourselves. I do hope you will see your way to some proposal that Bozzelli may consent to and the Council adopt.

1 Sept. Naples—11 Salita S. Anna di Palazzo

My Dear Sir Francis—You must excuse me for not having answered your letter sooner, but your proposal required some reflection, so I was very much surprised to read that you and the Council expected me to guarantee the peace between myself and Bozzelli in the case of my resuming at 36 Westland Row. For know that I could not take any step towards any such proposal to Bozzelli without acknowledging that I was wrong & he was right, and I can assure you it is utterly impossible for me to do so under the circumstances. The cause of my collision with Bozzelli was due to the fact of his declining to give up the training and direction of the Choir Class, on the ground of his having got the appointment of the post and as a proof of his pretension he showed the ordinary programme and the special report of the year 1881 with his name printed in connection with that class while my name had been withdrawn. I had to apply to the Council for the explanation of this highly irregular fact, but I could get no proper explanation from them, nay they thought fit to pass a resolution which I could not approve as it seemed to me that they wished to take no notice of my claims. I have made now my mind to never think to resume at the Academy unless a plain and clear answer does not fall from the Council on the following questions which I have the honor of submitting to them: 1st. Does it appear from the Minute Book previous to the 2nd or 3rd of May that

Signor Bozzelli's name has ever been mentioned with the choir class?

2nd And if such be not the case, how it did ever occur that his name did get printed in the programmes and the Report as instructor of the class?

Upon their answer which you will be good enough to communicate to me at your earliest convenience I will let you know whether I can find my convenience to resume my connection with the Academy putting it as a question sine qua non that Bozzelli or others who might have fault in this irregularity must apologise to me in writing.

28 September

My dear Signor Caracciolo—The first meeting of Council for the season was held this morning [actually the twenty-seventh] when your letter of the 2nd [actually the first] was read and considered [only Bozzelli, Jozé and Brady attending]. If you wish to return to the Academy the Council will form a class for you of such pupils as the Council may from time to time select. The Council think it better for the continued working of the Choir Class that you should be relieved from it and that it should remain under Sig. Bozzelli thus leaving you free for other engagements. The Council do not consider it necessary or desirable to enter into further controversy as to the instruction of the Choir Class during the interval from Novr. 1881 till May 1882 when you did not take part in its teaching, neither do they consider there is anything for which to apologise as required by you. They believe they have always treated you with the greatest consideration and desire to do whatever you asked as far as consistent with their duty.

This crossed in the post with the following:

24 September

Dear Sir Francis—As you will see by the envelope I enclose your letter did not reach here till this morning, on account of the terrible floods which have interrupted the communications with upper Italy. I did not mean to be unfriendly to you, but merely to save my character by having the unfortunate affair brought to light. You know it was utterly impossible for me to acquiesce with an imbroglio in which I, most unfairly, had been mixed with—as I did not receive any reply from you till today (22 days after my letter) I had to give up the idea of it being possible for me to obtain the satisfaction of having the affair properly discussed, so, I took some steps to settle myself elsewhere being utterly disgusted to return to a place where my best friends had turned all against me. By this time the Council must have had the opportunity to meet and discuss the matter. If their verdict is favorable to my request, I shall be delighted to return and resume at 36 Westland Row as if nothing had happened, but on no account can I consider my convenience to return to the Academy except in the full understanding that the affair must be properly discussed and whoever has acted wrong must accept the consequences of it. I shall be very obliged to you if you will kindly wire a few words of reply to this as I must take some urgent deliberation in consequence.

Napoli, 25th September

Dear Sir Francis—I thank you for relating to me the result of the meeting of the 28th inst. when my letter of the 2nd inst. was read and considered. As the Council do not consider it necessary to give me the explanation I thought myself entitled to receive from them viz.: to know how it could have ever happen that Signor Bozzelli's name had been printed in the report of the year 1881 as the instructor of the Choir Class, when it was I who actually held the post from the starting of the class till Novr. 23d. 1881 when I was obliged to leave Dublin on account of ill health, with the sanction of the Council, I regret to have nothing else to do now, but to insist on having my resignation duly acknowledged by the Council so that they might provide with the wants of the pupils for the forthcoming season.

With Caracciolo's departure Bozzelli wasted no time in cementing his own position in the Academy. In December 1882 he conducted *Messiah*, and in April 1883 we find him rehearsing *Sonnambula*—the first indication of a student opera production. In November 1884 the Academy purchased eighty copies of *Un ballo in maschera*, at a cost of £8 12s 6d, indicating that a production was contemplated.[103] However, in March 1885 Bozzelli tendered his resignation, was asked to reconsider, and withdrew it.[104] On 19 September he resigned again, this time without demur on the governors' part. He later applied unsuccessfully for a position at the RAM.[105]

Bozzelli's position was advertised in the Dublin papers, the *Times, Daily Telegraph, Musical Times, Gazzetta Musicale* of Milan, and Leipzig *Signale*.[106] By the twenty-third, applications had already been received, including one from Caracciolo, and on 30 September the governors considered these, together with those of one Tartaglione and four others unnamed, a decision being postponed for two weeks. On 14 October, Mayne and Levey having proposed the reappointment of Bozzelli (which was defeated), an alternative motion to reappoint Caracciolo was carried. He was also re-elected to the Council the following week, and was to remain in office until 1887.

Caracciolo's connection with the Academy had not only paved the way for the advent of Esposito but had also laid the foundations for a choral school, which would later feature Benedetto Palmieri and Adelio Viani. Its justification can be found in the fact that if it had not been for these cosmopolitan figures the great Irish singers and teachers later associated with the Academy, such as Renée Flynn and Michael O'Higgins, would probably not have emerged so easily.

The Robinson era was not, however, over. In October 1887 he was reappointed as professor of singing, to teach six pupils at nine shillings per hour; but the Council made it clear that there was to be another, parallel professor, 'who would be independent, not subordinate.'[107] The strategy adopted was to regard Robinson as the expert on British and Irish music and to appoint a 'foreigner' to the other post; English applicants for the vacancy were therefore turned away, and negotiations for the second position took place with Martin Roeder from Berlin (who had references from Arrigo Boïto and the director of the Milan Conservatory), Tartaglione, and one Sapio.

The position went to Roeder, but not for long. Whether he was a very temperamental man we do not know, but the tenor of the following letters, sent two years later, suggest that, at the least, he found it difficult to express his own mind in a foreign language.

11 June 1889—Dear Sir!

I am utmost sorry in not having carried out my intention as to have sent a letter to the Hon sec of RIAM which I keep in my desk since the 1st of May in which, after careful consideration of the existing conditions as to my appointment a senior professor of singing at the aforesaid institution, I was compelled to give my dismission after the session has expired . . . I never would have accepted the position at the academy held by myself since March 1888 would I have been fully aware and would I have foreseen in which an awkward position I was placed and that my artistic abilities could not possibly find an efficacious display, owing to many circumstances very well known to some of the members of the council. Before accepting and signing my first agreement I made careful enquiries about everything, writing purposely to the Hon. Sec. In reply to my inquiring I was told to have been granted by the council of *equal duties* and *rights* as the other professor of the vocal class. But I am most sorry to state how great my disappointment was in experiencing by degrees to be charged with duties to fulfil without any sharing of the *rights*. Amongst other things which would have led to equal rights (for myself) with my mentioned colleague one prominent was the *full disregard of that item of my first agreement* which granted me an alternating examination of the junior classes (as in the same way in the piano classes these examinations are shared amongst the three senior professors). Owing to the *advanced age* and social position of my colleague, I abstained from claiming my *granted* rights—always in the hope that forthcoming time would have brought change in my favour to this respect. This item and its complete disregarding to my disadvantage caused many other disagreeable things that happened afterwards. It would be of no special use whatever to mention them now again and again. By this *false* and *quite out of place* delicacy towards an elderly professor I gave up my rights and alas too late for me, I had to see the sad consequences of my gentle demeanour. Besides I think no doubt could be entertained with regard to the most peculiar and unexplicable treatment with reference to my choral class, after the most successful choral performance that the annals of the academy might record. I do not intend to give further unpleasant comments thereabout—everybody, sorry to state, is acquainted with them—only I have to state that this flourishing class has been destroyed piece by piece and I have been treated like a whimsical plaything—strong reason and enough for me as to come forward at the time with my dismission [i.e. resignation]. The

> only thing I really and heartily regret is to have endeavoured earnestly and made all possible efforts as to improve things at the RIAM witnessing afterwards that I did not find in the least the support I required, and which repeatedly had been promised to me. This dismission-letter as aforementioned was ready to be sent to you in your quality as Hon. Sec since the 1st of May and having not done so at the time I thought things would improve in my favour which I am sorry to say did not occur. *I must state again and most decidedly that it was my firm intention since then to withdraw my artistic services as a professor of the RIAM with the existing term.* I beg to consider this letter as an official act and you would greatly oblige me in laying and reading it before the council and the executive committee of the RIAM.

This was accepted by the meeting of 19 June, but immediately thereafter came another.

> Dear Mr. Cree!—Upon myself having been fully and duly informed of what happened at the Executive Committee meeting of the 13th which was held with the exclusion of the professors, which all were entitled to attend the meeting and besides having been specially invited to do so, *I herewith withdraw my resignation, sent in the 11th of June* and which you kindly wrote to me, you would have laid before the council at next week's meeting. At the same time I beg to say and eventually let it know to the members of the council that I am preparing the full report of the incident as I consider the proceeding the *greatest injustice* and *offence* and *damage of interests* which could have been done against me. I sent in my resignation at the time *with the intention* that it might have been discussed, which has not taken place, and as usually is done in similar cases; after which as well the resignant as the executive board has to decide upon the result. At any rate I beg to say to consider the matter in the way as if the letter of resignation I sent you, did not exist—*thus withdrawing my resignation.* And at the same time earnestly requesting you to be kind enough and lay this letter before the council next week.

What Roeder thought was going on is a mystery: there was no meeting of any committee on 13 June, and even if there had been he would not have been invited to it. However, all professors received a routine letter bearing that date from Jozé, pointing out that their contracts expired at the end of that term, and it is possible that this induced a state of unease in the excitable Roeder. The withdrawal of his resignation was not accepted, despite the almost undeniable fact that the elderly Robinson was misbehaving again.

Two years passed, and in 1890 Robinson, at the age of seventy-four, was making a nuisance of himself in the band room. Having alienated the horn professor, Brasfort, he resigned his conductorship of the orchestra and his chairmanship of the Board of Studies, on the grounds that Brasfort was a disruptive presence at rehearsals. Brasfort (writing under an Anglicised version of his name, Armstrong) had publicly attacked Robinson for his conduct of the Dublin Musical Society, and it was for this that Robinson was being vindictive. Brasfort explained:

> Towards Mr. Robinson I have felt nothing hitherto but respect, personally and in every capacity he fills with one exception . . . But I have always thought and said that as Conductor of the Dublin Musical Society he is in effect the worst enemy to music in this country, for the reasons which I have fully given. These views are held by very many; and as I have some knowledge and experience of orchestral matters in different countries . . . I was determined once for all to formulate what are very general objections and to protest openly against an intolerable state of affairs. This I have an unquestionable right to do, as a private person, as a Guarantor of the Society, and as a musician in my own line. No one will assure me that Mr. Robinson is to be considered above criticism—a provincial singing-master, immensely respected as such, who owes most of his reputation in the outer world to the licence (to use the mildest expression) which all his life he has permitted himself in criticising every individual and body he has ever had anything to do with, the RIAM included.[108]

The Academy clearly feared that even now the loss (again) of Robinson could be damaging, and they told Brasfort that 'they could not have a Professor in the orchestra at such issue with the Conductor, but hope the disagreement . . . will not long continue.'[109] Their trust in human nature was in this case an effective alternative to trying to resolve the dispute, and two weeks later Brasfort was writing:

> Nothing has passed, verbal or otherwise, between myself and Mr. Robinson, who I am merely told objects to being in the same room with me at the Academy. If that can be considered a disagreement on my part with the Conductor, I can only assure them that it is at an end entirely as far as I am concerned, with my letter of 18 January. I know what is due to the Academy as well as what I owe myself.[110]

However, Brasfort was to leave the Academy in 1892, having also secured teaching hours at the Municipal School of Music.

As we have seen (throughout chapter 3), Wilhelm Elsner was a stalwart member of the Academy's teaching staff and a central figure in Dublin music-making from his arrival in Ireland in 1851. Like many of his colleagues, he gave an annual concert, at one of which, in 1873, he was joined on the platform by Fanny Arthur, Robert Stewart, George Sproule, R. M. Levey, Grattan Kelly, and C. V. Stanford. The newspaper advertisement lists Brady, John Stanford, Cruise, Mahaffy and Yeo as ticket sellers. The programme included a trio by Mendelssohn, which Elsner would have played with the composer during a visit he paid to him before leaving Germany.

Elsner's career continued unabated until his tragic death on 15 July 1884, when he disappeared overboard from the Kingstown–Holyhead steamer 'on a dark, wet and stormy night,' as the governors recorded with melancholy the following September, shortly after his body had been washed ashore in the Isle of Man.[111] In their annual report for that year they stated:

> An admirable artist, his appearance in the orchestra at important public performances was a guarantee of all that perfect accuracy of intonation, a wide knowledge of music, and the steadiest attention, could ensure. As a teacher, his admirable method and untiring patience gained him a large number of pupils. It is needless here to remind his many friends of his genial social qualities, his quiet mirth, and unfailing good temper. No one who came into business relations with him could fail to be struck by his perfect probity and fidelity in discharging obligations . . . The manner of his death was peculiarly sad. He was going to Germany for his annual holiday . . . He left a large family, whom his care and industry enabled him to bring up to fill good positions in various professions, and some of whom are permanent residents in this, his adopted country. The Council have elected Herr Rudersdorff to the Professorship of Violoncello. An excellent artist and charming solo performer, the Council trust he will be found not an unworthy successor to Herr Elsner.[112]

Rudersdorff was to retain the post until 1890, when, after a disagreement with the Governors over the conditions of employment, he resigned.[113]

Elsner's 'method' referred to involved the unusual strategy of playing the cello without a spike, its base resting on the floor so as to achieve a tone more akin to that of the baroque era. It is recorded in the portrait of Elsner by Louis Werner.

There is a slight discrepancy between this account of Elsner's death and that contained in a privately kept family history assembled by his grandson, A. F. Elsner Stewart,[114] the eldest child of Alex Elsner, which records that he was on his way to Germany for a solo engagement when the accident happened. Whatever the cause, the loss of Elsner was grievous, not least for his large family of seven children, his widow, Elise, and Elise's two sisters, Margarethe and Josephine. They had followed the couple from Frankfurt about the middle eighteen-sixties and, after a short time as governesses (during which Margarethe nursed the infant Anna Parnell at Avondale), established the 'German School' at 6 Wilton Terrace, a famous teaching landmark until its closure with Josephine's death in 1895. After Elsner's death the family received financial support from W. Purser Geoghegan (1845–1934),[115] later a benefactor of the Dublin Orchestral Society, a pillar of the Feis Ceoil, and a donor of music to the RIAM, who was chief brewer at Guinness's and a very wealthy man.

Elsner Stewart tells us that his grandparents took a small house in Great Brunswick Street (Pearse Street) when they arrived in Dublin, which would have been convenient to the Antient Concert Rooms, where the Academy was then held.[116] We know that in 1856 they had taken rooms in 18 St Stephen's Green, clearly wishing to continue their proximity to the Academy, and it may have been at this time that Elsner rented rooms (which he retained for several years) at 16 Lower Pembroke Street. In 1863 the Elnsers took the big step of leasing a newly built villa in Leopardstown

Road, Foxrock, which they named 'Taunus', after the mountains near their native Frankfurt and whence they acquired the fir cones from which they grew the trees that still grace the site.

Of the children, five were musical, and in particular the eldest, Pauline (1851–1921), who became a senior piano student in the Academy in 1865[117] and gave several solo recitals, and Wilhelm (1857–1901), who became a violin student in 1865[118] before undertaking his military service in the Prussian army and becoming a doctor. Annie Patterson recalled that one of her earliest concert experiences was hearing Pauline Elsner accompanying her father in Mendelssohn's 'Spring Song',[119] and Patterson in fact studied cello with Elsner for a time.

Alexandrina (Alex) Elsner (1865–1942) was the most distinguished of the children, studying at the RIAM with Sir Robert Stewart and Joseph Robinson before being given a home from home by the Groves when studying at the RCM under J. H. Blower (with whom a fellow-student was Clara Butt) and undertaking private voice training with Alfred Blume and Carl Armbruster. She became a leading contralto, often accompanied by her sister Pauline,[120] and contributed to the family upkeep before, in 1898, marrying Abraham McCausland Stewart, the newly appointed harbour engineer in Derry, where she settled and became a founder of the local Feis the following year.

Alex and Pauline introduced the concept of classical song recitals, as distinct from vocal items in mixed programmes, which they gave at their aunts' house at Wilton Terrace and which featured novel lieder by Brahms (the 'Four Serious Songs'), Peter Cornelius (Christmas Songs), Strauss, Wolff, and the earlier Carl Loewe. As an accompanist Pauline had, in her sister's words, 'the gift of sympathy and self-obliteration, or effacement.'[121] They appeared at the Viceregal Lodge and other society venues, and, as Elsner Stewart put it, 'the rest of the family looked on Pauline and Alex as snobs and felt themselves to be an embarrassment to them as indeed they were, for Ida delighted to play the "enfant terrible". Alex used to come back from these visits to the mighty full of ideas she had just picked up and dying to use them for the reformation of the family.'

It must have been from his mother that Elsner Stewart received the family wisdom about his grandfather's character and home amusements.

> Wilhelm was a delightful but frightening creature. Returning to the bosom of his family on Saturday he was tired and inclined to be cantankerous, but when he was in form he was alarmingly boisterous and would invent games in which the children were expected to join. In this mood, table manners would go by the board and the rowdy behaviour of students in the Bier Keller would take over.

Elsner was responsible for one of the rarest and most convoluted musical jokes ever perpetrated, which took place at Westland Row railway station as a group of musicians were embarking for Bray, where they were to play in a concert by Stewart's Bray Philharmonic. In a smoking compartment were R. M. Levey, Elsner, and other members of the band. Just as the train was moving off, Dr Purefoy (a TCD student, later master of the Rotunda), 'rushed wildly into the platform in search of a carriage. Elsner at once cried out "Let him come in here, and he shall Purefoy the sons of Levey."'[122]

Ida Elsner (1867–1954) studied art at the Metropolitan School and was the longest-living sibling, dying suddenly after enjoying a recital at the RDS and a hearty meal. With Pauline, who became the head of the family and the chief breadwinner after their father's death, she ran a school and kindergarten at the family home in Foxrock, which included music in its curriculum and was fondly remembered for the mixture of good teaching and mayhem by its pupils, who included Beatrice Elvery (later Lady Glenavy and another prize-winning RIAM student) and Samuel Beckett, whose father had advised on the construction of the shed that housed the kindergarten.[123] It was with Ida that Beckett, who attended the school between the ages of five and nine, first began his study of French. Ida was known locally as 'Jack', because of her mannish and bossy nature, although in the family lore it was Pauline who was known as 'the sergeant-major'. Beckett's biographer James Knowlson suspects that Ida may have been a model for Maddy Rooney in *All that Fall*.[124] The Elsner family thus played a part in the early education of Samuel Beckett that another family, the Espositos, were to continue when, ten years later, he went to the school in 21 Ely Place where Bianca Esposito taught in the establishment run at that time by Pauline and Ida Elsner.

The youngest musical Elsner was Emily Vivien (1869–1954), who studied violin at the RCM under Parry and became a music teacher at a school near St Andrews. She inherited a Pietro Guarneri that had belonged to her father.[125] Grove seems to have cared for her but to have taken a poor view of her flighty behaviour, telling Edith Oldham in May 1891 that 'Emily is a nice girl but she's growing fat and (a trifle) coarse.'[126] A year later he wrote:

> I am sorry that Vivien Elsner behaved so absurdly. I talked to both Agnes Kitching and Delia Tillott about her, and they gave me to understand that she was much improved and solidified—but it will take a long time before her old thoughtlessness and flightiness disappear. I pitied her sister Pauline—but I never cared for her—there was always a certain something unreal about her—but poor thing how much she was to be pitied! and how imperfect the best of us are!'[127]

And, when in the thick of discussions about the rates of pay for teaching music in schools, he wrote in October 1892: 'I hear that Vivien Elsner is going to leave St. Andrews—at least she has asked for her pay to be increased: and as she gets at present £180 a year, I think there is no reason of increasing. Miss Dove tells me she is a good teacher but so intolerably silly and foolish that the pupils have no esteem for her.'[128]

Once the Academy was rehoused in Westland Row it could contemplate developments that had not been possible previously. It was determined immediately that the students would give frequent performances, to enable subscribers and others to estimate their progress. As with the earlier 'examination concerts', these were intended as 'educational and probationary tests [rather than] as concerts for display or public attention.'[129] Many of these were given in the afternoons; the following, on 25 November 1871, is typical:

Orchestra: Overture, *Semiramide*	Rossini	
Violin duet: Air no. 7	de Bériot	Masters Johnson and Levenston
Piano duet with horn accompaniment	Dussek	Adeline Wheeler, Miss Montgomery
Song: '*Assisa al pie*'	Rossini	Bessie Craig, harp accompaniment by Mrs Mackey
Piano Concerto in F minor	Sir W. Sterndale Bennett	Miss Wright
Orchestra: Selection from *Marta*	Flotow	
Songs: 'Winter' and 'Summer'	Joseph Robinson	Bessie Craig
Violin solo: First movement of Concerto	Rode	Master Byrne
Orchestra: Overture, *Le nozze di Figaro*	Mozart	

When, in 1873, the Lord Lieutenant requested a visit to the Academy, a special concert was arranged, and MacDonnell took the opportunity of emphasising that this was unusual, in that a very polished performance had been aimed at.

> The object of the usual concerts in the Academy is very commonly misunderstood. They are intended for purposes quite different from those of ordinary concerts. They are not meant to attract a large public, to make a showy display, to elicit applause and encores or to attain mere popularity in the programmes. They are meant to be educational, calculated to test and improve the power and taste of the pupils, and to give successful aspirants an opportunity of trying their powers, and of acquiring steadiness before an audience. Above all, the music is mainly selected from writers of a solid and classical style, and is such as is neither intended nor expected to tickle the ears of the votaries of Offenbach and Hervé.[130]

At the same time, with extra space and financial assurance, new classes were being introduced. In 1871/72 (as we have seen) a choral class was introduced, together with piano classes for men (taught by George Sproule),[131] harp (Mrs Mackey), Italian language, and elocution. As discussed in chapter 9 by Pamela Flanagan, the first official scholarships were awarded at this time, initial recipients being in 1872 Bessie Craig (voice) and Miss Wright (piano) and in 1873 Miss Bellew (voice), Philip Levenston (violin), and Anna Ellis (piano).

The ambition of erecting an organ was still professed, and this came to fruition in 1879, when Telford and Telford, of 109 St Stephen's Green, installed an organ 'suitable for teaching purposes,' at a cost of £200.[132] It had the following specification:

Pine case with speaking front pipes
Two manuals compass CC to G 56 notes and pedals   CCC to F 30 notes

The Great Organ	CC to G	
1. open diapason in front	8 feet	CC 56 pipes
2. Lieblich gedackt	8 feet	CC 56 pipes
3. gamba	8	C 44 pipes
4. Flute harmonic	4	CC 56 pipes
5. Piccola harmonic	2	CC 56 pipes

The Choir organ	CC to G	
1. Dulciana Wood bass	8 feet	CC 56 pipes
2. Lieblich flute	4	CC 56 pipes
3. Bassoon & oboe spotted	8	CC 56 pipes

The pedal organ	CCC to F	30 notes
1. bourdon	16 feet	CCC 30 notes

Couplers
1. swell to great
2. swell to pedals
3. great to pedals

Total	12 stops	466 pipes

Hydraulic blowing engine

David Lee has kindly supplied the following comments on this instrument. 'In the 150-year history of the Academy there appear to have been four organs built or rebuilt (it is, by the way, sometimes a moot point what constitutes a new instrument as opposed to a rebuild). There was also a move in 1891 to build a second organ in the Concert Room, but this did not come to fruition. The firm of Telford, founded in the mid-nineteenth century, was solidly in the mainstream of British and Irish organ building at a time when some fine instruments were being made, with ample specifications, rich in overall chorus development and including, for the first time in these islands, fully developed pedal departments. The mid-nineteenth century was, in fact, a vintage period of British and Irish organ building. Towards the end of the century, however, Telfords was a firm in decline, and the specification of the Academy's first organ, modest in scope anyway, reflects a sad deterioration in standard from the earlier fine instruments bearing the Telford name. The lack of upperwork and preponderance of eight-foot stops, together with a pedal department of but one sixteen-foot stop, is a far cry from the fine organs of Telfords' heyday twenty or so years earlier. In short, in this writer's opinion, it must have been a pretty dull-sounding affair.'

Stewart's opinion, expressed in 1891 when he was urging the installation of an organ in the concert room, supports this. 'The . . . organ was, and is, deficient in bass/deep tones from the necessity then felt by the former Council of being content with stopt pipes instead of open; the former are only half the length (8 feet high instead of 16 feet, &c.) but of course are very inferior in depth and sonority.'[133]

In 1873 further problems arose from a professional quarter when a meeting was held on 19 April at 105 Lower Baggot Street (the premises of Richard Smith), which passed a resolution deeply critical of the Academy's modus operandi.

> It is with surprise and regret that we have learned that the executive of the RIAM has departed from the true object of the foundation of that institution—namely: providing sound instruction for those gifted with musical talent, but who do not possess the means for its cultivation—or, as the Lords Commissioners of Her Majesty's Treasury put it, 'The training of professional musicians'—by receiving as pupils without objection the children of the gentry and high class officials of Dublin who manifestly cannot plead 'want of means' and who would doubtless get from their families high-class teaching. We believe that the President and Council of the Academy are not aware of, and would not sanction, such wide departure from the fundamental principle of its foundation and that though such objectionable admissions are many, they have been allowed through want of care and due consideration on the part of some members of the executive. Be that as it may, it is obvious that a continuance of such a practice would materially injure the prospects of the large body of Professors of Music in this country in whose interests we think we have a right to ask you to amend the error we complain of. Hoping that the future policy of the Academy will be defined and understood to be in strict keeping with the original object of its foundation, namely to form a school solely for the education of persons who intend to practice music as a profession in this country.[134]

The memorial might be taken as another fit of envy at the position of teachers in the Academy, especially since there is a blatant dichotomy between the idea of educating those destined for the profession and that of educating the less well off. But it was signed principally by Richard Smith, singer and son of the Academy's original professor, supported by, among many others (thirty-four in all), William Gater, Barton McGuckin, Charles Grandison, J. C. Culwick, W. Power O'Donoghue, Alban Croft, and Grattan Kelly, all of whom were of senior standing among music teachers in Dublin and many of whom were professionally associated with the Academy. More importantly, one of the signatories was J. H. MacDermott, a member of the RIAM Board, and he, together with the honorary secretaries, was deputed to investigate the matter.

Immediately they took action, writing to the RAM and other academies to ask what their admission policy was.

> We should be glad to know, whether in your Conservatoire any such law of exclusion, or any such declaration, exists; or whether the Examinations required, the severer discipline and more serious work enforced are found in practice to sufficiently limit the entrance of mere Amateurs? In case any difference is made in this respect between the classes taught gratuitously and those which pay, you will be good enough to explain it.[135]

Simultaneously they instructed Mrs Crean, the Lady Superintendent, to investigate the current roll of pupils. From her report they deduced that 'it is of course impossible for us to report as to the means of the persons appearing on this list to pay for private tuition; we think however that there are at least 4 on the list who judging from their position would seem clearly to be able to afford private tuition. The total number of pupils attending the pianoforte and singing classes this term is 217.' It acknowledged the fact that for some time the Academy had equivocated on the matter of whether amateurs were to be admitted but said that the practice of demanding a signed declaration of professional intent 'has long since been discontinued.'[136]

While this state of affairs was considered acceptable, it was decided that the Council would 'proceed to define more accurately the objects and scope of the Academy and make regulations with regard thereto,' to which MacDermott moved that, while the report showed 'but a small proportion of the aggregate . . . able to pay for private first class instruction,' it nevertheless 'proves that there are grounds for complaint—that there had been a departure from the principles of the institution in a few instances' and that therefore 'all possible care [should] be taken in future to make it generally understood that the Academy was designed to aid with sound instruction those who having a decided aptitude for music have not the means to pay for its due cultivation.'[137]

The curious fact is the intended or subliminal rewriting of history, since, quite apart from the issue of amateur versus professional, that of ability to pay had never been voiced formally by the Academy, either at its foundation in 1848 or its reconstitution in 1856 or in its applications for a government grant. Fees had been kept down and supplemented by subscriptions, to make tuition as widely accessible as possible, but with the exception of the *sub rosa* subvention of some pupils' fees, a deliberate policy of seeking out impoverished students had never been considered. When scholarships were introduced they were not means-tested but were awarded purely on grounds of musical merit.

In the meantime, replies were received from London, Florence, Paris, and Brussels, arguing a variety of approaches to the issue. John Gill of the RAM wrote: 'The RAM does not take pupils who are not intended for the profession. This is the rule on which the Institution is carried on: if students obtain admission who are not studying for the profession the Committee are not aware of it at the time of application.'[138] However, Luigi Casamorata, president of the Royal Institute of Music, Florence, had a quite different view.

> We do not concern ourselves to know whether they propose to practice music as a profession, or wish to learn it for the mere pleasure it affords. The object of the Institution is the diffusion & the advancement of the art; and that object is promoted, whenever good musicians are sent from the Institute whether they are Artists or Amateurs. Besides the case is not unusual that he who studies music as an amateur afterwards adopts it as a Profession, and vice versa, those who study it as an intended profession from some change in circumstances only use it as an amusement. Moreover, what use is it to make pupils at their entry into the classes of the Academy look to practice the art as a profession, because persons in more easy circumstances (from which class Amateurs are principally taken) prefer to receive lessons from private tuition, rather than submit themselves to the severe discipline of a public Academy.[139]

Two replies were received from Paris, one from the director, Ambroise Thomas, the other from MacDonnell's old friend Pauline Viardot. The former wrote:

> There are no class [*sic*] in the National Academy for which the pupils pay. The instruction is wholly gratuitous. The number of pupils is from eight to twelve in each class. The average total number is about 600. Admission is obtained by examination and competition; and the progress of the pupils is tested by examination every six months. The Directors impose no condition on the pupils they admit, and take no means to ascertain whether they intend to be artists or amateurs. They sometimes admit into the classes, under the title of 'auditors', such candidates as, not having passed at the entrance examinations, yet give promise of afterwards deserving admission.[140]

Viardot, for her part, wrote: 'Any person can be admitted if the examination be favourable, that is, if the voice and capacities are judged sufficiently good. All the classes are gratuitous. No pupil pays anything whatever . . . The Conservatoire does not enquire if the candidate wishes to become an artist. The pupils are perfectly free to do what they please with their abilities after having completed their studies.'[141]

Jaak Lemmens, who had resigned from the Brussels Conservatory and was living in London with his English wife, wrote:

> Concerning the admittance of students, it is my opinion that, in the competition for 'admittance', no regard should be paid to the social status of the competitors. Independent youths are generally better educated and instructed than their poorer brethren, and that is a great advantage for becoming a great artist. Moreover, an 'amateur' when successful has much more chances than a poor fellow who is obliged to give lessons from morning to night to sustain himself and his family.[142]

As a result of these investigations, a two-tier system of fees was reintro-duced, with those not intending to enter the profession paying 50 per cent more than those who did.

The incident must have impressed itself on the collective conscience of the Academy, as in 1886, when negotiations were under way with Dublin Corporation over control of the Coulson bequest, the Academy, in its formal submission, broached the issue of class in a characteristically straight-forward way.

> It has been objected that the Academy enables the richer classes of society to obtain education at a lower rate . . . The idea is entirely erro-neous . . . No restriction in this direction was ever contemplated, and the Government would not have given assistance to any such narrow scheme . . . While the Academy, as it does, enables the poorer classes of the citizens to obtain the best education at a comparatively small cost, any restriction of the classes to the students of any particular social rank would be most detrimental to its position as a school of music.[143]

A year later MacDonnell was on a similar errand, enquiring whether, in the Academy's sister institutions, pupils' concerts might legitimately call on the services of professionals. Gill of the RAM replied that 'at the Students Concert only students are expected to perform. In the case of an obbligato or some instrument for which the Academy has no pupils, a professional might be asked to assist, but this would be quite an extreme case. For violin and cello the pupils only would play.'[144] And Viardot bluntly answered: 'No. the Profs never play in the public *exercises d'élèves*, nobody but the pupils have to appear and perform in them.'[145]

And the following year he had yet another query, to which Viardot's reply was:

> No, my dear Mr. Macdonnell, the pupils have not the choice of the masters when they enter the Conservatoire. They may express their prefference to the Director—the Professors have a sort of right over the candidate presented and prepared by them—the Director alone tries to distribute the pupils so that each master may have some good pupils. Ah yes, but do not forget that the teaching is gratuitous here, and that your pupils in Dublin pay. I think that, in that case, they ought to have the choice of their professor.[146]

This has always been a difficult question for academy administrations generally; as we have seen, very talented teachers can suffer from freedom of choice if, for whatever reason, they appear unattractive to the prospective pupil. On the other hand, obligatory attendance with a stipulated teacher can alienate pupils through differences of temperament, method or style and can lose pupils to the institution or, indeed, to the study of music altogether.

Converse to the question of whether an academy's principal function was to seek impoverished talent was that of standards, and at this same period we find the RIAM enunciating a principle that had quite decidedly been part of its continuing ethos since its foundation. In its annual report for 1874, as reported by the *Irish Times*, it was stated that income had increased but that pupils' numbers had declined, which was attributed to the increase in fees during the year, 'with a view to procuring the best musical instruction, and of compensating the professors for increased demands on their time.' It had been a consistent feature of the Academy's income and expenditure account over the previous three years that fees had almost exactly met the cost of salaries (see the table below). That could no longer be contemplated as a reliable trend, the report pointing out that the growing divergence of the two was 'a necessary consequence of the inability of the Council to compass two objects at once—high teaching and cheap teaching.'[147]

The value of money had been fairly stable between 1860 and 1870 but had dropped by about $12\frac{1}{2}$ per cent in the next decade and by a further $12\frac{1}{2}$ per cent before 1890. It would be 1910 before money would have the same value as fifty years previously. It was the first indication to the Academy that previously reliable equations were no longer valid and a sign that it was not only politically and culturally that society was changing radically.

Main items of income and expenditure, 1870–72

	1870	*1871*	*1872*
Income:			
Subscriptions	£140 11s 6d	£101 3s 0d	£139 15s 0d
Government grant	£150 0s 0d	£150 0s 0d	£150 0s 0d
Tuition fees	£604 15s 7d	£993 15s 6d	£1,071 14s 8d
Expenditure:			
Salaries	£559 14s 6d	£731 3s 8d	£1,042 13s 0d
Premises	£126 10s 0d	£158 10s 4d	£275 4s 11d
Instruments	£31 2s 0d	£63 8s 4d	£41 17s 2d

Political change was, however, a factor in the Academy's relations with the government. In 1880 it was noted that the government grant had increased from £250 to £300—the level at which it was to remain for over seventy years. The rise had been effected by representations from the Duke of Edinburgh[148] and Lord Frederick Cavendish (then an MP and a Treasury minister), who was to die in the Phoenix Park assassinations in May 1882, shortly after becoming Chief Secretary for Ireland. After those assassinations, on 6 May, the Academy presented a loyal address to Earl Spencer, who had been sworn in for a second term as Lord Lieutenant on that day. The address had read originally: 'Notwithstanding the unfavourable state of the country this institution has made steady progress during the last two years and is now in a far more prosperous condition than it has hitherto been.' In the light of the murders it was amended to read: 'Although the circumstances of the country have for some time past been unfavourable to the encouragement of art, the RIAM has prospered and the number of students is greater than at any former period. The Council wish to state their detestation of the dastardly crimes which of late have disgraced the country, and they earnestly pray that Your Excellency may before long find Ireland restored to a condition of peace and security'—to which Spencer replied: 'I thoroughly share your detestation of the crimes which have been recently committed. Such crimes are opposed to the real spirit of the nation and are a hindrance to that tranquillity and peace without which no community can prosper.'[149] It was the only occasion on which the Academy formally referred to any political event with anything approaching explicitness.

It may seem ludicrous to follow such an expression with one of humour —and humorous doggerel at that—but the verse that Brady inscribed shortly after in the minute-book was caused by a change in the arrangements for the management of the Academy that must have seemed to him fundamental and was caused by social developments that induced the governors to move their time of meeting from morning (with breakfast) to late afternoon.

> In compliance with the wish of other members of the Council, the morning meetings at breakfast which have continued since the opening of the Academy in the year 1856 [*sic*] are given up.

> And has it come to this at last
> That I must breakfast all alone?
> Have all the friends of years long past
> Departed from me, one by one?
>
> How many mornings have we met
> While changing years have rolled along
> And here would other cares forget
> To teach the minstrel art of song!
>
> You all are gone, save those who fear
> To brave the early morning air
> Or grudge the moments buried here
> For some engrossing household care
>
> And I must join the rest and leave
> The task that morning made so light
> To finish, while the falling eve
> Is sinking into shades of night.
>
> Thus, one by one, in life's young day
> Companions crowd our footsteps round
> But, one by one, they fall away
> Till few along our path are found.
>
> These ties of friendship closer grown
> Must bind the friends remaining still
> If we would not be left alone
> To journey down life's evening hill.[150]

It was in a similar spirit that Brady wrote to Robinson in 1893 when the latter was elected a vice-president. 'Personally I feel a pleasure in having the old friends of the Academy still with us—Alas! the number is yearly growing smaller and I am the more anxious to keep together the few who still survive.' To which Robinson replied: 'My Dear Sir Francis—there was one, to me, very pleasant feature connected with the election . . . It was your exceedingly kind letter which I assure [you] I value coming as it did from my oldest friend in Ireland.'[151] It was a dwindling band of pioneers, most of whom were no longer so well suited to the new world evolving so rapidly around them.

The month after he had penned his verse, Brady found himself giving notice of a reorganisation of Academy business, which would mean standing down all teachers and re-engaging them on different terms.[152] Although the change did not occur until the re-establishment of the Academy and the implementation of the Blue Scheme in 1889, it was a sign of the need for a new style of management.

One of the factors affecting the future was the need to rationalise the arrangements for staff pay. It had been an assumption from the outset that the commitment by teachers to the Academy was a form of public service, in that a recognition of a social need was followed by a donation of professional time at a remuneration lower than could be obtained in private teaching. In the case of teachers working in Dublin this was no doubt a basic fact of life, which required no further elucidation. In the case of foreigners it did necessitate an explanation of what could be expected of the Academy, both overtly (by way of salary for hours taught) and invisibly (by way of introductions to private teaching).

In 1877 Herr Lauer of Frankfurt was appointed to teach violin, a post he retained until his death in 1889. On 18 October Henry Doyle wrote:

> I have to tell you that it is the custom that all the Professorships in the Academy are held by the year, and that each appointment is reviewed at the beginning of each session . . . The Council have no power to grant any pension or retiring allowance nor can they guarantee that you will receive further employment outside the Academy. However it has been roughly estimated that an efficient Professor should be easily able from other sources to make a sum at least equivalent to that offered by the Academy.

Similar letters—a mixture of warning and encouragement—were sent to most other foreign teachers contemplating a position in the Academy. In 1902 we find the secretary writing to Frank Broadbent (a candidate for the professorship of singing): 'While not engaged in the Academy the Board do not put any restriction on the Professors as to private tuition, and the fact of being a Professor of this Academy should materially assist him in getting private pupils. There is a fine opening for a good teacher of singing in this city.' He pointed out that at that time the Board was in a position to guarantee £150 a year from Academy teaching and expected the incumbent to earn 'a much larger sum.'[153] Up to the point in the nineteen-seventies when, for the first time, the engagement of teachers was recognised as being not merely their principal source of income but their single, full-time employment, the sums earned within the Academy from core teaching alone represent only a small fraction of teachers' incomes and bear no relation to salaries elsewhere. Even in the case of the lady superintendent, who was appointed in 1871, her salary of £120 hardly represented her real earning power, supplemented as it was by free accommodation and associated benefits for herself and her daughter, who assisted, and eventually succeeded, her.[154] Few teachers made the choice of Rhona Marshall and Dina Copeman, to teach exclusively in the Academy, when they could have commanded much higher incomes elsewhere.

In 1889 it was found that Miss Kelly (who had been teaching in the Academy since 1860), had sixty-seven pupils and received £172 4s 3d; Miss O'Hea had fifty-eight pupils, for which she received £133 3s 10d; and Miss Bennett, with thirty-three pupils, was paid £76 9s 6d. Jozé received £82 as professor of organ, £30 as professor of harmony, and £70 as secretary, a total of £182, in addition to which he received five shillings per hour for examining. There appeared to be no reason for the various rates of pay, other than the accidental way in which they had evolved, and it was decided to equalise the rates as well as the number of students assigned to each teacher.

In June 1889 the new rates of pay for those who were being kept on in the new Academy were decided on a double basis. Ordinary teachers were to receive a flat hourly rate, and professors were to receive this together with an annual salary (which we might today regard as a retainer, to ensure the continuity of their services and their contribution to the new Board of Studies). That there was a 'pecking order' is not in doubt:

> Robinson: 10s 6d
> Stewart, Esposito, Madam Frost: 9s
> Lauer, Rudersdorff, Scott-Fennell: 6s
> Jozé: 5s
> Ellard, Conroy: 4s
> Miss Bennett, O'Hea, Kelly, Barnewell: 3s 6d
> Connolly: 3s
> Miss Wright, Oldham, Hackett: 2s 6d
> Miss Irwin, Scarff, Mr May, Mr Boyle: 2s

The annual salary for a professor was to be sixty-five pounds. Though these rates were variable, with exceptional arrangements being made with a special teacher, they indicate that, in addition to rewarding 'star' teachers with higher pay, the rates for the less popular (and socially inferior) instruments, such as wind and brass, were comparatively low.

Actual incomes for the year 1889 indicate the huge differences that could arise:

	Hourly rate	Annual salary	Total	1998 equivalent based on price index
Sir Robert Stewart	£173 10s	£100	£273 10s	£11,120
Joseph Robinson	£226 18s 3d			£9,080
Michele Esposito	£174 9s 3d			£7,200
Alexandre Billet	£82 18s 9d			£2,920
— Rudersdorff	£92 6s			£4,487
Theodore Werner	£97 9s (one term)			£3,900
Mrs Scott-Fennell	£64 8s			£2,568
Dr Jozé	£108 3s 9d	£200 (£170 as secretary, £30 for harmony)		£12,320
R. M. Levey	£66 6s 10d			£2,647
J. Ellard	£14 8s 8d			£568
J. Conroy	£20 17s 4d			£837
J. C. van Maanen	£11 10s 8d	£30		£1,660
— Benvenuti		£40		£1,600
Miss Bennett	£76 9s 6d			£3,060
Margaret O'Hea	£133 3s 10d			£5,327
Miss Kelly	£172 4s 3d			£6,888
J. C. Connolly	£38 18s			£1,557
B. W. Rooke	£11 2s (one term)			£444
Charles Kelly	£7 15s (one term)			£310
— Brasfort		£40		£1,600
Miss Wright	£20 13s 4d			£826
Edith Oldham	£24 11s 8d			£980
Lucy Hackett	£10 8s 4d (two terms)			£422
Annie Irwin	£10 2s			£404
Annie Scarff	£9 6s 8d			£386
Mr Boyle	£35 4s			£1,408
Adelaide Barnewell	£81 2s 10d			£3,244

These represent the full complement of teachers in the Academy at the implementation of the Blue Scheme.

The chief benefactor of the Academy is a tantalisingly shadowy figure. All we know of Elizabeth Strean Coulson is that she was the daughter of John Coulson and his wife, Ann Strean. We can only guess at what the source of their wealth might have been, although we do know that in the late eighteenth and early nineteenth centuries, members of the Coulson family speculated extensively and successfully in land deals in the Rathgar area,[155] where a Coulson Avenue exists today.

Elizabeth Coulson's father had died in 1859. The following year, having inherited a considerable estate, she made her will and went to live abroad, in London at Park Street, Grosvenor Square (in the same vicinity as Lady Wilde) and in Paris at the Hôtel de Rivoli.[156] After specific bequests, the bulk of her fortune was left to trustees, who were to apply the funds to the founding of an academy of music in Dublin for the education in instrumental music of 'the sons and daughters of respectable Irish parents possessing natural musical talent,' particularly in piano, 'according to the incomparable method of the late master Frederick Kalkbrenner.' She further directed that the trustees were to join the Lord Lieutenant and the Lord Mayor of Dublin as joint trustees of the academy. This explains the presence to this day of Dublin Corporation nominees on the Academy's Board of Governors, which has occasionally been assumed to be due to the supposed pre-existence of a corporation grant to the Academy, whereas municipal funding was not provided until the creation of the new School of Music and the School Choir Competition.

When Miss Coulson died in Paris in 1880, her sole surviving trustee, Lt-Col. James Ward, set about the task of realising her ambition by founding an academy with the residue of the estate, which amounted to over £17,000 (today almost £600,000), chiefly in English, French and Dutch securities.

Miss Coulson may not have been aware in 1861 that an academy already existed in Dublin, or she may have considered the survival of the IAM— then only five years after its first big upheaval—as dubious. But her will created a serious problem for Ward, since he was required to *found* an academy, rather than give the money to an existing one. Furthermore, Miss Coulson's will envisaged an instrumental academy, whereas the RIAM was not exclusively such. And one of the two nominated trustees, the Lord Lieutenant, declined to have any part in the transactions, whereas the Corporation of Dublin became deeply involved in the ensuing discussions. Furthermore, long delays of a legal and administrative nature arose between the Commissioners of Charitable Donations and Bequests (CCDB), who were responsible for ensuring the application of Miss Coulson's funds to the appropriate end, and the Educational Endowments Commission, whose function it was to find a method of effectively employing them.

One suggestion came in a letter from Annie Curwen (née Gregg), the Dublin-born wife of John Spencer Curwen, who wrote to Brady:

> I wish that old lady's money were not tied up for instrumental music. It is well to be able to help young artists, but for the morale of the country at large choral music would have been better—Our people are full of music & it might be made the means of cleansing & refining them more than anything else. Choral classes for the 'people' would do much to reduce the number of 'public house patriots'—I always think of the Irish as a people without amusements, & that accounts for much of the mischief & misconduct, & if I were still an unappropriated female there is nothing I should like better than to undertake a Tonic Sol-fa crusade in the old country, as an antidote to Fenianism & Randolph Churchillism which is almost as dangerous.[157]

Brady's reply is not recorded.

In April 1884 the Commissioners of Charitable Donations and Bequests approached Dublin Corporation for an opinion on how best Miss Coulson's intentions could be carried out. (It was at this point that Hercules MacDonnell retired from the secretaryship of the CCDB, and—as if to show that the world is a very small place—he was succeeded by Arnold F. Graves, brother of Alfred Perceval and son of the 'Academy' bishop.) The Corporation advised that the funds should be 'administered through the RIAM, provided that it be kept as a separate foundation, and that the Lord Mayor and Council be adequately represented on the Council of the Academy.'[158] Thus began a complicated procedure that required an investigation into the *locus standi* of the RIAM and that proceeded along the projected lines of one academy (Miss Coulson's) being administered by another (the RIAM). The absurdity of such a situation was evident to all, but not so much that its contemplation was not pursued to a considerable extent before common sense prevailed.

At a meeting of the Corporation on 21 April 1884 several points were aired. The first, through Alderman Valentine Blake Dillon (who was to become a Governor of the new Academy), was that it lay within the power of the Corporation, under the Public Libraries (Ireland) Acts (1855 and 1877) to found an academy, employing the Coulson funds together with a sum of municipal money, which could now be applied at the rate of one penny in the pound. Secondly, Councillors Edmund Dwyer Gray MP and Thomas Mayne MP (the latter already a supporter of the RIAM) observed that Dublin could not support two such institutions. Thirdly, if the existing Academy were absorbed into a Corporation initiative, the private subscriptions would cease, and this in turn would extinguish the government grant, which was conditional on such independent funds.

It was generally agreed that the best way forward was for a joint working party, composed of representatives of the RIAM, the Corporation, and the trustees of the Coulson will, 'to ascertain how the intentions of the testatrix could be best carried out.'[159] However, this realistic plan was frustrated by the fact that the CCDB insisted that, for their function in the matter to be fulfilled, a 'scheme' had to be framed by them, which necessitated proceedings in the Court of Chancery, whereas the two chief parties to the matter, the Academy and the Corporation, wished it to be resolved by a scheme to be formed by the Commissioners of National Education.

Brady was the chief architect of the draft scheme, all the main features of which were eventually incorporated in the 'Blue Scheme'. The main differences between the draft and the result were that the Council was to consist of twelve members representing the subscribers and twelve representing the two constituencies of Dublin Corporation and the Coulson bequest (whereas the latter became a separate constituency); that a concert hall, to be known as the Coulson Hall, was to be built (whereas, as we shall see, a hall was built after many decades but it did not commemorate Miss Coulson); that the professorships of instrumental music were to be named after Miss Coulson; and that the Council (rather than the eventual Board of Studies) was to have control of educational matters. One draft clause stated that 'no teaching or discussion upon religion, or any matters connected therewith, shall be permitted to be given or take place by or between any member, teacher, or pupil of the Academy [except in connection with] any instruction which may be given in sacred vocal music.'[160] The draft scheme also envisaged the appointment of a registrar (amended at the insistence of the Corporation to 'secretary') and the capacity of the Council to award pensions. The previous attempt to exclude all teachers from the governing body was amended to allow the inclusion of members of the Academy staff.

In examination by the Educational Endowments Commission, Brady had to admit that, despite its significant assets—the Albert and Vandeleur funds in particular, and the house in Westland Row—the Academy had 'no corporate existence' and therefore 'could not have become a body that the Court of Chancery or the CCDB could treat as properly constituted to receive property.'[161] However, given that the RIAM was *de facto* the sole music school in Dublin, and that it had a proven capacity for music education over more than thirty years, it was clear to all parties that the only point of debate was the definition and constitution of the governing body that was to administer Miss Coulson's donation.

Here there were two points of difference between the RIAM and the Corporation. The first was whether the new board of governors would be composed equally of Corporation nominees, Academy nominees, and the trustees of the will; the second was whether professional musicians would be eligible for membership of the governing body.

The first point was easily settled, since it was accepted in principle that all three parties should be represented in equal proportions, which would reflect their financial contribution to the new venture. The second point gave rise to considerable discussion, as it opened up the question that had vexed those musicians in Dublin who were not associated with the existing Academy. As far as it affected the music profession, it hinged on two issues: whether an institution could have what are today known as 'worker-directors', and whether people with an interest in the business transacted in the institution, but not themselves engaged in the business of the institution, should have a say in its affairs. As Lord Justice Fitzgibbon observed, 'the professors could not be both masters and servants,'[162] which tended to quash any suggestion of inclusiveness. It was a problem that had vexed the RDS and the early school of art since the beginning of the century, and had been resolved by their exclusion.[163]

As it transpired, the first issue was eventually resolved by the inclusion in the Blue Scheme of professors acting as Governors—a feature since expanded to include non-professorial and non-teaching staff. The second issue was resolved by the exclusion of any person teaching music who was not a professor of the RIAM—a restriction maintained to this day. This decision allowed for the presence on the Board of Governors of musicians and those associated in a non-professional way with the practice of music, provided they did not teach music elsewhere.

During the proceedings before the Educational Endowments Commission, however, this point was examined in detail. Brady explained the exclusion of non-Academy professionals on the grounds that 'we believed that if professional teachers of music were to have a voice in the governing body, it would be placing them in a very unpleasant position with regard to the professors in the academy.'[164] The restriction was also necessary in respect of governors nominated by the Corporation, since otherwise the Corporation might appoint musicians from outside the Academy, 'and that would be considered very objectionable . . . Strangers come in the capacity of critics; one teacher comes in the capacity of the critic of another.'[165] A subsidiary point of difference then arose between the Corporation and the Academy, in that the Corporation wished the exclusion of musicians to be total: if it was debarred from nominating them, it wished the Academy subscribers to be similarly debarred; but this point was eventually settled in favour of Academy professors being included in the scheme.

At the point when a two-tier system was still envisaged (the new academy embracing, and jointly governed by, the existing Academy) Brady wanted the representatives of the RIAM to be nominated to the new Board of Governors by its Council, rather than by the body of subscribers, from whom they were to be drawn. As far as the representation of the Coulson trustees was concerned, the point was raised by Lord Justice Fitzgibbon whether 'Miss Coulson intended that there should be kept up trustees of her will, merely for the purpose of continuing to represent her on [the Board of Governors].'[166] Nevertheless, the three Governors representing the Coulson endowment continue on the Board to this day, the editors of the present book being two of them. While the capital sum in which the Academy found its principal financial base from 1886 has now been depleted, both by erosion of the capital and in real terms by inflation, and with access to new and larger sources of revenue to the point where it is now insignificant financially, the Coulson endowment continues to be represented because there remains a 'moral' dimension in ensuring that the general intentions of Elizabeth Coulson are observed. In recent years this has led to the amendment of her wish that education in her name be restricted to children of Irish parents, a wish that would not only be inequitable in a multiracial society but also probably contrary to EU law.

In evidence to the Educational Endowments Commission, Brady stated that it was the Academy's wish that the funds or assets of the existing Academy and those of the Coulson bequest be amalgamated into one new body. He insisted that the Commission had the power to frame a scheme to this end that was not enjoyed by the Court of Chancery, which had no jurisdiction over the RIAM.[167] This would lead to friction in the near future, since, under the scheme, the CCDB would have the power to dictate how capital might be applied and, indeed, how it was to be invested. The intransigence of the CCDB in the matter of investments in particular would cause the Academy serious loss of income, particularly over the next twenty years and again during the Second World War. For example, it was envisaged that a certain portion of the capital could be applied to building a concert room on the RIAM site,[168] but in the outcome this was steadfastly refused by the CCDB.

The hearing before the Educational Endowments Commission involved some very blunt speaking. Cree had spoken more openly than had Brady on the reservation about the level of Corporation representation and had sharply observed that the Academy, as it stood, was substantially larger than the assets it stood to acquire. Brady for his part had equivocated significantly on the question of how the scheme was to be framed, and by whom. The Lord Chancellor put it forcefully when he said:

> You are to a large extent a voluntary body, you have got a voluntary subscription, and the main portion of your income is derived from the instruction you give and from the fees of pupils. If that is so, I should be very slow, in any circumstances, to force a constitution on a body of that kind. It would be attended with no useful result. But, as I understand from you, it is the wish of the society that a constitution should be framed for it, and therefore, as far as we have gone, it appears to us that the proper course is for you to bring in and lodge with us a draft scheme, setting forth what you propose the scheme ultimately to be framed ought to be, and of course, before you bring that in, you should endeavour to come to an understanding with the Corporation and with the other persons interested.[169]

There was a palpable irritation not only with the equivocation of the Academy but also with the system of the administration of justice, in that the Court of Chancery and the CCDB were locked in to a proceeding to which the RIAM could not be a party. The Lord Chancellor therefore said:

> I would put it to all parties concerned, including the Commissioners of Charitable Donations and Bequests, that to found this academy of music, to put it on an assured basis, is a very useful public purpose, and that therefore the Commissioners . . . as well as all other parties should strive honestly to co-operate together with the view of making the best arrangements that can be made for the application of all the funds available for the purpose of musical education; and with no fancied idea that we are trying to interfere with the Court of Chancery or any feeling that we are trying to get up a contest with any other court and interfere with it.[170]

To which Lord Justice Fitzgibbon added:

> It would be very much deplored if after these six sets of parties had been settling a scheme in the Court of Chancery for a very considerable time, it turned out that that scheme was really only useful for the purpose of being incorporated in another scheme which we should settle for the RIAM.

From the point of view of public policy as well as that of efficiency, the Lord Mayor made a telling contribution.

> We think it desirable that a breath of outer air should, so to speak, be allowed to come in upon the strings of the instrument, and that public

opinion should be allowed to have some influence in the proceedings of the Academy . . . A society self-contained . . . and entirely self-governing, is hardly likely to keep pace with the progress of the times.[171]

Two significant points arise relating to the evidence of Dr Joseph Smith, purporting to represent the music profession in Dublin. The first is that although a public meeting of musicians had been held the previous year to discuss the issue, no organisation existed to promote their views as a profession. The second is that the hostility between Smith and Brady, and by extension between the non-Academy music teachers and the Academy, was obvious. Although the list of those attending the meeting (on 14 May 1884) has not survived, we can be reasonably certain that it would have contained many names appended to the earlier remonstration of 1873. The resolution passed at the meeting alleged that the teaching at the Academy was worthless, and its business was carried on by the honorary secretaries (Brady and Doyle) in a less than disinterested fashion. The Educational Endowments Commission clearly regarded it as an attempt to secure the Coulson bequest to those disaffected from the RIAM as a separate Academy, rather than its amalgamation with, and incorporation within, the status quo.[172]

Smith, who was professor of music at the Royal University, was almost exclusively interested in the fact that, in his opinion, 'the idea of any educational institution being conducted by . . . amateurs who have no special training or have undergone no special study in the special subjects' was highly anomalous.[173] Referring to the RAM, where musicians formed the majority of the management, as 'the headquarters of musical education in England,' he said: 'We have not been able to look up to the RIAM as the headquarters of music in this country.' Instead, its administration was 'calculated totally to frustrate or almost to frustrate the objects of musical education in this country.' Smith appears to have equated 'management' with 'education', in that he saw all decision-making as an educational function. On the other hand, he argued that the people actually engaged in teaching should not be their own masters[174] and to that extent looked for a managing body with a music director at its helm.

He criticised the Academy for its record in educational results and called for its reconstitution because decisions on educational matters had not been left to the teachers. To this end he further proposed the creation of a 'board of studies'—the first time the notion of an academic council had been so described—which would have sole responsibility for educational matters. Within this board would be a sub-board consisting of the director and two vice-directors, 'capable musicians and men of great experience, men of great repute from the point of view of success and fairness,' who would appoint the professors, 'because a body of amateurs . . . have no possible means of gauging the qualifications of any musicians.' In addition they would establish proper conditions for examinations and the diplomas, 'which hitherto has not existed . . . except in a nominal manner.'[175] The corporate board itself, in addition to the three chief parties already identified, should contain the professors of music in the two universities (on the grounds that the professors of Oxford and Cambridge were *ex officio* on that of the RAM) and representatives of the music profession 'to protect the interests of art.'

The lack of professional organisation among musicians in 1886 is underlined by the fact that, in evidence, Smith admitted that the only way in which he had been able to summon the meeting in 1885 was by taking names from the Dublin directory of the time, which was no guarantee of quality. 'I should think there are some thousands of people teaching music in Dublin,' he said, 'but we actually only find the names of forty or fifty in the musical directory.'[176] The meeting had excluded women, on the grounds that, although they were members of the profession, 'the position of women is always a very vexed one' in the matter of representation—this being the era of burgeoning female suffragism—but he conceded that 'if any lady proves her claim I would consider it.'

The period from 1886 to 1889 was transitional, in that disbursement of the Coulson funds by way of scholarships had already begun, while discussions on the final form of the scheme were still under way. It had been substantially agreed that the income from the Coulson funds would be used to finance a mixture of salaries and scholarships amounting to £300 or £400 a year, which was the approximate sum sought by the Academy as a grant when it first expressed its ambition to expand its horizons. This expansion envisaged increasing the award of a single annual piano scholarship to four; the employment of an extra wind teacher with responsibility for creating wind and brass sections in the Academy orchestra, with scholarships available up to a total of seventeen; renewal of the piano stock; and professional fees for examiners.[177] Many of these steps were implemented in anticipation of the Blue Scheme coming into effect, principally, one supposes, because the success of that scheme appeared to be assured by the good will evident on almost all sides.

The lasting success of the superbly drafted Blue Scheme is due to the twin facts of its having been a negotiated document and the result of academic pragmatism that had already put in place many of its essential provisions. In the first forty years of its existence the scheme remained intact, and in the last seventy it has only been found necessary to amend it on fifteen occasions, half of those being in the past two decades, as the speed and nature of change appear to dictate more serious revisions. When, in 1942, a thorough revision of the scheme was proposed, the view was easily formulated that 'there was no need to revise the Scheme [since] any required changes could be made within the Scheme.'[178]

The Blue Scheme was finally approved on 10 October 1889 by Order in Council under the Educational Endowments (Ireland) Act (1885). Having in its preamble rehearsed a brief history of the Academy and a lengthy exposition of Miss Coulson's testament, it established the RIAM as a body corporate with a president, three *ex officio* vice-presidents, six elected vice-presidents, twelve governors representing the subscribing members, eight representing the Corporation of Dublin, three representing the Coulson endowment, and one elected by the professors.

Anomalies have arisen in recent decades relating to the *ex officio* position of the Lord Lieutenant as president of the Academy (a feature it shared with the RDS).[179] As the representative of the crown (Queen Victoria continued as patron of the RIAM and was to be succeeded by later monarchs) he was followed in 1922 by the Governor-General of the Irish Free State, until the abolition of that post in 1937 with the introduction of the Constitution of Ireland. One might reasonably have supposed that the residual powers of that position would have been assumed by the new head of state (or, as with the RHA, by the head of government), but in 1938 and again in 1959 attempts to discover whether in fact the President of Ireland could become president of the Academy have been frustrated, and the Academy therefore lacks an official figurehead.[180]

The *ex officio* vice-presidents are the Lord Mayor of Dublin and his immediate predecessor and the High Sheriff of the City of Dublin; but the cessation of this last office means that the number of *ex officio* vice-presidents is in effect two.

The elected vice-presidents listed in the Blue Scheme were Bishop Donnelly, Lord Justice Fitzgerald, Sir Francis Brady, Sir Robert Stewart, Sir Thomas Jones PRHA, and Lt-Col. James Ward (being the executor of Miss Coulson's will). Lord Fitzgerald was at that time a Lord of Appeal; he had had a distinguished legal and political career, having served twice as Attorney-General, but he was to die within the year and was succeeded by Sir Patrick Keenan.[181]

The original twelve Governors representing the subscribing members of the Academy were William Bentham, George Cree,[182] H. Warren Darley, Henry Doyle, Dr D. B. Dunne, Richard Littledale, R. Wogan Macdonnell, Canon MacManus, Henry Mecredy, Dr Nedley, William Perrin, and Robert Sharp, almost all of whom were long-standing supporters of the Academy and many of whom were members of the outgoing Council. The significance of the members' Governors is due to the fact that, since the Academy's foundation, at any time up to a quarter of the subscribers had been actively involved in its administration.

Of the eight Governors appointed to represent the corporation, five at least—Alderman Dillon and Councillors Sexton, Sir George Owens, T. D. Sullivan MP, and Thomas Mayne MP—had been involved in the direction of the Academy or in the negotiations leading up to the Blue Scheme, the others being Alderman William Meagher and Councillors Wade and Dawson. In 1924–25 and in 1969 the Corporation was suspended and replaced with a commissioner, and the status of representative Governors during those periods went into a form of limbo, which has never been satisfactorily resolved (see appendix 1). Suggestions were made in 1973 and 1982 that the level of representation of the Corporation should be diminished, but these were not acted on.

The three original Coulson Governors were Capt. W. T. Ward (presumably a relative of Lt-Col. Ward), who disqualified himself straight away by non-attendance, James Drury, a long-standing member of the Council, and Robert Browne FRCSI.

Michele Esposito was elected by the professors to be their representative Governor, a position he would hold until 1911. We should note, however, that it was already eighteen months since the professors constituting the Board of Studies (which had been in existence as a result of earlier developments) had been asked, in anticipation of the Blue Scheme, to select one of their number. They had met on 28 May 1888, and the result of their first ballot was:

Joseph Robinson: 6 votes
Michele Esposito: 5 votes
R. M. Levey: 2 votes
Alexandre Billet: 2 votes
Martin Roeder: 2 votes
Total: 17 votes.[183]

On a second ballot, in which Esposito did not vote, Esposito received ten votes and Robinson six, suggesting that all votes previously cast for Levey, Billet and Roeder transferred to Esposito. In the light of later suggestions that the 'foreign' element among the professors used their numerical superiority to secure Esposito's election, it is salutary to note that of those present seven were 'foreigners' and ten 'native'.

In the case of the members' and Corporation Governors, a fixed proportion would retire each year and would be eligible for re-election. Detailed provision was made for the replacement of Governors who disqualified themselves by non-attendance during a twelve-month period or who died, resigned, or became bankrupt, insane or otherwise incapable of acting, either by election within a specified time of a substitute from the relevant constituency or, failing that, by co-option by the Board of Governors.

As we have seen, the sole restriction on membership of the Board of Governors was that 'no person who is engaged in teaching music in Ireland, except a Professor of the Academy,' might be elected. This was amended in 1995 to allow for the election by the non-professorial teaching staff of a representative Governor, and the franchise was further extended in 1996 by the inclusion of a representative of the non-teaching staff.

One of the continuing difficulties of the Academy in the years immediately following the Blue Scheme was that the scheme provides for the CCDB holding the Academy's endowment funds in trust, which in effect meant that the commissioners' agreement had to be sought when an unusual or very significant financial transaction was required. The Blue Scheme limited the application of funds to the maintenance of the premises and apparatus, including instruments and library, the payment of salaries, wages, and fees, and the provision of scholarships and other academic awards. It did not, however, envisage the use of capital of more than £2,000 for such purposes as the erection of a concert hall or any other building, nor did it provide for any pension scheme—each 'retiring allowance', as it was then called, having to be individually negotiated on the basis of the teacher's service and personal merits, until the amendments to the scheme of 1967 and 1969, which created a pension fund. Much more importantly in those early years, the Academy had (and still has) no right to manage its own investments, which was to cause serious disagreement between itself and the Educational Endowments Commission in the next few years, as the Academy sought to persuade them that more advantageous interest rates could be obtained than those paid on government stock, without going outside the portfolio of what would be regarded as 'safe' investments.

Before the Blue Scheme had come into force, a letter from the CCDB indicated the extent to which this problem could lead. The commissioners' secretary made it quite clear that even the use of the premises themselves was subject to the commissioners' approbation.[184] Within a year of its enactment, the commissioners were refusing to invest the funds as the Academy would wish, and the Governors were forced to write that

> they would not be discharging their manifest duty as trustees of the Charity, did they not again approach the Commissioners, and request that this matter may receive reconsideration, being confidently assured that the Commissioners will be, and indeed are, disposed to facilitate the carrying out of any proposal which the Governors consider to be for the good of the Academy, so long, as in this instance, as the Governors believe it to be, it is contemplated by legislation and free from serious objection . . . It is not only by the exercise of the most careful economy that, even with their increased resources, the Governors will be enabled to keep the expenditure of the Academy within its income, having due regard to efficiency. The Governors understand that the Coulson Endowment is represented by £17,447.7.6 Government New Consols and the Vandeleur Fund by £4,063.12.11 of the like stock: these together amounting to over £21,000.0.0. From inquiries they have made the Governors are satisfied that safe and undoubted stocks could be selected from among the various classes of securities enumerated in Sec. 46 of the Scheme of 10th Oct. 1889, which would yield at least one per cent more interest than the new consols and this would mean an increase to the Academy funds of over *£200 per annum*.[185]

Given the difference between income and expenditure at that time, the extra investment income that might become available to the Academy was crucial.

Over the past century, the real value of the Coulson and other endowments, held in trust by the CCDB, has been eroded, partly by capital expenditure, such as the installation of the new organ in 1905, and partly by inflation, which has made the dividend on investments almost meaningless in their capacity to finance the scholarships they were originally intended to support. Nevertheless, the CCDB remain the authority to whom the Academy must apply for any changes to the Blue Scheme. On only one occasion, in 1948–49, has there been any outright rejection by the Commissioners of a change, and that involved a fundamental revision (discussed in chapter 7).

One restriction that we have already mentioned in respect of Miss Coulson's testamentary intentions was that scholarships in her name should be awarded only to 'the children of respectable Irish parents.' In recent years in particular, this anachronism has prevented non-Irish students from competing for Coulson Scholarships and Exhibitions, and in 1982 the relevant clause was amended to open these to children 'one of whose parents is an Irish national or an Irish citizen'—the stipulation that the parent be 'respectable' being completely deleted. This of course only went so far as to extend eligibility to children of mixed parentage, and in 1997 the further decision was taken to remove the name of Coulson from the scholarships, so as to permit all Academy students to compete, regardless of nationality.

A special clause neatly overcame the problem identified in consequence of Miss Coulson's will, not only wishing the Kalkbrenner piano method to be the main focus of education but also restricting her academy to instrumental teaching.

> 23. Special provision shall be made for the study and practice of the pianoforte by the pupils receiving aid from the Coulson Endowment, and the Governors shall, in providing instruction in the pianoforte, have regard, if and so far as they shall find it advantageous to the pupils, to the method of Frederick Kalkbrenner.

This is followed by a clause allowing the Governors to afford 'systematic musical instruction of the highest class to pupils, both professional and amateur; such instruction shall be both theoretical and practical, and shall be given both in vocal and in instrumental music,' and giving them the power, envisaged and attempted right at the start of the 1856 Academy, to engage in teaching of modern languages or 'any other subjects of general education which they may deem useful to students of music.' This, for example, would allow the present-day Academy to introduce non-musical but music-related studies, such as arts administration or piano maintenance. However, in 1965 it was thought necessary to amend the scheme to establish a speech and drama faculty, although aspects of these subjects had been taught for many years as ancillary studies, such as declamation and elocution.

The constitution of the Board of Studies, under clause 26, 'to conduct the education given in the Academy,' originally envisaged a body consisting only of the professors, who in 1889 were Alexandre Billet, Michele Esposito, John Haveron, T. R. G. Jozé, Carl Lauer, R. M. Levey, J. C. van Maanen, Joseph Robinson, Martin Roeder, J. F. Rudersdorff, and Sir Robert Stewart. In 1989 the clause was amended to allow the election of three non-professorial members, and in 1995 a root-and-branch revision of the role and function of the Board of Studies was undertaken, which fundamentally changed its constitution. (This is discussed in chapter 7.)

From the inception of the Blue Scheme until 1996, it was the rule (under clause 30) that the president should take the chair at the Board of Governors and, in his absence, the senior vice-president present—an obligation that caused some vice-presidents to absent themselves until an amendment allowed them to attend but not preside if unwilling to do so. There was thus no identifiable chairman as such, simply an indication of how a chairman might be found for each meeting. Certain vice-presidents did regularly assume the chairmanship, both *de facto* and *de jure*—John F. Larchet, T. S. C. Dagg, Maud Aiken, John O'Donovan and Anna Brioscú most especially—but in 1995 it was felt that the Board needed a more defined sense of official continuity from one meeting to the next and one that would allow Governors other than vice-presidents to chair meetings, and the scheme was amended to provide that a chairman should be elected from among the Governors, to serve a two-year term.

The Blue Scheme originally provided for only one mandatory officer of the Academy—a secretary—and also permitted the discretionary appointment of a registrar or accountant and a lady superintendent (the latter having in fact been employed since the move to Westland Row). As described in chapter 7, a major alteration in the management of the Academy was effected in the late nineteen-seventies, culminating in the scheme being amended to allow for the appointment, at the discretion of the Governors, of a director. From 1889 the secretary was the principal officer of the Academy, responsible for implementing decisions of the Governors, acting as interface with the Board of Studies, assigning incoming pupils to teachers, organising concerts, managing examinations, and inspecting and maintaining relations with the Model Schools (and, within a few months, the Municipal School of Music), for which he was to be paid £150 a year. The lady superintendent was to keep the books, control the housekeeping, and arrange the teaching schedule, and was parallel to, and not subordinate to, the secretary, whose position was regarded as a part-time one up to 1954, whereas the (resident) lady superintendent was full-time.

At the meeting of 6 November 1889 to which the new Board of Governors had been summoned, T. R. G. Jozé was confirmed as the secretary of both the Board of Governors and the Board of Studies, and the new life of the Academy began.[186]

Intermezzo

Edith Oldham and George Grove

Edith Oldham (1865–1950) studied piano at the RIAM with Sir Robert Stewart. Her father, Eldred Oldham, had operated a business in Westmoreland Street, Dublin, that had gradually foundered until, shortly after his death in 1882, it folded up completely, leaving Mrs Oldham (who had herself been a member of the RIAM choral class in 1877)[1] and her many children in severely straitened circumstances.[2]

Edith was an extremely talented student. In 1882–83 she was faced with the choice of earning her living as a piano teacher in Dublin as a matter of necessity[3] or securing a scholarship to the newly created Royal College of Music in London—designed, unlike the academies, specifically to train music teachers. Successful in the latter course, she took up the scholarship in September 1883, thus coming under the care of the director of the RCM, Sir George Grove, then aged sixty-three. The meeting, and their ensuing relationship, was to have a profound effect on them both.

From the outset, Mrs Oldham and her family were apprehensive about Edith's move to London, on grounds of cost, propriety, and the possible effect it would have on her character. Her older sister Annie wrote:

> I hope it will indeed be the same Edith Oldham who went away that will come back, & not some knocked up with conceit young woman of English ideas & stupidity, for it is stupid to be conceited. Take care, shake it off before you come home.[4]

Edith began study with Ernst Pauer,[5] of whom Stewart wrote: 'I should esteem it a good thing to get under Herr Pauer's care; but no one can tell where the shoe pinches save the wearer.'[6] He was right: after the first year Edith transferred to Franklin Taylor. The unease with Pauer's style of teaching had been evident from the outset, her mother writing in her characteristic unpunctuated style:

> Alice . . . said Miss O'Hea had read your letter to her that she was very sorry you had gone to Herr Pauer that she had known him for twenty years & many of his pupils & that she always heard the same story about him that he will not teach, that he spends the whole time playing himself & that she never knew him make a good player, she says she does not think the College will do any good unless they get new foreign teachers[7] . . . I think it probable that you were spoiled by Sir Robert making so much of you but I dare say you will find the advantage of all the fault finding in the long run.[8]

Grove fully supported the change of teacher but cautioned: 'The change of master will be good for you—but of course in the end everything depends on ourselves; circumstances go for much, but one's own inner self is the thing which guides them—makes or mars.'[9] The note of concern, coloured by an insight that permeated his relationship with Edith, is characteristic of his side of the correspondence.

What Edith wrote to Grove we shall never know, since on at least one occasion he destroyed her letters. (The remainder were destroyed by Lady Grove after his death in 1900.)[10] 'I burned a great quantity of your letters last night. It's best I am sure. Such things as letters between those who love one another as you & I do are so obvious to be misunderstood; and even if understood right why should other people be reading the burning words we have said to one another?'[11] What exactly the nature of that 'love' was we can only speculate, but their relationship might be described as passionately platonic. Reading Edith's moving account of her ambitions for the Feis Ceoil (below, p. 220), in which she wrote of 'happiness, that intangible something we all desire and pursue, and which we so often seek in impossible places, and which so often eludes our grasp, because of this,' we can imagine the warmth and intensity of her letters and her capacity for self-expression.

In 1890 Grove wrote a typically fond and reflective letter, in which he poured out his truest affections.

> Dearest Edith
>
> I have just come indoors from one of the most memorable times I ever had. The others all went out to see the fireworks and left me sitting on the lawn with the trees all round me; a perfect summer evening sky overhead. It got darker & darker till the trees grew quite black: the giant elms like great solemn warders: the delicate foliage of the acacia, quite distinct against the silvery sky; the screen of limes like black lace shutting out the gradually fading after-sunset glow. It was exactly what is expressed in the poem 'In Memoriam'—'By night we lingered on the lawn'—Once before I saw it so, but not so beautifully, and not so solemnly; because the solemnity and the significance increase with one's years:—I could not *then* feel as I can & do now. Perfect stillness all around except the faint ghostly reports of the distant rockets. Oh how I longed for you! I thought 'my friendship with her is the last great event of my life. Love it *might* be but love it *can't* be, because there can be no sequel. Let it be Friendship then.' Oh that it could have been that you were with me![12]

One simple reason for Grove's attraction to Edith was that 'you are so much more cultivated & interesting than the ordinary run of girls.'[13] He admired her 'perfect simplicity, and your common sense and your readiness to be interested & amused with anything.'[14] He told her:

> I think we are a little alike. We each undervalue ourselves. I think so little of myself and so much of you that I naturally am anxious for your love and unable to understand that I have it, without assurance. You think so little of yourself that you can't understand the value I put on your affection. But seriously it is a mistake to undervalue oneself too much. I do it to such an extent that I can't imagine anyone valuing me or caring for me and so I am always craving for words.[15]

He also longed for reassurance, afraid that Edith could not reciprocate the depth of his feelings. 'I don't believe you care about me one tenth of what I do for you! No! That's nonsense—but really I am very insatiable when your letters come . . .[16] I think of you continually and long for you more than I can tell you—I know you are fond of me but you don't love [me] as I do you—do you dear?'[17] On another occasion he added somewhat pitifully but also with wry humour, 'Don't forget Aug 13 my buffday.'[18]

On the evidence of Grove's hundreds of letters to Edith, he poured out his heart to her on all matters—music, her study and later career, his plans for a new building for the RCM, his love of poetry, his unsatisfactory marriage, the various turns in Irish affairs, and, above all, his phobias and depressions. From Grove's comments on Edith's letters it is clear that she wrote as openly and as intensely as he, answering his 'craving for words,' and that she shared some of his psychological problems.

Grove threw himself wholeheartedly into his work, and this devotion may have been in part due to the fact that 'my wife is a dear wife but she has never taken interest in any of my pursuits public or private.'[19] He explained: 'It's a sad loss to me because one *must* talk & let out to someone, else one dries up; and there is nothing on which I can talk to her. The College she has no interest in. Music ditto. My friends do [ditto]. I have the nicest friends outside . . . but she knows and will care for none, and there is no inducement to have them here [his home in Sydenham] as a rule.'[20] When Edith told him of a disagreement with one of her sisters, he responded:

> How very hard it is to go on living day after day with no sympathy, no response, from those from whom one naturally expects it and ought to have it . . . Her thoughts are not my thoughts, nor her ways my ways. To have intercourse which ought to be full of love and spirit and confidence turned into a mere interchange of civilities, into a constant endeavour not to say the wrong thing, not to be misunderstood—do you know it's a most serious drawback & misery to life.[21]

In 1893 he reflected: 'Isn't it strange that 2 people should have lived together for 41 years (since Xmas 1851) and know so little of one another as we do—be as you said such *tombs* to one another.'[22]

From the outset Grove adopted a realistic note in his counsel in order to moderate his evident enthusiasm for Edith's musical and personal temperament.

Rev. Charles Graves,
Vice-Chairman of the
original Committee of
the IAM, 1848

Richard Michael
Levey, first violin
professor of the IAM

Two aristocratic supporters of the
IAM: the third Duke of Leinster
(*left*), and

the fourth Marquess of
Downshire (*below*)

Sir Robert Prescott
Stewart

Joseph Robinson

The Marmion family c. 1866
Standing: (*second from left*) Lizzie; (*centre*) Mary; (*right*) Flora

The Committee of the Dublin University Choral Society included several IAM supporters. Standing: (*second from left*) Sir Robert Stewart; (*fourth from left*) Sir Thomas Jones. Seated: (*second from left*) John Norwood; (*third from left*) Henry Mecredy; (*fourth from left*) T. M. Archer

The joint secretaries of the IAM from 1856:

Sir Francis Brady
(courtesy of the
Board of Trinity
College, Dublin)

Hercules MacDonnell

Michele Esposito, portrait by
Sarah Cecilia Harrison

Wilhelm Elsner, portrait by
Louis Werner (courtesy of
National Gallery of Ireland)

J. F. Rudersdorff

Guido Papini
with the celebrated double-bass player
Giovanni Bottesini

The RIAM orchestra, conductor T. R. G. Jozé, in the Royal University (today the National Concert Hall), 1899

18 St Stephen's Green, Dublin, the IAM's second premises, 1856–1870 (Irish Architectural Archive)

The Assembly Rooms, South William Street, Dublin, original site of the Municipal School of Music, 1890–1907 (Irish Architectural Archive)

Dublin Orchestral Society, leader Adolf Wilhelmj, conductor Michele Esposito (seated on his Erard piano), in the Royal University (today the National Concert Hall), c. 1900

Achille Simonetti

Clyde Twelvetrees

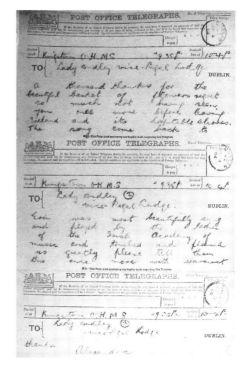

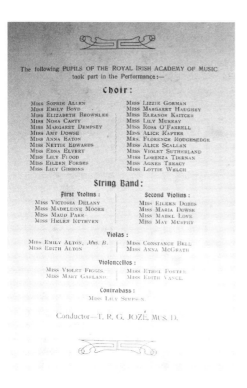

The following PUPILS OF THE ROYAL IRISH ACADEMY OF MUSIC
took part in the Performance:—

Choir:

Miss Sophie Allen
Miss Emily Boyd
Miss Elizabeth Brownlee
Miss Nora Carty
Miss Margaret Dempsey
Miss Amy Dowse
Miss Anna Eaton
Miss Nettie Edwards
Miss Edna Elvery
Miss Lily Flood
Miss Eileen Forbes
Miss Lily Gibbons

Miss Lizzie Gorman
Miss Margaret Haughey
Miss Eleanor Kaitcer
Miss Lily Murray
Miss Rosa O'Farrell
Miss Alice Kafter
Mrs. Florence Roughsedge
Miss Alice Scallan
Miss Violet Sutherland
Miss Lorenza Tiernan
Miss Agnes Treacy
Miss Lottie Welch

String Band:

First Violins:
Miss Victoria Delany
Miss Madeleine Moore
Miss Maud Parr
Miss Helen Ruthven

Second Violins:
Miss Eileen Dobbs
Miss Maria Dowse
Miss Mabel Love
Miss May Murphy

Violas:

Miss Emily Alton, *Mus. B.*
Miss Edith Alton

Miss Constance Bell
Miss Anna McGrath

Violoncellos:

Miss Violet Figgis
Miss Mary Garland

Miss Ethel Porter
Miss Edith Vance

Contrabass:

Miss Lily Simpson

Conductor—T. R. G. JOZÉ, Mus. D.

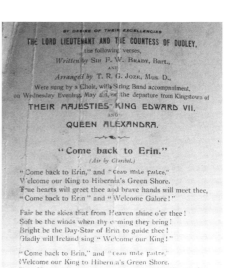

BY DESIRE OF THEIR EXCELLENCIES
THE LORD LIEUTENANT AND THE COUNTESS OF DUDLEY,
the following verses,

Written by Sir F. W. Brady, Bart.,
AND
Arranged by T. R. G. Jozé, Mus. D.,

Were sung by a Choir, with String Band accompaniment,
on Wednesday Evening, May 4th, on the departure from Kingstown of

THEIR MAJESTIES KING EDWARD VII.
AND
QUEEN ALEXANDRA.

"Come back to Erin."
(Air by Claribel.)

"Come back to Erin," and "Cead mile failte,"
Welcome our King to Hibernia's Green Shore.
True hearts will greet thee and brave hands will meet thee,
"Come back to Erin," and "Welcome Galore!"

Fair be the skies that from Heaven shine o'er thee!
Soft be the winds when thy coming they bring!
Bright be the Day-Star of Erin to guide thee!
Gladly will Ireland sing "Welcome our King!"

"Come back to Erin," and "Ceao mile failte,"
Welcome our King to Hibernia's Green Shore.
True hearts will greet thee and brave hands will meet thee,
"Come back to Erin," and "Welcome Galore!"

"Come back to Erin," our Queen Alexandra!
Never forgot be her goodness and love!
Happy and long may her reign and her day be!
Grateful and loyal all Ireland will prove!

"Come back to Erin," and "Ceao mile failte,"
Welcome our King to Hibernia's Green Shore.
True hearts will greet thee and brave hands will meet thee.
"Come back to Erin," and "Welcome Galore!"

The visit of King Edward VII and Queen Alexandra to Ireland in 1904 concluded with a rendition of verses written by Sir Francis Brady to the air of 'Come Back to Erin'. It was sung by a choir of pupils from the Academy under the baton of T. R. G. Jozé and drew warm praise from the Queen in a telegram to the Countess of Dudley, wife of the Lord Lieutenant of Ireland.

Class of Adolf Wilhelmj

Committee of the Students' Musical Union, 1910. Standing (*left to right*): Annie Lord, Amy Dowse, Bertha Dowse, unknown, Lilian Dowse. Seated (*left to right*): Hilda Dowse, Lily Simpson, two unknown, Marie Dowse

Henry Warren Darley

Patrick Delany

Adolf Wilhelmj

Annie Lord

Dear E.O.,

. . . If you will only be content to look on your practice playing as drudgery for a little while, you will reap the benefit. Bulow says the 1st thing in piano playing is technique & the 2nd technique & the 3rd technique—Quite true & how can technique be attained but by mere drudgery? Your mistake is in looking on it as an intellectual exercise— you really have nothing to fear . . . Hard, I know, when your heart is yearning for something higher—but to be done . . . Ever your affectionate friend.[23]

. . . It's part of that curious fact in music (alone of all arts) that technique has to be acquired by the practice of things which are so much over the head of the practiser . . .[24] Technique when perfectly attained is only analogous to the power which enables one to read with just accent & pronunciation—the groundwork on which expression and cadence of voice and all the other things that make good reading delightful—that preliminary process is far more difficult in music than in any of the other arts—I often think the attainment of it almost miraculous but there it is, and if one is to be a good player—to give real *interpretations*—it must be attained.[25]

He was a stern master and, in today's terms, strictly against the form of virtuosity that we today associate with the 'powerhouse' school of pianism.

I heard Paderewski on Saturday in the Schumann concerto—a very different version from Mad. S's [Madame Schumann's] but very interesting. I expected something very loud & smashing, but it was refined and delicate to a degree. He *can* smash however . . . coming down on a single note now and then with a *wicked vicious* force, that I can't bear. Nothing would make me in passing a bush tear off two or three leaves in a mutilating way; and so, nothing could make me *wound* a piano as these players do.[26]

He was also extremely affectionate and not at all without humour.

Athenaeum Club Friday evening $8\frac{1}{2}$ p.m.

Dear Edith

. . . I am very sorry to hear of your being so ill. I *order* you—recollect, I *order* you, as your Director—to stay in bed tomorrow and Sunday . . . Your precious health is beyond all. If you lie in bed for 2 clear days you will come out on Monday like a *lioness* . . . This is an *edict* and those who disobey it do so at their peril—Given at my court of South Kensington this 20th day of February 1885, George.

Always the tone is affectionate, warm-hearted, and—almost always— stopping just this side of sexual suggestion. He adopted a frank and incautious style of address, all the more striking when one reflects on his naïveté in assuming that such 'burning words' would pass the scrutiny of vigilantes like Mrs Oldham or indeed Lady Grove. The terms of affection are many and meant: letters begin 'My dearest Edith' or 'Darling Edith' or 'Dearest

Friend of friends' and end 'Ever your loving G.' or 'Goodbye darling, ever your fond G.' or 'Adieu cherie, je t'embrasse de tous [*sic*] mes forces et tout mon coeur.' Edith, for her part, was more reserved: as late as 1889 Grove was complaining, 'Couldn't you open your dear letters in some other way? That dreadful "Dear Sir George" is so horribly stiff. "Dear Friend", "Dear G" or some other less formidable way of address? Do try.'[27] The next year he calls her 'my clear headed and warm hearted friend' and tells her 'there are very few minutes of very few days that I am not thinking of you.'[28] Two years later, when he was seventy-two and Edith had been living in Dublin for the past four years: 'Sometimes a fit of longing for you comes on, so violent that I don't know how to resist it.'[29]

Despite his heavy duties (he was always fully occupied, not alone with the affairs of the RCM but also with preparations for his dictionary and other literary undertakings) Grove read prodigiously and eclectically, and he recommended poetry and memoirs to Edith—in particular his favourite poets, Tennyson and Browning (at whose funeral he was a pall-bearer), but also Newman, Turgenev, and Tolstoi. 'I have told them to send you Clough's poems and when I see your precious face again I will write your equally precious name in it . . . I am very much mistaken if they will not excite your immediate sympathy . . . You will revel in the book. It is nearer one's self than much other fine poetry—and the poet more of one's own stature and likeness (as Schubert is so much more intimate with one than Beethoven is).'[30] Later, Edith in her turn began to introduce Grove to contemporary Irish literature, exciting his interest in Emily Lawless's *Hurrish* and Somerville and Ross's *The Irish Cousin*.

Towards the end of Edith's time in London, Grove became solicitous for her welfare and future occupation—even though it caused a serious friction in the Grove-Edith-Mother triangle. Mrs Oldham had spent those years bombarding Edith with concern. The combination of poverty, late-Victorian propriety and middle-class prejudice brings a pathetic note to this side of the correspondence, and one cannot but reflect that Edith's affections must have commuted violently between the love showered on her by her mentor and these outpourings of her mother.

From the start, Mrs Oldham's money problems were evident.

> My dearest Edith A thousand congratulations. Your telegram both surprised & delighted us. From your letter to Annie we thought you had not much chances of the scholarship. The news put us in a state of wild commotion . . . If you have not got the maintenance you should make enquiries whether you could live at the College. I think the only possible way you can go up would be if you could live there on reasonable terms but at all events do not say anything about rejecting it until we can consult together about it . . . I am trying not to think of

myself in all this but one thing is certain whether you take it or not it is a splendid thing to have got it. God bless you & keep you whether you stay with me or go so far away . . .[31] I was reading an account of the Conservatoire at Cologne where Hiller presides & that certainly appears a wonderful place they have the most distinguished teachers in every branch & the whole charge is only £14 a year each pupil gets three lessons each week in the Piano & three in singing what would your College of Music say to this with their £40 a year.[32]

When Edith had eventually settled into her digs in London, the questions began.

You have answered some of my questions but there are still some unanswered will you put this letter before you & answer those I now ask . . . What do you get for breakfast you have breakfast so early & dinner at two that you would want a good breakfast how is it arranged for you to dine at the College the days you get your lesson there do you get a good meat dinner & what have you for tea have you a good sized room & a bed to yourself have you any time for reading & have you any books do the scholars in both houses dine & sit together if you answer all these questions I dare say I shall have another set next time.[33]

Her prejudice displayed itself in connection with Edith's predictable friendship with two of her Irish colleagues, both of whom appear to have been very lively and headstrong.

As to Miss Russell I think there is no doubt they are common people . . . I asked Mr Macran to make enquiries from his mother who lives in Limerick she said she did not know anything about the Russells but that the street & locality they live in is one of the worst in Limerick & that no respectable people would live in such a place. They may have money enough & Miss Russell may have been sent to a respectable school but from everything I can find out I would not wish to become intimate with them . . . I am very glad you seem to wish to keep clear of Miss Kellett she must be a very bad companion indeed the great drawback to your position is the friends you are thrown with it will take great care & good sense on your part not to be deteriorated by them.[34]

The chief irony of Mrs Oldham's warnings about keeping such company was that for much of the time it was Grove with whom Edith went about unchaperoned (a point on which he himself was constantly sensitive). After one account of an outing to a concert, Mrs Oldham complained:

I do not think it right for young girls like you & Miss McDonald to go about London late at night with young men of whom you know nothing except that they are students in the College. It also surprises me that there is not an escort provided to bring the girls to concerts when presented with tickets by musical societies that was one of the inducements held out in the prospectus of the college . . . I dare say there was no harm done but there might arise great mischief from mixing so freely with young men in a public institution where anyone who pays the fees would be received . . . The very candour with which you write shows there is not a thought of harm in your mind but . . . I cannot help thinking that many of those girls are what people would call decidedly fast & there is no character so despicable as a really fast girl hitherto I always thought you kept free from this fatal mistake but I also felt you were so lively & perhaps so thoughtless that a step further in that direction would make people think you fast although you yourself might have no idea you were going too far.[35]

When vacation time arrived in 1886 Mrs Oldham reported to Edith: 'Mrs Arundel was saying to Alice that you ought to stay in London but Alice said you did not know anyone there except Sir George that he was very kind & often took you to concerts. She was horrified at the idea of your going to concerts alone with him but Alice said you generally had some of the girls with you so as old as he is people will talk.'[36]

A couple of years later, Grove looked back on Edith's RCM career and commented on her one weakness: her lack of confidence, which made her afraid of performing.

That is the only thing you want, as far as I know—to be able *always* to command yourself, and I think you may be always very glad & proud, when you recollect what you were in this respect three years ago, to feel what an immense advance you have made. At both the two last examinations you have shown perfect control.[37]

It was a subject on which both Grove and Mrs Oldham were agreed. Grove wrote: 'I am sure that life can be kept in a teacher only by constantly playing in public and drawing thence constant new inspiration, new hints for expression & means of interesting the hearers,'[38] while her mother admonished her:

So far from trying to get out of playing you ought to be glad of every opportunity of playing in public, will you just for a moment ask yourself what you have been spending the last three years in London for, separated from your own family & giving your time exclusively to music, except that you might be able to play in superior style both in public & private & how can you bring what you have done to a test when you try to get out of playing when you are asked, I think you should realise more fully the importance of those opportunities you never can know what they may lead to.[39]

Serious differences between the parties occurred when the question arose whether Edith would return to Dublin to teach, hopefully at the RIAM, or take a position in England. In 1885 there had been a difference of opinion about whether Edith should return to Dublin to be in attendance at the visit of the Prince and Princess of Wales. Mrs Oldham was completely against the idea, not only on grounds of cost but also because 'there is a very lukewarm feeling about this visit amongst all classes the Nationalists will not have anything to say to him & the loyal people have lost so much by late enactments [principally the Landlord and Tenant legislation] that they have neither money or zeal to expend.'[40] The matter was partly resolved when Grove insisted on paying Edith's travelling expenses; but the seeds of division had been planted.

By 1887 an emotional tug-of-war had begun between mother and mentor in which the desperation of each is wholly evident. Mrs Oldham was anxious to have Edith at home, while Grove—whose selfishness begins to come through in his rather transparent machinations to keep Edith near him— fought to secure her a place in England rather than in far-off and (in his eyes) provincial Dublin.

> I don't altogether like your picture of your Dublin life and I dare say that even the good people there—like Doyle &c—are tainted with that absurd, inane, love of outside show . . . Keep up your own mind by reading and thinking and music and poetry and then you will always have your own position and your own mind to retire into however many foolish people you will have to endure as a necessary part of life. How are you off for books? Is there a Mudie in Dublin? Surely?[41]

> Dublin being what you describe it, are you always to throw away the best years of your life there, and waste the freshfulness of your charming self on a place and people so unworthy of you and out of reach of so much that makes life worth having?[42]

Mrs Oldham had already expressed her reservations about the renewal of Edith's scholarship at the end of 1885. 'It is a very serious question & involves more than another year's residence in London, for I feel if you remain and form a connexion there you will in all probability never come back to live in Ireland again.'[43] She too recognised the cultural shortcomings of Dublin for one whose eyes had been opened to the riches of London. 'You say everything is dull with you yet in every letter you tell us of some concert or Theatre you are going to what would you think of the life here . . .[44] When I read some of your letters I think how could you exist here without those splendid concerts you would feel out of the world.'[45]

Grove, for his part, seems to have put heavy pressure on both Edith and her mother to ensure that she completed her course. In July 1886 Alice Oldham wrote to her sister: 'Mamma sent me Sir G. Grove's letter about your finishing your scholarship. It shows the kind of man he is. No one who was a thorough gentleman could have written it. If I were you I would not trust or think much of such a person.'[46]

A year later, the battle lines had been firmly drawn. Neither Grove nor Mrs Oldham thought that the Academy was the right place for Edith (even though it appears that Sir Francis Brady was trying to secure her a position there). Mrs Oldham wrote: 'As far as the piano goes I think they are getting worse every year . . . Sir Robert Stewart is too lazy to do much and they all seem so much behind the times. Esposito is the man now most thought of.'[47] But Hubert, who had been partially supporting Edith, could no longer do so, and Mrs Oldham was convinced that she could get enough private teaching and perhaps a school appointment as an assistant to Quarry, Culwick, or Esposito,[48] whereas Grove, desperate to hold on to his confidante, begged her to take a position that he could secure for her at Hagley, the home of the Lyttleton family.[49] He adopted a hectoring tone that soon had the Oldham family in exasperation. To Edith he wrote: 'It seems to me terrible that your future should be sacrificed for your family claims when the two might be combined. Surely you will never make anything like what your brother says in Dublin; and, if you do only by starving.'[50] To Eldred Oldham (junior) he wrote:

> My dear Sir—It is a pity that your sister should give up so eligible an opening as that at Hagley if she can possibly combine it with her family claims. She will make a good income, live like a lady, and be in an excellent position in the place, and I have reason to believe that Lord Lyttleton's people would be kind to her. Could not your mother go and live there with her? . . . I do Edith all honour for her unselfish wish to sacrifice herself to her mother but the opportunity is one that can never occur again, and there is surely some consideration due to the College which has maintained and taught her during four years, and which looked to this post as a means of seeing its teaching put into practice in so advantageous a way.[51]

Although Mrs Oldham had been deeply offended by Grove's attitude the previous year ('I consider his letter ungentlemanly and in the worst possible taste . . . I always detested his letters and now I hate them worse than ever'),[52] she was prepared to recognise that 'it is very kind & considerate of him to be arranging all our private affairs for us'; nevertheless, 'he shows such total ignorance of our position & circumstances that his advice is valueless. I never got a letter from him yet that there was not something in it that hurt & vexed me.'[53]

Eventually Grove had to capitulate, and by 30 August we find him congratulating Edith on finding teaching at a convent school.[54] 'I fancy that if you once get into that sort of set you will go on getting more & more pupils—are they good pay? and do you see your way to making any good pupils out of them? Mere drudgery of teaching (even nuns) unless there was some chance of success must be hard work.'

Nevertheless, he never abandoned his hope that she would return to London, and as late as 1893 he was writing: 'I am not animated only by my tremendous wish to have you nearer me when I say that I do think it a great pity you shd be wasted at Dublin. London is the proper place for you.'[55] They were to meet again, on average, only once a year thereafter.

Following one such meeting he wrote: 'Do you remember our gig ride? and the good moments we had as we jogged along & as we went down the shady path down below that village? I felt 18, and you dear—you were Venus and the Virgin Mary rolled into one—an unforgettable time.'[56]

No doubt moving back to Dublin was a strain emotionally, as well as a time of apprehension as far as a career was concerned, as we can glean from the letters of both mentor and mother. In early 1888 Edith played at the Orange Hall, Rutland Square (Parnell Square), including in her programme Schumann's Carnaval, which she had played at an RCM concert just a year previously. Grove wrote: 'I want to know about the Carnaval. Did you play all the numbers? and did you leave out the Sphinxes? They ought not to be played. Madame S never does and laughs at those who do for shewing their ignorance—you will find something about them in S's letters. She leaves out Estrolle and the Lettres dansantes (besides the Sphinxes) but that is because the whole is so very long.'[57]

In less than two years, however, Mrs Oldham was dead. On New Year's Eve 1888 Grove wrote: 'Well dear here is another year gone & another beginning. May the new one be a good one to you throughout, in soul and body. I can wish you no more. In disposition and material you seem to me to want nothing. But may you be able to guide yourself right in all circumstances and be as wise as a serpent while you are harmless as a dove.' Three weeks later: 'I am so sorry for you: I know how you loved her and can well enter into yr feeling of satisfaction at having given up your prospects here to go back to her.'[58]

Shortly afterwards, Edith must have written to him about her grief, since Grove replied: 'I am *very much* interested in what you tell me of your mother. You always gave me the impression—or rather perhaps I got it in spite of you—that your feeling towards her was one of duty rather than of affection—but I now see how wrong that conclusion was, and I most heartily wish you joy of your feeling as expressed in your letter.'[59] On the other hand, both were obviously realistic about the pressures and tensions that families can embody and create. 'How exactly I agree with you about visits to relations. There's not one of my blood relations whom I can be on a decent footing with for more than 24 hours. I used to express it by saying that "water is thicker than blood."'[60]

In an undated letter probably written while Edith was still under his care, Grove wrote:

> Dear Edith, I am deeply sorry for your trouble and would do anything I could to comfort you. No one in the world knows the stress of those desponding states of mind better than I do—I can enter into every word, & feel every shade of your distress. They come from two causes: first the gift of a sensitive mind & a keen imagination—would you

> change? would you forego occasional suffering—even bitter suffering—
> for the inability to feel? If your sufferings are keen your joys are also
> keen—and how manifold! How many levels you and I enjoy—& live
> upon—which a lower duller nature knows nothing of. No! I have often
> asked myself the question and the answer is always emphatically no.
> Secondly these things mostly come—at any rate are always fed by
> physical causes—one is not well—tired, exhausted, overwrought—and
> then the fiend fastens on one . . . Always write or tell me of your
> troubles. You may have wiser counsellors but you can't have a firmer
> friend or a more affectionate one. G.

'The fiend' sometime becomes 'the demon' in Grove's letters: 'This
last week has been a bad one—an Egyptian darkness from Monday to
Saturday . . .'[61] I have been enjoying the company of the black dog (do you
know that infernal animal?) for the last 3 days. I am quite frightened at his
pertinacity the loudness of his bark & the sharpness of his claws. He is a
fearful inmate.'[62]

One of Grove's fears was 'a general dissatisfied sense of nothingness.'[63]
This stemmed partly from his own sense of inadequacy, partly from his fits
of depression, but also—and this may at first sight seem strange in one who
accomplished so much and communicated so strongly—from a feeling that
one is never truly represented by the chosen means of communication. 'Yes!
what strange things words are! and how much they mean or how little they
mean, according to the mind of the person who uses them. There ought to
be a mystical, deep, burning language for lovers—not to be employed for
ordinary people or things.'[64] 'For me', he explained himself to Edith,

> life seems to be that I find myself in contact with a lot of duties and of
> work & that an inward impulse (which I suppose is called conscience)
> urges and impels me to work till I drop to do these duties to the utmost
> of my power. Then, as an enormous help to this, there is in me some-
> thing which I call imagination or poetry which enables me to feel often,
> and sometimes almost to realize, things out of the ken of eye or ear—
> God and other ideals which give me a motiv for striving and hoping that
> nothing else could give me. But then would that sort of scheme do for the
> general run of men? If these spirits are ever to be awakened, must it not
> be by some *shock* such as that of being saved or of being lost?[65]

He wrote to Edith constantly about affairs at the RCM and his concern
for the students. 'College is beginning again . . . The difficult question of
the future of all these dear girls & boys committed to me—they must go,
in almost all cases—have I done all I can—have I been judicious, shall we
carry out our intentions and begin to work a good influence on the country?
You can understand how these things weigh on me.'[66] In excitement he
rushes to tell her: 'And now I must tell you a bit of real news. I have just
secured the money for building the new College! This day week I took a
rich Yorkshireman to the Prince [of Wales] and he promised HRH £30,000

and if 30 wasn't enough 40, and if 40 not enough, £50,000! . . . I am determined to have a building with the character of a college—that all the pupils shall remember with love and affection.'[67]

Two years later he goes deeper into the problem of balancing the needs of a college with those of a conservatoire.

> The College gives me great anxiety. I see evils, but do not know how to remedy them. I am sure it is too much a *school* All those *students* who come for a year, who have no gift or intelligence, and who will never do anything in music—surely a College ought not to teach those sort of people. In answer to this:— they get better taught by us than elsewhere and therefore it is better they should come: but that merely means to say that there ought to be a preparatory school, so that College may be devoted to serious work on those who are likely to repay it.[68]

He refused to take the easy route of cosy insularity, arguing against Franklin Taylor, who

> thinks the College quite self-sufficient—quite able to educate thoroughly a musician for any position however important. But I can't think that . . . I can't help feeling that abroad there are greater piano players and teachers, greater violinists, greater composers than there are in England and that our girls and boys would profit immensely by the opportunity of learning from Bülow or Joachim or Sarasate or Brahms . . . How very much we should profit if Bülow would come to us for a month a year as he does to Frankfort.[69]

He expresses his own musical prejudices—and displays his ability to transcend them—when he says of the College's syllabus: 'The modern music of Liszt and Tausig is hateful to them [Pauer and Franklin] and to me, but to a pupil it's absolutely necessary—the flood may be noxious, but one can't stop it, we can't dam everything back to Schumann or even to Brahms.'[70] Reporting on a performance of a Brahms symphony, he says: 'Very great and very interesting & often tremendously touching. But in all modern symphonies, even in Schumann's, I want the constant beauty of the orchestra and the grace and loveliness that I find in Beethoven & Mendelssohn. The moderns carry the portrayal of emotion so far that they disregard the means by which it is done; just as Browning does in poetry.'[71] The concern was not merely one of musical taste but (no doubt intimately related to his ruling fears and passions) also one of form:

> I am uneasy at the change in the proportions of the world, the disturbance of the old relations—what can be a better order than King, Lords, Commons?—what can be a better practical instrument than the Established Church? but in 25 years time all that will be bowled over. The Press will get more demoralised than it is now—more like the American model and everybody will be appreciably lower. Then the women—they will push their rights and their fads till, instead of fulfilling their own

place in the world, they try to take the man's place; and then what will become of the Race?[72]

Grove was concerned for Edith's future career, even though he was dismissive of Dublin as a cultural centre ('the desert in which you live').[73] In 1887 he had promised: 'I shall write to Sir R. Stewart about you. I fear it will not be much good, but still I shall do my best. I shall also write to Mahaffy. He is very clever & nice, where his own interest does not come in, & it *may* help you . . . Yes I am well prepared to love everything Irish. I have reason to my dear—don't you know that, you little Irish woman?'[74] That same year he approached Arthur Balfour, then Chief Secretary for Ireland, who replied: 'My dear Sir George, I really am extremely obliged to you for your letter, not merely on account of the kind wishes it contains for myself, but on account of your recommendation of Miss Oldham. If I get a chance, I will certainly ask her to perform.'[75] On another occasion, Grove tells Edith that at a Royal Academy dinner he had met Mahaffy and Charles Doyle, who 'said that he heard about you constantly and always in praise.'[76]

Grove was anxious on another count: that she would marry and that he would thus lose her affections; and together these two anxieties provoked several outbursts of a realistic but nonetheless selfish nature. 'I never was fonder of you or loved you more tenderly,' he wrote shortly after her return to Dublin. 'Never think anything else. I shall not alter—of course the time will come when someone of your own age will step in between us and absorb you. That's nature, & inevitable—but till then let me enjoy your affection!'[77]

There is a bitter and poignant tone one year later, which shows Grove's alarm that Edith's affections might have turned to another.

> I am very much amused & interested . . . by your 'real difficulty.' I am quite prepared to hear it. It is what often happens, and what in your case was sure to happen. Do you know dear child that you are a most attractive person? It is hard to find a face so charming and so simple or a character at once so intelligent and clever and so sincere as yours and you are sure to be fallen in love with . . . But dear don't give way till you feel yourself in love—were you ever? tell me. If not you have got the great event of your life to come. But wait till then, and may the man be worthy of you! It will be hard to find him . . . I can understand a woman being driven by circumstances—health, poverty &c into taking refuge in marriage and often such marriages may be very happy— happier than a marriage of passion, but still nothing can really make up to a sensitive man or woman for the absence of passion and when you think of the tremendous step that it is to surrender yourself (*se donner*) to another, it makes one hesitate to think of taking it on any other ground but that of real self-sacrifice & that only for passion's sake . . . You are not now contemplating any such step are you? Are you in difficulty? do you want money or rest? or anything which a devoted

friend can give you, a friend who loves you dearly and devotedly & quite unselfishly? Often and often I have repeated over & over all our interviews—I have you absolutely before me—your sweet dear face— your precious brogue, your sensible valuable words. I have them all. Dear, trust to such a tried friend and tell me how I can help you, before you take any rash step.[78]

Grove's powers began to wane markedly after his retirement from the RCM at the end of 1894, at the age of seventy-four. His last letters are a commentary on his 'constant deterioration' of mind and body, but he continues to rejoice in Edith's health and success. In 1897 he says:

You have got a long, lively, useful life before you. Don't forget what we have been to one another. No, I know you *won't* forget. You have been a dear friend to me; and though I shall never see you again, you are as much to me as ever . . . I must now say goodbye and I do it with the same affection that I have felt for you for an immense time—with love and thanks for all your goodness so much more than ever I deserved. G. Grove.[79]

At the close of 1898 Edith was on business in London with Esposito (who had become quite friendly with Grove), and she went to Sydenham— obviously to say goodbye to her mentor of over fifteen years.

Grove died in 1900, and Edith became a central figure in the Academy piano faculty and the local centre system, as well as the Feis Ceoil[80] and the Dublin Orchestral Society, although in 1902 there was a strenuous but unsuccessful effort by Elizabeth Bennett and Margaret O'Hea to prevent her promotion.[81] In 1906 she married Richard Irvine Best (1872–1959), a scholar who became director of the National Library of Ireland in 1924 and had been registrar of the Feis Ceoil. Edith Best retired from the Academy in 1932, receiving the FRIAM in 1938, and died in 1950.

In his will, Dr Best brought the story full circle by providing for the endowment of a scholarship at the RCM, 'to be competed for at the Feis Ceoil Dublin with which my dear wife was so intimately associated since its establishment . . . for an Irish student (female) of the piano.'[82] In the words of his executor, Terence de Vere White, 'nothing would have pleased him more than to see the letters published. He was keen to immortalize his wife as far as that was possible.'[83] The inclusion of some of this correspondence in Percy Young's biography of Grove has gone some distance towards putting this extraordinary relationship on the record; we believe that this *intermezzo* has completed that task.

5

Growth, 1890–1921

*Inauguration of the Board of Governors; nationalism and
internationalism; relations with Dublin Castle; development of
Academy functions; the 'Esposito era'; Esposito and his family; Esposito
as a teacher; Esposito and the literary renaissance; Irish music and
nationalism; Synge as a composer; RDS recitals; Esposito as a pianist;
Feis Ceoil; Dublin Orchestral Society; Municipal School of Music;
student and staff profile; the Woodhouse affair; Schools Choir Competition;
local centre examination system; proposed appointment of a director;
Esposito's resignations; wartime; the first women Governors.*

The inaugural meeting of the new Academy under the 'Blue Scheme' took place at 36 Westland Row on 6 November 1889. It ushered in the second phase in the life of Ireland's national school of music and signalled many departures. Partly because the RIAM was now a corporate body with statutory and charitable status, and partly because this development coincided with a resurgence in cultural nationalism, its future would be qualitatively different from its past.

This chapter (supplemented by those dedicated to the local centre system and the development of the internal examinations and scholarships) attempts to describe the educational, cultural and social changes that affected the Academy in this crucial period, and to indicate the main characteristics of the Academy's progress through it.

Although nothing in the minutes of the incoming Board of Governors even hints at the changes in the artistic or political environment, the Academy began to operate in an intrinsically different fashion. A subtle change in its governing personnel—partly, but not entirely, due to the advent of Dublin Corporation representatives—reflects this awakening of national self-determination. As the political complexion of Ireland changed with the increasing possibility of independence, the composition of the Academy's board now registered a swing from a liberalism with a separatist bias to a more overt nationalism. The meeting represented a veritable encounter between the old and the new: from the old Academy, Stewart, Jones, and

Brady, and from the new, Corporation nominees including three former Lords Mayor (Sir George Owens, Charles Dawson, and Alderman Meagher) and one future Lord Mayor, Valentine Blake Dillon,[1] the significant departure being the creation for the first time of representative constituencies. The next ten years would see the death of many figures associated with the Academy since its earliest days—Robinson, Levey, Stewart—and the advent of new faces, many of them to become equally legendary, such as Guido Papini, Adolph Wilhelmj, Benedetto Palmieri, Achille Simonetti, and Clyde Twelvetrees.

The swings in mood, from nationalism to internationalism, make the Academy, in parallel with the fortunes of the incipient National Theatre, a microcosm of Irish cultural life during the period 1890–1920, in which imperial events, such as the visits to Dublin of Queen Victoria (1900), King Edward VII (1907) and King George V (1911) and the First World War (1914–18) and, during it, the 1916 Rising (or 'Rebellion', as the Academy's records have it) emphasised the distinction between the existing Union and the ambitions, on so many different levels, for independence.

After its first forty years the Academy was ready to meet the challenges that had already been posed by the growing questions of national identity. How was Ireland to be governed, and by whom? How was a balance to be achieved between nationalism and cosmopolitanism? As with all its relationships, its approach was utterly pragmatic. Its loyal addresses to the three successive monarchs and to the Lord Lieutenants maintained an ostensibly unionist stance, but the realities of a vanishing ascendancy—and of an ebbing in Anglo-Irish power and presence in Irish society—dictated an accommodation between old and new in which the essential requirement was that the Academy keep its head.

Yeats, for primarily aesthetic reasons, regarded 1900 as the end of an era.[2] Others more prosaically identified 1901, the year in which Queen Victoria died, or 1914, the opening year of the world war, as the point at which an 'old order' of fixed and dependable values gave way to one of vortical and vertiginous change. Walter Starkie, for example, was of the opinion that 'the old world ended in 1914'.[3] Several other and earlier watersheds have given rise to a long history of reassessment and re-evaluation. The Famine, with which the founding of the Academy coincided; Disestablishment in 1869; the Irish Land Acts (1870 to 1903); the Phoenix Park murders of 1882; the Local Government Act (1898); the Home Rule Act (1914); and the Easter Rising of 1916—all punctuate the relationship not only of Ireland with England but also of Ireland with itself, as change began to take place of a much more radical nature than in most of western Europe. Educational changes, such as the introduction of a system of secondary schooling in the eighteen-seventies, the establishment of the Royal University in 1879, and the establishment of the Department of Agricultural and Technical Instruction in 1894, helped to create a Catholic urban middle class at first puzzled and directionless but by the eighteen-nineties increasingly vociferous and oriented towards participation in public affairs.[4]

In such revolutionary circumstances, it was impossible for any institution to remain stable, and the involvement of staff, pupils and governors in the cultural, political and social maelstrom—what Marie McCarthy calls 'a culture-conscious group of individuals concerned with reconstituting Irish identity'[5]—meant that the Academy too was affected in the way it saw itself and was perceived.

In a period that saw the exodus of so many families opting for the 'Anglo' side of their hyphenation, it is significant that those on the RIAM's Board of Governors decided to find themselves Irish. They include figures such as the playwright Lennox Robinson, a Governor for seven years, who wrote in his biography of his friend Major Bryan Cooper (a subscriber to the Academy): 'Two changes are taking place: the passing of power and . . . the realisation by a few sensitive and intelligent landowners like Bryan Cooper that their life and interests are inseparably woven in with the Irish people . . . In his change we see . . . the beginning of a change of heart of a whole class . . . The settlers are for the first time to merge into Ireland.'[6]

At this time, establishment figures such as Lord Arthur Hill—a descendant of the Marquess of Downshire, whose enthusiasm in 1857 had helped to set the Academy on its feet—would be assiduous in recruiting into membership of the Academy many members of titled families with Irish interests.[7] The upper classes, and Anglo-Irish landowners in particular, were an almost negligible minority whose power base had already been almost completely eroded by the Land Acts, culminating in that of 1923, and by the extension of education, to which figures such as W. J. M. Starkie and A. P. Graves had contributed significantly. Bruce Arnold makes the telling point that 'each issue was read and dealt with by the class most affected in the light of its immediate and long-term effects . . . While it was hard to predict just how the relatively new European spirit of nationalism would affect Ireland, there was no denying its early strength in the cultural field.'[8] The fact that many of the leading figures in the literary renaissance, and Esposito's collaborators, came from this class should not escape us.

One might be forgiven for thinking that the composition of the Blue Scheme would have set the Academy in concrete, its operations governed by a rigid modus operandi from which departure was difficult if not impossible. In fact it is at this point that we see the Academy becoming manifold. From the relatively monolithic institution of 1848 it now developed into a 'truly national' institution, its increasingly cosmopolitan teaching staff playing a prominent role in the creation of new institutions and stitching the RIAM itself more effectively into the fabric of Irish cultural life, at least as intimately as Levey and Elsner in the eighteen-fifties and sixties, and on a much broader scale. In this chapter we explore the tensions between the national and the cosmopolitan ambitions in the form of the initiatives taken, the personalities involved, and the issues negotiated.

The passing away of an old order, the creation of a new one and the intangibility of many of the Academy's achievements during this next period all serve to underline the fact that it is not only 'within its walls,' nor even in the lists of its graduates and laureates, that such an institution finds and determines itself. Increasingly, the Academy's activities grew beyond the concrete facts of Westland Row to confront more elusive realities, less defined concepts that were nevertheless felt to be somehow at the core of what music education had to achieve if it was to be 'truly national': serving the needs of an as yet unarticulated nation. How Irish musicians might be trained to play their part as musical citizens in the expression of that reality, in performance, or composition, or as an audience, was a new concern in the Academy, but subliminal and largely unspoken.

In Hamilton Harty's words, Dublin in the eighteen-nineties 'was still occupied in making . . . her tradition as a musical city' and 'important and influential enough to attract to herself some of the best contemporary musicians.'[9] But at the same time, in the words of Peter Goodman, an educational authority with whom the Academy would have substantial dealings in these years, Ireland in 1896 was still looking for its past: 'an entire nation has to be made once more musical. The lost character of the Land of Song has to be re-established.'[10] As a commentary on the continuing failure of both primary and secondary schools to develop music, this is probably an accurate reflection on the musical state of the country. It can be argued that, without a steadily increasing flow of students from the schools, the Academy could not develop its national character. But, as these remarks taken together indicate, despite the absence of such a flow, standards *were* maintained and raised, as the Academy grew more and more aware of its potential to meet an only imperfectly perceived need for a conservatoire.

The idea that there is, in addition to present reality, another reality that is inevitably *absent* is a commonplace of psychology. The 'shadow' side of the psyche is essential to the successful life of the organism as a whole, because it is only when both sides are fully integrated that creativity can be released (and here one is tempted to think of Frederick May's tone poem 'Sunlight and Shadow'). In the case of the Academy the job of inculcating musical knowledge and skills was affected, or 'shadowed', by a non-presence: that of a musical tradition important to the construction of the Free State but seldom acknowledged. In the expansion of the Academy, this other Ireland became increasingly manifest as examiners went out into the highways and byways to discover musical talent that had never been recognised, assessed, or given shape; likewise, its new function as an educator of working men in the Municipal School of Music took place in a building *elsewhere*; the career of Michele Esposito, prime mover of so many new departures, brought him as much outside the Academy as it found him within; and, in trying to touch the crock of gold that was the Irish musical heritage, the Academy met an indefinable entity without which its own existence would henceforth be only partly fulfilled. These reflections, hints and alternatives underline the fact that the provisional or tentative character of the Academy's early years never left it, that it would continue to be open to change, not merely responsive to but creative of the new.

Literature was the forum in which most of this transfer of meaning took place, Synge's *Playboy* being its epitome, and discussion of the issue continues to be predominantly literary. But in the three symphonies by Stanford, Esposito and Harty that their composers entitled 'Irish', an approximation to this exchange between two cultures also takes place.[11]

A pair of binary images, that of the circle and the straight line, helps us to understand the process by which the innate characteristic of one tradition may be given form in that of another. In this period the repetitive nature, the circularity, of an Irishness in which life was 'in waiting' for its true destiny, its fulfilment, met its antithesis: a narrative, linear sense of history that insists on a steady development or progression from one state to another. The meeting-place was a point of both fusion and confusion. But it was also a point of transformation, as the qualities of both circle and straight line attempted to accommodate each other.

From the 'symphonies' with which Stevenson sought to frame the melodies of Thomas Moore to the planxties in which Seán Ó Riada chose to re-present Irish music to a cosmopolitan audience, from the transfer of technique

A manuscript of T. R. G. Jozé, 1905, for Marie Dowse

between Geminiani and the native fiddlers of eighteenth-century Ireland to the baroque playing of the continuing Sliabh Luachra tradition, we have examples of movement between the seen and the unseen, the voiced and the silent.[12] Even the attempt to notate traditional music is both a reduction of something that will not easily lend itself to the record and an expansion of the possibilities of expression—an end to one form of absence or silence and a door on a new form of eloquence.[13] Stewart's archaeological approach (above, p. 120–21) may have been outdated even in the eighteen-eighties, but when students played 'arrangements' of traditional airs such as 'The Coolin' or 'The Lark in the Clear Air' by Jozé or Esposito, or Stewart's version of 'Cruiskeen Lawn', a form of translation was taking place that brought the 'hidden Ireland' partially inside the Academy and allowed some form of assessment, however cursory or ill-informed, to take place.

Mahler, hearing music by Sibelius, remarked: 'They are the same everywhere, these national geniuses. You find them in Russia and Sweden—and in Italy the country is overrun by these whores and their ponces.'[14] Slightly less vehement, but equally dismissive, is Adorno's comment that 'those musical languages that took national shape in the latter half of the nineteenth century can scarcely be understood beyond their own borders,' while of Sibelius he said: 'He has not acknowledged the Pan-European techniques of composition—his symphonic music combines the trivial and the mundane with things illogical and ultimately beyond comprehension; the aesthetically crude is put across to us as the voice of nature.'[15]

The remarkable parallels between Ireland and Finland to which we have already adverted recur here in Adorno's reference to 'things illogical and ultimately beyond comprehension.' This, to an ear attuned to logic and the linear progression of imperialism, strikes the note of superior cultural achievement, while to an ear accustomed to the notion of *difference* or *otherness*, to the experience of relegation or 'marginality', it immediately summons those shadowlands of Irish subliminal experience that writers like Yeats had brought to the fore in the notion of the 'Celtic twilight'—elements that made a positive virtue, rather than a disabling difficulty, of the illogical and the incomprehensible.

The terms *transition* and *translation* are so closely related etymologically that it is important to note that the former means a 'going across' whereas the latter involves a 'bringing across'. A society in a process of *transition* has its own internal momentum; and, however complex its machinery, Irish society and its leaders were making a *transitus* from one condition to another that relied little on external factors and owed much to the unique experiences of the Famine and subsequent fundamental social change. Yet a simultaneous act of *translation* was being undertaken by writers and critics who stood, at the one time, within and without that momentum. These 'translators' of Irish culture were bringing the sense of the past into a new relationship with Ireland and with the world, thereby meeting risk full in the face. They made many mistakes. Just as we say that 'something gets lost in the translation' between languages, so in the transfer of essential meaning between cultures something can become displaced.

T. W. Rolleston, a close associate of Charles Oldham, John O'Leary, and Michael Davitt, was one of the chief figures in the literary revival and a prime example of the displacement that can occur in the attempt at translation. With W. B. Yeats he had edited *Poems and Ballads of Young Ireland* (1888) and in 1892 had become the first secretary of the Irish Literary Society in London. Described by Yeats as 'serene' and 'the second Thomas Davis',[16] Rolleston (who edited the 1890 edition of Davis's works) had a practical side, working as secretary of the Irish Industries Association, and in this capacity he also played a role in the development of art education.[17] He believed that 'an art school . . . must endeavour . . . to familiarise its students with the past art life of their own country . . . The great need of modern Ireland is to be reunited with its past';[18] but he also argued that craft work needed a 'revolution in design' in order to become modern.[19] Both sides of the argument would be voiced in the debate on the development of Irish music.

Yeats himself sums up the ambivalence of the situation in wishing that Rolleston 'would devote his imagination to some national purpose. Cosmopolitan literature is, at best, but a poor bubble, though a big one. Creative work has always a fatherland.'[20] Yeats also said of Rolleston that he 'seemed always out of place';[21] and the same ironic fate was to befall Esposito. When he applied for the vacant directorship of the Naples Conservatory in 1909 in succession to his friend Martucci, Esposito was told that he was not sufficiently well known in Italy.[22]

The fate of a translator is not to be at home in either place but to be the load-bearing bridge between the two. It is also the fate of the translator to be pilloried when he fails to achieve the appropriate metaphor.[23] Beckett, employing an image both architectural and musical, says: 'I feel an outside and an inside and me in the middle . . . I am the tympanum . . . I don't belong to either'[24]—a condition that must also have been much lived by his mentor, Synge. When the translator fails to create this meaning between cultures, he is often regarded by both sides as a traitor, there being another semantic affinity between the 'trader' (he who 'hands over' the reins of continuity) and the 'traducer'. Mario Esposito, suspected (as we shall see) of being a double agent, and his father and his associates, must at times have sensed the danger, whether political or cultural, in what they were trying to achieve in the interest of causes in which they believed. As Séamus Deane has observed, where society was often at variance with the law of the coloniser, 'the Irish idea of tradition was naturally more inclined towards the notion of continuity betrayed than of continuity retained.'[25] More specifically, 'the whole territory of Irish music . . . is betrayed into print.'[26] As a result— and this would apply equally to the images and grammatical rules of a foreign musical idiom—the dominant tradition is one of *dis*continuity rather than steady attainment, and new beginnings and departures are usually the order of the day, searching both for their own grammar and syntax and their connection, or metaphor, with that of the past.

Part of the difficulty lies in agreeing a common acceptable vocabulary. Different outlooks give rise to differing expressions and, more confusing still, to differing uses of the same expression. While the call for a 'national school of music' might therefore have meant 'a school of national music', it also stood for the intention of establishing a 'national school' in which the entire science of music could be studied on a national basis. As Annie Patterson argued (citing her doctorate with her name at the head of her article, but signing it 'Eithne Ní Pheadair' at the end), 'ere we approach our superb native music whether as students or performers, we want a wholesome culture in musical science generally, as a particular comparison of our own native music and its possibilities with the music and musical output of the nations around us.'[27] It was simply not enough to uncover the wealth of the past, which included, on P. W. Joyce's estimation, five thousand distinct Irish airs[28] or, on Aloys Fleischmann's, ten thousand; nor was it enough to sing these unless the art of singing—rhythm, intonation, and meaning—had first been mastered.

By contrast, Brendan Rogers—speaking, we should note, to the National *Literary* Society—intended something that was at once more specific and more general than this: a 'class or style' rather than an institution or (rather pointedly) 'a learned academy of the grave and experienced signori'—a style that 'has sprung from a people's nature . . . the natural heritage of a people, the fittest medium for giving expression to the national sentiment.'[29] The fact that Ireland has never produced a figure equivalent to Bartók or Kodály, both of whom started their gathering of Hungarian folk music in the early years of the century, is in itself a commentary on the problems inherent in the subject. In 1902 W. H. Grattan Flood protested strongly at the 'un-Irish' character of the RIAM,[30] while in 1904 Dublin Corporation threatened to withdraw its support for the Academy unless it remedied its 'neglect of the study of native Irish music.'[31]

There are therefore several levels on which the act of translation can be considered: the carrying of Ireland's past across the divide of recent history into an unstable present and a dubious future; the translation of music, notated and inflected in one specific genre, into a qualitatively different genre; the translation of the 'Irishness' of Irish musical art into a universal musical language; and the meaning of different kinds of Irishness to different types of Irish men and women. The issue even had its quasi-comic side when Sir William Harcourt, then the leader of the Liberal Party, noticing Irish delegates at the Eisteddfod, exclaimed in dismay, 'Is there an Irish question in music also?'[32]

The question of what 'Irish' means is perhaps only now beginning to be painted on a sufficiently large canvas to allow us to comprehend some of the answers. J. S. Kelly, for example, observes most cogently that 'the developing objective reality of a nation is forever moving out of range of the subjective imagination that tries to encompass it' and that, between 1890 and 1916, writers 'who opted to speak for "Ireland" could give only a partial and biased interpretation of what they understood by the term.'[33]

When Patterson, therefore, says that Stanford in his 'Irish Symphony' introduces Irish melodies 'ingeniously but with a certain diffidence that probably arose from the composer's cosmopolitan principles,'[34] it enables us to realise that Stanford was perhaps escaping from a certain type of Irishness and a certain set of Irish circumstances into a different set of circumstances that nonetheless continued to have their Irish dimension.[35] This, as we have suggested, may be the compositional parallel with Yeats's intention of creating 'a national literature which shall be nonetheless Irish in spirit from being English in language . . . by translating and retelling in English, which shall have an indefinable Irish quality of rhythm and style, all that is best in the ancient literature.'[36]

The chief features in the concrete narrative of this period are the development of the Academy's curriculum, its management system, and its role in the community, the nationwide examination system being of prime and lasting importance. Those of its shadow-text are precisely these attempts (and usually failures) at translation and accommodation between three cultures: the Irish, the Anglo-Irish, and the cosmopolitan.

To transact these political and cultural issues with regard to music education, a new coalition of disparate figures, representative of the melting-pot of the next three decades, passed through the board-room of the RIAM, among them original members of the IAM, educationalists such as Patrick Keenan and P. W. Joyce, churchmen such as the Cecilian pioneers Bishop Donnelly[37] and Canon MacManus and the Dean of Christ Church Cathedral, William Greene,[38] artists such as Sir Thomas Drew[39] and Edward Martyn,[40] the rising breed of businessmen such as the paper manufacturer John Irwin[41] and the builder W. H. Beardwood, politicians such as the Sinn Féiner George Noble Plunkett[42] and the central figure of the 1913 lock-out, William Martin Murphy MP, and even, very briefly, W. T. Cosgrave, and women such as Sarah Cecilia Harrison and Kathleen Clarke, with the medical and legal professions continuing to be well represented by music-lovers such as Sir Francis Cruise[43] and Edmund Lupton, respectively. In the middle of these we find very significantly the figure of Michele Esposito.

Social change, including the growth of new professions and the development of new life-styles, affected the profile of subscribers to the Academy. Whereas in 1860 only 3 per cent of subscribers were musicians, in 1890 this had grown to 30 per cent, indicating a growing confidence in the profession. Lawyers continued to be heavily represented, constituting over 30 per cent of the Academy's supporters, while the representation of medicine had declined slightly. Those involved in trade and trade-related professions, such as the burgeoning insurance business, were on the increase. By 1920 the number of subscribers whose occupation we have not been able to trace increases, suggesting that a lower importance was placed on what positions people held in society or on their socio-economic status; instead of the titled and landed families (which were noticeably on the decrease), or even the well-known public figures, we find what one might refer to as a 'grey area' of ordinariness.

Concomitantly, their places of residence also change significantly. Whereas in 1860 subscribers lived in the closely defined area of the city centre, in 1890, despite a still heavy concentration in the axis of Merrion Square and

Fitzwilliam Square (40 per cent), a growing proportion (30 per cent) had moved to the increasingly accessible suburbs of Blackrock, Stillorgan, Kingstown (Dún Laoghaire), Monkstown, Killiney, and Dalkey. Terenure, Rathmines and Rathgar do not seem to have grown nearly as much as preferred locations, although Grosvenor Road, Rathmines, and Marlborough Road, Donnybrook, were favourite places for musicians themselves. As Mary Daly has observed, 'the move to the suburbs was initiated by the professional and upper middle classes seeking new residences which were physically removed from the dirt, smells and congestion of the city centre.'[44] It was also caused by rising prosperity, enabling people to build houses and to travel more easily, as well as to participate in local government through an extension of the franchise.[45] By 1920 this trend had been confirmed, with a marked drop in the numbers living around the city centre, a huge growth in the inner circle of Clyde Road, Herbert Park, and the South Circular Road, and a steady proportion (44 per cent) in the outer or satellite suburbs.

Accompanying this change was a concern for manners and morals, which manifested itself in several unusual ways in the Academy, chiefly in the areas of behaviour and sanitation, which were not as widely separated in people's minds as we might expect. For example, in 1897–99 a scarlet fever epidemic was followed by an outbreak of measles,[46] which would have given serious cause for concern in a place of collective study such as the Academy, with its growing orchestral and chamber music activity. Sir Charles Cameron (one of the Academy's subscribers) was responsible for public health, and he crossed swords with the institution when in 1892 an open cess-pool was discovered at the rear of the premises.[47] In 1891 the operation of a tyre manufacturing company was the subject of a legal action by the Academy to abate the nuisance of offensive smells, even though the Academy's solicitor, A. W. Baker of Clare Street, advised that 'there is no use my going to test the effect of the smells at the Academy as I am not able to smell at all.'[48] As recently as 1924 a complaint regarding the activities of the resident housekeeper was dealt with by the sanitary engineers, who stated that 'the premises are not suitable for the keeping of hens, and Mrs. Murphy is to be directed to immediately discontinue the keeping of any hens or fowl in or about the Academy.'[49]

Decent behaviour was insisted upon, and on two occasions on-the-spot dismissals for drunkenness—not at all uncommon in Dublin at the time[50]—were meted out. In 1900 'James Browne and his wife [hall porter and housekeeper, respectively] having been reported for drunkenness, the Lady Superintendent was authorized to dismiss James and his wife.'[51] In 1901 William Purcell, caretaker at the Municipal School, 'denied having been drunk,' as alleged by the Academy secretary, saying in his defence that 'his mother was eccentric and that the uproar arose from his endeavour to control her.'[52] On other occasions, derangement gave cause for dismissal: on 12 October 1892 it was reported that

> Dillon [the porter] was brought before magistrate today . . . and Messrs. Cree and Drury went to Police Office, Mr. Drury having charged Dillon last night as a dangerous lunatic. The magistrate, there being no evidence

before him of violence, refused to commit him. He returned to the house. Mr. Cree, Alderman Dillon and Mr. Perrin saw Dillon and his wife and after conversation they agreed to leave tomorrow. Dr. Jozé was authorised to engage two men to remain in the house tonight.

In fact, nurses were kept in the house to mind the unfortunate Dillon and his wife, who left the Academy with a payment for discharge of three pounds and a kindly if devastating note explaining their exit as 'owing to the serious illness of Dillon.'[53]

Improper behaviour on the part of Governors was also a feature at this time. It is quite likely that, because of the near-miracles that had been achieved in setting up and financing the Academy, figures such as Francis Brady may have acquired a certain arrogance, based on the assumption that they could do no wrong, or even that they had proprietorial rights in respect of Academy activity. Certainly bad feeling arose in relation to the Royal University, where, at an Academy prize-giving in 1902, the ageing Brady apparently gave serious offence to the university's secretary, Joseph McGrath, who complained that 'this is the second time Sir Francis Brady in his capacity as Chairman has publicly insulted me. As he made an apology on the former occasion I took no further notice . . . but his conduct to me last night passes all bearing.'[54] As the facilities at Earlsfort Terrace were essential to the Academy, the Governors took Brady to task, and it was resolved that in future the secretary (as administrator) and Cruise (representing the Board) would act for the Academy at all such Academy functions.

One of the curious aspects of the government of the Academy was the fact that, under the Blue Scheme, the Lord Lieutenant was its president and that Queen Victoria had accepted the invitation to be its patron. There was thus an institutional connection between Dublin Castle and the Academy, which saw the Lord Lieutenant (or sometimes his wife) presenting the prizes at the annual ceremony. In 1880, for example, Earl Cowper had thanked the Academy by assuring it of his interest. 'Even those whom nature has cruelly sent into the world incapable of appreciating the delights of music may well feel bound to contribute all they can to the cultivation of an art which affords such exquisite and inexhaustible pleasure to so large a portion of mankind.'[55]

Behind and beyond this, however, was a further set of facts that demonstrate the ambivalence of the Academy in its relations with both the Crown and its representatives. Formal addresses were presented to each Lord Lieutenant on his arrival in, and departure from, Dublin, but formality appears to have grown into warm regard in 1906–15 in the case of the Earl (later Marquess) and Countess of Aberdeen, who introduced themselves into the social and cultural life of the city more enthusiastically than many of their predecessors.

In March 1906, shortly after his appointment, Lord Aberdeen (who had held the position briefly in 1886 and had since been Governor-General of Canada) was told by the Governors: '[We] trust that during your term of office . . . we may be favoured with a relationship more personal than the term President ex-officio would imply' and heard in reply: 'Your . . . words . . . exactly express my own confident expectation and hope, namely, that this may be only the first of the opportunities afforded to me of coming into contact and communication with the RIAM . . . You will find in me not only officially but in a more personal sense, one who warmly appreciates, and will always desire to co-operate with you in, your important mission.'[56]

This ambition bore fruit in the next few years. In 1908 Lord Aberdeen told a delighted and gratified audience:

> To adapt an old proverb, hearing was believing, in the merits of both teachers and students . . . Only those who had some proficiency in the art could appreciate the amount of patience required before any proficiency in it could be obtained . . . Though all might not follow music as a profession, they all aimed at some real musical attainment, and he urged them not to rest satisfied with anything less than the highest efficiency which their talent enabled them to reach. Anything short of this would be unworthy of what had sometimes been called a divine art, because of its far-reaching influence, and the marvellous way in which it could go into the hearts of mankind.[57]

In 1912 Lord Aberdeen told them he hoped that in their music-making

> they would keep in view the far reaching essential element of sympathy. They had sometimes to listen to music that did not appeal to their hearts, because it was lacking in human sympathy. Simplicity was a thing they should aim at . . . There seemed to be an idea that simplicity meant superficiality, but he thought they could have simplicity without lightness . . . If they kept before them the necessity for sympathy, truth, reality, and depth of feeling in their renderings and competitions, their efforts as musicians were bound to be crowned with that measure of success which all present that evening wished them.[58]

The following year he

> related the legend of the girl who had a beautiful voice which was carefully trained. At last the great occasion of her debut arrived, and there was enthusiastic applause. The professor by whom she had been chiefly trained was congratulated, and asked if he was not greatly pleased. 'Yes,' he said, 'I am.' But there was something in the tone of his reply which prompted the questioner to say, 'But surely there was nothing lacking?' 'Well,' said the Professor quietly, 'she must first break her heart.' I am sure we do not want any young hearts to be broken (*laughter*) but there is no doubt a real meaning in that story.[59]

Formal communication between the Academy and the Viceregal Lodge was regular. The Academy (on the proposal of Canon MacManus) sent its condolences to the royal family on the death of the Duke of Clarence, eldest son of the Prince of Wales, in 1892.[60] In 1897, on the occasion of Queen Victoria's diamond jubilee, an address (drafted by Beardwood and Sexton) was presented in which the Board declared that they 'sincerely hope and pray that Your Majesty's life may be spared for many years to come, to benignly rule over the greatest Empire on Earth with the continued love and devotion of Your subjects.'[61] In 1900, during her visit to Dublin, not only was the Academy represented at the Viceregal Lodge but the Queen's daughters Helena and Beatrice were invited to visit Westland Row. On the death of Victoria in 1901 the Academy's condolences were sent to the new king, Edward VII, in 'expression of their loyal sympathy and . . . of the grief which has fallen not alone upon Your Royal House but also upon the Nation at large.'[62]

During Victoria's visit in 1900 Annie Patterson used the occasion to talk about the music of Ireland. Perhaps conscious of the lack of Irish music played and sung for the Queen in 1858, she asserted: 'The day is now gone by when it might be asked what Irish music is there fit to place before the Queen?' Citing the Bunting, Petrie, Joyce and Levey collections, and commending the current edition of Irish songs by A. P. Graves, she filled her page of the *Weekly Irish Times* with commentary without exhausting, or going beyond, the subject of folk-song.[63] It was well known that the Queen was not only attracted to Irish airs but was also 'at this time . . . indulging in an orgy of things Irish. She had decreed that all Irish troops in her army should wear the shamrock on St Patrick's Day.'[64] For many years the 'wearing of the green' had been a subject of discussion, if not dispute, within the Academy. In 1872 the *Evening Mail* had commented on the female members of the orchestra at the pupils' concert 'dressed in white, with handsome green sashes, indicative of the national character of the institution,'[65] while the *Irish Times* considered the sashes both 'chaste and national.'[66] This practice seems to have continued with some variation up to 1890, when it was temporarily decided to substitute rosettes for the scarves or sashes—a decision quickly rescinded by a motion to reinstate scarves 'dyed a deeper shade of green.'[67]

A 'deeper shade of green' may also have been intended in 1903 when, we are told, on the arrival at the Academy of the then Lord Lieutenant, the Earl of Dudley, to receive the loyal address, Dr Jozé 'played the National Anthem of England' on the organ.[68] Perhaps the point was made because on this occasion the presence of the Lord Lieutenant was more than symbolic. From the following letter it is clear that Brady had engineered the occasion for this purpose: 'I have reason to believe that Lord Dudley would like to visit the Academy . . . and that we could introduce matters into the Address, if presented at the Academy, that [he] would not so well appreciate if the address were presented at the Castle . . . I have written to Lord Plunket to let me know Lord Dudley's views on the subject.'[69]

Having been impressed by the Governors' reference in their address to their urgent need for larger accommodation—a point on which they had been pressing the Treasury unsuccessfully for four years—the Lord Lieutenant said:

> I sympathise with your desire for the erection of a fitting temple of music, but while I am ready to do all that I can to further your wishes, I fear that the Treasury, which is never over-eager to loosen the purse-strings, is not the best quarter to turn to at the present juncture. It

would, I think, be a more fruitful task to turn your energies towards obtaining from the Technical Education Committee of Dublin a grant out of the funds which they administer and which come partly from Imperial and partly from local sources.[70]

And perhaps the most telling point of all was in 1895 when the Lord Lieutenant attended the Royal University to present the prizes and the Academy was represented by Bishop Donnelly, Canon MacManus, Brady, Plunkett, W. R. Molloy,[71] Cree, Macartney, and Beardwood—a coalition of unionists and separatists that makes present-day attempts at similar diplomacy seem quite inadequate.

By 1890 the Academy had succeeded in establishing itself in the eyes of central and local government, the law and the musical public as the focus of Ireland's music education. In the previous twenty years it had brilliantly negotiated two government commissions of inquiry, it was incorporated under statute, it had secured an annual grant from Parliament and another from Dublin Corporation, and it was now made financially secure by a very considerable capital sum. These had been won largely from the traditional institutions of power and were to be applied to purposes that gradually drew the Academy, like Ireland itself, away from the ambit of that power and towards new forms of self-determination and self-expression.

There were, of course, highs and lows in the experience and performance of the Academy during the period, especially in the years around 1910, and some controversial and acrimonious episodes, without which no vigorous and ambitious institution is complete. But Harty's recollection of the RIAM in the eighteen-nineties stands the test of time:

> Good honest teaching and general integrity on the part of the principal teachers had begun to discourage that light-hearted facility and self-confidence which has always been the curse of native Irish musical talent. You were not really welcome at the RIAM, for instance, unless you were prepared to work hard and conscientiously at your chosen instrument, and to put self-respect and modesty before conceit and self-sufficiency.[72]

This comment helps to explain why, as in the Paris Conservatoire, virtuosity was not, as one might say, compulsory—rather the opposite: that while exceptional talent would be given its fullest capacity for development, the core values of the institution dictated an emphasis on musicality and the transmission of excellence in teaching and performance (underlined by an increasing tendency towards chamber music) that might or might not have a virtuosic dimension.[73] In 1919 Harty, as extern examiner, could write: 'Even those of no very outstanding talent had apparently been as carefully grounded in essentials as those with great natural gifts.'[74]

During this period the number and nature of the Academy's associations increased. The eighteen-nineties were an extraordinary decade, with the evolution of the Irish National Theatre under Yeats, Gregory, Synge and Martyn—the last two closely involved with the RIAM. Many writers and artists in the larger context of the 'literary renaissance' were related to the Academy through Esposito, not least A. P. Graves and T. W. Rolleston.

The creation by the Academy of the Municipal School of Music in 1890, and its subsequent development up to the point when, in 1905, it was able to take on a quasi-independent existence, is one indicator of the Academy's capacity to grow beyond the confines of its own walls. Another is the inauguration in 1893 of the singing competition for Dublin schools and, in 1894, of the nationwide local centre examination system. The involvement of Annie Patterson and Edith Oldham in the foundation of the Feis Ceoil and Esposito's pioneering of the RDS recitals from 1886 and his creation in 1899 of the Dublin Orchestral Society are examples of the Academy's growing awareness of the need to take part in and, where necessary, lead new initiatives that would bring Dublin and Ireland from a provincial to a self-determining and self-defining status.

Another example of the Academy's ability to bind together diverse and disparate forces is the inclusion of many members of the 'Cecilian' movement, which, from the eighteen-seventies, set out to promote authentic music in Catholic churches and in particular 'to banish from our churches what is certainly known to be profane music.'[75] The author of that statement, who was responsible for the impetus of the movement, was Bishop Donnelly, who at the time it was written had been a member of the Academy's Committee for ten years and who, at his death in 1920 (after sixty years as a governor), was its vice-president. Canon MacManus, his right-hand man in the movement, and Councillor Thomas Mayne MP, Edward Martyn and W. H. Beardwood, also staunch Cecilians,[76] were also Board members for many years, while Vincent O'Brien, a star pupil in the Academy, was deeply involved in church work.

It is ironic that central to this period of growth and development was the figure of Michele Esposito, whose fortuitous arrival at the Academy in 1882 was to set in train the creation of a piano school whose influence is evident in the present Academy and throughout Irish musical life today. Esposito's multifaceted career is reflected elsewhere in this history: in the assessment of Irish composers (chapter 7), in the unfolding story of the local centre examinations (chapter 6), and in the *catalogue raisonné* of Irish pianists and pianism (chapter 12). The mere fact that his work thus permeates the history —the 'Esposito era'—is proof of his paramount importance. Here, it is necessary to complement those aspects of his activity by referring to the ways in which he and his family were connected with educational and performance initiatives and with the cultural, social and even political developments of the times.

In particular, it is necessary to establish the context in which Esposito became such an enigmatic figure within the cultural revival, and such a persuasive figure as the creator of a piano school, because this in turn helps us to understand the complex commutation between national and international aspirations within the Academy and in the development of Irish music generally. We shall therefore discuss, firstly, Esposito's personal and family background, his place in the evolution of Irish music, and then his role in the inauguration of the RDS recitals and the Dublin Orchestral Society. We shall also describe the inauguration of the Feis Ceoil at this point in so far as the issues involved in its evolution relate to Academy personnel and preoccupations.

Michele Esposito was born in 1855 at Castellammare di Stabia, a small town in the environs of Naples, one of seventeen children of a small-time ferry captain, Domenico Esposito, and an illiterate peasant woman, Rosa d'Angelo. His grandson Mario would write that Domenico was 'an energetic, serious, severe man who easily lost, and just as easily regained, his temper.'[77] Michele seems to have inherited these characteristics. His musical abilities having been discovered early by a local schoolmaster, he was educated at the Naples Conservatory, where his teachers were Beniamino Cesi for piano and Paolo Serrao for composition. Here he befriended Giuseppe Martucci, who was to become a noted composer and director of the conservatory. Cesi was a pupil of Thalberg, and so we reach the first point at which Esposito's background fulfils a kind of pre-scripted role for him in Irish music: since Kalkbrenner had taught Thalberg, Thalberg taught Cesi, and Cesi taught Esposito, Elizabeth Coulson's ambition for an academy that would give expression to the 'incomparable method of Kalkbrenner' bore fruit in Esposito's presence in Dublin as professor of piano—a form of apostolic succession continued to this day in the teaching in the Academy by so many of Esposito's piano 'grandchildren'.

In 1879 Esposito eloped to London with, and married, his piano student Natalia Klebnikova, daughter of an émigré Russian scientist from the University of St Petersburg, Peter Klebnikov, who was living near Naples and whom he had met at a piano recital by Anton Rubinstein (who had been impressed with Esposito's playing). They moved to Paris, where he found teaching work and gave several recitals and where the financially independent Natalia established a salon at which Massenet, Gounod, Pleyel and Saint-Saëns (who became a friend and confidant of Esposito) were frequent guests. Esposito's brother Eugenio had in the meantime started what was to prove an unspectacular career in Russia. It was in Paris that Michele received news from Luigi Caracciolo, another Neapolitan contemporary, that there was a vacancy at the RIAM.

We have referred to the fortuitous nature of Esposito's position in Dublin. If Michael Quarry had not resigned in 1882, Esposito might have found permanent employment elsewhere. Like several of his compatriots, he might have come to Dublin for only a few years. (The short time spent by Busoni at the Helsinki Academy, 1888–90, is an interesting parallel, as it shows us that a colossal figure may have an influence out of all proportion to the space it occupies in his own biography.) Without Esposito, the remarkable piano school would probably not have been established. It is obvious that if he had not come to Dublin, some other teacher would have succeeded Quarry and might possibly have become central to the musical life of Ireland as Esposito did; but the most important fact about him, and about music in Ireland from 1882 to 1928 and beyond, is that he did teach piano, very effectively. Everything else to do with his life—including his astonishing energy and the way he channelled it—radiates from this.

Arriving in Dublin, Natalia Esposito re-established her salon, firstly at Ardenza Terrace, Monkstown; but the family was to live at several addresses, in Ballsbridge, Clonskeagh, and Ranelagh.[78] He seems to have accepted with equanimity the decision of Dublin folk to alter the pronunciation of his name (Esposíto) to a version of their own (Espósito), while his wife, who was conventionally referred to as 'Madame' and was, in her son's words, 'an atheist, indifferent—hostile even—to religion,'[79] associated with artistic circles in which she would later be followed by two of her daughters. In 1904 we find her translating Synge's *Riders to the Sea* into Russian and French, although neither version has survived,[80] and she was also wardrobe mistress for the play's first production. She died in Florence in 1944, aged eighty-seven, having outlived her husband by fifteen years.

The first of the Esposito children, Bianca, had been born in Paris in 1879. The others—Vera, Nina and Mario—were born in Dublin. Of Nina we know very little, except that she was expelled from Alexandra College for bad behaviour[81] and subsequently went to live in Italy, where she married Luigi Porcelli, moved to Milan, and had eight children, at least one of whom was alive in 1994.[82] Her three siblings, none of whom had any children, were, like their father, to play a significant part in the unrolling history of Irish culture and nationalism.

Bianca was the child nearest to her father. She stayed with him throughout the Dublin years and taught Italian both at the RIAM and at the Berlitz School in Dublin. Beside the Elsner sisters (above, p. 141–2), she has a place in the life and art of Samuel Beckett. It is clear that her knowledge of Italian literature was extensive, since she not only taught Italian to Beckett (at the Elsner sisters' establishment in Ely Place) but also opened to him a window on Dante's work; in his story 'Dante and the Lobster' in *More Pricks than Kicks* she is portrayed as 'Adriana Ottolenghi'. From 1912 to 1917 she taught Italian at the RIAM as part of the vocal courses.

Beckett kept with him throughout his life an edition of Dante on which he had worked with Bianca Esposito and in which he had inserted a 'get well' card she had sent him during a minor illness in 1926. When he stayed in the *pensione* of the real Signora Ottolenghi in Florence the following year he visited Natalia Esposito in her retirement at Via Fra Guittone near Fiesole and went on a walking tour with Mario, which he fictionalised in *Dream of Fair to Middling Women*.[83]

Beckett was also attracted to Bianca's younger sister Vera, who had been involved in the incipient Abbey Theatre. While Beckett was in Florence, Vera told him of the occasion when her father had been impressed by Joyce's singing (the Espositos had heard him sing several items at a private house on 15 June 1904, the eve of the original 'Bloomsday')—a compliment that Beckett in turn relayed to a gratified Joyce the next year in Paris. Beckett's biographer James Knowlson surmises that she would also have told him of the occasion four days later when she and her mother had had to step over Joyce's drunken and inert body when emerging from a rehearsal of Synge's *The Well of the Saints* in the Camden Hall.[84] Given their father's connection with three major figures of the literary renaissance, it is perhaps not surprising to learn of the Esposito daughters' relationship with Beckett, one of the descendants and subverters of that renaissance.

Vera's connection with the theatre was more than marginal. In addition to the fact that she was frequently called upon to act roles calling for a 'Continental accent', she appeared (using the stage name Emma Vernon) in the premieres of Synge's *Riders to the Sea*, produced by the Irish Literary Society in the Molesworth Hall in 1904 (she played Nora) and of *The Well of the Saints* in 1905 (as Mary Doul).[85] Having played the role of Mrs Tully in the premiere of Lady Gregory's *Spreading the News* in 1904,[86] she attempted unsuccessfully (like one of her colleagues, Synge's sweetheart Molly Allgood) to pursue a stage career in London but returned in 1906. With Lady Gregory, Yeats, Synge and Willie and Frank Fay she had been a signatory of the application for the registration of the National Theatre Society in 1905 but now joined the breakaway Theatre of Ireland, which involved Pádraic Colum, who told her: 'I never see a rose but I think of you.'[87] She also played in several productions elsewhere, including Lydia Languish in *The Rivals*[88] and on at least one occasion sang.

Vera was also an active sympathiser with the IRA—an affiliation suspected by Beckett.[89] On one occasion Michele had to be restrained from lighting the fire laid in the grate because, it was explained to him, there were guns stored up the chimney. Vera and Bianca related this episode to Éamon de Valera when they revisited Ireland in the nineteen-fifties.[90]

The youngest child, Mario, was the most enigmatic, a loner who espoused the cause of freedom. Originally intended by his mother to be a scientist, he became a mediaevalist, specialising in classical studies in the Ireland of the seventh to tenth centuries, to which he was introduced by Richard Best (husband of Edith Oldham)[91] and on which he became a profound and outspoken authority, contributing to *Hermathena*, the *Zeitschrift für Celtische Philologie*, the *Proceedings of the Royal Irish Academy*, and the first three issues of *Studies* (1912–14). He continued to pursue similar topics throughout his life and also became interested in natural sciences and mediaeval alchemy.[92] Elected a member of the RIA in 1913 at the early age of twenty-two, he has been described as having done 'more than any scholar before or since him to appreciate and define Latin learning in mediaeval Ireland.'[93] His career culminated posthumously in the publication in 1988 of *Latin Learning in Mediaeval Ireland*, a collection of thirteen of his most significant essays.

Mario was subsequently involved with the Italian resistance and in 1944 published an autobiography (of which almost all copies were destroyed by the Nazis) entitled *Montagne, Amore e Libertà*. In later life he was associated with the museum service in Florence, being particularly affected by the devastating floods in the city in 1966.

Mario's abrupt departure from Ireland for Italy in 1922, with his mother and Vera, must appear unusual for a scholar of such propensities, until one realises that, as a former agent of Sinn Féin, his status after independence would have been precarious. Natalia Esposito's apparent decision to quit Ireland on account of the climate, which she had tolerated for the previous forty years, becomes more understandable in the light of her son's and daughter's now unwelcome political history. Until now, Dublin gossip has labelled Mario Esposito as a gun-runner, and the family's involvement in politics has been so far exaggerated that Patricia Boylan, in her history of the United Arts Club, states: 'Maestro Michele Esposito, composer, pianist and conductor . . . would later become a Sinn Féin agent in France.'[94]

A TCD graduate and scholar who had corresponded with Arthur Balfour on mediaeval manuscripts, Mario Esposito may seem an unlikely Sinn Féiner. But we should recall that connections with revolutionary organisations were a feature of many of those involved in university life, among them Eoin MacNeill,[95] while within the Academy George Noble, Count Plunkett, director of the National Museum, a scholar and father of the 1916 poet, patriot and martyr Joseph Mary Plunkett, was a Sinn Féin MP.

J. Bowyer Bell recounts that in 1919 Mario Esposito had been entrusted by Count Plunkett (a Governor of the RIAM since 1891) with £500 to travel to Switzerland to promote the concept of immediate self-determination for Ireland, while simultaneously being entrusted with a separate mission by Michael Collins.[96] Meanwhile Robert Brennan, who in 1916 had commanded the uprising in his native Wexford, describes Mario Esposito (referred to as 'Jean Christophe') in his semi-fictional account of the times as 'extremely shy, sensitive and serious-minded . . . He anticipated that he would have little difficulty in getting Balfour's help in securing a passport, ostensibly to pursue his studies in Paris and Rome.' Brennan describes the fears of both sides of the revolutionary movement[97] that they might have inadvertently employed a British agent. The episode explains Esposito's precipitate exit from Ireland as due to his own fears of reprisal: 'He feared he might be shot . . . Jean Christophe left Ireland and so far as I know he never came back.'[98]

Whether or not the evidence on which this is based is reliable, further evidence has come to the attention of the present editors. Ulick O'Connor, in his biography of Oliver St John Gogarty, states that

> Gogarty had the highest admiration for Collins. He was always ready to help the IRA . . . When Mario Esposito was going as a Sinn Féin agent to France, and it was feared he might be conscripted because of his Italian parentage, Gogarty forged a medical certificate for him.[99]

It is clear, however, from a letter of 1969 from Mario Esposito to Maurice Dockrell (a Governor of the RIAM and nephew of Dr Maurice Dockrell, who had married Vera Esposito) that he had been merely a carrier of messages. Commenting on the appearance of the Gogarty biography, he wrote:

> [The] statement by Gogarty that he had given me a medical certificate to enable me to avoid conscription . . . is true in part, but the document was given to enable me to procure a permit from the police to go to London. De Valera was then in hiding and wished to send messages to

Collins and others in England. As I was not in any way suspected of being a rebel, the permit was immediately granted by Dublin Castle and I was able to carry the messages to Collins and other Sinn Féiners in London and Manchester. Gogarty was a friend of our family and studied Italian with my sister Bianca who found him an excellent student. I am surprised that he should have recorded the fact that he had given a false certificate! Another doctor, himself a Sinn Féiner, had refused to do this. I was never liable for conscription in any country![100]

In the absence of any other comment by him, this is the only evidence in his own words of Mario Esposito's political involvement. It is curious that Mario, whose mind remained active in old age (he was seventy-seven when this letter was written) should not have spoken more extensively about his secret diplomatic mission in 1919 if it was as serious and as consequential as these other accounts suggest. The fact that two of his children were actively involved in the revolutionary movement adds pungency to Michele Esposito's own connection with figures who were central to the cultural militancy of the period, most of all Douglas Hyde.

Esposito amplified the already considerable musical energy and cosmopolitanism of Dublin in the eighteen-eighties. The towering figures of Robinson and Stewart were in place, and his compatriots Caracciolo and Bozzelli had preceded him. The Leipzig-educated Quarry had conveniently left the space that Esposito was to fill so effectively for almost half a century, thereby transforming the Academy and, with it, the practice and perception of music in Ireland.

Yet what was this space? Despite the activity in choral music led by Robinson, there was little chamber music and no regular orchestral concerts. Despite the enormous advance in the educational infrastructure achieved by the Academy since its foundation, there was little visible flowering of the talent it had produced, and little had been done to cultivate the audience for classical music. In one sense therefore it was a green field to which Esposito came as the creator of institutions. As a teacher he filled a space that, with the sole exception of Margaret O'Hea, might otherwise have become a seriously depleted piano school, as we have seen suggested by Mrs Oldham.

It is important to look behind the affective resonance of the name Esposito, to establish exactly where his real significance lay. He was teacher, performer, composer, conductor, activist. He was not a *great* performer, yet his prodigious record of recitals, both solo and with the leading staff members of the RIAM, established his reputation as an undisputed centrepiece in Dublin music-making, as well as firmly placing these colleagues on the performing map. He was not a *great* composer, yet his compositions of the eighteen-nineties and nineteen-hundreds were a timely occurrence, establishing a nexus between the literary renaissance and the Academy, and are still performed and recorded.

It is easy also to accept Esposito's greatness as a teacher without examining how this was achieved. He did not teach composition, and one of the commonplaces of musical history is that he did *not* teach Hamilton Harty.

Yet in 1920 Harty not only called him 'the presiding genius of all that there is of music in Ireland' but said: 'I send him for criticism everything I write . . . he has always been right.'[101] That 'rightness' is the critical faculty that is rooted as much in intuition and instinctiveness as in knowledge and experience.

As a teacher, Esposito introduced the method of his own teacher (who was shortly to take up a position at the St Petersburg Conservatory), which was published in a series of fascicles. In this way Cesi's *Metodo per Pianoforte* became a standard text for Irish piano students. He also introduced the dual-teacher system, whereby a junior or assistant teacher took the pupils one week, concentrating on technique, and he, the senior, taught the second week, with the focus on interpretation—a system that still applies in the RIAM.

For each lesson the pupil was expected to prepare a prelude and fugue by Bach, a movement from a sonata by Beethoven, Mozart, or a similar master, and a study by Cesi, Chopin, Moscheles, or Esposito himself—his *Irish Sketch Book* being a late collection of pieces suitable for middle grade students. The study requirement was designed to introduce the student to as wide and as structured a repertoire as possible. The pupil sat at one grand piano, Esposito at his favourite Erard, sometimes playing in unison with the student and ready to demonstrate whenever necessary—a practice that became eroded over the years because of the prohibitive cost of replacing so many grands but that has recently been reintroduced.

He insisted on good phrasing, tonal gradations, and balance, and in the course of teaching inculcated an understanding of musical structure. At times he was irascible, once seizing a poker and violently beating time with it. At others he could be quietly sarcastic: Rhona Marshall (née Clark) recalled a fellow-student playing a piece by Brahms that she had insufficiently prepared; at the end, Esposito went to the mantelpiece, over which hung a portrait of Brahms, turned the composer's face to the wall, and said nothing.

A picture of Esposito as a teacher has been left us by Enid Starkie, one of a very talented musical family, who, after relinquishing her first love—music—as a career, became a distinguished French scholar at Oxford and an authority on Baudelaire and Rimbaud. (Her father, W. J. M. Starkie, was the last Commissioner of National Education before independence, and her mother was for many years a Governor of the RIAM, where her aunt Ida taught cello and her brother Walter was an outstanding student.) She writes in her autobiography, *A Lady's Child*:

> When we muddled a run or struck a wrong note he used to open his mouth wide, and horrible sounds gushed out from the back of his throat, as if he were gargling. 'Grrr! Grrr! Stop! Stop! Basta!' he used to roar . . . We never knew in what mood we were going to find him. Sometimes he was in a gentle and melancholy mood, and then he played with devastating sadness on his own piano and we were inspired to play better than usual.[102]

Starkie also recalls in the same passage that when, to strengthen her chances of a university scholarship, she was persuaded by her schoolteacher not to enter for the Academy's Vandeleur Scholarship, Esposito's rage was characteristic of 'the boiling lava of the Vesuvius of his native province.' As for his melancholy moods, a slight piece for piano entitled 'Vain Regrets' is thought to have been the embodiment of a particular emotional disappointment (perhaps an amorous one). The piece appeared at Academy concerts quite frequently in the nineteen-twenties and thirties but is seldom heard today.[103]

An idea of Esposito's working day can be glimpsed from the fact that over the average year he taught approximately sixty-five pupils for half an hour each week, besides teaching privately at the nearby Alexandra College (then in Earlsfort Terrace) and Loreto Convent in St Stephen's Green, and further afield at Loreto College in Rathfarnham, Sion Hill in Blackrock, and even the French School in Bray. In addition, meetings of the Board of Studies and, from 1889, of the Board of Governors consumed valuable time, as did work in connection with the RDS, rehearsals and performances of the Dublin Orchestral Society from 1899, and the Sunday afternoon concerts from 1905.[104] Considerable travel was involved when he was on local centre business around the country. Later, in 1915, he and the industrialist and music patron Sir Stanley Cochrane set up a music-publishing enterprise, CE [Cochrane-Esposito] Editions, which took up a great deal of Esposito's time and Cochrane's money and, commercially, was a decided failure.

It is little wonder that between 1882 and 1897 Esposito composed nothing, or that he had no time for practice. In 1901 Annie Patterson observed that 'the public and his professional brethren marvel at how this talented and untiringly active gentleman is able to accomplish all that he does . . . He is the soul of energy and verveful activity and invariably infects even the laziest and most apathetic.'[105]

With hindsight, it is surprising that it was to Elgar, rather than to Esposito, that Yeats and Moore had turned in their search for a composer of incidental music for their *Diarmuid and Grania* in 1900–01. By then, Esposito had written the cantata *Deirdre* and the prize-winning composition at the inaugural Feis Ceoil in 1897 and was working on the 'Irish Symphony', the suite 'Roseen Dhu' (to words by Alfred Perceval Graves), and, perhaps most significantly of all, Hyde's *The Tinker and the Fairy*. If there was, in the terms employed by both Anglo-Ireland and Irish Ireland, a 'battle of two civilisations'[106] between nationalism and internationalism, between indigenous traditions and an imported or imposed culture, then Esposito's position as a respected foreigner, with no ties to England, might have provided a bridge between them.

In one sense, music did not touch the literary renaissance, because the renaissance hardly concerned itself with music. And one reason for the comparative overshadowing of the Academy in public life was that when, in Joep Leerssen's words, 'living Irish culture was becoming the badge of nationality and nationalism,'[107] the musical branch of this culture was not to be found in the Academy. If institutional music was absent from the cultural palette of nationalism, the neglect lay on both sides; the epitome of hyphenation in the emerging sense of a national theatre was the production of *Diarmuid and Grania*, for which no Irish composer could be found to provide the incidental music.[108] It is a tantalising footnote to the history of the Academy that the only candidate considered for the task was one of its former students, J. M. Synge, whose musical legacy remains a presence in the Academy.

In both music and literature, Ireland had been diminished and impoverished by the imposition of English laws and manners, by the natural implosion of a culture geographically marginal, and by the haemorrhage of famine deaths and subsequent waves of emigration. Davis's schemes for raising literacy—the reading rooms, the 'Library of Ireland', and the *Nation*—succeeded in creating the essential base on which the 'literary renaissance' would build. Similar initiatives in the field of Irish music did not enjoy the same success. When, therefore, Yeats and others began to conceive a literature that could both reclaim an ancient Ireland and create a new one, latent energies could be brought to the task. If Stanford had stayed in Dublin he might have become the Yeats of Anglo-Irish music and so put composition onto a footing similar to the creation of a literature. As it was, in the musical initiatives that did take place—chiefly associated with the Feis Ceoil—and that ran parallel to the literary movement, the impetus came chiefly from figures closely connected with, and deeply sympathetic to, the Academy. Therefore, although music did not enjoy the same impetus, literature by no means enjoyed an automatic success—a success that at least in theory was also open to music. Nor, given the power of music as a medium of nationalism, was it by any means valid at the time to assume that a literary endeavour would gain popular momentum more easily than musical initiatives.

Furthermore, in both music and literature the field, however fertile, was at first bare. It will already be apparent that there were few Irish composers of any stature. Smith and Stevenson were negligible, Stewart largely spancelled by his church preoccupations; Balfe, Wallace and Stanford had chosen the European route; Esposito composed nothing between his appointment in 1882 and 1897, when *Deirdre* (described by Harry White as 'a major encounter between music and the literary revival')[109] becomes the first significant point in this stage of the history. By comparison, William Carleton, surveying the equivalent literary scene in 1863, could name only Griffin, Banim and himself as writers of merit in a 'transition state' that he presciently said would last half a century.[110] Into the eighteen-eighties the literary scene could still be described as one of 'paralysis'.[111]

The political ferment would have to die down before the arts could find the 'window of opportunity' presented by the death of Parnell and harness the energy no longer occupied with politics. 'The times are highly unfavourable for the cultivation of the intellectual faculties of Irishmen,' wrote *United Ireland* in 1889.[112] And when, in 1890, Justin McCarthy was asked whether there was a distinct national literature growing in Ireland, he replied that there was 'no great Irish poet, no great Irish novelist, no great Irish dramatist.'[113] This was due partly to the lack of infrastructure: 'Publishers and politics long ago killed literary activity in Dublin, and it does not look now that they will bring it back to life,' said Frank MacDonagh in 1892,[114] while another (anonymous) opinion held that 'there is no water in Ireland now which will turn the mill-wheel of letters.'[115]

Music, by contrast, had been moving forward during the period in which Home Rule occupied the hearts and minds of figures like Charles Oldham. But it was a progress towards the consolidation of a certain type of musical education and expression, which almost completely excluded 'Irish' music. It is this failure to join like with unlike, to bring the compositional skills and the orchestral palette to bear on Irish themes, that has permanently inhibited the evolution of a 'school' of Irish music and has left us with the small output of Esposito, Larchet and their successors at home, and of Stanford and Harty in the international context (as discussed by Jeremy Dibble and Axel Klein in chapter 8).[116]

Harry White makes the telling point that whereas in literature 'a dying culture was in part redeemed by the passage of one literature into the language of another . . . no such transition was available in music'[117] and that in addition to a 'language question' there was also a 'music question'— one that remained, and perhaps still remains, unanswered.

It must also be emphasised that it was not the function of the Academy to create a school of composition. It can certainly be argued with hindsight that the institution as a whole might have been more involved in whatever debate did take place in the eighteen-nineties. It was left to individual figures to become involved, and of these, Esposito was hardly likely to be predisposed to a debate on the nature of Irishness in art. As it turned out, however, he was more involved than most others—by action and example rather than through discussion—in the creation of Irish music. But the original IAM had no view of musical composition nor any ambition in that direction, and the constant problem of the presence or absence of theory teaching in its first four decades revolved around the question of the musicianship of its students as performers, rather than their capacity as creators.

It is significant that the discussion of Irish music should have been oriented towards opera and other text-based music, as distinct from purely chamber or symphonic music—opera being the popular idiom of the time. The referential combination of music and text is typical of the form of nationalism that would see Esposito's 'Irish' music intimately associated with the literature of the revival.[118]

The fortunes of Irish music-theatre composition were at this time resting on the narrow shoulders of O'Brien Butler and Robert O'Dwyer. The former (whose real name was Whitwell) wrote an Irish-language opera *Muirgheis* or *The Sea Swan* (1903) and the music to Thomas Mac Donagh's 'Marching Song for the Irish Volunteers'. In 1905 we find Synge writing to Lady Gregory: 'I tried to find out from the Espositos what is thought of O'Brien Butler's music, but I did not hear anything very definite. They evidently do not consider him a person of any importance, but I do not think Signor Esposito has ever heard his music.'[119] In 1910 O'Dwyer's Irish-language opera *Eithne* (with libretto by Father Tomás Ó Ceallaigh) was produced at the Gaiety Theatre, receiving a most unappreciative review in the *Evening Mail* by Harold White, headed 'Has Irish opera artistic value?' Although the work showed O'Dwyer to be 'a musician of distinct ability,' demonstrating affinities with both Verdi and Wagner, White was 'not quite certain . . . why anybody should compose an Irish opera . . . I entirely fail to see the wisdom, from a musical point of view.'[120] If opera were to be a vehicle for Irish, he thought popular operas such as *Carmen* or *Faust* could be translated. 'One cannot claim that the music is any more Irish than "Madame Butterfly" is Japanese or "La Bohème" is French.'

By contrast, Annie Patterson, committed to promoting the future of Irish music, saw opera as a way of promoting native talent. It was perhaps Stanford's own conviction of the necessity for a 'National Opera' in Britain[121] that persuaded her to see it within an inclusively 'British' context. In October 1900 she contributed three articles to the *Weekly Irish Times* on 'The prospects of native opera', 'How to aid British music', and 'The renaissance of British music'. In the first, she set out her views by stressing the need to regard music as an 'elevating and ennobling' art, identifying the Faust legend as 'an allegory of the human soul,' praising Wagner, in particular *Parsifal*. She then, by contrast, criticised the *libretti* of *Cavalleria rusticana* and *Pagliacci* as 'depraved and coarse' and, instead, praised Balfe's *Bohemian Girl* and Wallace's *Maritana* for their essential melody, symmetry, and rhythm.

Her vocabulary is ambivalent to the extent that, having stated that 'the old Gaelic legends teem with material for powerful and graceful *libretti*,' she then says that 'what we really want is a British Wagner—one of ourselves who understands the genius of our people.' Balfe and Wallace are not merely regarded as 'British' but are promoted to a place at the forefront:

> It really is a slur upon these islands that we have no School of Native Opera, and must, forsooth, draw upon Continental nations for our repertoire . . . For the honour of Great Britain let us not permit another century to pass without giving Balfe and Wallace some worthy, and perchance, still more distinguished companions.[122]

The meaning of Patterson's notion of 'British' music becomes clearer in her third article, where she says: 'We Kelts and Saxons can metaphorically shake hands with each other and consider ourselves the most gifted denizens of the globe'—except that in music 'we are playing second fiddle to the foreigner.' 'Can it be true that we Britishers are indeed unmusical? . . . We British people must arouse ourselves and unite in one common cause to rescue from oblivion the native musical art of our country.'

Bringing the argument nearer to the readers of the *Irish Times*, she then asks, 'Why not a British Bayreuth in Dublin?' She advocates establishing it at the Theatre Royal, and goes on to say that 'the burning question is, should a strong combination to launch Native Opera really be set agoing, will the public support a movement for the rise and encouragement of a school of indigenous dramatic musical production?' Not only in opera but throughout the musical spectrum she believed that a way must be found of creating employment for the graduates of the music colleges, thereby simultaneously stimulating conditions for the composition, performance and appreciation of contemporary music by 'British' composers but principally in an 'endeavour to work out a distinctive school of our own.'

'Either we have no musical talent worth exploiting in Great Britain and Ireland or else Native musical talent has no means of outlet.'[123] At home there were encouraging signs: 'Five years ago oblivion and scorn shrouded Irish music and the Irish composer. Now the Feis Ceoil is in full swing. Irish melodies, once termed vulgar, are to-day the fashion in our drawingrooms, and on our concert platforms.' Furthermore, she pointed to recent interest by the Carl Rosa and Moody-Manners opera companies in indigenous productions, citing *The Emerald Isle* by Sullivan (who was to die within the month, leaving the opera to be completed by Edward German) as a 'new Irish opera' of which much was to be expected, adding that 'a good opera upon topics of native interest is badly wanted on the British stage.'[124] But generally, London was asleep: operas were not sung in English at Covent Garden; Manns had been replaced at the modern-minded Crystal Palace concerts; and in contemporary music Bournemouth (where, since 1893, Dan Godfrey and the then Bournemouth Municipal Orchestra had been championing British music) had taken the lead, and continued to do so until at least 1939.

A year later, reporting the proceedings of the Pan-Celtic Congress in August 1901, Patterson made one of a very small number of references to a concatenation of cultural initiatives, in which the Society for the Preservation of the Irish Language, the Gaelic League, the Feis Ceoil and the Irish Literary Society are listed as the chief bodies involved in this awakening of the 'Irish Kelt'. It is pointedly stated that 'the unearthing of the Folk Music of the country' preceded the literary revival. The non-sectarian aspect of these departures is also strongly noted:

> At first our Saxon neighbours . . . looked askance at all such movements, and darkly hinted at all sorts of sinister outcomes; but when it became evident that the gatherings, and especially the musical ones, were bringing together on the one platform every possible shade of creed, caste, and politics, a different and more generous feeling became prevalent. In a prosaic and workaday world it is beginning to be recognized that the Kelt, from time immemorial, has been the presiding genius over the spiritual philosophy of Western Europe.[125]

The following week, however, Patterson was looking for a development from the basic and innate merit of folk music to a broader spectrum—one that has been constantly resisted not only by many traditionalists but also, it can be argued, by the material itself.

> Modern music, with its great polyphonic forms of the opera, oratorio, symphony, quartet, has taught us to look for greater breadth and more development than is to be found in a tune, no matter how delicious, of

eight to sixteen bars . . . We would not alter the folk song proper. Let it be as it is, in its native loveliness, and completeness of design, but let us remember it is a piece of music *in miniature* and that modern Keltic musicians, if they wish to make their musical art progressive, instead of multiplying the number of folk melodies, must build on the already existent basis a *new school* of composition which shall be as distinct as possible. The problem is to unite the *flavour* of Gaelic, or Kymric, melodic design with the *form* of the modern concert aria or song.[126]

Recognising, by now, that large-scale works such as operas and symphonies would be unviable for perhaps fifty years, she urged composers to concentrate on 'Gaelic chamber music', with Dvořák as their model.

Theo Gmür, the Swiss composer, organist and teacher resident in Cork, said in 1901 that 'the field is still open for the formation of a purely "Irish school" of native composition' but asked: 'When *will* Irish composers *believe* in themselves?'[127] Five years later Esposito echoed this point when he was interviewed for the *Freeman's Journal* by the writer and actor James Cousins, under the heading 'Irish music—a chance for Irish composers'. Here Esposito was described as having 'grown into our civic and national life more truly and firmly than many an individual who is Irish only by the accident of birth' and as having a 'grasp . . . of our heritage of melody and imagination compared with the puny knowledge possessed by many of us who think ourselves factors in the "movement".'[128]

Esposito took the lead in the interview by asking, 'What is 'Irish' music? . . . Is Brian Boru's March Irish music? . . . Well, give me the composer's score and I'll play it. But you can't. You can only give me a melody sixteen bars long; no harmony, no expression . . . Where is your Irish music, then?' Asked if he had little sympathy with 'an Irish School of Music', Esposito replied:

> On the contrary, I have every sympathy, but I think there is too much loose thinking on the subject. Some people want us to play or sing nothing but old airs. Others want us to harmonise according to ancient modes. We hear of certain pieces not being 'Irish' and we hear it said 'That's Irish' because something in a song makes one remember some other air which is regarded as Irish. But there is no standard and if there was a standard, why shouldn't modern music be as much Irish as single, primitive melodies . . . Music is a universal voice. Every development in the art belongs to the whole world. If your Irish composers use every modern device of the orchestra their music will be none the less Irish . . .
>
> [Irish music will not exist] because a composer has consciously restricted himself so that he may write in a special mode. Your lovely Irish airs are not Irish because they are written in a particular mode. They are Irish because they are the expression of the emotions of Irish people. You will not get a school of Irish music by mechanical means. The music that the future will call Irish will be written by Irishmen and will be Irish by virtue of something of his race—consciousness which his music will set free—no matter what his creed or political opinions may be. And your

composers will be recognised as Irish even though their music may differ as widely as Mozart and Wagner—both Germans. They will be 'national' in the same way that Dvořák and Grieg and Brahms are national. Their music reflects the spirit of their country, not because they have copied notes from the past, but because they have given themselves free expression as regards form and harmony, while at the same time utilising the rhythms and character of the folk-music of their country. My advice to Irish composers is to master their art as musicians to the fullest possible extent, then go back to the wonderful store of folk-melodies and build them into their music.

Here the figure of Synge represents a tantalising example of 'what might have been' in this transitional, or translational, phase. If Esposito in his many guises was the presiding presence in the Academy, Synge, in his absence from it, also has a ghostly relevance. Like most of his fellow-students, Synge was an enthusiastic amateur, studying violin first, privately, with Patrick Griffith and from 1889 at the RIAM with Theodore Werner and composition with Stewart. Unlike most of his contemporaries, however, he wished for a career in music. Werner is said to have told him that as a violinist 'he would never make a success . . . on account of his extreme nervousness.'[129] But as a writer his surviving compositions indicate that he was above average. These include a scherzo for string quartet, and movements of violin sonatas, which were performed at the RIAM in 1971 on the centenary of his birth.[130] On the strength of similar work, Synge was awarded a scholarship in composition in 1892. We know that he was working hard at a string symphony, a clarinet quartet, and, most interestingly of all, an opera, *Eileen Aroon*.

In addition to the lecture notes quoted in the preceding chapter, there is ample evidence in Synge's unpublished diaries of the composition studies and original work that he was undertaking at this time.[131] His literary and musical interests were proceeding in parallel—and, in the case of *Eileen Aroon*, merging, since he was working on both the music and the libretto. In January 1893 he was working on a violin sonata in G minor, which by February he had decided to arrange as a suite for string orchestra. By the end of February he had begun to refer to this as a 'string symphony'. On Saturday 20 May 1893 we find the statement 'Started words and music of an opera on Eileen Aroon,' on which he worked for the following month, up to the day he left Ireland for Germany. In the meantime he was going to the Academy to show Stewart his composition studies (mainly counterpoint, including one in twelve parts for two choirs) as well as to take lessons from Werner.[132] Works he studied included Wieniawski's mazurkas, Viotti's concertos, and Tartini's first sonata.

He also joined Francis Cruise's private Instrumental Club, which, on Henry Doyle's proposal, had been meeting at the Academy for some years, where he heard Mozart's Wind Quintet and Schubert's 'Unfinished' Symphony (on 22 February), the Mozart Clarinet Quintet and the 'Eroica' Symphony (on 15 March), the *Tannhäuser* march and Haydn's 'Kaiser' Quartet and Symphony in D (22 March), and Beethoven's First Symphony

and String Quartet, op. 18 No. 5 (23 May). On Saturday 25 March he heard
Sir Charles and Lady Hallé in recital at the Leinster Hall; his ticket cost him
a shilling (two pounds today). On 17 April his cousin, the pianist Mary
Synge, had given a recital at the Antient Concert Rooms, which he had
helped to arrange and at which he acted as steward. In addition to the solo
items (Beethoven's 'Pathétique' Sonata, a prelude by Mendelssohn, a capriccio
by Rheinberger, Schumann's Carnaval, a nocturne by Liszt, and 'Idyll' by
Jensen) she was 'assisted' in the programme with items by Werner and
Bast.[133] A few days later, Synge recorded having played Schubert's Violin
Sonata in D and Haydn's in G with her. Mary Synge had offered to give a
lecture at the Academy while in Dublin, but after her proposal had been
considered by Esposito and Jozé it was, rather surprisingly, declined.[134]

A typical day in Synge's life involved practice (usually two or three
hours at both piano and violin), analysis of prescribed work (Schubert's A
minor Sonata being a standard exercise), composition study, reading literature (Jonson, Dryden, Coleridge, and Shakespeare) and walking or horse-
riding, which would take him round the locality of Carrickmines, Foxrock,
and Glencullen. 'Practised on a dandelion stalk till I mastered the reed
sound, and brought three corncrakes across a field by it,' he recorded on 26
May.

In 1891 he joined the Academy orchestra, which at that time was a major
subject of interest to the Governors, who had been trying to stimulate
interest in cello, double bass, and wind (the wind under the tuition of van
Maanen, who was attached to the Constabulary Band). Synge's nephew
Edward Stephens recorded:

> He was shy at first when he began practising with his fellow-students,
> but he soon lost all self-consciousness and felt that, in the orchestra, he
> had become part of a composite body with one mind and one ideal. It
> was when he achieved this sense of identity with his fellow-students that
> he seemed to enter on a new stage of his life.[135]

Synge himself recalled:

> The collective passion produced by a band working together with one will
> and ideal is unlike any other exaltation . . . One is lost in a blind tempest
> that wails around one with always beautiful passion, the identity is merged
> in a symmetrical joy . . . yet one remains sane and a man[136] . . . When I
> found in the orchestra the world of magical beauty I had dreamed of, I
> threw aside all reasonable counsel and declared myself a professional
> musician.[137]

His mother was greatly disturbed by this declaration, and, by way of 'reasonable counsel', enrolled the help of her son-in-law, who advised Synge
'very strongly not to think of making it a profession. Harry told him that
all men who do take to drink. And they are not a nice set of men either.'[138]
Synge, however, saw it as part of the artistic life that he had recognised as
his future: 'Every life is a symphony, and the *translation* of this life into
music, and from music back to literature or sculpture or painting, is the
real effort of the artist.'[139]

But eventually he decided that it was to literature his talent should primarily turn. His musical longing, which was heightened by his experience of a dream in the Aran Islands, almost exclusively recurred in the form of music for strings. 'A resonance as searching as the strings of the 'cello . . . grew into an ecstasy where all existence was lost in a vortex of movement,'[140] and was set down on paper as 'Étude Morbide' (1899), an 'imaginary portrait' that encapsulates his passion for the violin and his fear of pursuing it. But he never abandoned music as a source of images and language: he continued to mark musical expressions in the margins of his work and, in a memorable episode in his Aran notebook, wrote of the changing sky in terms of symphonic movements; 'there is not any affectation in borrowing a term from music, no pictorial wording can express these movements.'

It was Synge's musicality, and his quest for an adequate 'music' to express his emotions, that led him to find a voice, and a literature, for the Irish national theatre, which placed the innate strophes and cadences of Gaelic speech within a Hiberno-English language of his own creation, similar to the voice that Sibelius gave to Finnish music, or Grieg to Norwegian. This 'soundscape', as Ann Saddlemyer calls it,[141] was described in an unpublished essay, 'The Duality of Literature', in which Synge says that folk melodies 'contain their own signature in a way complex art cannot do' and that original folk poetry has its own music, 'conceived with the words in [the poet's] moment of excitement.'[142] It was the immediacy of the musical speech achieved by Synge that enabled Vaughan Williams to give a literal note-for-word setting to his opera of Synge's *Riders to the Sea*—a speech so closely attuned to the music of original thought that it has a uniqueness, a signature, seldom found in composition. If Synge had realised his ambition of writing the opera *Eileen Aroon* it would have been more than a graceful footnote to Irish music and drama.

In a wry comment on the founding of the GAA in 1884, F. S. L. Lyons observes: 'It was necessary to give to Irish nationalism an intellectual basis more profound and exacting than an amiable enthusiasm for Gaelic pastimes or a less amiable detestation of "foreign" games.'[143] But 'foreign', whether it meant games or other cultural pursuits, remained anathema to many, whose unwavering predilection for things Irish would be encapsulated by 1905 in the term 'Irish Ireland' and the slogan 'The Gael must be the element that absorbs.'[144] The utopian vision of a Gaelic nation restored to unspecified conditions was still being articulated, albeit vestigially, as recently as 1969 by Máirtín Ó Cadhain, in speaking of 'the war for the repossession of Ireland.'[145]

Ironically, it was Irish Ireland that decried the genre created by Synge. Arthur Griffith fulminated against *In the Shadow of the Glen*: 'Cosmopolitanism never produced a great artist or a good man yet, and never will . . . If the Irish theatre ceases to reflect Irish life and embody Irish aspiration the world will wing its head away from it.'[146] Thus, if it seems as if music's secondary or tertiary position vis-à-vis the other arts, especially literature, pushed it into a limbo from which, as a 'creative intelligence' (in Harry

White's expression), it has never fully re-emerged, we must also recall that literature itself suffered an almost equally reductive transition. We do not know how Synge's work would have developed had he lived longer (he died in 1909, aged thirty-seven); but we do know that Yeats's own experiment with a literature open to foreign influences failed to capture the imagination of his audience, or indeed of his own theatre company, while the crushing experience of literary censorship, in the nineteen-thirties and forties in particular but continuing into the seventies, suppressed not only writing but the horizons of writers.

In 1900 Brendan Rodgers, writing in the *New Ireland Review*, said: 'We have amongst us those who consider that Irish music should stop short in its development, who ask us to remain content with traditional tunes and melodies, and who anathematise all such modern inventions as cantatas, overtures, symphonies, sonatas, etc. as . . . utterly unsuited to the Irish temperament and genius.'[147] The nub of the problem, then, is the question of confidence in relation to musical *form*. Clearly, without a sea-change in the approach to musical form in the RIAM, Irish musical energies could only be accommodated within the genre of mainstream art music—which therefore admitted only that kind of 'arrangement' of traditional airs acceptable to the *salon*.[148]

In 1902 Esposito had written the operetta *The Post-Bag*, subtitled *A Lesson in Irish*. It was his second collaboration with A. P. Graves—the first being 'Roseen Dhu'. Graves, an official of the Board of Education, was a friend of George Grove and the son of the bishop who had been a founder of the Academy. Frank Fay, one of the pillars of the early Abbey Theatre, objected that 'an Irish opera or operetta to satisfy us cannot be composed by a foreigner.'[149] The fact that Esposito wrote *The Post-Bag* and *The Tinker and the Fairy*, and that at one point he was collaborating with Moore, Cousins and George Coffey on a projected opera on the Deirdre theme,[150] suggests that Fay may have been in a minority, and it is possible to see Esposito, at least as much as Stanford, O'Brien Butler, or O'Dwyer, as a fulcrum in the attempted creation of a national, or nationalist, music-theatre. Of the composer of the cantata *Deirdre* (text by Rolleston), Harry White says:

> Esposito was an accomplished, if not especially original, composer whose piano music in particular comprises an authoritative meditation on the vocabulary and structures of a late nineteenth-century European tradition. That tradition speaks in *Deirdre*, but it does not speak to Ireland in any special way . . . Yet in its very emancipation from the burden of folk-song quotation and/or arrangement, Esposito's setting inherently argues the key question in Irish music at the turn of the century: whether or not an imaginative musical response to the myths of the revival could survive the ideological weight of the oral tradition.[151]

It is also instructive to note that White observes in relation to the song cycle 'Roseen Dhu' that the Irish air which forms the basis of each setting is identified beneath Graves's title, and the rubric 'arr. M Esposito' explicitly indicates the composer's secondary (even tertiary) role in the process of artistic production: first the text, then the pre-existent Irish air, then the arrangement by Esposito . . . Once again the arrangement of ethnic melody had come to seem like a *sine qua non* in Irish art music . . . The encounter between the European aesthetic and the ideological pull of the ethnic tradition which [Esposito's] work manifests is one which was destined to become central as Irish composers struggled to find a voice in the new century.[152]

Esposito's largest undertaking of this kind was with Douglas Hyde in the one-act opera *The Tinker and the Fairy*. Once again, the circumstances are as important as the achievement. The music first manifested itself as incidental to Hyde's play *An Tincéir agus an tSidheóg*, which was first performed (after much altercation between Moore and Hyde about its translation into English) on a memorable occasion in 1902 in George Moore's garden in Ely Place, Dublin, with a mixed audience partly composed of delegates to the Oireachtas.[153] Hyde played the part of the tinker and Sinéad Ní Fhlannagáin (later the wife of Éamon de Valera) that of the fairy.[154] This incidental music was subsequently arranged for concert performance and was given at least once by the RIAM Students' Musical Union about 1908. In 1909 the play was worked into an opera and performed the following year by the Dublin Amateur Opera Society (with Nettie Edwards in the principal role); it received lukewarm praise from the *Irish Times* and tepid criticism from Griffith in *Sinn Féin*.

Esposito, having resumed a compositional career interrupted by his teaching duties from 1882 to 1897, was to go on to write several other works with Irish themes or inspirations. His position continued to be ambiguous, and one would give much to know what reflections he might have made on subsequent attempts to synthesise the traditional and classical genres. But he had earned his place among Irish composers, if not as an Irish composer *per se*—so much so that in the nineteen-seventies Dublin Corporation included Esposito Road in the south-west suburb of Crumlin, along with roads dedicated to Bunting, Thomas Moore, Wallace, Moeran, Dowland, Percy French, O'Dwyer and O'Brien and avenues named for John McCormack, Harty, and Hardebeck, Balfe earning both a road and an avenue and Stanford a green.

Within the Academy board-room, the issue of 'national' music became divisive in 1896, when Brady, who had presented an annual prize for 'national music' for several years, offered to augment the award by means of two new prizes for performances of Moore's melodies 'as arranged by Sir John Stevenson and Sir Henry Bishop in order to preserve the memories of the past and musicians [*sic*].'[155] It is clear that opposition to this proposal had been mooted before the meeting, since a vote was called for—an unusual occurrence on an apparently uncontroversial matter. With Brady, Dean Greene, Molloy, Browne, Macredy and Beardwood voting in favour and Robinson, Esposito, Drury, Plunkett, Sexton and Cree against, Brady as chairman stated that it would be inappropriate for him to cast a deciding vote, and the offer was withdrawn.

At the next meeting Plunkett proposed a counter-measure, 'two prizes for Irish music (Instrumental) namely one given for the best performance of an Irish air on the pianoforte and one . . . on the harp. I am happy', he pointedly added, 'to leave the selection of the music to the judgement of the Board.'[156] Regrettably, we know no more of the reasons for the rejection of Brady's offer or of Plunkett's alternative.

Brady seems to have recouped some of his embarrassment three years later, when he 'handed in [a] cheque from Messrs. Matterson of Limerick [as a] prize of £2.2.0 annually for 5 years for best singer of an Irish melody from the collection of Moore arranged by Sir John Stevenson and Sir Henry Bishop.'[157] A decade later his son-in-law Col. Jervis White would make a donation that topped up the capital and allowed the National Music Prize to continue in existence.

Brady's advancement of Moore's works within the Academy should be seen in the light of the wider, and unfinished, contemporary debate over the status of Irish music in relation to nationalism. Harry White has argued that Moore provided 'the secular hymn book of Irish nationalism'[158] and that

> Moore's Melodies . . . endowed the repertory with a sense of dispossession which attained to conventional status; they supplied an influential precedent for the use of Irish music as an agent of political advancement and they confirmed a widespread tendency to regard the function of music in Ireland as an intelligencer of verbal feeling . . . The understanding of Ireland which Moore purveyed . . . was one which gained admission to the contemporary English mind through an arch-romantic synthesis of legend, political allusion, personal sentiment and domesticated Celticism.

It can be easily recognised that such a 'version' of Ireland would be acceptable to the social and political milieu predominant in the RIAM. It successfully translated an element of Irishness too raw—or unknown and unknowable—for the drawing-room into a tamer, more assimilable product that could recognise the sense of displacement from the creative heartlands in such titles as 'She is far from the land' or 'I wish I was by that dim lake'. There are two ways of thinking about this: if it thereby excluded or reduced its authenticity it did Irish Ireland a disservice; if, however, it introduced an otherwise hostile or distant audience to musical experiences that it might otherwise not have heard, it at least opened the possibility of creating awareness of and interest in the musical sources of the songs.

It is a commonplace that the chief audience for this 'translation' was 'the contemporary English mind', but in Brady's scheme we can see—and perhaps this is of even greater significance—that the Anglo-Irish mind was being introduced to something in its own cultural background and that that mind was in greater need of such introduction than its English counterpart. Moore was, after all, the only means of access to 'national' music for many decades.

In view of the connection between Moore and the Hudson family, who were so important in the inception of the Academy, it is salutary to remind ourselves of the common origin of so many of the Academy's founders in the O'Connellite and Young Ireland traditions and of the fact that nationalism, whatever its calibre, always has on its agenda the attempt, in Séamus Deane's words, 'to create a counter-culture and to define it as authentic to the nation.'[159]

The close association between the Academy and the concern for authenticity and the promulgation of traditional music is nowhere more evident than on the occasion of a lecture by A. P. Graves in 1912 on the work of Petrie. The occasion was the 'Margaret Stokes Lecture' at Alexandra College, at which the chairman was Sir Gabriel Stokes, a vice-president of the RIAM from 1912 to 1920, who reminded the audience that Graves had known Petrie as a visitor to the house of his father, the bishop. During the lecture, examples of Petrie's collection of folk music were played by Arthur Darley, himself a noted collector and one of an 'Academy family', who had been senior professor of violin from 1900 to 1903. 'Played without accompaniment and unharmonised,' the *Irish Times* reported, 'it was possible to realise the sheer beauty of melody which marks the old Irish music.'[160] The lecture coincided with an exhibition of Petrie's work at the National Museum organised by its director, Count Plunkett.

This is not the place to tease out the complexities of nationalism in music, at the centre of which Moore sits, but it is necessary that we are aware that it is not simply a matter of nationalism versus cosmopolitanism: there are deep ideological divisions within nationalism about how, or even whether, 'Irish music' was to be defined and communicated. Whatever the outcome with regard to the fate of an indigenous Irish school of composition, it is most likely that the Academy did well to have avoided any deeper involvement in the debate.[161] We hope to have indicated, however, that a sense of nationalism in musical affairs was not the exclusive right of those pursuing merely Irish Ireland preoccupations, and that a love of, and perhaps sense of responsibility for, the welfare of Irishness in music—whatever form it might take—was evident in the Academy and its associates.

The inauguration of the RDS recitals in 1886 marked the creation of a series that became the backbone of chamber music in Dublin and retained its central position until the advent of the National Concert Hall in 1981. It had been decided by the Council of the RDS that music should be 'systematically brought before the public as effectually as painting and sculpture are now in our public galleries.'[162] In addition to the income from ticket sales, the society would subvent the series to the extent of a further £100. Despite the appearance of domestic and visiting celebrities at other venues and under other managements, especially from the nineteen-sixties onwards, the weekly concerts in the society's original premises in Leinster House from 1886 to 1922,[163] at the Abbey and Theatre Royal from 1922 to 1926 and in its new home in the Members' Hall at Ballsbridge since 1926 have witnessed many of the world's finest solo artists and chamber ensembles.

Esposito—thirty-one years old and just four years in Dublin—was commissioned by the RDS to be the architect of the recitals, deciding programmes and artists, which allowed him to bring with him many of the Academy's teaching staff and, as one generation succeeded another, some of its most outstanding pupils. It was intended that the Monday recitals should feature the same core of performers for the whole season—a strategy that worked well in Esposito's favour both as a player and as an educationalist, since it enabled the audiences to hear a repertoire delivered in a single style.

Esposito's involvement demonstrates not only the remarkable breadth of his musical tastes but also his determination to educate. The inaugural season in 1886, performed by a quartet of RIAM professors—Esposito, Lauer, Griffith, and Rudersdorff—included works by Bach, Beethoven, Corelli, Handel, Haydn, Mozart, Mendelssohn, Marcello, Raff, Rubinstein, Schubert, Spohr, Tartini, and Veracini, designed to illustrate the historical development of chamber music. Mahaffy would sometimes introduce the items, and programme notes written by Stewart, and later Prout, were provided for the 400-strong audiences.

The intimacy of the Leinster House chamber encouraged an 'affectionate co-operation between the artists and the select public,' which, from 1891, included not only RDS members and their guests but also, to encourage younger people, a limited number of RIAM students, admitted free of charge.[164] This is clearly a concession that did not long continue, since in 1897 we find the Board of Governors instructing the secretary to write to the RDS requesting such a concession, which the RDS refused. A year later the Academy made the same request, again to be turned down.[165]

Esposito was responsible for the planning and organising of every recital from 1886 to 1900, in most of which he was also a performer, either in piano quartets or quintets or as a sonata partner. He also gave many solo recitals—usually three per season—again structured to demonstrate different keyboard timbres, from the baroque to the romantic, of which the following is typical:

'La Frescobalda' aria con variazioni	Frescobaldi
Minuet	Grazioli
Sonata in D	Scarlatti
Sonata in E flat, op. 31 No. 3	Beethoven
Carnaval	Schumann

A similarly structured programme from 1912 was:

Aria with variations	Handel
Rondeau 'Les Barricades mystérieuses'	Couperin
La Poule	Rameau
Sonata in C No. 6	Albanesi
Intermezzi from op. 119	Brahms
Preludes, op. 28 (Nos. 15, 23, and 24)	Chopin
Polonaise in F sharp minor	Chopin

Work by Scarlatti was included not only for historical reasons but because of Esposito's own local piety for, and championing of, the Neapolitan School, and for the same reason (as well as the fact that he was his almost exact contemporary) he included that of Carlo Albanesi. It is also significant that he considered it important to include nocturnes by John Field.

The RDS recitals also gave him the opportunity of playing his own music, chiefly solo piano works and duo sonatas, including, in 1908 with Sigmund Beel, the Second Violin Sonata (in E minor, op. 46), which had just won the Prix de la Société Musicale in Paris.

As Anthony Hughes has pointed out, programmes included works that we would today regard as unusual but were not so at that time—Raff, Rubinstein, Bargiel, and Mackenzie—as well as much contemporary music.[166] Brahms's Second Cello Sonata, written in 1886, was played at the RDS in 1891 and Franck's Violin Sonata of 1886 in 1898 (by Annie Lord); the Strauss Cello Sonata, op. 6, of 1883, the Arensky Piano Trio of 1894 and the Saint-Saëns Quintet were all heard in Dublin within a short time of their composition. As we shall see in the account of the Students' Musical Union, Esposito's example encouraged the study and performance of much contemporary (especially French) work well into the twentieth century. In 1912 Esposito and the Brodsky Quartet gave a legendary performance of the quintet by César Franck, which, although composed over thirty years previously, was, like most of his music, unknown in Ireland. Later, Dina Copeman would give the first Irish performances of works by Rachmaninov, while the availability of an organ in the rebuilt recital theatre in Leinster House brought to Dublin in 1908 transcriptions of orchestral works by the 42-year-old Sibelius, 'a Finnish composer whose work is being much discussed in England and elsewhere.'[167]

Walter Starkie recalled 'the look of horror that came into the faces of some of [the] steadfast Mozart and Mendelssohn lovers when Miss Annie Lord devoted most of her piano recitals to the works of Debussy and Ravel.'[168] In 1895 the critic of the *Freeman's Journal* took exception to Dvořák's Piano Trio in F minor: 'While, of course, one should feel grateful to the performers for novelties which involve on their part great additional study and rehearsal, the experience of one or two recent novelties is not attractive. Even the most hackneyed of the old classics would have afforded more pleasure than this trio,' which the critic considered 'formless, inchoate.'[169] The next year the same writer referred significantly to Mozart's D minor Quartet as abounding 'in beautiful and haunting melodies . . . with all the old-world elegance held essential to such compositions before the days when the Brahmses and Dvořáks infused into chamber music so much of the spirit of modern unrest.'[170]

Brahms (who died in 1897), because he was considered modern in the sense of being challenging, was particularly suspect. In 1910 Harold White, reviewing the Piano Quintet in A, said:

> I do not yet quite know whether he is a shallow poser or a profound thinker . . . His piano works are clever and interesting, and are original in treatment, if not in thematic material. His orchestral works are

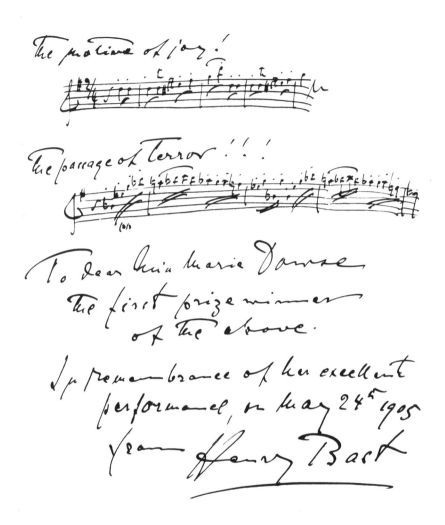

A musical joke by Henri Bast, 1905, for Marie Dowse

scholarly and even masterly, and yet they do not move me. His songs are poetic and refined, yet they seem to lack fire and life. It seems as if Brahms lived in a world of men where the sex question never occurred, because there was only one sex, and therefore the term was never defined.[171]

As a player, Esposito appears to have belonged to a school typified by Alfred Cortot, in which total accuracy and extreme virtuosity were of less importance than interpretation and communication. The *Dublin Express* reviewer of a recital in 1912, which included Esposito's three Ballades (op.

59), the Beethoven C minor Variations, the Chopin B minor Sonata, and Brahms's Romanze and Capriccio, commented on his 'breadth and passionate intellectuality.'[172] Beckett heard Esposito play the cycle of Beethoven sonatas and thought him 'a good, though not a great pianist' and praised his edition of Scarlatti sonatas. It is thought that Esposito was the model for the Italian music teacher in Beckett's radio play *Embers*.[173]

In 1891 Grove heard Esposito in London, when he reported to Edith Oldham:

> I heard the Finale of Op. 111—a sonata of his own for Pf & Violin and 2 of the Schumann Symphonic studies. They all gave me very much pleasure—there was so much more grace than one hears in this day of thumping & smashing so much more sympathy and care for the audience and love of the composer . . . There was plenty of force but no noise, also there was none of that absurd pretence of *accuracy* that is so hateful and absurd to an old fashioned man like me, and which offends me so cruelly in Paderewski, Stavenhagen & Co.[174]

Adolf Brodsky, with whom he was to work extensively, considered Esposito the greatest living interpreter of Brahms. Looking back from the nineteen-thirties, Walter Starkie recalled 'that dark-eyed, eager little man, who had such mysterious power of musical concentration' and in particular 'the subtle introspective qualities' of his performances of Beethoven's sonata, op. 109. 'Beethoven wrote below the finale with its theme and variations: *Gesangsvoll und mit inningster Empfindung* [with a singing tone (*cantabile*) and with innermost sensitivity] and these words might be taken as the description of Esposito's playing at its best.'[175] Starkie also commented on the partnership between Esposito and Guido Papini, who 'produced a golden tone from his Cremona violin and in his style laid stress on all that was emotional in the music.' From the 1887/88 season until 1896, Esposito and Papini formed a legendary partnership, which the *Freeman's Journal* called 'Papini the ever-beautiful, Esposito the never-failing.'[176] It led in 1892 to Papini, together with Grisard, Delany, and Bast, providing what amounted to the resident quartet (and, with Esposito, its quintet) at the RDS until Papini left Ireland in 1896.

In 1901, because of what had become 'overfamiliarity with the regular performers'[177] and consequently declining attendance, the RDS decided to look further afield, so beginning the reintroduction to the Dublin public of the world's top ensembles, of which the Verbrugghen Quartet was the first. The Belgian Henri Verbrugghen,[178] a pupil of Ysaÿe and Hubay, had been appointed to the RIAM staff in December 1899 (joining the Board of Studies immediately); but the arrangement, which involved Verbrugghen commuting weekly from London, was not satisfactory, not least because he was heavily involved in the entertainments at Colwyn Bay pier in Wales, and it was terminated by mutual consent in September 1900.[179]

The development was not greeted with unanimous approval, however. The *New Ireland Review* facetiously suggested that the plan would 'discontinue the employment in its theatre of musicians born or resident in

Ireland . . . to be replaced by artists free from any Irish taint,'[180] while the *Leader* called the development 'a piece of shameful anti-Irish snobbery.'[181] That the RDS recitals up to that point had heavily featured non-Irish (though resident) artists, such as those already mentioned, suggests that the departure was hardly as serious or as novel as the writer thought, but the comments do emphasise the aspiration to self-sufficiency, especially freedom from English influence, that underlay the xenophobic aspect of the slogan *sinn féin*.

Esposito was an important element in this development also, as he frequently played quintets with these groups, which included the Brodsky and Wessely Quartets (his own Quartet in C minor, op. 60, was dedicated to the Wessely Quartet).[182] His association with the Brodsky Quartet, who

A cartoon of Michele Esposito (artist unknown) from the SMU scrapbook

played thirty times at the RDS between 1901 and 1920, allowed him the rare opportunity of an appearance outside Ireland, when he played his Second Violin Sonata with Adolph Brodsky in Manchester in February 1910. It also brought the quartet into contact with one of his most talented pupils, Rhona Marshall, who was to appear with them on several occasions. Above all, Esposito's involvement with the RDS enabled him to introduce Marshall, Dina Copeman and many other academicians to a most important public arena, which became a showcase for the best Academy talent.

Academy people were central to the foundation of the Feis Ceoil. At early meetings of the Feis Committee, many of which were held in 36 Westland Row, letters of support were read from, among others, Elizabeth Scott-Fennell, Bishop Donnelly, R. M. Levey, Francis Cruise, and the daughter of Bishop Graves.[183] Count Plunkett took an active part in bringing the initiative to fruition as honorary treasurer, and Annie Patterson and Edith Oldham were heavily involved in its administration, as were Edith's brother and her future husband, Richard Best, the Feis's first registrar. Early subscribers to the guarantee fund included W. P. Geoghegan and W. R. Molloy, among many others whose musical sympathies were also aligned to those of the RIAM. The names of Sir Robert Sexton, George Cree, T. H. Drew, Joseph Robinson, Pauline and Alex Elsner (the latter soon to be a founder of the Feis in Derry), Jeannie Quinton-Rosse, Melfort d'Alton, Walter Bapty, T. R. G. Jozé, Alice Craig, Mary Garland and Margaret O'Hea occur in the lists of those attending public meetings. At the inaugural concerts, several of these, and in addition Lucy Ashton Hackett (a former pupil of Manuel Garcia), Mrs Scarff-Goodman and Charles Kelly (the father of Alice Yoakley) took part.

At an early stage it was even considered that the RIAM might be involved in the administration of the Feis. A deputation of the Feis Committee (Count Plunkett, Dr Sigerson, George Coffey, Mrs Culwick, Edith Oldham, Owen Lloyd, and J. O. Lindsay) had met Dublin Corporation in December 1895, as a result of which the Corporation considered it advisable to ask the Academy to divert 'such portion of [its grant of £300] as the Governors may consider best suited toward the holding of an Irish Music Festival in Dublin, as that object is calculated to further the purposes for which the grant . . . is made.'[184] Subsequently the Corporation asked the Academy if it were feasible for it to administer the Feis, an aspect that was overtaken by later developments.[185]

Here, however, we see a clear indication that the concept of the Municipal School of Music and the School Choir Competition, for which the grant was intended, was regarded as cognate with the Feis initiative. It would in fact be difficult to overestimate the positive response from all parties to this movement, or indeed the significance that was attached to it as a means of national revival.

The circumstances of the foundation of the Feis Ceoil bear out the remark attributed to Brendan Behan that the first item on the agenda of any Irish organisation is to have a split. In this case it was the simultaneous founding of the Oireachtas by those not satisfied that the Feis would sufficiently protect and promote Irish musical culture. It reflected the fact that, within the larger movement towards a celebration and revitalisation of Irish musical life, were the competing demands of nationalism and cosmopolitanism, with both Oireachtas and Feis having as their common figurehead Annie Patterson, the original proposer in 1894 of an 'Irish Musical and Literary Festival'. Harry White argues that

> in its emancipation from the constraints of cultural nationalism, the Feis created a mental (and physical) space for the cultivation (as against preservation) of music in Ireland. It provided an opportunity for public performance across the spectrum of musical endeavour, and it acted as a stimulus to composition. In these respects it filled a void in Irish cultural discourse: it transcended the nationalist symbolism of Irish music as a subset of the Gaelic League and it consolidated the movement towards music as a cultural preoccupation which might reduce the polarisation of native and colonial traditions.[186]

The Feis Ceoil was conceived in 1894, one year after the inception of the Gaelic League and two years after that of the National Literary Society and Vaughan Williams's pioneering Leith Hill Festival. The ambition, declared in *United Ireland*, of the literary revival—'We want our own literature made known to our own people . . . We want . . . to let the world know that intellectually and artistically the Irish are a distinct and distinguished race'[187]—is identical in tenor and syntax to that of the Feis Ceoil. Edith Oldham, addressing the Dublin Branch of the Incorporated Society of Musicians, said: '[It] is not a musical and artistic event only; it is the expression of the ideals and culture of a nation, and embodies its highest aspirations.'[188]

The firm assertion by the Feis Committee that 'it is generally recognised that the qualities in creative art, which distinguish the music of one country from another, are inseparably related to the individual genius of their respective peoples' was supported in the press not only by the signatures of the musical establishment but also by both Archbishops of Dublin and a cross-section of academic, legal and ecclesiastical life.[189] As Charles Oldham put it in 1897, 'in the movement they had a work for Ireland in which they could all join irrespective of party differences, creed or class.'[190] This was re-asserted in 1914 by W. P. Geoghegan: 'The committee has no intention of conducting the Association upon any but the non-political and non-sectarian principles which have guided it to the present.'[191]

The Feis in fact grew from within the National Literary Society, and it was at a meeting of the Gaelic League that Annie Patterson had urged the foundation of such a festival. If the twin ambitions contained in the original concept could have been achieved without division, the congruence between music and literature, as aesthetic equivalents, would have prevented the marginalisation of music as an aesthetic adjunct to literature and its reservation within the folds of a monolithic Gaelic musical culture. But in a sense the way the Feis developed was another demonstration of the pragmatic approach, or *l'art du possible*, which had characterised the coalition in the Academy and which pervaded almost all areas of cultural activity. Having seen a certain type of Irishness appropriated by the Oireachtas, the pro-moters of the Feis were able to develop the cosmopolitan aspects of musical life in Ireland without losing sight of, or contact with, the Irishness of such music-making. In this way, the original ambition to reconstitute—even to re-invent—the music of Ireland was translated in this institution into a festival of all music-making in Ireland.

From the correspondence of George Grove and Edith Oldham we can discover the views of an informed outsider on the ambitions for the Feis.

> April 20 1896—My dearest friend—Now that you are an Honorary Secretary I approach you somewhat with feelings of *hawe*. At least as much of it as I can feel towards one whom I love so much . . . I confess I take very little interest in the *antiquarian* part of it except as a mere matter of history. The 'concert of Antient Irish music' surely cannot be of any use. You cannot get the instruments, nor can you know what pro-portions &c they were used in—and the tunes played on the piano would probably give more pleasure. But the other numbers which deal with the future—the contests and prize compositions &c.—*those* I think will be practical & useful. They will not only help 'Irish music'—but they will bring people together and get them into the habit of co-operating. This I believe has been the tendency of the Eistedfodds [*sic*]—to drop the antiquarian side and strengthen the modern side of the undertaking.
>
> 3 June 1896—Dear E.O. . . . I saw Lord Monteagle in an omnibus yesterday and he asked me if I knew anything about your project, I told him it was in good hands—yours . . . He said he was afraid there were all sorts of difficulties from *jealousies and intrigues &c*. He feared the plan of an *Irish orchestra* would not answer at first: there would (for instance) be no wind. But why should you *not be content to have as many Irish as possible in the orchestra?* And *why should the conductor necessarily be a Celt?* Manns is conducting the fourth Wales festival, and I don't think that the Eistedfodds are (or were) so exclusive. The great point surely is to start the festival—get it into working order—*and then the Celtic element will increase every year.* This was very strongly borne upon me after I left Monteagle and I thought I would tell you.[192]

The Feis had twin—and ambivalent—models: the English festival, which had become such a marked feature of musical life since the early nineteenth century, advocated by Stanford, to whom the founders had appealed for guidance; and the Welsh Eisteddfod, which gave Edith Oldham the inspi-ration we have quoted.[193]

The ambiguities of the Feis are revealed in its attempts to be compre-hensive, to embrace all kinds of music and all kinds of Irishness. But these ambiguities became its strength, in combining the celebratory with the competitive. Its original aim—the millennial restoration of Irish musicality —was not obliterated by music-making of a non-Irish nature, but it was tempered by it. The *Freeman's Journal* remarked on the opening day of the first Feis that before it had begun 'the archaeological character of the Feis was almost swallowed up in the musical.'[194] But, as the paper went on to observe, this was a practical and positive aspect rather than a negative and defeatist one.

> At the start it seemed to be taken for granted that an Irish School of Music might emerge from a universal knowledge and practice of the old airs. Now the Committee saw that an Irish School of Music was impossible unless the Irish people themselves understood the elements of modern music. Thenceforward the object of the Feis was two-fold—first, to revive and resuscitate the old melodies, and, second, to teach the people the fundamental principles of music as an art.

This realisation is reflected in the programmes for the first three concerts, which encapsulated the Committee's thinking on what constituted a balance between ancient and modern Irish music and help us to identify the forces that influenced such thinking.

> The first concert is to be devoted exclusively to Irish music of what may be termed the ancient and middle periods . . . an Irish Cuoin [*sic*] or Lament (Bunting) arranged for solo, chorus and harp accompaniment; performances on Irish pipes, a band of harps, and Irish vocal solos . . . glees by Lord Mornington, Stevenson, Tom Crook and Moore . . . conclud[ing] with a quartet of harps playing a fantasia of Irish airs, specially arranged for the Irish Musical Festival by Oberthur. The second concert will include Sir Robert Stewart's overture 'Eve of St. John', symphonic poem (Augusta Holmes) and works by Robinson, Dr. Wood, John Field and Balfe . . . [and] Dr. Culwick's prize overture . . . The prize cantata by Signor Esposito will be performed at the third concert, as well as works by Villiers Stanford and Wallace.[195]

The commentary published by the Feis to accompany these concerts was extremely detailed and had as its principal aim the assimilation of these different manifestations of music in Ireland. The names of Bunting, Petrie, Pigot, Culwick, Stewart, Joyce, Moore (in the company of Stevenson and Bishop), Mornington, Rooke and Balfe are employed in an almost casual melding of styles, personalities and motivations into a 'common name'.[196] It was thus made possible to see the Feis, as the *Freeman's Journal* did, as 'in line with a movement of the day . . . the conception of a "nationality in music" as exemplified by the Welsh Eistedfodds [*sic*].'[197] This enabled the *Freeman's Journal* to see the Feis as epochal—'the institution of a musical renaissance in Ireland,'[198] which widened the field of musical experience beyond the traditionally 'favoured few' to an 'essentially democratic' condition that not only embraced Balfe, Wallace, Stanford and Stewart, 'who are universally recognized as Irishmen,' but also allowed them to discover William Michael Rooke, John Field, and Augusta Holmes.[199]

We can thus see that several different types of tension were present in the evolution of the Feis Ceoil, all of them also present in the RIAM since its inception: that between 'Irish Ireland' and 'Anglo-Ireland'; that within 'Irish Ireland' between those who were resolutely and exclusively Gaelic and those who admitted the heterogeneous nature of Irishness; between different approaches to the forms of musical expression; between those who favoured total independence for Ireland and those who could envisage an Ireland free but not completely autonomous. It also exemplifies the fact that it was quite possible for one person (as for a class or genre of people) to embody several of these tensions.

This complexity is embodied in a comment by the *Freeman's Journal* on the inaugural Feis, when it attributed the lack of musical tradition to 'the fact that in Ireland the transition from the old aristocratic order of things to the modern democratic spirit is not yet even complete.'[200] This neatly masks the fact that *two* orders, and *two* spirits, were involved. The 'aristocratic order' might be understood as the eighteenth-century Ascendancy, which had folded its tents and stolen away in the wake of the Act of Union and been succeeded by an emergent social order. Another is that conceived by Yeats as the true Celtic nobility of spirit and wisdom. One democratic spirit is that of universal suffrage (the audience) and self-determination without resort to external influences or attractions, but another is 'the filthy modern tide' of the new middle classes, so feared and despised by Yeats as a pollutant of the new intellectual aristocracy.

As we have already shown, all these elements met in the board-room of the RIAM and were to a greater or lesser extent present in the Feis Ceoil as it took shape. In 1900 the *All Ireland Journal* considered that the Feis 'has played [a] distinctive . . . part in the efforts which are going on in our time towards the reunion of all Irish folk on a non-sectarian national basis.'[201] Joseph Ryan comments that the Feis 'represented the first specialized and yet accessible forum which offered the opportunity of participation to a broad constituency.'[202]

To explain Esposito's creation of the Dublin Orchestral Society in 1899 it is necessary to refer briefly to the musical environment in Dublin at that time. The city's musical life from 1890 onwards shows a similar pattern of activity to the previous period, which we have described, with the notable exception of the Hallé concerts.

Solo recitals by international celebrities continued, the chief visitors— outside the opera seasons—being Paderewski (who first appeared in 1894 and thereafter on at least three further occasions, in 1895, 1899, and 1902), Arthur de Greef (in 1895 and subsequent years), and Vladimir de Pachmann, then considered one of the foremost players in the world. After several years' absence from the Dublin stage, Adelina Patti, advertised as the 'Queen of Song'[203] and described by the *Freeman's Journal* as the 'greatest of living vocalists,'[204] sang in 1891 and again in 1895, when she was on her worldwide cycle of farewell concerts. In 1895 the Dublin Musical Society announced a performance of *Elijah* with the participation of 'the new contralto' Clara Butt, who, the *Freeman's Journal* told its readers, 'is practically not known at all'[205] (she had made her London début in 1892) but who, it reported, 'has a fine voice . . . a cultivated style and plenty of intelligence.'[206] She was to return for further celebrity concerts in 1899. The young Eugene

Goossens conducted the Arthur Rouseby Opera Company's productions of *Cavalleria rusticana*, *Il trovatore* and *La sonnambula* and the world premiere of Pellegrini's *Mercedes* in 1897. And in 1899 Sir Hubert Parry conducted his own *King Saul* for the Dublin Musical Society.

Among local initiatives we note the foundation of the Dublin Choral Union, conductor Annie Patterson, in 1891, and of the Tonic Sol-Fa Society in 1896—the latter associated with the Dublin Glee Singers (among them the Academy student Agnes Treacy and professor Jeannie Rosse), conducted by Joseph Seymour with accompanist Vincent O'Brien. The début recital of Esposito's pupil Harry Charles[207] took place in the Antient Concert Rooms on 5 November 1898; and, as a result of the inaugural Feis, the opening concert of Culwick's Orpheus Choral Society took place on 7 December 1897, which featured music by Charles Grandison and performances by Gordon Cleather, with Harty as accompanist.[208] Simultaneously, the re-creation of the Dublin Glee and Madrigal Union, with Elizabeth Scott-Fennell, the Marchants and Melfort d'Alton to the fore, with assistance from Esposito, Bast, Papini, and de Angelis, was another important choral departure.

Arthur Darley, perhaps setting out to rival Werner's prodigious activity, gave a series of violin recitals in 1896 and another in 1897. In 1895 William Percy French, at the outset of his career as a singer-composer and raconteur, presented his 'High-Class, Refined, Well-Bred, Cultured, Select, Polite and Elevating Entertainment, "Social Absurdities",' at the Antient Concert Rooms,[209] perhaps sensing a niche in the market then occupied by George Grossmith, who was coming to the end of his career and who appeared at the same venue in 1896.

Denis O'Sullivan, better known by this time in the United States, appeared with the Carl Rosa company in 1895 and in 1900 was invited to sing at the Academy, an honour for all concerned if we take the delight expressed by both the singer and the institution at face value.[210]

The hitherto private Instrumental Music Club (whose 'at homes' with Edith Oldham, Octave Grisard, Melfort d'Alton, Arthur Darley and others resemble a formalised version of those discussed in chapter 3) gave its first public concert on 13 January 1897 with a 'large orchestra [seventy] and attractive programme,' featuring P. J. Griffith as leader and Grisard as conductor, performing Beethoven's Symphony No. 2 and overtures by Mendelssohn (*Son and Stranger*) and Thomas (*Raymond*) and a chamber item, Beethoven's septet, op. 20.[211] In 1897 the RDS marked the Schubert centenary with a quartet recital, to which Oscar May's double bass was added for the piano quintet 'The Trout', D667. The *Freeman's Journal* offered the opinion that 'in his way [Schubert] was a genius, but it was not a very large way, and his work does not promise to survive, like that of Schumann, the rapid development of the art of music.'[212]

In 1895 the Dubliner William Ludwig (after whom the Academy's Ludwig Cup is named), who, according to the *Freeman's Journal*, had not been heard for many years in Dublin 'save . . . in purely ballad concerts,'[213] sang in *The Creation* in aid of the St Vincent de Paul Society, with an orchestra led by Theodore Werner and conducted by Peter Goodman. In 1898, as part of the 1798 centenary commemoration, he organised a series of ''98 Concerts' with singers, pipers, harpists and dancers and 'songs of love and war, keenes and lullabies.'[214] Another prominent Dubliner, now a major figure internationally, was Harry Plunket Greene, who in 1898 sang the title role of *St Paul* with the Dublin Musical Society, which the previous year had marked Queen Victoria's diamond jubilee with a concert including 'The Mount of Olives', 'Zadok the Priest', Sullivan's oratorio 'The Light of the World' and, curiously, Hérold's overture *Zampa*.

The vogue for Sullivan's symphonic music was obviously considerable. In 1895 the Dublin Musical Society produced a concert performance of his opera *Ivanhoe* and in 1896 the dramatic cantata 'The Golden Legend', while the same year the composer himself was billed to conduct 'The Light of the World', but this was prevented by his illness.

In 1895 the Carl Rosa Opera Company gave *Jeanie Deans*, the new opera by the young Scotsman Hamish MacCunn and, two years later, Puccini's *La bohème*, which had been first produced in Turin the previous year. Also in 1895 the Dublin Musical Society introduced Dublin audiences to Dvořák's dramatic cantata 'The Spectre's Bride'. Stanford's 'national opera' *Shamus O'Brien*, featuring Joseph O'Mara, was given at the Gaiety in 1897, while another Irish opera, *Grace Darrell* by F. C. Collinge, was performed by the Carl Rosa company in 1896.[215]

Charity concerts continued to be a feature of musical life. A performance including Lucy Ashton Hackett, Alex Elsner, Walter Bapty, Harry Charles, Bast and de Angelis (all academicians) with the Dublin Glee Singers and the Dublin Metropolitan Police Band, conducted by Jozé, Joseph Smith, Seymour and James Conroy, took place at the Mansion House on 12 May 1898 for the 'Relief of Distress in the West and South of Ireland.' The popularity of the piano as the principal domestic source of entertainment was maintained by means of the 'three years' system' of hire purchase that Pigott's and Cramer's were strenuously advertising in relation to Bechstein, Schiedmayer, Kirkman, Collard, Broadwood and Erard instruments as well as many long-forgotten makes.

An index to the wider artistic life of the capital in these years is provided by the advertisement page of the *Freeman's Journal* in 1898 and 1899. In the former year, during the last week of March, Marie Lloyd was appearing at the Gaiety in a new musical, F. R. Benson's Shakespearian Company was playing in *Henry the Fifth* and *Julius Caesar* at the Theatre Royal, Ludwig's '98 Concerts were running at the Rotunda, the Dublin Musical Society performed *Israel in Egypt* and Mendelssohn's 'Hymn of Praise' at the Royal University, Paderewski played at the Theatre Royal, and Mrs Page Thrower was soliciting subscriptions for the 1898/99 concerts by the Hallé Orchestra.

In May 1899 the Irish Literary Theatre made its début with Yeats's *The Countess Cathleen* and Martyn's *The Heather Field*, while the melodrama *The Man in the Iron Mask* was playing at the Queen's. Clara Butt sang at the Rotunda, and the Dublin Orchestral Society was advertising the fourth concert of its inaugural season.

Between the two years a remarkable development had taken place, provoked partly by the Hallé concerts and partly by orchestral activity by the Dublin Musical Society. In 1896 the society introduced orchestral concerts to a city that, in the words of the *Freeman's Journal*, 'has had no orchestral concert of high class for very many years,'[216] the standard musical fare being the RDS recitals and the Dublin Musical Society's own cantatas and oratorios. 'How many Dublin concert goers of the younger generation have heard a Beethoven symphony?' it asked.[217] The Dublin Musical Society gave three orchestral concerts at the Royal University, starting in November 1896, with Joseph Smith conducting an orchestra of seventy-five, led by Arthur Darley. The opening event consisted of the overtures to *Der Freischütz* and *William Tell*, some vocal items, and Beethoven's Fifth Symphony. The *Freeman's Journal* complained about the new fashion of giving the symphony near the end of the concert, rather than the beginning,[218] but in retrospect it considered the initiative to have been 'a creditable but unhappy experiment.'[219] The situation was still what it had been in 1895, when Stanford had said that 'Dublin has of late had but little chance of hearing the great works of other nations properly performed.'[220]

Simultaneously, Theodore Werner and others, including the impresario and singer Mrs Page Thrower, announced the coming attraction of the Hallé Orchestra on 7 and 8 February 1897 at the Lyric Hall, also performing Beethoven's Fifth and, on the second night, Tchaikovsky's very recent Sixth, and with the vocalists Melfort d'Alton and Gordon Cleather. A letter was received by the Academy secretary from Mrs Page Thrower:

> Sir—I beg to request you to do me the favour to lay before your Board of Governors my request for their approval of an endeavour I am making to afford the Dublin music lovers and students of music an opportunity of hearing . . . the celebrated 'Sir Charles Hallé Orchestra' . . . I desire to obtain if possible permission to say in my notices in the papers that as a corporate body I have the approval of the Governors of the RIAM & shall be grateful if as individuals I may be allowed to add the names of my subscription list. The subscription of £1 will secure *two* 7/6 seats at both concerts, but single seats can be subscribed for at 7/6 or 5/− each. Trusting it may be possible I receive the permission I crave, I beg to remain, Yrs faithfully.[221]

A note (almost certainly by Brady) in pencil in the margin of the letter reads: 'doubtfull [*sic*] the A as a corporate body could accede to the request,' and it had to be declined.

The huge success of the Hallé venture, conducted in 1897 and 1898 by Hallé's successor Frederick Cowen and on subsequent visits by Hans Richter, prompted Esposito to consider how best he might establish a resident orchestra in Dublin. Discussing Harty's professional reasons for leaving Dublin, Raymond Warren has pointed out that 'a country with no full-time professional orchestra . . . was one of the factors militating against the establishment earlier in the century of an Irish national school of composition.'[222] Partly to fill this gap, and partly to broaden the educational base of the Academy's activities, Esposito founded the Dublin Orchestral Society. At the end of 1898 he wrote to Sir George Grove: 'My dream begins to be realized. I have played here almost all the sonatas of Beethoven and I want to give them the Symphonies and Ouvertures [*sic*] not only once but continually. It will be an uphill work for me but nothing will ever be done if one does not try and seriously.'[223] As with his programme-building in the RDS recitals, it is abundantly clear that he approached his work, with both the audience and the players, as a teacher—in order to create an awareness of music's historical development and the evolution of a sense of style.

With the assistance of Edith Oldham, W. P. Geoghegan, and Leopold Dix, a Dublin solicitor and accomplished musician who made arrangements for the Irish Church Hymnal, Esposito held public meetings at which the argument was that

> the splendid reception which has just been given to the Hallé band [in November 1898] shows that where good orchestral music is presented under the most favourable auspices the public here will gladly flock to hear it. It could not for a moment be pretended that a new orchestra here—or in any town in England for that matter—could attempt to rival the superb orchestra we have had the privilege of hearing this week . . . Nevertheless we do hope that with the necessary amount of support on the part of the public and of hard work on the part of the orchestra, we may at least give good concerts in our first season, and better ones in each succeeding year. Every good thing must have a beginning. When Sir Charles Hallé first thought of inaugurating his Manchester Band the people of that town would only have taken up a perfectly sound, logical position if they had said—'Oh, we can hear magnificent orchestras from London. We don't see our way to supporting a local orchestra as well.' They might have said this but for many reasons obvious to right-feeling citizens, they did not, and the wisdom of their decision is now best evidenced by the orchestra itself. We would urge on the citizens of Dublin to follow their example.[224]

Esposito was right to be optimistic. One public-spirited person who wished to remain anonymous, but who was probably either W. P. Geoghegan or Edward Martyn, had offered £500 to the projected foundation fund if the society raised £2,000 by New Year's Day.[225] A provisional committee, consisting of Margaret O'Hea, Leopold Dix, Geoghegan, and Martyn, had announced that a 'foundation fund' of £2,500 (£100,000 today) would be necessary to underpin the running expenses of the orchestra so as to avoid the necessity of calling in guarantees every year to pay the deficits. The proposed society would not come into existence until such time as the committee was assured of the fund, and then its control would be vested in the members.[226] The fund was invested in Bank of Ireland stock, and this was used to subvent the initial costs of the concerts, much of which consisted of the purchase and hire of scores.

The distinctive fact about the foundation of the Dublin Orchestral Society is that it was intended to be a professional co-operative orchestra.

Esposito was clearly behind the somewhat extensive and comprehensive rules of the new organisation, which was modelled on that of the Società Orchestrale della Scala in Milan, as a co-operative venture with a constitutional distinction between 'foundation' and 'performing' members and a pre-ordained minimum life span of seven years. The finances of the society were organised so that income from the sale of concert tickets, together with annual subscriptions and donations, would pay the costs of presenting concerts and a fee-per-concert for each player, on a three-tier system. Class A consisted of the leaders of the first violins, cellos, flutes, clarinets, oboes, bassoons, and horns; class B, receiving 20 per cent less, were the leaders of the second violins, double basses, cornets, trombones, and the second flute and piccolo players; and class C, receiving 40 per cent less than A, were what today would be called 'rank and file'.[227] In the event of the concerts being financially unsuccessful, the fund was structured in such a way that players would be guaranteed half their normal fees.

The accounts of the society are unclear about specific payments to players, but it would appear that the average payment was £1 8s per concert (£45 today). Additional players who were not members of the society would be hired for specific concerts. Esposito was to receive £20 per concert, and the society had a salaried secretary, C. W. Wilson, at £30 a year.

Committee meetings were held at first in a variety of places—the first at the Antient Concert Rooms, others at Pigott's premises, many at the Royal University after rehearsals—before settling mainly at the RIAM. The chief attenders, apart from Esposito, Dix, and Edith Oldham, were Edward Martyn, W. P. Geoghegan, J. J. Gleeson, P. J. Griffith, and John A. Ruthven.

Wilhelmj was to be leader, and the orchestra of sixty-one—below the full strength one would expect today of even a modest symphony orchestra—was to have intensive rehearsals before the first concert and several rehearsals (on average six or seven) for each subsequent concert. The orchestra included many academicians, including violins Patrick Delany, Victoria Delaney, Thomas Farrell, Constance Guinness, Ernest May, and P. J. Griffith, violas Grisard and Samuel Levenston,[228] cellos Bast and Richard O'Reilly, bass Oscar May, and wind Regazzoli, Ellard, and Conroy.[229] The *Musical Times* considered that 'with such splendid freedom from the bonds of mere financialism "the powers that be" should see to it that the music of native composers—using the word "native" in no narrow sense—should have its proper place in a scheme that is of a nature so distinctly national in its scope.'[230]

But that ambition was not to be realised. It was probably less of a priority with Esposito than the availability, as expressed to Grove, of a facility for performing the standard repertoire, and it was this that was greeted by the *Irish Times*, on the occasion of the inaugural concert on 1 March 1899, at which works by Gluck, Mozart, Mendelssohn, Beethoven and Wagner were performed: 'The creation of the Dublin Orchestral Society marks the opening of a new era in the history of Irish musical annals.'[231]

Since the *Irish Times's* report of the inaugural concert contains much argument bearing on the issues of Irish music and of contemporary creativity, it is worth examining in detail.

It has been said that the art of music in Ireland has fallen upon evil days—when not only has the well-spring of imagination failed, but when we are incapable as a people of sustaining that essential love and knowledge of music which once was conceded to be our intellectual quality as a right.

Here we find the two strands of thought that have concerned us in the preceding pages: the lack of 'native' composers, and the absence of a resident orchestra since the demise of the Antient Concerts Society and the Philharmonic.

While bemoaning these shortcomings, the writer proceeds to make pious genuflection to the ideals of innate Irish musicality and to the remnants of what we could be forgiven for calling 'ould dacency' in its modern audience.

Ireland has contributed much to musical literature. Never have its people lost touch with its essential qualities . . . There is not in any musical centre of the Three Kingdoms a more highly instructed or sharper audience than that of Ireland. There are those who say that we have fallen backward in our comprehension of what are the essential inspirations of art. But in that of music we are not prepared to yield the palm to any. By that art we stand. It belongs to us.

Between this and the final assertion, in a paragraph of increasing rodomontade, that 'we have raised ourselves above the reproach of incapacity and failure of enterprise,' there is a remarkable feat of legerdemain, in admitting, and at the same time ignoring, the faults that have brought Dublin its new musical departure. Tracing Dublin's musical greatness no further back than the middle of the eighteenth century ('the life-history of Handel is indissolubly bound up with that of Dublin'), the writer names Field, Stevenson, 'the school of Balfe and Wallace' and Stewart as 'links . . . in a series which every earnest and capable student will readily understand . . . There is no break in our musical annals.' It is doubtful if any reader at the time would have accepted this attempt to explain away the discontinuities in Irish composition, or indeed in Irish music-making. One can, however, understand the motive behind this curious argument: 'There is not any other [art] in which its associations are so close, not one in which those of its touches are nearer that make the whole world kin.' The weakness in the argument is that the flimsy emotional plank is insufficient to bring us across the gap between past achievements and current practice.

This is implicitly admitted in the next turn of the argument. 'We have been striving, not without success, to recover some of our own tone-dialects. But it is a greater and more important work still to grasp the language of the vast universal speech and it is this office which the Dublin Orchestral Society is striving to fulfil.' That 'not without success' betrays itself by pointing to the equal possibility of failure and in suggesting that, by trying to comprehend the mainstream repertoire, the audience might leave 'Irish' music behind—which is equivalent to the recognition by the leaders of the literary renaissance that Irish literature, to be modern and accessible to its readership, must be written in English.

A notable feature of the Dublin Orchestral Society, and of orchestral activity in Dublin generally, was the fact that its existence did not seriously change the situation in relation to wind and brass players. Right up to the foundation of the Radio Éireann Symphony Orchestra in 1947–48, these sections would continue to be regarded as somehow separate from, or adjuncts to, the rest of the orchestra, to be 'brought in' for the occasion—a situation that the original Academy had been partly set up, and had so far failed, to remedy. Even when, in the wake of Esposito's departure from Ireland, the new Dublin Symphony Orchestra and Philharmonic Society took up the reins, the situation was no better, in the sense that there was no attempt to integrate strings and wind, even though in this latter case the orchestra was largely under the direction of army personnel, Col. Brase and Cmdt Sauerzweig, who had the requisite forces at their command.

Annie Patterson drew attention to another dimension of the problem, that 'an instrumentalist, if at all capable, has to be feed, whereas a chorus singer usually gives his or her services gratis . . . When our young men and young women more generally favour orchestral instruments, it will be more possible to have good amateur bands; but until then, if we want a reliable band we must pay for it.'[232] The reason for this may be the Dublin custom of elevating the repertoire for piano, strings and voice at the expense of purely orchestral music, and it may also be that the Academy both responded to, and encouraged, such a taste. A social prejudice against the acceptance of wind instruments, which were characteristic of the 'city bands' of the lower classes, may have contributed to this lamentable ignorance. Therefore, even for the major choral works that dominated the concert scene, the wind and brass were regarded as necessary rather than indispensable, to be tolerated rather than encouraged. Esposito's wind and brass were mainly the teachers from the Municipal School, and this fact underlines the notion of these sections of the orchestra as somehow different, which was further complicated by the complete separation of the Academy and the Municipal School of Music in 1905. In fact it would not be until relatively recently (the nineteen-fifties) that a cadre of such teachers, drawn mostly from the principals of the RESO, was attracted to the Academy to develop this aspect of performance.

This predilection for, on the one side, private music of a restricted nature and, on the other, large shows of choral activity thus inhibited Dublin's capacity to accept and appreciate a symphonic repertoire, while giving it a reputation for discrimination in matters of singing and chamber music. This inhibition was to prove the undoing of so many orchestral initiatives, including the Dublin Orchestral Society and the Philharmonic, up to modern times.[233]

The first concert was given on 1 March 1899, at the Royal University. In the event, the audience was poor and in the opinion of the *Irish Times* not sufficiently capable of appreciating the programme, while the orchestra lacked the resources to fill such a large hall. The performance of the Mozart symphony received qualified praise; Harry Charles's performance of Mendelssohn's Serenade and Allegro Giocoso, op. 43, was dull; and

Wagner's *Faust* overture was marked by crudeness. But the *Freeman's Journal* was more optimistic and saw little room for criticism,[234] and the *Musical Times* concurred: 'In one night the reproach of years has been removed from musical Dublin.'[235]

In the next fifteen years, before the world war caused its demise, the Dublin Orchestral Society was to give over two hundred concerts, approximately five or six each season in the Royal University and later the Gaiety Theatre and, from 1905, over twelve each year at the Sunday afternoon concerts at the Antient Concert Rooms.

Musically, the concerts appear to have been a success, with a steady advance in ensemble playing noticeable from one concert to the next. But audiences were not as large as might be hoped, and receipts fell below the necessary level, even allowing for subvention from the fund. The opening concert in 1901 brought in only £24 in ticket sales,[236] and this was to prove the average, although a Tchaikovsky concert in 1903, in which Annie Lord was paid two guineas (£70 today) for her performance of the Piano Concerto No. 1, earned box office income of £38. At the end of the 1901/02 season the treasurer, Dix, reported that expenses amounted to £952, of which £922 had been covered by receipts, with the deficit made up by John (later Sir John) Nutting.[237] The same season saw Martyn making a personal contribution of £50;[238] other donors included Mahaffy and the Earl of Iveagh, while W. P. Geoghegan guaranteed the society against loss, which cost him dear, £150 being needed to make up the loss on the last two concerts in the 1902/03 season.[239]

Annie Patterson, noting the poor attendance, was forced to suggest that Esposito should introduce more attractive items as entractes to 'cater a little for the tastes of the public who are only beginning to understand what orchestration means and who must have *variety* in the preliminary stages of their study.' At the opening of the third season it was indeed decided to introduce such extra attractions, and Denis O'Sullivan was engaged to sing *'Ella giammai m'amo'* (Verdi), Esposito's arrangement of 'The Lark in the Clear Air', and Stanford's arrangement of 'Owen Roe O'Neill's Lament'.

Naturally Esposito involved RIAM personnel in every aspect of the enterprise. Besides the inclusion in the orchestra of staff and many former students of both the RIAM and the Municipal School of Music, important solos were given to figures such as Bast, while concerto opportunities were given to his students, such as Bessie Ruthven (playing the largo and rondo from Beethoven's Third Piano Concerto), Archie Rosenthal (playing the same concerto, with Rubinstein's cadenza), and, as we have seen, Harry Charles. By the end of the first year Annie Patterson was able to say that 'with Herr Wilhelmj, Mr. P. J. Griffith, M. Grisard, Herr Bast, and Mr. O. [Oscar] May as leaders among the strings . . . the complete artistic success . . . seems now fully assured to his orchestra.'[240]

On other occasions visiting artists were engaged. On 14 February 1900 the 24-year-old American Ernest Schelling (1876–1939), a pupil of Mathias, Moszkowski and Paderewski and 'an accepted virtuoso' with 'a powerful and brilliant technique,'[241] played Chopin's F minor Concerto and two solo items, Rubinstein's 'Barcarolle' and Liszt's Sixth Hungarian Rhapsody in a concert that also featured a repeat of the Gluck overture, Beethoven's Symphony No. 2 and Saint-Saëns's tone poem 'Le Rouet d'Omphale'.

By April 1901 the *Irish Times* was still complaining of the 'singular indifference'[242] of the public to the endeavours of the Dublin Orchestral Society, attributed to a form of inverted provincial snobbery on musical grounds. But one (anonymous) reader saw the problem as much more complex:

> Dublin, above all cities in the world, is divided into endless sections and sub-sections socially, and anyone who has had experiences of Dublin life could not fail to see how public assemblies, such as concerts, meetings, dances &c., &c. are hedged round by social considerations of the most marvellously minute character . . . Some friends of mine . . . 'did not care about those concerts, as they did not meet their friends there.' It is, doubtless, all very humiliating and provincial in the worst sense of the term, but I have not the faintest doubt as to the truth of my statements. Therefore what we want is patronage.[243]

The writer was of the opinion that if titled women were to lend their names to the enterprise the lower orders would attend for social reasons and continue attending for musical ones.

At the start of the second season it had been decided to ask for an audience with the Lord Lieutenant, presumably to request that he become the society's patron. This he apparently refused, although he did agree to attend concerts occasionally[244] and had engaged the orchestra to play at Dublin Castle on 6 March 1900. An application was also made to Dublin Corporation,[245] which resulted in 1901 in a grant of £50, later increased to £300.

A public meeting was held in the Mansion House on 11 April 1901, the purpose being to reconstitute the Society's finances. The meeting, which was addressed by Martyn and T. P. Gill, heard Leopold Dix explain that a loss of over £800 had been incurred in the running costs of the society's first three seasons, which had been financed out of foundation subscriptions. The Lord Chancellor, Sir Ignatius O'Brien (later Lord Shandon), a vice-president and benefactor of the RIAM, said that he

> did not believe that music should ever be narrowed to the dominions of class or party or creed. Good bands and musicians from all parts of the world were always welcome in Dublin. We listened to them with pleasure and sent them away with applause. But the citizens of Dublin, like Manchester, and other great cities, had a right to a good orchestral band of their own, and they should make an effort to have one established on a sure foundation.[246]

Mahaffy said that he too was 'strongly in favour of every home movement . . . which had no party, no politics and no creed in it,' while Heinrich Bewerunge supported 'music as a social and educational influence of the noblest kind.' On a more practical level, John Nutting offered to donate £100, provided it was matched by £1,000 from other subscriptions. (Five years later, in his interview with James Cousins, Esposito was to say: 'It cannot be expected that Mr. Geoghegan and Mr. Martyn will go on paying money out for the edification of an unappreciative public.')[247]

The Lord Chancellor's remarks were obviously intended to emphasise the imbalance between poor audiences for the Dublin Orchestral Society and the overflow crowds at the Hallé concerts, and this point was taken up by Patterson. Acknowledging the enormous success of the Hallé enterprise and the strenuous organisation by Mrs Page Thrower, which could hardly be expected to pay its way unless economic ticket prices could be achieved by means of a much larger concert hall, she stressed that the main benefit of the visits was educational. Richter's performances were 'invaluable lessons to student and professor alike.'[248] Turning to the Dublin Orchestral Society, she equally stressed that 'we are always glad to welcome and pay for the best foreign talent that visits our city . . . At the same time there is no reason why we should not possess, as do other great cities, a band of our own which puts fees into the pockets of our local musicians.' Patterson's article underlines the fact that Dubliners were doing themselves a disservice by ignoring such burgeoning talent: 'Years of study and patient rehearsal are always necessary before an ensemble . . . is attained.'

A marked improvement in the society over its first three years was an opinion agreed on by all. Since its first concerts, this improvement had been tangible. Although the inaugural night had been greeted with enthusiasm, it was generally agreed that standards could only go up. Harty, who played viola in some of the early concerts, said rather kindly that the orchestra 'was not superlative.'[249] The *Musical Times*, reporting on the fifth and final concert of the opening season, commented that, apart from the obvious need for better wind players, the orchestra was heading in the right direction.[250] Annie Patterson wrote in December 1899: 'Each successive concert . . . is a step in advance towards that perfect ensemble playing, with unerring attention to "attack" and *nuances*, to which the Hallé band performances have taught us to aspire.'[251] A class bias persisted, however, and one year after the society's foundation we find Patterson repeating her commendation of the string principals and adding that 'the wood and brass wind are similarly well supported, the horns and trombones in particular being in the hands of very *efficient* performers'[252] (emphasis added)—a term she would not have used of any of the string leaders.

We must reflect on the fact that the population was still declining, from 5.2 million in 1880 to 4.5 million in 1900, and that in the latter year the population of Dublin itself was only 250,000. Nevertheless, it was considered shameful that a European city of that size had no municipal orchestra. It was the view of Edward McNulty (educated at the RIAM and author of a musical, *Yo Sau's Choice*, performed by the Academy declamation class in 1906)[253] that the Dublin Orchestral Society 'resulted from the wave of enthusiasm due to the Hallé orchestra rather than to any widespread love of orchestral music.'[254]

Writing at the end of 1899, Annie Patterson surveyed the musical condition of Dublin in a benchmark article that observed that between the new local centre examinations and the curriculum at the RIAM (including Esposito's Academy orchestra) Irish students no longer had to consider emigration as a means of attaining musical education and accomplishments. The Feis also had an educational dimension, while musical activity by the Dublin Musical Society, Orpheus, RDS, Hallé and Dublin Orchestral Society provided 'a social . . . concourse.'[255]

In 1905 Esposito also started the Sunday afternoon concerts at the Antient Concert Rooms, with a band of thirty, which, Dix said,

> had caused a new class of people to become interested in orchestral music. There were hundreds of people who had never before heard of orchestral music who had gone to these popular concerts had acquired a taste for orchestral music and were now coming to the [Dublin Orchestral Society] concerts . . . The public taste for orchestral music had to be created, and it took years to do it.[256]

The fortunes of the society and of the Sunday concerts rose and fell until their demise in 1914, when it was considered impossible to continue. The world war has been identified as the reason for its closure, but since the war does not seem to have had such an impact on other musical activities, it is doubtful whether the society would have continued in any case.

The origin of the Municipal School of Music (later the City of Dublin VEC College of Music and today the DIT Conservatory of Music and Drama) lies in the need to provide a qualitatively different type of music education from that conducted in the RIAM, one that would take into account the social and cultural differences between the upper and middle professional classes and the burgeoning and increasingly articulate working class.[257] In 1885–87 research into the condition of the various bands in Dublin, resulting in a report by John O'Donnell, had revealed that this traditional element in the city's musical life was diminishing, for want of proper instruction. Simultaneously it was becoming clear that the Academy, for its part, was not responding to the needs of such bands, or of potential musicians from the lower classes, principally, one supposes, because its personnel were largely unaware of them. A similar initiative had occurred at the School of Art in the eighteen-fifties, with the provision of evening classes for artisans and with a different course of study (in design) from the eighteen-eighties.[258]

On 2 September 1888 a meeting of representatives of eight amateur bands,[259] numbering over two hundred men,[260] was held at the Working-Men's Club in York Street, Dublin, at which it was resolved to send a deputation to the Lord Mayor, the Corporation and the RIAM to demand the formation of 'a new School of Music for the Working Classes and Amateur Bands.'

> The late Council of the RIAM . . . never made any endeavour to give musical education to the amateur bands of the working classes of Dublin . . . The proposed future arrangements for wind instrument class sketched

out by the new governing body of the Academy is not satisfactory . . . It is proposed to establish a proper School of Music for evening classes for wind instruments in a suitable hall . . . Every amateur band . . . should have the privilege of sending three of its members to the School of Music to receive free musical instruction. This school to be under the joint management of the Corporation and the Academy.[261]

This was communicated the next day to the town clerk by John O'Donnell, a self-appointed spokesman for the bands, who was to become an important if troublesome figure in the subsequent development of the Municipal School of Music.[262]

A week later the deputation was heard. O'Donnell read the statement, which asked that a portion of the Coulson funds, which were about to be entrusted to the RIAM, should be allocated to the musical education of amateur bands, which he calculated to number over one thousand.

> The Academy of Music has all through studiously ignored this class. What the council have done was this: they have kept up a wind instrument class in the Academy for six boys from the Marlborough-street Schools, and also for such pupils as could attend from 10 to 12 a.m.— hours during which no working man could attend; and in 1876 they appointed Mr. van Maanen (conductor of the Constabulary band) to superintend this class at a salary of £40 per year. But what this council principally required of Mr. van Maanen was that he should provide a certain number of the Constabulary band for the pupils' concerts and other examination performances, to keep before the public the semblance of there being a wind instrument class in the Academy. During the past twelve years the members of the Constabulary have been thus brought before the public as pupils of the Academy, and this friendly deception on the public has in that time cost the Academy over £600, and not one player produced from amongst the pupils.[263]

The use of the word 'friendly' suggests that, despite the hard-hitting tenor of the statement, O'Donnell knew that the Academy had been genuinely struggling to maintain orchestral practice by such means. Van Maanen was not the first conductor from a band background to work in the Academy. And the cardinal point must be borne in mind that, even after forty years of the Municipal School (twenty-five of which were under the Corporation's direction), difficulties in the training of wind and brass players were such that, as we have already noted, successive orchestras, like Esposito's Dublin Orchestral Society and the Philharmonic, relied on army and police personnel, with the strings being recruited predominantly from the RIAM.

The statement continued to analyse in detail the alleged misdoings of the Academy in 'employing' bandsmen to masquerade as 'pupils'; but its main thrust was to urge the Corporation to ensure that a new departure took place.

> What this deputation . . . have come here for to-day is to respectfully urge your Lordship and the gentlemen of the Corporation who are

members of the new governing body of the Academy to energetically interfere in the management.

There were, however, at least two elements in the statement that indicate, firstly, that O'Donnell as spokesman was not merely the mouthpiece of the bandsmen but was also giving voice to a personal agenda and, secondly, that the bands themselves were more concerned with effecting a change in their own affairs than with securing a new form of education. O'Donnell rehearsed his own experiences of the Academy:

> The Council of the Academy have now circulated a report that they opened an evening class for the amateur bands last year, that they put it under my direction, and that it was a failure, because the bandsmen would not attend. Why, my Lord, the class was a great success. In the first six weeks I got in eleven pupils, and these pupils were so well up in their parts that the Council for the first time in the history of the Academy was enabled to dispense with the services of both police and military bandsmen for the annual pupils' concert.

One is entitled to wonder why, in the face of such success (which O'Donnell claimed would have attracted a further thirty pupils in the following year) any new initiative was necessary. The fact that the RIAM immediately acceded to the request from the Corporation to establish a separate school indicates that this was welcomed as a strategy that would prevent the Academy itself from becoming deluged by such an influx of students, to the detriment of its normal teaching. It was also a strategy that maintained the distinction between the genres of music played in the two schools, rather than the instruments taught. Eventually, the difficulties the Governors encountered as managers of the Municipal School of Music suggest that it was O'Donnell himself who was largely responsible for the personal frictions and failures of communication that led to the RIAM withdrawing from the Municipal School.

The second revealing point in the statement is the suggestion that, in addition to educating bandsmen, the Academy and Corporation together could 'assist them in the effort . . . to secure a portion of the open air engagements in the city and suburbs, which are at present altogether monopolised by the military band of the garrison.' At that time, military bands played sixty times each season in Bray and forty times in Kingstown (Dún Laoghaire); with engagements in Merrion, Blackrock, Dalkey, Clontarf, and Malahide, the total numbered over three hundred, while the annual running costs of St James's Band in 1887/88 were £150 and its income only £24.[264] In this respect the bands (and the Municipal School of Music) were singularly successful, and it is an indication of the type of instruction in the new school, and the direction it took, that by the turn of the century Dublin bands were giving a comprehensive series of summer concerts, principally in St Stephen's Green, St Michan's Park, and Halston Street Park, each performance earning the band four guineas.[265]

A nationalist sentiment can be detected in such a move: not only was it intended to have Dublin bands playing for Dubliners but they would also oust those of the garrison. But, in a lengthy digression at the end of his statement, with a strongly xenophobic attack on Esposito that echoes previous campaigns against foreign presences in the Academy, O'Donnell gives a hint that it was not simply the old enemy but new influences that were feared. Commending the work of Levey over the decades in training so many principal string players, O'Donnell turned to the facilities afforded to such 'Continental artists' as Lauer and Rudersdorff and the unnamed Esposito as the elected representative of the new Board of Studies on the Board of Governors.

> I do not see anything objectionable in [their] being engaged in Dublin provided they do not get an undue preference in competition with native artists. These gentlemen have been kindly received in this country by the public and the musical profession. I am therefore very much surprised that they should have been so indiscreet as to flout and insult the recognised head of the musical profession in Ireland, a gentleman held in the highest esteem by all classes of the public and the musical profession, both Irish and English. I allude to their electing a representative of the principal professors in the Academy to be a member of the governing body—taking advantage of their numerical superiority these Continental professors passed over the recognised head of the musical profession in Ireland and elected an Italian gentleman only recently come to Ireland. When I mention that Mr. Joseph Robinson is the recognised head of the musical profession in this country, I do not forget Sir R. Stewart. He is a great musical composer, one of a trio of musicians— Balfe, Wallace and Stewart, of whom any country might be proud.

O'Donnell betrays more than a dislike of Esposito in this diatribe. He displays an ignorance of the procedure by which Esposito had been elected and of the constitution of the Board of Studies. He also finds himself in such difficulties, having elevated Robinson above Stewart, that he has to join Stewart to the two indisputably international (as opposed to Anglo-Irish) musicians, a company Stewart did not merit.

A further point needs to be mentioned here. The emphasis was on the need for the improvement of bands rather than for individual tuition, an issue rightly corrected by the Academy when it opened the school.

On the proposal of the Parnellite councillor Thomas Mayne MP, the statement was referred to the Corporation members of the RIAM Board. Negotiations continued throughout 1889 and early 1890, which resulted in the grant of £300 mentioned earlier, the first payment being made on 28 October 1890.[266] The purpose of the school, as spelt out two years later, was 'to assist the RIAM in providing musical education at low rates for artisan and labouring classes and members of recognised trade bands first, and after for those whose position in life . . . renders them unable to obtain musical instruction if denied the advantages of the Academy.'[267]

It was agreed that the governing body of the school would be identical with the RIAM Board of Governors; that piano, organ and singing would not be taught; that string instruments would be taught in Westland Row and wind and percussion instruments at the new premises in South William Street; that members of trade bands would be taught at reduced rates; and that there would be two bands, each having twice-weekly practices. Some instruments were to be purchased for the students but others were to be hired from W. Higgins, 19 Essex Quay, at the rate of four shillings a month or ten shillings a quarter for brass, and six shillings or fifteen shillings for reed instruments.[268] The Corporation decided that the expenditure of £300 (£12,000 today) was warranted, although the sentiment was expressed that there was already a sufficient burden on the ratepayers.[269]

By September 1890 the Governors were in a position to ask Dr Jozé 'to submit a list of Professors for the Municipal School of Music and draft an advertisement as to opening of classes.'[270] A week later Jozé nominated the following:

> Flute & Piccolo, Mr. Ellard; oboe, Sgr. Regazzoli; clarinet, Mr. Conroy; bassoon, Mr. Haveron; horn, Mons. Brasfort; cornet, Mr. O'Donnell; trombone, Mr. van Maanen; drums, Mr. Trundle.[271]

ROYAL IRISH ACADEMY OF MUSIC.

DUBLIN MUNICIPAL SCHOOL OF MUSIC.

The following
CLASSES WILL OPEN
ON
WEDNESDAY EVENING, October 15th, 1890,
AT THE
ASSEMBLY ROOMS, WILLIAM-STREET :—

Flute and
Piccolo,   Professor, Mr G Ellard,   6 o'clock p.m.
Clarinet,   „   Mr J O Conroy,   8   „
Horn,   „   Mons E Brasfort, 8   „
Drums,   „   Mr W H Trundle, 6   „

Other Classes will be announced at a future date.

Fees—Five Shillings per term (two lessons weekly). To pupils paying into the fund of any existing city band half the above fee.

Intending pupils are requested to enter their names (stating instrument) at the Royal Irish Academy of Music, 36 Westland-row.

By order,

T. R. G. JOZÉ, Mus. D.,
Secretary.

7360

However, the newspaper advertisement that appeared on 6 October mentions specifically only flute and piccolo, clarinet, horn, and drums, stating that 'other classes will be announced at a future date.'[272] The fees were to be five shillings per term (ten pounds today) for two lessons per week, half price to pupils paying into the fund of any existing city band. Later, fees would be charged to 'non-artisans' or clerks at one pound per term (forty pounds today), provided they showed that they earned less than thirty shillings a week.[273]

It was not the first school of its kind. Cork had become the first municipality to inaugurate a school of music, in 1878, when, under the Public Libraries Acts of 1855 and 1877 (the latter influenced by the local MP Nicholas Murphy),[274] it became possible for a local authority to finance the employment of music teachers and the purchase of music and instruments. In London, the Guildhall School was to follow in 1880.

The school opened at the Assembly Rooms, South William Street, on 15 October 1890, with twenty-three pupils: six flutes, one oboe, five clarinets, two horns, four cornets, three trombones, and two drums. The accounts for the first full year of operation show that the grant was just enough to keep the school in existence, and that its expansion was obviously inhibited by the Governors' intention of staying within the budget.

Professors' fees	£176	
Cash prizes	£20	
Caretaker	£6	10s
Examiners' fees	£10	10s
Printing and posting	£13	10s
Advertisements	£12	
Petty cash	£1	10s

£240 (today, £9,600)

By March 1891, examinations were being organised with a jury consisting of Stewart, Robinson, and Thomas Mayne, with prizes of thirty shillings, twenty shillings and ten shillings for flute and cornet, thirty shillings and twenty shillings for clarinet, and one pound each for piccolo, horn, trombone and drums. The prizes were to be advertised 'at prominent positions in the City,' including the public libraries.[275] This had the effect of increasing the numbers on the register from twenty-three to thirty-three at the close of the third term (30 June 1891): flute and piccolo, eight; clarinet, four; bass clarinet, one; horn, one; sax horn, five; cornet, eight; trombone, two; drums, four. On 15 and 16 June, after the examinations, the following prizes were awarded:

Mr. Tallon, piccolo	20/–
Mr. J. McCluskey, flute 1	30/–
Mr. P. Cogan, flute 2	20/–
Mr. W. Kenny, clarinet 1	30/–
Mr. A. Lett, clarinet 2	20/–

Mr. W. Paisley, clarinet 3	10/–
Mr. J. Doyle, bass clarinet	10/–
Special prize—Mr. J. Murphy, drum	20/–
Mr. P. Murphy, trombone	20/–

By the fourth term (September 1891) the number of pupils had reached forty-four, with increases particularly in the study of clarinet, cornet, and saxhorn. The following year the total was fifty-three, and this rose in 1893 to fifty-eight.

In 1891 the Governors recorded that 'there is an evident wish amongst the public that classes for stringed instruments should be established in the Municipal School, and [they] would be glad to meet this wish did their income enable them, and could the classes be formed without interfering with those already existing in the Academy.'[276] In response to the addition of bombardon to the instruments taught, one was purchased for £6 from McNeill, together with an oboe for £4 10s and a flute for £1 10s.[277] Euphonium was also added to the curriculum; but already by April 1892 we find a committee of Stewart, Brasfort and Jozé recommending that numbers be limited to seventy, allowing an expected expansion of the clarinet faculty to twenty and of drums to eight but putting a limit on the flute-piccolo and cornet departments.[278]

In 1893 a tonic sol-fa class was formed under W. H. Nesbitt, with over thirty members, but it is not clear how many of these were learning instruments, for which there was a total of sixty-six. At the same time the Governors mooted the idea of forming a municipal band from the pupils as a way of demonstrating that a successful common identity had been established through the existence of the school. This elicited a rather surprising semi-rebuke from the Corporation's Finance and Leases Committee, which observed that the priority was to provide instrumental instruction in wind instruments, with the intention of forming a municipal band a subsidiary aim.[279]

A further objection to the idea of a municipal band was expressed by 'C.H.O.' (presumably Charles Oldham) in 1899. 'On the whole we would be sorry to see the amateur bands broken up to form a Municipal Band, the formation of which would be the putting up of a bribe to tempt the best players [in existing bands] to desert their comrades.'[280]

The annual reports for 1895 and subsequent years reiterated the Governors' intention of forming a municipal band, but irregularity of attendance at practice was blamed for the failure to achieve this. In 1899 this had been crystallised into the idea of a band 'to perform in such places as shall be sanctioned by the Academy'—the Mansion House and 'in the parks on Sundays' being particularly in mind;[281] but the success of individual bands under the aegis of the school seems to have worked against this civic-minded intention. At the same time, bands whose members had been trained at the Municipal School—most notably York Street and St James's —were becoming increasingly successful at the Feis Ceoil. In 1902, for example, the Lord Mayor, at the Municipal School prize-giving, drew attention to the fact that thirty out of the thirty-seven members of the York Street Band had been trained in the school.[282] In 1902 an attempt was made by the Academy (on the suggestion of John Irwin, who was also a councillor) to interest the Dublin Fife and Band Association in holding a contest for Dublin and county bands, with a top prize of four pounds, but nothing appears to have come of this.[283]

Another important development in 1902 was the decision of the corporation to require the Dublin Orchestral Society to divert fifty pounds of the municipal grant it received by way of the RIAM to the employment in its concerts of teachers or students from the Municipal School; this would

Municipal = School = of = Music.

BAND PROMENADE

— IN —

St. Michan's Park, Sunday, July 22nd, 1900,

FROM 4 TO 6.30 P.M.

Music by Band of Workmen's Club, 41 York St.

⮞ PROGRAMME. ⮜

MARCH	...	" The Last Stand,"	...	*Myddleton*
OVERTURE	...	"Poet and Peasant,"	...	*Suppe*
VALSE	...	" The Kiss of Love,"	...	*Karl Kaps*
SELECTION	... " Reminiscences of Scotland," ...	*Fred Godfrey*
INTERMEZZO	... "Old love is never forgotten," ...	*Vollstedt*
SELECTION	...	" American Airs,"	...	*Thos. Bidgood*
VALSE	...	" Angelo Mio,"	...	*Daniel Pecorini*
SELECTION	...	" Irish Airs,"	...	*Hartmann*

Conductor—MR. W. TRUNDLE.

⮞ Great Irish Composers. ⮜

WILLIAM MICHAEL ROOKE was born in South Great Georges-street on September, 1794. From his childhood he displayed a great aptitude for music, and studied alone and unaided. In 1813 he took to music as a profession and became a teacher of the Violin and Pianoforte, and among his pupils was Balfe. In 1817 he became chorus leader in Crow-street Theatre, and in 1826 he was Leading Oratoris in Birmingham. The same year he came to London, where he published his first opera " Amilu," which was a great success, and established his reputation. He also produced other operas. He died October 1st, 1847, and was buried in Brompton Cemetery.

DOYLE, Printer, 9 Upper Ormond Quay, Dublin.

'encourage and stimulate the efforts of teachers and students of such instruments at the Municipal School of Music as are needed in the orchestra over which Signor Esposito so ably presides.'[284] The Dublin Orchestral Society was told that 'having an earnest desire . . . to assist, as far as they were empowered, the objects which your Society have in view, the Committee have sought and have found a method by which . . . the efforts of the students of orchestral instruments at the Municipal School of Music to attain thorough proficiency in the use of the instruments which they are studying will be stimulated,' on the understanding that the society would 'receive and, subject to a reasonable standard of proficiency, employ in their Orchestra students of such instruments at the Municipal School of Music as are usually required in the performances carried out from time to time by the Society.'[285]

In any case, friction between John O'Donnell and Conroy in particular,[286] and between O'Donnell and the rest of the staff in general, seems to have grown during 1893 and thereafter, chiefly over who was responsible for conducting band practice. O'Donnell, who claimed that he was working a 27-hour week at the Municipal School, seems to have had the ear of members of the Finance and Leases Committee, since in both 1898 and 1899 the committee's report on the estimates expressed strong reservations about the management and even the *raison d'être* of the institution, while in December 1897 a special meeting between the Corporation and the RIAM had been called, apparently at O'Donnell's instigation, to consider the workings of the Municipal School.[287] So, despite the fact that the inspector's report by L. E. Steele (which, given his predisposition to favour the RIAM, one would expect to approve the arrangements at the Municipal School) recorded a total of 255 in 1899, including a successful new violin class,[288] the seeds of dissension had been sown, and it was really only a matter of time before a complete breakdown took place in the relations between the Corporation and the RIAM. That this eventually took a further five years to happen might be attributed in part to the simultaneous development of the Schools Singing Competition (another contentious event) and in part to the fact that, until the formation of the Technical Education Committee of the Corporation, there was simply no-one else to manage the Municipal School, thus making closure the only other option.

In March 1904 'the Board, having heard that the Corporation of Dublin have it in contemplation to withdraw the grant to the Municipal School of Music, it was resolved that a sub-committee be appointed with power to take the necessary steps to wind up the Municipal School of Music.'[289] The secretary wrote to the city treasurer to state that notice had been given to the teachers, administration and caretaker and that 'the Governors regret extremely that the Corporation should have felt compelled without previous notice to suddenly stop the grant to this most useful institution or at all events until such time as definite arrangements had been effected whereby the work of the School could have been taken over by the Technical Education Committee.'[290] Despite assurances that no such action was intended[291] and, a year later, an increase in the grant to £600,[292] the Academy clearly knew from other sources that a closure was imminent and proceeded towards an orderly withdrawal, including the preparation of an inventory.[293]

On the surface, however, the Board continued to operate the school as if everything were normal, even appointing Thomas Rowsome as a teacher of Irish pipes, and actively seeking the William Street Courthouse as alternative accommodation. But in June 1905 the city treasurer put the Academy on notice that the Corporation was likely to apply cut-backs in this area, in favour of expenditure on libraries.[294] If that was the case, the situation is likely to have been manipulated by O'Donnell, who had gone to the lengths of printing a pamphlet listing his grievances against the Academy's administration of the school, which, it is clear from the treasurer's letter, were receiving serious attention in City Hall. Finally, on 20 September 1905, the RIAM was curtly and officially told: 'I am to inform you that no further payment will be made for the maintenance of the Municipal School of Music to your Board.'[295] The Academy was asked if it was prepared to continue running the school under the supervision of the Technical Education Committee, which was unacceptable; and the control of the school, after fifteen experimental and instructive years, passed to that committee.[296]

A fruitful connection continued, however, with an interchange of teaching staff between the two establishments, including Arthur Darley, Florence Bloom, P. J. Griffith, and later Victor Love, John Larchet, and Michael O'Higgins, and this traffic helped to maintain unofficial good will between them, even though at management level relations were to become frosty in the nineteen-fifties and sixties.

There is an intimate connection between the development of the Academy curriculum, its staff and student profile, and the concert activity that was the chief means by which its work found public recognition. During the period under review in this chapter, all these aspects of the Academy underwent transformations, partly because of the external factors we have already adverted to but, more importantly, because of the internal dynamic with which music education was expanding.

Up to the incorporation of the RIAM under the Educational Endowments Act, the annual reports of the Committee stressed that financial stringencies had prevented the Academy from providing a fuller range of courses. The emphasis had remained on piano, strings, and singing (and, from 1879, organ). Thereafter, it became possible to engage in further pursuits, including orchestra and chamber music, without which a sense of collegiate musicmaking is much impoverished. Earlier attempts at forming a choral class— frustrated in part by the personality clashes between Robinson and his colleagues—gave way to better-established ventures. From 1905 the Students' Musical Union gave an entirely new dimension to concert life. Other instruments, such as the harp (the lack of which was considered an affront in an Irish academy), make their appearances in the curriculum, but they also make their disappearances, as student demand waxed and waned, the double bass and viola being especially noticeable in this regard.

The organ school in particular enjoyed a marked and growing success, although Stewart was unable to persuade the Governors to install an instrument in the new Concert Room, which he considered necessary for choral performances and would enhance its letting potential to outside bodies. It appears that this was deemed impossible on the grounds of cost (tenders were invited from Telford of Dublin, Forster and Andrews of Hull, and Conacher of Huddersfield) and also because accommodating the organ would have meant acquiring property beside the new hall, which was not at that time available for purchase.[297]

Nevertheless, the number of organ students multiplied, and teaching had a direct professional purpose. In 1898 Charles Marchant addressed the Governors:

> Would you have any objection to have the names of organ pupils who have received organ appointments (direct from the Academy) posted on the board in the hall [?]. There have been quite a large number of pupils who have obtained positions in churches within the last few years. I think it would be an encouragement to others to learn—besides been [*sic*] a recognition that the Academy is doing not only good but useful work.[298]

This was in fact a substantial source of employment, and in 1905, when the Academy organ was rebuilt by Conacher, a list of students successful in obtaining church positions was published.[299]

It became a feature of the prize-giving and pupils' annual concerts in the Royal University buildings that they were prefaced by an organ recital. In 1895 the *Freeman's Journal* commented on Stewart's achievement in creating the organ school, which became increasingly obvious in 1905 with a series of recitals designed to show off the new instrument in Westland Row. In all these public presentations the majority of performers were women (Marion Hilton being one of the foremost), and presumably their predominance means that they had a distinct chance of employment in both Catholic and Protestant churches. We should recall the ironic fact that in Joyce's story from *Dubliners*, 'The Dead', one of the Misses Morkan (modelled on the Misses Flynn of 15 Usher's Island) was the organist of Haddington Road church (where in real life Bishop Donnelly was parish priest). Those organists trained in the Academy who were not women were not negligible, but they were few, J. Desmond Fitzgerald, Godfrey Bird and W. S. Greig being some of the exceptions.

Marchant had been appointed in 1894 in succession to Stewart, as well as being appointed conductor of TCD Choral Society and of the Strollers and organist of TCD Chapel, and in addition had held the post of organist at St Patrick's Cathedral since 1879. He was succeeded by G. W. P. Hewson, whose international reputation was enormous. In 1905 five estimates were submitted for a new organ, by Telford, John White (Dublin), Conacher (Dublin and Huddersfield), Forster and Andrews (Hull), and Gray and Davidson (London), of which Jozé and Marchant chose that of Conacher, considering that Telford's submission was 'utterly inadequate'.[300] The new organ was inaugurated with a series of recitals that reflected the achievement of Marchant in building up the organ school. David Lee comments:

> The 1905 rebuild by Conacher represented a considerable enlargement of the original and almost certainly incorporated most, if not all, of the Telford pipe work. The original two-manual scheme was enlarged to a three-manual, with the addition of a reasonably substantial swell division which included a mixture and some reed stops. However, Conacher might well be described as a journeyman organ builder, whose work was reliable but uninspired, and the resulting specification does not give one much confidence as to the effectiveness of this instrument.[301]

The specification was:

		Feet	*Pipes*
Great organ, CC to A			
1. Open diapason (large scale)	Metal	8	58
2. Clarabella	Wood	8	58
3. Bell gamba	Metal	8	58
4. Harmonic flute	Metal	4	58
5. Principal	Metal	4	58
6. Harmonic piccolo	Metal	2	58
Swell organ, CC to A			
7. Violin diapason	Metal	2	58
8. Stopped diapason	Wood	8	58
9. Viol da gamba	Metal	8	58
10. Voix céleste	Metal	8	58
11. Waldflöte	Wood	4	58
12. Mixture (two ranks)	Metal	2	116
13. Oboe	Metal	8	58
14. Trumpet	Metal	8	58
Choir and solo organ, CC to A			
15. Lieblich gedact	Wood	8	58
16. Dulciana	Metal	8	58
17. Lieblich flute	Metal	4	58
18. Orchestral clarinet ⎫ enclosed in	Metal	8	46
19. Orchestral bassoon ⎭ swell box	Metal	16	46
Pedal organ, CCC to F			
20. Open diapason	Wood	16	30
21. Bourdon	Wood	16	30
22. Unison (derived from no. 20)	Wood	8	12

Couplers
23. Swell to great
24. Swell to pedals

25. Great to pedals
26. Tremulant

Composition pedals

Three to great organum, three to swell organ, two to choir organ
Thumb tremulant to swell organ
Melvin hydraulic engine
Tubular pneumatic action to choir and pedal organs
Radiating and concave pedal board

As a showcase for the talents of a career-oriented faculty the organ was perhaps more persuasive than it was as a provider of musical experiences *per se*. The Conacher instrument (with a rebuild by Willis in 1957) continued in use until 1987, when it was replaced with a new instrument commissioned from Prosser of Belfast (see below, p. 374–5). In 1914, however, there seems to have been a dip in standards, particularly where sight reading and extemporisation were concerned. The external examiner, Dr Kitson, pointed out that 'an organist may be called upon to transpose a hymn & play from a vocal score and extemporize . . . If he can do none of these things readily he is not fit for his post. What one desires is to see the musician with "gumption", full of resource and initiative, quickwitted for any emergency, rather than the mechanic who can play a piece well after much tribulation.' He called for the organ department to explore the works of Max Reger, Karg Elert and César Franck as examples of a more aesthetic style.[302]

Another area requiring remedial attention was the choral class, whose existence, in the vicissitudes of the post-Robinson era, had become tenuous. In 1895 Marchant agreed to institute a new choral class, which began on 15 March with forty-six sopranos, twenty-four altos, twelve tenors, and twenty-two basses. At the same time (and rather confusingly) a vocal class also started under Gordon Cleather, who had just been recruited from the RCM.[303]

The vocal faculty had problems different from those of the instrumental departments, as illustrated by Alice O'Hea, writing to the Board in 1900.

> I beg to bring the following statement regarding the junior vocal classes before you in the hope that you will favourably entertain the views set forth.
>
> These classes differ of course altogether from the instrumental classes inasmuch as the singing pupils being all grown up have views & opinions of their own & when they know themselves to be progressing well with a teacher they strongly object to have to compulsorily move to another teacher & method. This has caused the Academy to lose many good voices. At present I have a very promising pupil in my class who says she will leave the Academy if she has to move from me. I can positively assert that this desire to continue in the class where they think they are getting on springs entirely from the pupils' own wish—no influence whatsoever being brought to bear by me nor do I confidently believe by any of the other teachers.

> If I might make a suggestion it would be
>
> 1st. To let the pupils select a teacher & remain with that teacher as long as they wish.
>
> 2nd. To open the competitions for scholarship & prizes to all the classes as in the case of the National Music prize.
>
> 3rd. The pupils to rise to a higher grade in their own class & to pay a higher fee as they progressed sufficiently to compete for these prizes.
>
> 4th. The head master to examine the pupils in order to decide when they were fit to be raised to the higher grade.
>
> All the teachers I have spoken to on the matter including Mr. Cleather approve of the idea.[304]

There is no suggestion that there was any division within the voice faculty—simply that singing carried within it qualitatively different difficulties, partly because of the nature of the 'instrument' and partly because of the later age at which a singer became mature. A year later, Palmieri wrote to the Governors:

> With respect to the gentlemen's class . . . the drawback with them is that they know very little or nothing of music, otherwise there would be a better result . . . It is greatly regrettable that singing, generally speaking, is not taken as seriously as any other branch of the musical art. Pupils (and their parents specially) have the wrong idea that they could sing songs after having had a few lessons only. It is true that not everybody aspires to become a public singer; but how [much] more pleasurable it would be to listen to a well educated voice, small as it might be, instead of having a bad attempt to render a song without even the essential and most important knowledge of how to breathe?[305]

The problems in the voice faculty were to explode within the next five years, not least because of plain speaking from another of the professors.

The deaths of Stewart (1894), Robinson (1898) and Levey (1899) represented a break not only with the Academy's earliest origins but also with the forms and sites of musical activity that had been traditional in, and central to, Dublin society from the eighteenth century: the cathedral choirs and organ-lofts, the theatres and the large-scale choral works. Although these traditions would continue to be actively represented in the Academy—through the burgeoning organ faculty and through the involvement of academicians in the Abbey Theatre—the new personnel in the vocal and string faculties were more wide-ranging and more dynamic in their interests and influence, resulting in a fresher, more outward-looking student body.

These deaths were marked in time-honoured tones, recording the solid achievements of the three as the milestones that they were. But Stewart, despite his interest in European musical news, never in his own work stretched out beyond the social or musical horizons of cathedral close or glee club, and Vignoles's and Culwick's reverent memorials enforce, rather than liberate him from, those parameters. Levey had been largely inactive since the destruction of the old Theatre Royal in 1880 and was seen as almost synonymous with a long-lost monument.[306] Robinson's obituary emphasises his roots in the cathedral tradition, the friendship with Mendelssohn and the creation of the Antient Concerts Society and Dublin Musical Society and makes it clear that he had been a hard worker, determined to make the best of the resource available. Stewart's and Robinson's names were joined by the *Irish Times* in apostrophising the younger musical generation: 'It will be difficult to attain the standard of fame, and to win that same measure of respect, which the past masters in their art have attained.'[307]

Their successors did in fact achieve and enlarge on their standards. It is during this period that the names of teachers and students alike emerge from the mere records and take on life, rounded by still-living recollection. We are thus able to give a flavour (for that is all it can be) of the hundreds of musicians whose experiences and careers were moulded, and in many cases created, by the Academy.

From the eighteen-nineties onwards, we see the striking emergence of musical families in the student body, among them those of Starkie, Dowse, Alton, Bloom, May, Lord, Jephson, Potterton, and Vance,[308] all apparently innately gifted and some of whom became important members of the music profession, while others, after a period of conspicuous academic excellence, remained amateurs. Many of these are discussed in the *intermezzo* dedicated to the Students' Musical Union; but here we wish to suggest the way in which successive generations of teachers and students seemed to inhabit and gradually transform the Academy and its repertoire.

The huge number of Academy concerts (apart from those of the Students' Musical Union itself) given between 1890 and 1920 constitute four main categories: prize-givings, annual concerts, 'afternoon concerts', and specific chamber music events, of which the afternoon concert was the most frequent type, based on a decision of the Governors to encourage more public appearances by the students as a form of shop window. In addition, Esposito's efforts with the Dublin Orchestral Society seem to have borne fruit in the Academy, since the orchestra, which he took over from Werner, gave several impressive performances in this period, although consistency in orchestral activity was not a feature of the period and has only in fact been stabilised in recent years. Esposito and Jozé, who became the conductor of the Academy orchestra in 1891, succeeded in having as many as thirty-one first and thirty-one second violins, with eight violas, ten cellos, and six basses, and about thirty wind. Perhaps to avoid criticism such as that levelled at the Academy by John O'Donnell, the programmes explicitly stated which members of the orchestra were scholars, 'rank and file' students, members of staff, with those 'not connected with the Academy' invariably supplying the wind and brass.

A typical programme from 1891 is:

De Bériot:	Violin Concerto in D (Patrick Delany)
Beethoven:	Piano Concerto in C minor (first movement) (Mr. L. Buchanan)

R. P. Stewart:	Suite for Violins
Haydn:	'Clock' Symphony
Chopin:	Nocturne in G (piano solo, Miss Magee)
Auber:	Overture, *Fra Diavolo*

Another, from 1896, is:

Mozart:	Overture, *Die Zauberflöte*
Beethoven:	Larghetto from Symphony No. 2
Weber:	Overture, *Euryanthe*
Schubert:	Ballet music from *Rosamunde*
Mendelssohn:	War march from *Athalie*

In 1918 Esposito conducted the orchestra at a concert in the Mansion House in aid of the Red Cross, for which the programme was:

Leonardo Leo (1694–1744):	Concerto for four violins (Muriel Starkie, Rosalind Dowse, Rita Lynch, Primrose [?] Deane)
Elgar:	Elegy
Coleridge-Taylor:	Novelty in A minor, op. 52 No. 3
Weber:	'O Fatima' from *Abu Hassan* (sung by Constance Howe)
Mozart:	Serenade
Esposito:	Rêverie, op. 34 No. 7, arranged for solo violin (Vera Wilkinson)
Handel:	Minuet, Musetta and Gavotte (orchestrated by Martucci)
Gluck:	Aria 'O del mio dolce ardor' *(Paride ed Elena)* (Marion Dunne)
Grieg:	Spring Song, op. 34
Grainger:	Irish reel, 'Molly on the Shore'

If a report in the *Daily Express* is an accurate reflection of the time, the Governors succeeded in their aim, since the concerts at the Antient Concert Rooms and the prize-givings in Earlsfort Terrace were generally packed—no doubt partly on account of the attendance at the latter by the Lord Lieutenant—which 'afforded proof . . . of the wide circle of influence exercised by the Academy . . . and also supplied an appreciative indication of how its efforts are regarded and recognised.'[309] They demonstrate the emphasis on performance that permeated a young musician's life at that time. Alice Brough, who entered the Academy in 1916, told the editors that student life, and the life of a young professional on which she was then embarked, involved constant work in a wide variety of genres, including, after the advent of radio in 1926, sudden calls to the GPO for deputy work. She summed it up in the remark, 'You were always getting ready for something!'

Among those who were 'always getting ready,' in addition to the members of the *familles nombreuses* already mentioned, were the brothers Frank and Jack Cheatle (the latter to become leader of the RÉLO), Arthur Duff (a future conductor, composer and musicologist but then an organist and pianist), James Doyle (later head of the Army School of Music and first conductor of the RÉSO), Mina Davin and her sister Maud (who was by turns the director of the Municipal School and powerful chairman of the Academy Board in the nineteen-fifties and sixties), Laelia Fineberg, a singer, pianist and cousin of Samuel Beckett, the pianists Rhona Clark, Dorothy Stokes, and Dina Copeman (whose sisters Ivy and Iris were also prominent students), Kathleen Roddy (a singer who went on to become a Radio Éireann announcer), Frank Harrison (a musicologist), Mercedes McGrath (the mother and grandmother of Academy teachers), Rita Broderick, née Lynch (also the mother of a present-day Academy teacher, Maeve Broderick), and Thomas Hall (a remarkably accomplished singer).

The sex imbalance reflects the greater emphasis on music in girls' education generally, which was in turn a result of social prejudices about what was 'nice' and proper, strings being considered 'sissy' for boys. A feature remarked on by the *Freeman's Journal* in 1896, that 'the great majority of those who won prizes were ladies,'[310] continues to be a fact of life in the Academy today, although it has become more common than in earlier decades to find boys studying stringed instruments and girls those of the wind and brass departments.

A junior pupils' concert given on 24 June 1907 gives us some idea of both the number and the variety of items and the range of music, much of it from composers quite forgotten today:

Gurlitt	Overture des Marionettes (violin trio) (Masters A. Fitzgerald, Jones, and Meyerson)
Niels Gade	'Sylphides' piano solo (Zenobia Daly)
Pélissier	'Awake, Awake'—song (Sara Duncan)
Warner	Air de ballet—violin solo (Nora Weatherill)
Essipoff	'Tuber Rose'—piano solo (Maud Potterton)
Max Stenge	'Damon'—song (Alice McCarthy)
Van Biene	'Slumber Song'—violin solo (Walter Starkie)
Grieg	'Papillon'—piano solo (Annie Goldfoot)
Papini	'Idyll'—violin duet (Hilda Cowan and Phyllis Anderson)
Mendelssohn	'Spring Song'—piano solo (Agnes Brown)
Benedict	'In My Wild Mountain Valley'—song (Kathleen Ryan)
Mendelssohn	'Song Without Words'—for cello solo (Cecile Jephson)
Beethoven	Allegro molto from Sonata for Piano Duet, op. 6 (Frank Smith and Cecil Whelan)
Irish airs arranged by Jozé for orchestra	
Mendelssohn	'Song Without Words'—piano solo (Hilda Collins)
Goring Thomas	'Wind in the Trees'—song (Mary Delany)
Kirchner	Albumblatt—piano solo (Eileen Oulton)
Giordani	'Caro Mio Ben'—song (Eileen Brown)
Wagner	Albumblatt—violin solo (Hilda Dowse)
Schubert	Impromptu in A flat—piano solo (Annie Thompson)
Jacoby	Hungarian Dance—violin solo (Mollie Burke)

Brocca	'Canto del Ruscelletto'—piano solo (Gwen Lloyd)
Hiller	'Lord Whom My Inmost Soul Adoreth'—song (Minnie McConkey)
Beethoven	Minuet from Piano Sonata in G (Eileen Hopkins)
Böhm	'Moto Perpetuo'—violin solo (Janice Thompson)

German volkslied arranged by Jozé for orchestra

An 'afternoon performance' on 26 October 1911 had the following programme and artists:

Weber	'Moto Perpetuo'—piano solo (Annie Goldfoot)
Tosti	'La Serenata'—song (Grace Kennedy)
d'Ambrosio	Canzonetta—violin solo (Angela Clarke)
Allitsen	'A Song of Thanksgiving'—song (Edith Shaw)
Harty	Romance—cello solo (Cecile Jephson)
Gounod	'Far Greater in His Lowly State'—song (Mary Delany)
Schumann	'Des Abends' and 'Aufschwung' for piano (Olive Young)
Goring Thomas	'A Summer Night'—song (Maud Horne)
Brahms	Two Hungarian Dances for violin (Norah Byrne)
Woodforde Finden	'O Flower of All the World'—song (Charlotte Hobson)
Arr. Stanford	'Love at My Heart' (Ethel Nicholson)
Paganini-Liszt	Étude in E for piano (Miss F. Johnston)

During these decades an average of six or seven such concerts were given each year, allowing junior and senior pupils to perform in public as well as on the more formal occasions, when the scholars and prize-winners were the focus of attention. Without making a tedious compilation, we might mention items and performers such as Alice McCarthy and Nora Sidford playing the Franck Violin Sonata in A (1910), Thomas Hall singing the prologue to *Pagliacci* in the same programme as Victor Love's performance of the Chopin Ballade in G minor (1911), and Walter Starkie's characteristic playing of Sarasate's Zigeunerweisen (1914), which, judging by their subsequent careers, would have been high points of the calendar. One would give much to have been able to witness the evolving talents of the violinists Maud Davin (later Aiken) and Victoria Delaney (later Lupton) or of the great trio of pianists Dorothy Stokes, Rhona Clark, and Dina Copeman, or to have heard chamber music played by combinations of the Dowses and the Starkies.

In one of her articles in the *Weekly Irish Times*, Annie Patterson went out of her way to commend the work of the RIAM teachers, listing among others the Germans, French and Italians Bast, Wilhelmj, Grisard, Esposito and Palmieri, in the company of the Englishman Cleather and the Irish Oldham, O'Hea, Rooke, Jozé and Marchant, thus demonstrating her faith in 'foreigners' as well as the British, many of them receiving full-page feature articles from her pen in the remarkable series of over a hundred pieces in the *Weekly Irish Times* from 1899 to 1901.

The Italians, whose choral work we discussed in the previous chapter, and who also included the violinists Papini and his successor Simonetti, and Germans such as Bast, Wilhelmj, and Rudersdorff, met and leavened those of native stock such as Patrick Delany, Arthur Darley, and the remarkable O'Hea sisters. When Rudersdorff resigned in 1890, a cellist named Weinhardt (recommended by Clara Schumann) was offered the position but wrote somewhat strangely: 'Sir! I much regret that I cannot accept the place, because another cellist is living in Dublin. If I can be alone here, I would be very glad to live in Dublin.'[311] Where one might expect a recurrence of the chauvinism of previous decades, there was in fact an extraordinary interchange between Irish and foreign artists, which continues to be a feature of the Academy to the present day.

The centrality of the Academy staff to the wider music-making in Ireland continued, so much so that in 1895 the *Freeman's Journal* commented that Bast, Haveron and others, having performed in *The Creation* for the Belfast Philharmonic on one night, had made their way immediately to Dublin for *St Paul* by the Dublin Musical Society on the next.[312] Their work was not entirely of a serious nature—or at least they were not always to approach music-making with utter seriousness—as we learn from the fact that four musicians each contributed a movement to a 'toy symphony': Culwick (*adagio patetico*), Jozé (Er-in variations), Esposito (*scherzo fugoso*), and Joseph Smith (*stretta finale*), with instrumentation including 'timbrel in aspic', 'rattlesnake carnivora', 'zufola kodak', 'extra contra sackbut', 'foghorn in xx', 'gong furioso', and 'tuba e tremolo' (the last played by Esposito), which received at least one Dublin and one London performance in the years 1895–98, under the auspices of the Incorporated Society of Musicians.[313]

Indeed, when the Incorporated Society of Musicians met in Dublin in 1895 (the occasion of Margaret O'Hea's lecture), two-thirds of the Dublin teachers present were Academy personnel.[314] Many of them enjoyed considerable public success as solo artists. Bast was a regular performer, and at one of his recitals, in addition to a trio by Clara Schumann, his own fantasia of Irish airs for cello and piano was given, as well as a string quartet on Irish airs (Darley, Joshua Watson, Grisard, and Bast).[315]

Born in 1856, Bast (christened Heinrich but preferring to be called Henri) had brought to Dublin his experience as a member of the court orchestra in Munich and as principal cellist with the Hamburg Philharmonic, playing under Wagner,[316] Rubinstein, Liszt, Bülow, Brahms, and Saint-Saëns. As the forerunner of Clyde Twelvetrees, to whom so much of the success of the Academy's cello teaching is attributed, Bast should be acknowledged as another powerful influence. 'As regards taste and expression, the Irish student has a great deal more natural musical talent than any English learner,' he told Annie Patterson. 'The Irish would become infinitely better players than the English, if they would but spend as much time as the latter over technical development . . . The future musical progress of the country . . . will largely belong to Ireland's *female* intelligence, taste and love for music.'[317] Bast came to the Academy at the behest of Papini, and in preference to Carl Fuchs of the Brodsky Quartet, who, it had been hoped, would take charge of the orchestra as well as the cello school.[318] He died prematurely of appendicitis in 1907.

Arthur Warren Darley, who, as a solo performer of Irish airs, preceded the Abbey Theatre orchestra conducted by Larchet, gave many recitals. He was a member of a distinguished artistic, literary and medical family, which included Dion Boucicault; his father, Henry Warren Darley, an Academy Governor, was a violinist and player of the uilleann pipes. Darley was described by Katherine Tynan as 'God's violinist for ever.' He was not only a brilliant classical musician but also a dedicated collector and performer of traditional music. As Annie Patterson recalled on his death in 1929, 'he was a master; broad, convincing and sympathetic in his style . . . He identified himself with the culling and preservation of what music the country still possessed in a somewhat fluctuating and unrecorded condition.'[319] In the last year of his life he became the first designated director of the Municipal School of Music; he is commemorated in the Feis Ceoil by the Darley Prize for unaccompanied Bach. His son, also Arthur and himself a fine violinist as well as a doctor, was a friend of Samuel Beckett in the Irish Red Cross hospital at Saint-Lô at the close of the Second World War.[320]

Another distinguished fiddler whose work straddled the two traditions was Patrick Delany, who studied at the Academy under Jozé, Stewart, and Papini, playing with Papini in the RDS recitals. He was a prize-winning composer at the 1901 Feis and wrote the incidental music for Yeats's *The Countess Cathleen*. He taught in the Academy from 1896 to 1946.

We have already spoken of the remarkable O'Hea family. Mary O'Hea, who taught declamation at the Academy, began her career as an actress at the London Lyceum with Irving, became a teacher of elocution at the Marlborough Street schools, and acted occasionally at the Abbey (she appeared in 1910 in Casimir Markiewicz's *Mary*, produced by his own Independent Dramatic Company). In the later years of the nineteenth century she was famous for her 'declamation recitals', which included musical items. Like her older and younger sisters, Mary O'Hea lived—and worked—to a great age.

Long association with the Academy was (and continues to be) a regular feature of the teaching staff. Before compulsory retirement at seventy (now sixty-five), teaching careers of over fifty years were not uncommon, and where the teacher had previously been a student it was possible for him or her to have been associated with the Academy for well over half a century, as witnessed recently in the career of Seán Lynch, senior piano professor, who entered the Academy as a student in 1944 and remained until retirement in 1994. Thomas Weaving, who first enters the Academy 'hall of fame' in 1896, winning a junior prize for harmony, was still a member of the Board of Studies at his death in 1966; and Adelio Viani, appointed in 1917, remained until 1964. Several other teachers equalled or exceeded half a century, including Mrs Wright Barker, who retired in 1930 after fifty-six years as a teacher, having been a pupil before that; Annie Irwin, who retired in 1939 after fifty-two years; and Dorothy Stokes, who first entered the Academy's list of teachers as a pupil teacher in 1913.

Walter Starkie's praise for Papini was followed by his admiration for Achille Simonetti, another internationally acclaimed violinist, who took up a position as professor with the RIAM from 1912 until 1919. Starkie considered Simonetti, Esposito and Twelvetrees to have constituted one of the finest trios ever heard. After the Academy 'at home' in 1912 to welcome Simonetti, the *Irish Times* said that he 'produces tone of splendid fulness and "body" and his bowing is clean and expressive.' Of the trio it said: 'The three professors . . . are worthy to sustain the reputation of any teaching institution, and there are few in the United Kingdom that have professors in the three respective subjects of equal eminence.'[321] A pupil of Sivori (and therefore of Paganini), Dancla, and Massenet (for composition), Simonetti's first appearance in Dublin had been with Bottesini, and he was one of the first to tackle the daunting Brahms concerto, for which he wrote his own cadenzas. He wrote many elegant pieces for Academy students, several of which remained in the repertoire for decades and, typical of the work of a great teacher, are excellent vehicles for the pursuit of technique as well as interpretation.

Another distinguished addition to the string faculty was Adolph Wilhelmj, godson of Liszt and son of the German 'Violin King', August Wilhelmj, sometime Konzertmeister at Bayreuth, many of whose works his son introduced to the RIAM repertoire. He arrived in Dublin via Belfast in 1899 and became leader of the Dublin Orchestral Society as well as professor at the Academy and also became (with Bast and Esposito) a regular member of the Chamber Music Union, another forum in which the Academy professors became prominent in Dublin musical life.

Benedetto Palmieri, who taught at the Academy from 1900 to 1913, was one of those musicians who began in one faculty but moved to another quite different department of music. He had toured Italy and Greece as a child prodigy pianist, but after studying at the Naples Conservatory he decided to specialise in voice production, as a result of working as an accompanist with Patti, Sims Reeves, and Santly.[322] He thus continued the line of Italian voice teachers begun by Caracciolo and continued by Bozzelli and Cellini, which, after his own departure from Dublin, led to the appointment of Adelio Viani. In 1901, rather than attempt to boost Palmieri's income, which was necessary in so many other cases, the Governors had to take the opposite step and limit his earnings to £250 a year to ensure a greater spread of pupils among the other singing teachers.[323] For a brief period Palmieri taught James Joyce as a private pupil.

Despite, or perhaps because of, their eminence as musicians, some of the professors led colourful and not always commendable lives, Joseph Robinson's philandering being a startling example. Among these, it seems, was Guido Papini, whose virtuosic career has eclipsed what must be described as a discontinuous life-style. A child prodigy who became a friend of Vieuxtemps, through his interpretation of the latter's concertos, he was also a friend of Turgenev and a colleague of Sarasate, Bottesini, Piatti, Rubinstein, and

Bülow. Ill-health (alleged, at least) forced him to reduce his concert commitments in Europe and brought him to Dublin as a teacher, and of course performer.[324]

Shortly after his appointment, Papini had a heated altercation with the Board of Governors over his terms of employment, which, it seems, arose from a not uncommon misunderstanding based on linguistic differences, which have sometimes led to colourful eruptions in Academy tranquillity. On this occasion the Board retreated in the face of Papini's vigour and the correctness of his case. In 1896, however, he seems to have had trouble balancing his concert engagements, ill-health, and teaching duties. In January 1896 the lady superintendent, Susan Crean, drew the Governors' attention to the fact that two of the more senior pupils, Anna Kavanagh and Victoria Delaney, 'have had *no lessons at all from* Signor Papini since last May.' Both were pupil teachers, who taught juniors in exchange for their own free tuition.

> Signor Papini has been paid for the lessons up to Dec. 31st & is still marking his book as giving these two young ladies lessons. I asked him about the signatures on the 8th & 15th inst. and he replied that it was his affair. On Saturday 18th Sig. Papini was absent, he came on Tuesday 21st instead. Several of the pupils could not come on that day, yet they were marked as having had lessons, some of them have themselves made a declaration that they received no lesson. Perhaps it might be a good plan to confine Signor Papini's class to a limited number say 24 pupils selected from the most advanced of the class, that would give Signor Papini 4 hours teaching twice a week. In this way there would not be so great a chance of irregularities as at present. There are frequently eight or nine pupils in the class room at once, Signor Papini says it is necessary to have the pupils together. Perhaps if the number were limited to 6 it might be better and perhaps if one of the Committee would see Signor Papini & point out to him that the parents object to their children's lessons being interrupted by the talking of those pupils waiting in the class room. Miss Kohler who has recently been appointed pupil teacher also received lessons irregularly.[325]

A year later, other aspects of Papini's character began to catch up with him, in the form of a letter to the Governors from Hayes and Son, solicitors, enclosing a copy of an assignment of debt by Papini to the Standard Hotel Company (owners of the Metropole Hotel, where, it seems, Papini had been living), to which the Governors responded that they 'do not recognize the private dealings of Professors with their creditors.'[326] Hayes and Son, however, were persistent, and eventually the Governors agreed to make a monthly payment to them, which they held back from Papini's salary— their decision perhaps prompted by its coinciding with Papini's demand for an advance of pay, which they vehemently refused.[327]

Another Dublin teacher of singing, whose early career was overshadowed by that of Robinson, was the contralto Elizabeth Fennell (known after her marriage to the tenor John Scott as Scott-Fennell). She had studied at the

Academy with Robinson and Julia Cruise before going to London to study with Randegger, Poniatowski, and Costa, singing on the same platform as Tietjens and Sims Reeves and teaching Adelina Patti how to sing 'Kathleen Mavourneen' and 'The Minstrel Boy' authentically.[328] She was the sister-in-law of T. P. Gill, secretary of the Department of Agricultural and Technical Instruction, and mother-in-law of another RIAM professor, Gordon Cleather (1895–1901). Her obituary in the *Irish Times* said that 'her special forte was the singing of Irish songs and ballads, and never was the melody of our native music so delicately interpreted as through the medium of her charming voice.'[329]

A pupil of Charlotte Sainton-Dolby, Randegger, and William Shakespeare, Jeannie Rosse spent some time in grand opera, including the Carl Rosa company, before marrying a Dubliner, Harry Quinton, and beginning to teach in the RIAM, where she took responsibility not only for vocal tuition but also for declamation and deportment,[330] as well as pursuing a compelling sideline as a librettist for, among other projects, Charles Vincent's operetta *The Japanese Girl*. She later became managing director of the Leinster School of Music. Of her pupils she said: 'The great drawbacks in this country to turning out successful pupils are as follows: (*a*) the pupils' apparent inability to make a sustained and strenuous effort; (*b*) the want of richness and compass in voices, and the often delicacy of physique; (*c*) inferior musical education early in life, principally arising from the difficulty of hearing good music and good artistes, and (*d*) the young students' placid content with their own mediocrity.' To which Annie Patterson, her interviewer, added: 'The pity is that we Irish, in whom the higher instincts are so strongly developed, are failing in plodding qualities. But then, if we had *the will to work our way* we might be lacking in those qualities which go to keep us as a nation ever young and mercurial.'[331] Jeannie Quinton-Rosse was succeeded in the declamation class by Mary O'Hea.

A sad case was that of Alexandre Billet, who was regarded as one of the great piano exponents of his time; Grove listed him among the eighty-three greatest living 'executants on the piano.'[332] Appointed to replace Joseph Robinson on his dramatic resignation in 1875,[333] Billet became a member of the Council the following year.[334] His salary was fixed at £100 a year for five hours' teaching per week, with 10s 6d per additional hour (today, £3,000 plus £15.75 per hour).[335] After three years, however, he found that he could not make ends meet and wrote from 3 Lower Mount Street:

> Gentlemen—After a trial of three years I have the conviction that I cannot rely on a great number of pupils, so that my principal income ought to derive from the Academy. I apply for that purpose to the Council to have my fixed salary raised to £150 per annum. I would give $2\frac{1}{2}$ or three hours more lessons per week in consequence. I hope the Council will appreciate the reason of my request, and by agreeing to it secure permanently for the Academy an artist who, though wishing to settle in Dublin, could not do so without having a sufficient income.[336]

Brady replied on behalf of the Academy:

My dear Mons. Billet

The Council have most carefully considered your letter asking them to guarantee you a salary of £150 instead of £100 and I am sorry to say they do not feel that the circumstances will justify them in complying with your request. If the senior pupils were sufficiently numerous the Council would gladly place them in your class and thus be in a position to increase your income, but the pupils are not in the Academy and therefore the Council cannot afford the money. It is only by great care that the Council are able to support the Academy and avoid debt, at present as you can see from the minute books etc. our bank account is largely overdrawn and although we hope to balance the account before the end of the year still we cannot enter into an engagement which we do not see our way to fulfil without loss to the Academy. I enter into these details to explain to you why it is that with the greatest desire on our part to make your position more advantageous and remunerative it unfortunately is the case that the resources at our command do not give us the means. The Council will gladly by every means in their power facilitate your views and wishes and it is with very great regret they are not able to do so in the manner you ask them.[337]

Billet (now writing from 26 Northumberland Avenue, Kingstown), agreed to give the arrangement another year's trial, 'in the hope that some more advanced pupils may attend the Academy's classes,' but objecting to the fact that his pupils were transferred to another teacher (Stewart) when they progressed from second to first grade, 'as in Miss [Annie] Irwin's case who moreover wished expressly to join my class.' Billet had a constructive suggestion—even though the point was being made at the expense of another teacher—'that . . . all the new pupils would be preliminarily examined at the reopening of the classes. We would not then see the anomaly of pupils in second classes playing better and generally more advanced than many who are now in the first class.'[338]

It is possible that, despite his stature as a teacher, Billet was unable to attract private pupils, or that he was too choosy about whom he taught. Nevertheless, he persevered for ten further years at the Academy, until in 1888 he wrote:

21 Ely Place, 27 December 1888

Gentlemen—It is with sincere regret that I take the resolution of leaving the Academy. Since two or three years, everything has been done to diminish my influence there, and reduce the small salary which I accepted first when engaged in London to nearly nothing. I earn now 27 shillings [£52 today] per week, as I am still by special favor, no doubt, permitted to teach 9 pupils. You will agree with me that this position is not brillant [*sic*] enough for me to keep it any longer. I would certainly have preferred remaining in Dublin which I like and inhabit since 14 years, but this has been rendered impossible on such conditions.[339]

Clearly there was some bitterness on Billet's part, and a suspicion that someone within the Academy was working against him (could he have suspected Esposito?). A special meeting of the Executive Committee was held on 2 January 1889, resulting in a reply to Billet intimating that he might have been the victim of his own, rather than the Academy's, shortcomings. 'If your influence has been diminished and your salary in the Academy reduced it has not been through any desire or act of [the Council], and they cannot allow your remark on that subject to pass without notice. However considering your long connection with the Academy they would be sorry to be obliged to take your resignation as final, and they beg to refer it back to you for reconsideration.'[340]

The honorary secretaries were also requested to have an interview with Billet to explain matters more effectively. But by the end of the academic year things had not improved, and Billet again tendered his resignation, but again withdrew it, this time against an offer (without guarantee) of nine shillings per hour 'for such pupils as can be sent to you.'[341]

The exchange continued over the next four years, one letter containing the view of the Governors that they 'regret that pupils cannot be forced to join his class,'[342] until eventually Billet was offered a pension of fifty-two pounds a year, payable monthly in advance,[343] equivalent approximately to his annual income at that time. The Governors, in applying to the Commissioners, pointed out: 'Latterly his failing health has disabled him very much, and at his advanced age [seventy-seven] the re-establishment of his health must be looked on as very uncertain. During the long period of his connection with the Academy, Mons. Billet has given complete satisfaction to the Governors, who were very fortunate in securing the services of so eminent an artist.'[344]

When he accepted the offer of the pension, Billet wrote officially (and finally) to resign. '95 Lr Baggot St, 27 January 1894. Gentlemen—It is with the greatest regret that I beg to ask you to accept my resignation as professor of the pianoforte at the Academy. I will always remember with pleasure the ten or twelve years I first passed in Dublin . . .'[345] And two weeks later he was anxiously enquiring from Jozé, 'Let me know please, *how, when* and *where* this pension is payable.'[346]

Billet died three years later. This pathetic spectacle of a top-class professional who failed to capitalise on his talents, for whatever institutional or personal reasons, is somewhat extreme, but in lesser ways it was evident in others, reminding us that brilliance has its disadvantages as well as its rewards, and that perhaps seventy-seven was too advanced an age, especially at a time when the average life expectancy was forty-four.

A misfortune of a different kind arose in the case of a singing professor, Randal Woodhouse, who was appointed as a colleague to Palmieri in May 1902.[347] It was a move that, like so many in the voice faculty, was to disrupt Academy teaching and, in this instance, to lead to public scandal and legal proceedings. Woodhouse was a native of New Zealand, coming to Ireland by way of Australia after nearly dying of tuberculosis. 'A tenor of much power and of extremely pleasing quality,' as the *Freeman's Journal* called him,[348] he set himself, in the face of the existing staff, to expand and transform the teaching of singing. In addition to his appointment in the Academy, he also taught at the Leinster School and at the Loreto Schools in Rathfarnham and St Stephen's Green, as well as maintaining his own studio at 27 (later 116) Grafton Street. It was not so much his disruptive presence in the Academy as his double-jobbing at a rival establishment that caused his dismissal in 1906 and led to his instituting proceedings for wrongful dismissal.

On the face of it, Woodhouse's views on the musicality of the Irish take us back to the Academy's starting-point. 'Are the Irish people musical? Of course they are. But if you ask me are they a nation of musicians I must honestly tell you that they are not. As a matter of fact, they don't get the chance . . . As to the Irish voice, I am satisfied that there is no better in the world—all it wants is proper cultivation and a better musical environment than at present exists.'[349] He then went on to attack the musical establishment and, by implication, his own employers for the practice (and, one might read into his comments, the cultivation) of indifference that we have noted previously in connection with the audiences of the Dublin Orchestral Society. Criticising the low musical standards tolerated in Dublin, he also referred to 'the fact that so many excellent artists visit Dublin under great financial loss, while the public are induced to attend local functions by pestering ticket-sellers—all the time aware that the concert as a concert is "no good" . . . Dublin audiences are supposed to be and indeed claim to be critical. Until they really try to act up to this claim there is no hope for music; at present they don't.'

If Woodhouse had been the great authority on the art of singing that he claimed to be, and if he had been more circumspect in his method of inducing change, his views might have won some acceptance with the musical public and within the musical establishment. Many of his criticisms were well founded—for example his argument that it was inherently unfair that teachers with students competing at the Feis Ceoil should also sit on the committee selecting its test pieces—although given the smallness of the professional musical world in Dublin it is difficult to know how this might have been avoided. He stated in the interview from which these comments are drawn that he naturally could not criticise the Academy itself, and then proceeded to do so. 'It is doing a good work under difficulties. I should like to see those difficulties removed. I should like to see the Academy a really national institution rather than a merely local institution.' In singing, he drew attention to the lack of training in tone production, resulting in good voices badly projected, which was accepted by audiences 'in their good-natured Irish way—'Sure, it's not so bad, now.''

The first open sign of friction was a letter from Woodhouse to the Board of Governors shortly after his appointment, which was clearly aimed at the influence of Esposito (and, by inference, at the Italian component in the Academy).

At the request of Signor Palmieri I have pleasure in handing you herewith the enclosed lists of songs for the National Prize*—as we cannot agree upon the question of composers (or rather arrangements) we decided to send the lists to the Board, for them to select . . . The view I take of the 'National Prize' is that the test should be selected from the works of the best Irish musicians, and that until we have exhausted these, the question of foreign arrangements should not be considered. The term *national prize* implies to me Irish music, and, by an Irishman, if possible. When we have such musicians as Robinson, Stevenson, Stanford, Balfe, Molloy etc. (who have all arranged the melodies) to select from, it seems a slight to these native born masters as well as highly incongruous to select a foreigner's arrangement in preference . . .

*Soprano: 'The Little red Lark'—Standford [*sic*]
Mezzo-soprano: 'It is not the Year'—Stevenson
Contralto: 'No, not more welcome'—Stevenson
Tenor: 'The Coolin'—Robinson
Baritone: 'Avenging and bright'—Balfe
Bass: 'Avenging and bright'—Robinson[350]

Six months later, Woodhouse was attempting to have Italian discontinued as a compulsory subject for voice students.

With regard to the question of the Italian language a knowledge of which is required by the RIAM test, but by no other British institution, we [Woodhouse and Palmieri] are divided in opinion. Signor Palmieri desires to retain this test & I think it should be eliminated. No doubt a teacher would be better to know all languages, but Italian is not as much used in modern music as German & French & if it is demanded that the candidate sing any songs in the language they are printed I think the end will be met. This is all the English academies require. Making the tests of the RIAM more severe than the Royal Academy London— Royal College or Guildhall Sch. of Music will not tend to induce students to apply for the Certificate.[351]

He also insisted that singing required a grasp of the theory of singing, although the following argument does not make it immediately clear what he had in mind.

The only thing retarding their progress is want of theoretical knowl- edge—a very general failing among the vocal pupils; in the piano classes & also those of the violin, theory is acquired when mere children, singing on the other hand is mostly commenced by the girls when grown up & it is probably irksome for them to sit by little girls & have their igno- rance shown up—if the Board could see their way to have vocal theory classes I think it would be a distinct advantage.[352]

In March 1904 a special meeting of the Board, chaired by John Irwin, heard a complaint by Rooke about Woodhouse's behaviour, which seems absurdly trivial today but which expresses the sensitivities of people at the time, as well as bringing into the open what was evidently a deep hostility. The incident was caused by the way a violin pupil had been beating time. Woodhouse said to Rooke, the pupil's theory teacher, that it was 'silly'. The minutes recorded: 'Mr. Woodhouse admitted the accuracy of the statements as made by Mr. Rooke and he expressed his regret that in the heat of the moment he had used the expression "silly" . . . [and] stated that he did not mean to reflect upon Mr. Rooke's capability as a Professor.'[353]

But the concrete issue on which the Academy and Woodhouse parted company was his participation in the newly established Leinster School of Music, which was the first serious competitor for Academy business. (Others would be set up later, such as Robert O'Dwyer's school in Rathmines in 1907, at which Arthur Darley, Clyde Twelvetrees and Octave Grisard taught, and later still, in 1911, the 'Operatic School of Music' at 40 Dawson Street, 'musical director Richard Eckhold, formerly of Carl Rosa and Moody-Manners companies, professor of singing Vladimir Brodov.')[354]

On 28 September 1904 the Governors considered a motion 'that the attention of the Governors be called to the new School of Music & the advertised connection of certain Professors of the Academy therewith.' These were Clyde Twelvetrees, Annie Irwin, Victoria Delaney, T. H. Weaving, and Randal Woodhouse. There was an unwritten rule that assumed that Academy teachers would not take a salary from another teaching institution (other than a secondary school), whatever about teaching privately to augment their admittedly meagre Academy pay. Irwin, Weaving, Delany and Twelvetrees each replied in an even and conciliatory tone, pointing out that in their view there was no conflict of interest, and that the Academy had the prior call on their time, but gently underlining the need to supplement their principal source of income. Woodhouse did not.

Relations soured over the next eighteen months, and at the end of the 1906 summer term Woodhouse was dismissed. When he nonchalantly arrived for work at the opening of the next term, he was prevented from entering the building. He began proceedings for wrongful dismissal, on the grounds that the Governors who dismissed him were not in fact governors at the time, because they had not paid their subscriptions—a tactic that seems rather dubious if Woodhouse had a good case on grounds of natural justice. If these governors were acting illegally because they did not constitute a legal board, they must also have been incapable of appointing Woodhouse in the first place, a point brought up successfully by the Academy's counsel, Richard Littledale and Tim Healy, briefed by Daniel O'Connell Miley. Woodhouse lost his case.

He also parted company with the Leinster School, and in 1910 he publicly announced this. He also remained publicly in contention with the Academy, saying in a letter to the *Irish Times* in 1911 that 'this institution as at present constituted serves no useful purpose . . . Its closing down as a teaching body would . . . be a benefit to the public [and] to the professors . . . who not only receive no salary but have to contribute from 25 to 50 per cent of their earnings to keep the place going.'[355] That Woodhouse's arithmetic and his imagination were astray is further suggested by the assertion that 'the gross earnings of the Academy in one year only paid half the amount of the postage stamps.'

In May 1910 *Irish Society*, giving the results of the Feis Ceoil, reported that B. L'Estrange Graham had won the Plunket Greene Cup and stated that she was the pupil of Jeannie Quinton-Rosse. To this Woodhouse retorted that she had been *his* pupil at the Academy and then at the Leinster School.[356] Quinton-Rosse immediately replied that she had taught Miss Graham from October 1908 and that she had first won the Plunket Greene Cup in 1909, and further pointing out that she had been unsuccessful in the Feis in the two previous years. She added that she herself had introduced her to her winning aria, '*Lascia ch'ia pianga*', which Woodhouse had alleged he had taught Miss Graham.

In February 1912 *Irish Society*—which seems to have been a conduit for Woodhouse's rather hamfisted public relations activities—reported that Annie Irwin had been a pupil of his.[357] Considering that at this time she had been a scholar in 1886, a teacher at the Academy since 1888 and a professor since 1904, and that her brother, Sir John Irwin, had been instrumental in both recruiting Woodhouse to and barring him from the Academy, this was a curious strategy on Woodhouse's part. A week later Annie Irwin replied that 'it is to the late Joseph Robinson—whose pupil I was—that I owe any success I may have attained as a singer and teacher and it was upon the recommendation of that gentleman I was appointed as a Professor of Singing by the Governors of the RIAM many years prior to the advent of Mr. Randal Woodhouse to Ireland.'[358]

That should have ended the matter. But a week later Woodhouse retorted:

> This lady studied with me for nearly two years . . . I thought she was learning singing, if not, what was she paying the fees for? Furthermore, I have a number of letters from Miss Irwin referring to her tuition. Will she give me permission to publish them? I think not.[359]

A fourth occurrence, two months later, serves to underline the fact that Woodhouse was, at the very least, prone to overstate any valid claims he may have had to producing successful students. The *Daily Express* of 13 May 1912 carried a report that Mollie Keegan, the winner of the Feis Ceoil Blue Ribbon, was a student of Woodhouse for singing, 'physical culture and respiratory exercises . . . She is a deserving student of the Woodhouse School or method of singing.' That day, Woodhouse inserted advertisements in the Dublin *Evening Mail* and *Telegraph*:

FEIS CEOIL

Miss Mollie Keegan, winner of Ladies' Committee Prize and
Mezzo-Soprano Gold Medal, pupil of Prof. Randal Woodhouse.

The assertion was subsequently repeated in a report in the *Freeman's Journal*. This drew a chorus of protest from Mollie Keegan's then teacher, J. C. Doyle, and from Keegan herself. Doyle wrote to the *Evening*

Telegraph that the writer 'has been hoaxed by somebody . . . [Mollie Keegan] has been under my tuition for the past two years and under my tuition only.'[360]

Again, that should have brought the matter to a conclusion. But Woodhouse's determination to fight his case brought him back into the ring, with a letter quoting *Irish Society* of 19 May 1910 to the effect that Keegan possessed 'a mezzo-soprano voice of remarkable power and purity' on which he alleged he had worked 'for a whole year . . . week after week and month after month, gradually building up her voice and physique . . . Mr. J. C. Doyle comes along, puts a dash of whitewash over my vocal edifice, and claims the credit of it . . . Miss Keegan is quite blameless. She left me against her will and I insist that she is my pupil.'[361] In reply, Doyle stated that after less than a year with Woodhouse, Miss Keegan had come to him in 1910, following 'a very dismal defeat' in the Feis and with a voice 'quite uneven and shrill,' requiring seven or eight months of technical work, 'of which she assured me she had done little or nothing.' He then delivered the *coup de grâce*. 'Mr. Woodhouse wishes the public to know the whole truth. It is as follows: while under his tuition she entered for one competition with disastrous results. Under my tuition she entered seven competitions gaining six first prizes and one second prize.'[362] To this Mollie Keegan herself added the following statement:

> I did not leave him [Woodhouse] with any reluctance after being under his tuition about six months . . . I owe all my success in singing to Mr. J. C. Doyle's teaching, and it is my earnest wish to pay him the tribute. I have never gone through a course of physical culture under Mr. Woodhouse.[363]

Woodhouse continued to teach privately, until at least 1912. Interviewed again in 1911 by *Irish Society*, he repeated his criticisms in a tone that suggests that his impatience with Dublin was more a matter of his own temperament than of any particular local problem that might have been solved by his talents. 'Are the Irish people musical? They used to be, but are not now.' Reversing the popular view that political unrest had given way to cultural energies, he said: 'The political and religious troubles of the people have occupied their attention to the exclusion of music as well as the other arts.'[364] Some well-aimed observations on both musical composition and infrastructure followed. 'The digging up of some old tune from a dying fiddler, hastily finding some ready-made words to fit it . . . is regarded as a stride in art—a mummy in a hobble skirt. What is required is a drastic change in the musical leaders of the people in the first place, and then follow in the lines of Belfast and have a large town hall and organ.'

In view of the continuing problems encountered by the Academy in building a concert hall, and of the poverty of Dublin as a 'creative intelligence', it is hard not to agree with Woodhouse on both grounds. Nor is it easy to dismiss his earnestness as a teacher when one considers his insistence on knowing the anatomy of the larynx and the respiratory system and the importance of correct breathing and so of finding the correct way to tone production in what is essentially an 'imitative art'. It is therefore all the more disconcerting and disappointing that, instead of becoming a star teacher at the Academy and elsewhere, Woodhouse should have failed to attract the sympathy or the support of his employers or indeed, it seems, of his pupils.

In 1893 it was considered advisable to inaugurate a competition for Dublin school choirs. It has been suggested by Kieran Daly that this occurred at the behest of Dublin Corporation, after a similar initiative in Cork the previous year,[365] but evidence in the RIAM minutes points to the Academy having on its own initiative approached the Corporation for financial support, which was immediately granted to the extent of £150. In 1893 Peter Goodman recorded in his annual report that 'Sir Patrick Keenan [head inspector of the Board of National Education] gave me to understand that he wished a Public School Competition for Singing should be held in Dublin . . . under the auspices of the RIAM of which he is a Vice-President.'[366] (Keenan had become a vice-president in 1889, in succession to Lord Fitzgerald, who had died shortly after the implementation of the Blue Scheme.) Furthermore, the fact that two of the members of the RIAM committee established in 1892 to consider 'Vocal Music in Primary Schools and Local Examinations' were members of Dublin Corporation[367] points to a common interest between the two bodies.

Ten years later, when the scheme was coming to an end, Thomas Mayne claimed to the RIAM secretary, Charles Grahame Harvey, that he had 'induced the Corporation to make the annual grants,' using the argument that 'while vocal music was being taught in the Board Schools in England and Scotland it was being almost entirely neglected in Ireland, where from the temperament and natural tastes of the children it would probably be more successful than in either of the sister countries. At that time vocal music was being taught in only four primary schools in the entire Dublin district.'[368] The relevant minute is, however, decisive about where the initiative lay.

> Mr. Molloy having read some statistics as to recent examinations in Dublin schools, it was decided to recommend the Governors to adopt a plan for holding competitive examinations in vocal music in primary schools—to apply to the Corporation for an increased grant—to announce the scheme as soon as possible and to ask the senate of the RUI for the use of their buildings . . . The subcommittee also recommends the Governors to adopt a system of local examinations.[369]

The latter recommendation, appearing as it does almost as an afterthought, was to have repercussions out of all proportion to its significance here.

It is clear that all parties were concerned about the state of music education in primary schools and considered that a competition of this kind would help to raise standards of both teaching and learning. Donnelly himself, for example, had raised the matter directly at a meeting of the Cecilian Society, as it had a direct bearing on the quality of church music.[370] It is also clear that the introduction of the competition opened the way for trenchant exchanges of views on the exact nature of music education, which had been a subject of contention since the eighteen-thirties. If the competition provided an effective way of involving large numbers of homogeneous young people in the process of music-making, it also brought into question the methods of cultural transmission to be employed in training them.

Up to this point, the music education system in Britain and Ireland had revolved around the concept of the 'immovable *doh*', in which each note is identified by its sol-fa position. This method had been adapted by John Hullah from that of Guillaume Louis Wilhem in the eighteen-forties and introduced in Ireland through the Marlborough Street schools, its principal proponent being J. W. Glover. The application to vocal music of this method, which works effectively in relation to the keyboard, was always regarded as problematic. One of the main critics of the Hullah-Wilhem system was Patrick Keenan, who objected both to the method itself, which taught knowledge of the notes at the expense of 'melodic excellence', and to the song-book that illustrated it, which Thomas Davis had called 'English daubs'.[371] They 'do not pretend to any national character . . . are foreign to all sympathy . . . belong to no country . . . are sung in no home.'[372] There was thus a basis for both methodological and ideological dissent in the Hullah system as applied to a country that at that time was unconsciously looking for its own Kodály.

The replacement of this system with that of John Curwen—the tonic sol-fa method, which involved a different form of notation for those who could not read music and was based on the concept of a movable *doh*—became contentious, and in 1884 teachers in Ireland were given the option of employing either method. While there was no explicit case of pro or anti-nationalist ideology being aired during the years of the competition (1893–1903), the bitterness with which the debate between the two methods was conducted is palpable, and one can only surmise that at least some undercurrent of national feeling was present.

Marie McCarthy quotes Goodman's pointed comment that the competition would 'give voice to a most interesting display in itself—viz., a competition of methods—Tonic Sol-fa *versus* Hullah' and observes that 'one of the tacit aims of the contest was to prove the Tonic Sol-fa method superior to the Hullah method.'[373] The fact that Goodman himself had selected the schools to compete suggests that he deliberately set two 'Hullah' schools against eight with a tonic sol-fa background. Moreover, the fact that the sight-singing test had been devised by Curwen, and was judged at the inaugural competition by Curwen's wife, makes the bias towards tonic sol-fa more obvious. (The RIAM minutes record that Curwen himself had been invited to judge the contest but that he had deputed his Irish-born wife, a former student of Sir Robert Stewart, to do so, as he himself was deaf.)[374]

'I cannot help thinking', said one of the school inspectors, Newell, 'that if vocal music were generally taught in the National Schools, the songs learned would supersede those that the humbler classes now generally sing, which are for the most part vicious trash, hawked about by itinerant ballad-singers; in times of political excitement, often seditious, and frequently obscene and demoralizing.'[375] Keenan, influenced by Wyses's *Educational Reform* (1836), was particularly keen to promote singing as a medium of cultural transmission. As far back as 1855 he had said: 'We are unfortunately not only not disseminating Irish music but we are absolutely laying the foundations of its complete extinction from the tastes and habits of the people.'[376] His view led to the replacement of the Hullah song-book with one specially compiled by Glover, *School Songs* (1867).

McCarthy makes the point that the progress of music in the model schools was 'made visible through public approbation,'[377] and this is also evident in the warmth with which the press greeted, and reported on, the schools singing competition. But such progress seems to have been limited to the model schools and not to have percolated into the national school system as a whole, where, McCarthy tells us, 'parents' attitude toward "extra branches" of education such as music and drawing was not favorable and . . . parents showed apathy and disregard for subjects other than those which led to upward economic mobility.'[378]

By 1870 the situation caused Keenan to reiterate his belief that only by giving children the opportunity to sing Irish songs could the managers' and teachers' sympathy be enlisted.

At first, considerable money prizes were awarded: £20, £10 and £5 to the teachers of the best girls' and boys' choirs (today, £800, £400, and £200), together with certificates of merit. (Mixed schools competed in the girls' section.) This suggests an echo of 'payment by results', and in fact the competitive element of the project was suppressed in 1902, when the practice of announcing the placings of the choirs was replaced with a simple statement of the grades achieved. Thus, as the *Freeman's Journal* commented, 'the annual meeting of the choirs is an examination pure and simple,' and 'it is worth considering whether this departure from that competitive principle, which is so universal in educational institutions, is a wise one.'[379] The project was to die the following year without the point being resolved.

The competition went through a number of changes in its ten-year history, including division between larger and smaller schools in 1898, the year that also saw the introduction of a trophy, in the form of a shield, to be awarded to the school of the overall winner. The chief features of the competition are demonstrated in the competition in 1901:

> Tests—Smaller Schools' Division—Girls' and Boys' Schools.
> Each Choir Class will be required to sing:—
> 1. The Test Piece, 'When Evening's Twilight,' by J. L. Hatton, for three treble voices.
> 2. A Tonic Sol-fa Test in *two part harmony for girls, in unison for boys*.*
> 3. To take down the notes of an Ear Test, or simple musical phrase played on an instrument.†
> 4. A piece of its own selection.‡

*Should any Schools using the 'Hullah' method compete, the Sight Test will be printed for them in the key of C.

†The Ear Test will contain no chromatic tones.

‡The selected piece may be in any number of parts, but must not be in unison.

Tests—Larger Schools' Division—Girls' and Boys' Schools.

Each Choir Class will be required to sing:—

1. The Test Piece, 'In the Lonely Vale,' by Dr. Calcott, arranged for three treble voices.
2. A Tonic Sol-fa Notation Sight Test, in two part harmony.*
3. To take down the notes of an Ear Test or tune played on an Instrument.†
4. A Staff Notation Sight Test in two part harmony for girls; in unison for boys.‡
5. A piece of its own selection in any number of parts.

*The Sight Test in Tonic Sol-fa Notation will be of moderate length and difficulty, containing transitions to first sharp and first flat keys with phrases in the minor mode. (Should any school using the 'Hullah' Method compete, this Sight Test will be printed for them in Staff notation in the key of C.)

†The Ear Test will include easy chromatic tones, but no extended transitions.

‡The Staff Notation Sight Tests will be of the character of a simple hymn tune or simple song, but may be written in any key.

Tests for the Shield Competition.

Each Choir Class will be required:—

1st To sing the part song, 'To a Seagull' by Jos. Seymour, Mus B., to be found in Curwen's 'Choruses for Equal Voices,' No. 491.

2nd To sing a Staff Notation Sight Test in two parts of moderate length and difficulty.

3rd To take down an Ear Test, consisting of not less than 20 notes, and containing easy chromatics.

4th To sing a piece of its own selection.

Over the existence of the competition, certain choirs were conspicuously successful, that of North Strand National School (both boys and girls) conducted by W. H. Nesbitt (who taught sol-fa at the Municipal School of Music) being the most frequent winner, with St Mary's, Rathmines, and the Christian Brothers' School, St Mary's Place, conducted by Vincent O'Brien, also featuring in the placings. On one occasion Theodore Logier is mentioned as conductor of St Patrick's, Drumcondra, an unexpected re-emergence of this particular academician.[380] Another choir to achieve success (in 1898) was that of the national school in King's Inns Street, which caused the *Freeman's Journal* to comment sharply on the value of the project as a whole.

All the choirs . . . belonged either to ordinary National Schools or to Convent National Schools. This year the Marlborough Street Model Schools put in no appearance. In the earlier years . . . their performance had interest for the other competitors . . . But strange to say, the choirs did not prove to be 'models' at all . . . On the estimates for the current year there is a vote of £48 to the RIAM for the special benefit of the Marlborough Street schools and a sum of £140 is voted to provide two special teachers of music for them also. Yet the ordinary National School does as well, and the Convent School, which is paid on a still lower grade for its work, does vastly better.[381]

In fact in 1899 O'Brien won prizes with three different choirs (St Laurence O'Toole's, Christian Brothers, St Mary's Place, and Christian Brothers, Marino), leading in 1900 to his pointing out to the Academy, through Bishop Donnelly, that 'there will be no competition for the shield this year, no more than last year . . . as his choir remains in the field.' O'Brien's 'self-sacrificing' suggestion was that a three-in-a-row victory should not entitle the winner to outright retention of the shield and that the winner should in any case not be eligible for the next two years.[382]

While it might seem obvious that the RIAM examination systems, both internal and external, developed as a natural element of the overall education process, their evolution in relation to that process is by no means so clear. The first curious point is that the impetus for the local centre system (described below in detail by Brian Beckett) was not entirely *sui generis* but came as a development subsidiary to the decision to hold the schools choir competition. The second point demonstrates the complexity of the evolving status of music within the general development of education from the eighteen-seventies.

The Intermediate Education Act (1878), in particular, caused serious disruption in music education, since it reinforced the idea of education as a utility. The payment-by-results system, under which teachers in national schools received a nominal salary that was supplemented in accordance with their pupils' examination results, operated from 1882 to 1899. It had been introduced to ensure that expenditure on education would be cost-effective, and as a result music became peripheral as its usefulness in a career-oriented industry was diminished. On the introduction of this system, the Academy had protested to the Board of Intermediate Education that 'the consequences of awarding result payments to masters . . . for proficiency . . . in certain branches of education . . . will of necessity have the effect of concentrating the attention upon these branches, to the prejudice of others,' and that to omit music from the prescribed list would 'have the effect of . . . positively discouraging it.'[383]

Although in 1883 the fortunes of music within the system were enhanced, as its status shifted slightly from a 'non-compulsory' to an 'optional' category, Marie McCarthy has charted the complex situation as music became a stranger in the classroom and in the national curriculum,[384] a prominent feature of which was the declining value of certificates of competence in music in a system that discouraged their holders from using their qualifications. In 1874 only 12 per cent of national school trainees were trained in music, and by 1896 singing was taught in only 14 per cent of schools.[385]

The utility concept was not only apparent in the money prizes available to the *teachers* of successful schools in the competition (rather than to the school) but also began to permeate the Academy itself, where a profit-and-loss analysis of the violin faculty was undertaken in 1894. This showed that in the advanced class, where Papini was paid at the rate of 10s 6d per hour, the cost of tuition, at £12 19s, exceeded a student's fees of £12 per term, whereas in the lower grades, where Papini was assisted by a junior professor (Grisard at 6s or Rawlingson at 4s) or a junior teacher (such as Florence Bloom, who earned 2s 6d per hour), modest profits were made. The total picture was a profitable one, as the fees brought in £411 and the salaries cost £390, even though the £21 difference was more than taken up by awarding two scholarships to the value of £26.[386] (As this exercise, which unfortunately was not carried out in respect of the piano faculty, gives us an 'inventory' of the Academy's violin students at this time, their names are listed in an appendix at the end of this chapter.)

We also find the Academy at this time writing to the Commissioners of National Education, asking them 'to accept the Certificates of Competency awarded after examination by the RIAM as warranting teachers to earn result fees on satisfactory proficiency exhibited by National School pupils.'[387]

It appears that the payment-by-results system exacerbated existing imbalances in two areas: the urban-rural divide, which saw Dublin and Cork achieving far higher results than the rest of the country, particularly the smaller towns and villages; and the sex divide, which had traditionally seen a heavier and more successful concentration of music education in girls' schools than in boys'. So too did the new secondary system, which expressed Victorian prejudice about what was proper and desirable. Marie McCarthy suggests that the secondary system was permeated by a binary or dichotomous mentality that included those who were acceptable and attained prescribed results and excluded those who did not.[388] But this cannot be said to have been the case in the Academy, however oriented towards Anglo-Irish thinking it may have been in other respects. While it rewarded excellence, it did not discourage those whose principal interest was in music for its own sake.

With the 1878 Act in operation, the RIAM offered to participate in the devising of an examination system that resulted in theoretical aspects of music being included in the syllabus. It is not, however, accurate to suggest, as Marie McCarthy does,[389] that the Academy was responsible for the exclusion of practical musicianship: in fact quite the opposite was the case, with the Academy making strenuous representations to the Commissioners of National Education for the recognition of all-round musicianship.

Up to 1900 Peter Goodman was the Commissioners' examiner, responsible simply for assessing performance and monitoring payment of results fees. After 1900, when music became compulsory in national schools, he became an inspector, with scope to encourage the development of music education. But despite this change in departmental thinking, Goodman's was an uphill struggle against the low level of activity we have mentioned, with only a quarter of the country's twelve thousand music teachers holding any qualification. He therefore saw his task as the education of nine thousand educators;[390] but the fact that so many primary school teachers today are in a similar position to their predecessors suggests that there has been no consistency on the part of successive governments in respect of a policy on music education.

The decision of the Academy to start local centre examinations is therefore due to three factors: partly to combat urban-rural imbalance, partly to harness the Academy more closely and effectively to the music education system, and partly to occupy a strategic position that was already beginning to be taken by the Associated Board of the RCM and RAM.[391] (Later it would be calculated that £4,000 left the country in examination fees each year.)[392]

It was for this last-mentioned reason that, in January 1893, Esposito was added to the Governors' committee working on the schools choir project, 'with a view to considering a scheme for local examinations in music.'[393] This was the origin of the local centre examination system. The activity of the Associated Board had led teachers in 1892 to ask the Intermediate Education Board for an indigenous examination system. This was partly to avoid paying fees to the Associated Board and partly because Irish people wanted to be examined by Irish musicians. In the outcome, the RIAM's system was approved by the Intermediate Education Board. Although it did not absolve the schools from the obligation to pay fees (and the local centre fees continue to this day to be a very significant element of RIAM income), those charged were (and continue to be) significantly lower than those of the Associated Board.

The difficulty of music not being a productive subject became controversial in 1902, when it was decided to remove 'theory of music' from the curriculum. The RIAM told the Intermediate Education Board that the 'elimination of Music from the Programme would be a retrograde step & fraught with grave results to the study of music in Ireland.'[394] The board replied that '"Theory of Music" has been removed for the present from the Intermediate Programme but that the removal is subject to re-consideration in connection with the establishment by the Board of a system of permanent inspection of Schools.'[395] By the end of the year the Academy was still pursuing the matter, putting forward detailed proposals for an examination system geared towards the board's, rather than the schools', needs:

> The Governors of the RIAM think it is a pity that some examination in music should not be held under your intermediate system and would suggest that your Board should hold an Examination in practical as well as theoretical music. The Governors can see that such examinations might entail a very great deal of trouble and expense to your Board and . . . they would be happy to undertake the conduct of these examinations for you and to report the result to your Board. This Institution has special facilities for examining in music both practical and theoretical and during the last ten years have held examinations (similar to what your Board would require) at Local Centres and Schools throughout Ireland awarding honours and pass certificates to successful candidates.

The present terms are 10/6 each candidate for each subject (if not less than ten enter) 6/– each extra subject and a Registration fee for each centre of £1.1.0 with 25% reduction to pupils of the Preparatory Grade. The Associated Board . . . charge a fee of £1.1.0 for each pupil with 10/6 in theory + 15/– for Harmony.

As will be seen from our syllabus, our examination is a thorough one and includes an oral examination in the theory of music.

Our present fees are cheaper than those of the English and other similar examining bodies and our Examinations are conducted with a view to improving and encouraging music and not for pecuniary profit. The Govs. would be willing to dispense with the registration fee in the case of schools examined for your Board and would endeavour to modify as far as possible their examination and fees to meet your wishes. Should your Board consider that some such arrangement as is above suggested might be practicable a deputation from this Board would be glad to wait on them and my Board would be pleased to submit for your examination a detailed scheme for carrying out the examinations.[396]

Following remonstrations from all parties, the Academy was invited to submit a scheme whereby it would examine both theory and performance on behalf of the board. There is little clarity in the proceedings of the board in the next few months, but eventually the RIAM scheme was rejected in favour of that put forward by the Leinster Branch of the Incorporated Society of Musicians. Given that Jozé was the Irish secretary of the ISM, and that H. V. Yeo, a Governor of the Academy, was its local agent, it is confusing, to say the least, to find that Jozé was permitted by the Academy to have a hand in a competing project, and that Yeo was able to retain his seat on the RIAM Board. However, as the local centre examinations were experiencing very considerable growth at this stage, the Academy probably adopted a sanguine view of the situation. In hindsight, it is possible to recognise that, had the close association between the RIAM and the Intermediate Education Board been institutionalised to the extent necessary for the proposed system to be effective, it would most probably have been necessary also for the local centres to close down, as a superfluous duplication of resources. Moreover, an academy continuing to be independent of the government would have found it difficult to insist on, and to maintain, its own standards and examining methods and would probably have been drawn too far into the politics of music education in order to secure its continued independence.

The years 1906–14 witnessed a declining interest in the conduct of the Academy on the part of a large number of the Governors, so much so that in 1906–07 a large number of meetings failed to produce a quorum, and an unsuccessful attempt was made to reduce the quorum for Board meetings from five to three.[397] In 1908 only eight governors attended more than ten meetings out of the total of thirty-seven, and of these only four—Drury, Foot, Esposito, and MacManus—attended more than twenty. Some of the best attenders were the Corporation governors (Alderman Ireland and Sir

John Irwin in particular). This may be symptomatic of a general lull in the tide of cultural nationalism as interest in political and social affairs increased with the Liberal election victories of 1906 and especially of 1910.

It had become clear that the affairs of the Academy needed a firmer hand than the Board itself could provide. As far back as 1889 Brasfort had told the Board of Studies:

> There is not in the Academy a Director or Superintendent of Studies or functionary charged with the general supervision and control of the instruction given, to whom the Professors could report & by whom they would be consulted when necessary. Such an official exists in nearly all Conservatoires & Musical Schools & it is for him to decide whether a pupil can or ought to be permitted to take up further branches of study & if so what branches.[398]

On 27 January 1909 a meeting of the Governors was held (to which the press was admitted) for the purpose of receiving the report of a special committee that had recommended, among other things, 'that in the interests of the Academy, Signor Esposito should be invited to accept the position of Musical Director of the Academy.'[399] Because of the financial position of the Academy at the time, it was envisaged that the appointment would be a part-time one, entailing two hours a day during term and with a salary of £200 a year (today £6,000).

The argument in favour of creating the post was that it was 'essential that there should be some person responsible to the Governors at the head of the Academy possessed of musical knowledge and business habits . . . All other similar institutions of which the Committee have any knowledge have adopted the principle.' The committee itself had been split on the recommendation, and a minority dissented from the report and succeeeded in having the issue postponed for a year.

The £200—equivalent to Esposito's hourly teaching rate of 10s 6d—was to be found by effecting economies of £144 and by increasing some piano fees by £2 a year, to yield an extra £60. The economies depended on Esposito giving one lesson fewer per fortnight to some of his pupils (saving £66) and on merging the function of assistant lady superintendent and housekeeper (saving approximately £80). However, these reductions were not enough to convince the Governors that the financial position was sufficiently sound to facilitate the appointment. Sir Francis Cruise supported deferral, on the grounds that, 'though he yielded to no one in his personal respect for Signor Esposito,' his appointment was not warranted by the financial position. Behind this, however, was the unspoken feeling that, however eminent Esposito was as a musician, he did not possess the business acumen required. It is also possible that some of the Governors used the financial argument to mask their real fear that Esposito as musical director would enjoy too much power.

It was argued that such an appointment could not have been made previously, 'owing to the fact that though there were two Professors, either of whom would be suitable for the appointment, the appointment of either would probably have led to the retirement of the other. This was in the time of the late Sir Robert Stewart and the late Mr. Joseph Robinson.' Since Stewart had died in 1894 and Robinson in 1899, by which time Esposito had already been at the RIAM for seventeen years, one could be forgiven for wondering why ten further years had elapsed before the Governors turned their minds once more to the subject.

The issue had in fact been prompted by the death of the lady superintendent, Miss Crean, whose exercise of her function had largely made her the Academy's principal officer and during whose reign it would have been wiser not to attempt to create a superior position. Now the opportunity presented itself to redefine the functions of lady superintendent and secretary in the light of the envisaged post of musical director. This would also eliminate time-wasting procedures, whereby much of the business of the Academy was transacted by the Routine Committee, whose deliberations, however 'routine', were in turn ratified by the Board of Governors. The musical director would interview applicants, inspect classes, arrange concert programmes and examinations in conjunction with the Board of Studies, attend to daily business, and oversee the implementation of the Governors' decisions, thus ensuring the more efficient running of the establishment and attracting more pupils. It was particularly urgent to attend to this last-mentioned issue, since there had been an acute decrease in student numbers (and fees) in the previous six years.

Esposito was recognised not only as a fine musician and as someone with whom the staff would work well but also as a businessman, a capacity he had apparently 'exhibited . . . in his dealings with his own classes, at the Board meetings and also outside the Academy.' This reference was undoubtedly to his involvement with the Dublin Orchestral Society, regarding which Annie Patterson had referred to his 'keen sense of business management.'[400]

The proposal had the support of Bishop Donnelly, Count Plunkett, James Drury, W. P. Geoghegan, T. M. Gerrard and Philip Hanson and was opposed by Irwin, Ireland, and Brady. The objections seem to have been based partly on an unspoken feeling that Esposito, despite his pre-eminence as a musician, was already too busy and partly because, as director, he would overshadow the Board of Studies. It was difficult to give voice to such reservations, and so the objectors had to rely on much lesser arguments, such as the fact that the appointment was not permitted by the Blue Scheme—a point that the proposers rightly observed could be overcome by amending the scheme.

A further objection related to Esposito's current pay.

> Under the proposed arrangement with Dr. Esposito, the major portion of the time to be spent by him in the Academy must necessarily be devoted to individual teaching and examining, for which he is paid at the rate of 10s 6d per hour, and he does not propose to relinquish the Special fees which he also receives from the Academy for examining at various local centres throughout Ireland, which is based upon an allowance of five guineas per day when out of Dublin, and travelling

expenses, and amounted last year to about £70, a figure which is steadily increasing each year. Nor do we understand Dr. Esposito to agree that in future the fees which he receives for monthly and other examinations in the Academy should be merged in the additional £200 per annum—

the insinuation being that Esposito was motivated by fees as much as by the work that earned them. 'We are decidedly of opinion', said Irwin, Ireland and Brady,

> that a Musical Director of an Academy such as this should not be himself a member of the teaching staff but should devote his entire time and energies to the work of the institution, and be independent of fees so far as his remuneration was concerned, otherwise we are convinced that the appointment would be of no practical service to the Academy while increasing its liabilities. Dr. Esposito is a very busy man, his whole time is, as he has frequently stated, practically filled up at present between the Academy, certain Colleges and Schools, Orchestral and Operatic Societies and Concerts, and we fail to see how he could, while retaining his present engagements, render such special services to the Academy during the nine working months, as to warrant an additional payment to him of £200 per annum, always bearing in mind the fact that as a member of the Board of Studies, and in accordance with the terms of his contract with the Academy, he is bound in common with the other Senior Professors to render all necessary expert advice to the Governors.[401]

It was further intimated, privately, that Esposito had been the instigator of this recommendation, and one's inclination to believe this is increased by the fact that, immediately following its deferral, he resigned as the professors' representative Governor. The Board for its part immediately asked Esposito to reconsider this action, as did the Board of Studies, to which Esposito eventually agreed.[402]

We should take special note of the fact that the motion to defer consideration of the appointment was tabled by Albert Foot, since the next altercation to involve Esposito as a Governor and professor occurred two years later. (Foot was one of the most regular attenders at the Board, with twenty-eight out of thirty-seven meetings in 1910.)

On 25 January 1911, Esposito wrote from 7 St James's Terrace, Clonskeagh: 'Dear Mr. Harvey, After what has happened this afternoon at the meeting of the Board of Governors of the RIAM and in order to avoid being again insulted in the future, I write to ask you to kindly remove my name from the list of Governors of the Academy as I do not wish to act any more as such.'[403] What had happened was not an assault on Esposito's dignity but what can be bluntly described as a slanging match between Foot and Esposito, the consequences of which were the removal of Esposito from the Board of Governors for the next thirteen years and a severe rift between the Governors and the Board of Studies. It brings home to us that Dublin was, in the words of the *Freeman's Journal* (though in a very different context), 'a hotbed of histrionic ability.'[404]

The events within the board-room may be summarised in the impartial account that the Governors who had been present drew up shortly afterwards.

> Upon Mr. Foot's stating that the Board of Studies should in his opinion have dealt with [a specific report before the meeting] & expressed their views upon it, either agreeing or disagreeing with it—Dr. Esposito rising in his seat & raising his voice & leaning across the table towards Mr. Foot, in a loud voice called across the table (at the head of which the Chairman Mr. Irwin was seated) to Mr. Foot 'That is Mr. Foot's opinion'—& then laughed derisively & said, continuing in a loud voice, 'Who minds Mr. Foot'—or 'Nobody minds Mr. Foot'—whereupon Mr. Foot said 'We don't want any Italian tricks here' or 'any of your Italian tricks here'—Dr. Esposito then rushed over to the Pianoforte where his hat &c were & said 'I will not sit any more at this Board with Mr. Foot' & the Chairman endeavoured to calm Dr. Esposito, who ran to the door the Chairman urging him to come back, but Dr. Esposito again refused & went away.[405]

These minutes were signed by Irwin, Littledale, Ireland, Whewell, and Gerrard—all those (with the exception of Foot) who had been present at the meeting on 25 January. The matter would not be resolved until 10 May, and in the interim a series of painful manoeuvres would take place in an attempt to save the reputation and dignity not only of the chief participants but of the Academy itself.

Clearly the show of bad temper on both sides might be traced back to the way the issue of the directorship had been left unresolved. Equally clearly there was no room for such behaviour at meetings of the Board, however eminent the Governors involved might be.

Esposito's own account of the altercation was drawn up at the request of the Board of Studies, whose representative he was as a Governor and on whose behalf he had retaliated to Foot's original expression.

> I explained to the Board of Governors that the minute of the Board of Studies in reference to Mr. Boxwell's report was brief, because the report as it reached them appeared to them to furnish no ground of discussion . . . After this discussion had lasted about an hour Mr. Foot whose conduct and bearing will be within the recollection of the Governors present, cried out angrily 'Do you know that I am going to propose to make a clean sweep of all the professors.' It was in reply to this that I said, no doubt derisively 'Who cares?' Subsequently followed Mr. Foot's reference to 'Italian tricks'—unreproved by the Chairman— and the circumstances appeared to me to leave me no option but to tender my resignation to the Board of Governors.[406]

Having been requested by the secretary to retract his resignation, Esposito wrote on 6 February: 'Dear Mr. Harvey, I am in receipt of yours of the 3rd inst. and I fail to perceive in it anything that could make me alter my decision.'[407] He reported this to the Board of Studies on 3 March, when his action was approved by his fellow-professors. Two weeks later the professors were formally notified by the secretary of the vacancy for a professors' Governor, in response to which

> the Board of Studies unanimously resolved to bring before the notice of the Governors the difficulties in filling up the vacancy caused by Signor Esposito's resignation as the representative of the Board of Studies. Since the unfortunate incident which necessitated Signor Esposito's retirement there has been no expression of regret from the Board of Governors. Furthermore the Board of Studies have no wish to appoint anyone in Signor Esposito's place, nor would any other professor consent to act under the circumstances. The Board of Studies feel sure that the Governors will realize the position in which the former are placed and hope that the Governors may yet find a satisfactory solution of the difficulty.

The Governors met a deputation from the Board of Studies, consisting of Jozé (its chairman), Wilhelmj, and Rooke, who submitted the following statement:

> We . . . gladly avail ourselves of this opportunity to lay before you a frank and open statement as to the circumstances connected with Signor Esposito's resignation, as they have come before us, feeling assured that, by so doing, all danger of misunderstanding will be removed and a way possibly opened up, by means of which the present strained position of affairs may be brought to a speedy and welcome termination. Permit us to briefly detail the points above referred to: On Friday February 3rd 1911, at a meeting of our Board, Signor Esposito reported that on Wednesday 25th ulto. at the meeting of the Board of Governors . . . a Governor used insulting language to him, and that as he (the Governor) had not withdrawn the insulting expression, or been called to order by any member of the Board present at the time, he (Signor Esposito) left the Board-room, and that evening tendered his resignation, in writing, to the Secretary on the ground that he did not wish to leave himself open to further insult. The Board of Studies then made a minute embodying Signor Esposito's statement, and endorsed his action in resigning under the circumstances. We may add that the accuracy of this statement which went before the Governors on the occasion of their next meeting has never been questioned. On the contrary, Signor Esposito states that it was fully substantiated by two of the Governors who were present on the occasion of the reported insult while the incident was fresh in their minds. It was, therefore, with feelings of surprise (we say it with all respect) and disappointment that we learned from Signor Esposito, after the next meeting of the Governors, that he had merely received a formal letter from the Secretary, to the effect that the Governors unanimously wished him to reconsider his decision, but, as there was no suggestion of any regret at what had taken place, Signor Esposito replied to the effect that he saw no reason in the letter for reconsidering his decision.

At the next meeting of the Board of Studies we learned from the agenda that we were referred by the Governors to the article in the Scheme re the appointment of a representative Governor, Signor Esposito having resigned. We then passed a resolution pointing out to the Governors the difficulty of the position in which we were placed since no expression of regret had been received by Signor Esposito. We assured the Governors that we had no wish to appoint anyone but Signor Esposito, and that the difficulty which stood in the way of his remaining in office, stood equally in the case of appointing anyone in his stead. We at the time expressed our earnest hope that the Governors would be able to find a solution to the difficulty. To this the Board of Governors replied that the minutes would lie on the table for three months. Gentlemen, the foregoing is a brief résumé of the matter as we understand it, and, we add, that our desire from first to last has been to act rightly and fairly in difficult and most unpleasant circumstances. If it has seemed to you that we have acted in opposition to your views, or if we have failed to adopt the course suggested by you, we can assure you, in all good faith, that it is simply because it appeared to us that to adopt any course other than that on which we had unanimously decided would do an injustice to our representative.

Following this very even assessment of the situation, the Governors resolved that, 'having further considered the most regrettable conduct of two members of the Board . . . [they] are of the opinion that an apology is due to the Board of Governors by Signor Esposito Mus. D. and Mr. A. R. Foot.'[408] To this Foot immediately responded, neatly putting the ball into Esposito's court: 'Dear Mr. Harvey, I am in receipt of yours of 23rd inst. enclosing a copy of the resolution of the Board with which I quite agree. I deeply regret my conduct on the occasion referred to, & now beg the Board of Governors to accept my most sincere apology.'[409] The apology was accepted. Esposito, however, was prepared to play a waiting game: 'Dear Mr. Harvey, I have received yours of today . . . Will you kindly notify to the Board of Governors that I give three months notice of the termination of my contract as Professor of the RIAM.'[410]

The Board, for its part, was not prepared to see one Governor suffer at the hands of another, but above all it was concerned for the integrity of its own proceedings. At its next meeting, on 5 April, it was

> resolved that all the Governors present at the meeting of . . . 25th January 1911, other than Dr. Esposito and Mr. Foot, being now present, and stating their clear recollection that the regrettable language used by Mr. Foot was brought about by Dr. Esposito having first addressed him in regrettable language, the Governors are still of opinion that the behaviour of both Governors in indulging in personal recriminations at a meeting of the Governors is conduct for which an apology is due to the Governors by both gentlemen concerned.

Two days later, the Board of Studies expressed its extreme regret that the matter had not yet been resolved—the point here being that it was not only a matter of 'personal recriminations' between Foot and Esposito but one involving remarks made to the professors' Governor by another Governor. The Board of Governors, for their part, waited for three weeks for an apology from Esposito before instructing the secretary to acknowledge the receipt of Esposito's resignation.[411] The Routine Committee was meanwhile asked to draft an advertisement for a successor.

A week later a letter was received from Leopold Dix, which, setting aside the matter of Esposito's intemperate outburst, accurately summed up the position as far as the effect on Dublin musical life was concerned.

> Dear Mr. Harvey—I hear that Dr. Esposito is likely to sever his con-
> nection with the RIAM as the result of a severe vote of censure recently
> passed on him by a meeting of Governors. I can scarcely imagine an act
> more suicidal in the interests of the Academy than to force Dr. Esposito
> to leave it, as the Governors must do if the vote of censure is to remain
> unwithdrawn. He has been Professor there for nearly 30 years, and both
> by his own prestige, as the first musician in Ireland, and by the results
> of his splendid work in connection with his piano classes, he has done
> far more for the Academy than any other six people together. As a
> subscriber, I think I am entitled to ask whether, before the Governors
> finally force Dr. Esposito's resignation by refusing to withdraw this vote
> of censure, they will place before the subscribers their reasons for taking
> a position which, to say the least, calls for some explanation—I have
> spoken with other subscribers who agree with me, that to justify the
> vote of censure, the Governors who passed it would have to show that
> Dr. Esposito's behaviour on the occasion referred to was not only
> unjustifiable in itself but unprovoked; and also, that in forcing him to
> leave they would be acting in the best interests of the Academy.[412]

It is a pity that Dix had got his facts wrong, as it allowed the Governors to reply rather tartly that 'they regret he should have addressed them on what is manifestly imperfect and inaccurate information.' The point, however, had been made and was reinforced by another letter from W. P. Geoghegan, which said: 'Whatever may be the rights and wrongs of disputes leading to this state of things . . . nobody who knows anything of the progress of music in Dublin can regard the loss of Signor Esposito other than as a calamity to the City.'[413]

James Drury was deputed to speak to Esposito 'and inform him that the Governors would greatly regret the severance of his connection with the Academy.'[414] A week later Esposito returned to the fold.

> Dear Mr. Drury, referring to the interview which you had with me
> pursuant to the resolution of the Board of Governors passed last
> Wednesday, which was communicated to me by Mr. Harvey, Secretary,
> I am very glad to have your assurance, as the mover of the resolution of
> the 22nd March, that neither you nor the Governors intended the
> words 'most regrettable conduct' therein contained to apply to anything
> but the occurrence of the 25th January, and that they have no reference

whatever to me in my capacity either as a professor of the RIAM for the past thirty years, or as Governor since the date of the Scheme. I much regret the incident of the 25th Jan: and any part I took therein. I never intended to cause annoyance. Will you kindly convey this to the Governors at their meeting to-day.[415]

The next Governors' minutes record that 'it was unanimously agreed that . . . the Secretary convey to Signor Esposito the extreme satisfaction with which it has been received by every Governor present' (this included Albert Foot).

The matter was not, however, entirely resolved. At its next meeting the Board of Studies, on the proposal of Annie Irwin, seconded by Margaret O'Hea, unanimously re-elected Esposito as the professors' Governor—only to be told by Esposito when he arrived at the meeting that he could not accept the position. Dr Jozé was elected as his successor.

Wartime hardly affected the Academy. None of its staff or students was killed in action, although a few Governors lost close relatives. The first mention of the event that wiped out a generation of Europeans, and changed the course of politics and culture, is a vote of sympathy with T. M. Gerrard on the death of his brother in France in November 1914.[416] It was proposed by W. H. Brayden (owner of the *Freeman's Journal*), who was to lose a son himself in 1918. Later, in 1917, Sir Gabriel Stokes received similar condolences when his son Terence was killed 'in the service of his King and Country,' as, two months later, did Dr Cowan, whose 'gallant son Sydney Cowan MC . . . by his bravery had at the early age of 19 gained the highest distinction of the Military Cross with two bars.'[417]

In 1915 it was agreed, at the request of the Lord Lieutenant, to put up a recruiting poster in the hall, but only one member of staff joined up, and that was before the appearance of the poster. Of a much more serious nature was the notification from the Treasury that 'in view of the imperative necessity of restricting expenditure in all possible directions,' the government grant was to be suspended. The accompanying letter expressed the Treasury's confidence 'that the Governors will recognize its inevitability in present conditions.'[418] The Academy recognised no such necessity. Invoking the assistance of the Lord Lieutenant, it prepared a lengthy statement, redolent of those drawn up in the eighteen-sixties in pursuit of the original grant and asserting the status and usefulness of the institution, on the strategic grounds that it provided *technical* (as distinct from aesthetic) education, and submitting that 'even in these exceptional times, a grant which is wholly devoted to purposes of Technical Education, should not be discontinued.'[419] Perhaps as a show of petulance, the Board decided to refuse free tuition that had been requested on behalf of a refugee child from Belgium.[420] Dublin Corporation supported the application,[421] and by January 1916 the grant had been reinstated.[422]

The events of 1916 in Dublin were of some interest to the Academy. The premises of the RHA in Abbey Street had been destroyed by fire, and the minutes of 10 May record 'that the Governors . . . hereby express their deep sympathy with the President, Members and Associates of the Royal Hibernian Academy of Arts in the disaster which has befallen their Society in consequence of the recent disturbances.' The RHA was to have the use of the Academy premises as a meeting-place for several years to come.

Perhaps more alarming for the Governors than anything the war could effect was the announcement by the town clerk on 8 December 1914 that Dublin Corporation had appointed Sarah Cecilia Harrison as a representative Governor. From the Governors' minutes it appears that collective consternation broke out in the board-room at the idea of a woman being appointed—so much so that the secretary telephoned the Corporation to question the appointment. The town clerk's reply of 9 December was unequivocal: 'In answer to your inquiries by telephone this morning, I beg to state that the list forwarded to you . . . was a correct one. It may be useful to you to know, however, that Councillor Miss Harrison was appointed in room of Councillor Patrick Shortall.'

At the Board meeting the following week, the shock waves had hardly lessened. On 16 December 'it was decided to take Counsel's opinion as to the eligibility of ladies to be appointed or elected to the Board of Governors in view of the question having been now raised for the first time,' and a week later the town clerk was 'to be communicated with on basis of legal opinion.' Unfortunately we have no copy of the opinion, nor do we know what happened in the intervening month, but on 20 January 1915 Miss Harrison signed the statutory declaration of her willingness to serve as a Governor. Given the liberal inclination of the broad membership of the Board, and the movement towards an almost inevitable suffragist victory for women in the next few years, the mere idea of resistance to a woman Governor is surprising.

Born in 1863 at Holywood House, County Down, Sarah Harrison was a portrait painter of distinction, and the main point of interest in her involvement with the Academy is that she painted the portrait of Esposito that was presented to him in 1926, shortly before his retirement which is now in the National Gallery. A sister of Henry Harrison, Nationalist MP for mid-Tipperary and a secretary to Parnell, she lived at 16 Fitzwilliam Place from 1889, the year she first exhibited at the RHA, moving in 1905 to 33 Harcourt Street. She was involved in the campaign to build a gallery of modern art in Dublin, spearheaded by Hugh Lane, to whom she was engaged to be married. Her interest in civic affairs extended to the condition of the poor, and in 1912 she topped the poll in the Corporation elections for the South City Ward, so becoming its first woman member, exactly three years before she gained the same distinction in the RIAM. She remained a councillor for three years, forming an alliance with another local politician who was to become a strong figure in the Academy as well as a future lord mayor, Alderman Alfred Byrne.[423] As it turned out, Harrison was not to play a great part in Academy affairs. She attended twelve out of thirty-seven meetings in 1915, but in the aftermath of Lane's death in the *Lusitania* in May of that year she almost completely ceased painting for five years, left the Corporation, and attended only two RIAM meetings in 1918 and only one in 1919.

After Harrison, no woman was elected to the Corporation until 1920, when, among others, Kathleen Clarke (widow of the 1916 leader Tom Clarke and also a future lord mayor) was returned as an alderman. The significance is heightened by the fact that in 1921 she became the second woman appointed to the Board of the Academy, a position to which she returned in the nineteen-thirties.

The appearance of these two remarkable women in the RIAM board-room, one from a prosperous establishment family that had recognised the need for Home Rule, the other from a militantly republican background, is yet another sign of the watershed in the Academy's experiences of the period that this chapter has described. The presence of Kathleen Clarke, in particular, indicated that changes of a radical nature were taking place in Irish culture, society and politics that would inevitably affect the teaching of music and the life of the Academy.

The Violin Faculty, 1894

1st grade (advanced): Signor Papini, 10s 6d

Scholars

Miss Victoria Delany—Vandeleur Scholar, 1894
Miss Helen Irvine—Academy Scholar, 1894

Pupils

Name	Fee	Cost of lessons	Loss
Miss Gleeson	£12	£12 19s	19s
Miss D'Estene	”	”	”
Miss Miller	”	”	”
Miss S. Wood	”	”	”
Miss Grogan	”	”	”
Miss A. Kavanagh	”	”	”
Mr Miller	”	”	”
	£84	£90 13s	£6 13s

1st grade A: Signor Papini, 10s 6d, & Mon. Grisard, 6s

Pupils

Name	Fee	Cost of lessons	Loss
Miss Powell	£10	£6 9s 6d + £3 14s = £10 3s 6d	3s 6d
Miss Love	£10	£10 3s 6d	3s 6d
	£20	£20 7s	7s

1st grade B: Signor Papini, 10s 6d, & Miss Bloom, 2s 6d

Pupils

Name	Fee	Cost of lessons	Gain
Miss Kohler	£8	£6 9s 6d + £1 10s 10d = £8 0s 4d	
Miss Kevans	"	£8 0s 4d	
Miss A. Vance	"		"
Miss M. Vance	"		"
Miss Dodd	"	£6 9s 6d	
Miss Blood	"	£8 0s 4d	
	£48	£46 11s 2d	£1 8s 10d

1st grade C: Mon. Grisard, 6s

Pupils

Name	Fee	Cost of lessons	Gain
Miss Louth	£8	£7 8s + 10s 6d = £7 18s 6d	1s 6d
Mr Franklin	"	"	"
Mr Creevy	"	"	"
Mr Cluskey	"	"	"
Mr Byrne	"	"	"
Mr Hughes	"	"	"
Mr Horan	"	"	"
	£56	£55 9s 6d	10s 6d
Mr Rosaberg	£3	£7 18s 6d	net loss
	£59	£63 8s	£4 8s
Miss Ormity	£8	£7 18s 6d	

2nd grade: Mr Rawlingson, 4s

Pupils

Name	Fee	Cost of lessons	Gain
Miss Fottrell	£6	£4 18s 8d + 10s 6d (exams) = £5 9s 2d	10s 10d
Miss Tresillian	"	"	"
Miss Strangways	"	"	"
Mr Lawless	"	"	"
Mr Chancellor	"	"	"
	£36	£27 5s 10d	£2 14s 2d

Elementary grade A: Miss F. Bloom, 2s 6d

Pupils

Miss Curtis	£4	£3 1s 8d + 10s 6d (exams) = £3 12s 2d	7s 10d
Miss Middleton	”	”	”
Miss D'Harte	”	”	”
Miss McFenan	”	”	”
Miss Kohler	”	”	”
	£20	£18 0s 10d	£1 19s 2d

Miss L. Simpson	£4	£3 12s 2d	7s 10d
Miss Cresswell	”	”	”
Miss Lynch	”	”	”
Miss Henshaw	”	”	”
Miss Lyburn	”	”	”
Miss Sandall	”	”	”
Miss Holmes	”	”	”
Miss Evans	”	”	”
Miss Parr	”	”	”
Miss Gibson	”	”	”
Miss M. Simpson	”	”	”
Miss Macken	”	”	”
Miss Baker	”	”	”
Miss Newcomen	”	”	”
Miss White	”	”	”
Miss Lanigan	”	”	”
Miss Powell	”	”	”
Miss Stack	”	”	”
Miss Woods	”	”	”
	£96	£86 12s	£9 8s

Elementary grade B: Mr Delany

Pupils

Master B. Fair	£4
Master C. Powell	”
Master W. Harrison	”
Master Sheridan	”
Master Hamilton	”
Master Hayes	”
	£24

Mr Delany's lessons	£12 19s	
Exams, six pupils	3 3s	

Gain on B division	£7 18s	

Elementary grade C: Mr Delany, 2s

Name	Fee	Cost of lessons	Gain
Master Welsh	£4	£2 9s 4d+10s 6d (exams) = £2 19s 10d	£1 0s 2d
Master Cunningham	"	"	"
Master Lane	"	"	"
Master Fitzgerald	"	"	"
Master Curran	"	"	"
Master Deiphan (?)	"	"	"
Master Hayes	"	"	"
	£28	£20 18s 10d	£7 1s 2d
Master Honroy	£2	£2 19s 10d	loss 19s 10d
	£30	£23 18s 8d	£6 1s 4d

Elementary grade D: Miss Callaghan

Pupils

Name	Fee	Cost	
Miss Andrews	£4		
Miss Dot Foot	"		
Miss Garland	"	Miss Callaghan's lessons	£12 19s
Miss M. Dodd	"	Exams, five pupils	£ 2 12s 6d
Miss Harte	"		
Miss J. Dodd 1/2			£15 11s 6d
Miss Lambert 1/2		Gain on D division	£ 4 8s 6d
	£20		

Summary

Grade	Fees	Cost
1st advanced	£84 0s	£90 13s
1st A	£20	£20 7s
B	£48	£46 11s 2d
C	£59	£63 8s
2nd	£30	£27 5s 10d
Elementary A	£96	£86 12s
B	£24	£16 2s

C	£30	£23 18s 8d
D	£20	£15 11s 6d
	£411	£390 9s 2d

Fees £411
Cost £390 9s 2d
Gain £21 10s 10d

Cost of two scholars £25 18s
Free pupil
Miss Lily Lambert
Cost per annum about £7 15s

Intermezzo

DR ANNIE PATTERSON

I shall never forget the day when, a tiny mite of some seven years, having been entered as a pianoforte student, I was 'tried' by the authorities to see what class I was fitted for. There were two or three gentlemen professors present, whose names and faces were quite unknown to me; but one of them spoke kindly and encouragingly and lifted me up to the music stool, telling me to play the last piece I had learnt. This, I remember well, happened to be 'I'd Be a Butterfly' out of *Hamilton's Instructions*, and this I at once played gaily through with a child's easy confidence. At the time I was only a beginner, having been taught my notes at home. What my judges thought of me I do not know, but I came away with very pleasant recollections of what in later years I would have looked upon as a great ordeal.

The result was that I was placed with one of the lady teachers of the Academy, a Miss Kelly, under whose tuition I gradually made acquaintance with most of the classics in Charles Hallé's *Practical Pianoforte School*.

One incident when in Miss Kelly's class I still recollect with great pleasure, and it was probably a turning-point in my career. I was at my lesson and had been playing Jules de Serve's pleasing arrangement of Handel's Gavotte in B flat, when the door of the classroom opened and Sir Francis Brady, the most devoted and energetic of all the vice-presidents of the Academy, came in. He had heard my piece outside and he asked me to play it through again. I did so, not without a good deal of nervousness. But Sir Francis soon made me feel quite happy. First he praised the selection, making me repeat parts of it; then he spoke most encouragingly about my own performance. That was, perhaps, the first real 'spur' I got in my preliminary work. It was a great honour to be noticed by the revered vice-president; still more to be commended by him.

From that on I think I took redoubled interest in my pianoforte studies, and ere long I found myself under the tuition of no less a great professor than the late Sir Robert Stewart. But to the present day I can never forget, shall I say, that fatherly interest which, I have reason to believe, Sir Francis Brady never fails to take in the pupils of the Academy, no matter how tiny and insignificant they be.

My first meeting with Sir Robert Stewart! Ah, I remember that well also. It dates back many years now, and was possibly shortly after my admission to the Academy. I was entered as a very small pupil of his Harmony class, and diminutive indeed I must have been, for the kindly gentleman's first act was to raise me up in his arms and show me to the other students as a very little girl with a very large notebook. The subject treated of in class that day was the dominant seventh, and well I recollect my intense admiration of a big girl who sat next to me who was positively able to spell 'dominant'! Later on, to give a pictorial demonstration of the three kinds of motion in part writing, Sir Robert chose me and another very juvenile student to walk up and down in front of the class, sometimes together and sometimes in different directions, or else one quiescent and the other moving, to illustrate the 'similar', 'contrary', and 'oblique'. Such things make a great and lasting impression upon children, and, it is unnecessary to remark, I never forgot the facts taught in that, my first lesson in part writing.

There was a kindliness and enthusiasm about the late Sir Robert Stewart, a placing himself in sympathy with young intelligences—indeed he was a man that one could never call old—that won its way at once, especially with his child pupils; and when it was my privilege to study advanced work with him in later years, I always felt inspired and encouraged by the fact that, talented and distinguished as he was, he could yet enter into the initial difficulties of the inexperienced, and invariably bring out the best abilities that they possessed.

As his organ pupil I came to respect the genius of my master more and more. His own great powers as an executant, his marvellous ability at score reading and his wondrous memory did not prevent him entering, with admirable patience and geniality, into what I now realise was my most presumptuous ambition to excel at all which he did so well. To the present day I value, as one of my most precious possessions, some half-dozen original organ voluntaries in manuscript, which were written, in the first instance, for me. One of these, which Sir Robert permitted me to name 'Entreaty', was the piece chosen for my debut as solo organist at one of the Academy's pupils' concerts [on 2 May 1883].

This brings me to an important consideration with regard to the value of the RIAM as a training institution for the professional musician. The students are frequently required to perform in public, and so they have opportunities for 'first appearances' and getting 'known', which are absolutely essential to the intending concert artist. The programmes for those occasions are admirably drawn up, and those pupils alone are chosen whose abilities have either been well and carefully tested by their individual professors or else who, by distinguished merit, have won prizes and scholarships in their various departments. The value of these public performances, both in nerve training and as a means of exploiting deserving talent, is inestimable; and many an eminent Irish vocalist and instrumentalist, both here and in all parts of the world, will agree with me in saying that, if the RIAM did nothing else but organise its annual and other pupil concerts, its work would still be of infinite value as a factor in the practical development of the divine art.

The RIAM has, quite lately, still further widened its sphere of usefulness in this direction, namely by awarding certificates of proficiency in various branches, the examinations for which are held periodically over Ireland in certain local centres and schools. This is a most commendable step on the part of the authorities, and we may have every confidence that the examinations thus instituted will be carried on upon an upright basis and that an honourable standard of efficiency will be required from candidates entering for them.

Like most musical children, I was found to have a small voice and a good ear. Consequently I was placed under Miss Adelaide Barnewell at the Academy, and, through that lady's careful and able tuition, I learnt how tone should be produced, and eventually succeeded in interpreting songs correctly. Italian masters subsequently taught me a certain agility in the rendering of florid aria work; and, in short, I acquired enough technique to enable me to teach others and write for the voice; but I early realised that, beyond 'humming' for my own amusement, my solo vocal ability would never rise above mediocrity. Yet my culture at the Academy was thorough in every detail. Not only had I the advantage of the English and Italian methods referred to above but I was a member of Mr Joseph Mullen's then sight singing class, as also a soprano in the Academy choir, under Signor Bozzelli. From both of these instructors I gathered up much valuable knowledge and experience, the rehearsals of Cherubini's Requiem Mass and Bellini's *La sonnambula*—vastly opposite styles of work, by the way—being very pleasurable reminiscences to me.

Now I have not the smallest doubt that, had my voice naturally been worthy of it, the capable instruction I enjoyed at the Academy would have been ample to make me a 'star'. As it was I never cease to be grateful for the knowledge then acquired, because it has been useful to me in a hundred ways; and no professional musician, whether vocally gifted or not, should, in my opinion, avoid to add a course of voice training to his studies.

Sir Francis Brady, as I have hinted before, is as unfailing as ever in his devotion. In the past I recollect many proofs of his generosity to the institution. In my own time, in order to encourage violoncello playing among the girl pupils, he offered a free course of instruction to any student of the Academy who cared to present herself for the same, together with the loan of a cello for home practice. I was one of those who took advantage of this liberality and never regret my period of lessons in cello playing under the late Herr Elsner.

I hear lately that the Academy authorities hope to move the establishment into more commodious quarters. This is truly a step in the right direction and one which the public will gladly welcome. It seems also that the spacious premises of the College of Science will shortly become vacant. Now, were such a site chosen for our national music school, the advantages would be manifold and immediately evident to the most casual observer. The Academy would therein have better-apportioned space for class and concert rooms than has been possible within the limited resources of the Westland Row building. The position would be a commanding one; and, as 'birds of a feather flock together,' the proximity of the Royal University of Ireland, Alexandra College and School, the Catholic University College and the College of Surgeons would make St Stephen's Green, the munificent gift of Lord Ardilaun to the citizens of Dublin, a veritable 'academic grove' of the arts, sciences, and culture of all kinds.

Finally I would remark that, with such establishments as the RIAM within our city, musical students need not run abroad or elsewhere for their musical education. I have heard as good solo instrumental performance from the students of our Irish music school as from any scholars of the London Royal Academy and Royal College of Music. Of course it is not to be denied that, when students have gone through their pupilage at our Dublin conservatoire, a few London seasons of concert attendance and a taste of Continental opera are not to be despised in order to widen the intelligence critically and artistically. But by all means let Irish boys and girls not despise the boon, and that very estimable one, of having in the RIAM a thoroughly equipped music school at their doors.

Annie Patterson (1868–1934) was one of the first prominent women musicians in Ireland. She studied with Sir Robert Stewart (starting in the junior piano class in 1873), was the first woman to obtain a MusDoc from the University of Dublin, and became professor of Irish music at UCC. In addition to composing music (including two operas, symphonic poems and cantatas) and writing books on Schumann and on oratorio and The Music of Ireland, *she was a prolific journalist and campaigner for musical causes. In addition to the many articles she wrote for the* Weekly Irish Times *in 1899–1901, she contributed others on the basic issues of how to become a professional musician and how to appreciate music in the home, which eventually found publication in book form as* How to Listen to an Orchestra *and* The Profession of Music. *Probably her lasting achievement was the founding in 1895–97 (with Edith Oldham) of the Dublin Feis Ceoil. She is a noteworthy example of that extremely small group of writers on music who at that time embraced journalism as a way of creating an audience for the arguments of cultural nationalism.*

Intermezzo

Dr Walter Starkie

As I look back over the past fifty years [1906–56] many memories crowd before my inner eye and I am tempted to recall some of those dear old friends whose ghosts will haunt all of us this year when we celebrate the centenary [*sic*] of the RIAM.

Few people in these materialistic days realise how profound an effect environment and surroundings have upon the growing child. Gazing back in retrospect I see the personalities I have known against the background of the beautiful Georgian house at no. 36 Westland Row. For me in the past fifty years that building, with its organ room, its concert hall and foyer, its classrooms, its dark passages, its nether regions, becomes a vast theatre of memory, with stage, audience, green room and dressing-rooms inhabited by countless friends, who take part for my benefit in a continuous performance; but the curious thing about that performance is that there is no hierarchical precedence among the actors, and the call-boys, the supers and the walkers-on play as important parts in this drama of memory as the consecrated heroes and heroines.

My earliest musical memories of the Academy are strangely connected with toothache, teeth-pulling, and lawn tennis, because I used in 1906–07 to pay a number of visits to our family dentist, who lived in a house exactly opposite the Academy. While waiting in anxious apprehension for my turn in the chair of torture I used to gaze gloomily out of the window at the grey house opposite, and on a golden summer afternoon, when the windows were open, a medley of discordant sounds would break upon my ear: a cascade of piercingly shrill notes from some budding diva vocalising her Concone exercises, mingled with distant treble squawking of petulant fiddles and the hard, efficient rattle of scales on a number of pianos.

'Music has charms to sooth a savage breast,' but, alas, not in my case at the moment, for I continued to hear the shrill cacophony when I was seated on the stool of repentance and the man of wrath—or so he seemed to me—tried to direct my mind to thoughts of lawn tennis while he killed the nerve of my aching tooth. When the pain was over the man of wrath became transformed into the gruff, good-natured Olympian figure of F. O. Stoker, Wimbledon champion in the doubles with Pim, both of them heroes of my tennis-playing boyhood, in the days when I began to be bitten by the music mania and the craze for fiddling.

It was in 1907 that I caught the disease from the tone of the magic violin played by the wonderful boy prodigy Mischa Elman in the old Theatre Royal.* As a result I made life at home more hideous than it had been, for my catgut scraping, when added to that of my sisters, drove my parents so wild that they sought partial relief by sending me for systematic tuition to no. 36 Westland Row.

My teacher, Patrick Delany, was a miracle of patience, a truly Franciscan figure, who was entrusted with the teaching of all the aspiring boy fiddlers. The lady superintendent, Miss Crean, disapproved of boys in the Academy, calling them 'barbarous young brats', and Patrick Delany and his devils were relegated to one of the gloomy rooms in the basement next to the kitchen. The master devoted himself to us by turns, for he believed in class teaching, urging us to listen carefully to one another and begging each one to point out the faults of his companion. Alas, my memories of those classes picture various raw youths, milling, scuffling, pummelling in a corner while the master and the two best pupils fiddled conscientiously their Kreutzer study, completely oblivious of the boxing and all-in wrestling match that was going on around them.

Then came the yearly kermis of the Feis Ceoil, which was so excellent a stimulant in musical education, as it encouraged the virtues of ambition, self-criticism and self-confidence, as well as the corresponding vices of conceit, cheek, self-sufficiency and swollen head. Today I remember the ramshackle old Antient Concert Rooms, which was next door to the workshop of a stonecutter, who was busily engaged in chiselling tombstones. The stone-cutter was a sympathetic friend to us when we used to halt in his workshop on our way into the ordeal of playing in public at the competition.

The personality above all others who is stamped on my mind when I try to reconstruct those years is Michele Esposito—one of the greatest musicians of his time in Europe and one who left a name that will be forever hallowed in the annals of music in Dublin. By his piano playing, his conducting, his composing and his editing he has deserved his niche in the Temple of Fame. I preserve in my mind the image of that dark-eyed, dynamic little man playing ensemble music with Papini, Simonetti, Grisard, Bast, or Clyde Twelvetrees. When he entered the Academy it was as if a sea breeze had blown in the door, rousing the peaceful inmates from their slumbers; even the kitchen cat would arch its back and stretch itself, and the cherubic-faced porter, John, would motion us out of the line of fire as the little Maestro, overcoated and carrying his umbrella like a weapon, dashed up the stairs to his sanctum on the third floor with its two grand pianos.

*Starkie's memory was slightly amiss. On 26 October 1905 the *Freeman's Journal* carried a letter from Esposito asking the public to support a concert by 'the boy violinist, Mischa Elman', who was then fourteen and had just made a sensational London debut. 'He is not concerned with the exhibition of mere tours de force. His aim is not to display precocious powers, but to interpret the music of the composer.'

The group of budding pianists, most of whom were girls, gathered round the glass doors of the Maestro's sanctum like a frightened flock of birds when a hawk swoops into their ken, and they would cower away, each trying to avoid the blazing scrutinising eye and imperious command to play the Chopin study they had all practised. Those who were his pupils year after year never forgot those piano lessons or the music classes that built up the tradition of piano-playing in Ireland and gave to the world such artists as Sir Hamilton Harty, who, in addition to being one of the greatest conductors of his time, was one of the best accompanists in the world. Many pianists used to gather day after day in the Maestro's music room, listening attentively to his criticism, always expressed in a forcible jargon of Italianised English, or else sitting back dreamily, absorbing the music of Beethoven as the master played for them. Some of them, like Annie Lord, Edith French-Boxwell, Dina Copeman, and Rhona Clark, enriched musical life in Dublin and perpetuated the Esposito tradition.

And when we remember those student days we have a kindly memory of 'little Miss O'Hea', one of the talented sisters who were all connected with the Academy. I always used to call her the interceder, for she would protect the fluttering doves on the days when the hawk was swooping more fiercely than usual, and was a good-natured shock-absorber preparing the way for the timid pupil.

Those of us who had the inestimable privilege of studying chamber music with Esposito will never forget the experience of playing Brahms sonatas, trios and quartets for him. Not only did he open up vistas for us in the inter-pretation of classical music by his insistence on phrasing, tone values and balance of ensemble but he would enable us to understand the significance of sonata form and the structure of music as handed down from the early Italian violin composers, such as Corelli, Tartini, and Veracini, to Beethoven and Brahms.

When I was at the Academy in the years 1907–1908 I have vivid memories of the senior violin classes which were given by Adolf Wilhelmj, the son of one of the greatest violinists of the nineteenth century, August Wilhelmj, the friend of Wagner and leader of the orchestra at the first performance of the *Ring* in 1876. With bated breath we used to listen to his stories of life in German towns on the Rhine, of 'Wahnfried', the home of Richard Wagner at Bayreuth, of Frau Cosima, the widow, the daughter of Franz Liszt, and of Hans Richter, whom we all heard conduct in 1908 when he visited Dublin with the Hallé Orchestra. Wilhelmj brought Wagner influences with him to Dublin, and to cure his homesickness for his Wagnerian haunts he called his house in Sidney Parade 'Rhinegold Villa'.

In those days in Dublin there were certain families labelled as musical, and by tradition every member played an instrument, with the result that the Academy building of no. 36 Westland Row often became the scene of musical tournaments or joustings between rival families. There was one supreme family of fifteen children called the Dowses, where every one played an instrument and where musical talent passed from the older to the younger generation. The Dowses gave a great impulse to the study and appreciation of chamber music in Dublin, and some of them, such as Marie Dowse-Trimble, the violinist, were prominent in the Students' Musical Union, which used to meet in the Academy on Saturday nights to perform trios, quartets, symphonies, cantatas and even operas for the members.

The Students' Musical Union was founded in 1905 and it played a very important part in the years when I used to frequent the Academy. Two of the great pioneers were Miss Nettie Edwards, the singer, who later sang in the Quinlan Opera Company, and Miss Annie Lord, the pianist. The significance of the union was due to its crusading spirit in favour of contemporary music. Annie Lord in this respect was a valiant crusader, not only owing to her programmes of Debussy and Ravel in her recitals at the Royal Dublin Society before the Great War but also owing to her interest in modern ensemble music. Some of my most cherished memories go back to the early years when we played for the first time in Dublin the sonatas of [Guillaume] Lekeu [1870–1894], Roussel, Strauss, Debussy, [Georgy] Catoire [1861–1926], and Oscar Espla [1886–1976].

In those far-off days there was no radio, no television to distract us from performing music ourselves. In Dublin there was a regular craze for playing ensemble music, and there were brilliant musicians like Arthur Oulton, who literally devoured music. With him we used to play Mozart trios before breakfast, Bach double concertos before lunch, Beethoven after tea, and Brahms after supper. There were various musical tribes in Dublin, Foxrock, Rathfarnham, and Greystones, and occasionally the Crichton tribe from Sligo would descend upon Dublin with the Hamiltons and join up with the Orpens or the Dowses and become so immersed in music that I actually remember on one occasion that I was with them that we played a Haydn quartet in a railway station waiting-room while waiting for our train.

Whereas musical taste has developed greatly nowadays, owing to the gramophone and the Third Programme on the BBC, and everyone claims to be an expert listener, able to appreciate the finer beauties of Schoenberg's 'Pierrot Lunaire' or 'Wozzek' by Alban Berg, there are much fewer people who play for themselves and their private circle just because they are passionately fond of music and only discover its true meaning when they themselves play it.

Today the amateur, even when he or she reaches high proficiency, is afraid to play for others, because he feels that those who have been listening to the performances by the BBC or on the gramophone have reached such a high degree of hypercritical snobbery that they will turn up their noses at his home-spun effort. This has been the reason why I have found in the houses of many of my friends among the younger generation the latest type of radio or television sets but, to my sorrow, no piano, violin, or cello. And this saddened me when I remembered that some of those young married couples had been to the Academy and had reached a high enough standard to ride the musical hobby-horse.

In the Academy there was in the ancient days always plenty of encouragement given to the young performer, and many of us remember the old days of the Students' Musical Union when Dr. Larchet used to give soloists the opportunity of performing concertos with orchestral accompaniments. To Dr Larchet I personally wish to pay a warm tribute in the name of many of my contemporaries of thirty years ago. When I went first to the Academy, in the year 1907, I spent many a weary hour poring over the dry-as-dust manual of Ebenezer Prout on harmony, but when I came within the orbit of Professor Kitson and his disciple Dr Larchet, who taught harmony, counterpoint and the other subjects in association with ear training and made them eminently practical, harmony ceased to be mere mathematics and became living music, for Dr Larchet made us apply his teaching to the scores of the classical and modern composers.

To Jack Larchet I owe at the same time the privilege of having attended year after year, when a student, the full cycle plays at the Abbey Theatre in which he was the musical director. And with my countless memories of the Abbey Theatre first nights, from that of *The Playboy of the Western World* in 1907 to that of *The Plough and the Stars* of Seán O'Casey in 1926, I associate the music played by the Abbey orchestra as interludes, which, owing to Larchet's dramatic talents as piano-conductor and composer, were a very popular feature of the performances.

It is gratifying to know that in recent years the 'Academy Operatic Group', under the direction of Maestro Viani, continue to give excellent performances of the classical Italian operas such as *L'elisir d'amore*, for, ever since his arrival in Dublin from Milan, Maestro Viani has encouraged an operatic tradition in Dublin, a tradition which goes back beyond the days of Foley and Ludwig to the golden age when Mario and Grisi used to fill the Theatre Royal from floor to ceiling and the students would take the horses out of the prima donna's carriage and pull it triumphantly to the Shelbourne Hotel.

The musical atmosphere at the Academy in those days was predominantly Italian, not only because of the masterful personality of the Commendatore but because the greatest violin teacher the Academy has ever known was Achille Simonetti, violinist and composer, formerly member of the world-famous trio with Madame Amina Goodwin and Whitehouse. Simonetti was typically Italian but the exact antithesis to Esposito. Esposito came from Naples, Simonetti came from Turin: Esposito was nervy, fiery, passionate, and outspoken; Simonetti was gentle, ironical, indulgent, and long-suffering. Both made ideal partners in chamber music, because their varying qualities compensated each other. Esposito always dominated their arguments, because, when he did not convince with words, his eyes, blazing defiance, and his Olympian frown fulminated his opponent. Simonetti, when worsted in argument, would throw up his hands resignedly and pick up his fiddle. Their partnership at times reminded me of when Handel conducted and Corelli led the orchestra at Rome and the fiery German would abuse the lyrical Archangelo, whose playing was too soft and lyrical for the former's tempestuous music. But why, after all, expect Raphael to thunder like Michaelangelo? Both Esposito and Simonetti, however, had one accomplishment in common: like Rossini, they were past masters of the culinary art, and I could never make up my mind which of the two prepared the better dish of spaghetti.

Simonetti had absorbed the great and noble tradition of Italian violin-playing, for he was a pupil of Camillo Sivori, the only pupil of Paganini, and in his younger days, when his technique was at its best, one could note the characteristic Italian qualities of tone, legato playing, all the varieties of staccato and spiccato bowing and the close-knit virtuosity of the left hand. One felt, when listening to him playing on his beautiful Bergonzi violin, that the tradition of his playing descended from the days when Corelli, Tartini and Viotti played on instruments that had just come from the workshops of the supreme luthiers, Amati, Stradivari, and Guarneri del Gesù.

As a teacher he was at his best when facing a class with his violin in his hands, for, like Leopold Auer, he liked to play for the student and annotate in the margin of the violin parts the points that had to be watched and studied. Another of his great qualities was his insistence on ensemble music, and some of my precious memories recall the years when he, Twelvetrees (the professor of violoncello at the Academy), George Hoyle, the viola player, and myself used to meet in one another's houses to play the Beethoven and Brahms quartets. He was one of those violinists of whom the great Ysaÿe used to say that 'he had the religion of his instrument.'

In those days, too, the organists at the Academy were very enterprising in ensemble music, and I always feel personally grateful to Thomas Weaving, the organist, for the opportunity he gave me of playing the Handel sonatas with the organ and the violin concertos of Vivaldi with string orchestra and organ accompaniment. Such music was peculiarly suited to the majesty of that beautiful room, which suggests the graceful, intimate art of the eighteenth century.

Let us hope, as we celebrate this centenary of the Academy, that the Board of Governors of this august institution will in years to come not only turn out first-rate composers, singers, instrumentalists and teachers but also follow the motto which inspired the great old Dublin musicians a hundred years ago, Joseph Robinson, Sir Robert Stewart and Dr Ebenezer Prout, and which the Council of the Royal Dublin Society incorporated in their resolution of 1886 establishing the weekly classical recitals, namely, that 'music should systematically be brought before the public as effectively as painting and sculpture in the galleries.' Such art must be not only a means of earning a living through music but also an encouragement to the music lover to make music in the home instead of merely listening to it on the radio or the gramophone and to return to those ancient days which I remember in Dublin, London, Rome, Madrid and Budapest when people met once or twice a week in one another's houses to make music together.

Walter Starkie (1894–1976) was the son of W. J. M. Starkie, Commissioner of National Education, and of Mrs Starkie, who became a Governor and vice-president of the RIAM, and the brother of Enid Starkie. He was the godson of J. P. Mahaffy. He held the chair of Spanish and a lectureship in Italian at TCD, 1926–47, during the same period acting as director of the British Institute in Madrid, becoming a director of the Abbey Theatre, and living a peripatetic life among the gypsies of eastern Europe, which he described in his books Raggle-Taggle *(1933) and its successors. He was an extraordinary violinist as a student, winning the Vandeleur Academy Scholarship in 1913, and carried on his love of the violin among the gypsies, having early developed an affinity for the csárdás and other tzigane idioms. In 1924 he contributed the majority of entries on Irish subjects to Dent's* Dictionary of Music and Musicians, *including those relating to Stanley Cochrane, James Culwick, Esposito, H. Plunket Greene, Harty, Larchet, Levey, John McCormack, Edward Martyn, Joseph O'Mara, Annie Patterson, Joseph Robinson, Ethel Sharpe, and Sir Robert Stewart. In later life he held several visiting professorships in the United States. His autobiography is* Scholars and Gypsies *(1963).*

6

Tested Teaching: The Local Centre Examination System, 1894–1994

BRIAN BECKETT

The first reference in the minutes of the Governors to the holding of local examinations by the RIAM occurs in October 1892, when a committee formed primarily to consider the matter of vocal music in primary schools was also requested to consider the possibility of holding examinations in various parts of Ireland. The committee comprised George Cree, W. R. Molloy, Charles Dawson, Thomas Mayne, and later James Drury and, as we have seen, Esposito.[1] At the end of October the report of the committee recommended that the Governors adopt a system of local examinations, whose purpose would be, in the words of one of the system's later experts, 'a system of tested teaching.'[2]

This report was adopted by the Governors, and the committee was requested to draw up a scheme. In May 1893 the question of a local examination scheme was referred to the Board of Studies.[3] In June the scheme recommended by the Board of Studies for local examinations was approved,[4] and in September the secretary was directed to prepare proofs of the local examination scheme as soon as possible.[5] In January 1894 the prospectus for the local examinations as prepared by the committee was ordered to be printed and issued.[6]

During April and May 1894 examinations were conducted at Belfast, Bray and Rathfarnham (County Dublin) and in the RIAM. The maximum marks were to be 250, of which 80 were for performance of a piece, 50 for a study, 50 for scales, 40 for theory, and 30 for sight-reading.

In this first year, the examinations at centres outside the Academy were conducted by Joseph Robinson and Michele Esposito, while examinations in the RIAM were to be conducted by the senior professors. The payment to examiners was £5 5s per day (today, £210), with all travelling expenses paid.[7] Examiners in the Academy would receive 10s 6d per hour. A total of seventy-three candidates were examined. A 'centre' was either a school

where enough pupils were available in one place or a venue decided by the Academy itself, in which smaller numbers of pupils could be gathered.

In May of that year the Governors ordered that the results of the examinations be announced in the daily papers, a practice that was continued throughout the early years of the examinations, no doubt because the Associated Board had adopted the same practice.[8]

In 1895, 153 candidates were examined at eight centres, five of which (Rathfarnham, St Stephen's Green, Cabra, Merrion Square, and the RIAM) were in Dublin. It is significant that most of the centres were convent schools, since it is evident that throughout Ireland the teaching orders provided the only systematic and sustained source of music education. As Marie McCarthy has pointed out, 'communities typically had trained musicians among their members,' were 'rooted in or influenced by continental social and cultural ideals,' and were concerned for 'the all-round fulfilment of the child.'[9]

In March 1896 several motions relating to the local centre examinations were proposed by W. R. Molloy.[10] The third of these is of particular interest: 'That the Commissioners of National Education be invited to accept the certificates of competency awarded after examination by the RIAM as warranting teachers to earn result fees on satisfactory proficiency exhibited

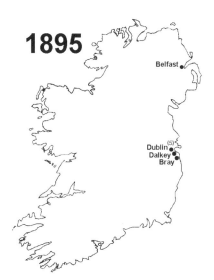

by National School pupils.' There is no evidence that the commissioners responded favourably to this proposal. If they had, it could have generated a considerable improvement in music studies in the national schools and knitted the RIAM examinations more closely into the national education system.

In 1896 examinations were held at seven venues, and a total of 126 candidates were examined. Of these only 16 achieved honours certificates, with 94 passes and 16 failures.

The examinations were conducted by Esposito, Jozé, and Bast. In May 1896 the Governors considered whether pupils of the Academy should be eligible to enter for local centre examinations, and decided that they should not. This decision was overturned some years later, and the present situation—whereby Academy students are eligible to enter for the examinations but not to compete for local centre scholarships—was established.[11]

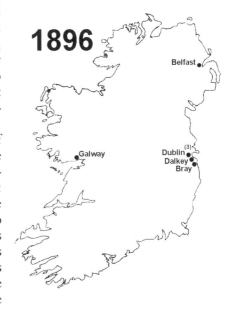

It was decided that the status of local centre certificates should be clarified, and accordingly the following note was added to the certificates: 'These certificates do not entitle the holders to append any letters to their names, nor are the holders thereof certified as teachers.'[12] This corresponded to similar statements on the certificates issued by the Associated Board on behalf of the RAM and RCM.

In 1897, 146 candidates were examined at seven venues, five of which were in Dublin.

The considerable contribution that Esposito made in the developmental stages of the examinations can be deduced from the following resolution at the Governors' meeting of 28 April 1897: 'That the Secretary with Signor Esposito be authorised to make all the necessary arrangements for the

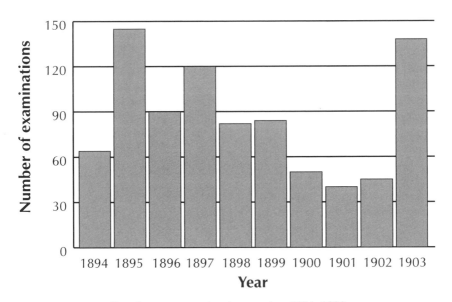

Local centre examination entries, 1894–1903

holding of the Local Centre examinations.'[13] By 1926 Esposito's influence
was so extensive that his appointment
as 'director' of the system was suggested by a committee established to
examine its workings.[14]

The years 1898–1901 saw a slight
contraction in numbers, despite the
addition of a new centre in 1901, the
Friends' School at Mountmellick,
which was to remain a loyal supporter
of the Academy for the next decade.
1902 saw a slight, but only slight, lift
in numbers, and it is possibly a reflection of the Governors' concern that
in December that year it was proposed
and agreed that the Academy write to
the Commissioners of Intermediate
Education about the possibility of the
Academy holding its examinations at various centres. A letter was sent,
including copies of the syllabus, and a meeting was arranged between the
commissioners and a deputation of the Governors.[15] It would seem that this
meeting did not produce a successful outcome for the Academy, as no further
reference to it appears in the records.

Despite the disappointment with the Commissioners of Intermediate
Education, 1903 was a promising year for the examinations, with a consid-
erable increase in numbers and new centres at Sligo, Kingstown (Dún
Laoghaire), Abbeyleix, Goresbridge, Clonmel, and Fermoy. 1905 saw the
inclusion of a centre at Armagh, the first centre in what is now Northern
Ireland since Belfast (1894).

In these early years, centres often presented a very small number of candidates, and the Academy faced some difficult decisions in considering
whether centres could be recognised where the entries were small. In 1907 a
letter from a Miss Roe is noted, asking if an examiner could be sent to
Roscrea to examine seven candidates.[16] The Board responded that it did
not feel justified in sending an examiner, as the fees were so small. Roscrea
is therefore absent from our map of centres in 1907; but the situation must
have improved in 1908, when Roscrea once more features as a centre, and
it remains so until 1911.

A similar problem arose in 1908 when a request for examinations was
received from the superior of the Presentation Convent in Tralee asking for
a centre. The Board informed her that no definite arrangement could be
made until it was ascertained whether there would be a centre at Killarney.[17]
In this case the outcome was positive, and Tralee joined Newtownbarry
(Bunclody) as a new centre for that year.

By 1909 the number of candidates had increased to 289. A change in the
system of marking was also introduced at this time. Previously 60 per cent

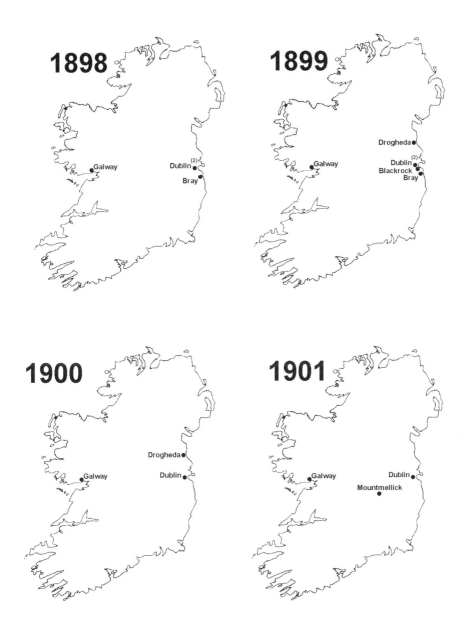

had been the requirement for securing a pass certificate and 80 per cent an honours certificate. Under the new arrangement, two different courses of study were offered, an honours course and a pass course. With this system, three types of certificate were awarded: an honour in the honours course, a pass in the honours course, and a pass in the pass course. Such a system would have the benefit of presenting the more talented students with a sufficient challenge, while lessening the likelihood of the weaker candidates failing to secure a pass.

By this time Esposito had come to occupy a position of considerable prominence in the examinations and indeed did almost all the examining work outside the Academy. This is reflected in the decision of the Governors' meeting of 24 March 1909: 'That the Board request Dr. Esposito to act as Examiner for the Local Centres recognizing as they do the special value of his services in that capacity.'[18]

The logistics of dealing with small centres continued to be a problem. Following enquiries from Bantry and Dungarvan, they were requested to send their candidates to Cork for examination in order to save expense. However, the schools were obviously not amenable to this suggestion, and Bantry and Dungarvan duly appear as new centres for that year.

In 1910 the government inspector, L. E. Steele, reported: 'It is pleasing to find that the Examinations held in various schools throughout the country known as Local Centres Examinations meet with good support, and that the certificates granted by the Academy on the results are highly valued.'[19] This hearty endorsement (although Steele was hardly impartial with regard to the Academy's activities) must have been very pleasing to the Academy authorities as they sought to establish their examination system in the face of stern competition from the various English examination boards. In this

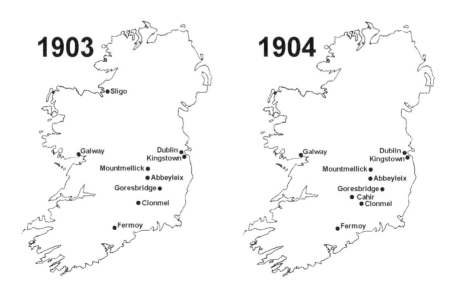

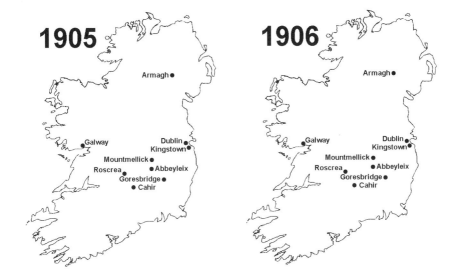

year the ban that previously prevented students of the Academy from taking the local centre examinations was lifted, and it was resolved 'that our Examinations shall be held annually in the RIAM in each grade of each subject of instruction, for which Examination every pupil, without any age limit, in such grade shall be eligible to enter.'[20]

It is inevitable that the administration of any examining body should attract a certain amount of complaint, and even Esposito was not exempt. In 1911 an indignant letter was received from a teacher in Nenagh (a new centre) alleging that 'a most glaring injustice' had taken place in the marking of his students. He asserted that higher marks had been awarded to the pupils at the local convent school and, furthermore, that this had

been done in order to 'curry favour' with the nuns. The Academy's response was to point out that 'after thirty years experience the Governors have good reason in reposing every confidence in their Examiner Dr. Esposito.'[21]

By 1911 the number of candidates had fallen back slightly, to 263, despite the addition of new centres at Birr and Nenagh. This gradual decrease was to continue until the pivotal year 1916.

In 1911 Esposito examined at all nine venues outside the Academy, including the new centre of Nenagh, accompanied at two of the centres by Wilhelmj, who examined the violin candidates. Wilhelmj also examined the violin candidates at the

Academy, while the piano candidates were shared between Esposito and Margaret O'Hea. In 1914 the Governors reported: 'We are pleased to be in a position to state that notwithstanding the adverse conditions prevailing during the latter term of the past year caused by the dreadful war in which this country is engaged the work of the Academy has been carried on in an eminently satisfactory manner'.[22]

In 1916 the Governors were able to report: 'The year showed a gratifying increase in the number of entries (from 185 in 1915 to 311), and it is hoped that the great care taken to maintain a proper standard of examination (thus making the certificates awarded a real evidence of merit) is being appreciated throughout the country.'[23] Appreciation for the work of the Academy in this area was readily forthcoming from the inspector, Steele, who stated:

> The Syllabus of the Examinations is so arranged that continuity of study is secured in the case of those candidates who having passed the tests subsequently join the Academy. They find the methods of the Academy no new thing to them, and are, therefore, all the better equipped to benefit by the instruction. This is only as it should be, and it would be well if the public more fully recognised that they can obtain

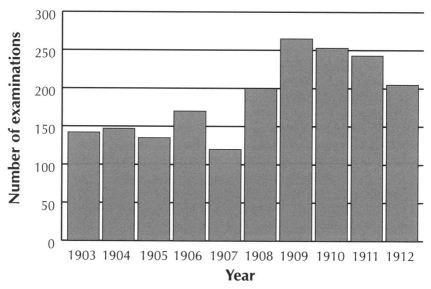

Local centre examination entries, 1903–1912

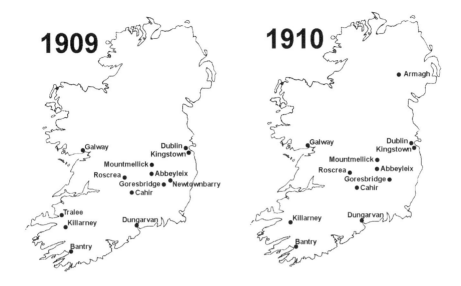

certificates of proficiency just as good as—in some cases much better than—those offered by English examination boards, which of recent years have extended their activities to Ireland.[24]

The increase in numbers in 1916 is largely accounted for by the addition of two new centres, the St Louis convent schools at Carrickmacross and Monaghan. The Monaghan centre in particular was a significant newcomer, entering in its first year a total of 74 candidates: 17 violin candidates (examined by Simonetti) and 57 piano candidates (examined by Esposito).

From 1916 onwards the growth and development of the examination system, which up till this time had been patchy and sporadic, becomes a rapid and steady expansion (see graphs on pages 312 and 317). Why this is so one can only speculate. Possibly Steele's hearty endorsement of the system had some impact; possibly the war situation made it more difficult for the English examining bodies to meet their Irish commitments; or possibly the political developments at the time caused a rise in support for Irish institutions. Whatever the reasons, 1916 was an important turning-point for the examination system, which thenceforward was well established as the leading system in the country.

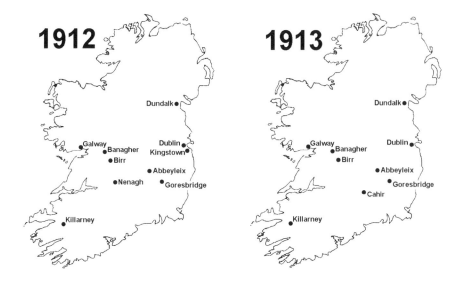

The growth continued in 1917, with the addition of centres at Bundoran (St Louis's) and Buttevant (St Mary's). Belfast reappears on our map for the first time since 1896. 1918 sees no new centres recorded but a steady growth in numbers, from 448 to 549. 1919 saw the addition of centres at Kanturk (Convent of Mercy), Kiltimagh (St Louis's), and Mitchelstown (Presentation).

In 1920 the influence exerted by Esposito in the development of the examinations is underlined by his appointment as examiner in local centres, with the additional proviso that he be authorised to arrange for 'such other assistant examiners as he may consider advisable.'[25]

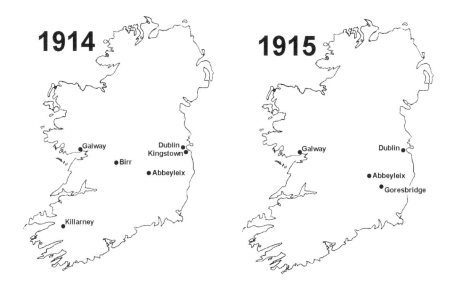

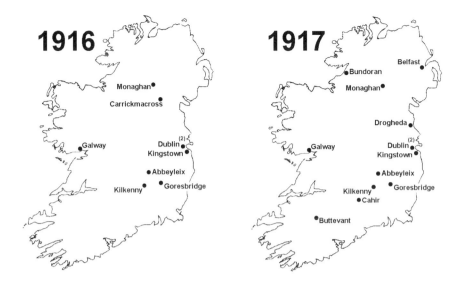

The annual report for 1921 records that

> it is pleasing to find the interest which is being evinced throughout the country, in the teaching of high class music, as well as in the increased use which is being made of the Academy as an examining body. The Syllabus for these examinations is prepared by the Board of Studies, and it may be accepted that the certificates awarded to the competitors represent real merit. The Governors can see no reason why any of the Irish Educational Establishments should send their pupils for examinations to centres organised by British Schools and Colleges of Music in this country while the Royal Irish Academy of Music is prepared to carry out this work by highly competent and impartial members of their staff.[26]

By 1922 the Academy could reasonably regard the examination as being firmly established, with entries for that year totalling over a thousand candidates from thirty-seven centres.

The Civil War, quite understandably, had an impact on the ability of examiners to reach their destinations. Esposito had already campaigned effectively to ensure that examiners had adequate means of transport; a week before the outbreak of hostilities it had been agreed that the syllabus would include a statement that 'in the case of all centres situated outside the town to which the Railway runs, the

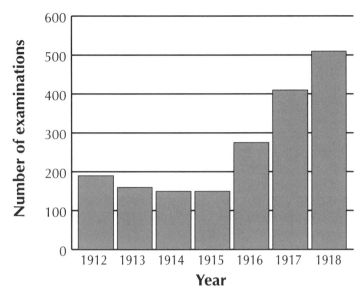

Local centre examination entries, 1912–1919

organizers of the Centres are expected to provide a suitable conveyance for the examiner or examiners to and from the station.'[27] It was a point to which they would return in 1926.

T. H. Weaving records that 'during the "Troubles" much of the travelling in the country districts was done in more or less decrepit taxis,' while 'the trains during the last war [1939–45] often arrived 8 or 10 hours late, leaving the examiners to extemporize some rearrangement of their tours.' Meanwhile accommodation was also somewhat variable: 'One night I arrived at my hotel at 10 p.m. after a heavy day's examining to find five pairs of boots outside the door of the room I had booked—there was a big cattle fair in the town next day.'[28]

The Civil War was another factor that deterred the external examining bodies. In 1923 the Board of Education was notified by the Incorporated Society of Musicians that 'last year the conditions under which the work was done were extremely unpleasant to say the least, and several examiners have already refused to act again.'[29] That year the Board of Education reported that examiners 'will have to go to Clare, Kerry, Cork, Fermoy, Waterford, in motor cars and be fired at impartially by both sides.'[30]

By 1924 the number of candidates entered for examination had risen to 1,675, entries being received from some forty-nine centres. Twelve examiners were required to cover the work, and these included such leading figures in musical life as Esposito, Larchet, Weaving, and G. W. Hewson. It was noted with satisfaction that there was a growing disposition by heads of schools to avail of the facilities offered by the Academy's examining body.

By 1928 the Incorporated Society of Musicians suspended its examinations, in order to become a purely professional musicians' society dedicated to safeguarding the professional interests of its members, and this led to a large proportion of its former adherents transferring their allegiance to the RIAM examinations, with a consequent considerable increase in the number of candidates. In 1928 the total number of candidates examined had risen to almost three thousand, and an idea of the widespread appeal of the examinations can be gained from the map for that year.

1932 saw an important step forward when it was decided to publish five sets of music books containing all the music necessary for the first five grades in piano. Until that time it would have been necessary for the students to acquire the set pieces individually, as was the case with candidates entering the higher grades. The popularity of this development is referred to in the annual report for the following year: 'In connection with the Local Centre Examinations the Governors published five sets of music books, for Grades one to five inclusive, containing all the Pianoforte music required in these grades. These books have further increased the popularity of the Academy's Local Centre Examinations owing to the excellence of the music contained in them.'[31]

In 1939 the Governors appointed a committee to consider the whole position of local centre examinations, the allocation of the work of examining, and the basis of payment for the examiners, and submit to the Board of Governors a report of their findings. The committee comprised Dermod O'Brien (chairman), Mrs W. J. M. Starkie, Mrs O'Hara, F. D. Griffith, and T. S. C. Dagg. The committee noted that at this time over 90 per cent of candidates examined were piano candidates. The committee suggested that local centre examiners should meet together and try to fix a standard of marking. Although various attempts were made in this direction over the years, it was not until the advent of the Senior Examiners in 1986 that regular meetings of examiners became an integral part of the administration of the system. The committee also recommended that examiners should not examine in the same centres for more than three consecutive years where possible: it is obvious that the interests of fairness are better served by rotating the available examiners among the different centres, and this principle has generally been applied since.

The examiners for the Academy at this time were Hewson, Weaving, John and Madeleine Larchet, Grossi, Biggs, and Viani. Two new examiners undergoing training that year were Rhona Marshall and Dina Copeman (herself an Academy student who had come to the attention of Esposito in 1921 as an examinee). It is interesting that at this time 'lady examiners' examined only on the Academy premises. The fee for examiners in 1939 was 10s per hour, and it is some indication of how little inflation pertained in this period that by 1952 the hourly fee had risen to the princely sum of 12s 6d (today, £9.50), with an overnight allowance of £1 5s (today, £19).

The war years caused no real interruption in the work of the examinations and were, curiously, a period of considerable expansion. In 1941 it is noted that 'in spite of all the difficulties of transport, the Local Centre Examinations again show an increase in the number of candidates examined. That these examinations are exercising a wonderful influence on the study of music is evidenced by the steadily improving standard exhibited by the majority of the 5,623 candidates examined.' The following year, however, it was noted that 'owing to the difficulty of travelling during the present emergency, centres must accept the dates we can arrange for them.'[32] By 1945 the numbers examined had risen dramatically to almost nine thousand, and the following tribute is paid: 'The various examiners deserve much credit and thanks for the loyal manner in which they ignored the difficulties, and in many cases the hardships, of fulfilling their appointments at the various Local Centres throughout the country owing to the continuing scarcity of suitable transport.'

Writing in 1950, Thomas Weaving, then chairman of the Board of Studies, noted that in 1949 over ten thousand candidates were examined at RIAM local centres. The subjects for examination included pianoforte (solo and duet), organ, harp, strings, string ensemble and orchestra, singing (solo and choir), elocution (later to become speech and drama), and theory and harmony. Interest in the theoretical side was increasing, with a considerable number of candidates entering for the written examination. Weaving comments:

> I think that we may thank the schools and teachers for the present renaissance in music; by their conscientious work in training pupils for examination, and again by the determination of the secondary schools in keeping their choirs and orchestras going during the dark war years, they preserved the spark of musical life from total extinction and prepared the way for our present promising and hopeful situation. So far as the choirs and orchestras are concerned however it has always seemed a waste of talent and training that so few of the students involved have an opportunity of continuing their ensemble work after leaving school. Our Vocational Educational Committees are in a position to remedy this sad state of affairs by making such opportunities available for their students, and it is to be hoped that they will strive increasingly to do so.[33]

Weaving was aware of the pitfalls as well as the benefits of adherence to a system of examinations.

> One feature of the use of examinations is disturbing, namely the habit formed by many teachers of allowing their students a whole year in

which to prepare the scales, study and pieces for a grade, so that they do practically nothing else. This is definitely bad for teacher and pupil. Instead of the examination being a test of the pupil's progress, it becomes the only progress. The student grazes in a restricted paddock containing sufficient musical food for about two months; when this is spread over twelve months the pupil suffers from musical malnutrition and it is a miracle if any interest in the art survives. It would be much wiser to lay down a systematic course of study as is done in the Music Schools and, as well, for all other school subjects, and let the pupils take the examination in their scholastic stride when they reach a standard equivalent to that of the tests of the grade for which they enter. Used in this way the examination is a real test of progress, and the student advances steadily along a well-planned path of study, instead of hopping insecurely from grade to grade.

Even the schools of music do not escape Weaving's warning in this regard. 'This form of examination madness has affected even our Schools of Music, where the course of study is disturbed, if not completely disrupted, by the students' habit of pot-hunting at Feiseanna, in addition to entering for their own Annual School competitions.' However, he concludes that 'examinations may not be an ideal way of testing a student's ability or progress, but they still must continue until some better method is suggested. They should be used as a means of spurring students on to good honest work and to the acquiring of a wider knowledge, a keener appreciation and a love of good music.'

In 1953 it was decided, in view of the high standard of many of the entrants, to inaugurate a system of scholarships, so as to encourage the more outstanding students to continue their studies at the Academy. This proved very popular, and scholarships are now offered every year, at junior, middle and senior level. This has attracted many talented young musicians to the Academy; some leading figures in the musical life of the country began their studies at the Academy after successfully competing for one of these entrance scholarships.

By 1958 the number of candidates had risen to more than thirteen thousand. With so much music teaching taking place, it was felt that many of the teachers might appreciate an opportunity to refresh and develop their skills, and accordingly it was decided to hold a summer school for teachers the following year. A total of 110 teachers from all parts of the country attended the first summer school, held in 1959, and were most appreciative of the assistance they received from the Academy professors.[34] It was evident that the summer school provided a very necessary opportunity for the teachers to improve their technique, and it was felt that it would make an important contribution to raising the standard of teaching throughout the country.

In the nineteen-sixties the scope of the syllabus was widened to include clarinet, concert harp, and public speaking, in addition to the established subjects. This led to a further increase in numbers, and by 1980 the number

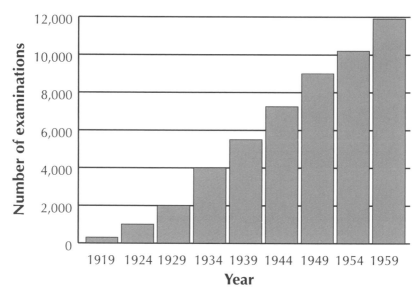

Local centre examination entries, 1919–1959

of entries exceeded twenty thousand. At the summer school of that year, demonstration lectures on the local centre examination music were begun and drew an enthusiastic response from the teachers who attended. These lectures would become a regular feature of Academy summer schools and were always both well attended and well received.

The principal blemish in the history of the local centres' expansion in recent decades has been the violence in Northern Ireland, which in 1971 had caused the Governors to decide that the examinations in Omagh and Enniskillen 'should only be held if an examiner, the risks having been pointed out, voluntarily undertook the assignment and provided a special insurance cover could be effected.'[35]

By 1986 the number and diversity of entries had increased so dramatically that the Board of Governors felt that a specialist panel of senior examiners should be appointed to oversee examining standards and to assist the Board of Studies in further developing the syllabus for local centre examinations. The first meeting of the newly appointed senior examiners (Brian Beckett, Arnold McKiernan, Eibhlín Ní Loingsigh, and Seán Lynch) took place on 30 September 1986. Brian Beckett was unanimously elected chairman, a position he was to occupy for the next eight years.

The senior examiners reviewed the existing panels of examiners for music and for speech and drama, and formal contracts were, for the first time, issued to examiners. These contracts laid down the conditions of service for local centre examiners and specified a minimum number of hours in each examination session that the contracted examiners were obliged to make available. Examiners who were unable to fulfil the terms of the contract but who had considerable examining experience were placed on a second list, known as the reserve panel of examiners. This ensured that valuable and well-practised examiners were not lost to the local centre examinations. The required number of examiners to fulfil the Academy's examination commitments had by this time far outgrown the resources of the Academy's own teaching staff, and a considerable number of examiners were enlisted from other teaching establishments or were suitably qualified private teachers.

As a means of establishing and maintaining regular contact between the committee of senior examiners and the examiners on the examining panel, it was decided to hold meetings of all examiners before each examination session. These meetings came to be known as briefing sessions and provided valuable opportunities for examiners to familiarise themselves with any changes in the syllabus or regulations and to conduct mock examinations to assist in the harmonisation of marking standards. They also gave the examiners the chance to express their views to the senior examiners on any difficulties or problems they might be experiencing and the views of the teachers with whom they were in contact.

The first meeting was held in the Dagg Hall in the RIAM on 12 November 1986. The senior examiners had prepared detailed guidelines on examination procedure and standardisation of marking, and these were discussed at some length. The guidelines on examination procedure emphasised the need for a friendly and relaxed but professional manner. Examiners were reminded of the importance of putting candidates at their ease and listening to all performances in attentive silence. Advice was given on tactful ways of handling queries from candidates or teachers, and advice was added on the interpretation of certain important regulations.

It was the view of the senior examiners that a unified approach to marking by all examiners would be a great asset in maintaining and enhancing the status of the RIAM local centre examinations. The relative smallness of the Academy examination panels, in comparison with much bigger examining bodies from abroad, should allow the Academy to achieve an advantage in this area. The harmonisation of marking standards was developed and maintained

—firstly, by issuing detailed guidelines to all examiners: these set out the overall requirements for obtaining distinction, honours, merit or pass and went on to provide detailed guidance on the marking in each section of the examination;

—secondly, by regular mock examinations of specimen candidates at briefing sessions; the specimen candidates were drawn from a wide cross-section of disciplines and abilities, and, following a mock examination, there was searching discussion between the senior examiners and the members of the panel on what marks would be appropriate in each section; and

—thirdly, by monitoring the percentage of awards in each category of each examiner and comparing these with the percentages of the senior examiners. Later, target percentages were established, based on the percentages of the senior examiners over several years. These percentages were applied within flexible margins, to allow for the natural variation in the standard of pupils examined during any one year. The senior examiners monitored the percentages of each examiner in each examination period and laid particular emphasis on the annual percentages based on the figures for all three sessions in the year. An examiner who appeared to be out of line would be contacted by one of the senior examiners, who would tactfully discuss this situation. If an examiner had persistent difficulty in adhering to the suggested standards, they might be monitored by one of the senior examiners, who would sit in on some of their examinations and offer advice on the marking of various sections. This system worked well and was instrumental in achieving a considerable improvement in this vital area of the examinations.

To provide the senior examiners with the required statistics, it was necessary for examiners to complete a detailed report form for each centre, listing the percentage of category awards and giving information on the facilities provided. In this way the senior examiners were able to form a clear picture of the quality of facilities at the many centres used throughout the country. While the great majority of centres provided a reasonable degree of comfort for examiners and candidates, there were some sorry tales of pianos a semitone flat, of damp walls and leaking roofs, and even of examinations being held in kitchens. As a response to these revelations, the senior examiners drew up guidelines for the minimum standard of facilities at local centres, for circulation to all intending centres.

In June 1987 a handbook was prepared to be issued with the syllabus, giving helpful advice to candidates, their parents, and their teachers. The introduction to the handbook states:

> The Local Centre Examinations of the Royal Irish Academy of Music were established to cater for the needs of music teachers, speech and drama teachers and their respective pupils. They are designed to provide a yard-stick to measure and assess the progress of students and to encourage a comprehensive approach to their development. Therefore in the Music examinations, in addition to the performing of the prescribed pieces, candidates are expected to develop scale-playing, sight-reading, aural training and theoretical understanding. Speech and Drama examinations are especially graded so as to encourage and develop the qualities requisite for a confident and successful oral communicator. The growth of interest in music and speech and drama in our society is reflected by the increasing number of entries and the expansion of the Academy's Syllabus. The programmes are so structured that a student who has successfully completed the course (Honours or Distinction in Grade Eight) will have established a good basis from which to proceed to further study. However candidates who hope to continue their musical studies to Diploma level will need to enter for the Academy's graded theory examinations to ensure that they have sufficient grounding in the theoretical sections which are part of all music Diplomas. The progression of grades should not be regarded as a complete course of study in itself. It is desirable that pupils undertake work outside the Syllabus in order to develop repertoire and technical ability.

The section on marking gave guidelines for the first time to candidates and teachers concerning the interpretation of the various category awards.

> Candidates sitting Local Centre examinations may receive one of four levels of certificate. For a mark of ninety per cent or more a Pass with Distinction is awarded indicating a high level of achievement. For a mark of eighty per cent to eighty-nine per cent a Pass with Honours is awarded, indicating that the candidate has performed very well and very competently, showing understanding. For a mark of seventy per cent to seventy-nine per cent a Pass with Merit is awarded, indicating that the candidate's performance was basically competent but not yet free from errors of understanding or execution. For a mark of sixty per cent to sixty-nine per cent a Pass is awarded, indicating that the candidate has made a reasonable effort. A mark below sixty per cent indicates that the candidate does not yet have the ability, or has not prepared sufficiently to meet the requirements of the Grade. In general it is recommended that a student who achieves less than seventy per cent should consider retaking the Grade after suitable preparation, as such a mark might not augur well for success in the next Grade.

In the advice to pupils and parents, the point was made that an examination is a means to an end, not an end in itself, and that the course of study should not become a mere working for one examination after another but rather a source of enjoyment and enrichment for the pupils themselves and for others.

Words of encouragement were included for the unsuccessful candidates.

> There are occasionally cases where pupils are entered for examinations for which they are not mature enough, and in such instances the results can be distressingly poor. It is urged that pupils should not take examinations for which they are not ready. On occasions pupils do less well than expected due to causes such as nervousness or self-consciousness. In these circumstances pupils should not feel discouraged. After consultation with their teacher they should either retake the examination or progress to a higher Grade. The preparation involved and the additional experience gained should help the pupil's confidence and assurance.

Teachers were reassured that

> the examiner will at all times be concerned to ensure that students are put at their ease in the examination room and given a fair and discerning assessment. The teacher's approach to examinations will inevitably influence the candidates' attitude to the examination experience.

And the following advice was included:

> It is recommended that Grades are taken consecutively and that the student be fully prepared, as failure to obtain a Pass could undermine self-confidence and perhaps discourage the student from further effort. Thus students should be entered for examinations only when they have

attained the desired standard in all areas of the examination. Naturally, teachers wish to obtain the best possible results for their students and to achieve this it is important to ensure that all the examination requirements as contained in the Syllabus are carefully adhered to and have been amply covered. It is always disappointing, when after the pieces or works have been well prepared and delivered marks are lost in the other sections through lack of preparation, resulting perhaps in the achievement of a bare Pass or Merit where an Honours could have been obtained. However, pupils who fail to obtain good results should not be discouraged from repeating the examination, or progressing to the next Grade, unless they are temperamentally unsuited to examinations.

In May 1987 the idea of introducing written comments on practical examinations was considered. It was hoped that these could be introduced by 1989. Although it took somewhat longer than this, and many reservations were expressed, written remarks are now an accepted part of the RIAM local centre examinations and are generally much appreciated by teachers and candidates alike. In October 1987 guidelines for the writing of remarks were drawn up by the senior examiners and later issued to all examiners. The guidelines pointed out that 'the main purpose of these comments will be to provide information for the candidates and their teachers as to why a particular mark or category award has been given' and stressed that 'it is important to avoid a tone of censure when making criticisms and that the pleasing aspects of a candidate's performance should receive favourable comment.'

At the pre-Christmas examination session in 1988 a trial run was organised, with all examiners filling out, in addition to the mark sheet for the local centre office, a further mark sheet incorporating written remarks for each candidate, solely for consideration by the senior examiners. This practice was continued in each session until written comments were officially introduced in 1991 and provided the examiners with an opportunity to become familiar with the writing of remarks.

One of the essential functions of the senior examiners is to constantly review the syllabus and to suggest appropriate expansion and modification where these are considered desirable. In January 1988, the senior examiners suggested to the Board of Studies that an easier starting grade would be desirable in the piano syllabus.

> We feel there is a need for the inclusion of an Elementary Grade for Piano, to be taken before our present Preliminary Grade. The addition of this Grade would recognise that children are starting to learn the Piano at an earlier age than heretofore. In our experience a large number of candidates attempt Preliminary Grade too soon after commencing tuition and consequently find not only this Grade too technically and musically demanding, but also the following Grades a big strain with increasingly disappointing results. We feel that an easier first step is required which candidates could approach with more confidence and which would focus on a more fundamental level of playing.

The elementary grade proved to be a popular and successful addition to the syllabus; and in 1993 the syllabus was further expanded by the introduction of a 'senior certificate' grade, which provided a useful bridge between grade 8 and diploma standard. This examination includes a *viva voce* section on technique and interpretation, which forms a useful preparation for candidates seeking to prepare for teaching diplomas. 1993 also saw the introduction of revised theoretical requirements for practical examinations, which focused more specifically on the candidates' understanding of the music performed.

In 1995 a complete syllabus for percussion was introduced, and senior certificate grades for bassoon, trombone, French horn, flute, euphonium and oboe were added.

The 1997 syllabus offered candidates an opportunity to present a recital programme of their own choice at any one of three levels, the first being the bronze medal category for a varied programme lasting between six and ten minutes, the second level (silver medal) for a programme of twelve to fifteen minutes, and at senior level (gold medal) for a programme of between twenty and twenty-five minutes. These examinations are purely for performance and do not include ear tests, sight-reading, theoretical questions, or scales.

Another aspect of the senior examiners' role was the organisation of seminars and workshops. The ending of the Academy's traditional summer school had left a void in several areas, particularly for teachers using the examination system who attended the summer school for guidance and advice on the preparation of candidates for local centre examinations. To fill this gap a series of summer weekend seminars was begun in 1990. For those seeking a more detailed coverage of specific areas, Sunday workshops were organised. The topics covered included theoretical questions at practical examinations, style and interpretation, theory and harmony, pedalling, fingering, and aural tests.

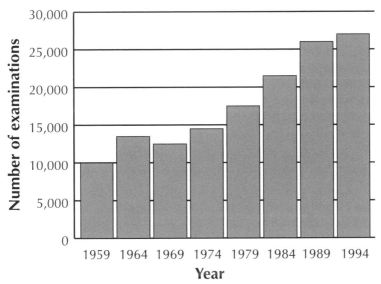

Local centre examination entries, 1959–1994

The work of preparing for the centenary of the local centre examinations began in 1989. A small steering committee, chaired by Anna Brioscú (vice-president and chairwoman of the Board of Governors) prepared an outline of the possible activities, which included local concerts to be held in each of the twenty-six counties and a final gala concert to be held in Dublin. It was envisaged that a souvenir edition of the handbook would be published and that special artwork, including a centenary logo, would appear on all syllabi, examination books, certificates and handbooks for the centenary year. It was also planned to offer three additional scholarships for four terms of free tuition at the Academy and to award extra local prizes.

A submission for sponsorship was drawn up, which included an outline of the management structure of the Academy, brief histories of the Academy and the local centre examinations, a costing of the proposed centenary celebrations, and a list of Governors for the current year. A list of possible sponsors was also drawn up, and this was circulated with the submission.

By 1992 the original committee had expanded to include Lindsay Armstrong (director), Brian Beckett (chairman of senior examiners), Audrey Chisholm, Thérèse Fahy, and Carol-Ann Scott, with Anna Brioscú as chairperson. In addition it was decided to co-opt Theresa Doyle (local centre supervisor) and David Lee (senior examiner). The ideas under consideration at this point included (1) a number of functions around the country; (2) a gala function in Dublin; (3) special logo for publications issued in 1994; (4) a reissue of the handbook, including a history of the local centre exam-inations, together with photographs of the Academy and senior examiners; (5) additional scholarships; (6) county prizes, with award-winners to play in a concert organised in each county; (7) Academy students to perform at venues around the country; (8) a number of grants to be made available for teachers to enable them to attend the Academy for a term's study (refresher course); (9) a centenary stamp to be issued by An Post; (10) a nationwide essay competition organised through the *Irish Times*; (11) a memento of the year to be given to teachers; (12) the printing of special centenary certificates and a special certificate to be presented to original or long-established centres; (13) a balloon launch by the Lord Mayor of Dublin to inaugurate the centenary year.

By April 1992 it had been agreed that both music and speech and drama candidates would perform at the county concerts; the number of speech items would be determined by the proportion of speech entries to total local centre entries per county. There would be twelve items at each county concert. It was proposed that the final or gala concert would be held on St Cecilia's Day (22 November) 1994.

In December 1992 it was decided that the county concerts would be held on weekends between 1 October and 20 November 1994. It was proposed that the President, Mary Robinson, be invited to the St Cecilia's Day concert to present certificates to the students selected to play at the gala concert. A sub-committee was set up to handle the detailed arrangements for the concerts, comprising Brian Beckett, Anna Brioscú, Lindsay Armstrong, and Theresa Doyle.

In February 1993 it was agreed that the following paragraph would appear in the next local centre regulations booklet: 'As part of the Centenary celebrations the Royal Irish Academy of Music will invite teachers throughout the country to apply to be considered for a small number of places on a refresher course of individual classes with Academy staff. No fee will be charged.' There was an enthusiastic response to this scheme from teachers throughout the country, and those eventually selected for the course found it a very beneficial experience.

In March 1993 it was noted that 1994 was also the centenary of the death of Sir Robert Prescott Stewart, a professor of harmony and a vice-president of the Academy, of whom there is a statue on Leinster Lawn. It was felt that some tribute to Sir Robert might be included in the centenary celebrations.

In September 1993 Ciara Higgins was engaged to act as public relations officer for the local centre centenary. This proved to be an excellent choice, as she made a considerable contribution in all areas of the centenary arrangements and attended most of the county concerts.

In October it was decided to launch the centenary on Monday 10 January with a balloon launch, to which the Minister for Education, Niamh Bhreathnach TD, would be invited. A caterer was asked to provide a cake in the shape of a grand piano. The party would be attended by about twenty children dressed in nineteenth-century costume, and the Minister for Arts, Culture and the Gaeltacht, Michael D. Higgins TD, would be invited to cut the cake. An ensemble of Academy students would provide suitable music for the occasion.

The climax of the centenary year was a series of twenty-six concerts held in venues throughout the country between Saturday 1 October and Sunday 13 November 1994. The programmes for the concerts were selected by the senior examiners from computer records of the top ten achievers in their subjects from each county during the previous three examination sessions (pre-Christmas 1993, pre-Easter 1994, and post-Easter 1994). From these concerts thirteen performers were chosen to play at the gala concert on 22 November 1994 in the National Gallery.

The concerts attracted considerable attention from the local press, and this extract from the *Kilkenny People* is typical:

> Musical and dramatic excellence were celebrated in Kilkenny at the weekend when the cream of the county got together for an exciting concert in Kilkenny Castle. The concert was one in a series of twenty-six marking the Centenary of the Local Centre Examination System of the Royal Irish Academy of Music. The concert featured students who distinguished themselves in the recent Local Centre examinations. And their talents were praised by a Governor of the RIAM, Dr. Anna Doyle, who also paid tribute to their teachers. Dr. Doyle said that music was a most important part of a young person's education as it opened up a whole new experience. And the introduction of Speech and Drama to the examination system broadened the contribution of the Royal Irish

Academy of Music to the art of performance. Talents cannot be discovered without participation, she said. Even if the young person does not proceed to a professional career in music or speech and drama, or reach a very high standard, nevertheless, the knowledge gained will enable him or her to become a member of a more discerning audience.[36]

The concerts were in general well attended and enthusiastically received, as indicated in the encouraging review of the Cavan concert in the Community College, Bailieborough, on Saturday 23 October.[37] 'The organisers were delighted with the excellent attendance, and the audience was treated to a most enjoyable and varied programme, performed mostly by young musicians from the county on instruments that ranged from piano to wind and brass. Most of these young players showed obvious talent and had already achieved the highest marks in their grades for the county. The concert provided them with the welcome opportunity to display their talent in public, something the audience clearly appreciated.' The review concludes: 'Each of the performers was presented with a Commemorative Scroll from the Academy in honour of the occasion, which they can display with justifiable pride and as a genuine achievement that may well be of use to them when it comes to preparing their future CV.'

The concerts also provided the Governors of the Academy with an opportunity to express their views on music education as a whole and, in particular, the Academy's role therein. This opportunity was enthusiastically grasped by Declan McDonagh at the Tipperary concert, in the Ursuline Convent School, Thurles, on Saturday 12 November, in an address that was reported extensively in the *Tipperary Star*.

A Tipperary born Governor of the Royal Irish Academy of Music has stated that early training in music is a gift which parents, teachers and educational planners ought not to undervalue. Mr. Declan McDonagh, a native of Gortlandroe, Nenagh, was speaking at the centenary celebrations of the Local Centre Examination System of the Academy in the Ursuline Convent, Thurles. The Ursuline hosted the County Tipperary Local Centre celebration concert featuring the highest placed students from the county who participated in the Local Centre examinations from November 1993 to June 1994. These distinguished students were presented with special Centenary Scrolls of the RIAM by Mrs Mae Quinn, Chairperson of Thurles Urban District Council and a member of the Ursuline Secondary Teaching Staff. Mr. Declan McDonagh, who now lives in Malahide, and who has been domiciled in Dublin for over thirty years said 'In any future planned educational changes in Ireland it is imperative that the intrinsic benefit of music education be fully recognised and capitalised upon rather than have music marginalised in the curriculum.' Mr. McDonagh added 'The Local Centre Examination System of the R.I.A.M. is uniquely placed to play a part, born of its experience over the years and its high standards of excellence, in any development.' Mr. McDonagh said that through the decades the system had been very much appreciated in rural Ireland and specifically in this county where, often against the odds, parents and teachers made major efforts and sacrifices to maintain a wonderful tradition.[38]

The culmination of the centenary celebrations was the gala concert in the National Gallery on St Cecilia's Day (22 November) 1994, attended by the President of Ireland, Mary Robinson. The programme of thirteen items included piano, Irish harp, flute, singing, recorder, concert harp, violin, classical guitar, clarinet, choral verse-speaking, and speech and drama. The participants ranged in age from eight-year-old Darragh Gallagher, a speech and drama student from County Wicklow, to the mature student Capt. Patrick O'Callaghan, a clarinettist from the Band of the Southern Command.

The ethos of the centenary year is aptly summed up in Anna Brioscú's address in the concert programme.

> The very small beginning pioneered by Michele Esposito one hundred years ago has grown probably beyond the wildest expectations of this great man. We proudly look back remembering teachers, students, examiners and Academy administrators who have contributed by their dedication to the success of the Local Centre Examination System throughout the past one hundred years. While we reminisce and indulge in a little nostalgia we must nevertheless look forward to the next century. The Senior Examiners appointed by the Governors are constantly monitoring and reviewing the system so as to enable us to give an even better service in the future. We look back with satisfaction and thanksgiving for our success while moving into the next century with confidence that the great work started by Michele Esposito will continue to flourish.

Intermezzo

The Students' Musical Union

The Students' Musical Union, affectionately known as the SMU, was founded in 1905, its object being 'the cultivation of classical and modern music.' This has given the SMU the chance to engage with the full gamut of musical forms. In addition, it has expanded its aims 'to assist and further the education of the students of the RIAM by providing concert experience and other facilities to such students calculated to equip them for a musical career.'[1] Very early, it became one of the chief focuses of music-making in Dublin by virtue of its guest nights; and by inviting members of staff and other experts to perform it gave students the experience of hearing interesting music played with accomplishment.

This *intermezzo* attempts to re-create some of the excitement and vigour of SMU activities during the first six decades of its existence—jumping ahead of our chronology to give an overall picture of the fortunes of the SMU.

The founder was Nita ('Nettie') Edwards, who had won the Vandeleur Scholarship for singing the previous year and had been appointed a teacher of theory (with Beatrice Elvery). She was to go on to a career as a singer, largely in the United States.[2] Although she is given sole credit in the SMU's records for the founding of the organisation, the inspiration was in fact shared with Tom Weaving, a past pupil who had been teaching theory and piano since 1902 (as well as teaching theory at the Municipal School of Music) and who was to become a pillar of both the Strollers and the Rathmines and Rathgar Musical Society (the 'R&R'), founded in 1913.

Looking back fifty years later, Nettie Edwards remembered 'the wonderful happiness of that period of my life' and her 'friendship and comradeship' with fellow-students such as Annie Lord, Madeleine Moore, Marie and Amy Dowse, Bessie Ruthven, and Arthur Oulton.[3] The proceedings of the SMU, she recalled, were 'very serious and business-like' and were marked by the fact that 'all the time a pattern was gradually being evolved.' It was one of the most exciting episodes in the history of the Academy, which saw the introduction of a body of music, especially to the chamber music repertoire, that was also a discovery—and a self-discovery—by the students themselves. This vibrancy of the SMU was maintained from its foundation up to the nineteen-sixties, when its continuation began to seem more fragile.

Nettie Edwards speaks of a collegiate spirit in which 'self-glorification was conspicuously absent' and in which Governors and staff co-operated in making facilities available and in providing music. The SMU had one inherent strength, and one inherent weakness. Its strength was the simplicity of its original objective. The students wanted something the RIAM curriculum could not give them: the right to choose their own music and their own performers and to introduce new music, as well as a new form of social intercourse. Its weakness lay in the fact that, although Nettie Edwards said that the SMU was 'most truly of the students, by the students and for the students,' there was a built-in temptation for students to rely on senior energies and guidance. As membership was open to all present and past pupils (which of course included many who had become teachers and indeed Governors), its membership would reflect a cross-section of the Academy. Staff members such as Tom Weaving and Jack Larchet only lent a practical hand when a conductor was required for new or unfamiliar music, or Clyde Twelvetrees when a cello part proved too difficult for student fingers. They were unobtrusive, and in many instances they benefited as much as the younger participants—Larchet, for example, acquiring some invaluable experience as a conductor. In later decades, however, and in particular the nineteen-sixties, an over-reliance on staff tended to produce a disappointing level of student activity.

Largely, however, the members of the SMU ran its affairs, independently and resourcefully, drawing up an elaborate set of rules and succeeding, very early on, in raising the purchase price of a Steinway piano (and in 1935 a Bechstein), which on occasion was rented to the Governors, with whom the SMU succeeded in negotiating a very amicable relationship of mutual respect. In March 1909 Annie Lord, in her capacity as treasurer of the SMU, circulated an appeal for donations for the purchase of a piano, the price being estimated at a minimum of eighty pounds, since it was recognised that hiring for each concert would be a prohibitive expense to be met out of the annual subscriptions. The Steinway was obviously obtained with ease, since it was played for the first time less than eighteen months later, on 8 October 1910.

The printed rules of the SMU in themselves mask the fact that it performed a vital social function, in providing a legitimate opportunity (for young women in particular) to find a social dimension beyond the home and the family and, indeed, beyond the strict repertoire and decorum of the Academy. SMU committee meetings, rehearsals and concerts were times of freedom as well as places of learning, while the emphasis on extracurricular activities, such as country walks and boating trips, and on contemporary music, should be seen in parallel, as attempts by young musicians to create an alternative life-style to that then available.

Another unwritten function was to teach the students the value of putting something back into the institution that nurtured them. Apart from music-making itself, this was achieved by substantial financial contributions to corporate activities. When, in 1924, the Academy was contemplating an enlargement of the band room, the SMU gave fifty pounds towards the project, and in the same year it subscribed a further fifty pounds to the Citizens' Hall fund.[4] Later, contributions would be made towards the purchase of chairs and other equipment in the Academy.

Practical aspects of social and political events, such as the Civil War, also pressed themselves on the attention of students. In 1922/23 the honorary secretary, Eileen Buckley, recorded that orchestral and choral items had been affected by 'the recent disturbed state of the city,'[5] while in 1939/40 Dorothy Stokes spoke of the SMU's consciousness of 'storm and tribulation . . . [and] dreadful happenings abroad,' which had 'threatened total blackout . . . Please goodness we shall be spared the horrors of this most awful of wars.'[6] This in itself was another form of education.

The most significant achievement was the introduction to the Academy of a new tier of concert activity, in the form of regular musical evenings, at which the members could hear, and take part in, music of their own choice. Added to the 'ordinary' nights, exclusively for members, there were special 'at homes' or 'guest nights', to which non-members could be invited. A typical programme from the early years of SMU concerts is this one for 5 June 1907:

> Rheinberger: Minuet and finale from Piano Quartet[7] (Misses H. Ruthven, Bell, Park, B. Ruthven)
> Brahms: 'Thou Art, O Queen' (Kathleen Smyth)
> Paganini-Liszt: Étude (Edith Coplin)
> Gounod: *'Nella calma'* (Mary Garland)
> Handel: Recitative and air (Elsie Warham)
> Liszt: Hungarian Rhapsody No. 2 (Annie Lord)
> Leoncavallo: 'A word, sweet ladies' (*Pagliacci*) (J. C. Browne)
> Hubay: Fantaisie Tziganesque[8] (Bertha Dowse)
> Saint-Saëns: Andante tranquillo and presto for quintet (Annie Lord, piano; Marie Dowse, Bertha Dowse, Constance Bell, Muriel Porter)

These were clearly 'occasions', as, according to *Irish Society*, the concert was attended by 'Mr. and Mrs. Edmund Lupton, the latter looking especially well in pale yellow silk, Miss Pauline Delany in white with touches of cigar brown . . . Mr. and Mrs. McHardy-Flint, the latter in a handsome black taffetus toilette . . . Miss Bertha Ellis in black net daintily fashioned . . . Miss Crean in a black lace robe,' and, in unspecified clothing, the Irwins, Dermod O'Brien, Leopold Dix, Professors Twelvetrees and Palmieri, Harold White, Sarah Purser, Reginald Montgomery, and Dr and Mrs Power O'Donoghue.[9]

On 6 May 1909 the programme was:

> Liszt: Angelus arranged for strings
> Hugo Wolf: 'Fussreise' (Alfred Johnson)
> Liszt: 'Waldesrauschen' for piano (Sophie Vance)

Verdi: '*Ritorna Vincitor*' from *Aida* (Eileen Forbes)

Saint-Saëns: Prelude to 'Le Déluge' for violin and orchestra (Madeleine Moore)

Chopin: Scherzo in B flat minor (Annie Lord)

Schubert: Serenade (Thomas Collins)

Wieniawski: Polonaise op. 21 for violin (Marie Dowse)

Twelvetrees: 'Come Back' (Nettie Edwards, with cello obbligato by the composer)

Gade: Sonata op. 59 [No. 3 in B flat] for violin and piano (Mrs Rawlingson and Mrs J. K. Toomey)[10]

A hallmark of SMU concerts was the introduction of contemporary, and particularly French, music. In 1910 Charles W. Wilson played 'La Cathédrale engloutie', 'La Fille aux cheveux de lin' and 'Minstrels' from Debussy's *Préludes*, composed in that year. In the same period Marie Dowse and Annie Lord introduced the Violin Sonata by César Franck, and in 1956 Frederick May recorded that the 'experience of hearing a great work [the Franck Piano Quintet in F minor] greatly performed was, without doubt, one of the most outstanding memories' and 'one of the most thrilling experiences I can recall from my student days at the Academy.'[11] Performances of May's music would become equally memorable in their turn. In 1936 Dorothy Stokes drew attention to an outstanding item in the previous year's calendar, a performance of May's 'Four Romantic Songs' for tenor with string quartet and piano, sung by Steuart Wilson with the composer at the piano, and a quartet of Nancie Lord, Arthur Franks, Petite O'Hara and Joseph Schofield.

In 1907 an evening was also devoted to the music of Esposito, including a string quartet, a violin sonata, a trio from *The Tinker and the Fairy*, two ballades for piano, and some songs.[12]

Other works played at SMU concerts at this time that we would today find unusual include piano duets by Adolf Jensen (1837–79), Simonetti's Mazurka for solo violin, songs by Frederick Rocke, 'Mia Piccirella' by the Brazilian Carlos Gomes (1836–96), and Sibelius's 'But My Bird' from the Six Songs of 1899.

Cui's cello solo 'Cantabile' was another unusual item, played on 8 November 1911 by Mary Gallagher. Others from 1911 include Larchet's incidental music, composed the previous year, for Synge's *Deirdre of the Sorrows* at the Abbey, and a piano sonata by Albanesi played by Victor Love. On 20 May 1911 the SMU presented a lecture by Esposito on 'The Origin of the Opera'—a project he had already realised at the RDS—with vocal illustrations by Nettie Edwards. In his official report on the RIAM in 1912, L. E. Steele commented on the excellence of the SMU concerts in 1911, and the Board of Studies commended the performance of *Messiah* on 16 December 1911, with seventy performers, of whom all but four were Academicians.

In 1916 May Lord (viola) played an andantino from a concerto by the Bohemian Hans Sitt (1850–1922), while Edith Boxwell performed two movements from the 'Grande Sonate Russe' by Felix Borowski (1872–1956), the English-born composer who made his career in Chicago. At the same concert Rosalind Dowse (violin), Nora Dowse (cello) and Mina Davin (piano) played the *allegretto con moto* from a trio by Stanford.

The Dowse family was remarkable for its contribution to the Academy. It was not at all unusual to find a quartet of Dowse sisters playing at a concert—for example the Schumann Quartet in A minor, op. 41. Altogether five of them featured as leading string players in the Academy (Marie, Bertha, Lilian, Hilda, and Rosalind); Marie was to become the mother of Joan and Valerie Trimble; Rosalind a member of the original 'Station Orchestra' of 2RN, later Radio Éireann. A sixth sister, Amy, a singer, was a member of the original SMU committee in 1905.

On 26 June 1909 we find the following playing the scherzo and finale from Spohr's Nonet op. 31: Alice McCarthy (violin), Richard Fleming (viola), Mary Garland (cello), Thomas Fleming (bass), H. M. Fitzgibbon (flute), R. Lea (oboe), Richard J. Butler (clarinet), Richard Littledale (bassoon), and De Courcy Miller (horn). It was not at all unusual to find works by Cyril Scott, Palmgren, Bantock, Moskowski, York Bowen or Taneiev on the programme. In 1925/26 several British works were introduced, including songs for voice and violin by Holst, Vaughan Williams's 'On Wemlock Edge', a two-piano work by Bax, a duet for violin and piano by Delius, and a vocal quartet with piano and violin accompaniment by Walford Davies.

By 1910 Nettie Edwards's reputation was sufficiently established for her to be giving concerts in venues outside Dublin. On 27 May 1910 she appeared with several SMU colleagues at the Town Hall, Galway (where she taught periodically). She sang the Jewel Song from *Faust*, 'For All Eternity' (with violin obbligato by Alice McCarthy) by Edoardo Mascheroni (1859–1941),[13] and a duet, 'Flight of Clouds', by Caracciolo, with Reginald Montgomery. Alice McCarthy with Nora Sidford played the finale of Esposito's Violin Sonata in G and a ballade and polonaise by Vieuxtemps.[14] Queenie Eaton sang 'Softly Awakes My Heart' from Saint-Saëns's *Samson et Dalila* and Tosti's ever-popular 'Goodbye'. According to *Irish Society*, which clearly found such details ever-important, 'she made a winsome figure in a pale blue diaphanous gown.'[15] *Irish Society* found that Reginald Montgomery's 'The Lord Is My Light' (by Francis Allitson)[16] 'could not be accounted a wise choice for a country-town concert, nor could the really beautiful Kashmiri melody "Pale Hands I Loved".'

A few months later, 'Nettie Edwards's New Operatic Concert Party', including Queenie Eaton, Madeleine Moore (soon to marry John F. Larchet) and, in his famous role of 'humorist', Sealy Jeffares (later to be the Academy's secretary), were entertaining Wicklow, where the programme included the third act of *The Bohemian Girl*.[17] Jeffares was a notable participant in the SMU's G&S activities, and later, as RIAM secretary from 1927 to 1949, he provided much unseen and invaluable support. In 1950 the SMU recorded that he had been 'guide, philosopher and friend' and, in wartime, had made gifts of scarce tea and sugar for SMU refreshments.[18]

By 1911 the *Freeman's Journal* was loyally asserting that the SMU concerts 'are perhaps the most convincing of proofs that the tuition at the [RIAM] can rank with the best in the three kingdoms.' Commenting particularly on the sextet by Rheinberger, two Beethoven sonatas, and Mary Gallagher's playing of Cui's cello solo 'Cantabile', the newspaper underlined the fact that 'the programme was not a conglomeration of drawing-room ballads and easy instrumental pieces such as are usually presented by a body of amateurs.'[19]

This departure was so significant that the *Irish Times* found itself commenting on the fact that the SMU's evenings seemed to have taken the place of Academy chamber music concerts. 'But for the tendency of pupils to leave the Academy just about the time when they should be getting seriously into this department of study, chamber music at the Academy might be in a good state . . . It is a pity that more of those who qualify themselves at the Academy . . . do not avail themselves of the excellent guidance of the Academy teaching staff in conjunction with [the RDS recitals]' to give practical study to chamber music.[20] In the same year the report of the Board of Studies mentioned an outstanding charity performance of *Messiah*.[21] In 1913 the *Irish Times* underlined the significance of these house concerts by pointing out the misfortune of those not able to attend the private gatherings at which such important contemporary works as Coleridge-Taylor's cantatas 'Hiawatha's Wedding' and 'The Death of Minnehaha' (1898 and 1899, respectively) were performed under the baton of T. H. Weaving.[22]

One of the SMU's remarkable early achievements was the production of Gilbert and Sullivan operas, which started in 1909 with *The Sorcerer*,[23] presented with three different casts on 9 and 13 February and 18 March. It was conducted by Richard Fleming, and the orchestra was led by Madeleine Moore. Young Kurt Wilhelmj played the part of a page, and one of the Governors, T. M. Gerrard, took the role of Dr Daly. On one of the three evenings Tom Weaving played Sir Marmaduke Pointdextre, an early signpost to his lifelong involvement with the R&R.

In the twenties G&S productions were to become an annual event, presented in Rathmines Town Hall, with *Trial by Jury* in 1927, *HMS Pinafore* in 1928, a double bill of *Cox and Box* and *The Pirates of Penzance* in 1930 and *The Mikado* in 1932 being especially memorable. This series of productions culminated in the SMU taking the Gaiety Theatre in 1933 for a week's run of *The Gondoliers*, which netted them a profit of over thirty pounds.[24] Apart from the enjoyment of staging the entertainment, it is significant that the activity was not regarded as in any way musically inferior. As Charles Osborne has recently observed, 'Sullivan's score for *The Pirates* is no less delightful than Rossini's for *L'Italiana* and his librettist . . . Gilbert, is immeasurably superior to the Italian composer's Venetian hack, Angelo Annelli.' And he points out that the patter song, which is especially successful in *The Sorcerer*, is not an original feature of G&S but derives from Haydn, Mozart, Cimarosa, Rossini, and Donizetti.[25]

In addition to G&S, the students also presented in 1912 a double bill of operettas by Lady Arthur Hill, *The Lost Husband* (for which she wrote both libretto and music) and *The Ferry Girl* (libretto by her mother-in-law, the Dowager Marchioness of Downshire); and in 1913 they produced Coleridge Taylor's 'operatic romance' *Dream Lovers* of 1898.

The SMU String Orchestra was formed in 1931 and won first prize in the Feis for three successive years, under the direction of Dorothy Stokes; but such activity became sporadic—mainly occasioned by the need for a band to accompany opera performances—and it was not until the fifties, under Max Thöner, that a similar venture was seriously attempted.

A further dimension of SMU activity was the introduction of lectures by staff and distinguished visitors. In 1923 Frederick Dawson, an extern examiner of the piano faculty, gave a lecture recital on the evolution of the piano repertoire, and in 1927 Walter Starkie spoke on the Russian Five. Two years later he gave an illustrated talk on a subject close to his heart, the *tzigane*, and in 1931 an illuminated autobiographical talk on 'Living the Life of a Gypsy'. A lecture of some curiosity was given by Larchet in 1936 on 'Stanford and his Works', during which, we are told, Larchet 'was able to tell us stories and incidents of Stanford's student days here at the Academy.'[26] As Stanford had not attended the Academy, this must have brought out Larchet's powers of invention.

These events coincided with the start of Dorothy Stokes's association with the SMU. She became secretary in 1927, having already been treasurer. Her long tenure as secretary, from 1927 to 1942, and later as president, proved to be invaluable. At the same time her dominating presence for over forty years curbed student involvement on the committees. Unlike the early days, committees became restricted to former students and staff, and current students tended to become spectators rather than activists.

The SMU was not without its share of controversy. On 10 February 1909 Nettie Edwards had the unpleasant task of writing as follows to the Governors:

Dowse family: back (*left to right*): Nora, Lilian, Hilda, Rosalind; front (*left to right*): Bertha, Amy, Marie

Students' Musical Union picnic, c. 1910. (*Left to right*) Nettie Edwards, Marie Dowse, Annie Lord, Lilian Dowse, Amy Dowse (in front, with cherry), unknown

Students' Musical Union guest night at the Gresham Hotel, 1931

Gilbert and Sullivan: SMU production of *The Yeoman of the Guard*, 1929. Back (*left to right*): Dorothy Griffith, Sealy Jeffares, Nancy Reilly, Biddy Kirwan, Mabel Home, Frank Cowle. Front (*left to right*): Paddy Byrne, Marcus Ruddle, Daphne Coote, unknown

Nettie Edwards in the role of Santuzza (*Cavalleria rusticana*) at the Theatre Royal, Dublin, in 1907

Dorothy Stokes in picnic mood, c. 1930

Michele Esposito, portrait
by Sarah Purser

Rhona Marshall

John Quinn, for fifty
years hall porter

Jean du Chastain

Adelio Viani

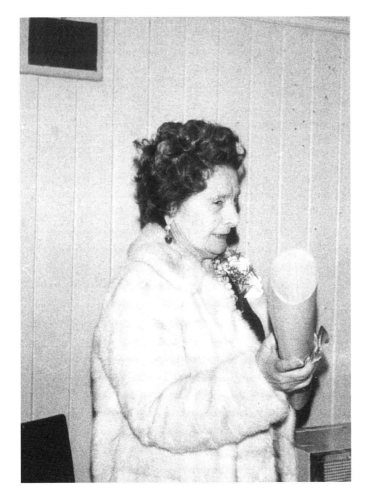

Dina Copeman

Frederick May

George Noble, Count
Plunkett, drawing by
Seán O'Sullivan

Bishop Nicholas Donnelly

Maud Aiken, centre, with Éamon and Sinéad de Valera, at a recital by
Joan and Valerie Trimble, Gresham Hotel, Dublin, 1965, in aid of the
Academy restoration fund

John and Madeleine Larchet receiving joint honorary doctorates at the National
University of Ireland, 1953

Hubert Rooney

Sealy Jeffares

Edith Best with her
teacher at the RCM,
Franklin Taylor

T. S. C. Dagg

The premises of Georg Wilhelm Hoffmann, violin maker and restorer, Lincoln Place, Dublin, frequented by generations of RIAM students. When Adolf Wilhelmj began teaching at the RIAM, he perceived the need for a first-class violin maker and, on the advice of his father, succeeded in attracting Gustav Meinel from London, who established himself in 1906 at 8 Westland Row and from 1910 in Lincoln Place, where the firm continued until 1972. Georg Wilhelm Hoffmann took over the business in 1919 on Meinel's death and, when he died in 1963, his son William Hoffmann continued the family business.

The Monteagle Library of the RIAM in its original location on the ground floor, showing the cases designed by Dermod O'Brien PRHA

Students' Musical Union, 1951. Standing (*left to right*): Seán Lynch, Valerie Walker, Audrey Chisholm, Louise Tate, John Benson, Minnie Clancy, Marjorie Nolan, Hilda McDonald, Peter Dodd. Seated (*left to right*): Janet Corcoran, Aoife Hanley, Mary Gallagher, Muriel Nolan, Florence Ryan, Maeve Broderick, Olive Boles, Margaret Hayes

RIAM prizewinners in the 1980 Feis Ceoil

Valerie and Joan Trimble

Joan Trimble and Havelock
Nelson receiving honorary
Fellowships, 1985

Karl-Heinz Stockhausen receiving honorary
Fellowship from the Lord Mayor of Dublin,
John Donnelly, 1991

Olivier Messiaen receiving honorary Fellowship
from the Lord Mayor of Dublin, Seán Haughey,
1990

At the launch of the RIAM
Local Centre Centenary, 1994:
Anna Brioscú, chairman of the
Board of Governors; Niamh
Bhreathnach TD, Minister for
Education; and Tomás Mac
Giolla TD, Lord Mayor of
Dublin

Governors at the award of honorary Fellowship to Anna Brioscú, 1995.
Seated (*left to right*): Declan McDonagh, Prof. Barbara Wright, Dr John O'Conor,
Anna Brioscú, Leo Gibney, Gabrielle Begg, Maurice Doyle. Standing (*left to right*):
Annraoí Ó Beoláin, Frank Murphy, Séamus Gaffney, Liam Fitzgerald, Desmond
O'Donohue, Unsionn Ó Farachtáin, Charles Acton, Richard Pine

Lindsay Armstrong,
Director 1982–93

John O'Conor, Director since 1994

Gentlemen—It has come to our knowledge that an anonymous letter has been sent to some of the Governors purporting to come from someone connected with the SU stating that Signor Esposito had arranged his concert and rehearsal for 9th and 11th inst. in order to upset our arrangements for the Sorcerer performance. While any anonymous letter should be treated with contempt, I still wish to disavow on behalf of the 'Sorcerer' company and the Union in general, any connection with this infamous production, and to emphatically deny the statement that the Dublin Orchestral Society's concert or rehearsal in any way interfered with the 'Sorcerer'. On the contrary the Students Union were afraid that owing to the Philharmonic Society's final rehearsal and concert being fixed for Feby 8th & 9th that we would have to postpone the Sorcerer but as Signor Esposito and the DOS consented to put off their concert until 11th Mr Marchant held his concert on 3rd which enabled us to carry out our original arrangements. It is a palpably malicious absurdity for anyone to suppose that Signor Esposito who has always been one of the warmest friends of the Students Union could in any way wish to injure it.[27]

Perhaps there *was* something in G&S that created intemperate situations, since twenty years later it was reported at a Governors' meeting that 'a junior teacher, Miss Dorothy Stokes, had, in a private conversation . . . said that he (Mr Prescott),[28] Lupton & Larchet are out to injure the Students Union and especially to baulk (or some such word) the performances of the *Pirates*. The Secretary was directed to communicate this complaint to the teacher concerned and ask for a reply in writing.' Dorothy Stokes denied using any such language.[29] As already stated, however, relations between the SMU and both the teaching staff and the Governors were generally free of any kind of bickering.

For guest nights the old band room eventually proved too small, and in the thirties the SMU took the Aberdeen Hall (also known as the Ballroom) of the Gresham Hotel for these occasions—the regular and almost only such venue for recitals in the thirties, forties, and fifties—often broadcasting live on Radio Éireann and thereby earning significant funds. 'The rough cost of a Guest Night there is about £23 [today, £450] so that it would be quite impossible for us to incur that expense without the relay fee,' Stokes recorded in 1934.[30]

Notable among these concerts from the thirties are the formation of a quartet by Nancie Lord and Alice Brough (violins), May Lord (viola), and Chrissie Fagan (cello); the solo harpist Sanchia Pielou, soon to win a scholarship to the RCM; and another group, the 'Irish Ensemble', consisting of Nancie Lord and Arthur Franks (violins), Petite O'Hara (viola), Ida O'Reilly (cello), and Rhona Clark (piano).

This was the era in which several present and past pupils began to forge reputations that would make them household names in the music world.

Apart from Nancie Lord, who was to become leader of the radio symphony orchestra, and those already mentioned, these included Madge Bradbury (renowned for songs at the piano), Kathleen Pollaky (cellist), Maud Aiken, née Davin (violist), Patricia Victory (pianist, soon to be involved in the world of theatre music), Dr Annie Keelan, née Brereton (pianist, medical doctor, vice-president of the RIAM, and one of the last inhabitants of Merrion Square), Myrrha Jephson (cellist), Madeleine Mooney and Ettie Mann (violinists), Violet Burne and Harold Hope Johnston (singers), and Alice Yoakley, née Bell (for many years conductor of the Culwick Choir, and a Governor of the Academy).

A typical programme from the first half of such a concert (broadcast by Radio Éireann) would be this one from 14 June 1933:

> Gordon Stutely: 'Salt o' the Sea' (String Orchestra, conductor Dorothy Stokes)
> Esposito: 'Remembrance'
> Schumann: ABEGG Variations (Una Kenny, piano)
> Brahms: Trio in C minor (Rhona Clark, piano, Arthur Franks, violin, Ida O'Reilly, cello)
> Coleridge-Taylor: 'Eleanore'
> Schubert: 'The Erl King', op. 1 (Michael Gallagher)
> Mozart: First movement from Sonata in D for two pianos (Eileen Buckley and Jean Russell)
> Bizet: Quintet from *Carmen*, act 2 ((Patricia Black, Ronnie Keary, Lucy Hamilton, Tadhg Forbes, Patrick Kirwan)

From the records kept we can see the way in which the SMU repertoire retained standard favourites over the years and also reflected changing musical tastes and preferences. Chopin, Beethoven, Debussy, Esposito, Liszt and Rachmaninov provide the basic fare for piano and Bach, de Bériot, Mendelssohn, Saint-Saëns and Tartini in strings, while Schubert and the contemporary English composers were the most-performed vocal items for men, Schubert and Brahms for women. A comparison of the catalogue of works performed in 1927, 1937, 1947 and 1957 provides the following insight into the less usual items (with dates of composition, where relevant, in brackets):

1927

> *Piano:* Glinka, 'L'Alouette' (Dina Copeman); Harty, Concerto [1922][31] (Hilda Shea)
> *Violin:* Stanford, 'Caoine' and 'Leprechaun's Dance' (Nancie Lord); Harty, Concerto [1908–9] (Eleanor Reddy)
> *Cello:* Bantock, 'Hamabdil' [1919] (Nance McLoughlin)
> *Strings and piano*: Hewson, Irish Rhapsody

1937

Piano: Rachmaninov, Fantaisie-Tableaux for two pianos (Annie Keelan and Rhona Marshall); Strauss: Gieseking, Serenade (Rhona Marshall)
Violin: Hurlstone, Romance and reverie (Una Kenny)
Cello: Glazounov, 'Chant du Memestrel' (Babette Kelly)
Duos: Paderewski, violin sonata (Nell Ronan and Posy Schreider)

1947

Piano: Byrd, John Bull, Gibbons (Anthony Hughes)[32]
Violin: Raff, Cavatine and Fiocco, Allegro (Joan McElroy)
Cello: Bantock, 'Hamabdil' (Emir Lang)
Ensemble: Purcell, Golden Sonata (Carol Little, Joan McElroy, Jean Meacock)
Organ: Stanford, Choral Prelude, and Stanley, Introduction and Allegro (Anthony Hughes)

1957

Piano: Fauré, Nocturne No. 7 (Carmel Lynch)
Voice: Wolf, 'Auch Kleine Dinge' and 'Auf ein Altes Bild' (Gráinne Ní Éigeartaigh)
Cello: Elgar, Concerto (Kathleen Pollaky)
Clarinet: Louis Cahuzac, Fantaisie Variée (Adolf Ganter)

Extracurricular activities were another feature of the SMU's social life. We have already referred to the early boating trips and their liberating effect. Under the vigorous leadership of Dorothy Stokes, who was secretary from 1927 to 1943 and remained a pillar of the union for over forty years, the SMU formed a hikers' club; and, as Stokes recalled, 'hail, rain or snow, each fortnight twenty or more members would take lunch and wander up hill and down dale, visiting places previously unknown to us.'[33] The inaugural hike, on 16 October 1932, began at Harcourt Street Station, where they took the 12:15 train to Carrickmines at a cost of 11d; they walked from there to the Golden Ball and Three Rock Mountain, coming home by Ticknock and Dundrum. Stokes's instructions read: 'Bring your own sandwiches & small thermos. Back about 5. Adverse climatic conditions will not deter us.'[34] Subsequent hikes brought them by way of the Terenure–Blessington tram to the Pine Forest and Kilmashogue; to Castletown demesne; to Bray Head and along the shore to Greystones; across the summit of Howth; to the waterworks at Glenasmole, Killakee, and Balrothery; to Roundwood and Lough Dan; and from Killruddery up the Little Sugar Loaf ('by easy stages!').

Activity in the forties was thin. Partly because of wartime shortages and restrictions, partly because of a general slump in Academy energies, few new departures are noticeable, and what did take place resembles an effort to keep things going rather than to breach new horizons. But mention must be made of the presence in the Academy of Brian Boydell, as a singing professor. In 1942 he sang Elizabethan songs with string quartet (arranged by Warlock) at an SMU concert, and in 1945 he sang the 'Songs of Death' (1928) by the Finnish composer Yryö Kilpinen. Boydell's emergence as a composer was noticed at this time, not least in the SMU, where in 1943 his Quintet for Oboe and Strings was premiered,[35] while in 1945 his Cello Sonata was played by Betty Sullivan.

In 1952 we find George (Seoirse) Bodley complaining of the lack of contemporary music on the programmes; but generally speaking, new music from within the Academy itself was performed regularly, and a large proportion of the programmes was occupied with foreign music from recent decades.

Another generation of students of truly national significance appeared in the fifties and sixties. The violinists Audrey Park, David Lillis, Mary Gallagher, Maeve Broderick and Elias Maguire, the singer and harpist Gráinne Ní Éigeartaigh, the singer Austin Gaffney and the pianists Anthony Hughes and Seoirse Bodley all feature in concert programmes of the time, alongside past pupils such as Renée Flynn and Dr Annie Keelan. Among the Academy staff, A. J. Potter took part, singing his own 'Ode to Dives' and songs by Vaughan Williams and Jeremy Johnston. The tenor Dermot Troy and soprano Eithne McGrath (soon to be married) sang 'Parigi o cara' and 'Unde felice' from Verdi's La traviata; and in 1960 a nonet in E minor, op. 5, by the youthful composer, cellist and aspiring conductor Proinnsias Ó Duinn was played.

An instructive innovation in 1951/52 was a 'serial' performance of the Franck quintet, with one movement played at each meeting and the whole work played at the end of the series. (The players were Joan McElroy, Eileen Parfrey, Kathleen Green, and Patricia Lavery, with Seán Lynch on the piano). A 'fun' occasion took place in 1953 when Rhona Marshall and Dorothy Stokes let their hair down and played Variations (or Paraphrases) on 'Chopsticks' by various Russian composers.

Again, musicality showed itself to run in families, with the progress through the Academy of many Healys, Staveleys, and Carneys. A programme of 1963 saw the appearance of two performers who would become a vice-president of the Academy (and professor of French at TCD) and a professor of singing, respectively: Barbara Wright played a Chopin nocturne and the Holst toccata, and Paul Deegan sang 'Una furtiva lagrima' and 'An Sylvia'. In 1966 the SMU congratulated itself that a 'galaxy' of members was now studying on the Continent: Maeve Broderick in Germany, Anne Cant in Vienna, Aisling Drury-Byrne in Paris, Maeve Foxworthy in Munich, Darina Gibson in Manchester, Richard Groocock in Hamburg, and Helen Healy and Colin Staveley (to become successively leader of the BBC Welsh Symphony and the RTESO) in London.

A notable piano duo was formed by Ann Clancy and Frank Heneghan, who became joint secretaries of the SMU and then husband and wife,

Frank going on to become director of the VEC College of Music. On 10 April 1968 they played:

> Franck: Prelude, Fugue and Variations, op. 18
> Mozart: Sonata in D, K448
> Bartók: Chromatic Invention from Mikrokosmos, Book VI
> Brahms: St Anthony Variations
> Rachmaninov: Suite No. 2, op. 17

In 1955 the SMU celebrated its fiftieth anniversary with a dance and concert attended by Nettie Edwards and by a newly elected Governor, Charles Acton, who wrote 'how very moving was Miss Edwards's emotion,'[36] while Annie Keelan reflected on 'the youthful promise of Maeve Broderick, the polished and sincere singing of Renée Flynn and Harold Hope Johnston and the superb piano playing of Rhona Marshall.'[37]

1955/56 was a very significant period for the SMU in its relations with the Academy, since it not only achieved its own golden jubilee in this manner but also gave a concert to mark the centenary of Esposito's birth and another to celebrate the Academy's own supposed centenary. This period also saw a number of events in which established musicians gave their services to foster a greater interest in SMU affairs. In October 1964 Charles Lynch, then a part-time member of the piano staff, gave a characteristic recital programme consisting of Beethoven's Appassionata sonata, three pieces by Debussy, a Rachmaninov prelude and the *Suggestion Diabolique*, the Third Sonata of Prokofiev, and Liszt's 'St Francis Legend' and 'Jeux d'Eau'. Two years later Werner Schürmann (accompanied by John O'Sullivan) sang Brahms's Four Serious Songs and a year later a recital of early songs by Mahler.

An important aspect of performance that has always presented difficulties was voiced at this time, when 'a request by the Governors that we encourage student members to participate more actively in accompanying at our concerts' was discussed. Rhona Marshall (then a member of the committee) suggested that the best way to foster this was to arrange that those interested be present at lessons given by professors of singing, strings and wind and 'take part in the accompaniments required at these lessons.'[38] This was, in fact, an informal feature of Academy life (as Carol Acton's *intermezzo* indicates), but its intangibility makes it difficult to describe, and today the scarcity of good accompanists (as opposed to those with a natural capacity for sight-reading) continues to be a problem.

As we have mentioned, one drawback of the SMU constitution was that the continuing participation of former students, many of whom became members of staff, put dominant figures such as Dorothy Stokes and Rhona Marshall into very influential positions. Despite the establishment of a Junior Branch in 1936, this reliance on Stokes, in particular, encouraged younger members to leave the organisation of musical and social events to their elders, thus depriving the union of a real student contribution. In 1934 Stokes commented that students needed to be coerced into activity,[39] and two years later she reported: 'I feel that a crisis of a rather serious nature is in our bones in the near future—it is not an artistic but a numerical one.'[40] In fact in 1935 student apathy was already evident: on the proposal that at least one member of the committee should be a present pupil, no pupil was actually elected.[41] By 1939 Stokes was saying: 'This apathy and indifference is like a germ and eats into the mind and outlook of the listener and transfers itself to the performer.'[42] In 1945 Michael O'Higgins, then secretary, pointed out that 'the SMU will fade out if steps are not taken to interest the younger members . . . in the management of the affairs of the Union.'[43]

In 1964 Charles Acton criticised the SMU for the low level of involvement of students in its activities,[44] which prompted the committee to organise a 'newcomers' concert'; but by 1966 the committee was expressing its own concern 'about the poor attendance at our concerts, and the general lack of interest by the members.'[45] In 1945 Michael O'Higgins had got to the nub of the matter when he advised that 'student members should control the destinies of the Union. It is their Union and it is a necessary part of their education to learn how to arrange and balance concert programmes.'[46] Twenty years later, in 1968, the AGM recorded that 'the discussion on [the] matter of having an all-student committee was lengthy and mostly incoherent enough not to be recorded in the Minutes. However, the staff were apparently in complete agreement to retiring from the committee and not putting their names forward for re-election[47] . . . It was then decided that this should be a year's trial . . . and it would be up to the students themselves to make a success of running the Union.'[48]

The next year the president, Anthony Glavin, noted that an all-student committee had brought 'fresh ideas, a reservoir of enthusiasm and a new lease of life generally to the somewhat arthritic activities of the Union.'[49] But he also asked 'whether the SMU should be run as an adjunct to the teaching activities of the staff, by providing platforms where exam pieces, Feis pieces etc. can be "tried out" so to speak on an unsuspecting public . . . or whether the SMU should be run as an adjunct to the interests and eccentric (or uneccentric) enthusiasms of the students.' Espousing the latter choice had brought a further decline in numbers, and by the following year the incoming president, John Gibson, was openly criticising committee members for lack of interest, despite the zeal of his predecessor, Anthony Lewis-Crosby.[50]

Despite attempts to introduce 'fun and frolics' in the form of quizzes, dances, picnics, visits to Dublin Zoo and a revival of the annual hike, the SMU never quite recovered the sense of excitement and endeavour of earlier decades. Nevertheless, 1968 also saw a renewed interest in presenting contemporary music, with a concert featuring Stockhausen's *Klavierstücke* and Seven Pieces (1968) by Yuri Schuldt, played by Anthony Glavin, a trio by John Gibson, a violin sonata by Derek Bell (both aspiring young composers at that time), and an aleatory octet (1961) by Cornelius Cardew, which was performed three times in the evening. Commenting on this, Charles Acton said:

> It does not matter a hang whether or not we elders like what the young are doing. What is vital is that the young should do it, should enjoy doing it, and that our schools of music should be in fertile contact with the living world of the future.[51]

The students still kept a more than respectful eye on the past, also commemorating in 1979 the fiftieth anniversary of Esposito's death with a concert that included a revival of *The Tinker and the Fairy*. The secretary's annual reports in the seventies also refer to notable activities such as John Beckett's chamber music class, which contributed a deeply appreciated sense of early music, and to student successes, including an Arts Council grant to the child prodigy Daire Fitzgerald to enable her to study with Rostropovich.

In 1974 the Governors noted with concern that the SMU was not functioning on any kind of regular basis, and its demise was expected[52]— an event that, as with so many bodies with an ephemeral membership, it succeeded in avoiding for the time being, playing its part in a new dimension of Academy life in hosting exchange visits between the RIAM and the Paris Conservatoire and RAM.

However, the death of Dina Copeman and more particularly of Dorothy Stokes in 1982 proved a near-fatal blow. The secretary's report records: 'It is often said that as far as our particular job is concerned we are all replaceable but for the SMU I am afraid that is not the case with Miss Stokes. As someone once said to me, she was the SMU and her constant hard work and loyalty have been responsible for keeping it alive for more years than many of us here can recall.'[53]

The picture that emerges from the first six decades of the SMU's existence is of an easily and early achieved plateau of performance followed by a regular pattern of involvement of, and presentation by, the student body, even though the presiding genius was that of a young-at-heart but increasingly senior figure. The picture of more recent decades suggests much less continuity and much more susceptibility to the strengths and weaknesses of student intake, which no doubt in its turn reflects social and economic changes outside the Academy. (In 1961 the then joint secretaries of the SMU, Bernadette Dowling and Seán Lynch, had observed: 'In these times of push-button entertainment the student is confronted with temptations and distractions which could very well deflect him from the serious study which is necessary to any form of achievement in the world of music.')[54] But it also suggests that the modern curriculum and its attendant exam pressures are such that the average student is less inclined to set foot outside the essential syllabus. By 1969 the committee had realised that 'the rôle of the SMU was somewhat outdated when compared to the position it was in many years ago, when there were far fewer organised concerts, e.g. RDS, St Francis Xavier[55] etc.—and it was thought that the general public had quite enough musical attractions without listening to students gaining experience on the concert platform.'[56]

Although it can never be said that student concerts (however volatile) are not a valuable experience for both performers and audience, it is true that fashions, and musical demands, do change. Today in the Academy the range of options within the new degree courses, for example, gives students many opportunities for performance under assessment conditions that did not previously exist, and this may have served to inhibit extracurricular activities and energies on which the SMU depended for its success. Equally, the social dimension of the BMusEd course perhaps supplies students with a sense of camaraderie previously to be found in the SMU; while the burgeoning opportunities for co-ordinated chamber music activities may also supply the need to explore the repertoire previously undertaken by students under their own independent line of enquiry.

Perhaps, therefore, the story of the SMU is a closed chapter, in that what it came into existence to achieve with great éclat and commitment has more recently been satisfied through other channels. One would hope, nevertheless, that the student body, with or without stimulus from its teachers, would continue in one way or another to show that sense of adventure, experiment and excitement in its approach to music-making that has always been the hallmark of the SMU.

7

Maturity
1922–1998

*Cultural identity in the Irish Free State; end of the 'Esposito era';
John F. Larchet; Dagg Hall; Academy orchestra; relations with
Radio Éireann; discussion of a conservatoire; changing role
of the Academy; refinancing of the Academy; appointment
of a director; expansion of activities;
reform of Board of Studies.*

On 24 February 1922 the secretary of the Academy wrote to 'Michael Collins Esq., T.D., Minister of Finance, Provisional Government of Ireland' at City Hall, Dublin, referring to 'the annual grant of £300 which the Academy has hitherto received from the British Treasury out of monies voted by the Imperial Parliament for this purpose . . . The Governors . . . desire to be informed if they may rely upon your Government continuing, and it is hoped increasing, this very inadequate grant to this the only National Academy of Music in Ireland.' The letter went on to ask for an appointment for a deputation to meet Collins 'to go fully into any matters which you might wish to have elucidated.'[1] Collins's reply, from Oifig an Uachtaráin on 13 March, was brief and to the point: 'The grant of £300 . . . will be provided in 1922–23 on the usual conditions. A deputation at the present moment would serve no useful purpose.'[2]

The exchange typifies the 'provisional' nature of the times. Within four months civil war had begun, and within six Collins was dead. To continue the provision to the Academy was, for the new government, a transitional necessity; to meet its administration was not. On the day his letter was written, Collins was meeting Lord Midleton to discuss the problems of the unionists living in the Free State. Two months later he received a deputation from the Church of Ireland, anxious to know 'if they were permitted to live in Ireland or if it was desired that they should leave the country,'[3] to which Collins replied that they were welcome to stay. If John Turpin's view, that the arts 'were associated with people from the Anglo-Irish minority, a politically marginalised social group in the new state,'[4] is even approximately accurate, then it is obvious that, having settled the broader issue of including the Anglo-Irish within the new state, its leaders would let related cultural matters take their course.

In any case, to the extent that the Academy's controllers had subliminally taken the decision to make common cause with the new state, no further action was necessary. It would be a matter of time for the rapprochement of the two to become effective, and when this happened, in the nineteen-fifties, the mutual recognition had a principally financial and utilitarian focus when the grant (still £300) was gradually raised to realistic levels.

In this chapter we consider the changing circumstances that saw a transformation in Ireland as great as that which had taken place between 1848 and 1920: a new way of governing the country, a new way of expressing that country's sense of identity, new means of cultural expression, such as the radio, and continuing anxieties about the purpose and methods of education. We shall see the Academy moving through troubled waters and doldrums, creating a new relationship with government and thereby renewing its role as 'the national academy', and expanding its services once more as it anticipated, and responded to, new educational needs.

This was the age in which, in John Hutchinson's term, 'the artist-creator is conceived of as the paradigmatic figure of the community,'[5] although with regard to music this was less true than it was with literature. Perhaps the sentiment expressed by Edith Best in 1897 about what music might achieve under the new arrangements was more apt:

> The mental and spiritual happiness of a people is a wonderful peace maker, and it should be the first effort of a wise Government to secure that state of mind in its subjects . . . To teach a people to stand firmly on its own merits . . . as a self-respecting and self-reliant entity in the civilization of the world, contributing its impetus to the progress of the human race, perhaps adding some inestimable gift which no other people can give—this is the true nationality.[6]

But the coming years would prove that, however strong the general will in the new Ireland to resist external influences and to develop inner resources, it was still necessary to look outside for guidance and inspiration. With regard to music, the Academy's need for such figures as Adelio Viani, who became professor of singing in 1917 and remained in that position for almost fifty years, did not change with the new dispensation.

Viani, who was born in Milan and trained at the Conservatoire there as a singer and flautist, and who had worked there and elsewhere as a teacher and examiner, was to become one of the legendary figures of the Academy. A friend of Puccini, he was an authority on opera, and, under his guidance, the Academy established and developed a new opera class, in which he would eventually be succeeded by Michael O'Higgins. Although there had been opera activity at the RIAM (as noted especially in chapter 3 regarding the early charity productions and in chapter 5 regarding some productions under his compatriot-predecessors), the Viani initiative was qualitatively different.

In 1922 the Governors received a letter stating that 'some of my pupils have expressed a wish to study singing on operatic lines, including acting. I feel sure that if a lesson of the kind requested were given when asked for, combined with the usual weekly lesson, which as a matter of fact is often of an operatic nature, it would give satisfaction for those preparing for the stage, and keep these students longer at the Academy.'

Rather surprisingly, the Governors were not immediately won over to the idea. 'The Governors do not see their way to undertake this at present and in any event there may be objection raised by the parents of some of the pupils. Meantime the Governors will be pleased if Signor Viani can increase the number of hours teaching in the Academy.'[7] But whatever influence he was able to exert, it achieved its aim a month later, and opera classes began. They were not, however, to be without their disadvantages, since the cost to the Academy was always considerable and at times could not be afforded. From time to time the classes were discontinued: in 1937 we find Joseph Holloway suggesting the introduction of a class for opera and ballet, as well as a dramatic class,[8] which makes it clear that its fortunes were variable. But while the official records indicate a stop-go type of activity, the folk memory of past staff and students suggests that Viani's achievements far outstripped these vacillations.

In 1933 the Board of Studies expressed its disapproval of Viani's scheme for vocal classes as being contrary to the Blue Scheme. It is difficult to see what was so very different in the proposals (which gave Viani complete control of the classes) from those previously accepted by the Board with regard to Palmieri, even though one can readily agree that it was in fact contrary to the scheme to interpose any educational authority between the two boards. It appears that the Governors overruled the professors on a matter that had clearly been under discussion for some weeks. In that year Viani had been elected a members' Governor and had received a fellowship of the RIAM, suggesting that he was in good standing both with the sub-scribers and the Board; yet an attempt was being made, with Raymond Victory as its ostensible leader, to set a limit to Viani's activities.

With Viani's scheme preferred by the Governors over that submitted by Victory, the secretary was notified by Edmund Lupton, the husband of Victoria Delany and an eminent lawyer, that in his view the Governors' actions were illegal. Although nowhere is the nature of the illegality spelt out, the letter—by which in effect Lupton ruled himself out of Academy affairs *sine die*—rhymes with the remonstration by the professors: 'The present position is ridiculous. It impedes the efficiency of the Academy and restricts the objects for which it is established. It is caused by honest beliefs which appear to me to be based on rumours and statements which have no valid foundations.'[9] By its nature, an institution of this kind lives partly in the shadow of such 'rumours and statements', and it is not surprising that this incident, like many similar ones, remains penumbral. Seldom, however, does such an incident retain the bitterness or pettiness with which it is often imbued at the time, and usually professional anxieties, coupled with personal dislikes and suspicions, exacerbate a situation to a point that it does not merit.

The incident is also part of the Academy's experience of finding its way in the new Ireland to what Marie McCarthy has called 'the music education process . . . in some way related to the construction of Irishness . . . of a sense of self in the world,' which in many ways is still continuing.[10] It may well be that some teachers in the Ireland of the thirties, when cultural restrictions on external influences were at their height, may have wanted to inhibit as far as possible the work of an expert who had not only reintroduced the work of Puccini to the Academy but had also voiced the same fundamental objections to voice training in Ireland as had Woodhouse and Scott-Fennell.

Viani, who in 1932 was created a *Cavaliere* of the Crown of Italy, had written extensively on the subject, and his essays, dating from 1925, were collected in 1945 in a volume under the title *Towards Music*, which underpins his reputation not only as a teacher but also as conductor of the Dublin Operatic Society (forerunner of the Dublin Grand Opera Society, now Opera Ireland), which he had founded in 1928.[11] In 1960, Academy students and staff performed a concert of works by Viani, including songs, a violin sonata, and a piano suite.

It would be pleasant to follow Frederick Corder in his view (at the conclusion of his history of the RAM) that 'it is not so entertaining to read about success and peaceful times as it is to peruse a record of struggle and strife'[12] and so to curtail this account by passing rapidly over the period since 1922. This chapter *is* shorter than its predecessors, partly because some of the events of the period are chronicled in other chapters (especially chapters 9 and 10) and partly because to have been all-inclusive in referring to recent history would have been impossible. But the period under review was not so much a successful and peaceful one, as one of continual re-negotiation and recharting of the Academy's critical path. Although in many ways the twenties and early thirties could be regarded as its golden age—with students of the order of Frederick May, Renée Flynn, May and Una Lord, Alice and Sheila Brough, Myrrha Jephson, Joan and Valerie Trimble, Havelock Nelson, Brynhilda Fannin, William Boucher, Walter Beckett, the three Larchet children, and Arthur Franks—there were still years of struggle and strife ahead.

The ambiguity of the Academy's situation after independence was due not so much to any political or ideological differences between itself and the government over the nature of the service it provided as to the failure to develop an effective and integrated system of music education of which the Academy could be part. This in turn is due to the failure of the British administration and its successor in identifying music as part of a dynamic (as opposed to a passive) creative intelligence. W. J. M. Starkie had pointed out the failure of the authorities to integrate the educational system. 'Impenetrable layers stretch between the different grades, and communication between the lower and the higher is almost as difficult as between this planet and Mars. It would indeed appear that in educational matters it is our cardinal virtue not to let our left hand know what our right is doing.'[13] It was within this situation, known today as the 'fractured continuum', that the Academy would have to find its way.

Brian Kennedy has pointed out that in Dublin over half the people lived in dwellings with two rooms or less,[14] but this helps to explain only the lack of material and financial provision for the arts, not the absence of any cohesive and comprehensive philosophy for aesthetic and cultural transmission or production.

The gradual recognition of the skills of teaching, performing and indeed listening to music had fallen short of the attention accorded to subjects such as literature, history, and the sciences. Music, like art education in general, had suffered because of its difference.

Music also suffered from the polarisation of the past and the present, which saw one tendency towards regression into the imaginative hinterland of pre-Famine folk spirit and memory and another towards modernisation and change. As we have seen, the Feis Ceoil succeeded in maintaining a balance in its early years between the original conception and what was actually possible. The Academy, because it was largely directed by the same, or similar, personnel, steered a middle course as far as the transmission of musical skills and values was concerned. But the Arcadian vision of Ireland desired by Irish Ireland (and still suggested by de Valera as late as 1943) did not in fact give way to modernisation until the 'Lemass era' of economic investment and expansion from the late fifties. Under the pastoral model, musical development was confined to a laconic, traditional agenda. Under the developmental model it was relegated to a position far behind the needs of an economics-driven and technology-driven school population.

Music performance, therefore, seems to have continued its growth in both the level and the standard of activity, with a renewed attempt to reconstitute a regular orchestra in the form of the Dublin Philharmonic (with the participation of the Free State army) and the emergence from the Academy of several generations of instrumentalists who would not only fill the ranks of this orchestra and its broadcasting successors but also provide the teachers of generations to come.

The Academy, by concentrating on the business of music teaching, and with its new subscribers, its intake from a changing student profile, its mixture of foreign and local teachers and a cross-section of the new Ireland in its board-room, avoided ideological confrontations either with the government or with the educational system and continued to display that pragmatism that had enabled it to survive unfavourable and stormy times in the past.

In *Writing Ireland*, Cairns and Richards, following Gramsci, observe that 'culture is the site on which the struggle for hegemony takes place' and that *discourses* are the means by which that struggle is exercised.[15] This, once again, helps to explain the astonishing, and today little-appreciated, phenomenon of Irish music-theatre and, side by side with this, the production of so much text-based church music. If the implementation of a set of rules implies that an instinctive opposition, with an alternative set of rules, will simultaneously come into existence, then music, as a discipline with strict givens, should in principle exemplify this process in its tolerance of a movement away from rules and their subversion by polyphony, jazz, aleatory and counterpoint as varieties of style. But the test cases in the cultural sphere took place in the area of film and literature, so that the 'music question' so innocently discovered by Sir William Harcourt remained unanswered and even largely unasked.

Ironically, the fact that music production failed to achieve a momentum or definition comparable to that of literature meant that composers escaped most of the problems experienced by writers, and audiences were not given the difficult choices forced on the reading public by censorship. The point is vital because, even more so than in the eighteen-nineties, it explains why Irish composition did not develop, and it explains why the Academy was able to proceed with its core business, unaffected by most of the cultural debate. Even so, because that debate had not been resolved, it was still being pursued in the thirties, with the twin basic themes 'What is Irish music?' and 'Whither Irish music?' continuing to make would-be composers doubtful of their cultural identity.

The explanation of this continuing dilemma is not hard to find. The dynamic of cultural nationalism in the earlier period involved the interpretation and presentation of various musical idioms, as well as their creation; we have seen this in relation to the Feis. After independence, creativity (and its control) was more important than performance. Therefore, if the mere performance of classical music was regarded as the purlieu of the Anglo-Irish (perhaps even the pro-Treaty) mentality and way of life, as personified in the audiences at the RDS recitals, and therefore marginal to the 'real Ireland', the question of the production of Irish music became more strongly focused. Thus, it could be said that composers had a simpler set of options than previously: either to embrace the corpus of traditional music holus-bolus or to reject it in favour of other idioms. They were hardly expected to steer a middle course between the two.

When some composers did make this attempt, they were faced with a near-insoluble dilemma: as Aloys Fleischmann put it,

> we have on the one hand a unique tradition in folk-music, on the other hand a half developed art-music which is for the most part alien to or at best no more than superficially connected with that tradition. What is needed is a Gaelic art-music which will embody all the technique that contemporary music can boast and at the same time will be rooted in the folk-music spirit, and will be as individual and genuine as that folk-music is individual and genuine.[16]

Music (but not necessarily the Academy) suffered the general fate of cultural life after independence, as the doors of Irish Ireland and sinn féinism were temporarily closed to the outside world as far as foreign influences in the arts were concerned. Fleischmann probably summed it up a little harshly, but expressed his own true fears, when he said in the thirties that 'unless his music is confined to arrangements of traditional tunes or at most to sets of variations on these tunes, he [the composer] may indeed risk being classed by the rank and file as Anglo-Irish, even as anti-Irish.'[17] Academy people like Frederick May, who broke these taboos to write works such as the 'Songs from Prison', seemed to be constituting a 'battle of two civilisations', as the debate since the eighteen-nineties had been called. The gradual deceleration and degeneration of creativity had a trickle-down effect on performers and, in time, on listeners. Stanford had emphasised that education must understand the listener, since, as he put it, 'the listeners are in immensely greater numbers than the performers. Without audiences we should have no performances; without intelligence in audiences we should have inferiority of performance; with an insufficiency of audiences we should have a minimum of performances.'[18]

This absence of an intelligent audience has been one of the greatest crosses Irish composers have had to bear. Whether or not it was greater than the general discouragement of creativity in the twenties and thirties is debatable. The suppression and exile of writers is relatively easy to quantify, but it is impossible, for example, to say whether any composer or other musician left Ireland because of censorship or the fear of ostracisation, although several (May, Boydell, Potter) found it necessary or desirable to go abroad to study. But it is clear that many more, like Larchet, experienced the same frustrations as Fleischmann and found their work confined to, rather than liberated by, Irish themes. Perhaps, if he was inhibited or repelled by conditions at home, May's exodus to Vienna and the nostalgic pastoralism that Axel Klein detects in his most important works (below, p. 421–2) could be seen as a musical parallel to the foreign sojourn of the novelist Francis Stuart.

But shutters *were* being brought down on the imagination, or rather on the power of the imagination to effect change. Burke, in his *Reflections on the Revolution in France*, observes that taste and morality are intimately related, and so the process of political, cultural and social change in the period 1890–1920 became more evident in the following thirty years, as both taste and morality became politically contested. It was Mario Esposito who, looking back from 1959 on his own exile from Ireland, summed up the two sides of the transitus: 'Under English rule there was a certain freedom of thought; today intellectual activity is suppressed by the priests who are as arrogant and domineering as they are ignorant and limited. De Valera and the opposition alike are completely under the thumb of the Maynooth hierarchy and the Jesuits. Liberalism and socialism are almost entirely unknown.'[19] If this seems somewhat abrupt and wide-sweeping, the close relationship of church and state in the management of national schools up to 1966—when a stronger emphasis was placed on the recognition of 'human needs'—should be recalled.[20]

There was a natural arrogance in Irish Ireland, which enabled Éamonn Ó Gallchobhair to say that 'the Irish idiom'—which was synonymous with 'the Irish mind'—'expresses deep things that have not been expressed by Beethoven, Bach, Brahms, Elgar or Sibelius—by any of the great composers.'[21] Ó Gallchobhair, educated at the RIAM (1927–35) and the composer of five operas and operettas in Irish, was a candidate for a vice-presidency of the Academy in 1951; significantly, one of the other candidates was

Sir Arnold Bax, who had been nominated on previous occasions. Noel Reid proposed Ó Gallchobhair, on the grounds that 'the Academy should honour composers who have been having a lone fight to develop and maintain Irish music,' while Edgar Deale proposed Bax, on the strength of his worldwide reputation, his Irish sympathies, and Irish influence on his music. In the event, neither of them was selected.[22]

But in an angry article entitled 'Academies and Professors' in 1937, Ó Gallchobhair had criticised the academies for turning out 'batches of amateur instrumentalists' rather than 'artists'. He also dealt with the issue of bringing traditional music into academe, not as an adjunct but so that it would redirect music education, and the approach to 'the great European tradition . . . would be governed by a set of values specifically Irish.'[23] Ó Gallchobhair turned on its head Esposito's analysis of Irish music by asking, in Yeatsian vein,

> what can the professor do with a perfect lyric like the 'Derry Air'; he can look at it, divide it into its component parts and so on, but technical analysis is useless before the complexity of its unity. All the technique of modern Europe will not achieve a thing like this lyric—its roots lie far underneath the superficiality of objective thought.[24]

The question is not entirely dissonant from Fleischmann's perception of a possible median course, but it is a million miles away from a resolution. Charles Acton would have both agreed and disagreed: in 1950 he wrote that 'traditional tunes as such are unsuitable themes for symphonies . . . They have too much character, unity and association to be moulded,'[25] which is presumably what Ó Gallchobhair meant. But Acton also wrote that Sibelius's music 'is so intensely Finnish . . . yet in whose music one could not find a theme which one could hold up as a Finnish folk-song.' The middle path, if it could be achieved, would therefore be found as indicated by Esposito in the interview quoted in chapter 5.

The perennial poverty of Irish composition is demonstrated by the following observations from the twenties to the sixties, and our adverting to them now is justified by Denis Donoghue's point that 'the future of Irish music depends on our composers.'[26] In 1924 H. L. Morrow wrote in the *Irish Statesman* that 'Ireland, we are forced to admit, has not produced a single symphony of any account; not even a piano concerto.'[27] Ten years later Frederick May, who had been one of the brightest students at the Academy in the twenties, wrote of cultural life in Ireland as stagnant, finding it ironic that a country such as Finland, with which, he stressed, Ireland had so many parallel points of interest, should have produced Sibelius, the archetypal 'national' composer.[28] He summed up the composer's dilemma succinctly, postulating a necessary connection between art and politics, which hardly existed in the Ireland of the time; instead there was a 'disastrous . . . cleavage' between art and life. It may indeed have been this impossibility of living a life in which the 'vital connection' required for a healthy musical environment was missing that caused May's short absence from Ireland and his long intellectual absence from the Academy, which, as far as his recollection indicates, was a favoured place.

After more than another decade (in 1947) May was to say that 'it is doubtful if any nation with such a wonderful storehouse of traditional music has made such a negligible contribution to art-music as we have.'[29] Three years later Charles Acton, in the article just quoted, referred to Ireland in 'the valley of contempt in which the musical world outside regards it' and urged composers 'who have in them the germ of creation' to harness 'the tools of modern music'; those who could not 'are in much danger of writing much competent music that will date as surely a Spohr's, however sincerely written.'

Another five years passed, and Denis Donoghue, a former music critic of the *Irish Times*, asserted that 'it is quite possible that Irish music may have no future existence.'[30] As an echo of informed opinions expressed by Annie Patterson over half a century previously, Donoghue's comments are profoundly depressing. 'The musical reputation of a country depends on her composers. Irish music will become internationally known and respected only if our composers can be trained to enter fully into contemporary musical activity.' Rejecting the notion put forward by Aloys Fleischmann that Ireland had twenty-nine composers ('No country in the world has twenty-nine composers worth listening to'), Donoghue reckoned that at most there were six established composers (he named only Boydell, May, and Deale) and three juniors: Victory, Potter, and Bodley. 'Internationally, contemporary Irish music does not exist . . . There is in Ireland today no composer whose works an intelligent European musician *must* know.' The reason was that Irish composers 'have fallen into the trap of folk-music,' which 'does not answer any of the problems of a composer.' The folk music that had been regarded as the life-blood of cultural revival was thus coming to be seen as, at the least, problematic and possibly a poisoned chalice.

Almost simultaneously, in *Music and Imagination*, Aaron Copland had described the conditions that would facilitate real achievement in a composer. 'The composer must be part of a nation that has a profile of its own . . . must have in his background some sense of musical culture, and, if possible, a basis in folk or popular art, and . . . a superstructure of organized musical activities . . . at the service of the composer.'[31] It can be argued that, given the neglect not only of composition but—and perhaps more importantly—of such a 'superstructure', it has only been in the last two decades of the twentieth century that those problems, identified in the last two of the nineteenth, have been solved by funding, direction, and an improvement in the built environment. Accompanying this amelioration of musical conditions has been a more accessible and generally agreed view of the multiplicity of 'Irishness'. When May wrote in 1935 of cultural life and cultural practitioners being equally fragile and vulnerable, by virtue of the fact that a nation did not exist, that there was 'a multiplication of private languages, but no vehicle of communication,'[32] such a sense of identity was not available to him.

All such commentators agreed on the need for a basic educational thrust in order to improve the situation, and this explains the concentration within the Academy on academic matters, including the development of diplomas (as discussed below by Pamela Flanagan). Other priorities, which we shall discuss in this chapter, were identified as the need for an adequate concert hall, the establishment of a full-time professional orchestra, and, a point raised vehemently by May, no doubt on the basis of his Academy experience, 'an infinity of chamber music.'

Faced with the near-impossibility of entertaining more than minimal composition activity, the Academy also found itself criticised for neglecting the Irish language. In 1934 the redoubtable Colm Ó Lochlainn attacked the Academy in a letter to the *Irish Press*, arguing, by means of a series of rhetorical questions, that the Academy had always ignored Irish and Irish music, that it had never introduced singing in Irish into its curriculum, and never 'recognised or patronised' Irish pipers or collectors such as Petrie or P. W. Joyce. 'If the Royal Irish Academy of Music is to enjoy a subsidy from the Irish Government, it must justify the second adjective of its title at least as thoroughly as it has hitherto justified the first.'[33]

The reader who has followed the argument this far will know that Ó Lochlainn was wrong on several points, but, despite the employment of Kathleen Roddy to teach singing in Irish, he was probably right to make the argument, if only to alert the Academy to the extent of concern and to remind it that its classical repertoire should not be pursued in isolation. It has been mentioned that Thomas Rowsome was employed by the Academy to teach at the Municipal School of Music. When the Academy was criticised by Dublin Corporation for its neglect of Irish music, Rowsome wrote a somewhat bitter note, which displays the fact that there are two sides to every dilemma of this kind.

> I should perhaps make you aware that there is at present no maker of the Irish pipes. Those whom we see self advertising of in the press have not been able to turn out even a single proper set of pipes, and for the rubbish they have produced they demand exorbitant prices. The instrument I refer to [for sale at ten pounds] was made by Egan the most celebrated maker of the pipes, but who is now dead for about 50 years . . . I have learned that the owner was about to communicate with the Museum Authorities who I have heard are anxious to obtain such specimens. It would be a crying shame that they should find a grave in a museum, but that seems to be the fate of everything Irish.[34]

A further point that was raised earlier reasserts itself here: that in order to teach traditional music one must also be able to assess the quality of both teacher and student by means of examination, and so in some measure to reduce a mode of expression that is essentially spontaneous and aleatoric to the dimensions of a system with which it is not in conformity.

In 1929 one commentator (who Turpin thinks may have been Dermod O'Brien) said:

> It is an unfortunate thing that the art of letters . . . has been fostered to a large extent at the expense of the sister arts of painting, sculpture,

music, architecture and consequently, not only are the young brought up in almost complete ignorance of these arts, but it is to be feared, their teachers and directors have had little or no opportunity for learning and appreciating the educational value of these arts before being first put in the position of so much responsibility.[35]

O'Brien is one of two figures (the other being Sidney Dagg) who represent the persistence of the old order and its transformation within the Academy. O'Brien (1865–1945), whose mother was a Spring Rice and whose grandfather was William Smith O'Brien, belonged to the 'Young Ireland' side of Anglo-Ireland. In 1909–11 his letters to his wife, Mabel (née Smyly), show how mixed his feelings were about Home Rule but how he nevertheless saw it as inevitable and even necessary. 'I doubt very much if we could live in this country under Home Rule because I don't see that as a class we can survive the years of revolution before we get a chance of being of use . . . If there is Home Rule, it is all the more essential that a leaven of our class should be left in the country.'[36] The concept to which he was determined to be 'of use' was not a faction or a faith but *Ireland*.

O'Brien was a landlord who became a farmer (and IAOS activist), a portraitist and landscape painter, and a musician. He was an unsuccessful candidate for the directorships of the School of Art and the National Gallery. His sense of Irishness, combined with his artistic interests, brought him into contact with Count Plunkett, and, he recorded, 'I . . . found that my ideas and his were practically the same about making the Museum into an essentially Irish one.'[37] We are once more obliged for these details to Lennox Robinson, who says of O'Brien that 'he was a hustler, a person who wanted to get things done . . . He wanted desperately to mould, and to get other people to help him to mould, an Ireland nearer to the heart's desire . . . an incorrigible dreamer of dreams.'[38]

An indication of the rite of passage that artists were experiencing in these decades was the dispute in 1942 over whether or not to hang Rouault's *The Passion of Christ*, in which O'Brien (who had trained at the Académie Julian in Paris) wholeheartedly supported Mainie Jellett, as he did in her attempt to create a 'national' Exhibition of Living Art.[39] From the turn of the century O'Brien had held musical 'at homes' in his house in Mountjoy Square, had befriended the Bests, Edith Boxwell, the Griffiths and Pursers, and had become involved in many music organisations, of which it seems inevitable that the Academy (once supported by both his grandfathers) should have been one. Already elected RHA in 1907 and PRHA since 1910, and president of the United Arts Club since 1919, he became a subscriber to the RIAM in 1920, was co-opted to the Board in 1923, and was elected vice-president in 1928.

Thomas Sidney Charles Dagg (1875–1964) was a barrister whose career began in the Congested Districts Board, with which he had travelled extensively throughout Ireland. Given the option in 1922 of transferring to another British assignment or remaining in Dublin, he chose to take a position in the Department of Finance, where he became a pillar of Ernest Blythe's administration. A talented cartoonist, writer of doggerel and punster, he was also passionately devoted to hockey, becoming an Irish international and selector and eventually president of the Irish Hockey Union. He left his estate to his alma mater, TCD, for the foundation of a scholarship in history.[40]

Each of these men in his own way endowed the Academy not only with time and wisdom but also with physical labour, O'Brien by organising the acquisition, design and installation of the Monteagle Library and the decoration of the Organ Room, Dagg by refashioning the old band room into the hall that today bears his name[41] and compiling the history of the Academy for its 'centenary' in 1956.

The twin facts of the second Dáil (1921–22) considering it necessary to appoint a Minister of Fine Arts (in the person of Count Plunkett) and of the short-lived ministry being abolished by the new government are indicative of the way inessential issues were decentralised. The only artistic (as distinct from cultural) issue that captured the popular as well as the political imagination was that of the Lane bequest, on which the Academy (at Dermod O'Brien's suggestion) joined with other bodies in petitioning for the return of Lane's pictures from London to Dublin.[42]

The strengths that had brought the country to freedom had been a concatenation of hotly debated energies in both culture and politics. Once freedom was achieved and stability established, a process of cooling off and consolidation took place as the new administration took stock of its resources. The Irish Free State was not the result of revolution. Nothing closed overnight. Even if there had been a national policy on a new form of music education, its implementation would have required years of trial and error. Ideologically speaking, the impetus towards an Irish School of Music espoused by the Feis would exhaust itself in speculation, because the 'revivalist dreams of an inner transformation' and the 'heroic impulse,' which John Hutchinson identifies as the dynamic of cultural nationalism, gave way to 'the task of constructing a stable order of citizens.'[43] The philosophy of Irish Ireland succeeded to a certain extent in effecting an *outer* transformation but failed to create any kinetic sense of a nation. Writers, musicians and painters continued to form communities of interest within a loosely conceived national framework.

There are suggestions that 1922 was as much a cultural watershed as 1800 had been. In 1958 Thomas Bodkin (former secretary of the Commissioners of Charitable Donations and Bequests and director of the National Gallery and later consultant to the Government on cultural policy) said that

> nobody in Ireland, with the exception of John Costello and very few others, is prepared to pay more than lip service to the cause of the Arts; a cultivated class in the full sense of the term has ceased to exist in our country, and the present methods of education are not likely to encourage the growth of one to serve us in the near future.[44]

But Bodkin himself had omitted music from the study commissioned from him in 1949 by Costello as Taoiseach,[45] perhaps because he was prejudiced by his personal interest in the visual arts, and perhaps because he subscribed to the belief in the innate musicality of the Irish. When, in 1953, the priorities of the Arts Council were under consideration as an outcome of Bodkin's report, music was thought to be more properly the concern of the Department of Education and Radio Éireann, with the main emphasis of the Arts Council on art and design.[46] It would not be until 1968 that a Minister for Education, Donogh O'Malley, would refer to 'my failure to provide adequately in our schools for music,'[47] but the personal tone of the admission was to prevent it from permeating either the Government or the department.

One problem facing the RIAM from the time when artisan education began in the eighteen-nineties up to the creation of the modern curriculum and the advent of its degree courses was the exact status of its activities. This had two aspects. One was the way the Academy was perceived by those who did not belong to the social classes that most frequented it (which we have seen in the events leading to the inauguration of the Municipal School of Music); the other was its relationship with funding bodies. In 1928 the Academy found itself addressing the Governor-General of the Irish Free State in terms slightly disingenuous but quite understandable for an institution uncertain of its standing with the new regime and anxious to improve its access to public funds (not least after its previous failure to secure support from the technical education authorities). 'The Academy is at once for all its pupils a school of culture in the noble art of Music and for many a Technical institute, qualifying them for the practical necessity of gaining their livelihood.'[48] It was a nice piece of legerdemain at a time when the institution was involved in a root-and-branch self-examination, which had its casualties as surely as the Viani affair, referred to above, and those involving Larchet, to which we shall shortly turn.

In 1924–25 a committee under Irwin had taken the opportunity presented by the retirement of Harvey as secretary (after thirty years' service) to look at all the functions of the Academy, including the local centre system, which had imposed on the structure administrative burdens that it was organically incapable of coping with, without a complete reorganisation. In addition, 'strained relations' between the lady superintendent (Ada Craig) and the new secretary (Gladys Tuite) made it imperative that one key member of staff be identified as the servant of the Board, and this was found to be the secretary (as implied, if not defined, in the Blue Scheme). At the same time, it was clear that it was Miss Tuite who was acting as 'irritant' to Miss Craig's 'counter-irritant' and that it was necessary that she be dismissed— a step never lightly taken by the Governors and certainly never taken in such a definitive fashion in the case of a senior administrative officer.

William Brayden proposed the dismissal of Gladys Tuite;[49] and, as in the case of Cmdt Connery, one of her successors, the proposal was carried on the strength (or weakness) of her accountancy practices. (Miss Tuite subsequently brought an action against the RIAM for wrongful dismissal, which was heard in 1929 and which she lost.) The case also lost to the

Academy the services of one of its most eminent (although least prominent) Governors, Raoul de Versan, who disapproved of the decision. The new secretary was Sealy Jeffares (previously known in the house as a humorist and a pillar of the SMU's Gilbert and Sullivan productions), and it was resolved that the position be part-time, the salary to be £180 a year—a retrograde step, which was reversed three years later, when Jeffares was confirmed in his post at £300 a year.[50] At this point the position of secretary was redefined, making it clear that the holder was also the Academy's accounts officer.[51]

We have seen (chapter 5) that Michele Esposito occupied a space in Irish musical life that was largely his own creation and of which the Academy's piano school was the centrepiece. Although in 1902 he had been seriously ill (the nature of the illness was not specified),[52] his apparently boundless energy belied the fact that since 1882 he had been the Academy's engine-room and that in 1927 he was over seventy years of age. He had received an honorary doctorate of music from the University of Dublin (TCD) in 1905 and became a *Commendatore* of the Order of the Crown of Italy in 1923. In 1924 he had been elected a vice-president of the RIAM in succession to Bishop Donnelly, thus rejoining the Board that he had left so tempestuously in 1911. It may have given him a wry satisfaction that Albert Foot, whose hostility had provoked that resignation, died in 1924 and that at the meeting at which his own vice-presidency was decided Raoul de Versan KC, a former pupil of Michael Quarry, was elected to fill Foot's vacancy.[53]

Esposito continued to take an enthusiastic interest in the career of Harty, and in 1924 he wrote to congratulate him on a recent appearance with the Hallé Orchestra.

> My dear Hay [Esposito's nickname for Harty]—Bravo! and with the Brahms 4! . . . The work is a hard nut for performers and public and you ought to be thankful to the band and take your rightful share in the success . . . I see in your letter a passing remark about 'health'—be a good boy and don't overwork yourself. I know the attraction of 'doing' everything that comes in one's way but try to get regular meals and sleep in bed and not in railways . . . My two pupils played your concerto very well the other day and I liked it more and more. Would you care to hear it when you come in January? . . . in which case I would tell the girls to keep it under their fingers . . . Love from Miche.[54]

The following year, 1925, Harty was knighted in London, and Esposito was instrumental in organising a reception at the Academy, at which Hilda Shea played his piano concerto, with Rhona Clark playing the orchestral part on the second piano.

Then, in 1926, the positions were reversed when a portrait of Esposito by Sarah Harrison was presented to him by Harty at a reception in Mill's Hall (a large coffee-house in Merrion Row) at which Sir Philip Hanson presided. Harty said that Esposito was especially valuable as 'an enemy of all that was false and unworthy.' 'He had never been a pupil of the Commendatore in the formal sense of the word, but in truth he had never been anything else.' Following the presentation, at which de Versan,

Leopold Dix, Viani and W. H. Vipond Barry also spoke, a recital of Esposito's music was given by Rhona Clark, Dina Copeman, Bessie Ruthven, Alice Bell (later Yoakley) and Harty (pianos), Clyde Twelvetrees (cello), and Eleanor Reddy (violin), with songs sung by Josephine Curran and P. J. Duffy. The list of subscribers is a catalogue of Irish musicians and a cross-section of Irish society.[55]

But Esposito was unable to take his own advice ('don't overwork yourself'). In 1926, in addition to his other commitments, he had examined the largest number of local centre candidates (1,067) at seventeen venues as well as at the Academy itself. On 8 February 1928 he suffered a heart attack while conducting an orchestral rehearsal. The Esposito era was over.

On 10 February a special meeting of the Governors was summoned to consider the situation, and by 7 March Esposito had recognised that he could no longer work. His official resignation was received on 23 April, and it was agreed that he would receive a yearly pension of £300 (£6,000 today). A fund was established for a further testimonial, to which all branches of musical life contributed. Robert O'Dwyer, A. P. Graves and Leopold Dix joined forces with Sister M. Berchmans of the Brigidine Convent, Abbeyleix, and many other of the convent schools, and the former organ scholar Marion Hilton wrote from Kirin (Jilin) in China, 'I have always thought of him as a real friend,' which probably best sums up the widespread feeling of loss and grief at his enforced retirement.[56]

The *Irish Times* published a summary of Esposito's career, headed 'A loss to Dublin'.

> He has been the head of the musical profession for so many years, and his energy and activity have been so continuous all the time, that one can hardly think of music in Dublin without him . . . To his pupils his reading of all music was so sound and so convincing that no other seemed to be worth considering . . . So notable was his success with the [Dublin Orchestral Society] that players leaving Dublin were always acceptable in orchestras such as the Hallé or the London Symphony Orchestra when it was known that they had served an apprenticeship under his baton . . . It is, however, as a teacher at the RIAM that [he] will be most missed. There patience and enthusiasm went hand in hand. He had a very high conception of the making of an artist. Any slipshod or hasty work was abhorrent to him. He has often said that it takes eight years of hard work to make a pianist.[57]

The paper's correspondent went on to quote a former pupil of Esposito who had written: 'He would sweep you completely out of yourself and fill you with his own inspiration, and actually make a musician out of you. That . . . was the great thing in his genius for teaching—he was always creating. He infected you with his great enthusiasm and he illuminated all music with his great understanding . . . His criticism was always forcible and humorous and often extremely abusive, but it never crushed you or made you despondent.'

Esposito's piano teaching was taken over temporarily by Frederick Dawson, and in October 1928 his position was awarded to the Belgian celebrity Jean du Chastain, in competition with Mme Grossi, Claud Biggs, Victor Love, and Eduard Beninger. Du Chastain gave an introductory recital on 8 March 1929, at which he played Beethoven's 32 Variations in C minor, pieces by Bach, Chopin, Debussy, and Liszt, and his own Mazurka in F sharp. It was not long, however, before he was giving his farewell recital, since on 9 October 1929 the Governors were told 'it is quite clear Mr. du Chastain does not wish to stay in Dublin even if he was given twice the salary. It is too far from his Trio. He does not get enough time for his practising and sees no future for a soloist in this country.' But Edmund Lupton recorded a conversation with du Chastain, who told him 'that, although he was leaving, he took a great interest in the Academy, & . . . volunteered that on the Continent the RIAM stood next to the RAM & RCM amongst musical institutions in England, Scotland, Ireland & Wales.'[58] He gave the farewell recital on 18 December 'as a compliment to the Academy,' at which it was said that 'unfortunately other countries offered greater attractions than they could offer in the City of Dublin.' Among the attendance were Ernest Blythe (Minister for Finance), Senator the Countess of Desart, Sarah Purser, Séamus Clandillon (director of the new radio service), and a very large number of diplomats.[59]

Jean du Chastain was succeeded by the Englishman Claud Biggs, who had been runner-up in the selection the previous year, at a salary of £400 (today, £8,000).[60] He came to Ireland with an impressive international reputation, especially for the interpretation of Bach and his contemporaries and of Schubert. He was to remain as senior professor, and a major influence in the Academy, for nearly twenty years.

In Florence, Esposito received the *Irish Times*, which told him of musical activities, and he kept up his friendships with Dublin during his short retirement. Writing on 13 November 1928 to Alice Bell, who had just been married, he joked: 'Dear Mrs Yoakley, I hope your husband has not begun to ill-treat you! but do you treat him well? . . . Life in Dublin must be very exciting now that I am out of it . . . I am now in a very lazy mood; I cannot make up my mind and body to do anything . . . Write often about everything in Dublin.'[61]

On 27 November 1929 the Governors received a letter from Vera Esposito Dockrell announcing her father's death on the nineteenth. Simultaneously Vera wrote to Harty: 'My dear Hay, Your Miche is no more . . . You have lost your best friend . . . And I hope you love him as well as he loved you or even half as much as he thinks you did . . . He had a wonderful little funeral, just a few very good friends and ourselves. There were English people, Germans, Italians, and one beautiful wreath sent by an Irishman resident here.'[62] As a relatively poor family, and with burial space at a premium in Florence, the Espositos had to settle for a *colombario*, a very narrow grave, in the cemetery of Trespiano, on which a stone was set with an inscription of three bars of Harty's music.[63]

The Governors elected Harty to succeed Esposito as a vice-president on 18 December 1929.

While Esposito's piano mantle fell eventually on Claud Biggs—who became a pillar of music-making in his own right—his position as the dominant personality in the Academy was assumed by John F. Larchet, who in 1912 had obtained the certificate of proficiency in harmony[64] and who had succeeded Kitson as senior professor of harmony in 1920. Esposito had never taught composition, so it is not strictly true to say that this aspect of his work accrued to Larchet, who had been teaching theory and composition since 1912 and was to take the lion's share in examination work, which had been Esposito's. Nevertheless, in every institution the sense of loss of one major figure is superseded by the emergence of another, and in the Academy's case it was Larchet who assumed and grew into the space relinquished by Esposito, becoming, in the year of the latter's death, the first FRIAM. As we shall see, he was also to become a controversial figure in the boardroom throughout the forties and early fifties.

Esposito and Larchet had in common one characteristic that fitted each for the role of supremo in the Academy: their apparently inexhaustible energy and capacity for continuous work, as well as, one suspects, the driving ambition that lay behind it. Energy was channelled into every form of activity, and their careers were remarkably similar in many respects. Both taught full-time in the Academy, as well as in several schools (Alexandra College, for example); both conducted and composed; both examined prodigiously throughout the country, Larchet not only for the RIAM but also as principal examiner for the Department of Education. Where Esposito was an organiser of concerts and recitals and an expert lecturer, Larchet held the professorship of music at UCD from 1921 until 1958—the only form of occupation that had eluded Esposito. Both attempted to become director of the institution, and—here the weaker aspect of their characters emerges—both displayed considerable pique when denied their ultimate goal. One difference might be mentioned: where Esposito, who had been supporting his family in Italy ever since his arrival in Dublin, retired into relative poverty,[65] Larchet became a considerably wealthy man.

Larchet demonstrated his fondness and admiration for Esposito in a radio broadcast in 1955, which we publish below as an *intermezzo*. As composers, each was involved with the literary renaissance—in Larchet's case, as the author of music for Synge's unfinished drama *Deirdre of the Sorrows* and Yeats's *Land of Heart's Desire* at the Abbey, where he became music director. Each was limited in his musical horizons by the inhibitions of trying to be an 'Irish' composer. Joseph Ryan has said of Larchet that he was 'to a great extent a prisoner of the age; the nationalist idiom he espoused was very much what was expected and what was fashionable, although it must be said that he was a willing disciple.'[66] Ryan has also pointed to Larchet's self-professed aim 'to encourage students to adapt the native musical idiom to modern harmonic developments and thus create a school of composers which would be truly evocative of the Irish spirit.' While the ambition was consonant with Esposito's view of where Irish composition should be going, the failure to found a 'school', or even to create an environment in which that evocation could become possible, is another disappointment in the saga of the musical renaissance. Perhaps Esposito's reference in 1924 to the cadre of Irish composers as 'Vincent O'Larchet' sums up what he himself thought about this side of Irish music.[67]

But Larchet's influence as a teacher was immense, and if Esposito was the creator of the piano school, and of much of the musical infrastructure of twentieth-century Ireland, Larchet can claim the credit for having taught almost every figure of significance in Irish composition up to his death in 1967. Much of his life would be spent trying to achieve a defined place for music in the educational system, based on fundamental principles. In addition he and his wife, Madeleine (née Moore), raised a family of three musically talented children, of whom two, Máire and Síle, became principals in the National Symphony Orchestra.[68]

Larchet had made attempts similar to Esposito's to encourage orchestral activity. He had been conducting concerts since at least 1910 with the Dublin Amateur Orchestral Society, but there had been, predictably, little continuity. In 1924, pinpointing the same type of gap that Esposito had set out to fill with the Dublin Orchestral Society, Larchet said: 'Except for occasional visits from some of the British orchestras, there has been no performance of any importance or educative value in Dublin for ten years. This means that most of the people have no knowledge of Strauss, Brahms, and the great volume of modern orchestral music.'[69] History was repeating itself. But Larchet went further, and onto less reliable ground. 'Little interest is taken in chamber music or choral music; a large percentage of music lovers in Dublin have never heard a string quartet [a fact that would be true of almost every city in the world, we might add]. Solo instrumental recitals, or classical song recitals, are few and far between, and are only attended by a small circle of enthusiasts or by those personally interested in the artist.'

While it may have been true that the impetus of the RDS and other recitals had diminished, the statement on its own would not be true of activity within the Academy, where, as we have shown, both the SMU and the general prize-winners' concerts and chamber music recitals were plentiful and of a high standard. But Larchet was correct in identifying the cause of the problem and in laying the blame at the door of the educational authorities.

> Our system of music education is not merely wrong, it is fundamentally unsound. From the primary and secondary schools all the way up through the circuitous paths and byways of individual teaching and private endeavour, the whole mental attitude is at variance with common sense . . . Music is generally pushed into the darkest corner of the curriculum.

At almost the same time (1927) Larchet contributed to the official handbook for Dublin Civic Week the view that 'aside from teaching we have been slowly feeling our way upwards within the last thirty years . . . Our main difficulty hitherto has been economic [which he blamed for the non-viability of Irish opera] . . . Even an artist must live . . . and if, through economic causes, he cannot obtain . . . bread and butter at home, he must seek it abroad.' It was not a scenario that encouraged civic pride: musically, Dublin had been reduced 'from a proud capital to a second-rate city.'[70]

In 1930 Dr Larchet informed the Board that 'he had been offered, and intended to accept, the position of Director of the Municipal School of Music.' At that point there was still a grey area, which had not been resolved by the Woodhouse affair and the emergence of the Leinster School, around the question of whether members of the RIAM staff could teach elsewhere. In particular, the status of the Municipal School of Music as a cognate institution may have added to the confusion, although in 1921 Larchet had already sought, and been refused, permission to teach in other schools.[71] In the event the Governors, on a vote, acknowledged (rather than acceded to) this application, although the fact that at the same meeting they received (and granted) a request from Viani to apply for the same position suggests that Larchet's new job was not as watertight as he may have thought.[72] He was to hold the post for only a year (other candidates had been Robert O'Dwyer, Harold White, and Petite O'Hara)[73] and was succeeded by Maud Davin (later Aiken).[74]

A month later a palpable, but obscure, row broke out both in the board-room and the Board of Studies, fuelled by what one suspects to have been bad feeling between Larchet and Weaving, possibly caused by Weaving's resentment at Larchet's larger share of the local centre examining work (and fees). The reason for the obscurity of the subject is that in the minutes of both the Board of Studies and the Board of Governors the statement by Weaving of his grievance against Larchet has been blacked out,[75] and only a fragment of a draft minute, referring to 'the impossibility of the present position,' survives.[76] Recognising the sensitivity of an issue such as this, we include it in our narrative in order to indicate both the volatile nature of personalities in a board-room environment and the important relationship between the Board of Governors, as the directors of the institution, and the professors as its academic council.

On 14 February 1930 the secretary wrote: 'At the meeting of the Board of Governors on last Wednesday I was directed to convene a special meeting of the Board of Studies to consider the matter of Mr. Weaving's protest which appears to have been adopted at a small meeting of the Board of Studies.' The meeting, convened on 18 February, agreed, by a vote of six to one, to adopt whatever motion Weaving had tabled. The single opposition came from Annie Lord, who believed that 'it is too personal and will lessen the confidence of the Board of Governors in the Board of Studies.' Weaving, however, did not believe that his protest was personal: 'he could have entered just as strong a protest against any member of the Board of Studies who acted as Dr. Larchet had done.'

One clue to the reason for the row is the opinion voiced by George Hewson that 'Dr. Larchet was mistaken when he said that he (Dr. Hewson) had not voted in favour of the degree of Fellow being conferred solely Honoris Causa.' Had Larchet breached some unwritten code of behaviour because he felt he had been slighted? Had words been exchanged, as they had between Foot and Esposito, or between Rooke and Woodhouse? Although it is well known that protracted disagreement was voiced between professors and Governors about whether the FRIAM should be purely honorary or might also be awarded by examination, as it was in the unique case of Larchet,[77] it does not help to clarify this particular incident. Rooke, however, as chairman of the professors, was 'authorised to deal further with the matter and make the position of the Board of Studies quite clear to the Board of Governors . . . as the Professors felt that the Board of Studies must have the complete support of the Governors if it is to function as their advisory Board in accordance with the terms of the Scheme.'

A further week passed, and the Governors received an offer of resignation from Larchet 'should [they] think that his action would be in the best interests of the Academy,' and he added that Edith Best was prepared to do the same. Naturally, and especially in the light of Esposito's resignation almost twenty years earlier, which would have been sharply in the minds of several present, such a development was unthinkable, as was the idea that the liaison between the two Boards might be ruptured.

It was at this point that the rumour voiced by Dorothy Stokes concerning Larchet's alleged antipathy to the SMU came to light. One can hardly credit Stokes with having deliberately manufactured such a rumour, any more than one can believe the rumour itself. But the entire incident, whatever its cause and whatever sides those involved may have taken, led to one concrete issue that has always dogged the Blue Scheme: whether teachers should be members of the Board of Governors. Sir John Irwin, the elder statesman of the Board, proposed that there should be no teachers on the Board other than the professors' representative Governor. In the event, the proposal was, sensibly, withdrawn, but Irwin insisted on making the point that he had not changed his mind—simply that 'his pressing the motion at this time might be misconstrued,' by which he probably meant 'misconstrued as an attempt to unseat Larchet as a Governor.'[78] That this was emphatically not the case is demonstrated by the fact that on 18 February 1931 Larchet was elected a vice-president (in succession to Lord Arthur Hill, who had died a month previously), a position he would occupy until his death in 1967.

Irwin's determination on the matter had in fact been manifested in 1925, when he had attempted to prevent a members' Governor from taking up her position, on the grounds that the Blue Scheme provided for *one* representative professors' Governor—his point being that, by implication, no other member of staff could act as a Governor. 'In my opinion it was never intended that such a thing would be possible as that 12 Professors subscribing £1 each annually could if they wished to do so gradually oust independent Members' Governors and constitute themselves a majority of the Governing body and I submit that the representatives of the Corporation and of the Coulson Bequest would in such an eventuality become powerless to exercise due control over the working of the Academy.'[79] It was a matter that would raise its head again in our own time.[80]

Clearly, the matter between Weaving and Larchet did not rest there, as it was not until July 1931 that Weaving proposed 'in the interests of the Academy . . . that my letter . . . be expunged from the minutes . . . its existence there having been referred to by Dr. Larchet as his reason for not attending our meetings.'[81] But this did not satisfy Larchet, and on receiving a letter from him three days later the Governors recorded their regret on learning of his decision, 'especially as they have done their utmost to meet him in the matter.' The Board of Studies was requested to reconsider the issue and agreed to remove all reference to the affair (which they did not). They recorded that 'the Board has no desire to unnecessarily keep on record anything calculated to cause friction and now that the cause of his non-attendance . . . has been removed . . . we will look forward to having him with us in the future.' There, it seems, the matter rested, and the Academy entered calmer waters, until the nineteen-forties, when personalities once again clashed.

One of the continuing sagas of Dublin musical life until 1981 was the lack of an adequate concert hall for symphonic music. The Academy, as the training-ground for orchestral players, was involved from the start in the perennial attempts to build one, and after its removal to Westland Row in 1870 it hoped to include one on its own site. The two main venues for orchestral concerts had been the Antient Concert Rooms and the hall of the Royal (later National) University, which had been built originally as a concert hall and eventually became the National Concert Hall. But for a variety of reasons—chiefly social and acoustic—neither of these was regarded as suitable. The Antient Concert Rooms was too small, and in the early days of the inexperienced and undersized Dublin Orchestral Society the Royal University was judged to be too large. It was also a matter of municipal pride that Dublin should have a venue comparable to Belfast's Ulster Hall, which the Round Room of the Mansion House only went part of the way towards fulfilling.

To go back no further than 1900, we find the *Musical Times* reporting that these needs were voiced at the AGM of the Feis Ceoil by T. W. Russell MP,[82] and we have seen Randal Woodhouse's appeal shortly thereafter for a municipal hall. What the term 'concert hall' might actually mean, however, was variable. When the Governors of the Academy contemplated (as they did at least once every decade from the eighteen-seventies to the nineteen-forties) the erection of a concert hall on the restricted Westland Row site, they clearly did not have in mind anything as spacious as the Theatre Royal in Hawkins Street, which had a capacity of almost four thousand. In 1908 Esposito said, 'What a great advantage it would be to those who are anxious to be present at concerts, with distinguished artists and a full orchestra, to have a building which would accommodate two or three thousand people,'[83] in which he was supported by Vincent O'Brien, Edward Martyn, and others. Halls approaching this capacity did exist in Dublin at the turn of the century—the Metropolitan Hall in Abbey Street being one—but the fact that they were dedicated to other uses prevented them from being principally a focus of music-making. Theatres such as the Gaiety, Olympia and Capitol were also used as concert venues, but, likewise, only when not required for their main function.

In 1910 Bishop Donnelly suggested that the Academy might become the nucleus of a scheme to provide a hall, and this remained an ambition—at times quite explicit, at others almost unvoiced—until the Academy's usual sense of reality forced it to acknowledge that such a project was beyond its resources as well as outside the scope of its core activities. At that time the building costs were generally reckoned to be between £30,000 and £40,000 (today, between £1.2 and £1.6 million); John Sweetman ironically suggested to readers of the *Daily Express* that the NUI, which had taken over the Royal University site, should be shamed into reconverting the hall to its original purpose rather than (as was mistakenly rumoured) demolishing it.[84]

Vincent O'Brien put the academic viewpoint very effectively when he said in 1912 that 'there are a lot of musical schools in Dublin and there is no culminating point in the form of a large hall in which to produce modern musical works with all the necessary detail,'[85] one such detail being an organ. The idea that a joint venture between interested parties, not unlike the moving force behind the original Academy itself, was the best way forward was not merely a matter of civic pride, since O'Brien pointed out that 'the money spent in the erection of numerous small halls by various organisations in Dublin during the last six years would have built one great hall, which would have been of general use to the city.'

When Hugh Lane initiated a similar controversy, by offering his picture collection on condition that Dublin provide a gallery to accommodate it, several saw this as an opportunity to create a multi-purpose house of the arts. 'J.D.A.J.', writing to the editor of the *Irish Times*, suggested that 'a fine hall or gallery where young people could dance and their olders listen to fine music, and admire beautiful pictures, is the ideal to be aimed at if Dublin wishes to lead in the emancipation of Ireland from its gloom.'[86] In 1916, after the destruction of the RHA premises, Lennox Robinson tells us that Dermod O'Brien 'dreamed of a great building that was to contain a concert-hall . . . a School of Painting . . . a home of all the arts.'[87] O'Brien himself was not yet involved with the RIAM, but in the same year Bishop Donnelly began to make enquiries about the possibility of obtaining a grant from the Carnegie Trust, established three years earlier.[88] Two years later another Governor, Frank Wynne, offered £100 for such a purpose, provided nine other people did likewise. At least one other, Sir Gabriel Stokes, matched his offer, but 'the Governors fear that having regard to the present conditions of the country it will not be possible to obtain such support as would enable them to claim his promised donation.'[89]

This did, however, prompt the Board into making a public statement to the effect that the Academy was prepared to build a hall on the gardens of numbers 36, 37 and 38 Westland Row (the adjoining two houses having been acquired in 1915). It was estimated that the cost would be between £5,000 and £6,000, of which £1,000 would be raised by subscriptions such as Wynne's and a further £1,000 from the Academy's building funds, which were held in trust, and that rental income from the hall would service a bank loan for the remainder. Here again the focus was naturally that of music education rather than concert-giving *per se*, and the extent of the costs envisaged suggests in turn a modest conception of what was to be built.

This scheme having failed to attract any further support, the Governors became still more modest and two years later 'decided that it was desirable that a Concert Hall be built on the Academy premises, not to exceed £3,000.'[90] Although the ambition to become involved in a larger scheme was never entirely abandoned, it is at this point that the Academy's sense of what could actually be achieved concentrated its mind on the bricks and mortar of the existing band room; but it was not to see any real movement until the forties. In the meantime, the scale of the projected building, or rebuilding, oscillated between £3,000 and £5,000.[91]

In 1942 the scheme became once more quite specific, with a projected hall measuring 75 feet by 42 feet and 23 feet high, with a gallery at one end, a seating capacity of five hundred, and a stage accommodating fifty performers, the cost to be £5,400, inclusive of electricity, ventilation, plumbing, and heating. Again this came to nothing, presumably because subscribers could not be found.[92]

There is an ironic touch to the circumstances in which the present-day Dagg Hall came into existence. Where in 1918 wartime conditions had inhibited the concept of a hall, in 1943–45 similar conditions had encouraged thoughts on the matter. T. S. C. Dagg, as an official of the Department of Finance, had been in 1937 a member of a departmental committee under H. P. Boland (himself an Academy subscriber) to consider the conversion of the Rotunda buildings into a cultural complex, at a cost that increased from an original figure of £175,000 (£3.5 million today) to twice that in the ten years during which the project was under review.[93] Dagg persuaded his fellow-Governors to support his proposal that 'as it appeared it would not be feasible to start work on the larger concert hall for some time . . . the smaller plan be proceeded with.'[94] Six months later he had personally begun to prepare the band room for extension and renovation, using timber from the recently installed air-raid shelter,[95] and within a year he had (as Academy lore has it) almost single-handedly finished the job,[96] with stage, orchestra pit and movable seating for two hundred giving it the potential for multi-purpose use. After years of prize-givings at which the intention of building a hall had been announced, the most recent being 1939—one could almost visualise the bricks and mortar going into place if the speaker could have been believed[97]—it was possible for the *Irish Times* to state that 'a concert hall to accommodate between 200 and 300 people is being built.'[98]

The hall was officially opened on 3 March 1945, with performances by Claud Biggs, Nancie Lord, and Michael O'Higgins, and three years later Dagg added to his benefaction by building and fitting out a 'restaurant annex', known today as the Foyer.[99]

The Academy continued to give its support to organisations such as the Music Association of Ireland (founded in 1948) in their campaign for a full-size concert hall, but at that stage its own needs for an orchestral venue and assembly hall had been met—at least until superseded by today's more pressing need for larger and improved facilities.

One reason for the vacillation in relation to the hall may well have been the condition of the Academy orchestra, whose fortunes seem to have been precarious throughout the period. Esposito's Dublin Orchestral Society had not encouraged Academy students to pursue orchestral activity, and successive conductors, right up to recent times—including Dorothy Stokes, Brian Boydell, Max Thöner, and Colman Pearce—had had to report inadequacy, indifference and failure in maintaining a collective sense of endeavour. If there was no effective orchestra in any given year, there was therefore no compulsion to give it a better home than it already enjoyed.

This was a general problem in Dublin, rather than one unique to the Academy, since we know that the Municipal School of Music experienced the same difficulties. It was not merely a question of shortage of wind and brass players, to which we have already adverted, but of ensuring that students attended orchestra practice. In 1974 Frank Heneghan, then principal of the VEC College (as it had become), reported that, despite regulations insisting on attendance at orchestra, students were reluctant to do so.[100] The Academy's regulations, which also demanded attendance by all competent players, had been formally in force since 1927 and were one of Esposito's last acts in the Academy, resulting from the suspension of the orchestra since 1923.[101] It had been thought in 1926 that compulsion was not the solution,[102] but Esposito was emphatic on the point, and it was probably this regulation that ultimately kept the nucleus of a band together.

The foundation of the Philharmonic Orchestra in 1927 (the same year that saw a short-lived attempt by Esposito to revive the Dublin Orchestral Society) indicated exactly the same problem with wind and brass as we have previously recognised; and it is also instructive to note that the same core of students, most of them about to make a career in orchestral playing, constituted the string sections. Its leader was Joshua Watson, Simonetti's successor as violin professor at the RIAM. One is tempted to attribute the reluctance of more string players to take part in the orchestra to the greater attraction of the burgeoning chamber music activity within the Academy, which we have already described; but a general shortage of string players has always been a root cause of orchestral problems in Dublin. Despite the existence of several amateur orchestras in recent decades (the Dublin Orchestral Players, the Dublin Baroque Ensemble and the Dublin Symphony Orchestra, for example) the proportion of Irish string players in the RTESO remained at approximately half until its repositioning as the NSO in 1990, with a consequent strengthening of numbers of Irish players; and even the reconstituted Irish Chamber Orchestra, a band of fifteen strings and the country's only professional chamber ensemble, has a predominance of non-Irish members.[103]

We have no consistent record of orchestral activity in the Academy, with the exception of the 'orchestral' items played at the SMU concerts, whose infrequency points to the problem being endemic, one that arose from both a natural shortage and a disinclination to take part. In 1946 we find the then conductor of the Academy orchestra, Dorothy Stokes, 'stating that she thinks it will be quite impossible to continue . . . owing to the lack of string players,' as a consequence of which Thomas Weaving 'was authorised to open negotiations with the Musical Art Society with a view to forming the nucleus of an Academy orchestra.'[104] The Musical Art Society was a new name for the Harding Orchestra, led and organised by Constance Harding (whose music found its way after her death to the Academy library), and was in turn to become the Dublin Orchestral Players. The attempt cannot have met with much success, as the following year Brian Boydell, who had taken over as conductor from Miss Stokes, had the same complaint,[105] and on this occasion it was considered advisable to identify a top string player such as Max Rostal (then a professor at the Guildhall) who might attend the Academy regularly, perhaps once a fortnight, to encourage string ensemble.

Four years later, in 1951, when Boydell resigned as conductor, Jaroslav Vaneček was encountering the same difficulties,[106] and at this point a short-lived development of extreme significance took place. The Minister for Posts and Telegraphs, Erskine Childers, requested an informal meeting to discuss the possibility of establishing a training orchestra to supply the RÉSO and RÉLO and to satisfy Radio Éireann's other broadcasting requirements. As part of the enlargement of the basic symphony orchestra in Radio Éireann in 1947–48 the secretary of the Department of Posts and Telegraphs, León Ó Broin, had encouraged the employment of newly recruited orchestral personnel as teachers in the Academy, and he, together with a Governor of the Academy, Edgar Deale, was responsible for this new initiative.

The training orchestra, which was to be directed by Vaneček (as string supervisor) and conducted by Eimear Ó Broin (son of León), was formed in 1953 and met at RÉ's Portobello studios (then the home of the RÉLO and later the RTÉ Singers) until its discontinuation in 1958. Many of the most prominent string players of the next generation, including Audrey Park and Mary Gallagher, were members of the orchestra. It was limited to strings, although originally all sections had been envisaged, along the lines of the BBC Academy; and a connection with the Army School of Music had been mooted. It was a small part of Vaneček's vision of a conservatoire that he had proposed after leaving the Academy and taking up a post at the College of Music.[107] It would be almost forty years before the notion of a national training orchestra would be seriously canvassed again.

The intimate connection between broadcasting, orchestral development and music education revolved around the figures of León Ó Broin, Patrick Little, Minister for Posts and Telegraphs, and one of his successors, Erskine Childers. While education was naturally the remit of another department, the fact that the attraction of foreign artists to the Radio Éireann orchestras depended on the availability of teaching to supplement the weekly wage of £5 (today £60) meant that Ó Broin could become involved in matters not immediately concerned with broadcasting. However, the department from which he had been promoted, Finance, was reluctant to countenance what it called 'subsidising places of amusement,' and this held back not only plans for the projected concert hall on the Rotunda site but also the creation of a national symphony orchestra, first considered by de Valera as early as 1936 and involving the participation of Sir Hamilton Harty. 'Is it any part of the State's duty', the Department of Finance asked, 'to resuscitate a Victorian form of educational recreation?'[108]

The Academy had enjoyed good relations with Radio Éireann since its inception, no doubt because of the involvement of Vincent O'Brien as the station's musical director, whose responsibilities were immense, given the policy of excluding almost all news and current affairs from the schedule.[109] A former pupil, Rosalind Dowse, was a member of its original quartet, which grew, acorn-like, into the orchestra, while Kathleen Roddy became station announcer. Within three months of the first broadcast of 2RN (its original name, from its call-sign) O'Brien had secured two broadcasts by Academy students. He had originally requested two one-hour programmes, the first of Bach, the second of Beethoven, which suggests that, however musical he might be and however devoted to the Academy, O'Brien was unaware of the tolerance of early radio listeners. He was persuaded by an anxious Board of Studies to modify his plans, but the Academy's support for the proposal was wholehearted, Sir John Irwin putting it very well when he said, 'I consider it the duty of a State-aided institution such as this to assist the Government Broadcasting Station . . . It is a favourable opportunity of appealing to a much larger audience than is in evidence at concerts given in Westland Row and giving the Irish public generally proof of the high standard of the teaching.'[110]

On Monday 15 March 1926, Rhona Clark became the second Irish student to perform on Irish radio (Dina Copeman had played on the opening night: see note 109), playing the *andante* and finale from the Appassionata Sonata, followed by Harold Hope Johnston singing Brahms's 'We Wandered' and Mendelssohn's 'On Wings of Song'. Alice and Sheila Brough concluded the programme with the *largo* and *allegro* from Bach's double concerto, with Rhona Clark playing the orchestral part on the piano.

At the end of that week (Friday 19 March) Mrs J. McDonagh (violin) and Mary Haimer (piano) played two movements from Beethoven's Sonata in C minor, Miss Curran sang Schumann's 'The Walnut Tree' and Debussy's 'Starry Summer Night', and Mary Haimer played Liszt's 'Waldesrauschen' and, again with Mrs McDonagh, the finale from the Beethoven sonata. The performers in each concert were paid a joint fee of five guineas. Later, as we have noted, concerts by the Students' Musical Union in the Aberdeen Hall were broadcast live by Radio Éireann, and later still the costs of drama productions directed by Ursula White would be met from broadcasting fees.

Parallel with these developments was the already mentioned opera class, which in the forties and fifties was increasingly in the hands of Michael O'Higgins, who, like Renée Flynn, combined an international teaching career with a prodigious output of pupils, including Dermot Troy and Austin Gaffney. (Flynn, who had won the Denis O'Sullivan Medal in the Feis Ceoil in 1920, went on to become a Wagnerian soloist at Covent Garden under Beecham, gave the first performance in London of Vaughan Williams's *Dona Nobis Pacem*, and taught at the RIAM in two separate periods, 1939–44 and 1951–52.) O'Higgins, to stimulate the unofficial side of opera study, collected a group known as the 'Thirteens' (from the number of his teaching room). As Carol Acton (née Little) records, 'Michael was too busy teaching to play the piano himself, so he would march up the passage into the Hall, find me basking in front of the fire (practising the violin in the unheated attics was a cold business) and he would commandeer me to play the orchestral score of *The Magic Flute* (or other Mozart operas) on the piano. I always agreed because it was fun and an extremely good way of learning the operas from the inside, without either having to sing or pay to hear them.' In addition to Troy and Gaffney, members of the 'Thirteens' included the sisters Eithne and Mabel McGrath and Martin Dempsey.

A further choral development during this period was the introduction of plainchant, which was taught by Hubert Rooney, a pupil of Jean de Reske and one of Dublin's foremost (private) singing teachers, who taught (among many others) Veronica Dunne and composed an opera for children, *Slumberland*. In Rooney's words, 'this subject furnishes valuable lessons for composer, vocalist and instrumentalist and in the days of the great classic masters, formed part of every musician's equipment.'[111] At first, from 1934, Rooney rented a room in the Academy as a business proposition, but in 1939, on the proposal of Mrs Starkie, his teaching was integrated into the Academy curriculum.

We return now to the events of the mid-forties to mid-fifties, to which, once again, John F. Larchet was central. In October 1945 the Governors referred to Larchet the question of 'a new Scheme for the government, administration and curriculum' of the Academy.[112] He was to take cognisance of the systems obtaining in similar institutions before making his recommendations, and this may account for the fact that it was over a year before any further discussion took place. We cannot be sure what exactly Larchet proposed, since no copy of the proposed new scheme exists in the RIAM archives or in those of the Commissioners of Charitable Donations and Bequests, to whom it was in course of time submitted. As far as we understand the situation, Larchet's own papers are no longer in existence; but from a minute of the Board of Governors of 20 November 1946, and from surviving correspondence between the CCDB and the Academy's solicitors, Miley and Miley, we can deduce the main elements in the new scheme. 'Dr. Larchet stated that the RIAM was the only Academy of its kind and standing without a Director. A Director must be a person of musical knowledge and teaching . . . There was not enough work in the Academy for a full-time Director.' The minutes go on to record: 'After considerable discussion Mr. O'Reilly proposed and Dr. MacNevin seconded "That the principle of a Director be approved".' This was agreed and referred to the Finance Committee. It would be over a year before the 'new scheme' was in any way completed and ready to be submitted for the Commissioners' approval, as it appears from the minutes that the separate elements of the new Scheme were introduced on an almost monthly basis.

The episode has all the signs of a repetition of the attempt to appoint Esposito as director in 1911. There is an interesting parallel between the two proposals in the role of the professors in the event of a director being appointed. A special Governors' meeting of 23 April 1947 considered a clause in the new scheme that proposed replacing the Board of Studies with 'an Advisory Board of Professors appointed annually by the Governors and/or the Director.' (It was not the first time that such a move had been contemplated: in December 1938 Larchet, Weaving and Viani had been asked to examine the workings of the Board of Studies and make recommendations for its future—apparently without result.)[113] A month later another special meeting approved (by eight votes to five) a clause that stated that 'no professor, teacher, member of the clerical staff or any other person in receipt of financial remuneration . . . shall be eligible to be or act as a Governor'[114]—a restriction that was later amended so as not to exclude vice-presidents. Larchet, if he had been successful in his scheme, would therefore have abolished the Board of Studies and eliminated all musicians and all other employees of the Academy from the Board of Governors, save himself.

A further consideration was whether the word 'Royal' should be deleted from the title of the institution. This deletion had earlier been proposed in 1940 and been defeated by the casting vote of Dermod O'Brien as chairman.[115] A decision to delete it was in fact taken in May 1947, by a vote of six to five, but in February 1948 Mrs Starkie was successful in having it rescinded. One can readily appreciate the validity of the intention, not least because it has been suggested that one obstacle to the position of president of the Academy being occupied by the President of Ireland has been the continued presence of the word 'Royal'.[116] Conversely, Academy lore has it that it was a sense of outrage among the convents, which threatened to transfer their students to the Associated Board if they could no longer deal with the *Royal* Irish Academy of Music, that secured the retention of the title.

Under Larchet's proposed new scheme, the President of Ireland was to be the *ex officio* president of the Academy, and the Government and county councils were to have the power to nominate representative Governors, which 'should contribute very materially to the welfare of the Academy.'[117] On the former point, the Commissioners of Charitable Donations and Bequests were told that 'the consent of His Excellency the President cannot be officially asked for until the proposed new Scheme for the Academy has been approved of by the Commissioners. Mr. McCullough, a Vice President of the Academy, has had conversation on the matter with His Excellency, who was considerably interested and requested that a copy of the Original Scheme and a copy of the proposed new scheme should be sent to him for his consideration.'

In reply to queries from the CCDB, the Board made the following points:

> The Governors desire to abolish the existing Board of Studies, and to appoint a Director, because the old system has proved unsatisfactory. The Board of Studies, in strictness, was only an advisory body, but

circumstances often arose in which it claimed for itself, or was forced by events, to deal with matters in which it had no authority. This often led to confusion and delay, and interfered with the smoothness and efficiency necessary.

The appointment of a Governor representing the Professors will be unnecessary under the new Scheme. From now onwards the Professors and the entire teaching staff will be represented by the Director and there is no occasion for dual representation.

The Governors propose to appoint a Director, because hitherto they had no responsible officer who could act for them in the administration of the Academy. The present system is unsatisfactory, the direction of the Governors being shared out, very loosely and vaguely, between at least four departments. The appointment of a Director is only following the precedent offered by every institution of its kind, and always works well. The best person to deal with musicians, and to interpret their problems and difficulties to the Governors, is himself a musician.

Furthermore, with the abolishing of the system of 'Senior' professor there is no 'head' for each class. The Director with expert advice when required from the Advisory Board, will, in future, act in this capacity. Thus, control and responsibility will be centred in one person.[118]

The proposed amended scheme went before the commissioners on 12 October 1948, with an explanatory memorandum (written presumably by their secretary) in which the other main points of change were identified.

The new amending Scheme abolishes all reference to Royal patronage and to the office of High Sheriff. An Advisory Board of Professors shall be appointed annually by the Governors. The Board, however, shall have no executive powers, and its object appears to be merely to confer with the Director on technical matters. Section 45 proposes to enable the Governors to make such leases of all or any of the property of the Academy with or without fine as after obtaining expert advice they shall deem expedient. This Section is entirely contrary to the provisions of Clause 44 of the Original Scheme under which the Governors are restricted to the making of occupying leases and letting of land for any term of years not exceeding 44 years, and leases of houses for a term not exceeding 99 years, and building leases for any term of years provided that such leases shall take effect within three years after the making thereof and shall be made on the highest rent and without fine.

The other amendments put forward to the Original Scheme are consequential to the new offices created by the proposed amending Scheme.

It can only be assumed that, despite the comparative narrowness of the vote on the exclusion clause, Larchet had the support of the Governors for the general thrust of his revolutionary proposals. Yet the attendance figures for Board meetings at this time indicate that the most regular attenders included Maud Aiken, Matt Costelloe, T. S. C. Dagg, Edgar Deale, Denis

McCullough, Mrs Starkie, T. H. Weaving, and Adelio Viani. Certainly the last two would have had little interest in voting themselves out of power, while Maud Aiken (aided by Costelloe) was an opponent of Larchet, in the sense that she regarded his increasing power within the Academy as ushering in a 'reign of terror'.[119]

There appears to have been at least some opposition to Larchet's intentions. An unattributed motion of 23 October 1946 proposed that 'the revolutionary proposals embodied in the Scheme being dependable [*sic*] on fugacious finance, which may be abortive for the fulfilment of material ends, the Scheme is abandoned.' It was defeated by ten votes to seven, and in 1948 the Governors proceeded to refer the new scheme to the CCDB, who asked 'that the views of the Board of Studies be ascertained regarding the abolition of the Professors' Governor and the replacement of the Board of Studies by the Director.'

A deputation consisting of Larchet, Mrs Starkie, Denis McCullough, Edgar Deale and T. H. Weaving (suggesting that these were all in agreement with Larchet's proposals, even Weaving, as chairman of the Board of Studies and a long-term combatant of Larchet) met the commissioners to discuss this point. They were supported by a letter from the Academy's solicitors stating that 'the members of the Board of Studies are the paid employees of the Governors and are concerned with the educational side only of the Academy. The complete control and management of the Academy is in the hands of the Governors and it has not been the practice to consult the Board of Studies in matters of administration.'[120] The letter suggested that the commissioners' need to consult the professors should extend only to matters concerning the curriculum.

The CCDB were adamant that the Board of Studies should express a view on the scheme as a whole, and they also referred the scheme for counsel's opinion, in particular whether they had power to alter clauses 26, 27 and 28 of the original scheme in the manner proposed. Counsel advised that they had not, and on foot of this advice the CCDB clearly felt that the proposed scheme was too far-reaching, since the annual report for 1949 records bluntly that it had not been approved, and no more was heard of the matter.

Of Larchet, however, the Academy was to hear more. A further series of incidents was to take place in 1953 that reflects badly on all concerned. As it became a matter of public record, we consider it legitimate to refer to it here, not least because it also reflects a curious and slipshod aspect of the then Academy administration.

Given the problems that we have seen arising with Joseph Robinson, Sir Robert Stewart, and Michele Esposito, one might be forgiven for thinking that such problems arise in direct proportion to the stature and importance to the institution of the personalities involved. There appears to have been a depth of unease surrounding Larchet, which is matched by the outstanding talents he undoubtedly devoted to the Academy. In particular, whatever occasioned the ill-feeling between himself and Weaving may possibly be explained as nothing more than serious rivalry in the area of local centre examining, in which Larchet held the lion's share, with Weaving coming a close second. There does seem to have been some resentment among other examiners that the work, which was extremely lucrative, was not shared out more equitably. For example, in 1939 it was decided to add Rhona Marshall and Dina Copeman to the examining panel, but only as far as examinations in the Academy itself were concerned, thus depriving them of the valuable expenses available to those—notably Larchet and Weaving—who travelled throughout the country. The following year, Larchet proposed that he and Weaving be appointed 'advisory examiners', with a minimum stipend of £200 a year in addition to their other income, to oversee the allocation of examination work,[121] a proposal that again was deeply divisive at the Board, being carried by a majority of five to four.[122]

Whatever the reason, Maud Aiken and Matt Costelloe in particular were conducting a campaign against Larchet, and at the end of 1953, when the secretary, Cmdt Matthew Connery (who had been in office since the death of Sealy Jeffares in 1949), resigned after the discovery of some irregularities in the finances, the veiled suggestion was made that Larchet had, at the least, condoned Connery's mismanagement of the Academy's affairs.

The outcome of this incident was that Costelloe, who was a keen advocate of what would today be called fiscal rectitude and had already quarrelled with his fellow-Governors over what he regarded as irresponsible spending, was appointed a 'Visiting Governor'. Visiting Governors, responsible for inspecting the Academy, receiving complaints and making recommendations to the Board, had been a feature of the Academy, on and off, for many years.[123] Six months after Connery's disappearance, Costelloe tabled a motion that read:

> Having regard to Dr. Larchet's recent unwarranted assumption of authority and his gross misbehaviour towards two of our senior administrative officers, he be asked to resign his position on the Board of Governors.[124]

The 'misbehaviour' complained of was suffered by the then secretary, Terry Blackledge, and the then supervisor of the local centres and eventual lady superintendent, Margaret Furlong.

Larchet had been very unwell with a gall-bladder problem, which in fact would require surgery within the fortnight, and, against his doctor's advice, had undertaken examining work in Cork, where he was taken ill on 26 May. In view of this the Academy arranged to send a deputy (Seán Lynch) to take over his work in Cork and to find another examiner to go to Limerick, where Larchet was next scheduled. Two days later, Larchet was back in Dublin, berating Miss Furlong for having given away his work in Limerick. He 'repeatedly stated that I had done him a grave injustice and that I had deprived him of £35 and had given it to Mr. Lynch . . . He then handed me some results sheets . . . and said "That finishes me now with Local Centres" . . . He terminated the interview by saying that there was something ugly behind all this.'[125]

There is no suggestion in Miss Furlong's report of the time of any unpleasantness but rather of Larchet's intemperate nature due to extreme annoyance. Miss Blackledge, on the other hand, stated that she was subjected to 'a tirade of what I can only call abuse,' which she found offensive, although she was prepared to believe that it had been caused by his illhealth.

The two members of the staff reported this incident to Costelloe, who three days later attempted to conduct an interview with Larchet, Furlong, Blackledge, and a clerical assistant to take notes. At this meeting, which took place in the library (today the board-room), Costelloe locked the door, to prevent eavesdropping. Larchet, however, refused to discuss the matter and, in Costelloe's words, 'gathered up his hat, coat and umbrella and protesting angrily hastened to the door . . . I had apparently automatically put the key in my pocket.' The rest of the details are too unpleasant to repeat, but after Larchet's repeated refusal to speak on the matter and after Costelloe had opened the door, having exercised what he mistakenly believed to be his power as a Visiting Governor to suspend Larchet from duty, the meeting, which had lasted between five and seven minutes, terminated.

A special meeting, chaired by the Lord Mayor, Bernard Butler, was called to discuss this highly unpleasant situation, not least because it had been reported in the press, with the additional information that Larchet intended to sue Costelloe for unlawful imprisonment and assault. This meeting accepted the reports of Margaret Furlong and Terry Blackledge (Larchet, somewhat predictably, 'protested that he was not in agreement with this action') and clarified the fact that Costelloe, although acting in good faith, had been misinformed by the Academy's solicitors that he had the power to suspend a member of the staff.[126]

Larchet proceeded with a legal action against Costelloe, which was not settled until March the following year, and in this period the matter was considered to be *sub judice*, with the effect that the matter of Larchet's alleged misbehaviour to the staff members could not be dealt with. On 30 March 1955, however, he was required in writing to apologise for his behaviour, and, although he remained recalcitrant, he realised that the time had come for the only end to the affair that the Board would find acceptable. After delaying almost two months, he wrote to Maud Aiken:

> I entirely agree with your sentiments that this 'unfortunate episode' should conclude harmoniously . . . I have however a most clear recollection of the entire episode but cannot remember any remark of mine which deserves an apology . . . I consider this decision of the Governors . . . to be an ill-considered judgement and one that, in the circumstances, is most offensive to me as a member of the teaching staff and unworthy of the Governors. For the last forty-two years I have given loyal and devoted service . . . In the face of this conduct of the Governors I have no wish to be further associated with the teaching staff and thereby subject myself to further possible similar ingratitude and I wish to tender my resignation . . . and would be very glad to be relieved of my duties at the earliest possible moment. I am not resigning my position as Vice-President however, as I wish to do whatever I can to further the interests of music in that position.[127]

The Board resolved by seven votes to six to ask Larchet to reconsider his decision; but the Larchet era had come to an end.

From 1880 to 1952 the government grant to the Academy remained static, at £300 a year, of which half was still conditional on the level of subscriptions reaching £100. In 1880 the grant was equivalent to over £10,000 in today's values; in 1952 it was equivalent to £4,500 today, a meaningless amount. In that year, in what must have seemed at the time a dramatic step, the grant was doubled to £600 (£9,000 today), of which £150 remained contingent on the members' subscriptions. The Academy was told that 'the Department of Education was being encouraged by the Department of Finance to take a more active interest in the future development of the Academy's activities' and that 'Mr. Ó Broin particularly emphasised the desirability of the Academy strengthening its teaching staff by obtaining the best possible Professors,' especially wind teachers.[128] It was made clear that 'the additional funds were being provided on the understanding that the Minister will have the full co-operation of the Governors in any arrangements he may make for the better musical education of the people.'[129]

The Victorian tone of this information is consonant with the thinking behind the increased grant. But León Ó Broin (1902–1990), as secretary of the Department of Posts and Telegraphs, with responsibility for RTÉ, was one of the most powerful figures in the civil service at the time and had been a major influence on the creation of the RÉSO in 1947–48. He was now involved in discussions on the formation of a national conservatoire, which might be effected by a merger between the Academy and the College of Music. Ironically, de Valera wanted to transfer Ó Broin to the Department of Education in the thirties, but he remained at Posts and Telegraphs, because his value as a supporter of music developments was highly valued. Ó Broin found the Department of Education (as well as the music institutions themselves) unsympathetic to the notion of a merger, which embodied a hint of 'Europeanisation' that would have been acceptable to pioneers like Hyde (and even to de Valera, who was responsible for bringing the mathematician Erwin Schroedinger to Dublin) but was anathema to the prevailing insularity.[130]

While the conservatoire remained a dormant dream, it did prove possible in the mid-forties to institute an international summer school of music, with participation by several of the major figures working at that time with the RÉSO, including Jean Martinon and Hans Schmidt-Isserstedt, and therefore underpinned by Radio Éireann and the Department of Posts and Telegraphs. It was intended that the impetus provided by such an influx of Continental musicians could be harnessed to the notion of founding a conservatoire. In fact in 1952 a memorandum on the subject was prepared by Vaneček and Engel but was set aside because of lack of funding.[131]

The International Summer School came to an end in 1956 with a change in Government and an economic cutback, and, after Larchet had temporarily introduced a summer school to UCD, it was partly to supply the lack of this valuable function that the Academy set up a similar venture in the early sixties, featuring lectures and recitals by Academy staff—in particular

A. J. Potter—and with financial support from the Department of External Affairs in recognition of its capacity to attract overseas students.

Since it was a period of stringency, it is not difficult to see that rationalisation of resources was uppermost in the minds of those administering, and indeed creating, what must have seemed to the needy to be luxurious commodities. There was in fact no resentment of the Academy among political figures. Alfie Byrne, for example, populist and popular Lord Mayor of Dublin (1930–39 and 1954–55), was one of the last ex officio chairmen of the Board to show any sustained enthusiasm for, or participation in, the Academy (another was his namesake, Mrs Catherine Byrne). It was more in a sense of national recovery that such pragmatism was developed. The fact that since the twenties the Municipal School of Music (which by then had become the College of Music) had grown into an institution complementary to the Academy meant that some duplication of resources took place. The lacuna caused by the absence of a conservatoire for the higher training of gifted players was starting to become obvious.

As Eimear Ó Broin puts it, 'the project of the Conservatoire was inseparable from the wider concept of promoting and developing music through public service broadcasting with the potential for creating wider sociocultural effects in society. The primary objective of the Conservatoire was to provide facilities for the advanced training of a new generation of Irish musicians to staff the orchestral expansion which was to come about in 1948 with the establishment of the RÉSO and RÉLO.'[132]

The existence in Dublin, for the first time, of a cadre of wind players who were not recruited from the army bands but who had immigrated in the wake of the Second World War, at the behest of Michael Bowles and Fachtna Ó hAnracháin, to become principals in the new RÉSO meant therefore that teaching potential was available of a higher order than had been enjoyed in recent decades. The appointment in 1952 of André Prieur (principal flute with the RÉSO) and in 1958 of Hans Kohlmann[133] at the rate of 15s per hour,[134] which was made possible by an Arts Council grant of £400 for wind scholarships, was followed in 1954 by that of Gilbert Berg (the RÉSO's bassoonist) as oboe, and subsequently saxophone, teacher[135] and in 1955 that of Victor Malirsh (horn) and Michele Incenzo (clarinet).[136] Other RÉSO players who became available in the same way were the cellists Maurice Meulien (1952–53) and Erich Eisenbrand (1955–58), and Heinz Jablonski (double bass, 1956–61), while the extra finance available to the Governors enabled them to appoint other major figures in the strings departments, the violinists François d'Albert (1952–55), Jaroslav and Kveta Vaneček (1949–55), Sydney Griller (1963–72), and Max Thöner (1955–63).

One of the internal difficulties of the Academy board-room at this time was the fact that the personal animosity between Maud Aiken and Larchet did not stop with his resignation. It did have one beneficial effect: in 1948 Larchet had succeeded in persuading the Board to divide the classes, and indeed the Academy itself, into a Senior (or Higher) School, staffed by the professors, and a Junior School, staffed by the teachers. This had become possible through the originally quite sensible practice of students taking alternate lessons, one week from a junior teacher and the next from the senior professor. Over the years, however, it had created too strong a distinction between them and inhibited promotion prospects for younger and newer staff. It is likely that a distinction along administrative lines, rather than serendipitous ones, would ameliorate this situation, but this did not happen, not least because, in the Junior School, talented teachers were limited to teaching beginners, who then advanced to the Senior School and could not retain their teacher. The situation was reversed in 1956, with all teachers being required once more to teach all grades.

Maud Aiken was determined to eradicate any lasting influence Larchet might have on the institution, and this unfortunately meant that she decided that Jaroslav Vaneček, a Larchet recruit, should be forced out. Despite serious opposition, she had her way, thus creating a rift in Dublin musical opinion that lasts to this day. Vaneček was a gifted teacher, to whose credit the string quality (and unanimity) of the ICO and its successor the NICO, and of course of the broadcasting orchestras, is due. To cause the departure of such a figure was also to play into the hands of Michael MacNamara, newly appointed principal of the College of Music.[137]

After Vaneček's departure from the Academy, Max Thöner, a member of the RÉSO, was recruited in 1955, at first at £1 an hour, increased in 1956 to an annual salary of £1,000,[138] and he in turn took on responsibility for a string class, although his broadcasting commitments gave him less time than might have been desired. In fact Thöner's widespread activities included leading the Dublin String Quartet and examining for the local centres. He both led and conducted the Academy orchestra and, on occasions, was soloist also. The dangers inherent in relying on one individual, however talented and multi-skilled, became apparent in 1962 when an Orchestra and Chamber Music Committee reported that the orchestra was 'not functioning satisfactorily due to Mr. Thöner's method of conducting rehearsals.' The senior students had objected to the juniors being coached while they waited, and as a compromise it was suggested that a chamber orchestra be formed for the seniors and that sectional rehearsals be held, in the interests of efficiency.

There had also been differences between Thöner and a junior violin teacher, Georg Gerike, over teaching methods. In 1960 Dame Ruth Railton expressed the opinion, based on the auditions of Academy students for the National Youth Orchestra of Great Britain, that 'no teachers of violin in Britain or Ireland approached this standard and she would recommend pupils from London and elsewhere to come to Dublin to take lessons from him.'[139] Thöner had succeeded in welding together an orchestra capable of giving a substantial programme, such as that which—under the baton of (then) Capt. Fred O'Callaghan of the Army School of Music—he took to Waterford in 1962:

> Vivaldi: Concerto Grosso op. 2 No. 8
> Beethoven: Violin Concerto (with Thöner as soloist)
> Haydn: Symphony in D No. 104
> Brahms: Hungarian Dances Nos. 5 and 6

This coincided with a number of contractual difficulties between Thöner and the Academy, which led to Labour Court intervention, and he subsequently left the Academy.

It would not be until the late eighties that the Academy orchestra, under the direction of Prof. James Cavanagh, became a more cohesive and consistent group, although still subject to the vagaries of the transient student population. To its annual concert at the NCH it has now added the increasing commitment to accompany the concerto performances of the Academy's candidates for performance degrees (BA and MMus), and in 1996 a historic joint concert was given by the combined orchestras of the Academy and the DIT Conservatory. In this period we also note the latest in a succession of chamber groups in the Academy, the Baroque Ensemble directed by Prof. Deirdre Ward from 1991 until her resignation from the Academy in 1997.

In 1953 the second substantive rise in the Government grant brought it to £1,000 (today, between £12,000 and £15,000) and in 1955 to £1,500. The Governors had become alarmed at the expansion of the staff at the Municipal School of Music, marked by the appointment of Michael MacNamara as principal, and, most significantly, of Jaroslav and Kveta Vaneček. This was so sharply felt that, in late 1954, Matthew Costelloe had proposed an examination of 'the critical position of the Academy as a result of recent developments in the Municipal School of Music which, if permitted to continue by the Dept. of Education and the Municipal authorities, must eventually result in the virtual extinction of the Academy.'[140] A committee consisting of Maud Aiken, Dagg, Alderman Butler, Costelloe, Deale and Noel Reid was appointed to investigate, and two weeks later Denis McCullough informed the Board that he (with three other Governors—Dagg, Deale, and Canon Richard Ross) had already had a meeting with the Minister for Education with regard to 'the parlous position of the Academy vis-à-vis the MSM.'

> I informed the Minister, inter alia, that in my view no continued progress could be made by the Academy, under its present Charter; that the composition of the Board of Governors was too large and unwieldy; that its membership was weakened by the inclusion of eight nominees of the Dublin Corporation, which body made no contribution to the income of the Academy and which now ran and financed liberally, from the public funds, what now promises to become a rival institution. These nominated Members of the Board . . . were able [to] and did influence its policy, by the weight of their voting power, thus reversing the old adage of 'no taxation without representation.' I further expressed the view that until this anomalous position was rectified, the Academy could not maintain the position which it was entitled to occupy in the musical life of our country.[141]

The minister had told the Governors that while he was sympathetic to their point of view, as they were meeting him on an unofficial basis he could only act when officially approached by the Board of Governors itself.

The committee charged with this matter recommended that a deputation be sent to the minister to stress the need for the Academy to be placed on the same footing as the Continental conservatoires. The action of McCullough in pre-empting this proposal was severely frowned upon by the Board, who strenuously objected to a suggestion that he be elected to a vacant vice-presidency, while the members of the committee dissociated themselves from the idea of a delegation if McCullough were to be a member of it.[142] Eventually the delegation was to consist of Maud Aiken, Alderman Butler, Costelloe, Councillor Byrne, and Noel Reid.

The minister's thinking became explicit in 1955 when the Governors held a special meeting 'in order to prepare a statement which the Minister for Education suggested should be submitted in order to show what steps should be considered for establishing the Academy on the lines of a National Conservatoire.'[143] This move was prompted by departmental thinking along the lines that, the attempt to create a conservatoire having failed, a compromise could be achieved by merging the Academy and the College of Music. It was not the first time such a move had been contemplated. In 1935 (a year after the Municipal School of Music had lobbied unsuccessfully to be called the National School of Music)[144] it was suggested that the Corporation Governors and the Board of Studies should meet 'to discuss closer collaboration between the Municipal School of Music and the Academy,' which prompted the somewhat unhelpful, if not disingenuous, query from the professors: 'Our Board would be greatly helped in its consideration of this matter if the Governors representing the Corporation would be so good as to supply the following information: What class of pupils does the Municipal School cater for? . . . is [it] self-supporting? . . . at what educational standards does it aim?'[145]

Such a reaction was hardly likely to make the educational authorities smile on the older institution when a rationalisation plan was needed. The fact that a merger did not take place is less significant than the fact that the need for such an institution was recognised. These were very difficult years for the Academy, as they were for the college also, as both sides resisted the merger.

The Academy was losing older, long-serving members of staff and of the Board. Larchet resigned in 1955. Mrs Starkie, a Governor since 1925, had been inactive since 1952 and died in 1961. In that year T. H. Weaving, at the age of eighty, received a presentation to mark his almost sixty years on the staff; he continued as a professor until his death in 1966. When Clyde Twelvetrees died in 1956, at the age of eighty-one, he had been connected in some way with the Academy since 1902 (he had returned to Manchester to play in the Hallé and teach at the RNCM in the period 1922–38). On his death Bianca Esposito wrote: 'Both Dr. Esposito and Sir Hamilton Harty held the firm opinion that Clyde Twelvetrees was as fine a cello player as any world celebrity of his time, not excluding the great Casals, and that his modesty and reserved sensitiveness had led him to choose the less spectacular but more serious career.' To replace these legendary figures would be no easy task.

But the Academy was also finding it difficult to cope with the need to increase salaries to attract top teachers, and to provide the facilities and conditions that such teachers would expect. The string supremos, in particular, all proved impossible to retain. André Prieur (flautist) followed Vaneček to the College of Music in 1958, partly attracted by the higher hourly rate available there.

A further expense was the need to renovate the Conacher organ of 1905, and this was undertaken in 1957. David Lee writes: 'Henry Willis undertook a rebuild which attempted to bring about a measure of "Baroque" style titivation. More upperwork was introduced and different actions were employed, tracker (mechanical) for the swell and great divisions and electro-pneumatic for the choir and pedal. This, to my mind, was a seriously misguided move as, apart from the extreme heaviness and insensitivity of the manual tracker action, the mixture of different action types within the one instrument was extremely confusing and unsettling for the player. As well as this, the organ was, by now, far too big for its cramped quarters in the organ room. The main shortcoming, tonally, was that an organ which had by now a very mixed ancestry and represented a hodge-podge of different tonal and aesthetic aspirations simply didn't add up to a satisfactory whole: the different stops and departments didn't blend and many, if not most, of the individual stops were either too loud or too soft. All in all, the Willis rebuild, however well-intentioned, failed, largely because it tried to be too comprehensive and inclusive.'

It therefore became necessary to undertake further work in 1984, and this time a more modestly sized two-manual instrument was built, of which David Lee says: 'Smaller in size but much more tonally comprehensive and adding up to a real artistic unity, it was the work of one man, Philip Prosser of Belfast. It had been decided not to try to be, musically, all things to all men, as it were, but rather to devise a scheme, that despite limitations of size and number of stops, could faithfully fulfil the demands of the high Baroque period of the early eighteenth century, with tracker action and low wind pressures throughout.'

Great organ
 CC to A 58 notes
1. Rohr flute 8
2. Principal 4
3. Nazard $2\frac{2}{3}$
4. Gemshorn 2
5. Tierce $1\frac{3}{5}$
6. Mixture III
 Tremulant

Choir organ
 CC to A 58 notes
1. Stopped diapason 8
2. Chimney flute 4

3. Principal   2
4. Quint $1\frac{1}{3}$
5. Krummhorn   8
    Tremulant

Pedal organ
    CCC to F   30 notes
1. Bourdon   16
2. Principal   8
3. Choral bass   4
4. Fagot   16

Couplers
Choir to great
Choir to pedal
Great to pedal

Mechanical (tracker) action throughout

The financial situation was not helped by the worldwide post-war depression, which stretched into the early fifties and in Ireland led to the decision by Seán Lemass and Dr Kenneth Whittaker to kick-start the economy with the 1958 Programme for Economic Expansion. But conversely, that depression, and the 1956 disturbances in Hungary and elsewhere in eastern Europe, brought to Ireland players of the calibre of Victor Malirsh, János Keszei, János Fürst, and Heinz Jablonski, refugees from different kinds of oppression and of all nationalities, which created a truly European sound in the RESO.

In December 1957 (a year after the Academy had celebrated its supposed centenary with a recital by the Trimble sisters and a concert by members of staff)[146] a deputation met the Minister for Education, Jack Lynch. It consisted of Maud Aiken, Matthew Costelloe, and a former official of the Department of Finance and the Academy's senior vice-president, T. S. C. Dagg. Their mission was to secure conservatoire status for the Academy and appropriate funding to carry out that function. The minister, although not acceding to this, recognised that a revision of music education was needed.[147] A year later, another delegation pressed the financial position more strongly, the minister being given to understand 'that the Board of Governors was not prepared to carry on under present conditions.'[148] This is redolent of the brinkmanship exercised by the then Committee of the IAM in the eighteen-sixties, when threats to close the Academy succeeded in securing the original government grant, and was repeated in 1962, when an Inter-Departmental Committee on the Arts, making a quasi-official visit to the Academy, was told that 'the Board of Governors were a voluntary body and were giving a service to the State. Their financial position was so bad that they had now come to the point of contemplating resignation and the surrender of their trust to the Commissioners of Charitable Donations and Bequests.'[149]

At the same time supporters of the Academy, such as the Fianna Fáil Alderman and TD Pat Cummins, who was (and remains) a member of the Board of Governors, spoke in Dáil Éireann about the financial plight of the Academy, pointing out the reality that such institutions 'cannot relate their fees to their running expenses' unless they were to 'render themselves inaccessible to hundreds of prospective pupils,'[150] thus emphasising the fact that there was a deficiency in respect of every pupil taught, since fees represented only a small fraction of the teaching costs. To which James Dillon—a nephew of the alderman (V. B. Dillon) who had been such an important contributor to the framing of the Blue Scheme—added: 'Institutions like the RIAM sometimes do not realise the volume of good will that exists in the Oireachtas for their work. Perhaps that is our fault if we do not sufficiently often give expression to our appreciation of the work they do.' He suggested that bodies such as the RIAM—'conservative and scrupulous'—might have 'inherited a tradition of self-restraint' in respect of making representations to the Government, 'a traditional reluctance to ask for more . . . a high-minded reluctance to constitute themselves a charge upon the public funds.' Dillon's ignorance of the Academy's lobbying tactics over the past ninety years can be forgiven; his suggestion that in the case of such bodies the minister 'has an obligation from time to time to query them as to whether their work is proceeding satisfactorily and as to whether any important work is being held up through financial difficulty' could still be welcomed.

As a result of these and other representations, the Government grant grew to £3,000 in 1959 (today, £30,000), and, for the first time, the stipulation relating to subscription income was dropped. One of the chief figures in obtaining this increase was Maud Aiken, who informed the Board on 14 January 1959 'that she had made personal representations to Mr. de Valera and to each government minister.' Her position as the wife of Frank Aiken, a former IRA chief of staff and a Government minister in every Fianna Fáil administration, including a period as Tánaiste (1965–69), would have been no barrier to her success, not least because the Board of Governors was at that time regarded as a Fianna Fáil fief, with Aiken and Costelloe in particular working closely together. Despite the Fianna Fáil hegemony, however, there was a departmental determination to resist support for the Academy, and Aiken's interventions would not have been so successful had a direct approach not been made to the *responsables* in the Department of Education, whose eyes needed to be opened to the fact that the Academy was *not* a private and outdated Ascendancy club, hoping to be bolstered by political hand-outs, but a public service institution capable of playing a part in the exponential growth in Irish society and culture that began at that time.

This fundamental change in the way the Academy and its work was perceived was as significant as that which had secured the original government grant in 1870. It brought the grant to £4,000 in 1960 and to £6,000 in 1962, and in the same period it encouraged the Academy to embark on a thorough renovation of the premises, including the historic fabric of number 36, which was to prove extremely costly.

More significantly, however, it enabled the discussion to continue regarding the question of a conservatoire. In February 1962, at the request of the Taoiseach, Seán Lemass, an Academy delegation met an inter-departmental committee attended by two representatives of the Department of Education, one representative of the Taoiseach, one of Finance, one of the Office of Public Works, and one of External Affairs, which focused on the expansion of the Academy outside Dublin.[151] This resulted in a recognition of the urgent need to appoint younger and fitter professors to replace those whose age and health had made them less useful. In particular, staff in the keyboard, strings and speech and drama faculties were to be augmented, and Seán Lynch (piano) and Dennis Noble (voice) were appointed.[152] János Fürst began a short and stormy association with the Academy as a violin teacher,[153] followed by Arnold McKiernan (organ and theory) and Vincent Pentony (organ),[154] and Charles Lynch was given a part-time piano position (see below, p. 507) with a guarantee of £500 a year.[155] With the retirement of Mercedes Bolger as harp teacher, Gérard Meyer was appointed to teach concert harp and Gráinne Ní Éigeartaigh to teach Irish harp.[156]

Throughout the seventies, representations were made to the Department of Education, and meetings were held with successive ministers on a twofold approach: the recognition of the Academy's role in music education (in particular the status of its diplomas) and the funding basis on which it operated vis-à-vis the service it provided.

The financial position up to 1974 had been static: the Academy had succeeded in balancing its books. But losses in 1974–75 began to appear alarming. They were due to three factors: the change in 1974 of the Government's accounts year, which had left the Academy with only nine months of its annual grant; the steep rise in teachers' salaries (along with most of the work force), which saw the Academy's wage bill rising from £60,000 to £90,000 in one year; and the Academy's desire to bring its teachers' salaries upwards into line with those of comparable institutions. (By 1968 the average annual salary of a senior professor in the RIAM was £1,500, supplemented by examining fees, which might amount to a further £500.) Increases in fees were, of necessity, constrained by market forces, and the Academy was faced with unpleasant choices as it contemplated an increasing bank overdraft. No change in the Government's attitude to the Academy was forthcoming.

In 1975 the extraordinary step was taken of proposing to double the fees, and an unprecedented meeting was held of Governors, staff, parents and senior students to discuss the serious nature of the Academy's finances. It was clear that a fundamental change might take place in the relationships of all concerned if any rise in fees were to approach the level of the real economic rate. Following this meeting, the increase was kept at a still painful and deeply regretted 50 per cent. There then followed a private meeting with Jack Lynch TD (then Leader of the Opposition) and John Wilson TD (Fianna Fáil's shadow spokesman on education), as a result of which questions were asked in Dáil Éireann of the minister, Richard Burke, among which was the following: 'Is the Minister aware that the Academy is running at a loss and has no means of coping with that situation other than by way of increased grant-in-aid?'[157] to which the Minister replied that the Academy had another source of income in its fees and that therefore the department could not be regarded as the only source of funding. Pressed on his future intentions, the minister said that he had no objection to consulting the Academy on matters of common interest but that a meeting to discuss a grant in aid was not conceivable. Despite being pressed by Jack Lynch, who argued that, as a minister, he himself had held consultations on the subject of a grant in aid with several bodies, and by a deputy from his own side, Maurice Dockrell (an Academy Governor), these questions failed to affect the apparently intractable position of the minister but led to a further meeting in May 1976.

The minister was told that the Academy's deficit was then over £60,000 and that the full wage agreement terms could not be paid without seriously increasing this figure. Salaries were still below those paid in the College of Music, even though fees were considerably higher. The grant to the Academy had increased much more slowly than the national wage agreements. It was stressed that the Academy functioned as a primary, secondary and third-level educator.

The submission drew the minister's reluctant agreement that there was some substance in the Academy's claim for a repositioning of its finances, which he asked his officials to investigate. He also made it clear that he intended to follow previous departmental thinking in relation to forming a systematic view of the Academy's role in music education. He pointed out, for example, that as his department had no jurisdiction over appointments or grading within the RIAM he could not be expected to be fully liable for salaries. On the other hand, he would welcome a submission from the Academy 'on the integration of music education in Ireland with reference to the Academy itself, the Vocational Schools, the Universities, and the National Institutes of Higher Education,[158] having regard to the desirability of preserving the autonomy of these institutions as much as possible,'[159] which the Academy agreed to undertake.

In the meantime, a thorough analysis of the Academy's finances was undertaken in the light of what can only be described as the spectacular upsurge in costs occasioned by the economic boom of the mid-seventies. It was probably the first time the Board of Governors had had to face such a novel situation, as the old equation of grants and fees, balanced by salaries and overheads, shot out of control. The task was deputed to a committee of Aleck Crichton (proprietor of John Jameson and Son Ltd), Desmond O'Donohue (an accountant), Séamus Gaffney (secretary of the Department of the Public Service), Anna Brioscú (mother of Colma and Orla Brioscú), and Leo Gibson (father of Darina and John Gibson), together with the secretary, James Callery.

The committee observed that most teachers taught a mixture of senior and junior pupils, ranging from twenty-seven to forty pupils during a working week of 27 hours (since reduced to 22). Some, however, whom we might today call 'workaholics', taught far more: Rhona Marshall at that time had forty-eight students (in itself a considerable reduction of her earlier quotas); Doris Keogh, flute professor and director of the early music Capriol Consort, taught a total of 113 (many of them, of course, in class situations rather than individually)—and did so of their own, unauthorised and unsupervised, volition.

There was a considerable difference between the costs per hour of teachers, some costing only £30 per pupil per year, others as much as £180 and in one case £275. Taking those taught by the full-time staff (659 students at a total cost of £61,000), the average cost per pupil per year was £93, while that for the part-time staff (519 at £30,000) was £59, the difference being attributable to the different rates of pay and associated costs between full-time and part-time staff.

It was essential to bring Academy teachers further into line with those in the VEC, who were approximately 10 per cent better paid for comparable hours. It was also essential to maintain a mix of 'star' teachers and a more general teaching staff. And it was essential, above all, to be giving value for money in a society that had rapidly become accustomed to the twin factors of inflation and consumer power.

A further meeting was held with the Minister for Education (now John Wilson) in July 1978, at which the Academy was represented by Maud Aiken, Maurice Dockrell TD, Aleck Crichton, and the secretary. A provision of £192,000 a year was sought, in addition to liquidating the Academy's liabilities, and it was stressed that without some elasticity it would be impossible for the Academy to maintain its standards, since staff training and new initiatives had to be constantly deferred. This, and subsequent meetings, meant that the Academy was able to keep pace with inflation, and by 1982 the Government grant had reached £300,000. Here, however, the question of expansion arose again, as it was proving impossible to do more than maintain the status quo. No new departures could be envisaged, and with the ever more pressing need to deal with the issue of third-level music education, the problem remained acute.

One consequence of the moratorium on non-essential expenditure was that the fabric of the building suffered from custodial neglect, and facilities for teachers and students became shoddy and even dangerous. The piano stock was extremely sub-standard. The administrative staff had come to rely heavily on voluntary assistance from Governors. The good will of staff was being trawled too deeply.

In 1982 the Academy took a step that had not been attempted since the days of sending deputations to the Lord Lieutenant: it made a submission directly to the Taoiseach. In terms that echoed the approach to the Intermediate Education Board in 1900, the Academy (through Lindsay Armstrong, director, Anna Brioscú, and Aleck Crichton) told the Taoiseach that its nationwide examination system was the only one available, 'none being provided by the Department of Education itself . . . The Department is thus saved both the expense and administration of organising such a scheme.' Meanwhile the grant from the department had fallen as a proportion of salary costs from 63 per cent in 1981 to 53 per cent in 1982. Bluntly put, inadequate funding by the Department has impaired development in musical education in the RIAM. This, together with the disadvantaged fees the Academy has to charge its students, giving the impression that the Academy is accessible only to an elite section of our population who can afford such fees, accounts for all the areas of neglect mentioned. These factors have produced an atmosphere of continual financial anxiety in which all energies are directed towards year-to-year survival, precluding any long term planning and development, and inhibiting day-to-day decision-making in relation to current musical matters and student/staff facilities.[160]

The Academy then went on to move away from current problems to deal with the environment it hoped to create in music education.

The RIAM sees its long term aims as consistent with the trends of the present decade and beyond. These are:

—Conservatoire-type facilities to cater for third-level studies . . . Coupled with these studies would be the development of library facilities including the employment of a librarian—the library to become a centre for research and study . . .[161]

—more broadly-based Junior and Middle Grade teaching through the expansion of teaching in the suburbs, either through specially set-up satellite colleges or in association with existing bodies . . .

—special teaching with recognised status of a junior college, to cater, on Saturdays, for young performers of outstanding talent likely to pursue a professional career in music;

—a Graduate Course in Practical musicianship, with separate modes for Teachers and Performers, with University association and recognized by the Registration Council . . . to involve the recruitment of at least one full-time member of staff qualified in music educational methods;

—full-time courses leading to LRIAM and ARIAM for other categories of students of music and speech/drama;

—Graduate and non-Graduate level speech/drama courses;

—in-service training courses for practising teachers;

—extra-mural courses in singing, speech/drama, history of music, ensemble work, for adolescents and adults, either in the context of 'second chance' education or in the context of leisure activities . . .

—a fuller back-up service for the existing network of Local Centre examinations (i.e. greater emphases on the pedagogical benefits of the examination structure and greater support given to teachers, particularly those working in rural areas);

—a course in Irish music, both modern and traditional, instrumental and vocal;

—an innovative curriculum in terms of jazz, ethno-musicology, electronic music . . .

—establishment of a school of studies for electronic music and acoustic research with University links and in possible association with the Dublin Institute of Advanced Studies;

—a premier International Summer School, which would continue to
attract numbers of highly-trained students from abroad, thus strengthening the external and international contacts of the RIAM itself, with
consequent benefits for its staff and students;

—modernisation of office equipment and procedures.

The submission resulted in a capital grant from the department of
£40,000 and another of £200,000 from the Fund of Suitors, which financed
the renovation of the whole building and the construction of an eight-room
suite of teaching rooms; in addition the arrears of staff pay under the
national wage agreements were met.

The significant fact is that, once it was put onto a secure financial footing,
the Academy was able to tackle all the items in its declaration of intent, and
almost all of them have been achieved in the intervening decade and a half.

As we have seen, the close working relationship of Governors, administrative
staff (chiefly the secretary and lady superintendent) and Board of Studies
had made the concept embodied in the Blue Scheme very workable. There
had always, however, been a nagging doubt that the lack of a figurehead, of
a personality among the staff who could be identified as the chief executive
of the institution, distinguished it from other academies in a not altogether
beneficial way.

We have also seen, with regard to Stewart, Esposito, and Larchet, that it
was possible for individuals to assume a mantle that was not theirs, chiefly
because this position did not exist. Whether the non-existent position was
that of a managing director or an artistic director was never made clear,
although, in the controversy surrounding the attempted appointment of
Esposito, there had been an outline of a new set of relationships that would
have both acknowledged the artistic leadership of Esposito, and provided
him with the authority necessary to give that leadership an executive role.

The abortive personality-led attempts to amend the Blue Scheme in
1911 and 1948 did not remove the Governors' anxieties about the nature of
the office they needed to call into existence. The lack of a director was
becoming increasingly anomalous, and it was felt that the Academy was
seriously inhibited by not having a single figure in the driving-seat. The
position of secretary was one subordinate to the Board—so much so that
until 1949 it was the chairman who took the minutes, and, until the death
of Sealy Jeffares, the secretary actually stood, rather than sat, in attendance
at the Board of Governors.

In particular, the new relationship between the administration (including
the Governors) and the teaching staff that had evolved in the seventies had
brought out into the open the real and acute need for direction in the
Academy that had been present, but undocumented, for over two decades.
If new curricula were to be introduced, and especially if new types of
student were to be entertained within the institution on degree courses,
then a new professional basis for administering and guiding it was also
necessary. It was also important that the Academy should have someone at

its helm who could effectively represent it in negotiations with the Government, the Arts Council, the universities and other teaching bodies and generally improve the status of the Academy in society. In 1977 this was formulated by a Special Finance Committee as 'overall planning and supervision by a qualified musician with attributes which would gain the support of teachers and pupils.'[162]

It would of course have been possible to secure a guarantee from the Government with regard to funding and to look no further than a year-to-year continuation of current activities, but the committee knew that this would be 'to risk a gradual lowering of Academy standards, and to risk the Academy becoming only a poor relation in the future musical organisation of Dublin.' The alternative, which it saw as a 'somewhat daring venture,' was to embark on a course of expansion, innovation and policy review, and 'we do not relish the prospect of starting an adventure without a leader.'

For the very financial reasons that made the appointment of a director so imperative, however, it was to prove impossible to put this into practice for a further four years, during which the Governors continued to fine-tune the arrangements they envisaged, in the light of their regularly developing realisation that their own work was far too technical, too onerous and too voluminous to be entrusted to a voluntary body meeting (then) twice a month, or even to an Executive Committee. In particular, the period between the acceptance, in principle, of the need for a director and the first appointment saw the parallel development of replacing the existing structure of ad hoc committees for finance, appointments, staff relations, premises and so on with a Management and Finance Committee, responsible for considering all business matters affecting the Academy and advising the Board of Governors accordingly. Henceforth, only in exceptional circumstances would any special committee be formed for an *ad hoc* purpose.

The Blue Scheme was amended in early 1981, and the Commissioners of Charitable Donations and Bequests accepted the change at the end of that year, at which time John O'Donovan, as chairman of the Board, wrote to his colleagues pointing out that a unanimous decision had been implemented and commenting that in 1964, when this had first been mooted, only he and Charles Acton had been in favour of such an appointment.

The search for a suitable director began. There was some unease on the part of James Callery, who considered that his own position as senior officer of the Academy was about to be jeopardised, and on one occasion, in January 1982, when the selection of a director was imminent, he attempted to cancel a meeting, on the grounds of the extremely inclement weather, by closing the doors of the Academy, an action that the Governors (who reconvened in Kildare Street in the office of one of the vice-presidents, Séamus Gaffney, secretary of the Department of the Public Service) 'noted with disquiet and disapproval.'[163] The following week the appointment was announced of Lindsay Armstrong, a former oboeist with the RTÉSO and founder-manager of the NICO, who had recently been the inaugural director of the NCH.[164] James Callery remained in his post for a further year, chiefly to facilitate the introduction of the new director to the workings of the Academy, and then retired. He died in 1997.

In the nineties the Academy has continued both to lead developments in music education and to respond to initiatives from other quarters. The institution has changed both internally, as far as its own modus operandi is concerned, and externally, in the public perception of its role. A fresher appearance, in the form of updated logos and literature and a revised prospectus, has underlined more significant changes, such as the appointments (following the retirement of the lady superintendent) of a Registrar, with responsibility for academic affairs, and of heads of the five faculties (keyboard, strings, voice, musicianship, and wind, brass, and percussion), with a consequent restructuring of the Board of Studies, all of which was regarded as vital if standards were to be maintained in the light of the new diploma and degree courses being offered, with graduates from the Academy forming a new phalanx of participants in the music education environment.

Internationally too the Academy has begun to play a more significant role. In 1990 Olivier Messiaen, visiting Dublin for the second time for, among other events, a performance of his *Turangalîla-symphonie*, was awarded an honorary fellowship—the first since those conferred on Joan Trimble and Havelock Nelson in 1985. The citation read as follows:

Maître, you have honoured the Royal Irish Academy of Music by coming here tonight so that we, in our turn, may honour you with the highest accolade which this institution can bestow—Fellowship *honoris causa*. We salute you in this way, as the most celebrated living composer, and as one of the most significant creators of the twentieth century. Furthermore, we greet a great organist, whose place in the historic tradition of this 'King of Instruments' is assured; a great professor, who has nurtured the genius of pupils such as Boulez, Stockhausen and Xenakis; and a great Frenchman, who stands alongside the most eminent of his compatriots.

In doing so, we acknowledge and celebrate three cardinal virtues which distinguish your work: First, your deep religious faith, which gives your music its incandescent spirituality manifest in your immensely moving opera, *Saint François d'Assise*. We cherish it especially in those of your works in which your veneration for Jesus Christ is so evident: *L'Ascension*, *La Nativité du Seigneur* and the *Vingt Regards sur l'Enfant Jésus*. We look forward particularly to hearing, in two days' time, *Le Livre du Saint Sacrement* for organ, receiving its Irish première in the beautiful ambiance of Saint Patrick's Cathedral.

Second, your love of nature, an exuberance and a humility in the presence of the natural world which you share with Beethoven and which you have recorded and translated into a new musical language in such works as *Le Merle noir*, *Le Réveil des oiseaux* and the monumental *Catalogue d'oiseaux*.

Third, we pay tribute to your own personal experience of the brutalities of warfare, which deepened and extended your fundamental love of your fellow beings, whom you served well and truly by creating one of the superlative pieces of chamber music in the history of our civilisation, the *Quatuor pour la fin du temps*.

Maître, all these qualities—your questing faith, your transparent humanity and your love of nature—are glowingly displayed in your epic work, the *Turangalîla-symphonie*. We anticipate with pleasure and excitement its performance this week, and we rejoice that it will be played in your presence, as it was on another memorable occasion in 1976 when you were also with us, with the same distinguished soloists, your wife Yvonne Loriod-Messiaen and her sister, Jeanne Loriod. In this work, you have celebrated the aesthetics of love in a marriage of East and West, and thus you demonstrate the technical prowess which has marked you as the formidable pioneer and teacher who has changed our conception of rhythm and instrumentation. You, *Maître*, have translated the divine and human love as portrayed in the great windows of Chartres to provide us with musical images for our own time.

Therefore, *Maître*, we rejoice that the occasion of your second visit to our country has given us the opportunity of saluting your magnificent achievements in the fullness of your years by welcoming and embracing you, in every sense of the word, into our Fellowship.

The conferring ceremony, which was conducted by the Lord Mayor of Dublin of the time, Alderman Seán Haughey TD, concluded with performances of a selection of Messiaen's music, including three movements of the *Quatuor* (performed by Aisling Drury Byrne, John Finucane, Geraldine O'Grady, and Gillian Smith), a work for flute played by Gareth Costello, and piano works performed by the Academy students Finghin Collins, Donagh Collins, and Orla McDonagh (soon to become the first Irish musician to achieve a place at the Juilliard School of Music in New York). The *Quatuor* was to be played in its entirety two years later, at the official opening, on St Cecilia's Day, of the Academy's new recital hall, named after Michele Esposito (on this occasion played by Deirdre Ward, John Finucane, Nora Gilleece, and Gillian Smith).

Later in 1990, fellowships were also conferred by President Hillery on Charles Acton, Walter Beckett, Brian Boydell, Aloys Fleischmann, Anthony Hughes and Gerard Victory and the following year on Karl-Heinz Stockhausen. (The complete roll of fellows is to be found in chapter 9.)

Other international connections arose through the selection of Academy students to participate in the then EEC Youth Orchestra, the visits by the Academy orchestras and by individual students to the Accademia Musicale Chigiana in Siena, the Paris Conservatoire, and the RCM, some of the most spectacular being the visits to Italy of the Capriol Consort of early music, directed by the flute professor, Doris Keogh. Darina Gibson (one of a generation in the sixties that included Albert Bradshaw, Colin Staveley, and Aisling Drury Byrne) won an international piano competition in London judged by Sir Malcolm Sargent, Solomon and Louis Kentner, while in 1977 Daire Fitzgerald was accepted to study with Rostropovich.

Exchange visits from corresponding institutions have given Irish music students a chance to hear and meet their colleagues from other countries and cultures, the latest of which has been the visit to the Academy of a youth orchestra from Espoo, Finland, in 1997 and, in the sesquicentenary year, the most ambitious such undertaking so far, a combined concert given in Birmingham and Dublin by the Academy Symphony Orchestra and that of the Birmingham Conservatoire.

The nineties have also seen the Academy reaching out into the community more effectively and extensively than before. As the infrastructure for music in Ireland (and particularly in Dublin) has developed since the opening of the NCH in 1981, there is a greater sense of excitement in music-making, and in this regard series of 'Meet the Orchestra' and 'Exploring Music', aimed at children aged between seven and twelve, featuring Academy staff and students under the direction of Prof. James Cavanagh at the newly opened Ark cultural centre for children in Temple Bar, Dublin, in 1996 and 1997 have been particularly successful in demythologising classical music.

On a similar note, a series of ten extra-mural classes on 'The Appreciation of Music', given by Prof. Brian Boydell in the Academy in 1993, were hugely successful and have been succeeded in later years by further series by Boydell as well as other topics such as opera, operetta, musicals, and jazz, given by experts such as John Allen and Ian Fox.

Behind these new ventures and activities stand years of critical self-evaluation by the Academy of its role and status. In 1990 a Long-Term Planning Committee was established to identify the Academy's needs over a rolling five-year period, and this considered four essential areas: curriculum development, financial management, community relations, and administration and internal relations. Preparatory work was put in hand to establish the performance degree course described in chapter 9 and the pre-instrumental classes for the very young, which were launched in 1997. The need for heads of department was seen as a significant development,[165] as was the creation of a constituency for Governors representing the non-professorial and non-teaching staff. Reviews of staff levels were set in train, and staff development opportunities were created.

Refresher courses for music teachers continued to provide the sort of service envisaged at the turn of the century by Peter Goodman. An inquiry into music facilities in the Dublin suburbs led to the Academy administering special schools in Leixlip and Tallaght for a number of years. The centenary of the local centre system was to be celebrated by the nationwide series of concerts described in chapter 6, as a way of bringing home to each county the wealth of talent the Academy had fostered among both students and teachers in the hundred years that had seen the system grow from four centres, examining 73 candidates, to its 1994 level of over 30,000 in 575 centres.

During this period the director, Lindsay Armstrong, who had played such a vital role in renewing and reinvigorating the Academy, indicated his intention of relinquishing his post at the close of 1993 to devote himself to performance. He had been the co-founder of the New Irish Chamber Orchestra in 1970–71, and since leaving the Academy he has created another chamber ensemble, the Orchestra of St Cecilia. After a period of some months, during which a new working relationship was developed for the posts of director, secretary, and registrar, more effectively defining their responsibilities, Dr John O'Conor, who had been professor of piano at the Academy since 1976, was appointed director after a public competition in 1994.

The period 1994–97 saw a marked increase in the scale and depth at which the music world was being considered by educationalists, politicians, and businessmen. The DIT began a consultative process with the Music Education National Debate (MEND), steered by a former Academy student, Frank Heneghan, who had become principal of the College of Music and later head of corporate affairs of the DIT. Elements in the music industry commissioned a consultancy report (mentioned below by John O'Conor), which gave considerable recognition and impetus to the concept of music-making as greater than the sum of its parts and as something 'tradable' in the world as a commodity.

The preparation of three documents in particular gave the Academy the opportunity to state the case for developments in education, finance and musical infrastructure, and to voice its anxieties, as well as its ambitions in each of these areas. In particular, the appearance in 1994 of the green paper *Education for a Changing World* caused the Academy to express its 'concern for the apparent lack of awareness of the role and status of music in Irish education' and to comment on the green paper's 'failure to identify music as a core subject in post-primary schools.'[166]

> While it is true that Ireland enjoys a vibrant musical life emanating from a strong cultural heritage, this is not currently translated into music in the classroom: the existing primary school curriculum is not being adequately sustained, with the real danger that some children may never experience music education during the primary years.

The fact that other experts, closer in some cases to the realities of the classroom, were voicing the same concerns with equal force did not exonerate the Academy from making such a submission. As an 'index to the health of Irish musical life,' by its teaching of the very young up to senior level, 'it views that health as threatened rather than enhanced by the intentions of the Green Paper.'

A further Academy viewpoint was expressed to the Arts Council, which invited submissions in advance of its own three-year plan for the arts, delivered to the Minister for the Arts in 1994. In speaking to the Arts Council, the Academy stressed the need for the council to 'act as a counterweight to what we perceive as a lacuna in the Green Paper.' Developing the arguments contained in the previous submission, the Academy put forward the view that

> there is a real need to promote equity in regard to access to music and to participation in the musical life of the nation. It is clear that such

equity does not presently exist. The diminution in exposure to a formal education in music as part of the normal school curriculum is particularly keenly felt in those schools which do not enjoy the enhanced facilities available in a minority of schools. If, as we believe, the foundations for an appreciation of music are laid at this stage, particularly in the case of music forms which presently do not have a large following, then this inequity in turn contributes to creating an audience which is socio-economically stratified . . . The Academy would wish to see this imbalance addressed through a national arts strategy which pro-actively promoted the diffusion of the appreciation of music in its many forms.[167]

Further aspects of the submission included the development of managerial capacity to lead the industry, and 'substantially expanded sponsorship of aspiring musical talent,' not in the form of subsidy but as an investment in young potential.

Another occasion for an expression of both views and intent was the establishment by the Minister for the Arts, Culture and the Gaeltacht, Michael D. Higgins TD, of a review group, 'Provision and Institutional Arrangements Now for Orchestras and Ensembles' (PIANO), chaired by John O'Conor shortly after his appointment as director of the Academy. The group reported in 1996, after a protracted period of discussion. Ostensibly the principal task of the group was to recommend (if considered necessary) new arrangements for the management and direction of the NSO, and it therefore had little to do directly with music education. But, in the course of framing its terms of reference, it was thought necessary to enable it to hear evidence relating to all aspects of music, and this had the effect of focusing attention on education. The report therefore includes elements beyond its initial remit (and, indeed, beyond that of the department that commissioned it), and the Academy saw it as a vital function to draw attention publicly to the fact that, for the first time since the fifties, attempts were being made on a bilateral basis with RTÉ to establish a national training orchestra, intended to embrace students from all music schools who aspire to a professional orchestral career.[168] While that aim remains an unfulfilled ambition, the first real seeds of such an association could be seen in the working visit on 19 April 1997 to the Academy's own orchestra of Alexander Anissimov, whose appointment as principal conductor-designate of the NSO had been announced the previous day.

Since its establishment, in the period before the implementation of the Blue Scheme, the Board of Studies had consisted of the professors of the Academy according as they were appointed by the Governors. What was in effect the Academic Council of the Academy was, therefore, in the hands of those whom the Governors thought suitable. There was no inherent system of promotion to professorship through merit; and although the various faculties were in general fairly represented, the situation could develop where one faculty unduly dominated the composition of the Board of Studies. Furthermore, although it was required by the Blue Scheme to meet regularly, there had been periods when that obligation was disregarded. In any case, there was no compulsion on individual professors to attend, and in fact some of them seem to have been quite cavalier in their attitude to meetings, particularly during periods when one or two personalities were pushing affairs in their own direction.

In 1994–95, therefore, the Governors took the parallel steps of appointing heads of faculty and amending the Blue Scheme to allow a restructuring of the Board of Studies to incorporate these new positions and that of the chairman of the local centre senior examiners.

A fitting point at which to end this narrative of the Academy's growth and maturity is the launch by the Nobel laureate Séamus Heaney of the Academy's *First Anthology of Poetry*, compiled and edited by Margaret Turley (local centre senior examiner) as a means of extending the considerable interest already shown in speech and drama in the Academy itself, and throughout the local centre system.

In greeting the appearance of the anthology, Séamus Heaney said:

> The recitation of poetry on festive occasions or in desperate conditions, repeating it silently or performing it in public, saying it to ourself or speaking it out—this has been a feature of human culture throughout recorded time. In Homer's account of life in Greece in the second millennium BC, for example, the bard Demodicus chants at the feast and as he weaves his tale of the fall of Troy into his metrical lines, Odysseus weeps at the emotional impact of the performance; in Ford Madox Ford's fictional autobiography that covers his experiences in the First World War, the novelist tells about finding himself automatically repeating lines of George Herbert's poetry while he's under bombardment in the trenches; and in Nazi Germany, prisoners in the bookless hell of the concentration camps used to piece together the words of poems out of their heads—re-membering them in every mental and bodily sense of the verb. The examples could be multiplied, from Anglo-Saxon England to Soviet Russia, but what they all add up to is evidence of the truth of one of the simplest and boldest claims that I know—the claim, namely, that 'poetry is strong enough to help.'
>
> The very circumstances in which this sentence was written is a guarantee of the reliability of what it is saying. It was noted down in Greece during the Second World War by the poet George Seferis, at a desolate moment in the course of the German occupation of the country, a moment when Seferis was reading the poetry being produced by his Greek contemporaries and measuring it by extreme standards, testing its worth by setting it in the balance against human suffering and human evil, and asking how it held up. And when he concluded that it *was* strong enough to help, Seferis was not talking primarily about the message that came from the poets' philosophy or patriotism, but rather about a strength that was intrinsic to the medium. It was the verification that came from the versification, from the art *per se*, that Seferis was giving credit to,

that feeling of being sustained at the foundations of your being by the experience of something totally satisfactory as an artistic whole. And it is the reality of that experience, its value and its meaning first of all within an individual's life and then within the life of a culture—in the end it is that which gives value and meaning to the practice and discipline of learning poems by heart and saying them aloud.

I like that phrase 'learning by heart' just as I like the phrase 'saying it into yourself.' They go together and they were often to be heard in the school I went to in County Derry. 'Say it into yourself and learn it by heart.' And when you think of the implications of the phrases, you have another reason for rejoicing in the publication of this anthology which we are gathered here to celebrate. The students who use the book, at whatever level and in whichever language, Irish or English, will be laying down words and rhythms in the very foundations of their ear which will eventually turn into a kind of fossil fuel for their inner life. Or, to change the metaphor, they will be establishing growth rings on their memory, marking their inner ear poem by poem, taking in lines that will be there like supply lines to their cultural identity for the rest of their lives.

This may seem a very roundabout and laborious way of saying that it is a good thing for young people to learn to speak poems aloud. But it is important to establish a plane of regard that sets the specific activities of Speech and Drama competitions within a much larger literary and philosophic context. Margaret Turley has obviously chosen many poems that are light-hearted and merry, more bagately than bardic, so to speak, especially in the Kindergarten and Preliminary Grades. But I was gratified to see poems here by Gerard Manley Hopkins and William Butler Yeats, for example, and Nuala Ní Dhomhnaill and Brendan Kennelly, and Seán Ó Ríordáin and John Keats. Anybody who learns these poems or any one of the scores of others which appear in the anthology will be furnishing their lives with the equivalent of what the Arctic explorers call base camps, fall-back positions and supply points for the journey. Once the poems are learned, there will always be that simple joy of recollection, the deep reassurance of coming home to a set of words that seem to have been yours in an almost pre-natal way; and there will be the inestimable enrichment of tapping into that great cable of language that carries the humming energies of human imagination, in this case the particular energy of metrical, rhythmical speech. Speech framed, as Yeats once said, 'to prolong the moment of contemplation.'

And the great thing is that the contemplation can come to you long after the moment when you learned the poem by heart. I am delighted to see in the anthology for example Keats's Ode to Autumn. It is one of the reasons why I am very glad to be here to launch the book and to congratulate all concerned. But I am also glad to be able to reassure any student who might at first be baffled by the sumptuousness and ritual of the poem that all will come out right in the end. When I learnt it by heart nearly fifty years ago in Anahorish School, I had no great sense of what I was repeating. We stood up in a ring around the master's desk and spoke the gorgeous lines out from the back of our South Derry throats without much sense of what the whole thing was about. But over the years the poem has rooted and grown and spread itself lavishly inside me until now it is a kind of bower of bliss. So I'd just like to end by re-membering it for you, or as much of it as I still have by heart.[169]

Throughout this history, the learning and contemplation of works of art, whether text or music, have revolved around the joy and the discipline of 'saying it into yourself,' of absorbing rhythm and cadence and setting up the 'supply lines' of which Heaney speaks. One feels that he would like to have known Margaret O'Hea, with whose vision this narrative opened, and shared with her—as indeed with the other truly great teachers around whom the Academy's students have gathered—the 'plane of regard' that finds us coming home to recollection.

Intermezzo

FREDERICK MAY

Going as a pupil to the RIAM wasn't an altogether strange experience for me, for two of the professors there, Dr and Mrs Larchet, had previously been my teachers privately, and Dr Larchet set my feet on the stony path that leads on and up to a knowledge of harmony and counterpoint. At the Academy Mrs Larchet taught the violin and not the piano, so that I never was her pupil again, and it was some time before I was sufficiently advanced to enter Dr Larchet's harmony class, but still their very presence seemed somehow familiar.

I well remember room no. 12, down the corridor on the left-hand side that leads from the office to what was then called the band room but has now been enlarged into the Dagg Hall; for it was in this room that I had my first piano lessons with Miss Annie Lord. From the outset her personality made the very strongest impression upon me; herself an immensely gifted pianist, she brought to both her playing and her teaching a truly wonderful creative energy and vitality. Sometimes she could be stern and even fierce, but for playing which pleased her, her praise was generous and unstinted. She it was who taught me to love César Franck, and his music was one of the abiding joys of her life.

I was a regular attender, and occasionally a performer, at the Students' Musical Union, and one of the most thrilling experiences I can recall from my student days was listening to a truly splendid performance of the great Franck Piano Quintet in F minor, in which Miss Lord played the piano and of which she was the driving force and inspiration; her niece, Miss Nancie Lord, played first violin. This experience of hearing a great work greatly performed was, without doubt, one of the outstanding memories of my student days at the Academy.

Another event at the SMU that meant a lot to me was a performance of Vaughan Williams' song-cycle 'On Wenlock Edge', which was organised by Miss Dorothy Stokes and in which the footballer Tommy Wallis sang the exacting solo tenor part. This was my first introduction to either the poetry of Housman or the music of Vaughan Williams, and both of them, especially the latter, have meant much to me since; after all, it is only in youth that one can make these fine discoveries.

Then there was the mingled awe and excitement of climbing the broad staircase to no. 5 to have piano lessons with Signor Esposito, afterwards to be honoured by his native Italy with the title of Commendatore. These were much more than piano lessons, and Esposito was, of course, much more than a mere pianoforte professor. He was a great musical scholar, besides being a fine conductor and a distinguished composer, so that lessons from him were a liberal education in music. His beetling eyebrows, hawk-like eyes and bushy moustache concealed a kindly nature, although he could be abrupt and sarcastic at times. He was steeped in the literature as well as the music of his homeland, and his eyes always softened when he spoke of the great Italian poets, particularly Dante, whose *Divine Comedy* he regarded as the greatest book ever written.

He managed to spare the time too to look through and advise on the juvenile efforts of a young would-be composer, and I remember his some-what sardonic answer to a query as to whether or not they showed any promise of future development: 'Some develop early, some develop late, and some never develop.' Although he lived in Ireland for so long, his English always remained strongly idiomatic, and once, when judging a band competition in Sligo I think it was, he remarked that he would not give a prize to the best band but to the band that was the least worst.

These two outstanding personalities, Esposito and Miss Annie Lord, form the core and centre of my memories of the Academy, although naturally I have others, many of them very pleasant, such as guest night in the Students' Union and that great annual event, the prize-giving. It is good to feel that the Academy is celebrating its centenary with its vigour and prosperity fully maintained.

Frederick May (1911–1985) was one of the most gifted musicians of his generation. At the RIAM he won the Coulson Scholarship for piano in 1925, the Vandeleur Scholarship for harmony and counterpoint in 1927 and 1929, and, also in 1929, the Arthur Oulton Prize at TCD and the Stewart Memorial Prize for composition, and was awarded a certificate in proficiency with 95 per cent honours. He went subsequently to study with Vaughan Williams, Gordon Jacob, and (after being accepted by Alban Berg but prevented by Berg's death from meeting him) Egon Wellesz. His main works, written before ill-health terminated his career, are the String Quartet in C minor (1936), Songs from Prison (1941), Spring Nocturne (1938), and Sunlight and Shadow (1955).

Intermezzo

MARIE TRIMBLE

I have a distinct recollection of my first day as a pupil of the RIAM, when I was brought by my eldest brother, who was an organ student. He explained to me that I must sign the time of my arrival in the large book on the counter in the office—I was very young, for I did not understand that 3.45 meant a quarter to four.

My first violin teacher was Anna Kavanagh, from whom I had private lessons. Then, at nine years of age, I entered the Academy and continued lessons with this most excellent teacher, who was a pupil of Signor Papini. I continued with her until I was twelve, and then had lessons from Henri Verbrugghen, who came over from Belgium once a week. I was rather young to be under such an advanced teacher, and I am afraid I did not enjoy my lessons.

Verbrugghen ceased coming, and I then started with Adolf Wilhelmj, of whom I have the happiest memories. He was a splendid teacher and a great friend. I continued having lessons from him and was appointed a pupil teacher, later on becoming a member of the staff.

Miss Crean, the lady superintendent of those days, seemed a very formidable person to young people. She was a perfect disciplinarian but did not seem to have any opportunity of becoming on friendly terms with us until the advent of the SMU, when she and Miss Alice Craig, her assistant, seemed to enjoy being on closer terms with the members. I then found Miss Crean to be a very amiable person and changed my view of her completely.

As a family I suppose we held a record. No less than eleven brothers and sisters studied there, and eight of us were scholars and exhibitioners for violin, viola, cello, piano, and organ.

I had a few chamber music lessons with Signor Esposito, when he took over from Herr Bast for a short time.

Lately I have been in contact with a contemporary of mine, Edith Vance. She was a very fine cellist who joined with me in studying chamber music under Henri Bast. I agreed with her when she said, on looking back, what a magnificent opportunity we had had with such a teacher. He was an inspiration to all of us, and my lifelong regret is that he did not live to give us the lessons we required when we had our own family string quartet.

Chamber music, harmony, orchestra, solo lessons—it was a completely satisfying life. Very pleasant were the orchestral rehearsals each Friday afternoon under Dr Jozé. When concert time came it was a certainty that you would be given a prominent front seat if you were pretty!

The SMU (of which I was a member of the original committee) gave us many opportunities of taking part in performances of chamber music, and indeed in most forms of music, including some of the Gilbert and Sullivan operas, which otherwise might not have occurred. It also brought students together in a social way and gave an opportunity of forming friendships.

The Academy concerts and distributions of prizes took place in my day in the great hall of the Royal University—now National University. The Lord Lieutenant of the time would present the prizes, and I have a vivid recollection of the late Duke and Duchess of Connaught, accompanied by two daughters, coming on one of these occasions. Would we have to make four curtseys? Miss Crean must have been especially worried about this, for she rehearsed us tirelessly. On the occasion of the visit of King Edward VII and Queen Alexandra to Dublin in 1907, a choir, accompanied by a small orchestra from the Academy, sang 'Come Back to Erin' to the royal visitors as they left Dún Laoghaire. This was an arrangement written for the occasion by Dr Jozé, a distinguished professor of the Academy.

Addendum by Joan Trimble

In this memoir my mother, Marie Dowse, says very little about her own career and achievements at the RIAM, which she entered in 1896. By the time she was eighteen she had won all possible prizes and scholarships, including the Coulson and Vandeleur exhibitions and scholarships in four consecutive years.

What chance had a young and talented musician to develop a career as a solo performer in those days, after the turn of the century? For a woman there was little to offer in the music profession, except as a teacher. Marie's friends Annie Lord and Madeleine Moore (later Larchet) had long and successful teaching careers at the Academy, Annie also performing as a soloist in Dublin musical circles. The SMU was their great chance to break out of the closed routine at the Academy—and they made the most of it. Marie also joined the staff, but envied her friends who had left for study abroad: the cellist Edith Vance, who went to Leipzig to study with Julius Klengel [who also taught Twelvetrees], and Helen Boyd, who became a violin pupil of Ševčik [the teacher of Vaneček] in Prague. In 1904 she was invited by an impresario to join other Irish musicians in St Louis, Missouri, at the World Fair, having become a Feis gold medallist. Two other gold medallists, John McCormack (tenor) and Lily Foley (soprano), were also invited. They accepted the invitation. Marie's father refused to allow her to go. She often wondered what chance she'd missed.

Her Feis Ceoil successes revealed her all-round qualities, both in chamber music and as a soloist; she had a formidable technique and innate musicianship. She heard all the great violinists who came to Dublin—Sarasate, Ysaÿe, Joachim, Kubelik, and Mischa Elman among others—

adding many of their programme items to her own repertoire. Before long she was getting regular solo engagements, along with other chamber music —her great love—and sometimes played in the Abbey Theatre for her friend Jack Larchet.

With three younger sisters—Bertha, Lilian, and Hilda—Marie formed the Dowse String Quartet. Ensembles like this were rare enough in those days; but a quartet of sisters must have been unique. At one lecture recital, on the Dublin violin-maker Thomas Perry, the quartet played on Perry instruments lent by the National Museum (they had been donated by Sir Francis Cruise). The work performed was a 'ballade' by the Dublin composer Harold White.

In 1912 the eminent pianist Fanny Davies was in Dublin, adjudicating at the Feis Ceoil. As a pupil of Clara Schumann, she gave a lecture recital and invited the sisters to join her in a performance of Schumann's Piano Quintet. (They had won the Bast Memorial Prize at the Feis that year.)

The quartet had to disband on the marriage of the two violinists. One went to India and the other to the north-west of Ireland. Marie's last memorable experience was to lead the orchestra for the first performance in Ireland of the Brahms Requiem, in Christ Church cathedral, conducted by Dr Charles Kitson.

After that, was her music to disappear? It took on a new lease of life instead, finding outlets in many ways. She was in demand for local concerts, and gypsy airs like Sarasate's Zigeunerweisen and Hubay's Hejre Kati were popular favourites, along with operatic fantasias—always a hit with Irish audiences. Country audiences loved the classical arrangements by August Wilhelmj, father of her own professor, Adolf. Encores would include Irish airs—arranged by Jack Larchet and Esposito—'The Coolin' and the reel 'The Wind That Shakes the Barley'. It was unsophisticated music-making, but it was live.

She conducted local choirs for Sligo Feis Ceoil, and performances of *Trial by Jury* (shades of her SMU youth). There were no longer any string quartets but the pleasure of other ensembles—piano quartets, duets, and trios—with her family. She never stopped adding new music to her repertoire. Her pupils at Portora Royal School included Vivian Mercier, the literary historian, and Terry (Walter) Beckett as a pianist.

She was once asked, 'I know you play the violin, but do you play music?' This, of course, meant the piano. And indeed she did: all music was a joy to her.

A final footnote: Thirty years after the St Louis fair and her American disappointment she met John McCormack once more. 'Tell me what it was like,' she asked. 'You were well out of it—they turned it into an "Oirish" fiasco,' was the reply. 'Lily and I walked out and came home. Your father was the wise man not to let you go.'

Intermezzo

JOAN TRIMBLE

Dublin in the early nineteen-thirties was still a Georgian city, filled with residential squares and streets, its centre adjacent to crowded lanes and decaying tenements. Trams crossed to and from Nelson's Pillar. Horses and cars mingled with bicycles. It was a familiar scene to us when my sister, Valerie, and I entered the RIAM together in 1931, as Coulson scholars for piano, violin, and cello. We were now to have regular music lessons for the first time—a new and exciting experience. We were fifteen and thirteen years old, respectively, at that time.

It was a warm welcome that greeted us on that first cold January morning. There was an open fire burning in the entrance hall—and a beaming smile from John Quinn, the Academy porter, who had known members of our family for just on thirty years. Everyone was very friendly, and we were made to feel at home.

The Academy itself we knew about from family tradition. It must have changed very little, if at all, from the days when our mother and ten of her brothers and sisters were pupils there. Eight of them were scholars and exhibitioners for violin, cello, piano, and organ. It was not surprising therefore that I already knew several of the professors who had been fellow-students and staff colleagues, including Dr Jack Larchet, his wife, Madeleine, Annie Lord, and Tom Weaving.

All our lessons had to be fitted in on those Saturdays. After harmony with Mr Weaving, followed by violin with Signor Ferruccio Grossi, I joined the orchestral rehearsal in the band room. We were really only a small body of string players, helped out by a single flautist, Mr Brown, who also played in the Gaiety orchestra, and Herbert South, organist of St Mary's, Donnybrook, who filled in the wind parts on the piano. The orchestra was led by a professor, Alice McCarthy, who played nightly in the Abbey Theatre with Dr Larchet's trio.

How competent we were I couldn't tell—never having heard a full orchestra 'live'. But ours was important in its own way, because Dublin had nothing else of the kind at that time, except for the short-lived Dublin Philharmonic Society, conducted by the army bandmaster, Col. Fritz Brase. There was only a piano quartet in the new radio station, 2RN. However, we rehearsed overtures and symphonic movements from Beethoven, Brahms, and Mendelssohn, swept along by Dr Larchet's enthusiasm. Above all, he encouraged us, and we needed that stimulus.

Our piano lessons ended the day's work. I regretted never having met Michele Esposito, whose spirit and reputation, as head piano professor for forty-six years, still seemed to be felt everywhere. Now that he was gone, musical Dublin had lost its dominant personality and the Academy its unofficial director. But I felt that I knew him—and his pupils were keeping his memory alive. There could have been no greater contrast than that between the volatile and legendary Italian, Esposito, and his successor, the equable and mild-mannered Englishman Claud Biggs. Where Esposito had played Beethoven's thirty-two sonatas in public shortly before his retirement, Biggs was known to have opened the BBC's famous 'Foundations of Music' series with all of Bach's forty-eight preludes and fugues. It was as a keyboard scholar and a fine performer that I was to learn so much from him.

What a contrast to my other piano professor, Annie Lord—perhaps the most talented of Esposito's pupils. It had been traditional since Esposito's day to have lessons from two piano professors, instead of one. This could cause problems at times, but I actually gained from the contrast. Annie Lord's great love for French music and her interest in the contemporary scene was a lasting influence on my own development. She could be terrifying—scathing in her reaction to what she considered careless work. But her wry sense of humour was never far away, and her lively mind would switch from art to literature and then back to music, as she described to me in vivid detail the conducting of Nikisch and Toscanini or the playing of Schnabel and Myra Hess.

Valerie achieved a nice balance between the intensity of Annie Lord and the stimulus of Rhona Clark. I was also fortunate to have some lessons from Rhona's teacher, Mrs Best (Edith Oldham). She had been Esposito's friend and colleague since the eighteen-eighties. Her influence on Dublin's artistic and musical world was far-reaching. Sadly, our association was short-lived, as she retired from the Academy in 1932.

The highlight of the RIAM year was the annual prize-winners' concert, held then in the Metropolitan Hall, Abbey Street. As president of the Academy, the Governor-General, James McNeill, accompanied by his wife and uniformed army aides-de-camp, would arrive to present the prizes. I remember it as an exciting occasion in which our orchestra played a prominent part. It was a real orchestra for these concerts, as wind players from the No. 1 Army Band joined us and made all the difference to the performances. We also accompanied some of the soloists who sang or played concerto movements and the Academy choir, conducted by Mr Weaving. Brahms, Haydn and Stanford were included in the choral items.

The programmes were long—surprisingly so—but nobody seemed to mind. The hall was always packed to the doors and the concerts reported at length in the Dublin papers. At our first prize-giving I was somewhat taken aback to find that all the string players (except the cellos) were expected to stand up while playing the national anthem. The wind players stayed in their seats! It was also traditional to wear emerald-green sashes with our white dresses, pinned diagonally over the left shoulder by the practised hand of the lady superintendent, Miss May Mageeney.

Before long there were changes. A new Free State government came into power in 1932, and the new Governor-General did not function as RIAM president. With the absence of James McNeill and his beautiful wife, Josephine, something of colour and ceremony also disappeared from the scene. No longer did we wear green sashes or drop curtseys to the President and his lady: we now shook hands with the Lord Mayor of Dublin, Councillor Alfie Byrne—a most popular figure. In my last year at the Academy the concert was given in the band room. There was no orchestra or choir; and the programme was a sensible length.

After two years of long weekly journeys from County Fermanagh I was able to stay in Dublin, having entered TCD as an arts undergraduate. This opened up my musical life at the Academy, as I could now join the SMU and take part in their activities. There was the joy of chamber music at last. String quartets were rare, but the ensemble included piano quartets, which I shared with Posie Shreider, Eileen Woods, and Myrrha Jephson. Our special guest nights were held regularly in the Aberdeen Hall of the Gresham Hotel and broadcast by Radio Éireann. At these events, friends and supporters of the Academy became familiar figures to me—personalities like Mrs Edith Boxwell and her great friend Mrs May Starkie, whose talented family had all been Academy students. They included Ida Starkie-O'Reilly, the cello professor, who taught my sister, and Dr Walter Starkie, distinguished both in literature and as a violinist.

The SMU members of those days who played on guest nights were a splendid lot of musicians, forming the core of Dublin musical life. The majority were past pupils. Instrumental players included Maud Aiken (Davin), Arthur Franks, and Annie Lord's three nieces, Nancie, May, and Una. There were singers like Dorothy Griffith, Patricia Black, Joseph O'Neill, and Patrick Kirwan. Pianists included Dina Copeman, Rhona Clark (Marshall), Madge Bradbury (Clotworthy), and Dr Annie Keelan. Dorothy Stokes, as secretary, always produced enjoyable programmes and played two-piano duets with Alice Yoakley, as did Havelock Nelson and Maureen Keegan, two of the youngest members.

Performers, committee and most of the guests wore full evening dress, making it a colourful affair. Dorothy also conducted the SMU string orchestra, in characteristic style. The press described the occasions and often sent photographers.

Twenty years after leaving Dublin, my sister and I returned to the Academy to give a two-piano recital at the end of a week's celebrations for the 1956 anniversary. In place of our old familiar band room, scene of so much music-making, there was now an enlarged and comfortable concert venue, thanks to T. S. C. Dagg, RIAM benefactor and vice-president. We met many old friends and had the added pleasure of sitting either side of Mr Dagg at the formal dinner in the organ room. It was an evening to be remembered, 'emphasising', as Charles Acton wrote in the *Irish Times*, 'the sociable side of music as a thread of grace and delight in the social fabric . . . What a pleasure it was to watch the large company in evening dress, mounting the grand staircase of this beautiful Georgian town house and dining amidst graceful eighteenth-century plasterwork in the light of scores of candles.'

That was forty years ago. Today, when so much of Dublin's historic fabric has changed, it's good to know the Academy is still in place, better than ever and still forward-looking.

8

The Composer in the Academy
(1) 1850–1940

Jeremy Dibble

Robert Stewart; T. R. G. Jozé; J. C. Culwick; C. V. Stanford;
Michele Esposito; Hamilton Harty; Arnold Bax;
E. J. Moeran; J. F. Larchet.

*I*t would not be an exaggeration to say that the socio-political conditions of nineteenth-century Ireland were barely conducive to the nurturing of musical composition. It is true that in many ways the lack of status of music as a cultural force largely reflected the general malaise in Britain. But at the same time Ireland, and particularly Dublin, was recovering from the upheavals of the Act of Union, which had deprived the country of an essential means of patronage and support.

London, on the other hand, was an economic centre that, with its beguiling powers of pecuniary advantage, was understandably seductive to Continental musicians. Dublin, while it maintained the ambience of a capital city, could not command the same prestige and was forced instead to rely principally on the enthusiasm of its 'professional aristocracy'—of physicians, university academics, lawyers, and clergymen—to promote music as an amateur pastime. Perhaps inevitably, those with compositional ambitions, most notably in secular music, chose to pursue much of their training and subsequent careers outside Ireland, either in England or on the Continent. The voluntary exile of Field, Balfe and Vincent Wallace bears this out, while others, such as George Osborne and Arthur O'Leary,[1] who both settled in London, under-line this tendency to seek an artistic environment more congenial to cre-ativity. Later the trend continued with the likes of Stanford, Charles Wood, Hamilton Harty, and Elizabeth Maconchy.

Those institutions in Ireland that could provide a modicum of musical education and opportunity for performance were essentially those of the establishment: the two metropolitan cathedrals of St Patrick's and Christ

Church, and, closely linked in aesthetic values and parameters, Trinity College. In mirroring Britain's predicament in the middle of the nineteenth century, the guardians of art music in Ireland were to be found in the Anglican church.[2] Ecclesiastical music was venerated as the highest and sublimest form of art, and this in turn was bolstered by the academic degree system, which, as at Oxford and Cambridge, promoted the Handelian, or latterly Mendelssohnian, cantata and oratorio as compositional paradigms to be emulated. This self-perpetuating system, by its very nature, existed therefore to nurture the church organist, who, within the province of secular music (where the lack of such things as a permanent orchestra was a powerful determinant), was naturally inclined to elevate choral genres such as the ode, cantata, part-song and glee over the symphony or quartet.

The inception of the Royal Irish Academy of Music in 1848, and its reorganisation in 1856, did much to focus nationally the importance of musical training within a secular setting. With its remit, however, 'to provide systematic instruction in instrumental music,'[3] the Academy's commitment to the teaching of composition was slow to develop. Indeed, 'creative' engagement with music was limited to the teaching of harmony, which was undertaken first by John Smith (1795–1861) and later by Robert Prescott Stewart (1825–1894) and Thomas Richard Gonzalvez Jozé. Of these three, Stewart was by far the most dynamic, although from surviving correspondence between himself and Sir Francis Brady (honorary secretary of the RIAM) it is clear that Stewart had reservations about his work. 'Harmony I don't care to teach, and I only engaged in it to accommodate you all, since few know and less care anything about it; however I decline to be shunted onto a harmony siding!' Brady responded: 'I am surprised to hear you condemn the study of Harmony. I would have expected you to be its warmest advocate.'[4]

Stewart's misgivings about the role and earnestness of harmony at the RIAM were nevertheless taken seriously, and a sub-committee was established on 17 April 1878, consisting of Stewart, Caracciolo, Jozé, Yeo, and Cree, 'to inquire into the present state of the harmony classes and report to the Council with a view to their encouragement and development.'[5]

Before he was twenty-seven years of age, Stewart occupied the three most prestigious ecclesiastical posts in Dublin, as organist of the Chapel Royal (Dublin Castle), Christ Church, and St Patrick's. In 1846 he succeeded Joseph Robinson as conductor of the University Choral Society, which he superintended for many years. As a recitalist he enjoyed a considerable reputation, and he was highly regarded as an educator. Indeed his influence, which was accentuated both by his position as professor of music at Trinity College and by his long career, was widely felt in Dublin. The testimonies of his friends Olinthus Vignoles and James Culwick, both of whom produced books about his life and work,[6] and the opinions of Stanford (his pupil) and Parry, bear witness to his achievements. Stanford spoke warmly of his teacher in his own autobiography, making particular reference to Stewart's powers of memory, knowledge of instrumentation, organ transcription, and abilities as a critic for the Dublin *Daily Express* (for which he provided an incisive account of the 1876 Bayreuth Festival),[7] though he bewailed the repressive environment of Dublin as a place in which Stewart could not flourish.

A little more dead-in-earnestness, and a greater grasp of the big things in life and art would have made Stewart an outstanding man. But his easy-going nature, and the sloppy laisser-faire atmosphere which surrounded him prevented his attainment of the highest place. It was hard, even for one gifted with so brilliant a brain, to live in a circle of half-baked musicians without being affected by their standard, and still harder to occupy a position in which he had no rival to excel or learn from. He left his mark however on the 'melancholy island', which was responsible both for his witty and versatile gifts and for the lack of opportunity to give value and effect to them.[8]

Parry, on receiving his honorary doctorate during the tercentenary celebrations at Trinity College, remarked how Stewart 'was evidently delighted with his own Ode, and appears to be thought quite a great man in Dublin.'[9]

As a composer, Stewart appears to have evinced a mixture of self-criticism and insecurity. Though leaving a modest list of works to posterity, he destroyed numerous others, including a symphony, two orchestral overtures, and a setting of Psalm 107 (his doctoral exercise). Among his most prominent surviving works are two cantatas, *A Winter Night's Wake* and *The Eve of St John*; the *Ode to Shakespeare*, written for the Birmingham Triennial Festival in 1870; and several *pièces d'occasion*, such as the Inaugural Ode for the Cork Exhibition of 1852, a fantasia for organ, orchestra and chorus on Irish airs for the Peace Festival in Boston (1872), and, perhaps of most musical interest, the Tercentenary Ode for Trinity College in 1892.

Stewart's music at its best suggests that he possessed a thorough understanding of the nineteenth-century harmonic apparatus, though his assimilation of later German developments was limited.[10] Indeed, though at times he has the ability to surprise—the opening chorus of his Tercentenary Ode ('The hallowed light the druid bore') contains several bold harmonic shifts —the governing stylistic conditions are generally those of Mendelssohn, Spohr, and S. S. Wesley. The Tercentenary Ode, as a deliberate 'commentary' on three hundred years of history, demonstrates his thorough grasp and knowledge of early music: the neo–Handelian bass solo ('The rugged chief in richer cell') is one such fine example, and the 'Symphony and Tenor Solo with Chorus' betrays his lifelong admiration for the seventeenth-century English school of Purcell, Croft, Wise, and Humfrey.

With so much of his time taken up with the provision of functional music, whether for church or choral society, Stewart had little time to come to terms with large-scale symphonic structures, and what he wrote in this genre appears to have been summarily destroyed through his own admission of weakness. Often he fell back on the 'doctoral' rubric of fugue and eight-part counterpoint, as exhibited in his *Cantate Domino et Deus Misereatur* for chorus and orchestra, and he invariably relied, as did so many of his organist contemporaries in Britain, on the dexterity of improvisatory technique.[11] In this he was S. S. Wesley's equal and was greatly admired by John Stainer; but this facility too readily rendered the content of his compositions sterile, directionless, and thematically indistinctive, which left only the cosmetic flair of colourful instrumentation. This was certainly Stanford's impression,[12] and one can adduce a similar perception from Parry's otherwise enthusiastic letter to the editor of Vignoles's biography.[13]

In many respects, Stewart's contemporary James Cooksey Culwick appears to have been a more accomplished composer. An Englishman by birth, Culwick settled in Ireland in the eighteen-sixties, where, after undertaking appointments as organist in Parsonstown (Birr) and Bray, he was elected organist and choirmaster of the Chapel Royal. In addition, he secured the position of professor of pianoforte and theory at Alexandra School and College. In recognition of his achievements, Trinity College conferred an honorary doctorate on him in 1893. Yet Culwick is little known as a composer and theoretician, in spite of his prolific and comparatively wide-ranging output.

A keen collector, he possessed at his house in Upper Mount Street an ample library of antiquarian works, including traditional music (conjectured to be the finest in Dublin), and this literary interest encouraged a steady production of papers for the RDS, the Church of Ireland Congress, the Incorporated Society of Musicians, the Musical Association, and various journals. His *Rudiments of Music* (1880; second edition 1882) was also widely used by students.

For Culwick, composition appears to have been as much a recreation as a compulsion, and a great deal of his work habitually took place during the summer vacations.[14] Besides the expected corpus of church music (much commended by Ouseley) and choral music (including the unpublished dramatic cantata *The Legend of Stauffenberg*, which brought his name to prominence in Dublin in May 1890), Culwick was notably productive in the province of orchestral and chamber music, though little of it was subsequently published. Perhaps most impressive is his Piano Quartet in E flat, op. 7, published by Breitkopf und Härtel and dedicated to the members of the Dublin Instrumental Music Club. The precedent for this work—Schumann's Piano Quartet, op. 44, in the same key—is obvious enough; but Culwick's essay demonstrates an assurance in the handling of the chamber idiom (in particular the lyrical 'Capriccio') that sets him apart from the traditional school of cathedral composers. Moreover, the work compares favourably with similar works by Parry, Stanford, and Mackenzie.[15] It is a pity that so much of Culwick's music, which included a concert overture, *Alice in Wonderland*, a suite for string orchestra, and a string quartet, was never published. Of his published works, most noteworthy besides the Piano Quartet are the Piano Suite and two organ sonatas,[16] the latter being modelled on those of Mendelssohn.

Stewart, Culwick, the Robinson brothers and Jozé dominated the musical scene in Dublin in the second half of the nineteenth century. As part of the loyal establishment, they duly reflected the unionist outlook of the city's professional classes. A prominent amateur member of this musical circle was the lawyer John Stanford (1810–1880). Indeed, as possibly one of the finest bass singers of his generation in Ireland, he sang many of the leading roles in oratorio performances in Dublin during the eighteen-forties and fifties and also sang some opera. Though he was forced to deny himself a musical career because of the puritanical objections of his family, he gave up much of his spare time to performance. Thereafter he channelled his passions into the setting up of the Academy of Music in 1848 and, most auspiciously, into the nurturing of his son's prodigious talents.

Charles Villiers Stanford (1852–1924) drew what he could from Dublin's musical life. His first harmony lessons were taken with Francis Robinson (brother of Joseph), violin lessons were pursued with R. M. Levey, and the piano with three different Moscheles pupils, Elizabeth Meeke, Henrietta Flynn, and Michael Quarry. However, the bulk of his formative training was undertaken by Stewart, which undoubtedly inculcated in Stanford a profound affinity for the Anglican church repertory. It was, after all, within Anglican church music—as organist of Trinity College, Cambridge—that Stanford found his first professional calling; but early on, fuelled by an indefatigable sense of ambition and self-belief, he was drawn to music of epic, monumental and dramatic forms, which lay beyond the bounds of what Dublin could offer. The seeds of this wider imagination, however stylistically inchoate, are evident in his early Rondo for Cello and Orchestra (written for Elsner), a Concert Overture (1870), and the incidental music for Longfellow's 'The Spanish Student' (1871), dedicated to Stewart. Together they demonstrate an ability that would have failed to flourish had he remained in Ireland. More to the point, as he embarked for England and Cambridge University in 1870, Stanford knew it himself.

Stanford's rise to eminence coincided almost providentially with the renaissance of musical interest and creativity in Britain in the eighteen-seventies. Though occasionally beset with disappointment, most notably with his second opera, *Savonarola* (1884), which resulted in (successful) litigation against the publisher, Boosey, his energy, single-mindedness, enterprise and ardour for public recognition continued inexorably. As organist and choirmaster at Trinity College, Cambridge (1873–1892), he raised the standard of the choir to a new level, which arguably rivalled that of Stainer's at St Paul's Cathedral, London. At the same time, he placed the Cambridge University Musical Society at the forefront of Britain's concert life in securing the first English performance of Brahms's First Symphony (March 1877) and, later, the participation of four Continental celebrities—Boïto, Bruch, Saint-Saëns, and Tchaikovsky—in the society's jubilee concert of 1893. In 1883, on the grounds of his achievements as conductor and composer, Grove appointed him professor of composition and conductor of the orchestra at the newly founded Royal College of Music.

At the RCM, Stanford was immensely successful as Britain's most eminent teacher of composition. The list of students who passed through his hands has become legend. One of his first students of composition was the Ulsterman Charles Wood, whom he did much to encourage both at the college and at Cambridge.[17] Stanford later recounted in some detail his recollections of the first intake of students at the college,[18] three of whom—Edith Oldham, Louisa Kellett, and Francis Bulkeley—were products of the RIAM. Edith Oldham (later Edith Best) was to become a close friend of George Grove, and in her he was frequently to confide his private thoughts about life at the RCM. Wood, a hard-working, co-operative colleague, is often mentioned;[19] Stanford, on the other hand, was subject to severe criticism.

> I came in from a very tiresome Board meeting at 11 last night where somehow the spirit of the d...l himself had been working in Stanford all the time—as it sometimes does, making him so nasty and quarrelsome and contradictious [sic] as no one but he can be! He is a most remarkably clever & able fellow full of resource and power—no doubt of that—but one has to purchase it often at a very dear price . . .[20]

Regrettably, Stanford possessed a short temper, an abrupt manner, and a quarrelsome temperament, which many found objectionable. Edith Oldham, who was busily active in the early planning stages of the Feis Ceoil, was one of many to experience the brusque side of Stanford's character and subsequently complained to Grove. 'I did not know how you felt towards Stanford before,' Grove replied.

> I am afraid the feeling is pretty general, someone said to me the other day that he was the most disliked man in England. He can be very disagreeable; but I have never yet seen that side of him towards myself. As to his music I cannot honestly say that I have ever cared for any of it. But on the other hand he is a very valuable member of College. His energy and vigour and resource are quite extraordinary. And above all he is so affectionate to me, and I am so fond of his wife . . . that I hope I shall never experience his rough side.[21]

In fact, Grove never fully trusted Stanford's irascible personality and was not favourably disposed towards the possibility of Stanford's appointments to either the professorship at Trinity College, Dublin (which went to Prout), or the directorship of the Royal College of Music (which went to Parry).[22]

Five years after his appointment at the RCM, Stanford was unanimously elected professor of music at the University of Cambridge. Such an academic accolade did not dampen his aspirations. The prestige of large-scale choral music drew him to the conductorships of the Bach Choir (1886–1902), the Leeds Philharmonic Society (1897–1909), and the Leeds Triennial Festival (1901–10), and he continued to direct the Orchestra of the Royal College of Music until after the First World War.

At Cambridge, his relationship with the university authorities was never more than cordial, but his radical reform in 1893 of the music degrees (particularly in establishing the condition of residence) was vital in elevating the subject to a level enjoyed by other disciplines. The changes proved controversial, as a somewhat acrimonious correspondence between Stanford and Frederick Bridge illustrated in the *Times* in 1898; but it did not prevent the like-minded Parry from attempting to introduce the same reforms at Oxford on his accession to the Heather professorship in 1900. Oxford subsequently refused to embrace the changes, which not only threw Stanford's sense of enterprise into relief (as well as Parry's bitter disappointment) but also prevented Oxford from modernising until after the war.

Stanford had clear, not to say dogmatic, views on matters to do with education, church music, and the role of government in the support of music. Perhaps his greatest disappointment was his failure to persuade both local and national government of the merits of a national opera based in London. This, Stanford believed with unswerving conviction, was crucial in popularising opera through the medium of English, as well as being a platform for indigenous composers and a means of employment for emerging native singers.[23]

Within the province of composition Stanford exercised his extraordinary fluency and versatility in all genres. Susceptible to the music of his Continental contemporaries—Brahms, Wagner, Verdi, Dvořák, Humperdinck, and Rachmaninov—his works can at times reveal a conspicuous stylistic opportunism. Nevertheless, his most assured works—the expansive choral essays (the Elegiac Ode, the Requiem, the Stabat Mater, and the Wellington Ode), the Fifth and Sixth Symphonies, the Irish Rhapsodies, the First Piano Concerto, the last two operas, *The Critic* and *The Travelling Companion*, and, arguably most original, his symphonic church music—exhibit the hand of a consummate craftsman. An ebullient if fractious personality, he never lacked the courage to put himself or his music forward, and this helped him to cultivate friendships and associations with the most prominent composers and performers in Europe.[24] This led not only to the successful staging of such events as the Cambridge Jubilee but also to the composition of works specially for celebrities such as Enrique Arbós, Leonard Borwick, Harold Bauer, Fanny Davies, Percy Grainger, Robert Haussmann, Fritz Kreisler, Alfredo Piatti, Moritz Rosenthal, and Frederick Thurston.

Stanford's intuitive compositional ability, evident early on in his career, proved a valuable tool as a teacher, even though his views hardened into intolerant conservatism as he grew older. At heart he was a classicist, inclining instinctively towards the intellectualism of Beethoven and Brahms, and it was this above all that he attempted to pass on to his pupils. As is evident from the censure in his primer *Musical Composition* (1911), there was no place in his output for programme music. For him, the nineteenth-century architectonic issues of absolute music were paramount; it is no accident, therefore, that he opted for the genres of symphony and rhapsody rather than symphonic poem.

In opera, Stanford was drawn in part, perhaps characteristically, to all the major nineteenth-century dramaturgical paradigms: to French grand opera (*The Veiled Prophet*), German music drama (*The Canterbury Pilgrims*), verismo (*Lorenza*), and *opéra comique* (*Shamus O'Brien*); but it was his predisposition to lyricism, the imperative of melodic content and his belief in the value of diatonicism that ultimately dictated his attitude to operatic structure. In this regard Stanford spent the best part of his creative life in the search not only for a satisfactory libretto (which largely eluded him) but also for an operatic style that could accommodate his natural lyric impulse. In the end, through an amalgam of techniques, he achieved this in *The Critic* (1916) and, debatably his masterpiece, *The Travelling Companion*, of which he only ever heard the overture.

In the mould of his establishment upbringing, Stanford, like Stewart before him, remained unwavering in his unionist convictions. In particular, he displayed that brand of Anglo-Irish patriotism espoused by the editors of the anti-liberal *Dublin University Magazine*, one that sought to challenge the monopoly of true patriotism claimed by nationalists and at the same time was not afraid of criticising the British government for its failure to understand the link between Ireland's prosperity and the role of its Protestant custodians.[25] As some of his pupils witnessed, he fiercely berated Gladstone's policy towards Ireland; and, as a series of letters to the *Times* reveals, he was a vociferous opponent of attempts to establish Home Rule before the outbreak of war. He became an earnest follower of Craig and Carson during the Ulster crisis of 1913–14 and was (according to Moeran)[26] a signatory to the Ulster Covenant. His support for Ulster unionism is also evident from the dedication of his Fourth Irish Rhapsody—'Dark and true and tender is the North'—and the belligerent song 'Ulster', written for the Union Defence League in 1913.[27]

Notwithstanding his hostility to change in the political status quo, Stanford was a proud Irishman with a deep love of his country and its culture, an attitude that evolved from the emerging antiquarian and cultural revival of his youth. Most influential was Petrie's founding of the Society for the Preservation and Publication of the Ancient Music of Ireland, which drew Stanford to the seminal collections of Bunting's *The Ancient Music of Ireland*, to Petrie's publication of the same name, and to P. W. Joyce's *Ancient Irish Music*. The variety and extent of Irish melody manifested in these collections chimed with Stanford's inherent lyrical instincts. His appropriation of the folk repertory for his own artistic ends was designed, essentially, to furnish his music with a sense of colour and character; added to which Stanford, forever aware of the possible commercial advantages, fully appreciated the widespread appeal of Irish music in Britain and on the Continent.

The fact that such regionally tinted music was already becoming popular in the concert hall was signalled by Mackenzie's two Scottish Rhapsodies, op. 21 and 24, of 1880. After the success of his first 'Irish' publication, the *Songs of Old Ireland* (1882), in collaboration with his lifelong friend and compatriot Alfred Perceval Graves, Stanford made continued use of folk material in all genres he confronted, whether in symphony, chamber music, opera, song-cycle, or the collections of arrangements he published (principally with Graves), including the editing of *The Complete Collection of Irish Music as Noted by George Petrie*, published under the auspices of the Irish Literary Society in London between 1902 and 1905. Much of this resulted in the wholesale quotation of actual melody, as in the last movement of the 'Irish' Symphony (1886) and in the later Irish Rhapsodies, though the assimilation of melodic types and contours is also detectable in his original thematic material. The opening cor anglais idea in the second movement of the Sixth Symphony is one of many such examples.

Stanford's engagement with traditional melody existed to serve his own cosmopolitan encounter with the Continental (and essentially Teutonic) aesthetic. In remaining deliberately apolitical, he directed the exotic element

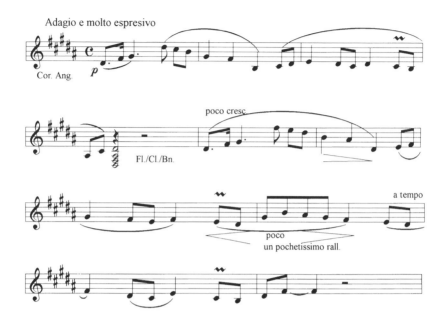

C. V. Stanford, Symphony No. 6, opening of second movement

of his Irishness at British and European audiences. *Shamus O'Brien*, a slick essay in the late nineteenth-century tradition of English operetta, replete with its once fashionable, though nowadays cloying, stage-Irishism, was a 'smash hit', receiving eighty-two performances in London in its first season alone, and toured the rest of Britain and Ireland until the end of 1897.[28] During that time it also received over fifty performances in the Broadway Theatre, New York, reflecting the appeal of Irish culture in the United States at the turn of the century. The same can be said of the Irish Rhapsodies, which enjoyed a vogue before the war, though, as mentioned above, the later excursions in that form came to symbolise an era whose end was imminent.

Stanford has often been accused of interacting with Ireland 'from the safe distance of the Savile Club.'[29] This may be true of the country's Catholic majority, about whom he knew relatively little, but it should not be confused with the common misapprehension that after his departure for Cambridge in 1870 he disengaged himself from Ireland completely. An only child, he lost his father in 1880 and in early 1892 lost his mother and two other close relatives. Shortly after this domestic cataclysm he would explain to F. J. H. Jenkinson, his Cambridge colleague:

I have been with my dear mother and saw the end at 6 o'clock this morning. Quite peaceful and gentle. Now all my links to the old country and blessed family are practically gone. You will be sorry for me. Three such losses in a fortnight.[30]

With little family to speak of, and with all his professional ties in England, there was no pretext to return to Dublin. Nevertheless, he did continue to take an interest in Ireland's musical affairs, principally through the agency of the Feis Ceoil, in which, according to its founder, Annie Patterson, he played a significant role as adviser.[31] He also took an active role as a vice-president (along with Charles Wood) of the Irish Folk-Song Society, founded in 1904. Moreover, Stanford's influence on art music in Ireland did not cease to be felt through his absence in England. As Patterson's regular articles for the *Weekly Irish Times* show, Stanford was very much perceived as a patriarchal figure in Irish musical circles, and in consequence his views and attitudes, particularly with regard to the folk repertory, were deemed axiomatic. Such a perception, in a growing age of national consciousness, was to encourage the part played by folk music (to the detriment of art music) in the formulation of a 'national' style. Indeed, as Harry White has pointed out,

> it was a habit of mind which grew independently of Stanford's own cultural assumptions and beliefs: indeed it served for long afterwards as the definitive arbiter of a work's being Irish in any meaningful way. The reliance on folk song was to prove acutely burdensome not only because it engendered a creative cul-de-sac (in terms of structural development), but also because it betokened the redundance of an art music thus circumscribed by literal representation of the indigenous repertory. And if the cult of nationalism which attached itself to that repertory was to have any address upon art music, it would only be in terms of repudiation on the grounds of irrelevance.[32]

By the eighteen-nineties, the arrangement and employment of Irish melody had become nothing short of a mannerism. Besides the central collections of Stanford there were those by Hoffman, Joseph Robinson, Stewart, Jozé, Culwick, and Charles Wood; and even Englishmen, such as Arthur Somervell, were to get on the band-wagon.

Other arrangements were to follow, though increasingly as part of the wider discourse of ideological nationalism. The Gaelic League, through Douglas Hyde's policy of de-Anglicisation, looked as far as it could to the precluding, or at least the tempering, of the European musical aesthetic, and in so doing sought only to advance traditional music as a cultural subordinate of the Irish language. This, so the League's proponents believed, would ensure the promotion of a genuine Irish culture. The league also sought to advance publications such as O'Brien Butler's *Seven Original Irish Melodies*, in which Irish was intended as the primary focus. Similarly, the league promoted operatic ventures—Butler's *Muirgheis* (1903) and O'Dwyer's *Eithne* (1909), composed specially for the Oireachtas—though both proved artistically unsuccessful. As Joseph Ryan has made clear in his article

'Nationalism and Irish Music', the consequences of equating linguistic and traditional musical components was, in turning one's back on the wider western heritage, to espouse parochialism.[33] Such a stance was deliberately taken by O'Brien Butler, Hardebeck, O'Dwyer, and Ó Gallchobhair.[34] Others recognised that—in taking the lead from Stanford—national music should find its home in art music; but, as White has explained,[35] the way ahead was uncertain. The policy of the Feis Ceoil found itself poised between those who wanted to adhere to more narrow nationalistic terms of reference (looking in part to the model of the Eisteddfod) and those, like Stanford, who wanted to see the festival promote the wider cause of music-making in Ireland. The outcome, thanks largely to the persistence of Michele Esposito, was for the broader spectrum and all that the RIAM represented, though this resulted in the withdrawal of support by the Gaelic League and the distancing of the National Literary Society.

Esposito's role in the development of Irish art music at this time is an important one. Compositionally he belonged to a group of stylistically eclectic Italian composers, including Giovanni Sgambati, Giuseppe Martucci, and Leone Sinigaglia, who more happily embraced a Teutonic aesthetic. Like both Sgambati and Martucci, Esposito was a fine pianist, with abilities as a composer and conductor. When he arrived at the RIAM in 1882 from Paris, he had already completed a substantial corpus of works, the majority of which were for piano. The presence, however, of an early symphony, op. 24 (1874), a piano concerto, op. 18 (1878), and two piano quartets, op. 12 and 17 (1877 and 1878), show that he possessed the technical capabilities for large-scale canvases.[36]

Esposito's musical voice in essence looks to Schumann, Chopin, and Liszt, though in later years he showed a willingness to embrace Wagnerian procedures in his operatic projects. His piano style, as John Wills has demonstrated,[37] shows a thorough assimilation of advanced keyboard technique and an assured handling of miniature forms, including the freer practices of fantasy and capriccio. Some of these works, such as the 'Tre Pezzi Caratteristici', op. 26, and the Impromptu in A flat, op. 6, merit revival; and it would certainly be instructive to hear his later Piano Concerto, op. 68, in the context of other lesser-known virtuoso concertos by Martucci, Scharwenka, Sauer, and Dohnanyi, not to mention those closer to home by Parry, Mackenzie, Stanford, and Hurlstone. Esposito's chamber works, which more fully show his interest in more discursive, intellectual musical argument (and for which he showed an increasing predilection, notably during the years 1898–1907), also earned some approbation from overseas.[38]

Between 1882 and 1897 Esposito composed nothing, as he devoted himself to the cause of piano teaching at the RIAM (which drew praise from external examiners such as Harty and Frederick Dawson) as well as to concert-giving in Dublin, principally in the form of the annual series of chamber concerts for the RDS. During this time, he began to establish himself as one of the most important and enterprising musicians, not only in Dublin but in Ireland, and it was undoubtedly through his personal magnetism that he was able to attract the likes of Arthur de Greef, Busoni, Backhaus,

Egon Petri, Fanny Davies, Leonard Borwick and Frederick Dawson to give recitals at the RDS. Esposito was himself a regular recitalist, and was frequently disposed to the production of unfamiliar seventeenth and eighteenth-century Italian keyboard repertory, including works by Pasquini and Scarlatti.[39] In pursuing this 'historical' dimension he continued the tradition established by Moscheles, Rubinstein, Ernst Pauer, and Dannreuther, who played an important role in the revival of early keyboard music. Esposito also played often with the Brodsky Quartet, whom he persuaded to give a complete Beethoven cycle, the first of its kind in Ireland; and his exploits as conductor of the Dublin Orchestral Society enabled the city to become acquainted with the symphonic works of Beethoven, Brahms, and Tchaikovsky.

As John Larchet intimated, Esposito settled in Dublin at a time when 'the old order [of Joseph Robinson, R. M. Levey and Stewart] was passing,' and after their deaths (Stewart in 1894, Robinson in 1898, and Levey in 1899) it fell to Esposito to assume the role of Ireland's most senior resident professional musician, a position recognised by the profile he received in the *Musical Times* in November 1903. Later, during the First World War, he was also to confirm himself as the pedagogical doyen of piano teaching in Ireland when he and Sir Stanley Cochrane established their own publishing company, CE [Cochrane Esposito] Publishers or CE Edition, in Dublin in 1915. To some extent Esposito achieved his aim (similar to that of the Associated Board) of publishing editions of the core piano repertoire at reasonable prices. However, it was not a successful enterprise financially, and it declined especially after the war, when Esposito returned to the concert platform. In June 1935 the company was taken over by Universal Music Agencies.

Esposito's creative energy seems to have been rekindled by the establishment of the Feis Ceoil. His cantata *Deirdre* was the prize-winning entry in its category at the inaugural Feis in 1897 and set a libretto by T. W. Rolleston based on the legend of the 'Slaying of the Sons of Usna'. In setting Rolleston's text, Esposito did not attempt to introduce folk material into the fabric of the cantata: rather, his work deploys a language drawn in part from Schumann and Liszt, as well as from the diatonic palette of late nineteenth-century English choral music. Part II of *Deirdre*, which makes use of a distinctive pastoral component, recalls the pentatonicism of the second part of Parry's *Job*, as does the 'lament' in part III.

Esposito's cantata was, however, to be a rare example of the composer's response to Irish subject matter, in which folk material was not a constituent part. In his output after 1897 there is a clear delineation between those works of a more classical nature (notably the piano music and concerted chamber works) and those that responded to Irish stimuli. The policy of the Feis Ceoil was to be particularly influential in this respect, for in 1901 the Feis committee announced that a prize would be offered in the 1902 festival for a symphony or suite based on traditional airs.[40] The successful entry was Esposito's Irish Symphony, op. 50. With the endorsement of the Feis, allied with Esposito's national cachet, this prescriptive approach to large-scale orchestral composition (which, if anything, considerably exaggerated the precedent of Stanford's 'Irish' Symphony) bolstered the view that a distinctive Irish voice in art music could only exist in conjunction with the folk repertory. Esposito's other 'Irish' works, written over the next twenty years—the *Irish Melodies*, op. 41, the narrative vocal suite *Roseen Dhu*, op. 49 (to texts by A. P. Graves), two Irish rhapsodies for violin and piano, op. 51 and 54, the 'Irish' Suite, op. 55, and *My Irish Sketch Book*, op. 71, for piano—intensified this perception. Similarly, his operetta *The Post Bag*, with a libretto by A. P. Graves, did much to consolidate the marriage of Irish tunes (on which the work is largely constructed) with Irish literature, a modus operandi sanctioned by the Irish Literary Society, under whose aegis the work received its first performance on 27 January 1902 at St George's Hall, London.

Perhaps only his one-act opera *The Tinker and the Fairy*, op. 53 (1903), with Hyde's bitter-sweet libretto, provided a more imaginative and challenging opportunity to fuse elements of folk material with a more overtly Wagnerian harmonic vocabulary. Esposito's opera, first performed in private in the garden of George Moore's house in 1905, is dramatically well constructed, making fertile use of the two main characters. The combination of simple, naïve, transparently diatonic thematic material with passages of more pathos—the Tinker's kissing of the Fairy invokes a Tristanesque move to B major (a most telling anagnorisis)—recalls the diversity of emotional levels in Humperdinck's *Hänsel und Gretel*, as does the inventive use of the orchestra in extended passages without the voices (notably the postlude).

The combined influence of Esposito and the Feis Ceoil was seminal to the formation of Hamilton Harty's compositional development at the turn of the century. In Esposito, Harty recognised a consummate technique and all-round experience that had not been available to him in Belfast. Although, on his own admission, he never became a regular pupil, Harty looked to Esposito as a mentor during the shaping of his early career.[41] 'Every work I wrote at that time was brought to him for his criticism and advice before ever it was produced. Everything he had learned during his own years of study at Naples, and afterwards as a concert pianist and conductor, was put freely and fully at my service.'[42] In addition, the Feis prizes provided Harty with an opportunity to secure good performances of his compositions, which he won annually between 1899 and 1904.[43] The culmination of these competition entries was his 'Irish' Symphony, which he conducted in Dublin on 18 May 1904, to great acclaim. The work conformed to an identical form of rubric (in accordance with the Feis committee's stipulation) as Esposito's symphony two years earlier, through its assemblage and arrangement of Irish airs within the characteristic movement types required of a nineteenth-century symphony.

The appeal of Harty's work appears not to have been generated purely by his (standard) deployment of Irish themes: rather it was the outstanding handling of orchestral forces that drew enthusiastic reviews from the *Irish Times* and the *Musical Times*.[44] Moreover, his fluent and rich harmonic resourcefulness demonstrated a broad and cosmopolitan eclecticism that lent his music a panache and freshness. At heart, he was conservative in his tastes, and throughout his composing career he showed, with single-mindedness, no desire to develop his musical language beyond the limits of late nineteenth-century romanticism. Like Stanford, Harty was prone to stylistic opportunism, and there are many instances where he drew freely, though unselfconsciously, on the rhetorical devices, developmental techniques and structural procedures of those he admired. His move to London in 1900 was crucial, not so much in amplifying his vocabulary but in affording him the greater opportunity of broadening his artistic horizons with regard to subject, unrestricted by Irish folk criteria. Moreover, in removing to England he recognised, with some regret, that Ireland could not offer him the employment or career that his talents as organist, accompanist, conductor or composer demanded.[45]

In London, Harty found himself within the lively maelstrom of British musical creativity. The pioneering Victorians Parry, Stanford and Mackenzie, having perhaps experienced their heyday in the eighteen-eighties and nineties, were nevertheless far from inactive in their production of large-scale works. Elgar was at the peak of his career; the individual voices of Delius and Grainger were being noticed; while the younger generation of composers emerging from both the RCM and the RAM—Coleridge-Taylor, Hurlstone, Vaughan Williams, Holst, Bridge, Ireland, and Bax—augured well for a promising future. In addition, London boasted as vigorous a concert life as any in Europe, and this infected the spirit of provincial music festivals in the rest of the country.

Harty was evidently swept along by the momentum of creativity, as can be judged from the quality of his larger works before the war. The *Comedy Overture* of 1906 and the Violin Concerto of 1908, with their employment of a more universal European language and assured structural handling, did much to enhance Harty's reputation as an orchestral composer, though it was the arresting Wagnerian potency of the extended 'Ode to a Nightingale' (1907), written for his wife, Agnes Nicholls, that made the deepest impression. In his setting of Keats's ode, lasting over twenty minutes, Harty demonstrated his powers of expansive melodic development, both of a lyrical and declamatory kind. The control of tonality within the episodic structure is impressive, as is the harnessing of chromatic and diatonic fluctuations, both of which create a powerfully emotional coherence at once comparable to the Wagnerian ruminations of Holst's *Sita* and *Savitri*. Harty did not rise to such a pitch of intensity again, though, like many of his British contemporaries,[46] he did find a heightened spiritual empathy with the poetry of Walt Whitman in three works: the fine song 'By the Bivouac's Fitful Flame' (1912), the choral ballad 'Come Up from the Fields' (1912), and, most substantially, 'The Mystic Trumpeter' (1913), composed for the Leeds Festival.

In his employment of a more universal musical language, Harty did not, however, turn his back on his Irish heritage. At the same time his more catholic stylistic outlook aided his attempts to conceive an Irish identity. In the unpublished 'Variations on a Dublin Air' (1912) for violin and orchestra he may have made allusion to his cultural background through the use of a

Hamilton Harty, 'The Children of Lir', wordless soprano solo

traditional air, but thereafter the choice of this material is incidental to the more compelling discipline of variation form, a genre that preoccupied many of his British contemporaries.[47]

However, the genre in which Harty was able to express his Irish affinities with the greatest success, and without the encumbrance of folk song quotation, was the programmatic symphonic poem. In his two essays, *With the Wild Geese* (1910) and the late *Children of Lir* (1938)—two works of great personality—he was able to exercise his considerable skill in thematic transformation (learnt from the example of Liszt, Tchaikovsky, and Wagner) and musical narrative. Moreover, the fertility of his symphonic treatment was enhanced by the contrivance of original material inspired by (but not drawn from) the traditional repertory. Both works are important landmarks in Irish orchestral music and stand out by the very distance their composer kept from the restrictive cultural discourse of nationalist ideology.

The exile of Stanford, Charles Wood and Harty underlines the fact that Britain benefited appreciably from Irish talent during its musical renaissance. Ireland, on the other hand, was too preoccupied with the metaphor and potency of its own literary revival to recognise art music as a significant element of the nation's cultural agenda. Indeed, poetry itself was seen to possess 'musical' properties in its own right, which for some, including Yeats, actually precluded music from consideration. As Bax recalled, Dublin at the

turn of the century was almost exclusively literary in its cultural preoccupations.

> In my early Dublin days I moved in an almost wholly literary circle.
> There was no talk of music whatever; indeed Æ never tired of relating
> in after time how I lived in the city for two or three winters before he
> discovered that I was a musician at all. Both Æ and W. B. Yeats were
> tone-deaf, though on one rare occasion the former expressed admiration
> for Tristan and Isolde (of all things!). Other than this the only comment
> upon music I heard from him was at an evening gathering in Rathgar
> Avenue when apropos of nothing in particular he suddenly remarked,
> 'There is a composer named Brahms. He aims at intense profundity,
> but all he achieves is an impenetrable fog!'[48]

Perhaps ironically, the richness of Irish poetry was, at the turn of the
century, to be most influential musically in England. After reading Yeats's
Wanderings of Oisin in 1902, Bax became possessed by the Celt within him,[49]
an obsession that resulted in an outpouring of literature under the pseudonym
Dermot O'Byrne and a substantial catalogue of 'Irish' tone poems. During the
First World War, Peter Warlock (who spent a year in Dublin between 1917
and 1918) was to be equally haunted by Yeats's symbolist collection of poems,
The Wind among the Reeds. Two highly original songs—'The Cloths of
Heaven'[50] and 'The Lover Mourns for the Loss of Love'—written under the
influence of Bernard van Dieren, date from this time and were part of the
preliminary sketches for his masterpiece, *The Curlew* (1922).

E. J. Moeran was also drawn to the work of James Joyce and Séamus
O'Sullivan,[51] but his strengths lay in the composition of instrumental
music. His Irish-inspired rhapsodic works from the early twenties enjoyed
a degree of popularity—Harty was especially fond of the First Rhapsody—
but in the thirties and forties Moeran's rigorous self-criticism led him to
the more abstract classical forms of the symphony and concerto, where he
produced his most imaginative and stylistically consistent work. Several of
these works, including the Symphony in G minor, the fine Violin Concerto,
and the Cello Concerto, were composed in Ireland. Two years after the
premiere of the Violin Concerto at the Proms on 8 July 1942 (with Arthur
Catterall) it was first given in Ireland, at Moeran's insistence, with Nancie
Lord (professor of violin and viola at the RIAM) at the Capitol Theatre,
Dublin, under Michael Bowles on 5 March 1944. Bowles also conducted
the world premiere of Moeran's Cello Concerto at the Capitol Theatre with
Peers Coetmore, Moeran's wife, on 25 November 1945.

With the establishment of the Irish Free State in 1922 and the realisation
of many nationalist ideological aspirations, it was perhaps inevitable, as White
has argued,[52] that attitudes to the composition of art music, and its relationship to an ever more culturally symbolic folk tradition, would harden. In line
with economic protectionism, there was a willingness among some musicians,
such as Hardebeck and Ó Gallchobhair, to adopt a similar cultural policy.[53]

There were, however, those with a more temperate outlook, who included
John Larchet. At the RIAM Larchet studied with Esposito and was greatly

influenced by his example, not least by his efforts to broaden the remit of the Feis Ceoil beyond the promotion of traditional music. This moderation characterised his approach to composition. Though greatly enthusiastic about Ireland's folk and literary traditions, one emphasised by his appointment as musical director of the Abbey Theatre (1907–34), Larchet hoped to infuse in new generations of composers a leaner sense of classicism imbued with folk colour. 'The aim', he declared, 'has been to encourage students to adapt the native musical idiom to modern harmonic development and thus create a school of composers which would be truly evocative of the Irish spirit.'[54]

As a teacher at the RIAM and UCD, Larchet's influence (and longevity) touched large numbers of aspiring young composers. First and foremost, he was a facilitator. He drew admiration from Bax for his work at the Abbey Theatre,[55] and he showed vision and tenacity in his efforts during the twenties to promote musical training for teachers at University College, Dublin, in order to tackle the infrastructural lacuna in the schools. Furthermore, as president of the Music Association of Ireland he did much to set the musical profession on a firm footing. Although Larchet may have adopted a less hard-line view of the role of European music in Irish culture, this is not evident from his creative output, which, like his contemporaries, reflects the familiar national preoccupation with native material. W. H. Grattan Flood may have detected some promise in the polished arrangements of traditional airs and dances,[56] but Larchet's talents ended up being tailored to the inter-war context of Ireland's national consciousness, in which music remained a conservative province.[57]

This conservatism was thrown into even greater relief by the conscious disregard of the indigenous idiom by Brian Boydell and Frederick May, who preferred to look to the potential of Continental techniques to fertilise their musical languages and, in so doing, in effect isolated themselves from an audience unsympathetic to their artistic aims. May was particularly candid in his assessment of Ireland's shortcomings in his essay 'The Composer in Ireland' for Fleischmann's symposium *Music in Ireland*. Besides the imperatives of a national concert hall, an established music publishing firm and, more radically, the integration (by legislation) of the various musical institutions, which in his view dissipated resources, into a national academy of music, May challenged the long-held shibboleth of the composer's mission in Ireland.

> Musical criticism must be creative and not destructive, and one of the most destructive and useless types of criticism is that which starts out from an unwarrantable premise, such as that all good music must be demonstrably national in feeling, and then proceeds to chain down the unfortunate composer on this ready-made bed of Procrustes. This is one likely way by which the bad may be exalted and the good abased, for there is no such infallible yardstick by which we may determine what is truly of permanent value. On the contrary, we must receive all-comers in a spirit of receptive enquiry, and only examine their credentials to the extent of asking if they have acquired the requisite technique to realise fully the expression of their ideas.[58]

As a fervent advocate of cosmopolitanism, May continued to pursue more universal artistic objectives throughout his creative life, at a time when Ireland preferred to look inwards; he also hoped to ignite belief in the search for an individual style, free from the constraints of outdated national stereotypes. In his music he attempted to be consistent with this idea, and several of his works, the fine String Quartet in C minor, the Spring Nocturne and the Symphonic Ballad (composed in the nineteen-thirties), not to mention the later, emotionally powerful Songs from Prison, demonstrate a stylistic vision well beyond those of other Irish composers of the inter-war period.

STRING QUARTET in C minor

Note: All accidentals hold good throughout each bar as the music is nearly atonal in places.

Frederick May, String Quartet in C minor, first movement

(2) 1940–1990

AXEL KLEIN

J. F. Larchet; Frederick May; Brian Boydell;
Walter Beckett; Joan Trimble; A. J. Potter; Aloys Fleischmann;
Gerard Victory; Seán Ó Riada; James Wilson.

The art of interpretation is a tremendous task. In art music in particular—
an art form that hardly exists without it—interpretation is vital in communicating between artists and audience. So, as with theatre, music needs
two kinds of artists. The interpreting artists are the musicians, for whom
the RIAM ideally caters. But where would these artists be without those
whose works they interpret—the composer? The creative input, speaking in
modern terms, is the source for the creative output, the music we hear and
play. But whereas the musician would be unemployed without the composer,
the composer would starve without the musician. A healthy dependence is
one in which both work together, and new music arises with new generations
of musicians. That is why the RIAM has always had close relations with
the creative part of music.

Composers have been employed by the Academy as well as originating
from it. A look into the biographies of many Irish composers of the nineteenth and twentieth centuries confirms this. From Joseph Robinson via
Michele Esposito and John F. Larchet to Walter Beckett and James Wilson,
there is a tradition of learning that is an integral part of the story of music in
Ireland. Even if every Irish composer of note had expanded their knowledge
and widened their horizons by studying elsewhere, possibly outside Ireland,
there is no debating the fundamental role of the RIAM in laying down the
basics for an individual voice. After this has been established, it is up to the
former pupil to develop it further or to treat music as an irrelevance.

Other chapters in this book have dealt with major personalities teaching
harmony, counterpoint or composition during the first half of the Academy's
history. But what was the impact of their musical children and grandchildren? Did they leave their mark on the Irish musical landscape or,
perhaps, beyond? Are they aware of their musical heritage, and do they
show it in their work? Or has the education in a universal language resulted
in an equally universal music? Is either better than the other, or more
desirable? These are just some of the questions I would like to touch on
here, without attempting to present a definite answer.

John Francis Larchet is in many respects the bridge between the nineteenth and twentieth centuries, between the first and second halves of the Academy's history. Born just a few years before Esposito began teaching in Ireland, he was a close friend and colleague as well as his successor at the Academy. So whereas 'Spotty' (as Esposito was lovingly called) brought the central European romantic tradition to Ireland, it was Larchet who embedded this idiom into the Irish context. Thereby he was allowing a music to originate that, although too late for the progressions in musical history, was a hitherto unheard sound in Europe. The happy wedding of traditional Irish tunes and dance rhythms with the sound of the modern symphony orchestra produced some fine music in its own right, fully aware of its timeliness. Works like Larchet's *Lament for Youth* (1939) and *By the Waters of Moyle* (1957) radiate an air of nostalgia not reached by composers such as Stanford and Harty, though they are often put into the same category. Larchet's song compositions too are an important part of this genre's Irish repertoire. 'Pádraig the Fiddler' (1919) and 'An Ardglass Boat Song' (1920) picked up elements from the folk as well as from the classical tradition and thereby established a unique musical voice at the dawning of Irish independence. And was it not Larchet who, in the fifties, asked when the great Irish composer for whom 'we all are waiting' will come? Perhaps through this question there sounds a note of awareness that he himself might have been the one, if he had been born earlier and if he had had fewer administrative duties. So nostalgia, the feeling for a time missed, remained as an artistic possibility, and Larchet took it and performed in it admirably.

It was the task of Larchet's pupils to take the next step. Now that classical romanticism had reached Ireland, there was no doubt that further development had to look out for a contemporary idiom. Few of his students in the basics of composition followed in his creative footsteps. However, as easily as differences can be detected, as quickly do the composers concerned applaud Larchet for his teaching. I have never heard one negative word about Larchet from any of his pupils. Of course they were critical, and he would be a bad teacher who would not teach them to be critical. But Larchet never left his pupils in doubt that the art of music embraced more (and newer) styles than his own. So, whereas every composer whose work I am going to discuss gained foreign experience in the course of his life, nobody would criticise Larchet for his neglect of modern music. As I have pointed out elsewhere,[59] the composers appreciated the immense value of Larchet's teaching in technical respects, acknowledging that Ireland's musical development at this stage could not provide for the central European avant-garde. So it is not by accident that all composers I am going to turn my attention to are pupils of Larchet and that it is impossible to include the many composers of note who sprang from the Academy since the late nineteen-sixties. The contribution to Irish music by many of the latter will be so much added to in the future that any advance comment at this stage would be too early.

One who strove for the European avant-garde, or who was at least fascinated by it intellectually, was Frederick May (1911–1985). He was the leading voice of Irish music in the thirties and early forties, until ill-health limited his creative output. May enrolled at the Academy at the early age of twelve and stayed until 1929, studying the piano and harmony and counterpoint with Larchet. His happily smiling boy's face decorated several prizewinners' posters for the Feis Ceoil, which compare sadly with the wrinkled and worried face of his later years, which he spent largely in hospitals. The story these pictures tell are impossible to convey here, and it must suffice to say that one of Ireland's greatest talents vanished when he eventually had to lay composition aside in 1955.

After his early education at the Academy, Frederick May went to study at the RCM, where his teachers were Gordon Jacob at the piano and Ralph Vaughan Williams in composition. May was, after Ina Boyle (1889–1967), one of the first Irish composers to be influenced by the Vaughan Williams school of thought. Certainly I think this influence was stronger than his other major influence, the later study with Egon Wellesz in Vienna. The Vaughan Williams influence I would like to describe as a more or less direct 'rubbing-off' of the teacher's style, a late romantic idiom with overtones of folk melody, occasionally tinged with modal harmony. One may argue my point, since May's most important works, such as the String Quartet in C minor (1936) and the Songs from Prison (1941), to words by the exiled German poet Ernst Toller (who died in New York in 1939 by his own hand), lead away from this very clearly. But since May's work of the early thirties reflects the great Englishman's style, and he later returns to it in the works of the fifties, I am not convinced that those more serious works really represent his deepest musical beliefs. I can even hear a traditional influence in parts of the String Quartet, a work widely regarded as his most international one in character. The first motif of the third movement, for instance, with its multiple variants in the course of the piece, is a clear reference to his Irish heritage:

Lento espressivo

Of course such references are much more overt in the Scherzo for orchestra (1933), his first orchestral work composed in London. This single-movement piece was his first success in Britain, and turned some critics' eyes towards the young Irishman. British, or rather Vaughan Williams-like, pastoralism returns in many pieces by May throughout his creative life. The most depressing parts of the Songs from Prison are relieved by such musical events, for instance at the point where the prisoner gains hope from watching a couple of swallows outside the prison building their nest. Here he takes up phrases from an earlier work, the Spring Nocturne (1938). This again demonstrates that May at no phase of his life was very far from pastoralism, although this influence was undoubtedly hidden for some years.

May attempted to study in Vienna with Alban Berg, the Austrian twelve-note composer, who indeed accepted him as his pupil. However, Berg was already too ill when May arrived in 1935 and died a year later. When looking back on his creative life in later years, May found that this was only the first of many ill-fated attempts to gain acknowledgment as a composer, interpreting his tinnitus and increasing deafness, as well as his desperate journalistic fight for a national concert hall and other things troubling him, as an indication that life did not favour him.

May's achievement in an Ireland just overcoming the aftermath of the Civil War cannot be overestimated. Together with Aloys Fleischmann and Brian Boydell he belonged to a group of composers believing in a future of composition in Ireland that would be oriented towards modern developments in Britain and on the Continent. During the thirties a debate was going on among composers in Ireland about the question of where the much-desired 'great Irish composer' should come from—from looking back to the past for models in the folk tradition, or from looking towards contemporary movements elsewhere.[60] As we know today, it was the latter group who succeeded and who spearheaded musical modernism in Ireland during a particularly difficult time, when the state for a while believed that 'classical' music was a Victorian art form on the verge of extinction and therefore not supportable.[61]

In particular, with his String Quartet in C minor, May succeeded in a style that—leaving aside Britain, which at that time had no equivalent idiom—made Ireland a member of contemporary aesthetic movements in Europe. Comparable in idiom to the middle quartets of Bartók, it is an immense achievement, reflecting the experiences of his foreign study, the deep impressions of Nazi Austria, the discovery of his growing deafness, and, as I have pointed out above, a glimpse of his Irish home, perhaps nothing but a passing shadow of memory. It would need more space to detect all this in actual notes in his music; but surely the desperate energy and the harsh discords, especially in the first two movements, and the glowing desire for peace, which eventually comes in the form of a quiet C sharp major chord at the end, are expressions of these experiences. Many other instances could be found throughout the piece.

The fact that this composition of 1936 was not performed in Ireland until January 1949 says much about the state of Irish musical life and the level of interest of Irish musicians in the creative voice of their compatriots during these years. Brian Boydell (born 1917), a good friend and sympathiser of May's, may have taken the Irish premiere of the quartet as a stimulus to write one himself. His String Quartet No. 1 (1949), in any event, is another milestone in Irish composition, which he had well prepared through earlier works in many genres. He too had been studying at the RCM (1938–39), where his composition teachers included Herbert Howells and Patrick Hadley. It is interesting that in Boydell's case the period at the RIAM came *after* the foreign stay. He studied with Larchet from 1940 to 1942. This may be attributed to his relatively late decision to devote his time mainly to composition, as Boydell already had a first-class degree in natural sciences from the University of Cambridge.

Many of Boydell's best-known works originated from another period at the Academy, namely his time as professor of singing, from 1944 to 1952. Pieces such as his Five Joyce Songs (1946), In Memoriam Mahatma Gandhi for orchestra (1948) and the String Quartet No. 1 were written during this time, which was therefore a particularly fruitful stage of his life. It was also the time during which he refined his technique of writing with a scale based on alternating tones and semi-tones, after discovering that he had already been using it more or less unconsciously. This scale, although known in musicology for a longer time, was lately termed 'octatonic'. It requires nine steps to reach the octave and maintains a comprehensibility without currying favour with sweetish tonality.

With this technique Boydell reached a modern idiom very much along the lines of contemporary western music.[62] Although in later years he found himself at a loss with regard to avant-garde 'plinkety-plonk' music,[63] in the perspective of the late twentieth century his music appears in a different light. I was astonished recently to hear a Boydell-like piece on German radio, only to hear the announcer say at the end that it was a piece by Karl Amadeus Hartmann, another composer who was just recently rediscovered and whose qualities were quite out of fashion as long as the Darmstadt or IRCAM doctrine dominated musical acceptance of what was modern. With the recent rediscovery of Hartmann, Goldschmidt, Frankel and Korngold, and the new attention given to Scandinavian composers such as Petterson and Rangström, we are slowly beginning to realise that, parallel to the Schoenberg-Webern-Boulez-Stockhausen line, other contemporary music existed that was not based on mechanical systems. Had this music been more listened to, and more critically acclaimed at the time it was written, perhaps the public would not have these problems with modern music that it has today.

So in my mind the music of Brian Boydell is, for its time, just as modern as it is sincere. Boydell remained 'in tune' with his style right up to the present, refining his music rather than changing it. At the same time his music appeals very much to European ears, reflecting his stylistic orientation and interests. The fact that by the end of the forties an Irish composer could be more moved by the death of an Indian pacifist than by the breaking of the last link with the British Commonwealth is a progressive example of today's cosmopolitan attitudes. His most 'Irish' work, the Violin Concerto (1953–54), is an exception and, as such, is much too often talked about. It is very much worth discussion, though, when it comes to the question of an Irish school of composition. Does such a thing exist? In what form? Can it be called a school? May, Fleischmann and Boydell show how very subtle this 'school' appears. One can glimpse it through some lines of May's String Quartet, and one can hear the melisma in Boydell's Violin Concerto, both rather exceptional works, seen from the stylistic view and from the public success they enjoy. Now if this is a school it needs a teacher, and an address. Perhaps it was Larchet at 36 Westland Row.

Other creative musicians followed more closely in Larchet's footsteps, traces of which can be found in the early *œuvre* of Walter Beckett (1914–1996). He studied at the Academy with George Hewson (organ) and John F. Larchet and received his piano teacher's diploma as early as 1934. In 1942 he gained his MusD by way of a composition at Trinity College. Beckett lived outside Ireland from 1946 to 1972, a long time, during which his music was hardly heard in Ireland, especially after about 1950. He virtually stopped composing seriously for about twenty years after 1960 and concentrated on teaching piano, writing music reviews, and being active as a musicologist. He wrote a book on Franz Liszt and contributed to the last volumes of the German encyclopaedia *Die Musik in Geschichte und Gegenwart* in the seventies. After he returned to Ireland in 1972 he began teaching harmony and counterpoint at the Academy, becoming full-time professor in 1974. He is also the author of a *First Harmony Course* (1975). Ill-health brought an end to his career in 1984.

Beckett's music before and after his years in Venice and Coventry is worlds apart. His many folk song arrangements permeated even much of his original works, such as his half-hour Suite for Orchestra (1945) or the Four Higgins Songs (1946). He composed a few more pieces in this direction until 1960, when he must have noticed that the public demand for this kind of music was small, and new generations of composers appeared. So his late masterwork, the Quartet for Strings from 1980— interestingly, another remarkable Irish piece in this genre—comes as something of a surprise. This work stands out even among his other late compositions, among which there is an Occasional Voluntary (1985) for organ and his largest piece, the Dublin Symphony (1989) for narrator, chamber choir, and large orchestra. Thankfully, a commercial CD recording of the quartet is available, so that any interested reader can make their own picture.[64] It seems as though Beckett's international experience made him turn away from traditional music as a source of creative ideas, because this is a truly international piece stylistically. It is beautiful music in its own right, but it comes seventy years too late to be considered 'modern'.

Apart from this reservation, the music is very well wrought and unashamedly romantic, without being kitschy in any sense.

So while Walter Beckett's late works do not apply any 'Irishisms', his earlier works surely do and thus constitute a part of what I am hesitantly calling an Irish school of composition.

With other composers, also associated with the Academy, one is on more certain ground. A prominent example is Joan Trimble (born 1915), equally known as composer and pianist, although at the Academy she studied piano and violin (1932–36). Unfortunately she did not compose much after the forties, with notable exceptions, such as the first BBC television opera, *Blind Raftery* (1957), and a very fine piece for wind quintet, the Three Diversions (1990). One of the reasons for Trimble's laying composition aside was the notion that her music did not fit any more in the contemporary musical language, which she used to perform in the piano duet with her sister Valerie. Her music between 1938 and 1949, which comprises some songs, piano duos such as the Sonatina (1940), and the song cycle *The County Mayo* (1949) for baritone and two pianos, reveals a most interesting facet of this Irish school. This music reflects her Irish heritage as much as elements of French impressionism. While the first may be attributed in parts to Larchet, the latter certainly is attributable to her piano teacher at the Academy, Annie Lord.

Another composer with obvious references to Irish traditional music (and to the Academy) was Havelock Nelson (1917–1996), a composer much better known for his many activities as pianist and conductor than for his rather conservative, if entertaining, original music.

One cannot write about the Academy, Irish composers, Irish music and originality without turning one's attention to A. J. Potter (1918–1980). Potter was born in Belfast and, like May, Boydell, and Trimble, was a student at the RCM, where he studied with Vaughan Williams from 1936 to 1938. After periods in east Asia and west Africa during and after the Second World War, he returned to Ireland in the late forties, and became one of the most influential teachers at the Academy. He first succeeded Boydell as professor of singing in 1953 and from 1955 to 1972 taught harmony, counterpoint and composition in succession to Larchet.

Potter remains known to many people as the composer who wrote probably the most entertaining Irish music of the fifties and sixties. For a while his name was virtually synonymous with the Radio Éireann Light Orchestra, for which he wrote unforgettable pieces like the *Overture to a Kitchen Comedy* (1950), the Variations on a Popular Tune (1955), and the Concertino Benino (1967) for trumpet and orchestra. As entertaining and as 'light' as these pieces may be, they never lose two distinct qualities that make them rise high above pure popular music. Firstly, they are perfectly shaped from the point of view of musical craftsmanship, and, secondly, they very often conceal a more serious side of the composer. This side sometimes peeps through the technical aspects of the music: for instance, who would notice from a hearing of the Variations that this is in fact the first Irish piece of music based on a twelve-note row? Sometimes the more serious side of Potter is very evident in moving pieces like the Concerto da Chiesa (1952) or the *Sinfonia de Profundis* (1969). Although again in his Sinfonia he uses twelve-note techniques, his music remains accessible to such a degree that one might doubt the dodecaphonic construction.

So with Potter there is a composer with hardly a European precedent. He picks up a technique that elsewhere has led to the most serious estrangement between music and the public, and achieves quite the contrary. Potter is thus the most outstanding example of a phenomenon in twentieth-century Irish music that includes a number of composers with a very eclectic list of works. I would like to mention Aloys Fleischmann (1910–1992), Gerard Victory (1921–1995) and Seán Ó Riada (1931–1971) among this group, composers who are predestined to misinterpretation and misunderstanding by anyone hearing a single piece.

Fleischmann, a former fellow of the Academy, is sometimes not even counted among the great names in early twentieth-century Irish music. This is surely due to the fact that throughout his life he wrote a very understandable music, trying unsuccessfully to bridge the gap between the taste of the well-meaning friend of 'light' classical music and that of the more discerning listener. I would advise the latter to listen to some of the small-scale music he wrote, and could single out many pieces that show a very different side of the composer who wrote orchestral choral music with audience participation.

Eclecticism is a characteristic often attributed to Gerard Victory, another former fellow of the Academy, whose outspoken desire to entertain produced many lovable works that had nothing in common with contemporary music. Friends of this music reacted quite disconcertedly to his very different other side.

And Ó Riada—what Irish composer could combine more misunderstandings in one person than he? If one thing is certain it is that his contribution to classical music in Ireland was much more limited than is usually assumed.

With these composers—and I am taking Potter as a representative example—it is difficult to understand the person from a group of works. Instead, one would have to divide their works into different groups, some written for a large audience, some for a small public audience, some even for a private audience, and perhaps some written for the composer's own taste and pretensions. If several historical eras and attitudes in music can be found in the *œuvre* of a single person, the documentation of contemporary history becomes difficult. It means that if I am asked about the importance of an Irish composer in a specific context, I must single out what I believe the composer would have replied, bearing in mind that the answer would be different if the question were asked in another context.

Why is this so? Pioneers like May, Fleischmann, Boydell and, ten years later, Potter had to 'educate' audiences to classical and modern classical music at the same time. This is a country where many people still think there is no indigenous musical history, and few composers worth hearing and playing. This was never true, but never less so than in the twentieth century. I believe that, quite apart from the sincere wish to entertain, there is an element of education in many works of the group of composers mentioned above, and this is a rare particularity of the Irish musical scene from the fifties to the seventies and sometimes beyond. But one should never condemn a composer who wrote 'educative' music as a pure 'educator'. This again conceals many other sides.

An educator in a different sense is James Wilson (born 1922). He was born in London and has been living in Ireland since 1948. As colleague and successor to Potter at the Academy from 1969 to 1980 and as co-founder of the Ennis Summer School of Composition in 1983 he is probably the most influential teacher of composition in Ireland in the second half of the twentieth century. With Wilson the teaching of composition in Ireland became fundamentally different. With the passing of time the importance of traditional music in the teaching of 'serious' music has diminished. And as an Englishman this reference had little meaning in Wilson's teaching at the Academy. He has a deep interest in Irish culture, but this has never permeated his musical thinking. So if he is setting to music a poem by Yeats it will sound very different from Larchet's and Trimble's, and also from Boydell's similar settings.

Nevertheless, Wilson is just as much an eclecticist as Potter. He has written in very simple, tonal styles, such as in his early success in Ireland, the opera *Twelfth Night* (1969), but at the same time he has written music using complex rhythms (Capricci, 1969) and harsh discords (Carrion Comfort, 1966). Moreover, he is a most prolific composer of stage music, including eight operas. The first of these, a children's opera after Lewis Carroll called *The Hunting of the Snark* (1963), received its first performance in January 1965 at the RIAM.

Wilson's music is very difficult to categorise; few names spring to mind when hearing his music. I sometimes like to think he could have become Ireland's Benjamin Britten, if Irish audiences were as receptive to modern music as those of other countries. So, although his music features on concert platforms very often, his impact as a teacher seems larger than as a composer. The way he copes with disappointment in the face of small audiences in his adopted country, and thereby continues to write music of the highest quality, such as in his viola concerto Menorah (1989) or the Concertino (1992), is impressive and admirable. It is to be hoped that through the medium of CD recordings the music of Wilson[65] (and, of course, other Irish composers) will eventually find the recognition that it could not yet gain in Ireland. For much has already been achieved in Irish music; but the majority of people interested in music still have to be led to their composers and forget that it is not the task of music to 'cater and comfort' in daily life.[66]

Today, we have pop music and 'folk' music to cater for different tastes; classical music lovers can turn to the romantic era and sweep the harsh present times under the carpet; and even symphonic shamrock music, like the Shaun Davey and Bill Whelan productions, has a following for a most outdated form of expression, often misunderstood as new Irish classical composition. The wish to raise standards of musical appreciation, so much desired by Larchet and others, is still felt today, and its necessity was never as urgent as now. The place of education and therefore the role of the RIAM cannot be overestimated. Irish composers have done their share. Now it is up to their interpreters.

Intermezzo

Michele Esposito

John F. Larchet

Broadcast on Radio Éireann, September 1955

It is my pleasure and privilege to speak tonight about one of the greatest musical personalities that ever lived in this country. The occasion is the centenary of the birth of Michele Esposito, an Italian pianist, teacher, conductor, composer, and authority on classical music, who came to Dublin in 1882 as a young man and who lived here without a break for forty-seven [in fact forty-six] years. These were years of the greatest activity devoted to the development of his own great musical talents and to the fostering of a love for good music in the Irish people.

Esposito was born in Castellammare, near Naples, on 29 September 1855. As a boy he obtained in public competition a scholarship to the Naples Conservatoire. He studied the pianoforte with Beniamino Cesi, a distinguished concert player and teacher of that time. Later he studied composition with Serrao. At the end of a brilliant scholastic career he left for Paris in 1878, bringing with him the highest testimonials from his professors and the director of the Conservatoire.

In Paris he began his career as a concert pianist and teacher. It was here that he first met Camille Saint-Saëns, who was one of the most famous composers of the time and a colossal influence in the musical life of France. He used to tell an amusing story about this first meeting. Musical Europe was then in a turmoil about the music and personality of Richard Wagner and bitterly divided into Wagnerites and anti-Wagnerites. When Esposito called on Saint-Saëns with a letter of introduction from the director of the Naples Conservatoire he was received rather coldly and was left standing while the letter was being read. Saint-Saëns then addressed him with the question, 'Are you a Wagnerite?' 'No,' was the reply. Thereupon Saint-Saëns said, 'Very good, sit down,' and, shaking Esposito warmly by the hand, struck up a pleasant conversation.

Saint-Saëns gave him a piece of advice which Esposito acted upon, and it was fortunate for Dublin that he did so. The advice was: 'If you wish to make a name in Paris as a concert performer you must first make a name outside it.' It is highly probable that this was the reason for Esposito's decision to come to Dublin to take up a temporary position teaching piano to boys at the RIAM as deputy for Signor Caracciolo, who had been granted leave of absence. [As we now know, Larchet was mistaken in this respect: see above, p. 195.] A few months later Caracciolo resigned, and Esposito was appointed senior professor of pianoforte at the Academy.

He arrived at the right moment, for at that time a very important era in the history of music in Dublin was drawing to a close. With the waning powers of Joseph Robinson, R. M. Levey, and Sir Robert Stewart, the old order was passing. In the most natural way the responsibilities of the future development of music in Dublin were placed and centred in Esposito. From the moment he decided to remain in Dublin his genius made itself felt, and almost at once he became the herald and leader of a new era in our musical history. His upright character and forceful personality dominated the entire musical scene in Dublin and eventually throughout the whole country until his death in 1929. So great a musician was Esposito, his passing closed another era, and his death was a staggering blow from which we have not yet recovered.

This new era, which we may term the Esposito era, brought with it developments that were progressive and entirely new. Firstly, the growth of the Academy as a great educational influence, emanating principally from the fine school of piano playing which he founded. Secondly, the inauguration of the music recitals at the RDS. Thirdly, the formation of a permanent local orchestra and the promotion of orchestral music through the performances of the Dublin Orchestral Society and the Sunday afternoon concerts, both conducted by Esposito. Fourthly, the Feis Ceoil, inaugurated in 1897, which was first started by the late Dr Annie Patterson and originally intended for the performance of Irish music only. Due to the enterprise of the late Mrs Best (then Miss Edith Oldham), a disciple of Esposito and one of the first secretaries of the Feis, it was extended to include all music.

It is stressing the obvious to say that the Feis Ceoil has been one of the strongest forces towards improving musical conditions in Ireland. Although Esposito was not a founder, his spirit hovered over its cradle and its growing years. He enhanced its prestige when he wrote the beautiful cantata *Deirdre* and the Irish Symphony especially for the composers' competition. Hamilton Harty, Esposito's most famous pupil [*sic*], also wrote his Irish Symphony for this competition.

There was no permanent symphony orchestra in Dublin until Esposito established the Dublin Orchestral Society in 1899. This was launched under great difficulties. It was easy to find string players in the Academy and elsewhere, but the problem was to find adequate wind players. They had to be gathered from the theatres, the local police bands, and from the bands of any British regiments that might be stationed in Dublin. Furthermore, the pitch of the wind instruments was the old concert pitch, that is, a semitone too high. To weld together such a motley gathering of sixty or seventy performers into a homogenous entity required a titanic personality like Esposito's. But he triumphed and formed an astonishingly good ensemble from the most unpromising material.

During the following fifteen years most of the great classical overtures, symphonies, concertos and orchestral pieces were heard in the hall of the Royal University in Earlsfort Terrace, many of them for the first time, especially those works of Wagner suitable for concert purposes.

Esposito also conducted Sunday orchestral concerts in the Antient Concert Rooms during the winter season. The Sunday orchestra numbered about thirty-six players, and the concerts were a great artistic success from the outset. At first there was some opposition to the idea, on religious grounds—a breach of the Sabbath Day—but this was successfully crushed by the action of the late Most Rev. Dr Walsh, Catholic Archbishop of Dublin, who attended them in person whenever it was possible for him to do so. These concerts were well attended and produced a profit up to Christmas, but from the New Year until Lent Esposito told me he invariably lost all he had gained.

There were two men who never missed one of these concerts during the nine or ten years of their existence; these worthy souls were to be seen mostly in the shilling seats, right behind the tympani. One was later to become the first president of the Irish Free State, the other the first Irish film censor. I refer to the late Arthur Griffith and the late James Montgomery.

Besides the activities directly associated with Esposito there was much interest and enterprise shown in the performance of music by semi-professional and amateur groups, such as choral and orchestral societies. Ballad concerts for charitable and other purposes were frequent, and large audiences greeted cross-Channel and favourite local artists. In those days there were four large concert halls in Dublin, as well as many smaller halls.

There was another form of music activity of which I cannot speak too highly: the great support, financial and otherwise, given so generously by music patrons like the late Sir John Purser Griffith, W. P. Geoghegan, Leopold Dix, Dermod O'Brien, Miss Maud Hutton, Sir Stanley Cochrane, and many others. Some of these had performances of chamber music in their houses. Sir Stanley Cochrane built a fine concert hall at his residence at Woodbrook, Bray, and brought over the London Symphony Orchestra, with Hamilton Harty as conductor. There was a concert every night for a week. The success of these concerts helped to put Harty on the road to fame.

This was the heyday of the Esposito era, and it was rudely halted in 1914 by the outbreak of the Great War. By 1918 the Feis Ceoil was the sole occupant of an empty stage. Music was in a sorry state, and, to add to the difficulties, our concert halls had become picture-houses or were utilised for other purposes. In the nineteen-twenties a big effort was made to revive our musical life. The RDS resumed its great work in the new concert hall in Ballsbridge. An outstanding event of the year 1927, the centenary of Beethoven's death, was a series of piano recitals given by Esposito in a hall in Upper Baggot Street, when he played from memory the thirty-two sonatas of Beethoven. He revived the Dublin Orchestral Society, and I had the honour to be his assistant. Thomas H. Weaving was the conductor of choral work.

There was one glorious week of festival music on the occasion of the first Tailteann Games, when the DOS, under Col. Fritz Brase, gave two orchestral performances. John McCormack gave two recitals. All this was in the Theatre Royal. We all looked forward to a rosy future, but right on the heels of this great triumph Esposito's health broke down, and the DOS was finally wound up. The Philharmonic Society struggled bravely on for six more years but eventually collapsed for lack of a concert hall.

I have mentioned some of the achievements of Esposito as a solo pianist, teacher, conductor, and organiser, and it will be agreed that it is remarkable that he could find the time for composing. His compositions are numerous and always of first-rate quality. His style is classical-romantic and displays the influence of Brahms. The orchestral works include an Irish Symphony, overture to *Othello, Irish Suite*, Poem for Orchestra, *Neapolitan Suite* for large string orchestra, two Irish Rhapsodies for solo violin and orchestra, and a piano concerto. The chamber music includes three very fine string quartets, three sonatas for violin and piano, and a sonata for violoncello and piano. There is a cantata, *Deirdre* (book by T. Rolleston) for soprano solo, chorus, and orchestra, and also two one-act operas, *The Tinker and the Fairy* (book by Douglas Hyde), and *The Post-Bag* (book by A. P. Graves). *The Post-Bag* was a great success in the United States, with a famous baritone of the day, Denis O'Sullivan, in the principal part.

In addition to much fine piano music Esposito edited five books of classical gems for teaching purposes, known as 'Students' Classics'. In his last years he edited and orchestrated a quantity of seventeenth and early eighteenth-century music for the Oxford University Press, and with Sir Stanley Cochrane founded the C. and E. Edition for publishing music.

In 1905 Dublin University honoured Esposito by conferring on him the degree of doctor of music (*honoris causa*), and in 1923 the King of Italy awarded him the Order of the Crown of Italy with the title of Commendatore in recognition of his services to Italian music.

Like all truly great men, Michele Esposito was a simple and lovable soul. Once you had penetrated the thin crust of a rather austere manner he was most approachable. His was a character of absolute integrity, unwavering truthfulness and fearlessness in upholding the highest standard of art at all times. I consider myself privileged and fortunate to have been his pupil and to have enjoyed his friendship, especially in his latter years. I cannot hope to meet his like again.

Intermezzo

John F. Larchet

ANTHONY HUGHES

Since he lived to such a great age, there may be some of the younger generation who fail to appreciate what a remarkable and beloved figure he was. Older people throughout Ireland will recall his spare, trim figure, his distinctive voice, and above all his consideration at choir examinations; some will have sung in the exquisite choirs he trained for many years at Loreto Abbey, Rathfarnham.

Many will remember his conducting the Dublin Philharmonic Society concerts; but most will have seen him in the pit of the old Abbey Theatre. He committed his whole life to the service of music in Ireland.

He taught at the RIAM for more than forty years and was professor of music at UCD from 1921 to 1958, when I had the honour to succeed him. I feel he would best like to be remembered for his teaching. The fastidious taste and careful craftsmanship we find in his own music impressed all his students. He had a great gift of human analogy, which ensured that any point or correction he made was indelibly engraved on the pupil's memory.

At UCD he moulded a stream of musicians who are active in many branches of music in Ireland and England. It was also a matter of pride to him that over the past fifty years every Irish-born doctor of music from TCD had studied with him, as had the vast majority of those Irishmen taking the MusBac there.

He served on many committees, in the RDS, DGOS, and elsewhere, to ensure that we in Ireland might be enabled to hear the world's finest musicians. Through more private committees he expressed his concern to relieve the plight of fellow-musicians who through illness or old age were in need. There were few who did not benefit from his advice in moments of difficulty or crisis.

His home life was supremely happy. His wife, Madeleine, was a most accomplished pianist and violinist, who even in her seventies sang with a beauty and freshness that could be the envy of a girl in her teens. Their three children grew up in an atmosphere of music. To their gracious home in Ballsbridge, musicians, artists and actors flocked to enjoy the glowing hospitality and his inimitable anecdotes. Here I gained my most treasured memories of him.

He could hold a company that included such brilliant talkers as Walter Starkie and Micheál Mac Liammóir entranced with his recollections of the

Abbey Theatre, among which his deep affection for Lady Gregory was clearly evident.

He frequently expressed his amazement that nowadays a student could hear the entire cycle of Beethoven symphonies, quartets or sonatas in a matter of days or weeks, while in his youth it was unusual to hear more than two or three in public performances in a whole year. He thought that was why in those days people made so many discoveries for themselves at home.

More than once he mentioned being overwhelmed when he first heard Wagner's music in reality, at a concert by the Hallé Orchestra under Richter in the Exhibition Hall in Earlsfort Terrace about 1903. He liked to recall that his friend Hamilton Harty brought the Hallé over many times in later years, so that when the orchestra came with Sir John Barbirolli, most notably for the Newman celebration of 1951, he claimed a long tradition was being maintained. Very often he would speak of his own teacher, Esposito, of Harty and John McCormack. It was a revelation, too, simply to hear him discuss the Dublin of the turn of the century with Dr Con Curran.

His involvement with Esposito was at all times one of master and pupil. He revered the great Italian musician and many times expressed his sense of gratitude and privilege at having studied with so great a teacher and mentor, of whom he said, 'He was a wonderful musician and a wonderful person, the greatest influence that a young student could have, not only about piano music but music generally and general behaviour. He was really a paragon.'

As the years advanced, Dr Larchet preserved his youth. He never succumbed to the closed mind. He maintained a lively interest in new musical developments and was delighted that his own former students should be so progressive in their style. His sympathies became more expansive, and he was ever ready to encourage young people to seek a new individual voice.

Only a small proportion of his own music is in print. It may be in what we now feel to be a traditional manner, but this was not true fifty years ago. His best work defies changing fashions. His own motets, sung by the RTE Singers at his Requiem Mass, came as a revelation to many. He was always modest about his own work and achievements. My abiding memory will be of his unfailing courtesy.

9

The Rewarding of Excellence

PAMELA FLANAGAN

*Certificates and diplomas; licentiates, associates, and fellows;
graduate diploma; bachelor in music education; BA in music
performance; diploma in music teaching and performance;
master of music in performance.
Scholarships: Vandeleur; Albert; Coulson; Esposito; Shandon;
Annie Lord; Aiken; Ruthven; Best; Marchant; Hewson; Rooke;
Irwin; Stokes; Burne; Papini; Wilhelmj; Nancie Lord; Delany;
Simonetti; Bast; Stewart; Larchet; Potter; Wilson;
Beckett. Cups, prizes, and medals.*

This chapter is intended as a survey of the various examination systems (with the exception of the local centre examination system) that have evolved in the Royal Irish Academy of Music during the 150 years of its existence.[1] Its direction is probably best summed up in the following 'snapshots' of the institution, taken from some of the main educational events that have occurred during that time.

In July 1857, the Executive Committee of the Irish Academy of Music met to consider the matter of awarding scholarships to the most deserving of the students studying at the institution.

In 1894, the first examinations conducted by the Academy for the benefit of students external to the institution were held in Dublin, Belfast, and Rathfarnham (County Dublin). Entrusted with overseeing this development, which was intended as a response to existing examinations held by the Royal Schools of Music, was Michele Esposito, a member of the Board of Studies and the Board of Governors of the Academy. The Governors reported that 'the result has been to fully justify their expectations.'[2]

In 1913 it was stated that 'the Governors are gratified to report that Mr. Larchet has succeeded in passing the very difficult examination prescribed in the Course, and securing the Diploma of the RIAM, a distinction which implies a very high degree of merit and carries with it the title of Licentiate of the RIAM.'[3]

In 1937, the Board of Governors announced that the diploma of associate of the Academy had been established to replace the former Certificate of Proficiency in teaching.[4]

In December each year, groups of students and their parents could be seen gathered around a notice-board in the Academy, as the results of the annual scholarship examinations were posted up by a member of the administrative staff. Animated discussions broke out as people craned their necks to see who had won the Annie Lord Scholarship for piano, the Guido Papini Exhibition for violin, the Joseph Robinson Memorial Prize for singing, the Sir Robert Prescott Stewart medal for composition, and others. Success in these competitions was greeted with surprise and delight, though the winners may not have been aware of the significance of the titles of the awards they had been given.

In July 1990, four students made their way to the podium in the Examination Hall of Trinity College, Dublin, to receive the degree of Bachelor in Music Education, the first group of students to receive this award, which is a tripartite degree administered and taught by TCD, the RIAM, and the DIT Conservatory. In January 1991, these students returned to the Academy to receive the diploma of graduate of the RIAM in recognition of their achievement.

In October 1996, the first student received the degree of Bachelor of Arts in Music Performance from the president of Dublin City University. The student graduated with first-class honours, a notable occasion marking an extremely successful association between the RIAM and DCU, a fact referred to in an address by the registrar of the university.

Encapsulated in these 'snapshots' is a testament to the Academy's policy of encouraging and rewarding excellence in music teaching and performance, the theme of the survey that follows.

> [The Board of Studies] beg to direct the attention of the Governors to Par. 25 of the Scheme (page 14) and to the authority given to the Academy of granting diplomas to competent students whether attached to the Academy itself, or to be found 'elsewhere in Ireland,' as a means of putting an end to touting advertisements which constantly occur, and are alike injurious to the Academy, and the art of Music and its professors.[5]

In 1890 the Academy took its first steps towards the rewarding of excellence in teaching, though at first the examination that became known as the certificate of proficiency was also intended to recognise excellence in performance in certain disciplines. Not surprisingly, given the composition of the Board and the link between the Academy and the RCM through their mutual pupil Edith Best,

> the Board had under consideration the question of a suitable course for examinations for Diplomas and Certificates of Proficiency . . . and suggest to the Governors one annual examination, and to adopt as far as possible the regulations laid down for similar purposes by the Royal College of Music, London . . .[6]

By the autumn a course had been drawn up, closely modelled on that of the RCM, and lists of suitable pieces were approved. In 1891, the first certificates were awarded to Annie Scarff (singing) and Ada Craig (piano teaching). Certain textbooks were prescribed for the theoretical component that was attached to the practical examination for this certificate, that produced by Stainer being a particular favourite. Six categories of musical disciplines were offered as examination subjects: piano and strings, organ, wind (performance only), singing (divided into two categories: public singing and teaching), theory of music, and composition. It is interesting to note the requirements for the examination during its early years: not all of them were musical, as can be seen from the following extracts from the rules and regulations.

> 2. Candidates intending to offer themselves for examination must signify their intention, in writing, not less than four weeks before the date fixed for examination, and must submit satisfactory testimonials of character . . .
>
> 4. All Candidates will be required, as a test of Literacy proficiency, to write a short essay in the Examination-room on some musical subject, of which previous notice has been given . . .[7]
>
> 6. No pupil of the Academy shall be allowed to enter for the Examination for Diploma or Certificate of Proficiency without permission of the Governors . . .[8]
>
> 7. Certificates of Proficiency may state that the candidate has a competent knowledge of branches of music other than the particular branch in which the Certificate is granted.[9]

A glance at the requirements of the practical component shows some notable differences from what is demanded of students today. The following is given as an example (italic type indicates requirements no longer demanded of candidates taking either of the Academy's instrumental diploma examinations):

(1) Pianoforte and String Instruments.
  (a) Solo Performance

   Each Candidate will be required—

   1. *To play one or more pieces, selected by the Examiners from the published list;* also scales and exercises as the examiners may require.
   2. To play a piece, selected by the Candidate, either from the published list or otherwise.
   3. To read at sight.
   4. To answer questions on the construction and treatment of the Instrument.
   5. *To harmonise a given figured bass in four parts. To modulate and to transpose; also to improvise an accompaniment to a given melody. (In the case of string instruments, equivalent tests will be given.)*

> *Candidates may, at their option, play from memory a piece chosen by the Examiners out of a list of three pieces submitted by the Candidate. Credit will be given for extemporisation.*
>
> *A knowledge of the entire of Stainer's Harmony primer will be required of each Candidate.*

(*b*) Teaching

1. *To play a piece of moderate length chosen by Candidate*, also scales and exercises as the Examiners may require.
2. To read at sight.
3. *To harmonize a given figured bass in four parts.*
4. To detect inaccuracies in the rendering of a composition well known to the Candidate.
5. *To answer questions on the construction of the Instrument.*
6. To answer questions on, and give an outline of a course of instruction in technique, studies and pieces.
7. Candidates for Certificates in teaching Stringed Instruments must be able to accompany on the Pianoforte . . .

Candidates will be examined in the following pieces:—

Pianoforte

Bach
First movement of Italian Concerto

Beethoven
Sonata in D minor, Op. 31, No. 3

Mendelssohn
Prelude and Fugue in E minor (Six Preludes and Fugues, No. 1)

Chopin
Scherzo in B minor

Schumann
Novellette in D major, No. 2

Liszt
'Waldesrauschen' Étude[10]

It would appear that candidates for the certificate of proficiency in performance were required to learn the entire list of pieces, with a guarantee that three of them would not be examined, while those who aspired to become teachers had the relatively simple task of performing one piece selected by themselves. Great emphasis, particularly on the part of the performer, was placed on the ability to improvise; and the candidate's theoretical knowledge appears to have been tested only through their proficiency in keyboard harmony.

Over the years certain amendments were made to the examination. At the behest of one of the professors of singing, Randal Woodhouse, for example, who considered that 'Italian is not as much used in modern music as German and French'[11] (and in the teeth of opposition from another professor, Palmieri), the compulsory examination in Italian for singers was replaced in 1903 with a test in Italian reading and translation (eventually abolished), while the knowledge of harmony for singers was also reduced. In 1905 honours and pass divisions in the certificate were instituted, with the further requirement that candidates in all disciplines have attained a minimum of 40 per cent in all requirements to be eligible for the award of the certificate.[12]

Precise specifications were also set down for a new paper on harmony, which every candidate in a practical discipline would now be expected to take,[13] though it was not until 1915 that a reference to separate sections of practical and theoretical requirements was incorporated in the examination regulations.[14] It was further recommended in 1911 that a paper in music history be added to the requirements, alongside an oral examination in the same subject.[15]

A proposal to abolish the certificate examinations was made by the Governors in 1919; but the examination, in a slightly altered form, continued until 1928, when the Board again began a review of the examination. In that year, again with an eye on the RCM and RAM, the Board of Studies proposed that

> candidates who pass the Academy Certificate of Proficiency examination as teacher or performer should be allowed to use the following after their name—Certified Teacher RIAM and Certified Performer RIAM which might if preferred be abbreviated to CTRIAM and CPRIAM, and that their right to do so should be stated on the Certificate they receive.[16]

The Board of Studies went further in making radical new proposals for the amalgamation of the certificate and LRIAM diploma examinations, to allow candidates who obtained 85 per cent to be considered licentiates and those obtaining between 75 and 84 per cent to be awarded certificates. It also recommended that those who had previously received certificates with honours be styled licentiates, without further examination, while previous holders of pass certificates would be required to sit a new theoretical examination. The Board of Governors refused to sanction the term CertRIAM, whereupon the Board of Studies withdrew the other recommendations in favour of maintaining the status quo.

Five years later, the Board of Studies tried again to abolish the certificate examination, as it was 'musically superfluous.'[17] There were no further awards after 1934, but in 1937 it was announced that 'the Diploma of Associate of the Academy (ARIAM) has been established. This Diploma will take the place of the former Certificate of Proficiency in Teaching.'[18] The first associate diplomas were awarded in 1938 to Sylvia Fannin (elocution teaching) and Nesta Vandeleur (cello teaching). Later, in 1943, it was decided that those who had already received the Certificate of Proficiency should be upgraded to the level of associate without any further examination.[19]

The associate diploma in teaching (musical subjects) endures to this day, relatively unchanged from its 1937 form, requiring three written papers (theory, rudiments, harmony and counterpoint; history; and aural training), performance (originally two, now three or four pieces selected by the candidate from a prescribed list), technical exercises (such as sight-reading and scales), and an interview (covering form, the particular instrument or discipline presented by the candidate, and the art of teaching).

The certificate of proficiency in performance was not replaced until 1991, when an associate diploma in performance was introduced (first awarded to Owen Lorigan in that year), differing from the teacher's diploma only in requiring a higher standard of performance. The first associate diplomas in bilingual speech and drama were awarded in 1964 to Eibhlín Ní Loingsigh, Finbarr Howard, and Máirín Uí Chathasaigh.

Apart from the written work being more extensive than in the earlier examination, the language in which the questions are couched has changed considerably, while the questions themselves relate far more to known works of classical composers than to the testing of rudiments in isolation.

Throughout the history of the certificate and associate diploma, candidates have never been obliged to be students of the Academy, though at first those who were students had to obtain the permission of the Governors before entering for the examination, a regulation that has since been abolished. Neither were those Academy candidates considered to be following a full-time course of study (though they might well have opted to take special classes of instruction in preparation for the examination). That specification was originally intended for the higher qualification of licentiate of the RIAM, and it is to this qualification that the discussion now turns.

Included in the petition of the Board of Studies to the Board of Governors in 1890 was the request that a higher-level diploma also be established. Turning its attention to such an enterprise, the Board drafted the requirements for what was termed later 'a very difficult examination'. These were as follows:

> I.—Each candidate must have been a pupil of the Academy for at least two years, and must satisfy the Governors of diligent attendance in the classes and application to studies.
> II.—Each Candidate will be required to pass an Examination in the following subjects:—
> (*a*) Elementary Acoustics
> (*b*) Harmony and Counterpoint
> (*c*) Canon
> (*d*) Fugue
> (*e*) Form
> (*f*) Musical History
> (*g*) General Musical Knowledge
>
> and in any one of the subjects in which Certificates of Proficiency are granted, to be selected by the Candidate, having special regard to that

branch of the musical art to which the Candidate has devoted particular attention. A knowledge of Orchestration will be tested by an examination in the full scores of such works as the Governors shall from time to time prescribe.[20]

The diploma of licentiate of the RIAM was considered to be a much more academic qualification and not a little influenced by degree-level thinking, quite possibly emanating from the then chairman of the Board of Studies, Sir Robert Stewart. It also attempted to establish as near as possible a full-time course of study by insisting that such aspects as regular attendance and application to homework (as outlined in regulation 1) be taken into account.

Royal Irish Academy of Music.

36, WESTLAND ROW, DUBLIN.

HARMONY EXAMINATION.

Dr. GATER.

VANDALEUR QUALIFYING EXAMINATION.

Maximum of marks, 90. Time allowed, 3 hours

November, 1909.

---

1. (*a*) What are leger lines?

   (*b*) What is the value of ♩ . . ?

   (*c*) Write a Breve and its rest.
   (*d*) Write the signs for double sharp and double flat
   (*e*) Explain Ped, and *   10 marks.

2. Write this passage at the same pitch, using (*a*) the Alto, (*b*) the Tenor clef :—

                                          10 marks.

3. Write the various forms of the minor scale on D.
                                          10 marks.

4. Describe the following intervals :—

                                          8 marks.

3

2

5. Harmonize this melody, using only common chords in root position.

                                          12 marks.

6. Describe the following chords, figure each, and add resolution when required.

                                          10 marks.

7. Work the following for four voices, indicating the modulations :—

                                          30 marks.

A committee was set up to review the requirements in 1910, as a result of which special classes in harmony and counterpoint for the certificates of proficiency and the diplomas in theory and composition, under the instruction of Jozé, were introduced. The review of the examination system carried out in 1928–30 resulted in the division of the licentiate award into teacher and performer categories (for instrumental licentiates and vocalists), a considerable reduction in the theoretical requirements for this examination, and the elimination of questions on history and form for the performer's diploma. Other stipulations for the performer's diploma included that at least one of the pieces selected by the candidate be played from memory; but by far the most significant recommendation was that the requirement for full-time study be abolished.[21]

The first licentiate diploma awarded under the new format was obtained by Muriel Graham in 1930, while the first licentiates in elocution were Noreen O'Connor and Kathleen O'Neill, in 1935. The first LRIAM in bilingual speech and drama was awarded to Eibhlín Ní Loingsigh in 1966. For a brief period in the forties the licentiate diploma in musical subjects was awarded to performers only, the associateship being considered sufficient as a teaching qualification, but by the early fifties the two categories had been restored. The LRIAM retained (with occasional slight amendments) the format of practical examination, interview (for teachers), aural tests and two written papers (covering theory, harmony, counterpoint, history, and form) until 1996, when it was decided that written requirements for the performer's diploma should be abolished. It was also decided, for the first time in its history, that an honours category for this examination be instituted.

The LRIAM remained the highest award the Academy could bestow through examination (and the only qualification awarded by the Academy recognised by the Department of Education—after many years of application—as the equivalent of the higher diploma in education)[22] until 1986, when the degree of bachelor in music education was established, thus restoring to the Academy's curriculum a full-time course of study. (Up to 1986 the LRIAM was recognised by the Northern Ireland Ministry of Education, and by its British counterpart for 'qualified status'.)

The review of the diploma and certificate examinations carried out in 1910 also called for the establishment of a 'higher distinction'[23] and recommended that the award of fellowship be inaugurated. In 1920 it was announced that

> the Governors have further considered the proposal to apply for the necessary authority to vary the Scheme, the principle of which was approved at the last annual Meeting, in order to, inter alia, establish Fellowships of the RIAM. A special resolution in connection with this matter together with details of the proposed new Diplomas of Fellowship and Licentiate, will be laid before the forthcoming annual meeting of members for adoption.[24]

Nothing was done until the review of 1928–30, concerning which L. Edward Steele reported that the Governors had taken an important step which cannot fail to raise the status of the institution. An Amending Scheme has been sanctioned by the Commissioners of Charitable Donations and Bequests which enables the Governors to grant Diplomas carrying the titles of 'Fellow' and 'Licentiate'. The conditions on which these are granted are stringent and enhance the value of the distinctions.[25]

The first fellow of the Academy was John F. Larchet; but what was not apparent was that the requirements for the awarding of fellowship had by no means been agreed on. As late as February 1930 the Board of Studies, having debated long and hard the merits of an award by examination against those of an honorary award, were petitioning the Governors 'that the Diploma of Fellowship should be an honorary one in the gift of the Governors.'[26] The Governors responded with a request that a formal examination be instituted. The Board of Studies carried out its instructions and presented a syllabus nine days before Steele wrote his report but in doing so reiterated its plea that

> it should be simply an honour conferred at the discretion of the Governors. Our Board while submitting a course as requested, ventures to hope that the Governors may see their way to adopt our recommendation for the following reason. It is unusual to have two Diplomas obtainable by examination, as the higher depreciates the value of the lower. In both the Royal Academy and Royal College, the Licentiate of the former, and Associate of the latter can alone be obtainable in this way. They are in fact the Diplomas of the Royal Academy and Royal College, the Fellowship being an honour conferred by the Council in cases of special distinction. Our Board feels very strongly this view of the matter, the adoption of which, by the Governors, would bring the Royal Irish Academy of Music into line with the Royal Academy and Royal College.[27]

In time, the Board of Governors took the advice. Although it remains within the power of the Governors to prescribe an examination, fellowship of the RIAM since its inception (save for Larchet) has always been conferred *honoris causa* on those who have made a major contribution to musical excellence, in the Academy itself as well as nationally and internationally. A list of those so honoured will be found at the end of this chapter.

One of the most recently instituted diplomas, that of graduate of the RIAM (GRIAM), was inaugurated in 1990 as an award for those students who had successfully completed a course of study for the degree of bachelor in music education and was awarded that year to Martin Fahy, Paul Glynn, Patrick Scarlett, and Caroline Senior. With the advent of the degrees of bachelor of arts in music performance and master of music in performance (in 1992 and 1995, respectively) it was decided to extend this award to all students who graduate from the RIAM.

This discussion of awards now moves to a consideration of the last twelve years of the Academy's history, during which time the most rapid developments in the evolution of its examination system have taken place.

The most recent history of the Academy has witnessed an astonishing expansion of courses at third level, to a situation where no less than three degree courses, validated by two Dublin universities, the University of Dublin (Trinity College) and Dublin City University, have been established, with plans at the time of writing for a fourth degree course. Established in response to a demand for professional qualifications at the highest level, and a recognition of the extraordinary musical talent that Ireland's young musicians possess, and also with a view to competing with the best overseas musical institutions, these qualifications have resulted in a huge increase in the numbers of full-time students pursuing third-level courses at the Academy.

Motivated by its pursuit of excellence in the provision of music education, mindful of the changes occurring throughout the country, and following recent proposals to re-establish a full-time course of study in the RIAM,[28] the Academy inaugurated the degree of bachelor in music education in 1986, following three years of negotiation between the RIAM, the College of Music (formerly the Municipal School of Music, now the DIT Conservatory of Music and Drama), and TCD. A tripartite course of four years' duration, taught and administered jointly by the three institutions, it represents at once a new departure and a renewal of old connections. Designed primarily for those students who wish to pursue a career in secondary school teaching, it remains, at the time of writing, unique in its field in the co-operation of three of Ireland's foremost musical institutions, and is the first full-time course ever to be established in the Academy.

The wording used to describe the aims of the course, as encapsulated in the following extract from the education component (drafted by the School of Education, TCD) could not be in greater contrast to that of the first licentiate diploma syllabus, and illustrates how far the institution has travelled.

> General Aims: To assist the students to understand
> 1. the meaning of musical sounds as a means of artistic and aesthetic expression,
> 2. and develop their own view of the nature of music education and its contribution to the curriculum,
> 3. how children develop skills in the cognitive, affective and psychomotor domains and the factors which enhance or impede learning, with particular reference to the learning of music,
> 4. how teachers design for and manage learning and instruction in the classroom and the school,
> 5. and develop the basic skills in music essential for effective music teaching,
> 6. the significance of their performance in the education of children through the practical acquisition of a vocal technique independently of their instrumental specialisation,

7. the differing needs of children in rural and urban environments in respect of their indigenous folk materials especially those in the Irish language and their maintenance and significance in their respective cultures,

8. the importance of research in music education and the potential as well as the limitations of different methods of investigation.[29]

Lectures in the written and practical aspects of music are provided in alternate years by the RIAM and the DIT (with music history lectures being supplied by the School of Music, TCD), while lectures in education are supplied by all three institutions, under the overall guidance of the School of Education, TCD. A third subject, history, is taught by the School of History, TCD. The course is unique in another way, in that students complete their teaching practice within the four years of their training, rather than pursuing a separate course of study at the end of their degree course. Having begun as a qualification for secondary school teachers, the course has, during its brief history, provided a springboard for students to continue to study music at postgraduate level in such varied areas as research, performance, and music therapy.

Notwithstanding the success of the bachelor in music education course, the Academy was acutely aware that, since the time of Edith Best's success, many of its young students were travelling abroad to complete their studies in music performance. With the BMusEd degree firmly established, the time was therefore ripe to consider establishing the Academy's own degrees in music performance, a process that started in 1987. Following the first graduation ceremony for Academy students in 1990, events moved rapidly, and a new link was forged with DCU, the city's most recently established university. A happy meeting of minds resulted in the institution of the bachelor of arts in music performance course in 1992, from which the first student, Stuart O'Sullivan, graduated in 1996. A full-time course of four years' duration, it trains its students in all aspects of performance through classes in solo performance, chamber music, accompaniment, orchestra and opera, and academic studies. Despite its extremely short existence to date, its students have represented the Academy, and Ireland, with distinction in international competitions, concerts, and television and radio broadcasts.

Established in 1995, the diploma in music teaching and performance represents one of the Academy's plans for the future. Ever conscious of its role in the wider community, and of the need to encourage a love of music so that its appreciation is not confined to those students who are lucky enough to have access to music through a secondary school, the Academy has designed a course to bridge the gap between its teaching and performance degrees. The DipMusRIAM is a one-year full-time course that trains young students to become teachers and performers in the community, whether this be in private practice or a specialist music institution, or as a peripatetic teacher. The course (which provides a comprehensive training in all aspects of music, such as performance, ensemble activity, academic studies, and the psychology of music teaching) is at an early stage in its history, but its first graduates, Sarah Moffat and David Reilly, have acquitted themselves well in their subsequent musical careers. It is intended that this diploma will eventually develop into the Academy's fourth full-time degree course.

The success of the Academy's undergraduate performance degree formed the basis for the establishment in 1995 of one of the other projects for the future, the postgraduate qualification of master of music in performance (also validated by DCU). And so the tide has turned: not only are Academy students remaining to complete their studies at the very highest level but other students are now coming from abroad to study at the Academy, reversing the trend of previous years and reinforcing the Academy's reputation as a centre of musical excellence, not only nationally but internationally as well.

The educational system of the Academy has, from its earliest days, been founded on a basic three-tier system, called originally first, second and third classes (first class being for the most senior students), then senior, middle and junior grades. Some minor modifications to this system took place over the years, particularly with regard to beginner students (at various times termed elementary, beginner, and preparatory grade), though one of the most radical alterations was the division of the Academy in 1948 into two schools, Senior and Junior, the former incorporating senior and middle grades. From the outset, the grades of the teachers, and their salaries, were linked to the three main grades of the students. Until 1961, the majority of the teaching staff operated on a system that allowed them to teach only to a certain level before their students were obliged to undertake an examination or be sent to a teacher in a higher grade or a senior professor. All junior students were examined at regular intervals by the senior professors or by such examiners as the Board of Studies appointed, and this was supported by a system of reports on all pupils, sent in the early days of the institution to the Board of Studies, and later to the parents of each child.

This system, which had endured since the nineteenth century, was finally abolished in 1961, together with the two schools, though the sending of reports continued until 1974. At the present time, the Academy's assessment procedures are once again under review.

A hierarchy of scholarships existed parallel to the diplomas described above (in some disciplines these were originally incorporated in the system), with attendant qualifying examinations based on technical requirements, aural tests, and the theory of music, for which prizes were also available. Awards for excellence were regarded as an essential stimulus for the students, whether in the form of prizes, medals, books, cups, or scholarships. Then, as now, the different grades and categories of scholarships were determined by a combination of age and ability, though (with the exception of those awarded at entry) the first scholarships were awarded to senior students of widely differing ages.[30] As the number of scholarships and awards increased, they were extended to include the lower grades, and consequently the age bands narrowed. The awards also came to be regarded as a commemoration of excellence, reflected in titles honouring distinguished members of staff and students of the RIAM as well as its benefactors.

It is interesting to observe how the sources of such awards have altered, beginning with the first annual prize, the Begley Prize (for singing, instituted 1873, from the estate of Maria Begley, a former singing teacher, and bestowed by her brother) and including such awards as the Countess Cowper Prize (for singing, 1881), the Lord Chancellor's Prize (for piano, 1917), those bestowed by governors and friends of the Academy, such as the Hubbard Clark Cup (for singing, donated by Alderman Hubbard Clark in 1944), the Briscoe Cup (for the most promising student, donated by Mr and Mrs Robert Briscoe in 1962), the H. K. Edwards Bursaries (1974), and the Margaret Furlong Award (for the best young piano student from either junior or middle grade, donated by the former lady superintendent in 1991), and those commemorating exceptionally talented students, such as the Arthur Oulton Memorial Prize (for advanced piano sight-reading, 1919), the Caroline Reilly Scholarship (for middle grade piano, 1927), and the John Benson Cup (for the best rendition of a set keyboard work by Bach, 1952; John Benson, a pupil of great talent, especially in the music of Bach, was killed in an aeroplane crash, and the fund was subscribed by his friends).

The Academy has also been deeply appreciative of the help it has received from others, such as Pianos Plus, Andrew Tynan and Max and Judith Segal (formerly Shreider) in donating cups for concerto and repertoire performance (piano), Dublin Corporation, for its donations to the scholarship fund, and Philip Kavanagh (voice), the Mary Burke Memorial Fund (piano and violin), McCullough-Pigott (piano), the Actors' Church Union (speech and drama),[31] and Petrof (piano), in establishing entrance scholarships to enable promising young talent to begin studying at the institution.

In the survey that follows, the growth of the earliest-established examination system in the Academy is outlined through consideration of those scholarships and awards commemorating its most significant benefactors and members of staff.

While one of the first references to the awarding of scholarships is contained in the minutes of the Executive Committee for 7 July 1857, it was another five years before the committee, 'having considered the report of Mr. Levey as to the highly deserving conduct of Thomas Farrell, his diligence, talent and proficiency, resolved that Thomas Farrell be elected a scholar of the Academy.'[32]

This fact, however, is not stated in the first of the annual reports of the Council (1872), where the first recipients of Academy scholarships are recorded as Susan Wright (pianoforte) and Bessie Craig (singing). Before this date, excellence was recognised through prizes of books and medals or, for exceptional students, monetary awards, known as premiums. The date of this decision is significant, coming as it did a year after the Academy moved to its present premises and in the year in which Queen Victoria became the Academy's patron, bestowing on it the title 'Royal'.

The Academy's improved financial position is reflected in the fact that the awards were guaranteed a slightly more regular and dependable income by the Treasury in 1870. The categories of award reflect the most popular subjects in the institution at that time, even though the Academy employed teachers of other musical disciplines, such as violin, cello, and harmony. Proficiency in the piano allowed the widespread transmission of popular musical classics (either specifically written or arranged for that instrument) into a middle-class home as a popular form of entertainment, a worldwide phenomenon, frequently in parallel with vocal performance; while public performances of newly written operas had raised much-needed funds for the Academy.[33]

The sex of the recipients also reflects the greater number of women students in the Academy at the time (the listing of classes and instruments in the prospectus under the separate headings 'Ladies' classes' and 'Gentlemen's classes' persisted well into the twentieth century). The categories also illustrate, however, a slight educational bias, in that while classes in piano, singing and harmony were provided for women at this time, instruction in other instruments, such as violin and cello, was being offered to men only. Violin classes for women began in 1878, followed by classes in organ, cello, and harp, but it was to be some time before classes in wind instruments were available to all students; many times during its history the Academy was unable to offer classes in any woodwind or brass instruments.

The piano school of the Academy has long been one of its greatest strengths, due in no small part to Michele Esposito, whose influence as a teacher endures to this day and whose name will be found among the list of scholarships below. It would therefore seem appropriate to continue our survey with a consideration of the awards available for this school.

> The most important circumstance in relation to the Academy has been the bequest by the late Mr. Ormsby Vandeleur to the Academy of a legacy of £5,000, and some Musical Instruments. Of this legacy £1,000 is at the absolute disposal of the Academy, and £4,000 is to be invested, and the interest applied towards the education of Students . . .[34]

Thus, in 1879, the Council announced one of the most significant donations to the institution in its history. Two years previously, the Academy had advertised 'an Examination for Voices, open to all Ireland,' with the purpose of awarding what were in effect entrance scholarships (see below).[35] In 1880 the examination was repeated, and some of those elected to scholarships received their award under the Vandeleur title. At first awarded to three singers, with two instrumentalists selected from within the Academy, the range of the Vandeleur scholarships was extended to include piano, singing, violin and (briefly) cello by 1887, though for some years a distinction was made between those who received their tuition under the terms of the Vandeleur bequest and those who were titled Vandeleur scholars, presumably to distinguish between those who were entrance scholars and those who were current students.

In 1897, because of the reorganisation of the scholarship system, the Vandeleur bequest was divided (one part being combined with the original Academy scholarship awards) to form the 'Vandeleur Academy Scholarships' for senior grade students and 'Vandeleur Scholarships' for middle grade students.[36] By 1900, the range of disciplines had been expanded to include organ and harmony, counterpoint and composition as categories; to this day the Vandeleur Academy scholarships and Vandeleur scholarships are only awarded in piano, organ, singing, violin, viola (Vandeleur only), cello, composition, and harmony and counterpoint. Until 1977, the scholarships also carried with them gold and silver medals (Vandeleur Academy and Vandeleur, respectively).

Since 1985, all Vandeleur Academy scholarships in instrumental and vocal disciplines (for which there are no age limits) are awarded on the basis of a recital, which is open to the public. The Vandeleur scholarships in these disciplines (with an age limit of twenty-two) retain their technical requirements of scales and sight-reading, with the exception of the violin, where another recital is required.

> Upon the completion of the Albert Memorial Group on Leinster Lawn—one of Foley's masterpieces—the Dublin Prince Consort Memorial Committee presented to the Academy a sum of £940 Government three per cent. stock, being one half of the surplus remaining in their hands. This donation, known as the 'Albert Fund', provides a scholarship and prizes for student of the Academy.[37]

Mention has already been made of the examination for voices held on 8 and 9 November 1878 to select 'so many of the candidates as [were considered] deserving, and give them the advantage of free instruction in the Academy for one year.'[38] The title disappeared from the list of scholarships quite soon after the bequest was made (though it continued to be awarded as a prize) and did not appear again until 1934, in the middle grade for piano. Today, the Albert Scholarship is the first of the three senior grade scholarships for piano, with an age limit of twenty.

> That £52 be allocated towards the remuneration of Professors of the Pianoforte in the Academy. That four Pianoforte Scholarships, open each year to public competition, be founded in connection with the Academy. The sum allocated these Scholarships is £18. That an Organ Scholarship be founded in connection with the Academy. The sum allocated for this Scholarship is £12. That £30 be allocated towards the remuneration of the Professor of the Violoncello and Double Bass in the Academy. That two Scholarships for proficiency in the above instruments be founded in connection with the Academy. The sum allocated for these Scholarships is £20. That £30 be allocated for, or towards the remuneration of Professors of Wind Instruments in the Academy. That in pursuance of the scheme . . . £50 per annum be allocated in or towards the remuneration of the Professor of Harmony, Composition, Musical History, and other theoretical branches of Musical Education in the Academy.[39]

Perhaps the most significant educational development for the Academy in the nineteenth century, the first scholarships to be advertised under the terms of the comprehensive scheme that was the Coulson bequest, were awarded in May 1887 to seventeen students, including performers on flute, clarinet, bassoon, horn, and trombone. Thereafter Coulson scholarships appear to have been restricted to students of piano, organ, violin, and cello, though open to all 'sons and daughters of respectable Irish parents, possessing natural musical talent,' either internal or external to the Academy. (This latter distinction was not applied to the Coulson Academy scholarships, which were confined to Academy students only and, at various stages in their history in the piano school, to those who had not won a Vandeleur or Albert Scholarship.)

As with the Vandeleur bequest, a distinction appears to have been made at first between those who received tuition under the terms of the bequest and those entitled 'Coulson scholars', while in 1900 the scholarships themselves were divided into 'Coulson Academy' and 'Coulson' categories. Further sub-division came in 1920 when the 'Coulsons' (as they had become affectionately known) for piano acquired senior and junior status, though, rather confusingly, the former category eventually became part of the middle grade scholarships. The 'Coulson Academy' scholarships also found their way into the middle grade. For many years the 'Coulsons' retained a slightly separate identity from other scholarships on offer, in that the examination required proficiency not only in pieces, scales and sight-reading but in theory and aural tests as well, thus reflecting their dual status.[40]

The Coulson theory and aural requirements were abolished in the late seventies, by which time another problem had emerged, namely that a sizable proportion of students were being excluded from competing as a result of the ruling on Irish parentage. Having been temporarily suspended in 1976, the Coulson title disappeared from the entrance scholarships in 1987, and finally the Board of Governors in May 1996 decided to remove the Coulson name from the annual scholarship examinations, while reasserting its intention to apply the Coulson bequest, for so long such an important mainstay of the Academy's educational system, in other areas pertaining to musical instruction.

> The Board of Studies recommends that two scholarships giving free instruction in the Senior Pianoforte class for one year, and in a suitable theoretical class for the same period, be given by the Governors to be competed for by those Local Centre candidates who in Grades V, VI and VII obtain a minimum of 90% marks at the Local Centre examinations . . . The Board of Studies further suggests that these scholarships be known as the 'Esposito Scholarship,' the Commendatore having, with the approval of the Governors, inaugurated the Local Centre examinations. They would also serve as a fitting commemoration of his long association with the Academy and of the services he rendered to Music in Ireland.[41]

Esposito's influence has continued to affect the Academy in many different ways: as a piano teacher, with the school of piano teaching and performing that he founded persisting to this day, being perpetuated by his pupils (themselves commemorated through awards being named after them); as a composer, whose compositions are still set for competition as a test of both virtuosity and interpretation; and as a music editor, whose well-loved and now sadly extinct *Student Classics* was the staple diet of many a young pianist, myself included.

> Signor Esposito has . . . been the Director of the Pianoforte Class for male Pupils. The Council cannot speak too highly of the pains so able an artist has taken to improve the Class, which has fallen away considerably from the state of efficiency to which it was brought by Mr. George Sproule . . . The Council cannot doubt that when the advantages of the Class become known it will be as before, a very important class and well attended.[42]

This was one of the first of many tributes during a long and immensely distinguished career, which, as we have seen, was not solely confined to the Academy.

In time, the proposal of the Board of Studies was amended (in 1932) to provide three entrance scholarships for junior students, such a benefit persisting until recently.[43] The lack of an internal scholarship commemorating Esposito was rectified in 1941, and the Esposito Memorial Scholarship, for middle grade piano students (under sixteen), remains one of the most keenly contested awards at the annual scholarship examinations.

In 1929, the year in which Esposito died, Lord Shandon (the former Sir Ignatius O'Brien), a vice-president of the Academy since 1917, was in mourning for his wife. His association with the examination system of the Academy had begun that year when, as Lord Chancellor, he 'most kindly gave two prizes—1st and 2nd—to Junior pupils of the Piano, who, in the opinion of the Professors, exhibited most sympathetic spirit in their playing in accordance with Schumann's instruction to young players' and 'who exhibit the most "taste" in their musical performances.'[44] Lord Shandon did not long survive his wife; in 1930 it was reported that he had bequeathed £1,000 'for the purpose of founding a scholarship to be known as "The Lord and Lady Shandon Scholarship" for competition annually in the Junior Pianoforte class.'[45] The professors at first considered instituting two scholarships, one for junior grade students under thirteen, the other for middle grade students under fifteen, both to be open to internal and external students. It was also decided to retain the Shandon Prize. However, following further representations from the Governors, the Board of Studies revised its recommendations in line with the terms of the original bequest. The scholarship was therefore to be awarded to the best student under twelve who was eligible to compete after only one term of instruction before the examination, a stipulation it shared with the 'Coulsons', but unlike other scholarships offered by the Academy. At that time the scholarship, which provided free tuition for a year, could be renewed for a further period at the discretion of the Governors. Today, the age limit has been raised to thirteen, and the scholarship is tenable for a year only.

In Annie Lord we have the first of Esposito's students to be commemorated by such an award. She was a distinguished member of a distinguished musical family. Nancie Lord (also commemorated by a scholarship bearing her name) was a superb violinist and Academy scholar who became one of its most notable professors; Kevin Lord was the winner of the Coulson Scholarship for cello in 1917; and May Lord was an accomplished viola player who, in winning the Vandeleur Scholarship for viola in 1915, became not only the first student to win a viola scholarship but for many years afterwards the only student to do so. A pupil also of Margaret O'Hea, Annie Lord is recorded as a Coulson scholar in 1893, becoming a pupil teacher in 1896, one of those Academy students who were considered to be of a sufficiently high standard to be assistants to the main teaching staff and who received free tuition in return for their services. So began a teaching career that lasted forty-two years.

Annie Lord's name next appears on the roster of scholarship winners in 1899, when she is recorded as having won the Vandeleur Scholarship for piano; in the same year she was awarded a certificate of proficiency as a piano teacher by the Academy and in 1900 followed this by winning the Vandeleur Academy Scholarship. By June 1902, Annie Lord was listed among the members of the main teaching staff, though it was not until 1926 that she was eventually made a professor. Her foresight was remarkable: she gained a reputation as a champion of 'modern' music (see p. 391, 397); she was also conscious of the need to open the Academy still further to the general public; and one of her first recommendations on becoming a professor was that scholarship and prize examinations be conducted in the presence of an audience. In this she was only partially successful: the Arthur Oulton Memorial Prize (now no longer awarded) was the only competition so designated by the Board of Studies until the ruling on the Vandeleur scholarships in 1985. Her contribution to the musical life of the Academy was recognised by the Board of Governors in 1936, when they awarded her the diploma of FRIAM 'in recognition of long and untiring work on the Professorial staff of the Academy and in furthering the Art of Music in Ireland.'[46]

Annie Lord resigned her position in 1938 because of ill-health, and died the following year. By 1942 the Annie Lord Scholarship had been instituted, at first in what was then known as the preparatory grade. Today, transferred to the junior grade, it is one of the first scholarships available to students under twelve.

The other scholarship available in this category is the Maud Aiken Exhibition. Maud Davin is recorded as a Coulson scholar in 1914, as a Coulson Academy scholar in 1915, and as winning the Vandeleur Scholarship as a violinist in 1916. Again a member of a musical family, her sister Philomena Davin had also won Coulson scholarships for piano and cello in 1912 and the Coulson Academy Scholarship for piano in 1913; both sisters studied piano with Margaret O'Hea. Some years were to elapse (some of which she spent as director of the Municipal School of Music) before Maud Davin's name was to appear again in Academy records, this time in 1939 as Maud Aiken, wife of the future Minister for Foreign Affairs, when she joined the Board of Governors as a Corporation governor, becoming vice-president in 1950. She was made a fellow of the Academy in 1961 at a ceremony that included the President, Éamon de Valera, and the Lord Mayor of Dublin, Robert Briscoe, among those present, and also received an honorary ARAM.

As chairman of the Board of Governors, Maud Aiken presided over many a prize-giving ceremony in the Academy and was a formidable presence at many concerts given in the institution. It was largely through her efforts that another award, the Tibor Paul Medal, was instituted in 1968.[47] As a tribute to her unstinting work on behalf of the Academy, it was decided that one of the junior piano scholarships should be renamed the Maud Aiken Exhibition; this scholarship was first awarded in 1972.

Margaret O'Hea resigned from the teaching staff in 1928 after a teaching career of some fifty-five years. Her departure, together with Esposito's resignation, caused something of a crisis in the piano school, which was deprived of two of its finest professors at a stroke. Margaret O'Hea was made a fellow of the RIAM in 1931. Having worked alongside Esposito as professor and local centre examiner, she shares with him the distinction of having two awards named after her. Following her death in 1938, her friends and former pupils presented the Margaret O'Hea Memorial Cup for competition in the annual examinations for piano; by 1942 the Margaret O'Hea Memorial Exhibition had been instituted. Both awards endure to this day, the former for the best performance of a complete sonata by a student aged sixteen or over, and the latter for the best competitor under ten.

Bessie Ruthven, who was a student of Margaret O'Hea (and one of the first secretaries of the Students' Musical Union), provides us with an example of a slightly less prominent but nonetheless worthy teaching career. She is first mentioned in Academy reports in 1891, when her success in the rudiments of music examination is recorded; three years later she is listed as one of the pupil teachers of piano. Having won the Vandeleur Academy Scholarship in 1897, she obtained the certificate of proficiency in piano teaching in 1902. She and Annie Lord were given the status of teachers of third-grade classes in the same year. Thereafter she appears to have maintained a somewhat low profile as a teacher and, for a brief period in 1925, as a local centre examiner before she resigned her post in 1926, moving to Edinburgh but remaining a member of the Academy until 1930. The first scholarship bearing her name was awarded in 1971 and is the second award for competitors under ten.

By now the reader will have gleaned the fact that long association with the institution is a hallmark of many teachers of the RIAM. Edith Best, née Oldham, was connected with the Academy for some seventy years. The sense of enormous pride in her first major achievement as a scholar at the RCM, and indeed the first such achievement by a pupil of the Academy, is quite evident (other students, such as Sancia Pielou and Valerie Trimble, were to follow in her footsteps), and her career at the Academy did indeed fulfil the expectations of the Council, as has been recorded elsewhere in this book. It is perhaps worth noting that she was the first professor to be listed as the holder of a diploma in music in 1887, the ARCM (indeed the

only holder of that particular diploma among Academy staff until the temporary sojourn of the cello professor John Mundy in 1919), and her contribution
as teacher and governor was recognised by her peers in 1938, when, together
with Annie Irwin, she was made a fellow of the RIAM. The first Edith
Best Scholarship was awarded in 1968, eighteen years after her death, and
is the first scholarship on offer in the piano school, being given to the best
young competitor under eight, in recognition of the woman whose own
distinguished musical career began at an early age.

> The Governors have for some time past felt that the Organ Classes were
> handicapped by the old and somewhat out-of-date instrument which
> had been in use in the Academy for the past 26 years, and accordingly
> they obtained estimates for the building of a new organ . . . they are
> pleased to say that the new instrument has proved in every way satis-
> factory, and is now one of the best organs to be found in any teaching
> institution in the United Kingdom.[48]

The provision and maintenance of an organ in the Academy had been a
continuing expense since 1879, when one was installed under the terms of the
Vandeleur bequest. Organ classes for women and men were then instituted
under the tutelage of Sir Robert Stewart, assisted by Dr T. R. G. Jozé and
Charles Marchant. The construction of the 'new' instrument referred to above
in 1905 was made possible by the funds accumulated from the other major
bequest in the Academy's history, that of Elizabeth Strean Coulson.

While the first Academy organ scholar is officially recorded as having
been Charles Byrne in 1893, the first scholarships for organ were awarded
as entrance scholarships under the terms of the Coulson bequest in May
1887, two of the recipients eventually becoming major personalities in
Ireland's musical life, Annie Patterson and Vincent O'Brien. The first
scholarship awarded bearing the Vandeleur title was granted in 1897, to a
student who again was to become a major figure in the Academy's history,
Thomas Weaving, who also won the Vandeleur Academy Scholarship in 1899.

In an effort to encourage students to take up the instrument, extra prizes
were instituted in 1896 for playing at sight, and at one time, in the late
nineteen-forties, the number of students studying the instrument was so
great that a total of six scholarships was on offer. Today that number has
been reduced to five: the Vandeleur Academy, the Vandeleur, the Charles
Marchant Exhibition, the Hewson Exhibition, and the Rooke Memorial
Exhibition, the last of which is an entrance scholarship to the organ school.

In anticipation of the numbers expected to flock to the Academy after
the installation of the organ in 1879, Charles Marchant was engaged as an
assistant to Sir Robert Stewart in 1880, and as a piano teacher. However, the
expected deluge never arrived, and Marchant's services were dispensed with
after a year. He was appointed to succeed Stewart following the latter's
death in 1894, alongside Jozé, and represents one of the links between the
Academy and other venerable institutions, in this case St Patrick's Cathedral,
where he was organist. For a brief period the conductor of the Academy's

choral class, he frequently acted as examiner for the Coulson entrance scholarships; and while the number of organ students was never overwhelming during his tenure, a steady attendance of between twenty and twenty-five was maintained. The excellence of the teaching they received from Marchant and Jozé is attested to by many extern examiners' reports of the time and the professors' own accounts of their students' successes. One, William Hopkins, became assistant organist at St Patrick's in 1916, while Thomas Weaving (about whom more will be said later) was successful in obtaining the post of organist to the Chapel Royal (Dublin Castle).[49] Charles Marchant, meanwhile, obtained his doctorate in music from TCD in 1910 and, following the resignation of Jozé in 1918, became senior professor of organ at the Academy. His health began to fail in 1919, and he died the following year.

The first Charles Marchant Exhibition was awarded in 1961, and for a time it was twinned with the Coulson Academy Scholarship. However, in view of the difficulty referred to earlier concerning the regulations governing the Coulson scholarship, it was decided in 1996 to restore the Marchant Exhibition as the sole award available to middle grade students under twenty. Marchant's successors as professors of organ, B. Warburton Rooke and George Hewson, have also had awards named after them.

George Hewson represents another link with St Patrick's Cathedral, where he was trained and where he became organist and choirmaster in 1920 (in succession to Marchant). He also renews the connection, begun by Dr John Smith (and continued by Sir Robert Stewart), with Trinity College, Dublin, where he was awarded a doctorate of music in 1914 and where he was appointed professor of music, in succession to another Academy professor, Charles Kitson, in 1935. Dr Hewson retained his position as professor of organ and member of the Board of Studies of the Academy for forty-seven years, though he was succeeded as professor of music at Trinity by a former member of the Academy staff, Brian Boydell, in 1962; in the same year he became a fellow of TCD. Dr Hewson retired from the Academy in 1967, and died in 1972. When it was decided in 1996 to rename the Coulson Scholarship (under twenty) for organ, George Hewson's name was the immediate choice. This was not the first honour accorded him. He and Esposito are the only two members of staff to have had a teaching and recital room named after them; in Hewson's case, not surprisingly, it is the room that has housed the Academy organ since its installation.

B. Warburton Rooke is recorded as having won the first scholarship awarded for harmony in 1881. One of the many examples of Academy teachers who taught in several departments, Rooke joined the staff as a teacher of piano in the men's classes in 1889, in succession to Blüthner, who resigned his position to take up an appointment in Canada. Rooke is listed as an examiner for the annual rudiments of music examination two years later and by 1893 had started teaching harmony as a junior teacher alongside Jozé. He was appointed official teacher of junior harmony two years later, while retaining a piano post. In 1898 he became a member of the Board of Studies. Having established a special class for sight-singing, with himself as its sole teacher, in 1908, he became vice-chairman of the Board of Studies in 1913 and an examiner for the local centre examination system in 1918. Having temporarily taken over Marchant's classes in 1919 because of the latter's illness, he became joint professor of the organ (with George Hewson) in 1920, the year in which he became professors' Governor. He retired as governor in 1930 and was awarded a fellowship the same year. Following a long term of office as chairman of the Board of Studies, he retired from the Academy in 1937, and died five years later. The first scholarship bearing his name was awarded in 1946; it was open to both internal and external students until 1986, when it was decided that it should be confined to external students only.

> In the Vocal Department the Council thought it of great importance to engage a Professor from the Italian Schools of Singing, and with this view they communicated with some of the most important of the Italian conservatoires. They decided, after much enquiry, on the appointment of Signor Luigi Caracciolo, from the Conservatoire of Naples, considered among the very first of the Italian Schools of the present day. The Council have every reason to be pleased with the appointment made, and, in the short time that has elapsed, the progress of the pupils in the Classes under the direction of Signor Caracciolo has been most satisfactory.[50]

The quotation illustrates the Italian influence exerted on the vocal department, the second faculty in the history of the Academy to award scholarships, in its formative years. Indeed, until 1965 the singing school was largely dominated by Italian professors: Caracciolo, Bozzelli, Palmieri, and Viani. The Governors took this factor so seriously in the training of young singers that classes in Italian were also established and were the longest-lasting of the language classes (which at one point included French and German also), though the number of students attending them was very small. When the line of Italian singers was temporarily broken in 1887 with the death of Caracciolo and the reappointment of Joseph Robinson in his place, the Council

> thought it desirable that a colleague to Mr. Robinson should be chosen, who should specially represent the foreign schools of singing . . . Herr Roeder resided for a considerable time in Italy, where he studied the Art of Singing under distinguished Professors . . .[51]

Despite this, the titles of three of the singing scholarships commemorate three Irish professors associated with the vocal faculty, who between them encompass almost a hundred years of teaching: Annie Irwin, Dorothy Stokes, and Violet Burne.

Annie Irwin was one of the first pupil teachers employed in the Academy, being mentioned in the records as an Academy scholar in 1881. A pupil of Joseph Robinson, her ability was apparently not confined to singing: having won a scholarship in harmony in 1881, she was reported as receiving tuition under the terms of the Coulson bequest as a cellist in 1887 and 1888. She was made a full member of the staff in 1889 and became a junior professor and member of the Board of Studies in 1903. The distinction of fellowship was conferred on her in 1938, and she resigned from the Academy in the following year. After her death in 1945, the Governors founded the Annie Irwin Memorial Exhibition 'as a permanent memento of her worth.'[52] It was first awarded in 1946 and is today considered a middle grade scholarship (under twenty-three).

Like Annie Irwin, Dorothy Stokes was multi-talented. Another student of O'Hea and Esposito, she had a distinguished student record as a pianist (Coulson scholar 1914, Coulson Academy scholar 1915, Vandeleur scholar 1917, Vandeleur Academy scholar 1918, Certificate of Proficiency 1919, and Arthur Oulton Memorial Prize 1921), which was supported by an equally distinguished record in harmony (Vandeleur scholar 1918, Vandeleur Academy scholar 1919). The minutes of the Board of Studies of 1 March 1921 record that she was the student singled out for special praise by Hamilton Harty. 'He expressed himself absolutely delighted with the one pupil who was in for the Arthur Oulton prize and who got all her training in the Academy saying that he had never heard anything like it before.'

It was as a teacher of theory and harmony that the greater proportion of her energies was engaged early in her teaching career in the Academy. She was appointed to the main staff as a theory teacher and rehearsal pianist in 1928, while also teaching in Alexandra College. She found time to become secretary of the Student's Musical Union and took over the direction of the RIAM Orchestra from her old teacher, John F. Larchet, in 1941. She was appointed a professor in 1951, serving the Academy in the administrative capacity of professors' Governor (1966 and 1977) and chairman of the Board of Studies (1976), and continued to teach piano and musicianship after she had retired from the Board in 1978, up to her death in 1982. She is commemorated in the awards of the vocal faculty by virtue of her greatest strength as an accompanist and répétiteur. Her work with singers is attested to many times in external examiners' reports: 'May I add a special word of praise to Miss Dorothy Stokes for her really outstanding work as accompanist,'[53] and 'I hope that the various candidates fully realise the enormous help supplied by Miss Dorothy Stokes as accompanist. In many cases they have her to thank for the grand total of their marks!'[54] It was for this reason that it was decided in 1988 to rename the junior vocal exhibition (under twenty) the Dorothy Stokes Memorial Exhibition.

Writing in the 1956 'Centenary' brochure, Dorothy Stokes said of her time as secretary to the Students' Musical Union that she felt 'very proud, as I had so much enjoyed the work and in a way the success of the Union . . . I handed on the torch, so to speak, to Havelock Nelson, Michael O'Higgins, Betty Sullivan, Molly Concannon, and later to the joint Secretaries, the first pair being Violet Burne and Agnes Murphy . . .'[55]

Violet Burne—a descendant of the owners of one of the premises that now houses the Academy, number 38 Westland Row—was appointed a singing teacher to replace Kathleen Roddy, who resigned from the staff in

1946. She became a professor and member of the Board of Studies in 1964, resigning her position in 1979. She was the dedicatee of E. J. Moeran's last song cycle, and her many pupils included Gráinne Yeats (née Ní Éigeartaigh). Following her death in 1988, a new junior singing scholarship (under nineteen) was designated the Violet Burne Scholarship, in tribute to her. The following year a silver cup for lieder singing was donated to the Academy by her sister, Dorothy Woodham, and it was first competed for in 1990.

> Hitherto the Pianoforte and Harp have been almost the only instruments taught to ladies, but the Violin is, even more than these, an instrument suitable for domestic cultivation. Its wonderful power of expression, its portability, and convenience of price, render it available for all classes of musicians, while the resources it opens for Part Music and performance of the works of the Great Masters, are calculated extensively to promote the introduction of musical works of a concerted character into the circles of private and family society. The Council hope that this branch of musical instruction in the Academy will become a useful and popular addition to its Classes.[56]

The first string scholarship, for violin, is recorded as having been awarded to Philip Levenston in 1873. While classes in violin, cello and wind had been well established for male students in addition to classes in singing, piano and harmony, women were confined to these last three subjects. Despite the optimism of the Council, which clearly regarded this announcement as breaking new ground in 1878, its expectations appear not to have been fulfilled, as three years later it reported that

> the number of ladies attending ordinary Violin Classes not having increased as the Council had hoped, a class was opened towards the close of last season for instruction to pupils already in the Academy. This class has been very successful so far, the number of pupils being thirteen. A similar class for the Violoncello has been established and is attended by five Pupils. The Council desire gradually to encourage the study of Orchestral Instruments by Ladies, thus largely developing the resources for home music, at present limited almost entirely to the Pianoforte.[57]

In this endeavour the Council appears to have been eventually successful, though the expansion of cello classes referred to presumably applied to male students only; cello classes for women were not established until 1885. The number studying both instruments showed a steady increase; and the string school received a welcome boost in 1887, when scholarships for both cello and double bass were established under the terms of the Coulson Bequest, with the consequent extension of the duties of the professor of cello to include the teaching of double bass.

The presence of double bass players no doubt added greatly to the regular orchestral practice that had been announced the previous year, and the Council proudly reported that among the various performances given by students in 1887 there was a 'Concert of Chamber Music on which occasion J. S. Bach's triple Concerto for three violins, three violas, and three violoncellos [Brandenburg No. 3], was performed for the first time in Dublin.'[58] It is not clear whether the viola players required for this performance were students at the Academy, as formal viola classes were not announced until the following year, with no indication of which professor would be in charge. This situation was rectified with the appointment of Theodore Werner as professor in 1889 as a successor to Carl Lauer, not only teaching violin and viola but assisting with orchestral practices alongside Joseph Robinson.

These names indicate another fact concerning the string school in its early years, namely the preponderance of German professors associated with it: Berzon, Lauer, Stein (violin), Werner (violin and viola), Elsner, and Rudersdorff (cello and double bass). In the eighteen-nineties this influence was modified somewhat by the appointment of Octave Grisard and the first of the Italian teachers, the internationally renowned soloist Guido Papini.

In 1891 Theodore Werner asked for a 50 per cent increase in his wages if the Academy wished to retain his services. The Governors refused, and following his resignation they appointed John Dunn, who stayed only a few months.

'Signor Papini was well known to the Public, and he was engaged as Instructor of a limited class of advanced pupils, the Governors providing for his remuneration by an enhanced term fee.'[59] Born near Lucca, Papini received his musical education in Florence and made his performing debut at the age of thirteen. By the time he came to Ireland he had been court violinist to the Queen of Italy, a soloist at the Philharmonic concerts in London, and a member of a distinguished quartet that numbered Sarasate and Wieniawski among its members, and had shared the stage with such musicians as Rubinstein and Hans von Bülow. In the Academy his stature was recognised not only by the high fee his lessons commanded but by the introduction in 1892, for the first time in the institution, of the practice of 'alternate lessons' from him in tandem with Grisard (who may have acted as a type of assistant and who was clearly regarded as the junior partner, as evident from the lower fee charged for his classes). He also specified a junior teacher, Florence Bloom, for the women's classes and a future full-time member of staff, the pupil teacher Patrick Delany, for the men's classes.

By 1895, pupils of any teacher in the violin school could apply for alternate lessons from the senior professor, and the success of the violin school is reflected in the number of students, recorded as 118 in 1896.[60] The following year, however, the Governors were reporting a slight decrease in numbers, caused by 'the regrettable intermittent illness of the head professor, Signor Papini.'[61] In an attempt to keep Papini on the staff, the Governors engaged yet another assistant, Gerolamo de Angelis from the Conservatory of Milan, but to no avail: within a year both men had resigned their positions. Papini retired to London, where he concentrated on composition and private teaching.

By 1936, the number of scholarships available to violin students had dwindled to three, but from 1939 onwards the number of awards began to increase once more. The first Guido Papini Scholarship (the first of the senior grade violin scholarships for students under twenty) was awarded in 1951. Adolf Wilhelmj was appointed to succeed de Angelis in December 1898. He was the distinguished son of an even more distinguished father, the violinist August Wilhelmj, a friend of Wagner and leader of the orchestra at Bayreuth. Adolf Wilhelmj, the violin professor most referred to in the Academy's previous commemorative publication, was clearly influenced by his father's association with so great a composer; his Dublin home in Aylesbury Park (from 1908 onwards) was named 'Rhinegold'. He is listed as a Coulson examiner from 1901, in which capacity he worked alongside his eventual successor, Achille Simonetti, and he also acted as a local centre examiner. He resigned his position to return to Germany in 1912. The first Adolf Wilhelmj Exhibition was awarded in 1951, and today it is the first scholarship on offer to middle grade students of the violin under sixteen.

Nancie Lord, a niece of Annie Lord, is first mentioned in Academy records as a Coulson scholar in 1917.[62] Thereafter, she proceeded to sweep the boards at Academy examinations by winning the Coulson Academy (1918), Vandeleur (1920) and Vandeleur Academy (1921) scholarships and obtaining her certificate of proficiency (honours) as a violin teacher in 1922. Appointed to the staff of the Academy in 1925 to succeed Mrs Lang, who had resigned, she pursued a dual musical career in Dublin as a teacher and as a member (and sometime leader) of the Radio Éireann Orchestra (later the RÉSO). She was made a professor in 1948. Nancie Lord died in 1966. The first scholarship bearing her name was awarded in 1972 and is the most senior of the scholarships available to junior grade students (under fourteen).

The Board of Governors' tribute to Patrick Delany on his retirement in 1946 refers to a connection with the Academy as 'an unbroken span of over 60 years, and never had any institution such a loyal and devoted friend.'[63] A pupil of Guido Papini, he won Academy and Vandeleur scholarships (1891 and 1892, respectively), becoming a pupil teacher in 1892 and being promoted to full staff member in 1896, with responsibility for the men's junior and elementary grades, and evening classes. Like Bessie Ruthven, he appears to have had a somewhat quiet if worthy Academy career, in which he also acted as a local centre examiner. The first Patrick Delany Exhibition, for the best young violinist under twelve, was awarded in 1949.

We have seen Walter Starkie's memories of Simonetti, written in 1956. Born in Turin in 1857, Simonetti, like Papini, enjoyed an international reputation as a soloist and chamber musician, having studied in Turin, Milan, Genoa, and Paris, where he not only studied violin with Dancla but also studied composition with Massenet. Having been the leader of a quartet in Nice, Simonetti went to England to tour as a chamber musician, taking up residence in London in 1891. While a member of the London Trio (1901–12), he was engaged by the RIAM to act as examiner for the Coulson Academy scholarships in 1906, and he returned in 1907 to examine jointly with Wilhelmj for the Coulson scholarships. Following his appointment in 1912, he also became an examiner for the local centres, a position he occasionally filled even after his connection with the teaching staff of the Academy had been severed. That the number of students studying the violin declined during his tenure is not a reflection on his teaching but probably a sign of the war in Europe, as many Academy students went off to fight in Flanders.

Simonetti resigned his position in 1920 to return to London, dying there in 1928. The first Achille Simonetti Scholarship was awarded in 1951 and is the middle of the three junior scholarships (under ten) available to young violinists; the first scholarship in this grade provides a second tribute to Maud Aiken.

The first scholarship for cello is recorded as having been won in 1880 by Joseph Edwards. The first Vandeleur Academy scholarships were awarded in 1897 to Kathleen Gibson and Mary Gallagher. The only other named scholarship awarded in the cello school commemorates a professor of that time, Heinrich (or Henri) Bast. He was the last of a line of German professors of cello appointed to succeed Rudersdorff in 1892, and, like his predecessors, was required to teach men the double bass, should any pupil for that instrument present himself (it was six years before Bast acquired his only student of this instrument). Becoming a Coulson examiner on his appointment, Bast, like Papini, adopted the practice of alternate lessons in the men's classes in 1894, expanding this to all students in 1897, and it was to him that the task of revitalising chamber music classes was entrusted in 1899. In this he appears to have been extremely successful, as recorded by the number of prize-winning ensembles from the Academy in the annals of the Feis Ceoil from 1901 onwards, and this despite the complete lack of viola students in the institution. A serious illness in 1902 resulted in the temporary appointment of Clyde Twelvetrees to take over the cello classes, and he was then appointed a full-time member of staff, and professor, on Bast's return. It was Twelvetrees who succeeded Bast as senior professor following Bast's death in 1907. The Henri Bast Exhibition, which is given to the best junior cello competitor under fourteen, was first awarded in 1961.

The first scholarships to be awarded in the Academy were given, as we have seen, in the keyboard, vocal and string faculties; the next faculty to award scholarships (1881) was known variously as 'harmony and counterpoint' and 'theory', what we now know as musicianship. In common with these other faculties, the musicianship school has bestowed Vandeleur Academy and Vandeleur scholarships, the first winners being again Thomas Weaving for the former and Gretta Gillespie and Margaret Gallagher for the latter, in 1900; but the commemoration of its distinguished teaching staff has been through the award of prizes for composition.

One of the dominant figures in musical life in the nineteenth century, Sir Robert Stewart came late in his career to the Academy, in 1872, the year in which he received his knighthood. Like Charles Marchant, he represents a link with not one but practically all the major musical institutions of that time. In 1894 it was stated that it is an interesting circumstance in relation to . . . his character, that from among the pupils of the Academy has been, at their own suggestion, collected in small sums, a fund from which an annual medal will be given as a Prize for competition. The public at large have contributed liberally to establish a monument to his name and genius, but this spontaneous work of affection and esteem from those who, most immediately, were able to appreciate his powers as a teacher, speaks perhaps more eloquently than any other monument to his memory.[64]

Sir Robert's reputation endures still. On the centenary of his birth, further tribute to his legacy was paid by the Board of Governors,[65] while more recently, in 1994, the statue of him that stands on Leinster Lawn was restored to its former glory in commemoration of the centenary of his death.

The requirements for the award of the Stewart Memorial Prize tended at first to vary from year to year; today, silver and bronze medals are awarded for the best original composition submitted by either present or past students of the Academy, the only award in the Academy with this distinction.

For many years the Stewart Prize remained the only prize for composition, along with three scholarships: the Vandeleur Academy, Vandeleur and Junior scholarships. (The latter two were transferred to the category of harmony and counterpoint in 1975.) In 1996, the Board of Governors decided to institute four prizes for young composers in the Academy, commemorating four of its most recent professors of harmony and counterpoint.

Having obtained his certificate of proficiency in harmony with honours in the previous year, Larchet was appointed to succeed Nita Edwards as a junior teacher of theory the same year. The distinction he achieved in obtaining the LRIAM was not to be repeated for another seventeen years, when Muriel Graham was awarded the diploma in 1930; until that time, Larchet enjoyed separate listing in the lists of scholarship and certificate holders printed each year in the annual report of the Board of Governors. Born in 1884, Larchet also studied with Esposito and was appointed musical director of the Abbey Theatre when he was twenty-three, a position he held for twenty-seven years. He was awarded the degrees of MusB (1915) and MusD (1917) by the University of Dublin and was appointed senior professor of harmony, succeeding Kitson at the Academy in 1920, thus joining his old teacher Esposito on the Board of Studies. He also succeeded Kitson as professor of music at the National University the same year; and so when George Hewson became professor of music at Trinity College (also in succession to Kitson) in 1935, the Academy could boast the distinction of having the professor of music from both Dublin universities on its board of education.

Larchet achieved a further distinction in 1929 when it was announced that

during the year, with the consent of the Commissioners for Charitable Endowments and Bequests, the Governors instituted the Diploma of Fellow of the Royal Irish Academy of Music and named John F.

Larchet, LRIAM, MusD. TCD, the first Fellow of the Royal Irish Academy of Music, he being the first pupil of the Academy who ever presented himself for and passed the examination for the Diploma of LRIAM.[66]

Larchet's influence in the Academy was widespread, ranging from his work as a local centre examiner, senior professor of harmony and conductor of the orchestral class to membership of the Board of Studies (where he was frequently entrusted with the overseeing of various projects not necessarily connected with his own post) and of the Board of Governors, who entrusted him with the task of restructuring the administration of the Academy in 1948. He became a vice-president in 1931 and vice-president of Trinity College of Music, London, ten years later. He was awarded a second doctorate in music by the NUI in 1953. He retired from the teaching staff of the RIAM in 1955, though he remained a vice-president until his death in 1967. In tribute to him, and to the enormous influence he exerted on Irish music, the John F. Larchet Prize is awarded for the best arrangement of a traditional air for instrument or voice with piano accompaniment submitted by a student under the age of fifteen.

In the year in which Larchet received his second doctorate, Archibald James Potter received his MusD degree from Trinity College, Dublin. Born in Belfast in 1918, Potter received most of his musical training in England, having had Ralph Vaughan Williams among his teachers, and for a time his musical career was focused on two areas, singing and composition. It was as a singer that he obtained his first post at the Academy, in 1952, when he was appointed professor of singing; three years later he was appointed professor of harmony, in succession to Larchet. Like Larchet, he held a number of positions in the Academy: local centre examiner, chairman of the Board of Studies (1957–62), and member of the Board of Governors (1959–71). A prolific composer, he also combined his work at the Academy with a career in broadcasting and is the only member of the Academy staff to have received a Jacob's Award. He retired from the Academy in 1971 and died suddenly in 1980. It was thought appropriate that someone who was a skilled and sympathetic teacher, and who encouraged young composition students, should be honoured through the award of a prize for best original composition submitted by a student under fifteen. The first A. J. Potter prize was awarded in December 1996.

James Wilson acted as an external examiner for the annual scholarships in composition at the Academy in 1970, before being appointed a teacher of composition in 1971, following Potter's retirement. Wilson was born in England and studied composition at Trinity College, London, before settling in Ireland in 1948, though he has also worked in Denmark, and his music reflects his travels in Europe generally, particularly in the use of rhythm. A member of Aosdána, he has been associated with most of Ireland's principal music festivals and institutions in connection with performances of his works, including RTÉ, Wexford Opera Festival, Cork International Choral Festival, and the International Summer School of Composition held in

Ennis each year. In a tribute to his work at the Academy during his brief tenure (he resigned in 1974), the James Wilson Prize is awarded for the best original composition for solo piano, instrument and piano, or voice and piano, submitted by a student under eighteen.

A student of both George Hewson and John F. Larchet, and a member of a distinguished artistic family,[67] Walter Beckett is first mentioned in Academy records as the winner of the Coulson Scholarship for organ in 1932. This he followed by winning, in successive years, the Coulson Academy and the Vandeleur and Vandeleur Academy scholarships for organ, together with the Vandeleur scholarship for harmony in 1935. Having obtained the diplomas of LRAM (piano teaching, 1934) and ARCO (1936), he was appointed organist of St Canice's Cathedral, Kilkenny, in 1938, a position that has subsequently been held by other members of the Academy staff, such as Arnold McKiernan and David Lee. Walter Beckett was awarded the degrees of MusB and MusD by the University of Dublin (1936 and 1947, respectively), and, following a period of residence in Italy as conductor and composer, returned to Ireland to pursue a career as teacher, author (his biography of Liszt remained the standard work for many years), and composer. He was appointed professor of harmony, counterpoint and composition at the RIAM in 1974, and retired from that position ten years later. During his tenure as professor he also acted as chairman of the Board of Studies and of the musicianship faculty, the professors' representative Governor, and local centre examiner. He was made a fellow of the RIAM in 1990. A superb teacher and an unfailingly kind and courteous chairman of faculty, his death in 1996 was keenly felt by all those associated with him during his Academy career. The Walter Beckett Prize (awarded for the best arrangement of a traditional air for instrument or voice with piano accompaniment, or small chamber ensemble, by a student under eighteen) is a tribute to his skill as a teacher, as well as a recognition of his interest in Irish music and chamber music.

Mention has been made of the various prizes offered by the Academy; some commemorating past members of staff have already been referred to. But of this category, five such awards deserve special mention.

The Joseph Robinson Memorial Prize (instituted in 1900 to commemorate one of the most prominent founders of the Academy, who died in 1898 and whose contribution to the history of the institution is documented elsewhere in this book) is awarded for the best performance by a singer of a recitative and aria from an oratorio.

The Rita Broderick Cup (donated 1974) is awarded for the best performance of set and own-choice repertoire by a middle grade violin or viola student, in tribute to another student of Margaret O'Hea, a distinguished professor, member of the musicianship faculty, and member of staff of the music department of University College, Dublin.

The Weaving Cup (instituted 1962) is awarded for accompaniment and sight-reading as a tribute to Thomas Weaving, who was appointed to the Board of Studies in 1925 (and was still a member of the Board when he died in 1966) and who was associated with the Academy (as student, organ and harmony scholar, co-founder of the Students' Musical Union, local centre examiner, professor of organ and teacher of harmony, chairman of the Board of Studies and professors' Governor) for seventy years, from 1896 onwards, and musical director of the Rathmines and Rathgar Musical Society for many years.

The Dina Copeman and Rhona Marshall Cups are two of the most recently instituted awards, commemorating more of Esposito's students, two of the most eminent members of the keyboard faculty, whose careers were closely intertwined over a period of some seventy years. A student of both Margaret O'Hea and Esposito, Dina Copeman won the Vandeleur and Vandeleur Academy scholarships for piano in 1915 and 1916, respectively, and obtained her certificate of proficiency (honours) as a piano teacher the following year. In 1919 she was the first winner of the newly instituted Arthur Oulton Memorial Prize for advanced piano sight-reading. Rhona Clark (Marshall) is first mentioned as a Coulson scholar in 1915; she subsequently won the Coulson Academy (1916), Vandeleur (1919) and Vandeleur Academy (1920) scholarships, obtaining the certificate of proficiency (honours) in 1921 and the Oulton Prize in 1922.

Thereafter, the careers of the two women progressed along parallel lines. Both were appointed teachers of the junior grade classes in piano in 1926 and were among the first Academy students to give many radio broadcasts as performers in the early years of broadcasting. Ten years after their appointment, they were both promoted to teacher of middle grade classes, while in 1948 both were appointed professors.

The similarities in their Academy careers was signified in 1963, when fellowship of the RIAM was conferred on them, virtually identical wording being used in the tributes that appeared in the Governors' report of that year.[68] Both served the Academy as local centre examiners, as chairwoman of the Board of Studies and as professors' Governor many times during their professorial careers. They both retired from the Board of Studies in 1978, though continuing to teach, Dina Copeman until shortly before her death in 1982 and Rhona Marshall until she retired in 1985.

The Copeman Cup, which is awarded for the best performance of an own-choice programme (all or part of which must be works by Chopin) by a student aged sixteen or over, was first awarded in 1980. Rhona Marshall died in 1994; in 1996 the trustees of the fund established in her name donated the Rhona Marshall Cup for the best performance by young students of a sonata for string and piano duo, in tribute to her work as a teacher and her love of chamber music.

In this review, three categories are missing: wind, brass and percussion; speech and drama; and chamber music. While all have figured in the Academy's history from the late nineteenth century onwards, expansion of the range of scholarships, awards and grades has only occurred within the last forty years, and few commemorative awards have been created.

As noted earlier, the first Coulson scholars included wind and brass players, but it was not until more recent times that the foundation for today's awards was laid by the sponsorship of scholarships by the Arts Council (1952–57) and entrance scholarships sponsored by the Irish Federation of Musicians (1963–64). The range of scholarships has continued to expand, the most recent being that for percussion, which was first awarded in 1994. The named award in the wind, brass and percussion faculty is the Raymond Cavanagh Award, established in 1995 in memory of a talented young French horn player, awarded for the best performance by a student under eighteen of original repertoire for brass.

One of the first prizes for declamation is mentioned in 1902.[69] In that year, the Academy received a donation of five volumes of Shakespeare as a prize from the renowned actor Sir Henry Irving. Prizes and cups for declamation, elocution and speech and drama continued to be awarded subsequently by the Board of Governors (and through the generosity of Ursula White, professor of speech and drama, who donated the senior grade and advanced senior grade cups for competition); but it was not until 1964, following the establishment the previous year of the School of Dramatic Art (no longer in existence), that scholarships for speech and drama were listed for the first time. These were added to through the provision of the first award (a gold medal, 1963) and first scholarship (1965) for *deaslabhra agus drámaíocht*, and major restructuring of the syllabus in 1974 resulted in the comprehensive scheme of awards that exists today.

'This [chamber music] Class has been formed during the year and placed under Herr Bast. The results are already most encouraging and the Governors confidently expect that Chamber Music will in future form an important branch of study in the Academy.'[70] Though this statement appeared in the Governors' report of 1899, the class was, as we have seen, a reinstitution of an older one, which is recorded as having been under the tutelage of the piano professor, Billet, in 1888.[71] The tradition of a tutor or co-ordinator for chamber music continues today, two of the most recent incumbents being Professor Seán Lynch and Sheila O'Grady.

The first prizes for chamber music in recent times were awarded in 1958; in the following year it was reported that 'Mr. Joseph O'Reilly very generously made a donation to provide a scholarship for a Chamber Music Group,'[72] which was awarded to a string quartet in the same year. Joseph O'Reilly, who, like L. E. Steele, was a Government inspector and a member of the Academy, continued to donate prizes for chamber music until 1964. In 1970 the Joseph O'Reilly Award reappeared as a named prize, and further funds were provided in 1976 by a member of his family, John O'Reilly, to enable the competition to continue.[73] Today the award is maintained by the Academy in tribute to yet another of its benefactors. The competition is open to ensembles drawn from middle and senior grade students, with the exception of piano duettists, for whom separate prizes are available.

The Beethoven Cup was presented to the Academy by the German government in 1970 in commemoration of the bicentenary of the composer's birth. Originally shared between the faculties (with the exception of musicianship) as an award, the competition is today confined to students of strings and piano, in all grades.

The Dorothy Moulton Mayer Memorial Trophy commemorates Dorothy Moulton, who died in 1974, an author and singer (who sang in the first performance in Britain of the second string quartet of Schoenberg) and wife of the renowned businessman and music patron Sir Robert Mayer. The fame of both rests on their founding and patronage of an annual series of children's concerts in Britain, which began in 1923; and Lady Mayer, who was of Irish ancestry, is further remembered in Ireland for establishing the Dorothy Mayer Foundation for musical projects in 1958. The trophy is unique, in that it is offered for competition between students of the RIAM and the DIT Conservatory of Music and Drama, being held in the two institutions in alternate years. Inaugurated at a ceremony held in the Academy in 1974 in the presence of President Erskine Childers, it was first awarded to Academy students in 1978.

The primary schools competition has been discussed earlier (chapter 5). Professor Marie McCarthy has shown how the Academy drew on the model provided by the British music colleges in establishing such a competition and how the motives behind such an enterprise owed as much to the competitive payment-by-results system, prevalent among music teachers in schools of the time, and the imposition of the tonic sol-fa method of sight-reading developed by Curwen (through the use of the 'carrot' of a substantial monetary award and a subtle downgrading of the alternative Hullah system) as to any well-meaning desire to foster a love of music among the Dublin school community in general.[74]

Nonetheless, the Academy was clearly proud to be associated with such a project, as is evident from the Governors' report.

> The teaching of Vocal Music in the Primary Schools of the Dublin District . . . is a subject of much importance, and likely to tend to very great improvement in musical education. It is a branch of instruction which the financial resources of the Academy would not enable the Governors to undertake. The Corporation, recognising the need of such education, considered that the citizens would heartily support them in promoting it.[75]

> The Governors report with much pleasure that the Corporation of the City of Dublin have voted a grant of £300 yearly towards the maintenance of a School of Music in connection with the Academy. The grant is made in pursuance of the Public Libraries Act. Some time must elapse before any important results can be expected, as efficiency is to be attained only after a considerable period of study. The pupils are increasing in numbers, and the citizens of Dublin, it is hoped, will, at no distant date, reap advantage from the expenditure of their funds.[76]

The history of the RIAM's involvement with the Municipal School of Music is discussed elsewhere in this book, beginning with its origins as an institution where mainly wind, brass and percussion instruments were taught, with the addition, not surprisingly, of a course in tonic sol-fa, which was being taught in its parent institution. It then expanded to include classes in violin, cello, and theory. Some members of the Academy staff, such as Arthur Darley and Thomas Weaving, were employed at both institutions. Annual examinations were conducted, and small monetary prizes awarded, but references to these are scarce in the reports of the Governors at the time. In 1898 L. Edward Steele made the following recommendation:

> I would venture to suggest that, now that there is some balance to the credit of the funds of the School a series of more valuable prizes should be instituted, frequent and more public advertisements of its advantages be made, and that some connection between its pupils and the Academy be formed. This latter might be effected by founding some small scholarships, carrying free instruction in the Academy for the more deserving pupils of the School.[77]

No significant developments resulted in response to this suggestion (which was reiterated in 1902), though in 1900 it was decided to inaugurate an annual prize-giving ceremony, with the Lord Mayor presiding.[78]

With the Denis O'Sullivan Medal, the Academy is linked to some of the principal music festivals. Denis O'Sullivan was an Irish-American baritone and actor who was born in San Francisco in 1868 and who studied singing in his home city and in Florence, London, and Paris. He first came to the attention of Irish audiences when he made his operatic debut in Dublin with the Carl Rosa Opera Company in Verdi's *Il trovatore* in 1895, and thereafter he pursued an operatic career on both sides of the Atlantic, while finding time to appear in a number of plays by Dion Boucicault on the American stage. He died in Ohio in 1908. His connection with the Academy comes in the person of Esposito, in whose opera *The Post-Bag* (1902) Larchet says that O'Sullivan played the principal role in an American production. Esposito first suggested that the Academy become associated with such an award.

Funds for the Denis O'Sullivan Medal were originally donated by his widow to the Feis Ceoil, the committee deciding to award a gold medal for a competition open to baritones only, and with set test pieces.[79] The Academy was then prevailed on to continue the award, and to administer a trust fund in his name. A memorial fund was eventually established in the Academy in 1909 with an initial sum of fifty pounds, increased to seventy pounds the following year, the interest being used to purchase silver and bronze medals. The fund was invested at first in the Merchants' Warehousing Company, but it was decided in 1911 to reinvest it in the British government's India stock at $3\frac{1}{2}$ per cent, so as to place the award on a sounder footing.

In its first year under Academy auspices, an award was made to a competitor at the Sligo Feis only, those competing at the Feis Ceoil being deemed not to have reached the standard. In its report of 1912, the Board of Governors announced plans to award a bronze medal at the Derry Feis the following year, though it was not until 1949 that the award was extended to include the Limerick Feis. Gradually the original requirements were altered, and the competition was expanded to include all singers, who must present 'two Irish songs of contrasting character in English or Gaelic, ancient or modern, original or arranged, provided the spirit and form are Irish.'[80] The award continues to this day (a silver medal being awarded at the Sligo Feis, a bronze medal at the Feis Ceoil), a visible reminder of the Academy's commitment to performing excellence, as well as of the brilliant career of a fine artist.

Fellows of the RIAM

1929	Dr John F. Larchet	1990	Olivier Messiaen
1931	Margaret O'Hea		Charles Acton
	B. Warburton Rooke		Walter Beckett
1932	Vincent O'Brien		Brian Boydell
1933	Adelio Viani		Aloys Fleischmann
1936	Madeleine Larchet		Anthony Hughes
	Annie Lord		Gerard Victory
	Thomas H. Weaving	1991	Karl-Heinz Stockhausen
1938	Annie Irwin	1993	Doris Keogh
	Edith Best	1994	Lindsay Armstrong
1954	Dr J. J. O'Reilly		Dr John O'Conor
1961	Maud Aiken	1995	Valerie Walker
1963	Dina Copeman		Audrey Chisholm
	Rhona Marshall		Seán Lynch
1985	Joan Trimble	1996	Anna Brioscú
	Havelock Nelson	1997	Deirdre Kelleher
		1998	Terry de Valera
			Richard Pine

Intermezzo

HAVELOCK NELSON

It seems that I was meant by Fate to go to the RIAM at an early age. I was first taught the piano (and viola) by Jeanie Russell, who had been there in the great Esposito's regime. She lived near us in Sandycove. In addition to her piano teaching she was also a violinist and violist. When I was ten she enrolled me into playing piano trios, me on the piano, with her on the violin and an elderly neighbour on the cello. Thanks to her we explored all the Haydn and Mozart trios.

Those early incursions into chamber music continued weekly for about twelve years and ended when I finished university. They were never meant for public hearing (thanks be to God!) but they were a musical joy to the three performers—music making as it should be.

Alas, Esposito had retired back to Italy and died just before my father enrolled me as a student, so that I never had a lesson from him. However, I had the next best thing: nearly everyone who taught me came from his stable. When I was twelve my parents sent me to St Andrew's College, then in St Stephen's Green. That meant a journey by train to Westland Row station and a walk past the RIAM. I had noticed that many people made the sign of the Cross passing St Andrew's church in Westland Row. My father was most amused when, one day when we were together, I did the same thing when passing the Academy.

In spite of the headmaster of St Andrew's College trying to persuade my father to make 'Havelock give up this musical nonsense,' it continued to be my absorbing interest, and I was enrolled in the Academy.

My principal piano teacher, who took the place of Jeanie Russell, was a dedicated lady called Dina Copeman, who had given up a promising career as a performer to devote herself to teaching—she had in fact been the pianist chosen to play at the inauguration of Ireland's first broadcasting station, 2RN, later Radio Éireann and now Radio Telefís Éireann. She and Dorothy Stokes were major figures and I owed a lot to them, especially in the chamber music field from Dorothy Stokes, she being a splendid theory cum harmony teacher.

Miss Stokes was undoubtedly the 'character' on the staff. Despite the fact that she was one of the famous Stokes medical family and related to the Guinness banking family, and had been educated at a high-class ladies' school, she had a fierce Dublin accent. One got the impression that she must have been brought up to sell bananas in Moore Street. Even though she could be quite astringent at times, I was very fond of her. Short and rotund, she directed our theory and harmony class from the piano with a lighted cigarette dangling permanently from her lower lip. We used to watch with eager anticipation to see the lengthening ash drop off and fall down the front of her ample bosom. Strangely enough, I cannot remember it ever happening, but there was always the hope.

It was Miss Stokes who encouraged me to start composing, and I sketched out the music for an opera early on. Where I got the libretto from I have no idea.

One thing with Miss Stokes that I did hate was sight-singing tests, and I somehow managed to develop laryngitis on the days when the tests were held. I don't think I fooled her for a minute, but she passed me over as quickly as she could. Later in my time Dorothy Stokes and I used to compete in feiseanna with student orchestras, but it was usually a good-natured battle.

Dina Copeman was a different kettle of fish: you either worked for her or there was trouble ahead. She was a real tyrant who terrified any pupil who had not done sufficient practice. I don't think that I would have had any success but for her driving force. But she certainly got results. Even after I had left her officially, I used to return for refresher lessons, until I left TCD in 1943. I remember once a distinguished English adjudicator called Ambrose Cobiello stopping me in a piece and asking me where I got my lovely singing tone from—Dina Copeman of course.

She was broad in her teaching approaches and sent me to Rhona Marshall on several occasions, because she said the latter knew the test pieces better than she did. Prof. Anthony Hughes was at the Academy with me, and I found she had done the same with him also. I still remember seeing her in St Michael's Hospital at the end of her life, and she analysed all the lessons I had had from her as though they were yesterday.

Though not so in name, the virtual director of the RIAM in those days was Dr John F. Larchet, a gentle, kind, helpful musician who was loved by all his pupils. He was an admirable composition teacher who never imposed his own musical personality on them. He was lucky in having as organiser a delightful colleague, Sealy Jeffares, the secretary of the Academy, a man who was helpful and kind on every occasion. He was never surpassed in his particular field.

Then there was the Quinn family, who ran the porter and domestic services of the Academy. John Quinn, the father, was 'just' the porter but, with his beaming kindness and unaware but unquestioned authority, seemed to preside over the place. One of his sons (also John) became the first Irish maker after the war of the real Irish harp. He had a real craftsman's love. A friend of mind once asked him how he gauged the thickness of the soundboards. He answered, 'I just go on planing until God tells me to stop.' I am told that it is only a very few years since his daughter Sheila retired, thus ending a family connection going back to the very first year of this century. They were an essential part of the RIAM's make-up, especially at exam times.

Exams, and the excellent scholarships, were an integral part of the musical year, and we would have been sadly off without them, and the Quinn family looking after us like motherly hens. We picked our orchestras from the exam results and laid the plans of future 'bands'. Many of us aspiring conductors were born from these efforts. People were anxious to get experience and to do things for love and enthusiasm—something sometimes remote from today's scene, where the good players expect to be paid from the start.

People have asked me was the Academy a good thing. *Yes!* Within its restrictions it definitely was. One remembers all the encouragement it gave to students, especially through the Students' Musical Union, which was run by Dorothy Stokes for many years and whom I followed as hon. sec. The Dagg Hall, originally the band room, where the SMU events took place, was also the venue for other ventures; one recalls the first performance in Ireland of Britten's *Let's Make an Opera* (presented by the Music Association of Ireland, and conducted by me). That was the inspiration of James Wilson's *The Hunting of the Snark*.

One could go on remembering events which came to fruition in the Academy; suffice it to say that Ireland and Dublin would have been a much poorer place without it. And recently Joan Trimble and I were recalling that it was one of the few places where one could practise two-piano duets.

Havelock Nelson (1917–1995), born in Cork, educated in Dublin, and working professionally in Belfast, claimed thereby to be the 'real United Irishman'. In addition to a MusB at TCD he took an MSc, and a PhD in bacteriology, before devoting himself full-time to music. As a composer he had over a hundred published original works and arrangements, and as a conductor he worked with most Irish orchestras as well as acting as the station accompanist at BBC Northern Ireland. He was the founder and conductor of the Studio Symphony Orchestra and the Studio Opera Group (and later the Trinidad Opera) and became much sought after as an adjudicator, and in later years was often accompanist for the violinist Geraldine O'Grady.

Intermezzo

BRIAN BOYDELL

When Michael O'Higgins retired from his position as a singing teacher at the Academy, I applied for the post and was very glad to be appointed to what was my very first securely paid job as a struggling young professional musician. That was just after my marriage in 1944, when I was very glad of the £32 2s 10d I was paid in the first year. As the number of my pupils grew, I earned what was then the princely sum of £193 7s 10d in the year before I retired in 1948. I was then teaching about twenty-seven hours each week, with just two dozen pupils on my roll.

My room was above where Maestro Viani taught in the large front room next to the organ room. I still have ringing in my ears the sound of large operatic voices going through their exercises. Five notes rapidly up and down—a two-chord modulation up a semitone—same again—and then again, with ever increasing strain until I imagined them totally exhausted and no longer able to respond to the next upward modulation.

Spending so much time in my rather bleak room, I resolved to add a touch of humanising cheerfulness. I was given permission to redecorate it over the summer holiday, which I did with the help of Frank Keyte, armed with brushes and a bucket of distemper. He was one of my more senior pupils, who had come over with his wife from England to the well-paid position of vicar choral at St Patrick's Cathedral. My wife and I formed a lasting friendship with the Keytes—as indeed with some other pupils of mine, including Denis Donoghue, who eventually went on to become a very distinguished literary critic and academic.

My activities at the Academy were not confined to teaching singing. I was appointed conductor of the student orchestra and took an active interest in the Students' Musical Union, where pupils had the opportunity to perform in public. My young singers would normally be accompanied by that wonderful character Dorothy Stokes, whom I visualise in memory with a cigarette permanently dangling from her lips.

If Dr Larchet could be thought of as the 'prime minister' of the Academy in the forties, there is no doubt but that the 'president' was John Quinn, the caretaker and hall porter. His warm and cheerful smile welcomed all who entered, from shy little children to formidable senior members of the teaching staff.

Intermezzo

CAROL ACTON

'You don't know how to practise! How long were you up there?' (i.e. in the attic above her room in the older house—my friend Joan McElroy was in the other one). 'Three hours? And how long exactly did you practise?' Mentally I worked it out and answered, 'Ten minutes.' I was still in my teens, and 'she' was my violin teacher, the diminutive and formidable Nancie Lord. The time spent not practising was used for gazing out of the window at the traffic far below in Westland Row or, when the cold defeated me, mooning around the blazing coal fire downstairs in the entrance hall, well fuelled by either John Quinn or his son Paddy.

The fire was large, glowing, beautifully hot, and a meeting place—in fact it was the hub of the Academy in the late forties and early fifties. The secretary, Sealy Jeffares, a large, amiable gentleman, would pass by and make enquiries about the state of our studies. Michael O'Higgins would sail rapidly into the hall on a scouting expedition for a répétiteur for his 'Thirteens', who were rehearsing *The Magic Flute*. He often found me, a piano pupil of Rhona Marshall (my two instruments were equal), to our mutual delight, because I was a good sight-reader and avid for experience.

The singing pupils Denis Donoghue, a tall and handsome baritone (and future world academic) and Anne Woodside (singer but also organ pupil of Prof. George Hewson and who later married Alan Bliss) came looking for somebody to accompany them in Vaughan Williams's *Songs of Travel*, or Duparc.

If the hall got too crowded close to the fire, some of us would move out to Johnston, Mooney and O'Brien's for a coffee and a cream bun, often sharing these when money was short (£2.50 was my weekly allowance for digs, food, bus fares, postage stamps, cinema, etcetera).

If you lived far away and were in 'approved' digs and piano was one of your instruments, then finding one to practise on was a problem. Friendship with Paddy helped, and I used to turn up in Westland Row at 8:30 in the morning to find Paddy doing the brasses on the front door; a little chat and I was in, with no teachers about and my choice of pianos.

Paddy helped again when we wanted to rehearse in what is now the Dagg Hall, rigging lights or showing us how to. We hated that stage, with the yawning wide gap of a pit between us and the audience.

Working down in the pit was a different matter. Playing fiddle there for one of Maestro Viani's operas had its own hazards, as our inadequate sounds often caused him to dance with rage on top of his small table. Still, we learnt a lot of Donizetti and Bellini, from the inside out; our pianist was Gertie Leahy, a gifted jazz player and now living in the USA.

Chamber music was frowned upon in my day; pianists would ruin their muscles if they took up the cello; time spent on the classical Brahms and Mozart quintets (with those rather unacceptable wind players) cut short our practising time on solo concertos, sonatas, and scales. It's no wonder we sneaked away from assignations made by the fire to play all sorts of lovely music that had nothing to do with our scholarship and exam requirements. To say nothing of playing for a week's *Mikado* in the Holy Faith Convent in Glasnevin, with black ice on the ground and no buses from the Pillar, all for ten shillings (old style) per week. That was part of being a student of classical music (two practical instruments plus harmony and counterpoint) at that time.

10

The Special Collections of the Academy Library

PHILIP SHIELDS

*Establishment of the library; Antient Concerts Society collection;
Anacreontic Society collection; Monteagle bequest; Hudleston
guitar music collection; Academy composers; vocal music;
chamber music; methods and tutors.*

D ermod O'Brien, the person most responsible for establishing the new Monteagle Library in 1939, described what previously existed as follows:

> A good many years ago, on the occasion when the appointment of a senior Professor of piano was under consideration, I was struck by the request of one of the candidates to be allowed to see the library. Such a request seemed to be a natural one, for this Academy is not merely an examining body or a school of technique, but is primarily an educational body . . . At that time there was a small room at the top of the house with locked presses and many paper parcels of music on top of them. In another room there were more shelves with music on them, and many parcels on the floor which represented Signor Esposito's collection. Elsewhere there were also many unopened parcels of music bequeathed by the late Lord Shandon. Very little of this music was catalogued or available for use or reference.[1]

Although the library was not officially opened until 1939, following the substantial bequest of books and scores from Thomas Spring Rice, Lord Monteagle, the history of its collections extends as far back as the end of the eighteenth century. The great bulk of the Academy's collection was obtained by donation or bequest; only in the last fifteen years has music been purchased systematically according to the teaching requirements of the institution. As there is no detailed record of accession lists (donations being merely recorded briefly in the Governors' minutes), the provenance of much of the material is difficult to establish, although some collections are identifiable by a stamp or owner's name on the flyleaf. Occasionally the donation was recorded inaccurately, as with a private collection comprising over sixty-five volumes of bound guitar music received in 1877 and recorded as 'orchestral music from Mrs. Hudleston.'[2]

For most of its existence, the library has not been served by a comprehensive catalogue and has remained hidden from musicologists and researchers. As a result, a rich and varied collection has built up that has not received the attention it warrants. Of particular interest are the libraries of several orchestral and choral societies active in Dublin in the eighteenth and nineteenth centuries (the Anacreontic Society, Sons of Handel, Antient Concerts Society, and others), and many more private donations of vocal, instrumental and chamber music containing early printed editions of works by Handel, Corelli, Haydn, Mozart, Beethoven, Pleyel, and Spohr.

Some items of interest previously believed to be lost or unpublished have been found in these collections. Apart from their interest as source texts, these items have a value as historical documents, being a record of the musical activities of individuals or societies. With regard to private societies, such as the Anacreontic Society, they are probably the most substantial record of their activities. The Hudleston Collection contains an astonishing range and wealth of solo and chamber music for the guitar dating from the nineteenth century.[3]

Clearly there was no continuous effective library service until the opening of the Monteagle Library in 1939. Previous attempts had been made to deal with the accumulating collection of printed music. J. E. Geoghegan, a Governor, was reported in 1929 as undertaking the 'onerous task of overhauling and re-cataloguing the Academy Library.'[4] When Thomas Spring Rice, Baron Monteagle, died in 1934, his cousin Dermod O'Brien, an Academy vice-president, approached Monteagle's uncle with a view to securing the donation to the Academy of Monteagle's substantial private music collection.[5] This was granted, on the condition that the music be properly housed and maintained.

O'Brien originally undertook to provide for the building of an annexe (at no extra expense to the Academy) to house the collection.[6] A library committee was set up to advise on the establishment of the new library, and after some deliberation it was decided instead to use the front room of number 36 (previously the secretary's office and now the board-room). O'Brien organised a subscription concert among Monteagle's friends and associates, given by the Hungarian violinist Jelly d'Aranyi and Donald Tovey, from which he managed to raise almost half of the £1,200 expended on the establishment of the new library.[7] One of the respondents to O'Brien's requests for funds declined, remarking, 'If you do build a library your Govt. will probably confiscate it—or your anti-govt. burn it down . . . I gather that you are considered to be "foreign" by people with such distinctively Irish names as de Valera and Blythe.'[8]

Later, the Academy sought guidance from an expert in the National University,[9] and two cataloguers were employed to sort the holdings before the library's opening.[10] Alice McCarthy, a former RIAM violin teacher, was appointed librarian, receiving a remuneration of £52 a year.[11] The Academy clearly regarded the new library as a source of pride: the Governors' Annual Reports mentioned 'use of the very fine Library of Music' when outlining Academy membership entitlements.[12]

Interest in the library led to an increase in the number of donations, which at first were conscientiously acknowledged in the Governors' annual reports. The same level of commitment was not maintained, however: the published acknowledgments became routine and generalised, and the use of the library was no longer proudly proclaimed as a conspicuous advantage of Academy membership. When Seán Lynch was librarian, as a student in the period 1951–52, he received just one pound a year, from which he was also obliged to pay for postage.

Following an extensive restoration of the eighteenth-century stucco work,[13] the rooms in the building were reallocated, and the library was moved into two basement rooms. In more recent years, the position of the library has improved markedly: it was reopened and extensively reorganised under John O'Sullivan in 1982 and today provides a comprehensive service to staff, students, and researchers.

The performance of oratorios and orchestral works by amateur societies was a central part of concert life in nineteenth-century Ireland. This is perhaps most evident in the growth of choral societies such as the Sons of Handel (founded 1790),[14] the Antient Concerts Society (1834–63), and the Dublin Musical Society (1873–98).[15] These societies maintained a continuous, thriving choral tradition throughout the nineteenth century, central to which was the involvement of the Robinson family, in particular Joseph Robinson, who conducted the Antient Concerts from 1834 until 1863. Substantial portions of their libraries are to be found in the Academy. In 1872, the Academy purchased the entire collection of the Antient Concerts library (which comprised also the parts for the Sons of Handel), for the purpose of running a choral class.[16]

The collection yields an insight into the repertoire of the society and, assuming the collection of choral parts to be relatively complete, the size of the choir at various stages of its development. The status of the Antient Concerts, as direct successor to the Sons of Handel, is confirmed by the presence of copyists' parts of Handel's *L'Allegro, il Penseroso e il Moderato* stamped 'Sons of Handel', with the stamp of the Antient Concerts from 1835 overlaid. Connections with societies or individuals are revealed elsewhere: there are a number of parts of Beethoven's *Fidelio*, Haydn's *Seasons* and Mozart's *Don Giovanni* printed specifically for 'Dublin Subscription Concerts, 1834,' which were evidently presented to the Antient Concerts Society in that year by William Hudson, who had been instrumental in organising the Dublin Grand Musical Festival in 1831.

The repertoire is also revealing. A large part of the collection is taken up with printed scores and parts of Handel's oratorios, with the society's stamp indicating the date of acquisition in the middle to late eighteen-thirties but also as late as 1859.[17] The full scores include a number edited by John Clarke in the early nineteenth century, and later some of the Handel Society editions; other editions have a curiosity value, such as *L'Allegro*, published by Surman with 'additional accompaniments by G. Perry,' including clarinet parts. While the preponderance of such works in the collection testifies to the continuing popularity of Handel's oratorios well into the nineteenth century, there are also four volumes of Purcell's works in nineteenth-century editions by Novello.

Of interest also are the early editions of Locke's *Macbeth* in Boyce's revision of 1770. This work was performed by the society in 1849 at a concert in aid of the new Irish Academy of Music.[18] Mendelssohn's music is particularly well represented: it includes the psalm settings, oratorios and sacred and secular cantatas, many of which are in the original German Simrock edition, obtained shortly after their publication. Among these can be found the oratorio *St Paul*, which the society performed on a number of occasions in the late eighteen-forties and early fifties.[19] A Novello full score of Mendelssohn's *Hear My Prayer* contains a note stating that the composer orchestrated the work expressly at the request of Robinson for a performance by the Antient Concerts Society.[20] Large-scale oratorios and cantatas by contemporary English composers, such as Horsley, Benedict, William Gardiner, and William Sterndale Bennett, also make up a substantial portion of the collection. The Antient Concerts Society held an annual competition for composers, the winning composition being performed by the society.[21] The collection contains a manuscript copy of the 1838 winning composition in full score, *Remember O Lord* by Thomas Atwood Walmisley (1814–1856), an English cathedral composer of some note.[22]

The Sons of Handel collection consists entirely of manuscript parts in a copyist's hand of works by Handel such as *L'Allegro, il Penseroso, ed il Moderato, Judas Maccabaeus*, and *Acis and Galatea*. All these have watermark dates of 1820, indicating their probable date of production and acquisition by the society to be between 1820 and 1825.

The Academy's collection contains a number of sets of bound orchestral parts from the late eighteenth and early nineteenth centuries. At least three of these have some connection with the Anacreontic Society (*c.* 1740–1865), an orchestral group that consisted mainly of amateurs, although its leaders and conductors were usually professionals. It hosted a number of visiting virtuosi, including Kalkbrenner in 1824, Liszt in 1840, and Thalberg in 1842.[23] The society was essentially private, and did not advertise or gain publicity, records of its activities being confined to cursory newspaper reports, which rarely detailed the music performed.[24] These bound part-books are probably the fullest record of its activity and repertoire.

The first collection contains a dedication on the flyleaf of the *principale* part: 'Presented to the Anacreontic Society in 1837 by Captain Speedy

MILITARY PIECE's

FOR

TWO CLARINETS TWO HORNS

&

A BASSOON

COMPOSED (BY THE LATE)

I.. C.. BACH

AND MOST .RESPECTFULLY DEDICATED

TO THE

RIGHT HONORABLE

LORD O NEILL

COL: OF THE ANTRIM MILITIA

PRICE 8.. 1h

DUBLIN

PUBLISHED BY B: COOKE at his PIANO FORTE HARP & MUSIC WAREHOUSE (4) SACKVILLE sT.

Who Supplies MILITARY .BANDS with Instruments Music &c. &c. &c.

[Royal Barracks, Dublin] for many years a member and recently voted Honorary Secretary.' There are indications that they were bound a decade or so earlier, possibly the middle eighteen-twenties, suggesting their prior use by another orchestra.[25] The repertoire comprises mostly concertos for violin and flute by leading virtuosi of the late eighteenth and early nineteenth centuries, such as Devienne, Drouet, Kreutzer, and Rode, although Beethoven's violin concerto is included. Interestingly, there are a number of concertos by Ivan Mane Jarnowick (Giornovichi) (*c.* 1740–1804) and Feliks Janiewicz (1762–1848), both of whom visited Ireland as celebrated performers between 1796 and 1821.[26] Other items include Weber's *Overture to the Celebrated Opera Der Freischütz*, in a copy dating from around 1823 (indicating the immediate assimilation of the work in the repertory) and even an orchestral arrangement of Handel's 'The Harmonious Blacksmith'.

Although this is primarily a collection of orchestral music, there are two sets of military quintets. The first is the only surviving copy of J. C. Bach's four *Military Piece's* [*sic*] *for Two Clarinets, Two Horns and a Bassoon . . . Dedicated to the Right Honourable Lord O'Neill, Col. of the Antrim Militia*, published in Dublin by B. Cooke in 1794. The dedication almost certainly originates from the publisher, not the composer, who died twelve years previously. These pieces were rediscovered in the Academy by Stanley Sadie in 1956, and he edited them for publication by Boosey and Hawkes the following year. He described them as being comparable to 'the lighter and less ambitious wind divertimentos of Mozart's Salzburg period . . .'[27] The second collection of quintets is a set of twenty short pieces (probably also a unique copy) for the same forces by Johann Bernhard Logier (1777–1846), unfortunately lacking a title page and any indication of the publisher or date.[28] Logier, of German extraction, settled in Ireland from 1809 and was to gain notoriety for his controversial teaching method, based on the 'chiroplast', discussed in more detail below. These military pieces are a reminder of his rather less exalted musical origins as a bassoon player in the Tyrone Militia. Hitherto they have been considered to be either unpublished or lost.[29]

A separate set of incomplete parts contains the wind sections of two symphonies dating from 1821 by Paul Alday (1764–1835), another foreign musician who settled in Dublin around 1805 and who was active as a composer and publisher, taking over Francis Rhames's music shop in 1810.[30] He was also for many years leader, secretary and treasurer of the Anacreontic Society. When these symphonies were reviewed on publication in 1821, they were claimed to be the first works in this genre composed and published in Ireland. Writing of the second symphony, the reviewer declared that 'on the whole it contains so many beauties that it must always be a desideratum to the selection of every lover of instrumental music.'[31] All the parts of the symphonies were previously believed to have been lost without trace.[32]

A very different range of repertoire is covered in another bound set of parts, each of which is clearly identified as part of the society's library, comprising overtures and symphonies by Auber, Spohr, Beethoven and Mendelssohn and seven concert overtures by Johann Wenzell Kalliwoda (1801–1866), a composer much in vogue in the eighteen-fifties.

One set of orchestral parts exists whose original ownership cannot be determined; these were bound by Rhames's music shop, probably in the last years of the eighteenth century.[33] They contain eight Haydn symphonies in editions by Longman and Broderip and by Imbault published in the seventeen-nineties, and sixteen *sinfonies périodiques* by Adalbert Gyrowetz (1763–1850), a composer active in London between 1790 and 1792. Gyrowetz had the curious distinction of having one of his symphonies pirated by the publisher Sieber and published under Haydn's name, through which it became a favourite in the repertory.[34]

A number of manuscripts in a copyist's hand are marked 'Anacreontic Society, 1823' and contain parts of accompaniments to arias from Mozart's *Don Giovanni, Figaro, Così fan tutte*, and others. Other copyists' parts of *Messiah* can be dated to *c.* 1815. A range of activities, other than purely orchestral concerts by the society, is indicated by the presence of Haydn's string quartets and manuscript part-books of glees in its library.[35]

Thomas Spring Rice, Baron Monteagle (1883–1934), had a distinguished career in the British diplomatic service, being posted at various stages to St Petersburg, Washington, and Paris; he was attached to the British delegation at the Peace Conference in 1919. His interest in music was lifelong. An overriding appreciation of Bach is revealed in the forty-six volumes of the complete *Bach-Gesellschaft*, as well as the many other volumes of Bach's organ music owned by him. While in Russia he took a keen interest in the country's contemporary music, represented here by a full score of Scriabin's *Prometheus* in its original 1911 edition, Stravinsky's *Petrushka* in the composer's piano duet version (1911), and full scores of four Glazunov symphonies. Some volumes of flute music (incomplete) belonged to Thomas Rice, an ancestor of Lord Monteagle,[36] dating from 1812 and including many contemporary editions of flute music published by Monzani and a flute solo by Louis Gianella (1778–1817) 'composed for and dedicated to Thomas Rice.'

Texts and treatises are represented by Helmholtz's treatise on acoustics in an English edition (1875) and Hopkins and Rimbault's work on the history and construction of the organ (1877). The most outstanding item is a finely bound 1789 edition of Burney's *A General History of Music from the Earliest Ages to the Present Period*, a landmark of music historiography in England but one that also has an interesting contemporary outlook on the works of Haydn and Mozart.[37] Monteagle's interest in European folk music is shown by a collection of French folk songs collected by Bujeauld (Nice, 1866), as well as a collection of Breton folk songs.

In 1877, the wife of Josiah Andrew Hudleston (1799–1865) donated his entire collection of over sixty bound volumes of guitar music, in printed and manuscript form, to the Academy.[38] Hudleston had lived for many years in Madras, where he worked for the civil service of the East India Company, rising to the position of chief revenue collector, before retiring to Ireland in 1857. He was an amateur of considerable accomplishment, judging from the difficulty of his own guitar transcriptions. While in India, he purchased his substantial collection of guitar music from Europe through a publisher in Madras and a bookseller in Calcutta. The printed collection is comprehensive, covering all the major guitar composers of the early nineteenth century, including the complete solo works of Giuliani and many by Sor, Carulli, Legnani, and other lesser figures. The editions were published mostly in London and Paris, a centre of interest in the guitar and home to Sor and Carulli at various times. There are many chamber works, including duos for two guitars or guitar and flute and other instruments, and even a work for guitar and string quartet. Notable also is the quantity of tutors and methods for flute, violin, piano, and harmony (strangely, none for guitar), as well as the chamber works for clarinet and other instruments. Apart from the printed editions, there are a great number of items in manuscript. Most of these are compositions and arrangements by Hudleston himself, as well as a short tutor by him on the production of harmonics on the guitar. His arrangements are of most interest: they include selections from the *Water Music* and a collection of airs and choruses from *Judas Maccabaeus, Solomon*, and *Messiah*. There are also selections from operas by Donizetti, Verdi and Rossini and the entire second act of Bellini's *Norma* in Hudleston's arrangements. These are quite faithful to the originals and of uncompromising difficulty, sometimes having entire passages in harmonics, and were clearly intended for virtuosi rather than amateurs.[39]

The popularity of this music diminished greatly towards the end of the nineteenth century, and only in recent years has it begun to be played widely again; as a result, this private collection is a valuable resource, containing rare or unique copies of publications that have been used recently as the source for a number of forthcoming editions. An interesting feature of this collection is the fact that it belonged to a guitarist who was a contemporary of many of the composers represented and who in fact knew some of them.

There have been numerous other donations of music from individuals throughout the Academy's history; the more substantial are listed in the note at the end of this chapter. The most notable are the Shandon Bequest (1930), comprising volumes of opera scores, nineteenth-century piano music, and popular songs; the Edith Best Collection (1951) of piano music; and the Emily Knox Collection (1952), mostly parts for orchestral and chamber music discussed below. More recent donations have been from Joan Trimble (two-piano music) and Heather Hewson (songs and vocal scores).

The Academy contains a substantial portion of the *œuvre* of Michele Esposito (1855–1929), whose varied career is discussed elsewhere in this book. He conducted the Dublin Orchestral Society from 1899 to 1914 (whose orchestral library he donated to the Academy in 1929)[40] and in 1915, with Stanley Cochrane, established a publishing house, CE Editions, which operated until his death in 1929.[41]

While his works encompass a variety of genres, including piano and violin sonatas, string quartets, symphonies, and songs, piano music forms the greater part of the Academy's collection. The style of these works is firmly entrenched in a romantic idiom, deriving in part from Brahms and Fauré. Also of note is his cantata *Deirdre* (Dublin, 1897), which he dedicated to his pupil Edith Oldham. In 1909 he composed the opera *The Tinker and the Fairy*, to a libretto translated from the Irish by Douglas Hyde.[42] Like many of his contemporaries, he arranged traditional airs for both violin and voice with piano accompaniments. As well as composing, he produced a considerable number of editions of piano works by Mozart, Beethoven, and Chopin, all published by CE Editions, as well as Italian Baroque composers such as Marcello, Galuppi, and Paradisi. His edition of Beethoven sonatas compares favourably with other contemporary editions, with only a minimum of editorial markings overlaid on the original text. The Academy holds none of Esposito's manuscripts, still the only source for many of his works.

There is a handful of works by Sir Robert Stewart (1825–1894), professor of harmony and organ, in the collection, in both manuscript and printed form. So also are those of T. R. G. Jozé, who taught in the Academy from 1870 and who was professor of harmony from 1894 to 1919.[43] Many of Jozé's are in manuscript, including his composition submitted for a University of Dublin BMus and DMus in 1877, *The Prophecy of Capys*.[44]

Other Academy teachers feature as composers in the library; these include Achille Simonetti (violin professor 1912–19), Guido Papini (violin professor 1893–96), and Adelio Viani (singing professor from 1917 and a Governor from 1931). The Antient Concerts collection contains the cantata *God Is Love* by Fanny Robinson (a teacher of piano and Joseph Robinson's first wife), which was the first item to be performed by the Irish Academy of Music choral class in 1872[45] and which received favourable reviews. Her output is also represented here by a number of ephemeral piano pieces and songs. Joseph Robinson produced a number of choral arrangements of Irish airs, as well as a *Magnificat* and *Nunc Dimittis* and elementary choral exercises, all to be found in the Academy's collection. There are also a number of songs by Sir Francis Brady. Stewart and Jozé collaborated on producing arrangements of Irish airs,[46] as did Sir Francis Cruise and Guido Papini.[47]

A number of other Irish composers not directly connected with the Academy feature in the collection. These include C. V. Stanford, whose works here comprise songs, opera, oratorio, and many other genres; James Culwick, who founded the Orpheus Choral Society in 1898 (later the Culwick Choral Society). An opera by a virtually unknown composer, W. Harvey Pélissier, *Connla of the Golden Hair*, was a Feis Ceoil prize-winner in 1903 and is of curiosity value in that the composer provided a detailed table of leitmotifs, in the manner of Wagner, at the beginning of the vocal score; and a number of works by Benedetto Palmieri, Joyce's singing teacher in 1903 and professor in the Academy, are also extant.

Vocal music, particularly solo song, comprises a very considerable part of the Academy collections. Many of the nineteenth-century editions are of popular songs no longer in the repertory. A copy exists of the *Celebrated Death Song of the Cherokee Indian* (Dublin, *c.* 1780) by Tomasso Giordani, an opera composer who settled in Dublin from 1779, as well as a number of other Dublin publications of songs from the period. Opera is well represented by a collection of over three hundred vocal scores from the nineteenth century, including much mid-century French opera.

Earlier publications include six volumes of operatic *pasticcios*, published in London by Bremner and Walsh in the early seventeen-sixties. In a practice prevalent in London in the eighteenth century, operas were presented not as originally conceived but as assemblages of airs by different composers, with inclusions or substitutions of arias, often at the whim of the singer. Gluck's *Orfeo* was heard in London in 1770 and in Dublin in 1784 as a *pasticcio*, with additional airs and modifications by J. C. Bach and others.[48] There is a copy of this version in the library.[49] In a separate volume is a selection of English *pasticcio* operas in contemporary editions, including *The Maid of the Mill, Lionel and Clarissa*, and *The Beggar's Opera*, all of which were performed regularly in Dublin at the time.[50] A bound volume contains a copyist's manuscript of nineteen arias from *Crispo* and fifteen from *Ciro* by Bononcini (1670–1731). Active in London as an opera composer from 1720, Bononcini was seen there as a rival to Handel, his style being acclaimed for its lyricism and sensitivity to text, in contrast to the highly virtuosic style of his contemporaries. As the original score for *Ciro* was destroyed during the Second World War, this aria collection is the most extensive source for the London performances of the work.[51]

There are quite a number of volumes of collections of Irish and Scottish folk song. Notable are early editions of Bunting and Moore, including Bunting's second collection of 1809,[52] which attempted to compete with Moore by including twenty airs with songs written by Thomas Campbell and others. A volume of the original *Selection of Irish Melodies with Symphonies and Accompaniments by Sir John Stevenson* (which Moore produced between 1808 and 1834) is here, as well as the 1838 edition of *The Melodies of Scotland with Symphonies and Accompaniments . . . by Pleyel, Haydn, Beethoven, Weber, Hummel &c.* in six volumes, collected and commissioned by George Thomson.

Chamber music parts include London editions of Haydn string quartets from 1795, published as opp. 1 and 7,[53] as well as an early Pleyel edition of the complete eighty-three quartets published in Paris. Thirty of Pleyel's string quartets are contained in bound part-books, in editions published in London in the seventeen-nineties (the composer paid a visit to the city in 1791–92). Flute quartets by Pleyel, Devienne and Eler (all published in the seventeen-nineties) are included also.

Most striking is the number of arrangements of symphonies by Haydn, Mozart and Beethoven for chamber ensembles ranging from three to seven players, dating from the early nineteenth century, perhaps indicating a favoured means of realising such orchestral works in a private setting before the later popularity of the piano duet.[54] These include the adaptations of Haydn symphonies for trio and quintet made by Salomon, who had secured Haydn's visits to London in 1790–91 and 1794–95. Of two volumes of Handel's keyboard music, one contains the eight 'great' *Suites de Pièces pour le Clavecin* (1795) published in London by Wright, who succeeded

Walsh, Handel's original publisher, in 1785. The other comprises arrangements for solo keyboard and duets with keyboard of Handel's overtures, organ concertos, and *Musick for the Royal Fireworks*, all in the original Walsh edition.

There is also music for the newly invented English concertina (as well as music for its predecessor, the mouth-blown 'symphonium', patented by Sir Charles Wheatstone in 1829), taken from the German *konzertina*, invented in 1834, and composed and published by Wheatstone and Company, who held the patent for the instrument. These are specimens of some of the earliest music written for this instrument and include some remarkably virtuosic works by Giulio Regondi (1822–1872), who in fact performed on this instrument in the Antient Concert Rooms in 1854.[55] The music includes the *Fantasia on Airs from Lucia di Lammermoor for Concertina with Accompaniment for the Piano*.

A substantial donation of harp music from Louisa Cane (1901) contains, among other things, an autograph manuscript of Charles Oberthür's *Meditation: A Musical Sketch for the Harpe, Composed and Dedicated to Miss Louisa Cane . . . op. 149*, which Oberthür presented to her during his visit to Dublin in 1858.

The collection of methods and tutors, mostly dating from the early to middle nineteenth century, is impressive. A number of these are in the Hudleston Collection. They include John Gunn's *Essay . . . on . . . Thorough Bass [Applied] to the Violoncello* (London, 1802), historically interesting in advocating the harmonisation of a bass line through multiple stops and arpeggios on the instrument; John Gunn's flute method (1793); tutors by A. F. C. Kollmann on thorough-bass (1807), harmony, and fugue (1822); and a clarinet tutor by Lefèvre in an early edition. Hudleston also bequeathed piano tutors by Kalkbrenner, Hummel and Czerny in contemporary editions. Outside his bequest can be found violin tutors by Spohr (1832) and Campagnoli (1824) in their original editions.

A copy of the sequel to the *First Companion to the Royal Patent Chiroplast or Hand-Director* dates from 1820. The 'chiroplast' was an invention of Logier, whose military music was discussed previously. This device was a wooden frame extended over the entire keyboard, on which were placed movable slotted 'finger-guides', which positioned the hand and blocked all finger movement except for the vertical. Logier used this bizarre instrument to drill a dozen or more pupils playing separate pianos simultaneously. This system was adopted in a number of 'Logierian academies' of the early nineteenth century. Kalkbrenner was an enthusiastic follower of the system and produced a modified version of the chiroplast (later mistakenly gaining credit for the invention); elsewhere, however, Logier's system met with much opposition and was lampooned by Cruikshank in a caricature captioned *A German mountebank blowing his own trumpet at a Dutch concert of 500 pianofortes* (page 487).[56]

Major donations, acquisitions, and bequests, 1848–1998

Anacreontic Society (n.d)	Orchestral parts
Antient Concerts Society (1872)	Choral and orchestral parts
Best, Edith (1951)	Piano music and song
Boydell, Brian (1996)	Books on music
Cane, Louisa (1901)	Harp music
Copeman, Dina (1984)	Piano music
Dublin Orchestral Society (1926)	Orchestral parts
Feddersen Library (1912)	Piano music and song
Feehan, Fanny (1995)	Books on music
Heller, Madame Coslett (1940)	Music by C. V. Stanford
Hewson, Heather (1995)	Keyboard and vocal music
Hudleston, J. A. (1877)	Guitar music
Joy, J. H. M. (1892)	Opera vocal scores
Knox, Emily (1952)	Orchestral and chamber music parts
Lloyd, E. (1898)	Vocal music and *Harmonicon*
Marshall, Rhona (1993)	Piano music
Baron Monteagle (1934)	Bach complete works and other music
Lord Shandon (1930)	Songs and piano music
Stockhausen, Karl-Heinz (1991)	Volumes of the composer's writings on music
Trimble, Joan (1996)	Music for two pianos
Weaving, Thomas (1964)	Vocal scores

Intermezzo

Valerie Walker and Audrey Chisholm
IN CONVERSATION WITH ARMINTA WALLACE

Valerie Walker came to the Academy as a pupil in 1944, studying piano with Dina Copeman and theory with Rita Broderick. Audrey Chisholm, who joined in 1951, studied piano with Rhona Marshall and theory with Dorothy Stokes.

What sort of place was the Academy in those days?

Valerie: It was a pretty dreary old building at that stage, with a terrible rickety old wooden porch inside the hall, and the stone staircase, which I remember being washed down regularly by Nan Bethel, our general factotum. But there was always a lovely fire in the hall, so everybody used to congregate there, and John Quinn, the porter, would be at his desk in the corner—a genial man; he was like everybody's father. It was very cold. There were fires in the teaching rooms and a coal bunker on each landing. I had my lesson at two on a Friday. Miss Copeman was always late, and Nan would be there trying to get the fire going with sticks. Oh, we used to battle with that fire—and if we didn't have it roaring up the chimney by the time Miss Copeman got in, there'd be real trouble. She felt the cold; my goodness me, she used to wear jumper on jumper. And if things weren't going well at the piano she'd go over to the fire and give it a good rattle and a bang . . . I think all our lives as students really revolved around Mrs Marshall, Miss Copeman, and Miss Stokes.

Audrey: Nan was a unique character. When I came to the Academy it was a lively institution, and I can remember us all congregating round the fire in the hall. There was another cleaning lady called Connie—she was engaged to John the porter's son (also called John), who made harps. She had a grandmother who lived down in Pearse Street, and she wouldn't marry John while the grandmother was still alive. John, unfortunately, died very suddenly, and when her grandmother died she left the Academy and went to work in Wales. The Quinn family, who were the caretakers, lived in the basement and had bedrooms at the top of the building. John's daughter, Sheila, prepared morning and afternoon tea in the kitchens and carried trays up to the teachers' rooms.

Valerie: As a teacher, we used to get tea to our room on a tray. You could hear it coming up the stairs. It was a great sound, the rattle of the tea—and you could get biscuits, or bread and butter. Mrs Broderick, who used to teach late in the evenings, would get her supper here. A boiled egg would arrive! Yes, it was a small place, but I didn't really get to know the other pupils at all. It was just in for my lesson and out again, and that was it—until I was involved with concerts and the SMU.

Audrey: Well, when I came in here the Students' Union was very active. As my home was in the midlands I lived in a bed-sit, and I practised in the Academy, so that's probably why it was more of a way of life for me, as I spent a large part of the day there. I loved the SMU. We took part in concerts every fortnight, and at the end of each term there was a guest night, when the items were chosen from the best of the fortnightly concerts. There was always a large audience, and the press and music critics came along. There was a great buzz at those end-of-term concerts, and refreshments for everyone afterwards. Then it was 'holding our breath' until the next day's *Irish Times*, and usually congregating in the library for a general read of 'What the critics said'! I mostly practised on my teacher's piano—one of the best. But one evening I thought I'd try Miss Copeman's piano. She always locked it, but, having been to a boarding school, I knew how to pick locks. Normally she'd be gone home, but this night she was walking down Westland Row with a friend and saw her light on. In she came and up the stairs—I'll never forget it, it was dreadful. 'How did you get the piano open? Have you broken it?' and then I was hauled up the next day before the lady superintendent. My bravery of the night before flew out the window, and I stuck to pianos that were open after that.

Valerie: Miss Copeman? Oh, she was flamboyant, though she had a very hard life. Her family lived in South Circular Road. They were Jewish; her father came over as a refugee to Dublin. There were about nine or ten in the family. She was always very grateful to the O'Hea family: they more or less adopted her. I don't know how much schooling she could have had. She was a very fine pianist—really passionate, I suppose you'd call it, and full of flair. She really loved music, and she could impart that to you too, but she could murder you: you'd come out feeling you couldn't take any more and would never go back. But you did go back, and the next time she'd have you walking on air—very inspirational.

Audrey: We had some hilarious times. I remember one Saturday morning I had been up having a chamber music class with Jaroslav Vaneček (who was a wonderful violinist and teacher), along with Seán Lynch, Molly Concannon, and Joan Miley [McElroy], and a couple of others. John

Quinn's son Paddy, who was on duty, was an experienced backer of horses. There was a race on that day, and he gave us a 'sure bet'. I had never in my life backed a horse and didn't even know how you did it; but there was a bookie's across the road, so we all put a shilling each way on the horse, and Paddy placed the bets. Then we all got into Molly Concannon's car and went up the mountains and listened to the race on the radio. I made twenty-one shillings, and all the others got something too—we all made money. It was exciting and scary all at once. I'll never forget it, and spent all the money. Luckily, I never felt like taking up the hobby.

Mrs Marshall was a real live wire. She had a house out in Glenageary called 'Moelvra', and she was very generous to her students—we all used to end up going out there at weekends, and we became almost part of her extended family. It was a sort of ritual coming near Feis time especially; if you went out for a lesson in the morning you had lunch there.

She used to service her own car—she had a little Ford—and she rode on a bicycle from her house to the station. Vaneček and Mrs Marshall were an excellent chamber duo and gave concerts at the RDS and around the country.

Vidor L'Estrange was a student of Rhona Marshall. He was practising a piece by Chopin for the SMU and was sliding off all the notes, making a dreadful hames of it, and Mrs Marshall told him on no account to play the piece at the concert. But he did play it—and not only did he play it, he turned up in a velvet jacket with his hair slicked back, and powder on it, trying to look like Chopin. We were all quite taken with his looks, but Mrs Marshall was 'not amused.' He was ostracised for a few days, and we weren't allowed to talk to him. But Mrs Marshall relented, as she always did, when her students got out of hand occasionally.

Valerie: You're getting a picture, are you, of these two matriarchal figures who almost ran the place? Even when I became a teacher myself I couldn't put a stamp on a letter without consulting Miss Copeman. If you did something wrong you'd be told in no uncertain terms. They were formidable even to look at—both of them: they had quite a presence. Miss Copeman had fantastic hats, and loved her fur coat . . .

I had a car, and Miss Copeman hadn't, so when we went away examining about the end of the nineteen-fifties I was brought along more or less as the chauffeur. She knew every nun from Galway to Donegal. She used to bring all her laundry—and this is odd, because nowadays you hear so much about the Magdalen Laundry—well, there was one attached to the Mercy Convent in Galway. And they would give us a wonderful supper there, and Miss Copeman would leave all her skirts, coats and dresses for cleaning. There was one place where we used to go in Louisburgh; it was before Easter, so it would be March—ugh, the cold—and as we drove up the avenue to the convent, there were all the little ones lined up along the avenue, most of them in little white dresses, with their music under their arm and the wind howling and the rain. And us in the car like royalty as the poor little kids shivered outside. There was an old Reverend Mother there, Mother Michael—she was well over ninety—and she had them so well drilled that they'd come into the room and babble off their name and their grade and do a little curtsey to Miss Copeman and sit down and begin to play. And then when it was all finished they weren't allowed to turn their back on the examiner, so they had to back out of the room! But they were very good—and there were some wonderful nuns. If it hadn't been for them there would have been far fewer local centres. There was a nun in Tuam Mercy Convent, Sister Attracta, who had been a pupil of Esposito, and in Clifden there was an orphanage school with orchestras.

There was never a dull moment with Miss Copeman around. She was a bit accident-prone too: she fell off a donkey in the Aran Islands and broke her ankle; she had her leg out with a plaster on it—that would have been about 1948. She used to play for the cinema; for the silent movies she had to do all the effects—the cowboys and the rest of it. I remember her mother. She used to come into the Academy to the concerts—a very kind distinguished-looking lady.

Several academy students found their way into the theatre orchestras
of the time.

Audrey: Seán Lynch was asked by Micheál Mac Liammóir to go up for an audition to Harcourt Terrace, and he was asked to get somebody else, as he needed two pianists. So we got work playing six nights of the week at the Gate Theatre. We got seven pounds a week—a fortune in the late fifties. We could play whatever we liked, but it had to be timed so that the curtain came up just as we finished. I know we played Schumann's theme and variations, and we started off with the Arrival of the Queen of Sheba. We also had to play the national anthem. We played at the start and at the interval. The start was the Queen of Sheba, then the first act, then the Schumann—it had to be the same thing every night because of the timing.

I remember the night that Seán didn't turn up. Hilton came along, and then Micheál came along and said, 'Can you cope?' and I said, 'Well, I'll do my best.' So I was sitting at the piano when I heard Seán's footsteps coming up the stairs—what a relief! It was a wonderful time. We did a season; *Tolka Row* was the play—it was on every night. I remember one night Orson Welles came, and we had a little peephole, so we peeped out at Orson Welles. Well, it was a very funny play, but at the funniest part of it he was sitting with a poker face. He never laughed the whole way through. I couldn't get over that.

Audrey: I started as a part-time teacher—I didn't teach every day—and what I remember most was we were paid in arrears. We started in September and got paid at Christmas; then we got paid at Easter, then in June, and not another penny until the next Christmas—that's what I remember most. It was a big lump, but by the time September came it was all gone. At that time, though, the MAI was successfully organising tours around Ireland with soloists and chamber groups, so that was a way of earning extra money, as well as having a 'platform'.

My favourite partner was the violinist Margaret Hayes, and we played in venues from Donegal down to west Cork. The worst piano was in Clifden, and at the rehearsal we had to change a phrase in a Brahms sonata where there were no notes sounding at all at one of the biggest climaxes. When these occasions went well it was really very exhilarating. Broadcasts from RTÉ and the BBC in Belfast also filled in the time, and concert engagements with the Symphony and Concert Orchestras, and the Dublin Orchestral Players were also very generous in offering young people engagements. One also had the opportunity of working with outstanding musicians, including Brian Boydell, who was a very entertaining conductor with the DOP at that time. They were halcyon days.

Valerie: Six and sixpence an hour, and you had to fill out a book with all your hours. The pupils came in twice a week, even the little ones, for fifteen minutes; it was nose-to-tail, with no time between each one, though it was a better system for the children, the twice-weekly lesson.

In the late forties and early fifties the music scene in Dublin—and therefore, of course, in the Academy—was dominated by a small but colourful cast of characters, many of whom were of European origin, having fled the Continent during or after the war.

Audrey: Mrs Vaneček was very artistic, and she used to do caricatures. They'd be up on the board out in the hall—Mrs Marshall on the bicycle down to the train, and do you remember Francis Engel from Switzerland? He was very thin and very delicate. He had to go back to Switzerland for the air, but while he was here there was a restaurant called the Cherry Tree in Nassau Street, and everybody went there, and Mr Engel would be sitting up on a stool at the bar, and drank about three glasses of milk—there was a caricature of him too, and Dorothy Stokes with her cigarette. And Mr Weaving was a great character too—he taught organ and piano, and the Italian Maestro Viani who used to come in the door—he always had a hat and an umbrella, and he'd come in the middle of the afternoon and say, 'Good morrrrrning,' and tip his hat.

And the Cork pianist Charles Lynch taught here for a while. He used to go round the country giving recitals, but he didn't take to teaching really.

He lived down in the Grosvenor Hotel for a while. He never had any money. He never owned a piano: he'd come to someone's house for a weekend, and several years later he would be still there.

Francis Engel—the man who drank all the milk—used to teach up in what used to be a bedroom at the top of the house. He used to hold a class called eurhythmics—we'd be lying on the floor, squirming to music. I'm afraid it was not taken too seriously, and eventually on one occasion we couldn't stand up for laughing. He was actually a very nice man, but I remember going upstairs one night, looking for a room to practise in, and there he was talking away to himself—communicating with something or someone. And there was a caricature of Ursula White, an ebullient speech and drama teacher, crashing through a door with the doorknob left in her hand. She had a heart of gold and was always in a hurry.

Valerie: François d'Albert—he was another colourful character. He came from behind the Iron Curtain—he had been a wonderful violinist in, I think, Budapest. His father had been sent to Siberia, so they never heard from him again. He managed to smuggle his mother and his sister out of Hungary to join him. Nobody knew anything about him, but he was a very fine violinist, and in no time had galvanised everyone—Charles Lynch, Tony Hughes, and Michael O'Higgins, and of course Miss Copeman—into performing all over the country. He used to organise series of celebrity concerts in the Gresham Hotel, with lists of patrons from the embassies and cultural establishments—a real entrepreneur. He gave me six Bach violin sonatas to learn for some recitals—just threw you in the deep end and expected you to swim—a bit like Miss Copeman. Eventually he went to Canada and set up his own conservatoire. I owe him a lot. He was very encouraging; in fact I was going to be a secretary, and he said to my parents that I should be a musician.

Audrey: Esposito was a very fatherly-looking man, and Mrs Marshall and Miss Copeman always spoke very affectionately of him. They had studied with him in the early part of the century. Now Valerie and I, our contemporaries and our students have the privilege of carrying on this great tradition.

11

From Kalkbrenner to O'Conor

CHARLES ACTON

Friedrich Kalkbrenner; John Field; George Osborne; William Wallace; Sir Robert Stewart; Elizabeth Meeke; Henrietta Flynn; Michael Quarry; Fanny Arthur; Arthur O'Leary; Michele Esposito; Ethel Sharpe; Hamilton Harty; Annie Lord; Margaret O'Hea; Edith Oldham; Rhona Marshall; Dina Copeman; Ella Rosenthal; Victor Love; Tilly Fleischmann; Bridget Doolan; Charles Lynch; Micheál O'Rourke; Philip Martin; Hugh Tinney; Barry Douglas; Patricia Read; Mabel Swainson; Geneviève Joy; Dorothy Stokes; John O'Conor.

S trangely enough, one of the most important pianists to affect the history of the Academy had nothing to do with the place at all—Frédéric Kalkbrenner (1785–1849), whose 'method' Miss Coulson wished to be used.[1]

Friedrich Wilhelm Michael Kalkbrenner was originally a German, born while his parents were en route from Kassel to Berlin.[2] Apart from his father's teaching, his musical education was entirely at the Paris Conservatoire, from 1799 to 1801, whence he emerged with two *premiers prix*, and he became essentially a French musician. His influence on Miss Coulson could have come in one of four ways. He lived and taught in London from 1815 to 1824; he toured Ireland in 1824; she could have spent a period in Paris after 1825; or she could have been taught by someone according to Kalkbrenner's *Méthode pour Apprendre le Piano-Forte à l'Aide d'une Guide-Mains* (1831), which had an immense popularity for years.

The first generation of 'great pianists' as such (following Mozart and Clementi, whose principal fame is as composers) consisted of Hummel (1787–1837), whose life was in Austria, Germany, and Hungary; Kalkbrenner, the French pianist; and John Field (1782–1837) from Ireland, whose career was in Russia. They stood between Mozart and the generation of Chopin, Liszt, and Thalberg.

John Field gave his first recital in Dublin, at the Rotunda, when he was ten (although, in the time-honoured fashion, he was billed as being only eight). The family emigrated to England, first to Bath and then to London, where he was taken up by Clementi, who both taught him and used him to demonstrate Clementi pianos. In 1802, Clementi went on a business tour of Europe, taking Field with him, primarily to demonstrate pianos but also genuinely to advance his pupil's international renown. Eventually they reached Russia, where Field stayed on after Clementi left, and he lived the rest of his life there, mostly in Moscow, making his living as a fashionable pianist and fashionable teacher.[3]

In Russia, as Nicholas Temperley has put it, Field was the inventor of a style of piano playing that differed strikingly from the prevailing virtuoso mode.[4] His compositions—the nocturnes (a form that he invented)[5] and the piano concertos—reflect his own playing. He was famed for his 'singing' tone (and on instruments with far less sustaining tone than ours). His melodies are likened to those of Bellini—twenty years his junior.

In 1832, Alphonse Marmontel observed that by 'his expressive touch and extreme delicacy Field obtained sonorities of exquisite colour. His lightness in rapid passages was incomparable: singing phrases took on, under his fingers, a sweet and tender feeling that few virtuosi are able to achieve.'[6] He was also famous for the clarity of his part-playing in the music of Bach.

Although it is unlikely that Field and Kalkbrenner ever met, or heard each other play, it seems that the latter's playing was extraordinarily like Field's, characterised by restraint, dexterity, and singing lyricism. And their teaching seems to have been extraordinarily similar, though Kalkbrenner was a dedicated, hard-working and enthusiastic teacher, while Field taught by example—and was often downright lazy.

So, it seems that Miss Coulson was advocating piano teaching remarkably similar—though she did not know it—to that of her compatriot.

During the half century before the Academy's foundation, there were a number of locally eminent Irish pianists, such as Philip Cogan (born Cork, 1748; died Dublin, 1833)[7] and Sir John Stevenson, who has been too much reviled for his harmonisations of Moore's *Melodies*.[8] These were not so much pianists as general musicians. The most eminent of these pianists internationally was George Alexander Osborne (1806–1893). His father was organist of St Mary's Church of Ireland Cathedral in Limerick. George received all his piano education in Ireland from his father and at nineteen became organist of St John's Catholic Cathedral, while his father remained organist at St Mary's. Osborne left Limerick in 1825 for Brussels, to study under Fétis and Pixis. There he found a home with the Prince de Chamay, friend of Cherubini, who introduced him to the German musical literature. In Brussels, Osborne also taught the future King of the Netherlands, by whom he was decorated.

In 1826 Osborne left for Paris, continuing studies with Fétis and Pixis but also with Kalkbrenner. He became one of the major Parisian pianists and a close friend of Chopin and Berlioz, coaching the latter in writing for the piano. According to a notice in the *Freeman's Journal* in 1848, his style (in a performance of the Mendelssohn Concerto) resembled that of Madame Pleyel, to which he added 'an exquisite delicacy that no other performer . . . ever reached.'[9] In 1843 he moved to London, where he became 'one of the most esteemed and genial teachers.' He was musical director of the Philharmonic Society and a director of the Royal Academy of Music.[10]

Osborne was very favourably disposed to the Irish Academy of Music, giving a recital in January 1874 'for the sole purpose of improving and encouraging the pupils.'[11] In 1872 he gave the Academy a bust of himself by Dauton, at the request of MacDonnell and Brady.[12] He was also elected a member of the Council of the Academy (the then equivalent of Governor) as a representative among London professors.[13]

A thoroughly maverick pianist was William Vincent Wallace (born Waterford, 1812; died in the Pyrenees, 1865), whom we all know for *Maritana*. Wallace was by all accounts a magnificent pianist, even though we think of him more as an operatic composer. But he also seems to have been a Baron Munchausen in his alleged adventures, whose accounts eclipsed his undoubted pianism. Few pianists have received a fee of a hundred sheep for a recital.[14]

Continuing the idea that, throughout the nineteenth century, musicians were of course pianists, we come to Sir Robert Stewart (1825–1894), who was appointed organist of Christ Church Cathedral and of Trinity College, Dublin, at the age of nineteen, to which he later added being a vicar choral in St Patrick's Cathedral, professor first of piano and then also of theory of the RIAM, professor of music of TCD, and conductor of various bodies. Everyone in Dublin then was well aware of the formidable pianist underlying his other activities, including composition, in connection with which he was commissioned to write a work for the Great Peace Festival in Boston in 1872. His statue is on Leinster Lawn, near the National Gallery. In the 'centenary' celebration of 1956 a pupil of Stewart's, George Harrison, who was organist of St George's Church, Hardwicke Place, for the remarkable period of seventy-five years, played one of Stewart's pieces on the RIAM organ and told me about his piano teaching at the RIAM.

The names of Miss Meeke and Miss Flynn keep cropping up together as though they were as inseparable as the Ladies of Llangollen. In the middle of the nineteenth century, both seem to have been formidable pianists and teachers. According to Stanford's *Pages from an Unwritten Diary*, his first piano teacher after his mother was Elizabeth Meeke, his godmother (who was always called 'Meeke' by her friends). She had been one of Moscheles's favourite pupils in the days when he lived in London (1825–46). She was 'an ample lady with a sweeping and swishing silk dress and hands of exactly the same build and type as Madame [Clara] Schumann's, whose style she closely resembled in touch and interpretation. As a disciple of Beethoven's, Moscheles grounded her in all Beethoven's piano works,'[15] and he passed on many of Beethoven's own sayings. One of these, in particular, was his insistence that *acciaccature* must always be played *before* the beat, which of course is very important, as in the beginning of the last movement of Beethoven's quartet, op. 18 No. 6. She passed on the message that the player should 'sit at a sufficient height to keep the upper line of the forearm absolutely straight to the first joint of the fingers.' This, Stanford writes, contributed to the 'velvety tone which distinguished her playing.'[16]

Miss Meeke apparently left Dublin, and Stanford then learnt from 'a curious, clever and somewhat eccentrically clothed lady, Miss Flynn.'[17] She had also been a pupil of Moscheles, but in Leipzig, and had also studied under Mendelssohn, 'a most impatient teacher.'[18] In that connection, Stanford's addition that Mendelssohn rigorously insisted that everyone should play from the music is interesting, bearing in mind present-day practice and the fact that Clara Schumann was much blamed in her day for playing her late husband's music from memory.

Miss Flynn lived at 31 Harcourt Street and studied with W. S. Conran,[19] and there is a long report in *Saunders's News-Letter* of Thursday 24 January 1856 of her *matinée musicale* at her home on the previous Saturday, 'which may be called her first public appearance before a public audience.' 'While still almost a child . . . [she] journeyed into Prussia for the purpose of placing herself under the gentle and refined Moscheles and that still greater . . . Mendelssohn and she returned only when the latter . . . told her that she might now go forth and play the finest music of modern times in a way that no one could surpass.' On the advice of one of her pupils, the Countess of Charlemont, she went to seek her fortune in London, but ill-health prevented her progress. She was still living in 1900.[20]

Returning to Stanford: 'When this excellent dame left Dublin, I found my last Dublin master in Stewart . . . and in yet another pupil of Moscheles, then fresh from Leipzig, Michael Quarry,' who had also learnt from Miss Meeke and Miss Flynn. Michael Quarry was born in Cork in 1840, the son of a John Quarry MA DD (1809–1899), Archdeacon of Cork and Rector of Donoughmore and grandson of John Quarry MA LLD (1777–1837), Rector of St Mary's, Shandon.[21] Quarry studied with Moscheles at the Leipzig Conservatory from 1862 to 1866, where he played the latter's concerto for his diploma. Stanford wrote:

> He opened my eyes to Schumann, whose music I had never seen; to the choral works of Bach; and to Brahms. We spent hours over the four-hand arrangements of the Serenades, the Sextets . . . and he taught me the Handel Variations and even the D minor Concerto. It was a new world which opened to my eyes, when I first read the score of the St Matthew Passion, which till then had never penetrated to Ireland.[22]

We do not now think of Stanford as a pianist but as a composer and, in London and Cambridge, as the teacher of almost every British composer (and many Irish ones) until 1924; and yet that great singer Plunket Greene said that 'Stanford's touch was the most delicious thing imaginable, impossible to define, and he always said that it was to Quarry that he owed whatever he was as a pianist.'[23]

Quarry taught at the RIAM from 1880 to 1882, as well as at Alexandra College (where one of his pupils was Violet Martin, the 'Martin Ross' who

was the writing partner of Edith Somerville). The Governors' minutes record that he resigned following an acrimonious correspondence.[24] It was as a result of his departure that the professorship was advertised, and after some negotiation Esposito was appointed to the vacancy. In 1896 Quarry returned to Dublin for a recital at the Antient Concert Rooms.[25]

Joseph Robinson is by now a familiar figure. Equally familiar should be his first wife, Fanny Arthur, one of the leading Dublin pianists of her day. Liszt had invented the idea of the 'recital', adapted from the contemporary practice of poets reciting their work, an event of a single performer only (himself) instead of the normal 'concert' from the early eighteenth century until early in the twentieth, when performances were given by soloists and groups of musicians of various sorts.

The first 'recital' in Ireland was given by Fanny Arthur on 9 April 1856, in the Antient Concert Rooms. According to *Saunders's News-Letter*,

> last night a concert of a very unusual character was given by Mrs. Joseph Robinson. It is not long since a similar *soirée* took place at her own residence, but this is the first time that a regular pianoforte recital has been attempted in a Dublin concert room. It consisted exclusively of pieces on the pianoforte played by Mrs. Joseph Robinson herself.[26]

One would like to have space to quote the whole piece, but suffice it to say that 'an audience, composed of the most cultivated and refined lovers of music, was assembled, listened with profound attention, and testified their pleasure no less by their homage of silence, than by the frequent bursts of applause: Never, indeed, was a pianist subject to a more trying ordeal.' Her programme appears to have been Mozart's Sonata in C minor, K457, a suite by Bach, a sonata by Hummel, Beethoven's 'Moonlight' Sonata, *The Lake* and *The Fountain* by Sterndale Bennett, Chopin's Berceuse, and *Les Arpèges* by Kullak.

An Irish pianist, or at least a pianist (and composer) of Irish parents who had emigrated to Paris, was Augusta Holmès (1847–1903). (When she became a French citizen, at the age of thirty-two, she adopted this spelling of her name, corresponding to the French pronunciation.) As a pianist she was a child prodigy (to her parents' annoyance), and she later studied with César Franck. Her work as a composer, however, eclipsed her pianism. As a composer she is entirely French, although, as Adolphe Jullien has pointed out, her symphonic poem *Irlande* is her most complete work. Alas, we virtually never hear her music.[27]

In the eighteen-thirties and forties County Kerry was hardly a hotbed of international musical achievement, in spite of its various remarkable schools of traditional music, still celebrated by the musicians of Sliabh Luachra. But in 1834 there was born in Tralee Arthur O'Leary, who learnt the piano at home and, in about 1842, was noticed by Wyndham Goold, who had him sent to the great Leipzig Conservatorium (thanks to which, presumably, he escaped the Great Famine). There Mendelssohn gave a dinner in his honour. He studied with Moscheles and Plaidy (and studied composition with Richter and Rietz) and was befriended by Robert and Clara Schumann.

Eventually, he settled in London as professor of piano at the RAM, where he died in 1919. As so often, the gifted performer became a famous teacher.[28] He also seems to have been a composer, since we read in *Saunders's News-Letter* of 3 April 1856 (when he was twenty-two) that, a week before Mrs Robinson's piano recital, she had been the piano soloist in the Philharmonic Society's concert, one item of which was the overture *The Spanish Student* by A. O'Leary.

Although, as so often, major individual pianists seem to arise independent of the leading schools and teachers, an Irish pianistic event was the arrival in 1882, as professor of piano-playing at the RIAM, of Michele Esposito, who was born near Naples on 29 September 1855 and died on 26 November 1929.[29] Like pianists of a previous age, Esposito was a musical polymath, teacher of a century of Irish pianism, conductor, composer, *animateur*, administrator, and general inspiration. It is probably fair to say that he not only changed the Academy, making it close to what it is today, but that he transformed the face of all music in Dublin; and it is certainly fair to suggest that almost every pianist from Dublin since the eighteen-eighties has owed something to Esposito.

In 1916, the extern examiner Frederick Dawson commented on 'Dr. Esposito's thorough and well-planned scheme which covers the whole course of music education, a gradual and complete system which, commencing at the lowest classes, works up to the highest classes where one finds the pupil fully equipped as a teacher and soloist, a most gratifying and convincing showing of the value of correct "grounding".'[30]

Apart from teaching, composing, and examining, Esposito's personal contribution as a pianist to the musical life of Ireland was immense. He was a central figure in the early years of the RDS recitals, and continued as such until almost the end of his career. He appeared in the inaugural season in 1886 with a quartet composed of professors of the RIAM, and from 1888 he gave solo recitals, often as many as three each year. These included much of his own music and the first complete cycle in Ireland of the Beethoven sonatas, as well as a prodigious amount of chamber music, not only with Irish or Irish-based performers but also with visiting ensembles, such as the Brodsky Quartet, who gave what was probably the first Irish performance of all Beethoven's quartets.[31]

One of Esposito's earliest pupils was Ethel Sharpe (born 1872). After the RIAM she went to the RCM in London and became a pianist of remarkable accomplishment. On the recommendation of Grove (who referred to her affectionately as 'E♯')[32] she received the Musicians' Company silver medal in 1891, and she played several well-received concerto and recital performances in London. In 1892 Richter was impressed with her playing of a Brahms Rhapsody, when she also accompanied her fellow-student Emil Kreuz in his Viola Concerto.[33] She gave an outstanding recital in Vienna in 1894, enjoying there the friendship of Brahms (whose work she had already played in Vienna in 1893)[34] and other notable musicians. In 1895 she married Alfred Hobday, a leading English viola player, after which she gave many recitals with her husband and became a specialist in concerted chamber music. She was also the mother-in-law of the great violinist Albert Sammons.[35]

Now we come to a very underrated pianist and musician, Sir Herbert Hamilton Harty, whose family came from Limerick and who was born at Hillsborough, County Down, in 1879. As a conductor, he was world-famous between the wars, making the Hallé Orchestra one of the leading orchestras in the world. As a composer, he has lately been regaining some of the recognition that he deserves; but in our context he was not only a superb pianist but one of that smaller band of superb accompanists. He was never a pupil of Esposito, but after he had come as a young man to Dublin (and as a parish organist in Bray), Esposito was his friend and mentor. Before the days of Gerald Moore, he clearly demonstrated the sort of qualities that Moore showed supremely in his day. Just as, in the middle of this century, we have to acknowledge that Britten's greatness as a composer stood in the way of his being a magnificent pianist, an outstanding conductor, and an accompanist of genius (and his essays into those fields prove the points on record), so Harty's concentration on conducting left only summer holidays in Ireland for composition, and virtually no time for his remarkable pianism.[36]

If one is a world-class musician, the world may be one's oyster, but growing on one's original roots, or finding other beds for them, or else swimming rootless, is a problem. Harty would have liked to work and live in Ireland. He came back to it, to Antrim and Sligo, whenever he could, but in 1901 it was entirely clear that his native country could not offer him a living, and certainly not one commensurate with his remarkable gifts. In my view, John Field inaugurated a personal style of pianism but Harty was at least his equal in every part of music and deserves far more of our national respect than he has ever been given.

Today, with radio and television broadcasting, and recordings available in so many forms, we know a great deal more about musicians than before the electronic age. It is hard to realise, for example, that throughout the last century 'recitals' were the more or less eccentric prerogatives of a handful of top performers, whereas the usual event was a 'concert' with many players, such as solo pianists, singers or violinists with accompanists, ensembles, perhaps a concerto or a vocal ensemble. Before the gramophone, famous virtuosi could (and did) tour the world, and especially the United States, for years with only one programme; and pianists performed far more for society hostesses (going in by the tradesmen's entrance) than before the public. Even up to the last war, a recital by such a great player as Kreisler would consist of a first half of two sonatas (such as Beethoven and Brahms) and a second half of light or 'encore' pieces, such as his own admitted ones and his 'classical manuscripts'.[37] It is to the credit of people like Esposito and Joseph Robinson that they struggled to put on more serious concerts in the Antient Concert Rooms and in the Great Exhibition Hall in Earlsfort Terrace.

We know of our nineteenth-century pianists primarily as teachers, therefore, because of the anecdotes and achievements of their pupils. Annie Lord compiled a scale book for the Academy that was still the standard into the fifties, until the Associated Board produced the present standard, which is in fact more useful.[38] Annie Lord had two nieces, Nancie and May. May was a semi-professional viola player of very great quality. Nancie was leader of the RÉSO and was designated by E. J. Moeran to give the first performance of his violin concerto, commissioned by the BBC. Nancie was for many years professor of violin in the Academy, and I recall her coming into the hall of the RIAM after a day of teaching saying, 'My aunt Annie used to say that you don't earn your living teaching geniuses.'

As Joan Trimble has written to me of her, Annie Lord was a fierce personality, a soloist to her marrow, temperamental and hidebound by her view of Catholicism of that period; hence her veneration for César Franck. But she later venerated Debussy and Ravel, and in fact introduced contemporary French music to Ireland. She and Marie Trimble (née Dowse, mother of Joan and Valerie) gave the first performance of the Franck Violin Sonata in Ireland. She was also the teacher of one of our most potentially gifted composers, Fred May, and of the pair of sisters of worldwide renown, especially during the forties and fifties, Joan and Valerie Trimble, each of them a formidable pianist and teacher in her own right but famous as a two-piano partnership.

In the thirties there were two pairs in this unusual field, the Peppin twins and Ethel and Rae Robertson. Then the Trimbles took over, and the 'Jamaican Rumba' was written for them by the Australian composer Arthur Benjamin and became, thanks to them, one of the most popular twentieth-century classical pieces of the world. Percy Scholes wrote of the rumba: 'The original and genuine . . . rumba is erotic and confined to the lower classes—not suggestive, as has been alleged, since it leaves nothing to suggest.'[39] There was a time when Benjamin's exciting piece was very nearly their signature tune. Valerie died in 1980. Joan is a significant composer and the formidable owner-editor of a remarkable newspaper in Enniskillen. In 1986 she was awarded a fellowship of the RIAM.[40]

Margaret O'Hea ('little Miss O'Hea', as she was affectionately called) was another outstanding pianist who devoted her life to teaching in the RIAM.[41] She was a pupil of Miss Flynn and afterwards Fanny Arthur. Her pupil, Dina Copeman, herself one of the greatest of our piano teachers (whose pupils will be named often hereafter) and the piano recitalist chosen to perform on the opening day of Irish radio in 1926, described Miss O'Hea: 'Like all great teachers she had the admirable qualities of patience and enthusiasm and took a deep personal interest in each of her pupils.'[42] Among her many pupils were Annie Lord, Edith Boxwell (née French, a relation of Dorothy Stokes), Madeleine Larchet, Bessie Ruthven, Alice Yoakley, Maud Aiken, Annie Keelan, Col. James Doyle, Dorothy Stokes, and many members of the Starkie family. Enid Starkie suggested that 'it was she rather than Esposito who was responsible for the musical education of Annie Lord and Edith Boxwell.'[43] She taught at the RIAM for fifty-five years and only retired (in 1928, aged eighty-five) because Esposito retired (after forty-seven years there).[44]

Under Esposito there were two streams of teaching, which survive to this day. One is Margaret O'Hea's, the other Edith Oldham's. She, better known by her married name, Edith Best, was one of the very first scholars of the Royal College of Music in London in 1883, after her studies at the

RIAM, but instead of a solo career she returned to the RIAM in 1887, where she taught until 1932.[45] 'She had a wonderful influence over her pupils, by all of whom she was greatly loved.' Among them was Rhona Marshall (née Clark), and in her and her pupils, as in other Best pupils, can be heard a dedication to music rather than only technique. Rhona Marshall indeed was a noted performer in concert and on the wireless until her enthusiasm for teaching absorbed her.[46] Both in performance and teaching, her penetration into the essence of the composer's thought and her discovery of inner, secondary and tertiary melodies was uncanny. As well as that, one can only regret, as with Britten, that her chamber-music gifts, especially in sonata duos, were rarely exploited.

For half a century, from the thirties on, Copeman and Marshall dominated piano teaching in the Academy. Though each had her separate lineage (O'Hea and Best, respectively), they were both stamped by Esposito, because of his practice of giving all senior pupils (and many middle grade ones) one lesson a month himself. They made a remarkable pair of opposites. It seemed to the outsider that Copeman was primarily a technician, while Marshall put the music first. Dina suffered from the cold and had the disused fireplace in her room blocked up and even stuffed paper in the keyhole and surrounded herself with electric fires. Rhona, with a rural upbringing, was impervious to the cold, and pupils would find the windows of her room opened wide, even during snowstorms. While Copeman and Marshall, naturally, were friendly and courteous to each other in public, a deep and often bitter rivalry was very visible, only forgotten when they combined to ostracise Charles Lynch when he temporarily joined the Academy staff. But deep below their rivalry was a strong foundation of mutual respect and friendship.

In the late nineteenth and early twentieth centuries there was an important Jewish community in Dublin, sadly decreased by now. It is curious that not more of them became more famous, although we note Posie Shreider and her sister Judith, now emigrated to Israel, and, in the early years of the twentieth century, Edith Coplin and Rachel Levin. One member of this community, who married a Catholic, Daniel O'Connell Miley (a descendant of Daniel O'Connell and at one time a Governor and the Academy's solicitor), was Ella Rosenthal (1886–1938), one of several siblings who studied at the Academy (including a violin student, May) and whose father, J. D. Rosenthal (1833–1907), a lawyer, was a subscriber to the Academy from 1860. I am proud to possess her copy of the Mendelssohn G minor Concerto. She seems to have had the Jewish commitment to music and, as well, the musicality that so many foreign adjudicators are surprised to find in Ireland. She was taught by Samuel Spencer Myerscough, an English organist who came here to Loreto Convent, Rathfarnham, who founded the Leinster School of Music and died in the thirties and whose descendants, in insurance and horse breeding by profession, are dedicated musicians in private.

Another member of the Rosenthal family, possibly Ella's brother, was Archie Rosenthal, who flourished from the end of the nineteenth century, giving an RDS recital in 1910 (including Edward McDowell's 'Sonata Tragica' and works of his own, of which the *Irish Times* commented on 'his now infrequent visits to his native city.'[47] He also appeared as a soloist with the Dublin Orchestral Society. He married the violinist Hilda Gee.

A remarkable patron of music was Sir Stanley Cochrane of Woodbrook, near Bray, where he built an opera house. The estate is now a golf club, the opera house now an auction room. Both Cochrane and his brother, Sir Ernest, were Governors of the Academy. On 11–16 August 1930 he engaged the London Symphony Orchestra, 'conductor Mr. Hamilton Harty,' to perform there, and Victor Love was the soloist in the first performance in Ireland of Rachmaninoff's First Piano Concerto.

Victor Love (1890–1946), another pupil of Esposito, won first prize for sight-reading in an Academy exam in 1910, was active as a pianist, organist, composer and teacher between the wars, and was a member of the Academy staff from 1938 to 1944, joining the Municipal School of Music in the latter year. His programmes show that he must have had a fine technique—he played quite a lot of Albeniz, as well as Liszt, and then modern composers such as Dohnanyi, William Baines, and Debussy.[48] He performed often in London with the London Symphony Orchestra and the London Philharmonic Orchestra—and in those years neither the LSO nor Beecham and the LPO engaged second-rate soloists.

I have mentioned the importing of Esposito. Another most significant import was Aloys Fleischmann senior, and his wife, Tilly. He was part of that wave of Catholic organists from Germany and the Low Countries at the turn of the century who came into the cathedrals and important churches of Ireland. Tilly Fleischmann (née Schwertz) was born in Cork in 1879 and was sent by her father to the Hochschule für Musik in Munich, where she studied with Bernhard Stavenhagen. She gave a number of successful recitals in Munich and was invited to give a recital to the King of Bavaria at Nymphenburg. She married Aloys Fleischmann in 1906. Thereafter 'she was the first Irish pianist to give a BBC broadcast, the first to introduce Bax's piano music to Irish audiences, presenting an all-Bax programme at the Clarence Hall, Cork, in 1929,' and all-Liszt programmes to commemorate his anniversaries in 1911 and 1936.[49] She was in Cork a pianistic force rather like Esposito in Dublin.

In 1986 the Adare Press in Cork published *Aspects of the Liszt Tradition*, edited by Michael O'Neill from Tilly Fleischmann's writings. Her teacher, Stavenhagen, was as a young man 'the last pianist to work consistently under Liszt's guidance in Weimar, Budapest and Rome. He succeeded Liszt in Weimar . . .'[50] Her transmission here of Liszt's views of Chopin's and of his own works, as well as of his legacy of practical and technical advice, makes this an important book. She transmitted in Cork Liszt's tradition, especially to that lazy, jazzy genius Seán Ó Riada, but sadly she found few pupils who could receive her full spirit. One was Gerard Shanahan, who became a dedicated piano teacher in the Dublin College of Music, a lovely man who collected all sorts of things, including memorabilia of Sir Robert Stewart and Mendelssohn and paintings by Jack B. Yeats. In my many recollections of Schumann's 'Dichterliebe', no performance was greater than that of Gerard Shanahan and Claus Ocker in St Canice's

Cathedral, Kilkenny—and such a cycle is as much an affair of the pianist as of the singer.

Another pupil was Bridget Doolan, a fine pianist and the enterprising principal of the Cork Municipal School, until she decided that teaching is more important than administration and moved to Waterford RTC, where she taught until her sudden death in 1997.

Thanks to the kindness of Prof. Aloys Fleischmann, son of Tilly's and himself 'Mr Music' in Cork for more than half a century, I have studied a host of programmes from early this century by Tilly Fleischmann's pupils. At a time when concerts included a lot of very light music, her pupils all played what we would now regard as works of a proper standard.

Among Tilly Fleischmann's pupils was my dear friend and colleague Geraldine Sullivan, later Geraldine Neeson, who was herself a dedicated piano teacher in Cork, music critic in Cork for the *Irish Times* and critic of most arts for the *Irish Independent* and *Cork Examiner*. Professor Fleischmann lent me a programme of 24 February 1927, where she and her future husband, Seán Neeson, performed together. Her solo items were Debussy's 'Children's Corner', Mussorgsky's 'Pictures at an Exhibition', and Schumann's 'Études Symphoniques'. As I knew her, with a fund of stories of the national movement, and a most piquant wit, but an extremely just appreciation of a critic's job in Cork, and a very fine teacher, I now feel ashamed not to have been aware of her formidable musicianship and pianism as a performer.

Now we come to another pianist of real international importance, and one who was enormously loved by the concert-goers of Ireland and England but who, sadly, did not secure the recognition to which his gifts entitled him, because of his 'inability to cope with life in its practical aspects,' as Richard Pine wrote in September 1984 in an appreciation in the *Irish Times*.[51] Charles Edgeworth Cagney Lynch was born in Cork in 1906, with a reasonably silver spoon in his mouth, but showed himself very early to have real pianistic ability. His first public recital (in Greenock, when he was nine) included Beethoven's 'Moonlight' and 'Pathétique' sonatas and Chopin's 'Fantaisie Impromptu'. Between the wars he was a 'phenomenon' in London. Everyone in that world knew him as 'Charlie Podge'. Rachmaninov, who never willingly taught anyone before Charles,[52] wished to, and did, coach him in the first sonata before he gave the first British performance.[53] Bax dedicated to him his Fourth Sonata, of which he gave the first performance. His effortless technique and fantastic sight-reading ability betrayed him into many performances (and I promoted some) where he did not give enough time to working out the deep significance of his music. But during the war years he largely kept Ireland going for solo and concerto pianism. And, with a curious arrogant modesty, he achieved a very great deal.[54]

In the years before wireless, gramophone or weekly symphony concerts, Liszt laboured for about twenty-five years to transcribe for the piano all nine Beethoven symphonies, and did so with a worshipping fidelity to the composer. In 1987 it was claimed in *Classical Music* that some pianist had played all nine in a series for the first time, but already in January 1971

Richard Pine[55] had presented Charles Lynch playing all nine in a surprisingly short number of weeks, and the experience was fascinating, teaching me a great deal about Liszt, Beethoven, and Lynch.[56] Pine also promoted him in 1972 to give us the complete centenary series of Scriabin's sonatas. In Cork in his later years he performed the complete piano music of Debussy and Ravel in a short season.

Lynch was a large man, in every way, with the weight to perform Brahms, and I was privileged to present him in a series of recitals in 1950, each of which had a major Brahms work and a major modern work. And I shall always be grateful to him for introducing me to the Holst Toccata, and I wish people would revive it.

When it was found that Lynch wanted to teach seriously, he was appointed to a part-time post at the Academy in 1963. Unfortunately, quite apart from the ostracism he met from Marshall and Copeman, he did not last long; neither teaching nor punctuality were among his fortes.

In *A History of Irish Music*, Grattan Flood wrote: 'It is risky to mention persons still living, but . . .' That is precisely how I feel, but I will stick my neck out some little way. At the moment we have several pianists of international renown. Three of them, all Dubliners, are of the same age, having been born in 1947, all with quite different personae. John O'Conor I will treat of later. Micheál O'Rourke, who first studied with Elizabeth Costello, one of Esposito's last surviving pupils, is now based in Paris. Essentially a romantic pianist, he gave a complete Chopin recital that made me compare him to Cortot (but without the latter's wrong notes).[57] In recent years he has developed an international career, largely in Poland (where he was awarded the Chopin Medal) and in Russia (where he has given the premieres of the Britten and Lutoslawski concertos and where his researches have discovered previously unknown works by Field). He is particularly noted for his recordings of the complete works of Field (for the Chandos label), and in 1996 his performance of the First and Second Concertos with the London Mozart Players was a best-selling disc. 1998 saw the release of his CD of piano music by Esposito.

Philip Martin is in the polymath tradition. He accompanies his wife, the singer Penelope Price-Jones, as sympathetically as Britten accompanied Pears. He is an admirable composer. He specialised in modern American music during his tenure of a Bicentennial Fellowship there; he was the soloist in 1988 in the premiere of his first piano concerto with the then RTÉSO at the NCH. Almost anything good is grist to his mill, and audiences love him for his obvious enthusiastic enjoyment of getting out onto a platform and playing for them. He has recently pioneered a revival of interest in the piano music of Louis Gottschalk.

The other two famed international pianists are of a decade later. Hugh Tinney (born 1958, of a notable Dublin musical family) was a pupil of Mabel Swainson (a superb teacher, who was a member of the Academy staff from 1985 to 1987) and then of Louis Kentner and Maria Curcio and won the Paloma O'Shea competition in Santander—one of the most rewarding of all competitions, because it provides two years of work throughout the Latin countries. Such an opportunity is significant if it leads to return visits. In Tinney's case, the demand for return visits is enough to keep him working for years; but he was also a prize-winner in the Leeds competition, which now assures him considerable work in the northern hemisphere. He joined the Academy teaching staff in 1995.

Barry Douglas of Belfast (born 1960), also a pupil of Maria Curcio, was the first western pianist to win the complete first prize at the Moscow Tchaikovsky Competition (1987) since Van Cliburn won it in 1958. Hearing him here, it seemed to me that he had the firm granite of his native County Antrim and can combine the evocative poetry of Mussorgsky's 'Pictures at an Exhibition' (which he played at the Moscow competition) and the scale of Beethoven's 'Hammerklavier' Sonata.

These pianists, in their two generations, are of world quality, all different, all clearly set on personal careers.

A remarkable succession of teachers is associated with the Read School. Patricia Read was born in the eighteen-sixties and studied with Carlo Albanese at the RAM in London. Sadly, she never realised her potential as a performer, because in her twenties she developed severe arthritis in her hands, but she became an extremely fine teacher, starting in the Leinster School of Music and then forming her own important school. Among her pupils there were Rhoda Coghill, George O'Neill (an especially brilliant pianist, who died very young in the 1918 Spanish flu epidemic), and, so much later, Mabel Swainson, who came to Dublin only to learn from Miss Read when the latter was eighty-four (she died when she was ninety-three). Miss Read's pupils included many famous pianists, teachers, organists, and other musicians, including Frederick Stone, who succeeded Ernest Lush as the BBC's London accompanist.

Among Miss Read's staff was Elizabeth (Lily) Huban, an equally famous teacher, who studied in the Cortot school in the École Normale in Paris and taught many pianists of note. Miss Read's pupil Mabel Swainson is one of our leading piano teachers of the present day, her pupils including Philip Martin and Hugh Tinney.

It is easy to forget talent that has emigrated. Geneviève Joy, born in Dún Laoghaire, daughter of a flautist and niece of the singer Samuel Joy, emigrated when young to Paris, where she became a distinguished teacher in the Conservatoire, a well-known adjudicator in international piano competitions, with Jacqueline Robin a world-famous two-piano team, and wife of the important French composer Henri Dutilleux. Among her pupils are Philippe Cassard, the winner of the first Dublin International Piano Competition in 1988, who has gone on to be a much-loved visiting artist here.

Deirdre McNulty married a Dutch-Hungarian cellist, Victor Harsanyi, and has become a Dutch specialist in modern piano works, of which she is a formidable exponent. Sadly, we hear her too seldom here. Veronica McSwiney, who joined the Academy staff in 1998 and with a high reputation on music-oriented cruise ships, made the first recording of the complete Field nocturnes (for Claddagh Records), was the first Irish pianist to tour extensively in the Soviet Union, and was one adjudicator of the GPA and later Guardian Dublin International Piano Competitions in 1994 and 1997.

Frank Llewelyn Harrison (1905–1987), a notable student of the Academy, was expected to make a brilliant career as a pianist (and paid for his studies in the University of Dublin by working as a cinema pianist in Dublin in the days of the silent films) but instead became a leading pioneer of mediaeval music as the lively performable art we know today, before moving on to become one of the world's leading ethnomusicologists.[58]

Though we have up to now been considering solo pianists and teachers, it would be wholly wrong not to write about accompanists, in whom Ireland and especially Dublin has been rich for a long time. Repeatedly adjudicators at the Dublin Feis Ceoil praise our accompanists, compared with their experiences elsewhere.

I have already referred to Sir Hamilton Harty's superb qualities as an accompanist. Kitty O'Callaghan (née O'Doherty), born in Derry, was always in great demand. She was 'station accompanist' in Radio Éireann, until the then civil service marriage bar forced her to retire. Thereafter many international artists coming to Dublin made it a condition of the engagement that Kitty play for them. She was succeeded in Radio Éireann by Rhoda Coghill, who for many years was loved by all for whom she played and is a highly regarded poet as well.

All her life associated with the Academy, Dorothy Stokes only taught the piano there in her last few years, preferring to teach in private practice just round the corner in Lincoln Place. But she was first appointed to the theory school of the Academy at the age of thirteen and, as an accompanist, guided generations of Academy singers and instrumentalists.

Jeannie Reddin, the favourite accompanist of Mattio Battastini, is an outstanding coach and répétiteur. She has an extraordinary gift for receiving on the very platform the vocal score of an obscure Italian opera aria from an Italian tenor, and not only playing it for him with instant sympathy but conveying the whole orchestra on the piano as the composer meant it.

Havelock Nelson, another musical polymath (composer, conductor and *animateur* as well as accompanist, and PhD in biochemistry) was Rhoda Coghill's opposite number and equal at the BBC in Belfast, and I recall with great pleasure his splendid playing of Messiaen's 'Harawi' (no easy music!) with Veronica Dunne. In 1985 he received the fellowship of the Academy, and we are very glad that he contributed his *intermezzo* to this book just before he died in 1996.

From Ballinrobe, County Mayo, comes Courtney Kenny, for many years principal répétiteur at Glyndebourne and the Wexford Festival. The succession goes on. Like Harty, Ingrid Surgenor comes from County Down and has emigrated, being now one of the handful of the world's top accompanists. We should also include Frank McNamara, serious pupil of Rhona Marshall at the RIAM, who plays for many RTÉ programmes, especially the 'Late Late Show', accompanying a pop group, a ballad singer, an opera singer, all in his relaxed stride. There are many others, but I take refuge in Grattan Flood's disclaimer—except for John O'Conor, who neatly rounds off the ideas in this chapter.

The exact contemporary of Philip Martin and Micheál O'Rourke, John O'Conor studied with Dr J. J. O'Reilly at the College of Music. He had the ambition of becoming the best piano teacher in Ireland; to that end he obtained an Austrian government scholarship to study with Dieter Weber at the Hochschule für Musik in Vienna. When he won the Beethoven Competition there, and then the Bösendorfer Prize, he felt that he had to give performing life a trial; and, as a result, he now regularly tours America, Japan, Korea and Europe and has recorded the complete Beethoven sonatas and the Field concertos and nocturnes for the Telarc label in the United States. Among other important events, he has performed the complete Beethoven piano sonatas as a cycle at the National Concert Hall. He is an extremely fine chamber music player and accompanist as well as soloist.

O'Conor was to have become Dieter Weber's assistant at the Vienna Hochschule, but he was devastated by Weber's sudden death and returned to Ireland. It was an important day for the Academy when he joined its teaching staff in 1976. As professor of piano, he is realising his original ambition, as can be seen in such pupils as Ruth McGinley (piano section winner of the BBC Young Musician of the Year in 1995) and Finghin Collins, RTÉ Musician of the Future in 1994, who reached the semi-finals in the 1996 Leeds competition and the 1997 Guardian Dublin Competition.

After long preparation, O'Conor launched the triennial Dublin International Piano Competition in 1988, which was immediately recognised as one of the top handful of piano competitions in the world, and has remained so ever since. He is much in demand as adjudicator of prestigious piano competitions, including Leeds, Vienna, Munich, and Sydney.

In 1994, the Governors of the Academy appointed John O'Conor to succeed Lindsay Armstrong as director. With his virtually definitive recordings of Field's works, he brings us back to the first great Irish pianist. His Beethoven sonata series brings us back to Esposito, who was hailed as a pioneer when he gave the cycle. Through Dieter Weber in Vienna he is part of that apostolic succession going back to Bach and Sweelinck. Through his studies with J. J. O'Reilly his musical ancestry goes back to Esposito, and thence to Kalkbrenner. Though he is not a conductor or composer, the Dublin Piano Competition and his enthusiastic and inspiring direction of the Academy has made many feel that he will be the Academy's Esposito of the twenty-first century.

Intermezzo

Anna Brioscú

I attended my first Board meeting in January 1974. Maud Aiken was the senior vice-president and chairwoman. She welcomed me but cautioned that it would take three years to become attuned to the affairs of the Academy; she advised that I should not speak at meetings during that time. I was rather taken aback, and decided there and then not to take her advice.

Maud Aiken had done trojan work, but she had become proprietorial and was reluctant to listen to others. She was also rather elderly, and, as the vice-presidency is for life, there was no indication that she would retire.

At the reception to mark the opening of the summer school in 1977 we heard that Maud Aiken had been killed in a motor accident en route to the Academy. It was a traumatic and very sad occasion, truly the end of an era.

I had been nominated to the Board by John O'Donovan. He had a somewhat irascible personality, which did not endear him to many people, but he had a sincere commitment to the future of the Academy as a vice-president and a long-serving member of the Board. A financial crisis was looming, and it became obvious to me that membership of the Finance Committee was essential if I were to have detailed knowledge of the workings of the institution. John proposed me for this committee—also chaired by Mrs Aiken—and then the work became really interesting.

A Special Finance Committee was appointed, consisting of Desmond O'Donohoe, Séamus Gaffney, John O'Donovan, Aleck Crichton, and myself, which had two priorities: to appoint a director, and to persuade the Department of Education to put financing on a more realistic level to meet the just and rightful demands of the staff. When I became vice-president and ex officio chairwoman of the Board in 1980, these became my immediate goals.

In 1982 we achieved both objectives. The grant was increased, and the Board appointed Lindsay Armstrong as director. Both were brought about by magnificent teamwork; and I am proud to have been associated with John O'Donovan, Aleck Crichton, Leo Gibney, Liam Fitzgerald, Séamus Gaffney, Barbara Wright, John O'Conor and Charles Acton in bringing about a revitalisation of the Academy.

The biggest sponsors of the Academy have been the taxpayers, through the Department of Education. The annual grant in 1974 was £47,000; it is now over a million pounds.

In addition to its main function, the Academy has a social dimension. There is a dedication and a sense of responsibility towards their pupils among the teaching staff that is unique. The coming together of young people from diverse backgrounds in pursuit of a common interest is very important. Dedication to work, punctuality and team spirit through orchestral involvement, or playing chamber music, are cultivated. Friendships are made and continue through life.

During my time as a member of the Board there were many new developments. The restructuring of salary grades for both academic and administrative staff, the setting up of procedures for recruitment and the general improvement in conditions of employment, the introduction of degree courses—all opened up new perspectives.

The decision of the staff to become unionised was something I welcomed very much. It may seem strange for an employer to favour unionisation, but to me this was a strengthening of the Board's hand when pressing for adequate funding. Credit is due especially to Anthony Glavin and Brian Beckett, as representatives of the Teaching Staff Association, for building bridges between the staff and the Board at a very sensitive time.

I was a Governor when the Academy had the good fortune to persuade John O'Conor to join the teaching staff on his return to Ireland from study in Vienna. His coming here cleared away many cobwebs, and I was delighted to chair the interview board that appointed him the second director of the RIAM in 1994.

I enjoyed my twenty years as a Governor. I have a great interest in people—in what makes them tick, and sometimes in what makes them thick. The Academy is a wonderful place, to the non-musician a very complex institution, both in its people and in its workings. I have learnt a lot. Even after the most heated debates and discussions, once a meeting closed people were able to be warm and friendly, returning to the next meeting without rancour.

I have learnt a lot about politics (with a small p) since becoming a Governor. Artistic endeavours are often fraught with jealousy, intrigue, one-upmanship, and petty nonsense. Cliques lead to unrest and suspicion. I am confident that that is not the case in the Academy. It is important always to strive for harmony, and if musicians cannot achieve that, there is little hope of achieving it elsewhere.

When I decided to bow out as chairwoman of the Board, I also decided to relinquish my vice-presidency. The honour was one that enabled me to contribute whatever skills I possessed to furthering the Academy's interests. An institution, to continue in a vibrant state, must have the benefit of new people, with fresh vision. I left the RIAM in the happy knowledge that it was in a healthier state financially, administratively and academically than when I had become a Governor. Long may it continue to flourish.

12

The Future

JOHN O'CONOR

In many ways, the history of an institution is also the story of its future: in part because history tends to repeat itself, and in part because a dynamic and vibrant organism carries within it the seeds of its own growth and renewal. The original prospectus for the Irish Academy of Music referred to 'an always beginning, never ending labour,'[1] and no-one would disagree with that or, indeed, wish it otherwise.

In charting the inception and progress of the Academy, we have seen many peaks and valleys. In the spirit of optimism that has steered the RIAM through its past, we must look to the future and the chance of building on our achievements and capitalising on the extraordinary human and physical resources available to us, in extending the frontiers of music education, not only at home but also internationally.

That future includes the remarkable achievements of the past 150 years, because we carry them forward, knowing where we have come from, what we have learnt, the environment in which we operate, and what we can achieve. There is a sense of corporate identity that gives the place its dynamic forward thrust and this comes from a family of teachers, Governors, administrative staff—the 'social partners' without whom we would have no social connections—and above all the students (and their parents), who are the ultimate test of our effectiveness.

Wordsworth said (I am paraphrasing) that to be great we must create the standard by which we are to be judged. People like R. M. Levey, Joseph Robinson, Sir Robert Stewart, Michele Esposito and John F. Larchet, backed by a strong board of management, with figures like Francis Brady, Hercules MacDonnell, Dermod O'Brien, and Maud Aiken, created these standards in the past. By doing so, they have helped to bring into existence not only a national musical institution but also an environment in which all forms of musical expression can flourish. These pioneers who established the IAM would, I think, be gratified by the way the institution has developed.

There is, however, one major deterrent to all our endeavours in planning for the future. Reading through the record of the Academy's leading role in music education, we find that in the eighteen-sixties the Commission on Science and Art in Ireland reserved their comments on the status of the IAM, 'pending the organisation of a complete system of musical education.'[2] One hundred and thirty years later, we still await the design and implementation of that system. The scandalously low level of importance accorded to music in primary and secondary schools, compared for example with Finland, continues to deny Irish children the chance to develop what is widely regarded as a national talent.

We have an abundance of this talent, and we now have the training that was so conspicuously lacking 150 years ago. But it is still not underpinned by the true infrastructure that we are entitled to expect if music is to be a real expression of our full cultural identity as a people. We have a huge musical heritage of world importance, and we also have a future role to play, again of world importance. We have the resources to do so, but we do not have at our disposal the means to deploy those resources in the best possible way.

Despite this, Ireland has made huge advances in music education in recent years, which is part of the increasing centrality of music-making to Irish society and a raising of the profile of the music professions. At the time of the Academy's conception, Thackeray, on a visit to Ireland, saw advertisements for a Dublin concert by the Limerick-born Catherine Hayes before her departure and noted: 'Only one instance of Irish talent do we read of, and that, in a desponding tone, announces its intention of quitting its native country.'[3] That was the fate of Irish-born musicians for many decades. I myself had little choice, almost thirty years ago, but to emigrate in search of advanced musical education. But today, not only are there many Irish singers and instrumentalists performing frequently in our towns and cities but these young musicians no longer need to go abroad to study. Within the walls of the Academy, a student can progress from junior level, through the teaching and performing diplomas, to undergraduate and post-graduate degrees in education and performance. Our first master in music performance graduates this year, and, given the necessary finance, we now have the wherewithal to provide the first doctorate in music performance ever offered in Ireland.

In recent years, we have seen within the Government a greater commitment than ever before to the well-being of the arts and of education, but we cannot automatically expect this to be translated instantly into bricks and mortar, or flutes and fiddles. However, the intellectual environment of the Government has undergone a major change, which is unlikely to be reversed, and we can expect that the climate in which the development of cultural life and identity in Ireland is appreciated will ensure that music education receives its long-awaited significance.

The acceleration of processes whereby music is being recognised as central, rather than peripheral, to Irish society and its expression is marked. It comes less from the conventional channels of the music profession than from walks of life that have not hitherto openly acknowledged this centrality or even seemed to be aware of music and musicians: the accountants, management consultants, public servants and financial institutions that, in various combinations, have spoken of the cultural dimension of Irish society and, more importantly, of its development in a way we have seldom heard before. They have told us that Irish cultural life has an innate merit and also has an economic identity, and a social vibrancy, with a role to play in the development of Ireland as an internationally traded commodity. They have pointed to the exponential growth in Irish achievements in popular music, to the international acceptance of Irish traditional music as one of the major genres of the folk revival, to the contribution of Irish orchestras to the film industry, to the capacity of Irish soloists to beat a path to the doors of the world's greatest concert halls and opera houses.

One influential report has referred to music as a defining national characteristic and, therefore, a facet of our national experience that not merely cannot be excluded from the future equation but must be included.[4] Such recognition, however belated, puts an entrepreneurial emphasis on the aspirations for national musical revival that has been a leitmotif of this history.

Two points in this history strike me most forcibly. One is the discovery that I myself, along with many of my colleagues in the piano faculty, have inherited the mantle of Kalkbrenner, as it has been passed down to me through generations of teachers, of whom Michele Esposito is the most famous. This in itself shows that in the past two hundred years music has been an 'internationally traded commodity', and that Ireland at one time enjoyed—and is now beginning to enjoy once more—its full share in this commerce, both taking lessons from Europe and giving back expertise in the form of great Irish musicians to the world market.

The second discovery was the 'magical beauty' that dawned on J. M. Synge as he sat here, in the Academy, in our student orchestra. Naturally, not every student sees the orchestral experience in such glowing terms; but the fact that a writer as great as Synge could see concerted music in such terms suggests to me that there is a greatness in the experience itself that transcends the hard work and the constant repetition and that fills our young people with a kind of joy they may never find elsewhere.

It is one of the great assets of the Academy that we have been able to maintain and develop our commitment to fostering the love of music in young people who will not necessarily enter the music profession but who, through the Academy, will achieve an appreciation of music that will last their whole lives and who, through this education, will swell the ranks of the audiences of the future.

We have also, through over a hundred years of the local centre examination system, spread our influence to all corners of Ireland. The task of developing that system to present-day and future requirements is of enormous importance, not only to the more than thirty thousand students who take our examinations annually but also to the many private teachers who do such sterling work throughout the length and breadth of the country.

But to return to my initial expression of frustration: the real difficulty in progressing the work of the Academy is that we do not have an integrated system of education. The PIANO committee identified the lack of educational initiatives in music as the most serious factor affecting the health of musical life in Ireland. One after another, submissions to the PIANO committee identified the education system as the place where the deficiencies in music appreciation originate, and the place where they must be rectified.

The RIAM in the past few years has not only extended its diploma and degree programme but has also demonstrated its accumulated expertise by making detailed and sustained arguments in response to the Green Paper on Education, in respect of the Arts Council's development plan for 1994–97, and to the PIANO report, the last-mentioned including a realistic proposal for the establishment of a much-needed national training orchestra.

Through our strategic alliance with the University of Dublin (TCD) in music education, and with Dublin City University in performance, we have established degrees that are on a par with the best that are offered throughout the world. Each year our students continue to win the majority of prizes at the Dublin Feis Ceoil and other feiseanna and to win significant plaudits at international competitions. The work of a great teaching institution, however, is largely invisible and undocumented, and even an exhaustive history, such as the present one, cannot hope to give voice to more than a fraction of these unspoken achievements.

These, then, are the strengths that the Academy has to trade in a market that increasingly recognises and accepts the value of our core activities and applauds and encourages the growth of that core and the development of ancillary services. We have a collegiate spirit among staff and students that animates music-making in a very special way, despite the fact that the facilities could hardly be termed glamorous.

In 1898, Annie Patterson expressed the ambition 'that there might be founded in Ireland, through public or private enterprise, a Free National Conservatoire of Music, such as exists in Paris and other Continental cities, for the admission and free culture of all deserving native students. No more superb achievement of the twentieth century for the glorification of Ireland could be imagined.'[5] The twentieth century has passed without that ambition being realised, yet the potential for such an institution exists. The transformation of the RIAM into such an institution, within a short span of time, is more than a remote possibility. That challenge, and any similar challenge, could hardly be greater than that faced by the Academy people of 1848, and, once again, it is this accumulation of wisdom and vision that gives us our present confidence. But whatever happens, the 'always beginning, never ending task' of finding and nourishing musical talent continues to be a labour of love, grit, and joy.

Appendix 1

Governors of the RIAM

1. Members of Committee, 1848–1856

Walter Berwick QC (chairman), Rev. Charles Graves (vice-chairman), William Hudson, Wyndham Goold, Prof. John Smith, Henry Bussell, Walter Sweetman, Joseph Robinson, Richard J. Greene, George Schoales, Samuel Pigott, Francis Robinson, John Stanford

2. Members of Committee and Council, 1856–1889

Up to the introduction in 1889 of the RIAM's constitution—the 'Blue Scheme'—approximately a quarter of the Academy's members were involved in its management. There was no strict procedure for the election of its Committee, and members who joined it generally tended to remain in position unless incapacitated by reason of death, the exception being a rule introduced in 1876 debarring professors of the Academy who were members of the Council (as the governing body was called from 1875 onwards) from continuing to serve if they ceased to be professors.

The following list includes all those whose names appear either in the minutes of the Commitee or Council or in the annual reports as having been elected governors.

(*a*) Original Committee of reconstituted IAM, 1856

Chief Baron Pigot, Baron R. J. Greene, Walter Berwick, B. C. Lloyd QC, T. M. Archer, Henry Bastable, Dr Thomas Beatty, Cheyne Brady, W. G. Dubedat, Henry Bussell, R. Exham, F. Elrington, Rev. C. Graves, J. H. Glover, T. Maxwell Hutton (*resigned 1879*), Dr Evory Kennedy, E. Latouche, A. R. Levey, Hercules MacDonell (*resigned 1866*), T. H. Macdermott, J. Macgrath, J. E. Pigot, Francis Robinson, Joseph Robinson, J. R. MacRory, J. Norwood, John Stanford, F. W. Brady, R. M. Levey

(*b*) Members of Committee elected subsequently

1860:   D. G. Griott, Capt. (Sir) John Esmonde Bt MP
1861:   Percy Fitzgerald, Edward Lysaght Griffin, John Reilly
1862:   Sir Jocelyn Coghill Bt, Rev. James Daniel, Sir T. A. Jones PRHA, Dr Thomas Nedley, Rev. Myles Macmanus, William Roper
1864:   Hon. H. Caulfield
1865:   W. R. Bruce, William Griffin, Luke Macdonnell
1866:   Rev. J. P. Mahaffy
1868:   Rev. Nicholas Donnelly
1869:   R. P. Stewart
1870–71: Henry Doyle, Rev. J. H. Monahan, Thomas Fagan, Hon. Sidney Skeffington, P. Hayes, (Sir) Francis Cruise, Michael Merriman, Nicholas Murphy MP, James

Owen RHA, Randal Macdonnell QC, Edward Kinahan, P. W. Joyce, C. Dollard, George Cree, William Bentham, John Harris, B. Rooke

1872: G. E. Sproule, H. Vivian Yeo (*resigned 1881*), J. K. Toomey, Wilhelm Elsner, George Benson

1873: Edward de Selvier, Michael Gunn, Joseph Mullen

1876: Augustus Burke RHA, Hugh Kennedy, Rev. W. Martin, Alexandre Billet, Carl Berzon (*debarred 1877*), Luigi Caracciolo

1878: George Delany, G. H. Irvine, T. R. G. Jozé, Carl Lauer, W. B. Martin, Thomas Mayne MP, George Osborne, E. H. Telford

1880: Raoul de Versan, Richard Farrell, Maurice Brooks MP

1881: J. C. van Maanen, Martin Kirwan, George Macartney

1882: Giuseppe Bozzelli

1883: Dr D. B. Dunne, H. Warren Darley, Robert Sharp

1886: Michele Esposito, R. W. W. Littledale, R. Wogan MacDonnell, Charles Miller, H. S. Mecredy, Arthur Patton, J. F. Rudersdorff, Charles Tichborne

1887: William Perrin

3. Board of Governors, 1889–1998

The Board of Governors consists of six elected vice-presidents and three vice-presidents acting ex officio, together with representative Governors from several constituencies—originally four (Members', Dublin Corporation, Coulson Endowment, and the professors) and today seven (Members', Dublin Corporation, Coulson Endowment, Board of Studies, teaching staff [non-Board of Studies] and administrative staff). The ex-officio vice-presidents are the Lord Mayor of Dublin, the immediate past Lord Mayor, and (until the position became obsolete) the High Sheriff of the City of Dublin. The president of the RIAM was the Lord Lieutenant, and since the abolition of this position the presidency of the RIAM has been vacant.

The symbol '. . .' indicates that there was a hiatus of one or more years between the cessation of one Governor's tenure and the election of his or her successor.

Elected vice-presidents from 1889

Bishop N. Donnelly –1920, . . . 1924, Michele Esposito –1929, Sir Hamilton Harty –1942, Denis McCullough –1968, A. P. Healy –1978, . . . 1981, Anna Brioscú –1994, Declan McDonagh

Baron Fitzgerald –1889, Sir Patrick Keenan –1894, Lord Ardilaun –1914, Sir Stanley Cochrane –1949, T. S. C. Dagg –1964, John O'Donovan –1985, Leo Gibney

Sir Francis Brady –1909, Lord Arthur Hill –1931, J. F. Larchet –1967, Charles Burgess –1968, . . . 1971, Noel Reid –1990, Liam Fitzgerald

Sir Robert Stewart –1894, Very Rev. William Greene –1909, George Cree –1910, Rev. Canon M. MacManus –1918, Sir James Campbell –1921, Lord Glenavy –1930, Edmund Lupton –1942, Mrs W. J. M. Starkie –1960, . . . 1963, Dr Annie Keelan –1982, Séamus Gaffney –1997, Joan Trimble

Sir Thomas Jones –1893, Joseph Robinson –1898, Sir Francis Cruise –1911, James Drury –1928, Dermod O'Brien –1945, . . . 1950, Liam Paul –1951, Timothy Walshe –1953, . . . 1954, M. J. Costelloe –1962, James Dowling –1974, D. J. O'Donohue –1998, Charles Acton

Lt-Col. James Ward –1897, Lord Justice Holmes –1916, Sir Ignatius O'Brien –1930, Count John McCormack –1945, . . . 1950, Maud Aiken –1978, . . . 1981, Aleck Crichton –1987, Prof. Barbara Wright

Governors representing the members

The symbols [vp], [m], [c], [d] and [p] following a Governor's name indicate that he or she became a vice-president, a members' Governor, a representative of the Coulson Endowment, a representative of Dublin Corporation, or a Professors' Governor, respectively, and ceased to represent the constituency from which he or she was originally elected.

William Bentham –1889, George Macartney –1907, P. C. Cowan –1923, J. E. Geoghegan –1932, William Lemass –1942, Percy Greene –1950, Noel Reid [vp] –1970, Mercedes Bolger –1975, Anna Brioscú [vp] –1981, John O'Conor –1994, Maurice Doyle –1998

George Cree –1908, R. W. W. Littledale KC –1917, Edmund Lupton KC [vp] –1929, Edwin Bradbury –1936, Lorcan Sherlock –1938, J. J. Nolan –1944, P. J. Kinsella –1947, J. A. Hurson –1949, Harvey Lyon –1961, Jack Griffith –1975, John Appleby –1982, Leo Gibney –1986, Pamela Flanagan

H. Warren Darley –1891, George Noble Count Plunkett –1916, Hayes –1917, George Prescott –1921, Dermod O'Brien [vp] –1927, T. S. C. Dagg [vp] –1949, James Callery –1958, J. M. P. Higgins –1979, Annette Perry –1981, Liam Fitzgerald [vp] –1990, Frank Casey

Henry Doyle –1891, William Martin Murphy –1905, Sir Ernest Cochrane –1908, Sir Stanley Cochrane –1915, Alexander Williams RHA –1925, Alice Griffith [c] –1931, Judge Cahir Davitt –1934, J. J. Mooney –1948, Dr Pádraig Breathnach –1951, Seán Breathnach –1953, Dr Annie Keelan [vp] –1963, D. H. Brocklesby –1964, K. G. Brady –1975, M. Minehane –1989, Seán Lynch –1990, Brian Aylward

David Dunne –1892, Michael J. Dunn KC –1907, Sir Philip Hanson –1910, the O'Donoghue of the Glens –1920, Sen. James Moran –1925, Mrs W. J. M. Starkie [vp] –1941, . . . 1943, Michael Dalton –1953, J. Quinlan –1957, C. Kennedy –1959, William Lemass –1963, Victor Leeson –1971, Amy Jagoe –1983, Charles McCarthy –1984, Peter Doyle –1990, Thomas Brosnan

Richard Littledale –1896, J. G. Pollock –1904, Albert Foot –1924, Raoul de Versan –1927, J. Hubbard Clarke [d] –1930, Raymond Victory –1936, A. E. Smith –1939, J. J. Shiel –1954, W. R. McDermott –1966, Dr Desmond Carney –1969, Desmond O'Donohue [vp] –1974, . . . 1976, Aleck Crichton [vp] –1981, . . . 1984, J. J. Kiernan –1986, Muiris Mac Uistin –1996, Liam Mac Uistin

R. Wogan Macdonnell,—Russell, Judge Daniel Browne –1911, W. de Courcy Millar –1926, Lennox Robinson –1932, Joseph Holloway –1944, Timothy Walshe –1950, Hugh Smith –1960, Anne Byrne –1965, A. Drury Byrne –1978, Sen. Michael Yeats –1980, Walter Beckett –1985, Hylda Beckett

Canon Myles MacManus [vp] –1910, Col. Sir William Taylor –1926, Denis McCullough TD [vp] –1942, Rev. Richard MacNevin [c] –1949, M. J. Costelloe [vp] –1954, Charles Acton [c] –1956, Albert Healy [vp] –1968, Gabriel Fallon –1975, P. Heffernan –1977, K. G. Brady –1979, Eric Sweeney –1980, Eugene Horgan –1994, John Casey

Henry Mecredy –1891, W. R. J. Molloy –1909, Maj. Arthur Whewell –1926, Edith Best –1931, Adelio Viani –1964, A. Broderick –1982, Christopher Fitz-Simon –1985, Unsionn Ó Farachtáin –1995, Anne Fuller

Thomas Nedley –1899, T. W. Gerrard [c] –1920, Frank Wynne –1924, George Prescott –1942, A. E. Smith –1945, J. J. O'Connor, Christopher Burgess [vp] –1967, M. A. O'Sullivan –1977, Eibhlín Ní Loingsigh –1984, Audrey Chisholm [p] –1986, Loretta Keating –1991, Annraoi Ó Beoláin –1995, Frank Murphy

William Perrin –1921, William Ireland [c] –1925, J. F. Larchet [vp] –1932, Gerald Horan –1933, M. W. O'Reilly –1953, J. E. Dowling [vp] –1962, A. J. Potter –1971, Desmond Carney –1975, Séamus Gaffney [vp] –1982, Charles Barrett –1988, Declan McDonagh [vp] –1995, Ian Fox

Robert Sharp –1890, Charles Tichborne –1904, W. P. Geoghegan –1911, J. P. Wrenn –1915, W. H. Brayden –?, Liam Paul [vp] –1950, John O'Donovan [vp] –1964, P. L. Gibson –1979, Barbara Wright [vp] –1987, Gabrielle Begg

Governors representing Dublin Corporation, 1889–1923

The records of Dublin Corporation and the RIAM are at variance in many respects regarding the dates on which representative Governors were appointed by the Corporation and, more particularly, the dates on which they retired or were reappointed. Many corporation Governors disqualified themselves by non-attendance, and this was not always accurately recorded by the secretary of the RIAM. The following is therefore a reconstruction from the archives of both institutions and is not entirely dependable.

Ald. William Meagher –1894, Valentine Blake Dillon –1897, Ald. Laurence Mulligan –1898, Thomas Kelly –1905, Joseph Hatch –1908, James Crozier –1916, Charles McGuinness –1917, W. T. Cosgrave –1919, J. Russell Stritch

Ald. Valentine Dillon –1892, M. J. Losty –1896, Joseph Hatch –1897, Ald. W. Doyle –1899, Ald. Thomas Lenehan –1903, J. J. O'Meara –1916, Sir Patrick Shortall –1917, Ald. William McCarthy –1921, Ald. Kathleen Clarke

Cllr Sir Robert Sexton –1900, Sir John Irwin [c]

Cllr Robert Wade –1891, Thomas Sherlock –1899, J. P. Cox –1904, — Cole –1905, Michael Doyle –1910, Sir Patrick Shortall –1915, Sarah Harrison

Cllr Sir George Owens –1896, Richard Jones –1902, J. Coghlan Briscoe

Cllr T. D. Sullivan MP –1891, Daniel O'Connell Miley –1896, William Ireland –1905, E. P. Monk –1908, William Ireland

Cllr Thomas Mayne MP –1895, P. J. McCall –1909, Joseph Gleeson –1912, W. H. Brayden [m] –1915, P. Meehan –1918, William Paul

Cllr Charles Dawson –1893, Cllr John J. O'Meara –1893, W. H. Beardwood –1907 — Cahill –1911, Gerald O'Reilly –1915, Dr Myles Keogh –1916, Ald. W. T. Dinnage –1921, Richard White –1922, Ald. B. F. Shields

In May 1924 the Executive Council of the Irish Free State dissolved Dublin Corporation. After an initial uncertainty whether the sitting representatives of the corporation were entitled to retain their positions, the three commissioners appointed to administer the city—S. Ó Murchadha, P. J. Hernon, and Dr Dwyer—represented the corporation in the capacity of Governors until October 1930, when the Corporation was reinstated.

Governors representing Dublin Corporation, 1930–1969

Cllr — Caffrey –1934, Mrs Frank McDonnell –1948, Cllr Thomas Doyle –1949, Patrick Coughlan –1951, Denis Larkin –1952, James Kelly –1955, Dr T. B. Herlihy –1964, Noel Coughlan

Ald. Hubbard Clarke –1948, William J. Colman –1962, Cllr G. McLoughlin

Frank Cluskey –1932, David Coyle –1934, Sen. Kathleen Clarke –1938, J. J. Byrne –1950, Cllr Harold Douglas –1953, Margaret Fitzsimons –1961, Desmond O'Donohue [m]

Mrs David Glasgow (Terry O'Connor) –1932, Ald. Robert Benson –1933, Ald. Ernest Benson –1939, Maud Aiken [vp] –1949, Cllr Annie Byrne –1967, H. M. Dockrell

Mrs W. O'Hara –1949, Fr Leo McCann

Cllr J. Ryan –1932, M. Fitzpatrick –1939, Rev. J. Fennelly –1945, Ald. Bernard Butler –1957, Cllr C. Keeble –1964, Cllr M. Long

Lorcan Sherlock –1934, John McCann –1939, James Kennedy –1943, J. Keogh Clarke

Dónal O'Sullivan –1934, Martin O'Sullivan –1944, Joseph Brown –1948, Cllr J. J. Phelan –1957, Cllr Daniel Morris –1960, Ald. Patrick Cummins

In 1969 Dublin Corporation was suspended by the Minister for Local Government, and until 1973 its powers were exercised by a Commissioner.

Governors representing Dublin Corporation, 1974/75–1998

Rev. T. Blennerhassett –1975, P. J. Malone –1981, T. Duffy –1987, Eric Byrne TD –1992, Dr A. Doyle

Cllr Pat Cummins –1986, Pat McCartan –1987, Pat Cummins

Miss M. McAuliffe –1979, Cllr Mary Freihill –1986, Cllr Peter Burke –1991, K. Downey 1993, . . . 1994, L. Mooney

Rev. Leo McCann –1977, M. Humphreys –1978, Vincent O'Neill –1981, . . . 1986, Ben Briscoe TD –1988, . . . 1989, Mary O'Donnell

John Keogh-Clarke –1988, P. Carey –1990, Ben Briscoe TD –1992, Maureen O'Flynn –1996, E. Quinlan

Rev. J. Larkin –1986, Dr Dermot Fitzpatrick TD –1991, . . . 1995, Aidan Meagher

Cllr S. Kelly –1977, Cllr Kevin Byrne –1981, Mrs Purnell Barry 1993, . . . 1994, Thomas Rowan

Cllr B. Lynch –1975, . . . 1983, Ald. Alexis Fitzgerald

Governors representing the Coulson Endowment

Capt. W. T. Ward –1890, Frank Browning –1921, Sir John Irwin –1934, Nora Sidford Fannin –1948, Rev. Dr R. MacNevin –1955, Rev. Canon John Ross –1970, Hon. Mark Hely Hutchinson –1975, Dr Judy Shepherd –1989, Richard Pine

James Drury –1911, A. W. W. Baker –1925, William Ireland –1931, Frank Wynne –1939, Alice Yoakley –1944, Richard Midgeley –1956, Charles Acton –1998, Tim Thurston

Robert Browne –1911, Sir Gabriel Stokes –1920, Capt. T. M. Gerrard –1928, — Whewell –1930, Alice Griffith –1938, Frank Griffith –1939, Edith Boxwell –1944, Edgar Deale –1977, Maurice Dockrell –1985, Philip Jacob –1990, David Byers

Governor representing the professors (since 1997, the Board of Studies)

Michele Esposito –1910, T. R. G. Jozé –1914, Clyde Twelvetrees –1919, R. W. Rooke –1930, T. H. Weaving –1951, Rhona Marshall –1953, Dina Copeman –1959, Dr A. J. Potter [m] –1963, Rhona Marshall –1966, Dorothy Stokes –1967, Dina Copeman –1977, Dorothy Stokes –1978, Seán Lynch –1981, Paul Deegan –1983, Maeve Broderick –1987, Audrey Chisholm –1988, Paul Deegan –1994, James Cavanagh –1997, Deirdre Doyle

Governors representing the non-professorial teaching staff, 1996–1998

1995 Marion Hyland –1996, Carol Ann Scott –1998, Anthony Glavin

Governors representing the administrative staff, 1996–1998

1995 Grace Hickey –1996, Ellen Whelan –1997, Teresa Doyle –1998, Wendy Davis

Appendix 2

Teaching and Administrative Staff

1. Members of teaching staff, 1848–1998

The names are arranged in chronological order of the opening of the faculties.

The symbol ◊ has been employed to indicate each individual post. The symbol ¶ after a teacher's name means that he or she was a staff member at the time of publication of this book.

Names in bold type indicate members of the staff who were appointed professors of the RIAM and therefore served as members of the Board of Studies, or were elected to the Board of Studies as representatives of the non-professorial teaching staff.

In the case of the principal teachers in the Academy, a distinct line of succession can be traced from one teacher to the next. This is especially so in relation to the chief professors (such as the succession of senior violin teachers) and is emphasised below by sequential post-holders who were also members of the Board of Studies. In other cases, teaching posts were established additional to the main professorships (as indicated, for example, in the cadres of extra piano teachers recruited in 1938 and 1944), some of which were suppressed after the tenure of the first incumbent.

Where a member of the staff had previously served as a pupil teacher (receiving free tuition in exchange for teaching junior grades), this is indicated by the symbol [p] and the years in question, e.g. [p 1901]. Those pupil teachers who did not go on to become members of the staff have not been included in this listing.

The symbol '. . .' indicates that a hiatus of one or more years may have existed between the cessation of one teacher and the appointment of his or her successor.

The editors have made every effort to ensure that these lists are complete and accurate. In some cases, however, where staff records are not extant or are ambiguous, members of the staff may have been inadvertently omitted or may have incorrect dates assigned to them.

Violin

◊ 1848 **R. M. Levey** –1897, **Gerolamo de Angelis** –1898, **Adolf Wilhelmj** –1911, **Achille Simonetti** –1919, **Joshua Watson** –1925, **Feruccio Grossi** –1947, . . . 1949, **Jaroslav Vaneček** –1955, **Max Thöner** –1963, **Sidney Griller** –1972, **Maeve Broderick** –1991, **Deirdre Ward** –1997, . . . 1998, Eyal Kless¶

◊ 1858 John Hughes –1859, James Wilkinson –1860, Charles Grandison –1865

◊ 1874 C. Berzon –1877, **Carl Lauer** –1888/89, **Theodore Werner** –1891, **Guido Papini** –1898, . . . 1899, **Arthur Warren Darley** –1902, [p 1899] Mabel Love –1905

◊ 1876 C. Stein –1877

◊ 1884 J. C. Connolly –1891, **Octave Grisard** –1912

◊ 1890 E. Rawlingson –1900

◊ 1892 [p 1891] Florence Bloom –1894/95, Victoria Delany (Mrs Edmond Lupton) –1916, Edith Kelly-Lang –1925, **Nancie Lord** –1966

◊ 1895 [p 1892] A. Callaghan –1903

◊ 1895 [p 1894] Anna Kavanagh –1900

◊ 1896 [p 1893] Patrick Delany –1946
◊ 1898 [p 1897] Aileen Grogan –1899, Henri Verbrugghen –1900
◊ 1902 [p 1897] Maud Parr –1909/10, [p 1907] Marie Dowse –1912, [p 1908] Alice McCarthy –1949, Carol Little –1952, François d'Albert –1954, Savino Agnoli –1955, Georg Gerike –1973, Patricia Higgins –1989
◊ 1903 P. M'Cready –1905, [p 1901] **Madeleine Moore (Larchet)** –1945, Arthur Franks –?
◊ 1949 Kveta Vaneček –1955
◊ 1952 Una Fox –1953
◊ 1958 David Lillis –1967
◊ 1959 Íde Ní Raghallaigh (de Búrca) 1971, reappointed 1977¶
◊ 1962 János Fürst –1965
◊ 1962 Margaret Murphy
◊ 1964 Una Kenny –1972
◊ 1970 Kevin Kiely –1992
◊ 1970 Geraldine O'Grady –1974, reappointed 1985¶
◊ 1971 Ruth David –1982
◊ 1975 Colin Staveley –1979
◊ 1976 Ian McKenzie –1977, 1978–79
◊ 1979 Camilla Gunzl –1980
◊ 1980 William Shanahan –1989
◊ 1981 Thérèse Timoney –1990, Margaret Hayes¶
◊ 1994 Michael d'Arcy¶
◊ 1994 Sheila O'Grady¶
◊ 1997 Maeve Broderick¶

Cello

◊ 1848 Joseph Lidel –1851, Wilhelm Elsner –1884, **J. F. Rudersdorff** –1891, **Henri Bast** –1902/03, **Clyde Twelvetrees** –1919, **John Mundy** –1919, **J. Schofield** –1930, **Ida Starkie O'Reilly** –1944/45, **Clyde Twelvetrees** –1956
◊ 1890 [p. 1888] Richard O'Reilly –1900, . . . 1901, [p 1900] Mary Garland –1903
◊ 1900 Mary Gallagher –1940, Dorothy Clifton –1945, Betty Sullivan –1946, Molly Concannon –1949, Caitlín O'Byrne –1953, Betty Sullivan –1957
◊ 1952 Maurice Meulien –1953, Wolfram Henschel –1954/55, **Erich Eisenbrand** –1958, **Coral Bognuda** –1967, **Albin Berky** –1969, **Aisling Drury Byrne** –1979, reappointed 1994¶
◊ 1960 Elizabeth Barrett –1986, **Nora Gilleece**¶
◊ 1985 Mihai Dancila –1986, Olwen Lewis¶
◊ 1994 William Butt¶
◊ 1994 Annette Cleary¶

Woodwind and brass

◊ 1856 — Weizig –1856, — Clements –1862
◊ 1856 J. A. L. Rungeling –1860, J. Reilly –1862, Harry Hardy

Brass

◊ 1868 Bernard Dwyer –1879

Woodwind

◊ 1868 William Woods –1879, **J. C. van Maanen** –1892
◊ 1888 John Haveron (bassoon and oboe)
◊ 1890 George Ellard –1917

Cornet and trumpet

◊ 1886 J. O'Donnell –1888, **J. C. van Maanen** –1892

◊ 1949 Novemo Salvadore –1963, Giulio Sfingi –1965, David Fetter –1966, Carey Donaldson –1969, Victor Malirsh –1975, Joszef Csibi –1980, **James Cavanagh**¶
◊ 1980 Charles Parkes

Trombone

◊ 1888 J. C. van Maanen –1892
◊ 1949 Novemo Salvadore –1963, . . . 1965, David Fetter –1966, Carey Donaldson –1969, Seán Cahill¶

Flute and recorder

◊ 1889 George Ellard –1917
◊ 1931 H. J. Leeming –1952, André Prieur –1958, Hans Kohlmann –1964, Patricia Dunkerley –1972, William Halpin –1980, Jenny Robinson –1985
◊ 1974 Rosemary Hill¶
◊ 1978 Elizabeth Gaffney –1980, Margaret Caffrey –1989, Aedin Halpin¶
◊ 1977 **Doris Keogh** –1993, **Adrian Brett** –1995, William Dowdall¶
◊ 1995 Susan Doyle¶

Clarinet

◊ 1890 James Conroy –1912, J. L. Toole –1917
◊ 1924 William German –?, ? –1940, Joseph Murphy –1951, . . . 1953, Michele Incenzo –1961, . . . 1963, David Lloyd –1966/67, James Daly¶
◊ 1996   John Finucane¶

Bassoon

◊ 1888 John Haveron
◊ 1949 **Gilbert Berg** –1961, Michael Rogers –1980, Michael Jones –1987, Michael Rogers¶
◊ 1996 Michael Jones¶
◊ 1996 Rachel Nolan¶

Oboe

◊ 1888 George Ellard –1917
◊ 1948 Léon Thonon –1949, Roland Dufrane –1952, **Gilbert Berg** –1961, **Helmut Seeber**¶
◊ 1996 Ruby Ashley¶
◊ 1996 Matthew Manning¶

Horn

◊ 1888 **E. Brasfort (Armstrong)** –1893
◊ 1919 A. C. Busby –1921
◊ 1948 Leopold Laurent –1955, **Victor Malirsh**¶

Singing

◊ 1856 J. Smith –1858, Julia Cruise –1869, **Joseph Robinson** –1875, **Luigi Caracciolo** –1882
◊ 1864 Richard Smith
◊ 1868 **Elizabeth Scott-Fennell** –1872, 1875–1877, 1881–1902
◊ 1868 Bessie Herbert –1879/80, J. Ward –1885
◊ 1871 J. Dunne
◊ 1871 **Adelaide Barnewell** –1912
◊ 1871 J. C. Culwick
◊ 1871 W. Power O'Donoghue

◊ 1873 Joseph Mullen
◊ 1876 — Bellew –1881
◊ 1878 A. L. Cowley
◊ 1881 Giuseppe Bozzelli –1885, **Luigi Caracciolo** –1887, **Martin Roeder** –1889, Lucy Ashton Hackett –1926
◊ 1880 — Swanwick –1885
◊ 1880 **T. R. G. Jozé** –1881
◊ 1886 Lizzie Connell –1888, **Annie Irwin** –1939, **Michael O'Higgins** –1946, Brian Boydell –1948, Michael O'Higgins –1951, Renee Flynn –1952, A. J. Potter –1973
◊ 1886 — Erskine –1889, Charles Kelly –1894, **E. Gordon Cleather** –1900, **Benedetto Palmieri** –1912, **Charles Tinney** –1916, **Adelio Viani** –1964
◊ 1887 Joseph Robinson –1895
◊ 1888 Annie Scarff (Goodman) –1921
◊ 1889 [p 1888] Alice O'Hea –1936
◊ 1901 **Randal Woodhouse** –1905
◊ 1902 George Ellard –1903
◊ 1937 Kathleen Roddy –1946, **Violet Burne** –1979
◊ 1939 Renee Flynn –1944, Violet Pearson
◊ 1944 Brian Boydell –1946
◊ 1961 **Denis Noble** –1965, Elizabeth Downey –1968
◊ 1966 Austin Gaffney –1969
◊ 1967 **Paul Deegan**¶
◊ 1967 John Carolan –1969
◊ 1967 Jacqueline Pomeroy –1969
◊ 1969 **Michael O'Higgins** –1973/74, **Maciej Smolenski**¶
◊ 1978 Patricia McCarry¶
◊ 1995 Veronica Dunne¶
◊ 1995 Irene Sandford¶

Harmony/composition/rudiments/theory/musicianship

◊ 1856 J. Smith –1861
◊ 1869 **Sir Robert P. Stewart** –1892
◊ 1876 **T. R. G. Jozé** –1918, **Charles Kitson** –1920, **J. F. Larchet** –1955, **A. J. Potter** –1973, **Walter Beckett** –1984, **Pamela Flanagan**¶
◊ 1891 — Bevan
◊ 1896 **B. Warburton Rooke** –1930
◊ 1908 Nettie Edwards –1912
◊ 1910 **Thomas Weaving** –1965
◊ 1928 **Dorothy Stokes** –1977
◊ ? Agnes Murphy –1955, **Arnold McKiernan** –1987, John O'Flynn –1989
◊ 1937 **Rita Broderick** –1962
◊ 1963 **Bernadette Marmion**¶
◊ 1963 Frances Moore
◊ 1966 Noel Curtin –1983
◊ 1971 James Wilson –1982
◊ 1971 John Beckett –1983
◊ 1972 Jean Archibald¶
◊ 1972 Joseph Groocock –1997
◊ 1973 Muriel Dagg –1975, Leslie Yorke Calvert –1980
◊ ? E. McGowan –1980
◊ 1977 John Gibson –1978
◊ 1977 Denis Ferguson –1987
◊ 1978 **Annette Perry**¶
◊ 1978 Brendan Murray¶
◊ 1978 Evelyn O'Sullivan –1997
◊ 1986 Marie Moran¶

◊ 1994 Martin Barrett –1998
◊ 1995 Helen Haughey –1996

Languages

◊ German 1856, — Weizig
◊ French 1857, — Blum
◊ Italian 1880, — Morosini –1888, — Benvenuti –1893, Armand Loup –1895, Christina Doyle –1897, Mary Story –1912, Bianca Esposito –1917

Piano

◊ 1856 Joseph Robinson –1875, **Alexandre Billet** –1894/95, [p 1892] Charles Wilson –1928
◊ 1856 Fanny Arthur –1879
◊ 1857 **Elizabeth Bennett** –1901
◊ 1860 — Kelly –1893 . . . 1894, A. Robertson –1905
◊ 1869 **Sir Robert P. Stewart** –1892
◊ 1871 G. E. W. Sproule –1879, . . . 1880, — Volkmer –1881, Michael Quarry –1882, **Michele Esposito** –1928, **Jean du Chastain** –1929, **Claud Biggs** –1948, **Francis Engel** –1953
◊ 1871 — Gayrard –1873, **Margaret O'Hea** –1928
◊ 1872 **T. R. G. Jozé** –1882
◊ 1875 — Broderick –1883, — Douglas –1886
◊ 1875 — Ellis –1882
◊ 1875 T. Moore –1876
◊ 1883 Susan Wright (Mrs Wright Barker) –1930
◊ 1883 — Cruise –1884, — Hogg –1886, **Edith Oldham (Best)** –1932
◊ 1883 Charles Irwin –1885, A. Blüthner –1888, **B. Warburton Rooke** –1929
◊ 1887 Clara Bloom –1895, [p 1894] Daisy Bloom –1924/25, **Alice O'Hea** –1936
◊ 1887 Albert May
◊ 1895 [p 1891] Ada Craig –1914
◊ 1895 **Mary Ellen Robinson** –1907
◊ 1898 [p 1896] Edith French (Boxwell) –1925
◊ 1901 [p 1894] Bessie Ruthven –1926
◊ 1901 [p 1896] Annie Lord –1938, Victor Love –1944, Nell Ronan –1979
◊ 1902 **Thomas Weaving** –1956
◊ 1926 **Dina Copeman** –1982
◊ 1926 **Rhona Clark (Marshall)** –1985
◊ 1938 Marjorie Brunskill
◊ 1938 Margaret McNamee
◊ 1938 Audrey Tonkin
◊ 1938 **Carmel Turner** –1977
◊ 1944 Dympna Connolly
◊ 1944 Irene Nabarro –1950
◊ 1944 Patricia Victory –1950
◊ 1944 Margery Watson –1946
◊ 1948 Gráinne Ní Éigeartaigh –1951, **Seán Lynch** –1994, Patricia Kavanagh¶
◊ 1949 Gertrude Leahy –1953
◊ 1949 Rita O'Brien –1956
◊ 1949 Anthony Hughes –1958
◊ 1954 **Valerie Walker** –1998
◊ 1955 **Audrey Chisholm**¶
◊ 1956 Sheila Ryan
◊ 1957 Ann Clancy (Heneghan) –1973
◊ 1963 Charles Lynch –1965
◊ 1975 Dorothy Stokes –1982

◊ 1966 Judith Shreider (Segal)
◊ 1969 **Anthony Glavin**¶
◊ 1970 Darina Gibson –1971
◊ 1971 John Beckett –1983
◊ 1971 Marie Whyte¶
◊ 1973 Brian Beckett¶
◊ 1975 Walter Beckett –1984
◊ 1975 Patricia Herbert –1991, **Anthony Byrne**¶
◊ 1975 **Carol Ann Scott**¶
◊ 1976 **John O'Conor**¶
◊ 1977 John Gibson –1978
◊ 1977 Denis Ferguson –1987, Therese Fahy¶
◊ 1977 David Lee¶
◊ 1978 Peter Dains –1989
◊ 1978 **Deirdre Doyle**¶
◊ 1979 Sheila McCabe –1989
◊ 1984 Gráinne Dunne –1986, Colma Brioscú¶
◊ 1985 Mabel Swainson –1987
◊ 1988 Áine Quinn –1996
◊ 1989 Gillian Smith¶
◊ 1991 Brian MacNamara –1993
◊ 1993 Réamonn Keary¶
◊ 1995 Hugh Tinney¶
◊ 1998 Veronica McSwiney¶

Concert harp and Irish harp

◊ 1871 — Mackey –?, ? –1888 Priscilla Frost –1889, Josephine Sullivan –1894, Esther Corless –1895, Angela O'Connor –1897, Miriam Bernard –1898, Norman Summerfield –1900, Annie Scarff Goodman –1917
◊ 1930 Annie Fagan –1954, Mercedes Bolger –1963, Gráinne Ní Éigeartaigh (Yeats) –1967, Elizabeth Hannon –1972, Denise Kelly –1981, Helen Davies –1989, Áine Ní Dhubhghaill¶
◊ 1954 Gérard Meyer –1963
◊ 1964 Pauline Nevin
◊ 1971 Anne Crowley
◊ 1978 Orla Brioscú –1987

Organ

◊ 1880 Sir Robert P. Stewart –1892
◊ 1880 T. R. G. Jozé –1917
◊ 1880 — Volkmer –1881
◊ 1880 **Charles Marchant** –1881, also 1894–1918, B. W. Rooke –1937, Thomas Weaving –1966
◊ 1918 **George Hewson** –1967
◊ 1962 Arnold McKiernan –1987
◊ 1966 Vincent Pentony –1975
◊ 1975 **David Lee**¶
◊ 1975 Walter Beckett –1984

Chamber music

It was only periodically that specific appointments were made to teach chamber music. At other times the subject was offered and all members of the teaching staff were encouraged to teach or coach it.

◊ 1880 Sir Robert P. Stewart –1888, Alexandre Billet –1892, T. R. G. Jozé and Charles Marchant –1899, Henri Bast –1905, Clyde Twelvetrees –1918, John Mundy –1919, Michele Esposito –1927, Feruccio Grossi –1929, Jean du Chastain –1930
◊ 1984 Seán Lynch –1994/95, Sheila O'Grady¶

Choir

◊ 1881 Giuseppe Bozzelli –1885
◊ 1883 T. R. G. Jozé –1885
◊ 1887 Martin Roeder –1890
◊ 1894 Charles Marchant –1918
◊ 1928 Thomas Weaving –1965, . . . 1977, Denis Ferguson –1987, James Cavanagh –1998, Mark Duley¶

Orchestra

◊ 1881 R. M. Levey –1884, J. F. Rudersdorff –1885/86, Carl Lauer –1888/89, Theodore Werner –1891, T. R. G. Jozé –1916, Michele Esposito –1917
◊ 1881 Wilhelm Elsner –1883
◊ 1881 J. C. van Maanen –1884
◊ 1889 Joseph Robinson –1894
◊ 1926 Madeleine Larchet –1928, J. F. Larchet –1940, Dorothy Stokes –1982
◊ 1948 Brian Boydell –1951, Max Thöner –1961?, 1966 Colman Pearce –1977, Denis Ferguson –1987, **James Cavanagh**¶

Double bass

◊ 1887 **J. F. Rudersdorff** –1892, Henri Bast –1906, Clyde Twelvetrees –1908, Zachariah Lee –1945, Robert Bushnell –1952, Rudolph Frei –1954, . . . 1956, **Heinz Jablonski** –1961, Helmut Engemann¶
◊ 1997 Dominic Dudley¶

Viola

◊ 1888 Theodore Werner –1890, E. Rawlingson –1900, Octave Grisard –1912, George Hoyle –1937, Feruccio Grossi –1947
◊ 1980 Séamus O'Grady –1985, Anne Gilleece –1987, Séamus O'Grady –1989, **Elizabeth Csibi**¶

Declamation and deportment/elocution/speech and drama

◊ 1890 Jeannie Quinton Rosse –1901, **Mary O'Hea** –1936
◊ 1937 **Ursula White** –1977
◊ 1951 Christopher Casson –1953, Sylvia McCormick (Noble) –1965, **Nora Lever** –1966
◊ ? Bláithín Ní Chnáimhín –1965
◊ 1965 **Eibhlín Ní Loingsigh**¶
◊ 1965 Máirín Uí Chathasaigh
◊ 1966 Anne Crowley
◊ ? Aileen Harte –1991
◊ 1995 Ann Russell Weakley¶

Opera

◊ 1891 Jeannie Quinton Rosse –1898
◊ 1917 Adelio Viani –1957, Michael O'Higgins –1973
◊ 1977 Paul Deegan¶

Plainchant/liturgical music

◊ 1937 Herbert Rooney –1958, Seán Hayes –1970

Saxophone

◊ 1954 Gilbert Berg –1961
◊ 1996 Fintan Sutton¶

Percussion

◊ 1961 Kurt Goedike –1964, János Keszei –1966, . . . 1970, Henning Knöbel –1975, Joachim Wieland –1976, Dan Breen¶
◊ 1996 Richard O'Donnell¶

Harpsichord

◊ 1967 John O'Sullivan –1995
◊ 1971 John Beckett –1983, Malcolm Proud –1986
◊ 1989 David Lee¶
◊ 1993 Gillian Smith¶

Classical guitar

◊ 1963 Jack Gregory –1971, Arthur Dolsen –1972, Andrew Robinson –1980, Cecile Gormley –1987, **Marion Hyland**¶
◊ 1971 Ernest Earley –1973

Euphonium and tuba

◊ 1969 Seán Cahill¶
◊ 1996 Rory Boyle¶

Accompanists

◊ 1963 John O'Sullivan –1995, Dearbhla Brosnan¶
◊ 1975 Rosemary Hill –1980
◊ 1995 Patrick Zuk –1998, Dearbhla Collins¶

Viol

◊ 1976 John Beckett –1983, Andrew Robinson –1986, Honor Carmody –1998, Andrew Robinson¶

Conducting

◊ 1992 James Kavanagh¶

Classical accordion

◊ 1997 Patricia Kavanagh¶

2. Administrative staff, 1856–1998

Secretary (termed Assistant Secretary from 1856 to 1889)

◊ 1856 S. H. Sloane –1857, — Powell –1858, Robert Wheeler –1868, Mervyn Browne –1875, E. M. Crean (combining duties of lady superintendent and secretary) –1886, T. R. G. Jozé –1894, C. Grahame Harvey –1924, Gladys Tuite –1927, Sealy Jeffares –1949, Matthew Connery –1954, Terry Blackledge –1959, James Callery –1982, James Forde –1986, Dorothy Shiel¶

Lady superintendent

◊ 1875 E. M. Crean –1900, Susan Crean –1908, Alice Craig –1930, May McGeeney –1955, Margaret Furlong –1990, Margaret Hickey. (This post was suppressed in 1992.)

Registrar

◊ 1882 John O'Rorke –1885
◊ 1992 Anthony Madigan¶

Librarian

◊ 1888 J. H. Trundle
◊ 1939 Alice McCarthy –1949, Bernadette Carbery –1950, Seán Lynch –1953, Aileen O'Hanrahan –1955
◊ 1992 Philip Shields¶

Director

◊ 1982 Lindsay Armstrong –1993, . . . 1994, John O'Conor¶

Heads of faculty, 1995

Keyboard: Deirdre Doyle¶
Strings: Elizabeth Csibi¶
Woodwind, brass, and percussion: James Cavanagh¶
Voice: Paul Deegan¶
Musicianship: Pamela Flanagan¶

Notes

Sources

In 1980–81 the Academy decided to transfer the greater part of its archives on loan to the Public Record Office, and these are now in the National Archives, where they are catalogued as collection 1120. These contain minutes of the governing body, the Board of Studies, and various committees, accounts, student records, and press cuttings. Reference to these in the notes is made by citing, in the instance of the Board of Governors and its predecessors, 'Minutes of [date]' and, in other cases, the name of the relevant committee or board; this is followed by a statement of the location within the collection, e.g. NA 1120/1/1. Material outside this collection is cited as, for example, 'RIAM', 'NLI', or 'TCD'.

The newspapers cited in the notes have been abbreviated as follows:

DE:	*Daily Express*
DEM:	*Dublin Evening Mail*
FJ:	*Freeman's Journal*
IT:	*Irish Times*
SNL:	*Saunders's News-Letter*
WIT:	*Weekly Irish Times*

Chapter 1 (p. 1–11)

1 McCarthy, 'Music Education', 71, in discussing this milestone development, also refers to the fact that 'an intriguing network of private and voluntary education agencies was in operation in Ireland prior to . . . 1831.'

2 Augustus Frederick Fitzgerald, third Duke of Leinster, 1791–1874; educated Eton and Oxford; succeeded father in 1804. Nephew of Lord Edward Fitzgerald; supporter of Catholic Emancipation and parliamentary reform; Grand Master of Freemasons in Ireland; first chairman of Board of Commissioners of National Education 1831–50, vice-president of Royal Academy of Music, president of RIAM.

3 O'Connell's use of this term was not original but derived from Sir Robert Inglis: 'A gigantic scheme of Godless education.' Quoted by John Molony in *A Soul Came into Ireland*, 302.

4 Quoted by John A. Murphy in 'Queen's College, Cork: beginnings', *Irish Review*, no. 17–18, 1995.

5 Cf. White, *The Keeper's Recital*, 7. 'It has scarcely been recognized that if there was a language question in Irish cultural affairs, there was also a music question.' The point is shared by Joseph Ryan in 'Nationalism and Music in Ireland', 3: '[This study] is predicated on the basis of the symbiotic relationship between nationalism and the artistic life,' and by McCarthy, 'Music Education', 3: 'Music in education, education in music, and music education, are conceived in, of, and through culture on the one hand while also contributing to its transformation on the other. In this sense, music education is both culturally determined and culturally determining.'

6 Lee, *The Modernisation of Irish Society*, 89. 1848 was the year chosen by Lee as the starting-point for his invaluable study.

7 *Nation*, 23 Aug. 1845. Sixty years later Douglas Hyde would refer to a vision of Ireland 'self-centred, self-sufficient, self-supporting, self-reliant' (quoted by Dunleavy and Dunleavy in *Douglas Hyde*, 267).

8 McDowell, 'Ireland on the eve of the Famine', 83.

9 See Ryan, 'Nationalism and Music in Ireland', 180, where he identifies the problems of musical activity in early nineteenth-century Ireland as 'musical literacy, in maintaining some measure of enterprise and thereby promoting a consciousness of the art and in encouraging broader participation.'

10 To say that there was an ideology among its founders to be teased out in writing a history of the RIAM is to beg a full history of music in Ireland that would relate

music to the whole culture and relate that culture to politics and society—but that is a task for other hands.

11   The minutes of 5 May 1857 record his subscription (NA 1120/1/1).

12   Hutchinson, *The Dynamics of Cultural Nationalism*, 80.

13   Ibid., 3–4, 66.

14   McDowell, 'Ireland on the eve of the Famine'.

15   Namier, *1848*, 33.

16   Woodham-Smith, *The Great Hunger*, 15.

17   Sir Randolph Routh to Deputy Commissary General Hewetson (quoted ibid., 67).

18   Lewis Namier, 'Nationality and liberty' in *Avenues of History*, 47–8.

19   Joyce, *Ulysses*, 329.

20   Ibid., 330.

21   Quoted by Boyce in *Nineteenth-Century Ireland*, 46–7.

22   Kearney, *Postnationalist Ireland*, 2–6.

23   Ibid., 99–107, and *Crane Bag*, vol. 1, no. 1, 1977.

24   White, *The Keeper's Recital*, 12.

25   Namier, *1848*, 29.

26   See Leerssen, *Remembrance and Imagination*, 9: 'From 1800 onwards, we see a sudden increase in the tendency to view Irish history as unfinished business, as a set of outstanding grievances waiting to be redressed.'

27   Three Bloom sisters (Florence, Clara, and Daisy) studied and taught in the Academy. They were the daughters of Marcus Bloom (originally Blum), a dentist practising at 2 Clare Street, Dublin, and a founder of the Dublin Dental Hospital who had become a Catholic on marriage (Hyman, *The Jews of Ireland*, 175–6). Another daughter, Beatrice, was also a musician. Florence taught violin from 1894 to 1895, resigning on marriage (she was known in later life as Mrs Bloom Pollock); Clara taught piano from 1887 and also resigned in 1895, being succeeded by her sister Daisy, who had previously been a student teacher and a pupil of Esposito and Margaret O'Hea. Daisy also studied the harp, which she played in the Dublin Orchestral Society.

28   Lee, *The Modernisation of Irish Society*, 165.

29   Ibid., 13.

30   Ibid.

31   R. D. Lyons, *Intellectual Resources of Ireland*.

32   Joseph Ryan, 'Nationalism and Irish music' in Gillen and White (eds.), *Irish Musical Studies, 3*, 102.

33   Woodham-Smith, *The Great Hunger*, 179, 202, 372.

34   Boyce, *Nineteenth-Century Ireland*, passim.

35   Quoted by Woodham-Smith in *The Great Hunger*, 321.

36   Ibid., 373.

37   Ibid., 36.

38   Like the St Stephen's Green Club—which was being formed at that time and which had several Academy founders among its membership (including Walter Berwick, Maziere Brady, Henry and W. E. Hudson, David Pigot, and Walter Sweetman)—it was if anything 'liberal nationalist in politics' and 'non-sectarian in religion' (Smith and Share, *Whigs on the Green*, 40–1).

39   'Shock of the new' was originally the title of a study of modernism by Ian Dunlop (1972) and subsequently adopted by Robert Hughes in *The Shock of the New: Art and the Century of Change*, London: BBC 1980.

40   See Namier, *1848*, 31: 'The "Revolution of the Intellectuals" exhausted itself without achieving concrete results: it left its imprint only in the realm of ideas.'

41   O'Hegarty, *History of Ireland under the Union*, 374. In respect of the 'revolt' the following year by James Fintan Lalor, Joseph Lee writes (*The Modernisation of Ireland*, 36) that the rebellion 'failed so farcically that few realised that there had even been an attempted movement to abolish landlordism and establish an independent Ireland.'

42   Namier, *1848*, 3.

43   Lewis Namier, 'Nineteenth Century European History' in *Vanished Supremacies*, London: Hamish Hamilton 1958, 204. Elsewhere (*1848*, 110) Namier said that 'by

1848 O'Connells had arisen also in East Galicia, and demanded to be heard on behalf of its peasant people.'

44 On 18 March 1843 the *Nation* reported that Ireland was larger than Portugal, Bavaria and Saxony, Naples and Sicily, Greece, Switzerland, and Holland and Belgium. On 8 January 1848 it opined: 'Plainly we have no hope of any conclusive political achievements for Ireland for 1848 . . . From Constantinople to Washington we are known not as a vital nation but as a beggared community.'

45 See Maurice Colgan, 'Young Ireland in Literature and Nationalism' in Barker et al., *1848*, and Mansergh, *The Irish Question*, 95–7.

46 Quoted by Boyce in *Nineteenth-Century Ireland*, 284.

47 *Dublin and London Magazine*, May 1825, 128. In 1831 James Hardiman stated: 'That this country, from an early period, was famous for the cultivation of the kindred arts of poetry and music, stands universally admitted' (*Irish Minstrelsy*, vol. 1, iii); 'music is the first faculty of the Irish,' said Thomas Davis (preface to *The Spirit of the Nation*); while P. W. Joyce said that the Gaels regarded music as fundamental to human life (*Social History of Ireland*, vol. 1, 572).

48 See Nettel, *The Orchestra in England*, 243: 'Since there could be no doubt about the superiority of nineteenth-century German music over its contemporary British cousin, there was a growing contempt for *das Land ohne Musik* about the time when Wilhelm II came to the throne.' Turner, *English Music*, 7: 'In the sixteenth century England was known abroad everywhere as "Merrie England". In the nineteenth century it was referred to on the Continent as "The Land without Music".' See also Rainbow, *The Land Without Music*, passim.

49 Cf. McCarthy, 'Music Education', 6: 'In a statement to the Select Committee of the House of Commons in 1835, Richard A. Blake, reporting on education in Ireland, promoted the introduction of music since "it would tend very much to civilisation."'

50 Stanford to Stewart, 2 Jan. 1881 (RIAM).

51 Sir Arnold Bax, foreword to Aloys Fleischmann, *Music in Ireland*, iii, Bax having said that 'Stanford was not Irish enough. An Irishman by birth, he belonged to that class abominated by Irish Ireland, the "West Briton".'

52 Vignoles, *Memoir of Sir Robert P. Stewart*, 95. It was Stewart who said, 'Ireland is not a musical country. The people, of course, will tell you she is' (ibid., 189).

53 *WIT*, 20 Oct. 1900.

54 Walter Scott, quoted by Cecil Woodham-Smith in *The Great Hunger*, p. 24.

55 For Giordani see Hogan, *Anglo-Irish Music*, 96, and for Logier, ibid., 98.

56 Quoted by Hogan in *Anglo-Irish Music*, 57.

57 Ryan, 'Nationalism and Music in Ireland', vi.

58 Brian Boydell, 'Music, 1700–1850' in *New History of Ireland*, vol. 4, 568–628.

59 Boydell, *Dublin Musical Calendar*; 'Music at the Rotunda Gardens, 1771–91' in Gillen and White, *Irish Musical Studies, 1*; *Rotunda Music in Eighteenth-Century Dublin*.

60 Aloys Fleischmann, 'Music and Society, 1850–1920' in *New History of Ireland*, vol. 6, 500–22. See also Collins, 'Music in Dublin'.

61 Brown, *Ireland: A Social and Cultural History*.

62 A role more fully addressed in his lecture 'Music: The Cultural Issue' in Pine, *Music in Ireland*.

63 Sheehy, *The Rediscovery of Ireland's Past*.

64 Richards, *Provision for the Arts*.

65 Litton, *Unequal Achievement*.

66 Kennedy, *Dreams and Responsibilities*.

67 Cairns and Richards, *Writing Ireland*.

68 Kiberd, *Inventing Ireland*, especially chap. 7, 'The national longing for form'.

69 Leerssen, *Remembrance and Imagination*.

70 White, *The Keeper's Recital*.

71 Ryan, 'Nationalism and Music in Ireland'.

72 John O'Donovan, 'Classical' in Coogan, *Ireland and the Arts*, 176–85.

73 Akenson, *The Irish Education Experiment* and *A Mirror to Kathleen's Face*; McElligott, *Education in Ireland*; Coolahan, *Irish Education*.

74   Benson, *The Place of the Arts in Irish Education.*
75   Herron, *Deaf Ears?*
76   McCarthy, 'Music Education'.
77   *'PIANO' Report.*
78   See Harris and Freyer, *The Achievement of Seán Ó Riada.*
79   Aloys Fleischmann, *Music in Ireland.*
80   Groocock, *General Survey of Music in the Republic of Ireland.*
81   See Thomas Davis lecture series 'Music in Ireland' (Richard Pine, editor), RTE radio, 1998.
82   In nine years of the *Crane Bag* (1977–85) only two issues (vol. 5, no. 2, 1981, 'Irish music defined' by Micheál Ó Súilleabháin, and vol. 8, no. 2, 1984, devoted to popular music) were directed towards music.
83   White, 'Musicology, positivism, and the case for an encyclopaedia of music in Ireland', in *Irish Musical Studies, 1*, 84.
84   The condition of Irish music has also been addressed by Charles Acton in a series of articles in *Feasta* and *Éire-Ireland* and by various writers in the journal of Comhaltas Ceoltóirí Éireann, *Treoir.*
85   Quoted by Boyce in *Nineteenth-Century Ireland*, 86.

Chapter 2 (p. 12–27)

1   R. V. Comerford, 'Ireland, 1850–70: post-famine and mid-Victorian', *New History of Ireland*, vol. 5, 375.
2   See Brian Boydell, 'The Dublin musical scene, 1749–50, and its background', *Proceedings of the Royal Musical Association*, vol. 105, London 1978–79, and 'Music, 1700–1850' in *New History of Ireland*, vol. 4, 568–628. op. cit.; *Dublin Musical Calendar, 1700–1760*; 'Music at the Rotunda Gardens in Dublin, 1771–91' in *Irish Musical Studies*, Dublin 1990; *Rotunda Music in Eighteenth-Century Dublin*, Dublin 1992. See also Walsh, *Opera in Dublin*, and Hogan, *Anglo-Irish Music.*
3   See Collins, 'Music in Dublin'.
4   Neal Zaslaw, 'Music and society in the classical era' in *The Classical Era*, London: Macmillan 1989, 1 and 2, also 'Chronology', 390–5.
5   This society, known more fully as the Irish Musical Fund Society for the Support of Decayed Musicians and Their Families, was incorporated by an act of Parliament in 1794. Boydell, 'Music, 1700–1850' in *New History of Ireland*, vol. 4, 585.
6   The 1857 performance was of Handel's *Messiah*. See MacDonnell, *Book of Dates*, 23.
7   *FJ*, 19 Mar. 1901; *DJ*, 10 Apr. 1902; *FJ*, 2 Apr. 1917.
8   Except for 1800, 1801, and 1803, when they performed in the Theatre Royal, Crow Street.
9   *FJ*, 4 Apr. 1895.
10   See Collins, 'Music in Dublin'.
11   See Collins, 'Music in Dublin'.
12   Hogan, *Anglo-Irish Music*, 54.
13   For an account of the background and events that led to Emancipation see Beckett, *The Making of Modern Ireland*, 295–305.
14   From a general impression of the most frequently used venues. For further detail see Collins, 'Music in Dublin'.
15   McCarthy, *St Mary's Pro-Cathedral*, 15. *FJ*, 21 Dec. 1813, 13 Feb. 1832, 11 May 1833, 28 Jan. 1834.
16   William Weber, *The Rise of Musical Classics in Eighteenth-Century England*, Oxford: Clarendon Press 1992, 103–42.
17   Entertainments included three oratorio performances given in St Werburgh's Church and three concert performances given in the Rotunda, from 8 to 16 August 1814 (*FJ*, 2–17 Aug. 1814).
18   *FJ*, 22 and 29 July 1830.
19   *FJ*, 5 Aug. 1830.
20   *FJ*, 3 Sep. 1830.

21 *FJ*, 4 Mar. 1831.

22 *FJ*, 7 Mar. 1831.

23 For patrons see *FJ*, 27 Aug. and 4 Sep. 1831.

24 *FJ*, 13 Aug. 1831 and 9 Sep. 1831; Boydell, 'Music, 1700–1850' in *New History of Ireland*, vol. 4, 613.

25 Boris Schwarz, 'Paganini' *NG*, vol. 14, 86–91.

26 Paganini was paid £682 10s to appear in the Dublin Festival (*FJ*, 11 Nov. 1831).

27 Kalkbrenner also gave concerts in Belfast and Cork and in Scotland as part of this tour (*FJ*, 12 and 24 Aug. 1824, 2, 4, 6, 7, 11 and 18 Sep. 1824).

28 *FJ*, 9, 12, 13, 17, 23, 24 and 27 Jan. 1826.

29 *FJ*, 30 Jan. and 5 Feb. 1828.

30 *FJ*, 29, 30 and 31 Oct. 1834, 4, 7, 8, 15, 19, 24 and 25 Nov. 1834, 1, 7, 16, 22, 25, 28 and 30 Nov. 1836, 2, 6, 7 and 9 Dec. 1836.

31 Nicholas Temperley, 'Bochsa', *NG*, vol. 2, 831–2.

32 *FJ*, 1, 4, 6, 7, 9, 16 and 17 Feb. 1837.

33 *FJ*, 2 Feb. 1837.

34 *FJ*, 11, 12, 14, 15 and 20 Dec. 1837, 2–6 Jan. 1838.

35 MacDonnell, *Book of Dates*, 14, 15, 17.

36 For details of this tour of Britain and Ireland see Walker, *Franz Liszt*, vol. 1, 353–62.

37 *FJ*, 17, 22 and 24 Dec. 1840, 5, 7, 8, 11, 12 and 13 Jan. 1841.

38 Walker, *Franz Liszt*, vol. 1, 355–7.

39 *FJ*, 29 Jan. 1828.

40 *FJ*, 14 and 16 Aug. 1838.

41 I am indebted to Dr Roy Johnston for this point and for providing information contained in *Grove I*, vol., 4, 507, 'Zeugheer'.

42 *FJ*, 2 Apr. 1830.

43 *FJ*, 10 Dec. 1847.

44 The designation 'band' was applied as a generic term to a variety of groups, not only reed or brass ensembles. In the context of an oratorio performance the 'band' could include the orchestra, soloists, and chorus.

45 Hogan, *Anglo-Irish Music*, 195–6. David Charlton, 'Logier' *NG*, vol. 11, 132–3.

46 *FJ*, 16 July 1810, 13 May 1811.

47 *FJ*, 11 Dec. 1811, 4 Feb. 1813.

48 *FJ*, 25 Jan. 1806, 16 Oct. 1809, 20 Feb. 1810, 22 July 1813, 2 Aug. 1813, 13 May 1814.

49 *FJ*, 12, 24, 27, 29 and 30 Dec. 1847.

50 This title had already become fashionable at large-scale events in London and Paris. For further details of the New Music Hall see below.

51 This demonstration involved an estimated 250,000 people (Boydell, 'Music, 1700–1850' in *New History of Ireland*, vol. 4, 610).

52 The managers of Portobello Gardens had recently 'erected a new orchestra,' what would now probably be termed a bandstand (*FJ*, 16 May 1840).

53 *FJ*, 11 Mar. 1818.

54 *FJ*, 15 Mar. 1822.

55 *FJ*, 31 Jan. 1820. He may also have been one of two violinists called Wilkinson who appeared in 1827 and 1828 (*FJ*, 10 Apr. 1827, 4 Dec. 1828).

56 *FJ*, 16 Apr. 1839, 15 May 1840.

57 *FJ*, 17, 20, 23, 24, 27 and 28 July 1840.

58 These were given on 28 August, 8 and 14 January, 16 March, 28 May, and 18 February, respectively.

59 8–12, 14 and 15 June 1841. See *Freeman's Journal* on these dates.

60 Keith Horner, 'Jullien', *NG*, vol. 9, 748–9; Grove, 'Jullien, Louis', *Grove III*, vol. 2, 797–9.

61 Performances at the Theatre Royal were from 1 to 5 June. The term 'band' again means orchestra (*FJ*, 1–5 June 1841).

62 *FJ*, 7 June 41. Note that the exact number of musicians involved in these concerts, though logically the sum of each group, is not actually stated.

63   *FJ*, 17, 21 and 22 June 1841, 26 July 1841, 10, 12 and 16 Aug. 1841.
64   *FJ*, 18, 21, 25 and 28 Sep. 1841.
65   See *Freeman's Journal* between these dates.
66   *FJ*, 5 Jan. 1853.
67   *FJ*, 3 Feb. 1841, 3 Nov. 1841.
68   Robinson conducted, Conran occasionally accompanied at the piano, and Barton, who was a violinist, acted as leader alternately with Mackintosh.
69   The performances took place on 2, 5, 9, 12, 19 and 27 February and 5, 19 and 26 March 1841 (*FJ*, 29 Jan., 5, 8, 9, 12, 17, 18 and 25 Feb. and 4, 19 and 26 Mar. 1841).
70   *FJ*, 17 Feb. 1841.
71   These concerts were held on 12, 16, 19, 23 and 30 November and 2, 4, 6, 7, 9, 10, 13, 16 and 20 December 1841 (see *Freeman's Journal* of these dates). Mackintosh continued his series in January 1842, beginning with six concerts per week.
72   This figure excludes eight performances of Italian opera at the Theatre Royal between 30 August and 11 September, thirty-six at Robinson's Music Shop, Westmoreland Street, and six at the Rotunda by the harpist Miss Gregory, a Dublin infant, three years and seven months old, beginning on 8 March. Curiously, only one performance appears in October (*FJ*, 6 and 29 Mar., 12 Apr., 4, 30 and 31 Aug. and 1, 3, 6, 7, 9, 10, 11 and 13 Sep. 1841).
73   In some cases sources should be treated with caution, as what seems like an important premiere or the appointment of a conductor, for example, may have taken place well before observations in the press.
74   This society is reputed to be the oldest surviving in Europe.
75   From Anacreon, sixth-century BC Greek lyric poet and musician. This society predated those of London (1766) and Belfast (1816).
76   A rare indication of the size of the society is given in 1825, when twenty-six performers appeared at the Rotunda on 14 April. Even though membership may have varied considerably over time, this would seem smaller than usual, given their repertoire (*FJ*, 18 May 1825).
77   Nelson's Pillar, formerly in O'Connell Street (*FJ*, 10 June 1794, 14 and 15 Jan. and 20 Feb. 1806).
78   These took place at the Rotunda on 14 and 20 May and the Theatre Royal, Crow Street, on 21 May 1821 (*FJ*, 7, 12, 16, 20 and 21 May 1817).
79   *FJ*, 3 May 1819, 8 Nov. 1824, 16 Apr. 1828, 9 Nov. 1830.
80   *FJ*, 3 May 1819, 2 Feb. 1822, 10 Dec. 1825, 14 June 1826. Singer and choirmaster of the 1831 festival with William E. Holden (*FJ*, 24 Feb. 1831, 24 Jan. 1834), pianist and composer (*FJ*, 23 Jan. 1839).
81   *FJ*, 2 Feb. 22 and 1 Apr. 1822, 16 Apr. 1824, 14 June 1826, 16 Apr. 1828.
82   *FJ*, 6 Mar. and 26 and 29 June 1822, 6 Oct. 1823, 17 Jan., 3 Apr., 6 July, 16 Oct. and 14 Dec. 1824.
83   Not to be confused with a previous Philharmonic Society, first mentioned in 1742. (See Boydell, 'Music, 1700–1850' in *New History of Ireland*, vol. 4, 580, 620–1.)
84   The first mention of Bussell as a professional violinist appears in May 1829 and as a pianist in January 1834; a single mention of him playing viola appears in December 1837. However, his significance remains as a conductor (*FJ*, 6 May 29, 24 Jan. 1834, 20 Dec. 1837).
85   *FJ*, 24 Feb. 1831, 24 Jan. 1834, 3 Mar. 1836.
86   In the absence of firm evidence this is speculation.
87   *FJ*, 25 May 1833, 17 Dec. 1835, 3 June 1841, 1 Feb., 26 Apr. and 8 June 1848, 27 Feb. and 1 Mar. 1849, 6 June 1850.
88   MacDonnell, *Book of Dates*, 16.
89   Joseph Robinson began his remarkable career as a singer as a chorister in St Patrick's Cathedral at the age of eight (W. H. Grattan Flood, 'Robinson, Joseph', *Grove III*, vol. 4, 408–9).
90   This building remains (as the former Academy Cinema) in what is now Pearse Street but is almost derelict.

91 Philharmonic concerts had been held until this point at the Rotunda.
92 The society gave further performances of *Elijah* on 13 April 1848 and 19 April 1849. Excerpts from the work remained popular in their programmes (*FJ*, 7 Dec. 47, 14 Apr. 48, 12, 19 and 20 Apr. 49).
93 Conductor: Joseph Robinson. Vocal soloists: soprano, Mrs Frith, Miss Searle; alto, Mrs Wilkinson, Miss M'Dermott; tenors, Dr Smith, Mr F. Robinson, Mr Geary; bass, Mr Stanford (amateur), Mr Smith. Chorus: 75 sopranos, 16 altos, 26 tenors, 33 basses. Orchestra leaders, Mr Levey and Mr Barton; 4 first violins, 6 second violins, 3 violas, 3 cellos, 3 basses, 2 flutes, 2 oboes, 2 clarinets, 2 bassoons, 4 horns, 2 trumpets, 3 trombones, kettle drums, organ *(FJ*, 10 Dec. 1847).
94 *FJ*, 18 Feb. 1848, 24 Feb. 1849, 9 Feb. 1850.
95 About this time Levey was leader of the orchestra of the Theatre Royal, Hawkins Street, where he occasionally conducted concerts. See *FJ*, 12 Oct. 1839.
96 Women were admitted only as associate members as late as 1870 (C. W. Wilson, 'Dublin', *Grove III*, vol. 2, 97–100).
97 *FJ*, 17 Dec. 1847. This report goes on to remark on the great improvement in the abilities of the society and suggests that 'more practical benefit is conferred on young men by the existence of such humanising institutions . . . than all the lectures and instructions that fines compel them to attend.' Stewart was appointed organist of the two cathedrals in 1844.
98 *FJ*, 27 and 29 Jan. and 2, 5, 6, 8, 9, 12 and 13 Feb. 1847; MacDonnell, *Book of Dates*, 16.
99 From a graph illustrating the Dublin music trade, 1650–1850, quoted from an unpublished study of the music trade undertaken by Brian Boydell, in 'Music in Eighteenth-Century Dublin', 35.
100 *FJ*, 23 Nov. 1815.
101 *FJ*, 25 Feb. 1820. In 1826 the figure of 30,000 pieces is advertised (*FJ*, 30 Jan. 1826).
102 *FJ*, 30 Mar. 1836.
103 Moses began trading on his own in 1836, having worked for twenty years with Willis (*FJ*, 28 Mar. and 28 Nov. 1836, 17 Jan. 1837).
104 In 1850 these firms were still operating independently. See Grafton Street listing in Shaw, *New City Pictorial Directory*; *FJ*, 7 and 11 Nov. and 31 Dec. 1836, 16 Mar. 1839.
105 Gerard Gillen, 'Church Music in Dublin, 1500–1900' in Boydell, *Four Centuries of Music in Ireland*, 23. The earliest provision of vicars choral at St Patrick's Cathedral was by Henry de Loundres in 1220 (Grindle, *Irish Cathedral Music*, 3–6).
106 Grindle, *Irish Cathedral Music*, 61–2.
107 Grindle, *Irish Cathedral Music*, 49, 50, 64–6, 71.
108 Ernest Walker, 'Degrees in music', *Grove III*, vol. 2, 35.
109 William H. Husk, 'Stewart', *Grove III*, vol. 5, 137–8.
110 Husk, 'Smith, John', *Grove III*, vol. 4, 792. Temperley, 'Mornington', *NG*, vol. 12, 586.
111 Peter Ward Jones, 'Corri', *NG*, vol. 4, 802–4. *FJ*, 6 Feb. 1821.
112 *FJ*, 20 Nov. 1821, 1 and 28 Jan. and 20 Aug. 1825, 18 Sep. 1826, 5 Nov. 1827.
113 For example Signor de Vescovi's guitar method and Haydn Corri's singing tutor (*FJ*, 10 Feb. 1827, 31 Oct. 1829).
114 *FJ*, 11 July and 17 Aug. 1835.
115 *FJ*, 6 Apr. 1835.
116 *FJ*, 16 Dec. 1834, 7 Sep. 1835.
117 First advertised for sale in 1815 (*FJ*, 13 Jan. 1815).
118 *FJ*, 19 June 1815, 9, 15 and 20 Mar. 1816.
119 *FJ*, 16 Sep. 1815, 2 Feb. 1816, 19 Mar. 1816, 25 Nov. 1816, 26 June 1818, and 10 Nov. 1818, respectively.
120 *FJ*, 29 Aug. 1816, 13 Nov. 1817, 16 June 1824.
121 These were published in the *Freeman's Journal*, 29 Aug. 1816.
122 *FJ*, 22 Nov. 1827.
123 This latter version had been adapted by Kalkbrenner. See David Charlton, 'Logier', *NG*, vol. 11, 132–3.

124   *FJ*, 20 Apr. 1819, 4 Feb. 1833.
125   *FJ*, 5 Jan. 1829.
126   *FJ*, 21 May and 24 Dec. 1830.
127   Only in 1856 was the provision of military bands financed by the War Office (Aloys Fleischmann, 'Music in nineteenth-century Ireland' in Boydell, *Four Centuries of Music in Ireland*, 41).
128   *FJ*, 19, 21, 23 and 24 Nov. and 1, 8, 12, 15, 19, 22 and 29 Dec. 1814.
129   *FJ*, 10 May 1815.
130   These were given at his house, now at 46 Upper Sackville Street (O'Connell Street). Admission, one-and-a-half guineas (£1.58), professional musicians one guinea (£1.05) (*FJ*, 31 Jan. 1829).
131   *FJ*, 6, 14, 15, 19, 20, 27 and 29 Jan. 1824.
132   Previously the law required a tax scaled from 40 to 75% for the lower class and from 1 to 10% for the upper class on newspaper advertisements (*FJ*, 9 Aug. 1853).
133   Five piano makers, four organ builders and four other instrument makers, including one bagpipe maker, are also listed (Shaw, *New City Pictorial Directory*).
134   *SNL*, 29 Jan. 1848.

Chapter 3 (p. 33–95)

1   *FJ*, 13 May 1851.
2   *SNL*, 29 Jan. 1848.
3   *FJ*, 13 May 1851.
4   On a parallel note, we find a reference in 1809 to the incipient school of art at the RDS as 'a National establishment' (Turpin, *A School of Art*, 85).
5   *SNL*, 7 June 1849.
6   *IT*, 10 Mar. 1869 Almost contemporaneously, the secretary of the Dublin Working-Men's Club was asking in relation to art education, 'When shall we have the control of the industrial education of our country in our own hands?' (quoted by Turpin in *A School of Art*, 183).
7   See M. A. G. Ó Tuathaigh, 'Ireland and Britain under the Union, 1800–1921: an overview' in Drudy, *Ireland and Britain since 1922*.
8   Ryan, 'Nationalism and Music in Ireland', 174.
9   Ryan, 'Nationalism and Music in Ireland', 173.
10   *IT*, 7 Feb. 1861.
11   See Hogan, *Anglo-Irish Music*, 77; Boydell, 'Music, 1700–1850' in *New History of Ireland*, vol. 4, 583–4.
12   See Turpin, *A School of Art*, 1, 9.
13   See Kelly, 'The Political, Intellectual and Social Background to the Irish Literary Revival', 28: 'The *Nation* with a Catholic as its editor and a Protestant as its main contributor tried to set an example to a country where, only fourteen years after Catholic Emancipation [1844] and with the Penal Laws still a living memory, religious segregation was built into social and political life.'
14   The argument is contained in a memorial of 1867 addressed to Benjamin Disraeli, Chancellor of the Exchequer, in the RAM directors' minute book, p. 92–7 (RAM).
15   MacDonnell, *Book of Dates*, 16.
16   *FJ*, 2 Feb. 1852.
17   *FJ*, 10 Dec. 1866.
18   In 1868 it was reported in the *Freeman's Journal* (4 Feb.) that the musical world expected Francis Robinson to be knighted by the Lord Lieutenant.
19   Stanford, *Studies and Memories*, 118.
20   Ibid., and MacDonnell, *Book of Dates*. Joachim first appeared in Dublin in 1847 at the age of almost sixteen, having made his London début three years earlier.
21   Stanford, *Studies and Memories*, 122.
22   It was performed on 21 December 1848.
23   Stephenson, 'The Antient Concert Rooms', 5.
24   'We regard her playing as in a style only surpassed by Osborne' (*FJ*, 20 Dec. 1851).

25 *Dublin Evening Post*, 15 Jan. 1848. In June they published an endorsement by Thalberg of an Erard grand 'which, for magnificence of tone, is equal, if not superior, to any instrument I have ever played on' (*Dublin Evening Post*, 3 June 1848). On 12 May 1852 the *Freeman's Journal* reported that the Broadwood piano to be played by Mme Pleyel at the Philharmonic concert that night could be seen at the premises of Robinson and Bussell.

26 Stephenson, 'The Antient Concert Rooms'; G. Osborne, 'Musical Coincidences and Reminiscences', *Proceedings of the Musical Association*, 2 Apr. 1883, 95–113.

27 Anon., *Recollections of Dublin Castle*, 278–9.

28 MacDonnell, *Book of Dates*, 14.

29 Levey and O'Rorke, *Annals of the Theatre Royal*, 82–3; for Robert Lindley see *NG*, vol. 11, 3–4.

30 See *Letters of Daniel O'Connell*, ed. Maurice O'Connell, vol. 5, 303.

31 See *Letters of Daniel O'Connell*, vol. 5, 51–2.

32 See *Irish Monthly*, vol. 14 (1886), 202.

33 McGlashan, Dublin (co-publishing with Bussell and Novello's of London), 1853; the IAM purchased six copies of the book in 1856 (minute of 14 Mar. 1856, NA 1120/1/1).

34 See Hogan, *Anglo-Irish Music*, 197.

35 On his death in 1861 *Saunders's News-Letter* (13 Nov. 1861) said: 'He was . . . the author of a clever work on composition and vocalization, and innumerable ballads. But valuable and attractive as these were, his fame will rest on his Church music . . . If not an Irishman, he has enriched the music of the country.'

36 Secretary's day book, 6 Dec. 1858 (NA 1120/7/1).

37 However 'safe' the seat may have been, Goold remarked sarcastically, 'I did not follow the hounds, therefore I could not be a good representative' (*Dublin Evening Post*, 12 Dec. 1850). For his death see *FJ*, 28 Nov. and 8 Dec. 1854.

38 Lablache's *méthode de chant* was in use in the Academy at least as late as 1883.

39 Luigi Lablache sang in Dublin in 1841 and 1842 and Federico Lablache in 1838 and 1852; Jenny Lind and the younger Lablache sang together in the 1848 season, Balfe conducting (Levey and O'Rorke, *Annals of the Theatre Royal*, 97–8; MacDonnell, *Book of Dates*, 17).

40 *Illustrated London News*, 5 Sep. 1868, 234.

41 Smith and Share, *Whigs on the Green*, 59.

42 Catherine de Courcy (in *Foundation of the National Gallery*, 95–101) lists David and John Pigot and Maziere Brady as members of the first informal meeting of the Irish Institution, October 1853, Robert Callwell, F. W. Brady, John Lentaigne, J. E. Pigot and Walter Berwick as attending its first meeting on 1 November 1853, Maziere Brady and William Dargan as being appointed vice-presidents and Berwick, F. W. Brady, Callwell, Rev. C. Graves, Thomas Hutton, Lentaigne, Alexander MacDonnell, William Stokes and J. E. Pigot as Committee members (of whom Callwell, Brady, Pigot, Berwick, Graves and Hutton were appointed to various sub-committees) at that meeting, and J. E. Pigot, Maziere Brady, Hutton and Callwell as members of the first Board of the Gallery.

43 DD, DCL, FRS; Bishop of Limerick 1866–99; FTCD 1836, professor of mathematics 1843, dean of Chapel Royal (Dublin Castle) 1860, dean of Clonfert 1864, president RIA 1861; distant cousin of Rhona Marshall (née Clark).

44 Graves, *To Return to All That*, 15, 22.

45 *SNL*, 31 Jan. 1852.

46 O'Connor and Parkes, *Gladly Learn and Gladly Teach*, 10–11.

47 Ryan, 'Nationalism and Music in Ireland', 175.

48 McCarthy, 'Music Education', 63.

49 Lyons, *Ireland since the Famine*, 236.

50 See Corder, 4.

51 Quoted by McCarthy in 'Music Education', 90–1; but in 1845 Wyse stopped short of advocating the establishment of a music institution within a system of professional

education in science and art (*Notes on Educational Reform*, 94–6). McCarthy (p. 89) says that while Wyse's ideas on educational reform in music 'did not find explicit expression in the practical workings of the National School system, they were, however, recognized internationally as a significant contribution to music education philosophy . . . [and were] drawn upon in the introduction of music into American public education.'

52   *Speech of Thomas Wyse MP* [House of Commons, 19 May 1835], Dublin: Richard Milliken 1835, 5, 6.

53   in F. S. L. Lyons's paraphrase (*Ireland since the Famine*, 239).

54   'John Eglinton', *United Irishman*, 23 Jan. 1902.

55   R. Kane, *The Industrial Resources of Ireland* (2nd ed.), 1845.

56   See John Turpin, 'The Irish Arts and Industries Exhibition movement, 1834–1864', *Dublin Historical Record*, vol. 35 (1981), no. 1.

57   See A. B. Philip, 'European nationalism in the nineteenth and twentieth centuries' in Mitchison, *The Roots of Nationalism*, 3–4: 'A feature of almost every nationalist movement in Europe has been the common pattern according to which it has developed. The first stage in this process is the revival of interest in a nation's past, a taste for antiquarianism and the discovery of local history, acquired perhaps by members of the gentry and indulged in as a hobby with no ulterior political motive in view. The second stage reflects the transformation of this aristocratic interest into an intellectual movement with a nationalist perspective . . . The third stage sees the transfer of this new perspective, as a result of education, literature and social changes, to the civic and political leaders.'

58   Quoted by John Turpin in 'Arts and Industries exhibitions', 4.

59   Cf. Gavan Duffy: 'When a people have the boundaries and history, the separate character and physical resources, and still more, when they have the virtue and genius of a nation, they are bound in conscience, in prudence and in wisdom to assert their individuality, no matter how conciliation may lure or armies threaten.'

60   *Reports of the Parliamentary Committee of the Loyal National Repeal Association of Ireland*, vol. 1, Dublin 1844, 103.

61   See Inglis, *The Freedom of the Press in Ireland*, 189.

62   1796–1871; devilled for Louis Perrin; appointed Commissioner to Investigate Municipal Corporations 1833; Solicitor-General for Ireland 1837, Attorney-General 1839, Chief Baron of the Exchequer 1840, judge of Irish Court of Chancery 1846, Lord Chancellor of Ireland 1846–52, 1853–58, 1859–66 in the Liberal administrations; member of the National Board of Education and first Vice-Chancellor of the Queen's [Royal] University 1850; baronet 1869. At a meeting in 1869 he moved the erection of the 'Gough Memorial'. Noted for his 'firmness and impartiality' (*Times*, 15 Apr. 1871). Amateur geologist and conchologist. Brady's relative Robert Maziere was secretary of the Antient Concerts in 1852. Wills and Wills (*The Irish Nation*, 33) suggest that 'it was a rare thing for a young Protestant barrister, connected . . . with the Ultra-Tory Corporation of Dublin, to throw himself heartily into the ranks of the Liberals.'

63   See Kenny, *Tristram Kennedy*, 208.

64   1824–1909. Son of Sir Maziere Brady; QC 1860, chairman of Quarter Sessions, King's County (Offaly), 1861–63, Roscommon 1863–72, judge of Co. Tyrone County Court 1872–1908. In his edition of Petrie's collection, C. V. Stanford mistakenly referred to Brady as president of the RIAM; as honorary secretary, trustee and eventually vice-president he must indeed have seemed to many to have been the presiding figure during the sixty-five years of his involvement with the institution.

65   See Kelly, 'The Political, Intellectual and Social Background to the Irish Literary Revival', Conclusion, ii.

66   Leerssen, *Remembrance and Imagination*, 4.

67   IAM to Gladstone, 27 Apr. 1870 (NA 1120/1/5).

68   Ryan, 'Nationalism and Music in Ireland', 180.

69   1794–1875; no relation to Hercules; winner of Newdigate Prize for poetry (Oxford, 1816); Resident Commissioner of National Education in Ireland (predecessor of W. J. M. Starkie).

70 The coalition between Protestants and Catholics is also strikingly reflected in such initiatives: cf. Gavan Duffy, *Young Ireland*, 692–3: 'The Protestant hated the Catholic and oppressed him, the Catholic hated the Protestant and refused to trust him. Any plan which would strengthen the soul of Ireland with knowledge and knit the creeds in liberal and trusting friendship [he is here referring to the Queen's Colleges] would be better for her than if corn and wine were scattered from every cloud.' Cf. also Brian Boydell ('Music, 1700–1850' in *New History of Ireland*, vol. 4, 609). Even in 1825, when political feelings were running high, the *Freeman's Journal* wrote: 'This society [Anacreontic] affords the best proof of gentleman-like feeling and of practical conciliation. The protestant and catholic here do truly play in concert, and it has never been known that in the Anacreontic Society aught of political discord has occurred to put so distinguished a body out of tune.'

71 Levey and O'Rorke, *Annals of the Theatre Royal*, 166.

72 Charles Petrie, 'Introduction', in Stanford, *The Complete Collection of Irish Music*, vii.

73 'Irish music and poetry', in *Prose Writings*, 188.

74 Ibid., 190.

75 White, *The Keeper's Recital*, 60.

76 Ryan, 'Nationalism and Music in Ireland', 4.

77 *FJ*, 10 Feb. 1868.

78 White, *The Keeper's Recital,* 6.

79 Oberthür played with the Philharmonic in 1854 (*FJ*, 10 June 1854) and gave a recital on 1 February 1858, accompanied by Henrietta Flynn (MacDonnell, *Book of Dates*, 24); he returned to Dublin occasionally, and in 1892 a visit to the Academy was mooted but did not transpire (minutes of 11 May 1892, NA 1120/1/12). In 1894 he asked for £15 to come to Dublin to examine four harp students, but this was considered excessive (minutes of 4 Apr. 1894). It was in 1858 that he presented the manuscript score of his 'Meditation', op. 149, to Louisa Cane, and it may be that it was through her it reached the Academy library, since in 1901 she donated, in addition to a quantity of music, an Erard Gothic harp and much ancillary material, including 'peg of 5th F catgut string which was removed when the F metal string was placed on my harp by Herr Oberthür, like there was on his own harp' (minutes of 6 Nov. 1901, NA 1120/1/18).

80 Anon., *Recollections of Dublin Castle*, 281.

81 On 23 Feb. 1855 the *Freeman's Journal*, in a review of the Dublin Philharmonic Society's concert of the previous evening, referred to 'a quartet and canon from an unpublished opera by Robert Tennant.'

82 A privately bound series of these programmes has been made available to the editors from a private source.

83 Sir Robert Stewart recalled Mahaffy, Elsner and himself playing a Mendelssohn trio in 1866 in TCD (Vignoles, *Memoir of Sir Robert P. Stewart*, 86). Mahaffy is quoted as saying: 'At one time, I had thought of becoming a violinist, but when I realized that I could not become a great violinist, I decided to remain a musician, just a musician' (Stanford and McDowell, *Mahaffy*, 14).

84 The Close family also included Alan (a composer, who sang in the IAM performance of *Don Giovanni* in 1858 and wrote the music for Sir Jocelyn Coghill's opera—see above, p. 73) and Rev. M. Close, who was a supporter of the *Gaelic Journal* in the eighteen-nineties (Kelly, 'The Political, Intellectual and Social Background to the Irish Literary Revival', 135). Thomas Rice Henn of Paradise, Co. Clare—ancestor of T. R. Henn, English scholar and late Master of St Catherine's College, Cambridge—was a lawyer and brother-in-law of John Stanford. The Henn and Spring Rice families (and thus Monteagle, Dunraven and O'Brien) were closely related. A minute of the governors of 13 January 1857 records that a letter had been received from John Palliser regarding an original unpublished manuscript of Mendelssohn that he had authority to print, donating the proceeds equally between the Academy and the Artists' Fund (NA 1120/1/1).

85 Stephenson, 'The Antient Concert Rooms', 6.

86 That same day (5 February) the *Freeman's Journal* reprinted a report from the *Tuam Herald* observing that 'the poor are dying of starvation—the gentry and rate payers,

as if paralyzed, patiently surrendering themselves to their fate—the apathy that prevails is astonishing, and if there be not a mutual co-operation between every class and creed universal ruin is inevitable.' Unable to have any effect on this distressing front, the Academy's founders were nonetheless able to take the idea of 'mutual co-operation' to other spheres.

87 Stanford, *Pages from an Unwritten Diary*, 34.
88 *FJ*, 24 and 31 Dec. 1856, 10 Jan. 1857.
89 Stanford, *Pages from an Unwritten Diary*, 34.
90 Barrett, *Balfe*, 23–4.
91 John O'Donovan in Coogan, *Ireland and the Arts*, 181.
92 *NG*, vol. 10, 702. W. H. Grattan Flood, who is often unreliable, says (*Introductory Sketch of Irish Musical History*, 888) that Levey taught both Robert Stewart and C. V. Stanford; but as neither of them mentions it in their memoirs the assertion may be discounted.
93 *FJ*, 31 Jan. 1856.
94 We are indebted to Mr John F. Levey for this information.
95 *FJ*, 9 May 1848.
96 See Woodham-Smith, *The Great Hunger*, 386–7.
97 MacDonnell, *Book of Dates*, 17, 20.
98 *FJ*, 14 June 1849.
99 *SNL*, 7 June 1849.
100 See *NG*, vol. 16, 400.
101 It would be gratifying to know that the *Macbeth* in question was Verdi's work, scarcely two years old; but the Verdi opera was not to receive its Dublin premiere until 1859, and in any case, from the programme of a private at-home at the same period at which the Witches' Chorus from *Macbeth* by Matthew Locke (1621–1677) was rendered, it is clear that the earlier, long-established work was involved.
102 *FJ*, 6 Apr. 1848.
103 *IT*, 31 May 1867.
104 Cf. Corder, 15–16: 'The initial display [1823] made by the students was, oddly enough, called *An Examination*, and was given before a select party of some thirty or forty members of the musical and fashionable world.'
105 For example in 1851 'Lutzow's Wild Hunt'.
106 *FJ*, 13 May 1851.
107 Stanford, *Pages from an Unwritten Diary*, 33. Elsner may not have come directly from Frankfurt to Dublin, however: the Elsner family history suggests that by 1851 he had moved to London in search of work to support his young wife and incipient family (A. F. E. Stewart, 'The Elsners of Taunus').
108 Stewart, op. cit., 1–2.
109 *FJ*, 10 May 1851.
110 *SNL*, 13 May 1851.
111 Étienne-Nicolas Méhul (1763–1817) was a significant accessory to the revolutionary environment in France, and the fact that music from his *Joseph* (1807), even though it was an *opéra comique*, was performed in Dublin at this time and in this company was significant, not least because his overtures after 1800 'point the way stylistically to the symphonies' (David Charlton, *NG*, vol. 12, 64), which have a distinctly nationalist character.
112 *SNL*, 13 May 1851.
113 *FJ*, 16 June 1851.
114 For Rainforth see *NG*, vol. 15, 547, and MacDonnell, *Book of Dates*, 14 ff.
115 *SNL*, 18 June 1851.
116 *FJ*, 18 June 1851.
117 *FJ*, 24 Jan. 1852.
118 *FJ*, 2 Feb. 1852.
119 See Turpin, *A School of Art*, especially chap. 5, 'Problems after the Act of Union', chap. 9 'The School's struggle with Henry Cole's system', and chap. 10, 'The South

Kensington system in Dublin'. Also Turpin, 'Exhibitions of Art and Industries', 3: 'A new alliance of science (they meant technology) and art (they meant design) would overcome the acknowledged ugliness of industrial mass production.'

120   Ibid., 146.
121   See Turpin, *A School of Art*, 493.
122   *FJ*, 12 Feb. 1853.
123   *FJ*, 20 Sep. 1853.
124   *FJ*, 21 Sep. 1853.
125   *FJ*, 2 Oct. 1854.
126   *FJ*, 25 June 1855. Several senior artists, including Grattan Kelly, supported the programme.
127   Ibid.
128   *FJ*, 27 June 1855.
129   NA 1120/1/1.
130   *FJ*, 27 June 1854.
131   *FJ*, 19 Oct. 1849.
132   *FJ*, 22 July and 1 Aug. 1848.
133   *FJ*, 26 Aug. 1850, and 18 Apr. 1853.
134   *FJ*, 12 Jan. 1850, 21 Oct. 1854.
135   *FJ*, 7 Jan. 1852.
136   *FJ*, 15 Nov. 1854.
137   Cf. *FJ*, 21 Feb. 1852.
138   *FJ*, 9 Dec. 1854.
139   *FJ*, 23 Nov. 1854.
140   *FJ*, 29 Dec. 1849.
141   *FJ*, 14 June 1850.
142   See McCarthy, 'Music Education', 15; Stephenson, 'The Antient Concert Rooms', 11.
143   *FJ*, 14 Dec. 1849. He also composed an opera, *The Deserted Village* (1880), and an oratorio, *St Patrick at Tara* (1870). He was the grandfather of Jimmy Glover, conductor at Drury Lane.
144   *FJ*, 20 Oct. 1853.
145   *FJ*, 24 Mar. 1851.
146   *FJ*, 28 Nov. 1851.
147   *FJ*, 11 Aug. 1853, 26 Apr. 1854.
148   *FJ*, 27 Sep. 1855.
149   *FJ*, 16 Oct. 1856.
150   *FJ*, 3 Apr. 1856.
151   *FJ*, 6 Aug. 1855.
152   *FJ*, 1 Feb. 1848.
153   *FJ*, 18 Feb. 1848.
154   *FJ*, 12 Mar. 1850.
155   *FJ*, 13 Feb. 1858.
156   *FJ*, 3 Feb. 1854.
157   *FJ*, 28 Mar. 1855.
158   *FJ*, 21 Mar. 1855.
159   *FJ*, 20 Mar. 1855,.
160   *FJ*, 15 July 1854.
161   *FJ*, 3 and 4 Aug. 1854.
162   *FJ*, 3 Mar. 1852.
163   *FJ*, 28 Mar. 1848; *DEP*, 4 Apr. 1848.
164   *FJ*, 30 Aug. 1848.
165   *FJ*, 27 Feb. 1849.
166   *FJ*, 16 Jan. 1855.
167   *FJ*, 5 Mar. 1852.
168   *FJ*, 13 May 1852.
169   *FJ*, 27 Feb. and 3 Mar. 1855.

170   *FJ*, 10 May 1852.
171   *SNL*.
172   *FJ*, 1 May 1852.
173   *FJ*, 24 Oct. 1853.
174   *FJ*, 1 Jan. 1850.
175   *FJ*, 28 Mar. 1850.
176   *FJ*, 23 Apr. 1852.
177   *FJ*, 6 and 9 Mar. 1854.
178   Croker, *Researches in the South of Ireland*, 13.
179   John Hutchinson (*The Dynamics of Cultural Nationalism*, 93) refers to the simulta-
      neous failure of Samuel Ferguson 'to form an Irish school of poetry in English' as
      'symptomatic of a more general failure of the second revival [of cultural nationalism,
      1830–48] to reconstruct a creative Irish spirit in any brand of culture.'
180   White, *The Keeper's Recital*, 99.
181   NA 1120/1/1.
182   *Educational Endowments (Ireland) Commission, Minutes of Evidence, 1886*, 7 June 1886,
      346, para. 8111–12.
183   Corder, 3–4.
184   *Educational Endowments (Ireland) Commission, Minutes of Evidence, 1886*, 16 Mar. 1886,
      para. 2722.
185   The meeting was attended by Rt Hon. Baron Greene (chair), Thomas Beatty, J. E.
      Pigot, E. Digges La Touche, Robert Exham, Cheyne Brady, H. MacDonnell, H.
      Bussell, Prof. Smith MusD, Henry Bastable, Emory Kennedy MD, Joseph Robinson,
      F. Robinson, A. R. Levey, and F. W. Brady.
186   *FJ*, 2 Jan. 1856.
187   1787–1867. FTCD 1808; professor of oratory 1816–52; regius professor of Greek,
      1843–52.
188   His father once wrote to Daniel O'Connell that 'he has every quality suited to an
      appointment save in his being the son of a wicked Anti-Repealer' (*Correspondence of
      Daniel O'Connell*, vol. 8, 130–1).
189   C. V. Stanford refers to MacDonnell's articles for the *Irish Times* (*Interludes*, 143) and
      to Robert Stewart's for the *Dublin Daily Express* (*Pages from an Unwritten Diary*, 50).
190   *IT*, 21 and 24 Aug. 1876; letter from Desmond Shawe-Taylor to Charles Acton, 23
      Mar. 1976.
191   L. E. Steele in MacDonnell et al., *The Story of the Strollers*, 3; TCD ms. 10560/120.
192   *FJ*, 11 Mar. 1853.
193   L. E. Steele in MacDonnell et al., *The Story of the Strollers*, 5.
194   Stanford, *Pages from an Unwritten Diary*, 25–6.
195   L. E. Steele in MacDonnell et al., *The Story of the Strollers*.
196   *IT*, 27 Aug. 1909.
197   As neither Brady nor his brothers had any male offspring, the baronetcy that he
      inherited from his father passed to his brother Robert, who died within the month in
      1909, then to his youngest brother, William, who died in 1927, and then became
      extinct. Brady's daughter, Marian, married a later benefactor of the Academy, Col.
      Jervis White. Like his father, Brady married twice, and like his father he married for
      the second time a daughter of Dr George Hatchell, who provided him with his last
      home, Sorrento Cottage, Dalkey, which she had acquired from Hercules MacDonnell
      and which in turn passed to Lennox Robinson.
198   Maria Glancy (in *The Rise and Fall of the Dubedats of Dublin*) speculates that Frank
      Dubedat (1851–?; died after 1896), a director of W. G. Dubedat and Sons, JP (Dublin)
      1889, and president of the Dublin Stock Exchange 1890, convicted of fraud 1891, was
      the model for Shaw's Dubedat in *The Doctor's Dilemma*. Frank Dubedat was known
      by his relatives as 'the actor'. The National Archives (1120/7/2) have evidence of a
      Miss Dubedat of 8 Herbert Road, Sandymount, becoming a senior vocal student in
      1867.
199   Foster, *W. B. Yeats*, vol. 1, 15.

200 Author of the highly influential monograph *Obstetric Auscultation or Means of Detecting Life or Death of the Foetus Before Birth*, 1833.

201 Later, *c.* 1912, the *Irish Times* recorded a production at the Kunstler Theatre, Munich, of *Liebespiel* by Digby La Touche, son of Lt-Gen. William Paget La Touche and a great-grandson of the music patron David La Touche of 52 St Stephen's Green, who brought Peter de Grée to Dublin, thus contributing indirectly to the decoration of the Academy's premises and so entering yet another name in the as yet uncovered history of Irish opera writing.

202 *Letters*, vol. 7, 276 (no. 3100) and 280 (no. 3103).

203 See Molony, *A Soul Came Into Ireland*, 228–9, 233, 325–7.

204 *Letters*, vol. 6, 56 (no. 2852), 74–5 (no. 2874). Yeats would equally find that although his separatist leanings 'cut him off from his own Ascendancy class . . . the Irish Protestants were a necessary part of his scheme for a comprehensive Irish literature in that they had qualities of taste and discrimination not so far to be found in the emergent Catholic classes' (Kelly, 'The Political, Intellectual and Social Background to the Irish Literary Revival', 234).

205 Quoted by Cooke in *Ireland's Premier Coachbuilder*, 27. The company later engaged in building Daimler and other prestige marques.

206 *IT*, 6 Feb. 1896.

207 NLI ms. 14056.

208 See Denis Gwynn, 'John E. Pigot and Thomas Davis', *Studies*, June 1949, 145–57.

209 'Letters of Thomas Davis', *Irish Monthly*, vol. 16 (1888), 179.

210 Carlyle, *Letters and Memorials of Jane Welsh Carlyle*, 230.

211 Quoted by Gwynn in *Young Ireland and 1848*, 112.

212 Ibid., 146.

213 'Letters of Thomas Davis', *Irish Monthly*, 266.

214 *Correspondence*, vol. 7, 292–3.

215 *Irish Monthly*, vol. 24, 275, May 1896.

216 *Nation*, 8 July 1871.

217 De Courcy, *Foundation of the National Gallery*, 3.

218 NA 1120/1/1, circular dated 4 Jan. 1856.

219 The fact that wind and brass instruments were the preserve of the military bands is well established; the fact that at that time the bandmasters were almost entirely of German origin is not. In 1856 those posted in Ireland were directed by Schmuck, Hartmann, Rothe, Elsen, Forkert, and Stoeckel (*FJ*, 23 Apr. 1856)—as in later years the incipient Army School of Music was to be directed by Fritz Brase and Friedrich Christian Sauerzweig.

220 *Daily Express*, 12 Apr. 1856.

221 The fourth Marquess (1812–68) and his wife, Caroline (d. 1893), were members of the Hill family, which had built the town of Hillsborough, Co. Down, and were patrons of the church where Hamilton Harty's father was organist. Their great-grandson, Lord Arthur Hill, was an active vice-president of the RIAM in the early twentieth century. The Marchioness of Downshire was also (from 1864) a subscriber to the RAM to the extent of £5 5s per year (minutes of RAM, 11 Mar. 1864, 102). Ironically, it was the Downshires' presence in Ireland at that time, in connection with the militia regiment stationed at the Curragh, that enabled them to aid the institution that was pledged to eliminate the need for militia bands.

222 There is no evidence of a further donation from Lady Downshire, but a reference by F. W. Brady to the investment of this sum (*First Report of the Educational Endowments (Ireland) Commission*, 1885–86, 129, para. 2604) was understood by Dr Michael Quane to mean that a straightforward gift of such a sum had also been made in 1858 ('The Royal Irish Academy of Music', *Dublin Historical Record*, vol. 20, 42–56). Brady was in fact subject to a lapse of memory when he informed the Commissioners (para. 2719) that 'we never got an account of what that concert cost. The Marchioness of Downshire who gave it, gave us the amount of receipts but never told us what it cost her.'

223 *SNL*, 9 Feb. 1856.

224   *SNL*, 16 Feb. 1856.
225   *FJ*, 24 Jan. 1856.
226   *FJ*, 25 Feb. 1856.
227   MacDonnell, *Book of Dates*, 18.
228   Ibid. 29–30.
229   MacDonnell et al., *The Story of the Strollers*, passim.
230   Ibid., 38.
231   TCD ms. 10560/1/1.
232   *FJ*, 19 Jan. 1855.
233   *SNL*, 24 Apr. 1858.
234   *FJ*, 15 May 1860.
235   *FJ*, 2 June 1860.
236   Ibid.
237   The complete list was: Mrs Loftus Bland, Mrs Blane, Mrs F. W. Brady, Mrs Howe, Mrs Emily MacDonnell, Mrs R. M. Williams, the Misses Blake, Miss H. Blake, Miss Carroll, Miss C. Courtney, Miss Dunlop, Miss Drury, Miss Fannin, Miss C. Fannin, Miss Fox, Miss Susan Hort, Miss Howley, Miss E. Howley, Miss Howley, Miss Kane, Miss M. Kane, Miss Kelly, Miss Kirwan, Miss A. Kirwan, Miss H. Kirwan, Miss Kyle, Miss L. Kyle, Miss Mary MacDonnell, Miss Emily MacDonnell, Miss Prior, Miss A. Prior, Miss Shaw, Miss Seymour, Miss G. Seymour, Miss Stokes, Miss H. Stokes, Miss Trulock, Miss Thornhill, Miss F. Williams, Mr Holt, Mr W. Archer, Maj. Bagot, Mr Carroll, Mr Crosthwaite, Mr D. Crosthwaite, Mr R. Exham, Mr Fleming, Mr J. Graves, Mr William Griffin, Mr J. Haysted, Mr Henry Hogan, Mr J. Hill, Lt-Col. Hume, Mr A. H. Jacob, Mr Allan Johnston, Mr T. A. Jones, Mr J. Kennedy, Mr H. W. Lloyd, Mr John Mahaffy, Mr Martin, Capt. Murphy, Mr G. H. Major, Mr R. Orpen, Mr A. Preston, Mr B. W. Rooke, Mr Robert Reeves, Mr L. Studdart, Mr Trench, Mr Webber, Mr Webber. From this it will be seen that nineteenth-century conventions relating to names, particularly of women, make it very difficult to identify individuals. The practice was to refer to a female student as, for example, 'Miss White'; only if her younger sister enrolled would she be identified by an initial ('Miss A. White'), while the elder sister continued to be identified purely by her surname.
238   *FJ*, 31 May 1860.
239   The author of *Recollections of Dublin Castle* (p. 281) confirms this: 'The MacDonnells were intimate with the great Italian opera set, Costa, Grisi, Mario, Tamburini, Lablache.'
240   Also in 1858 Rosina, Fides in Meyerbeer's *Le Prophète*, Desdemona, Donna Anna, and Yelva in Balfe's *La Zinagra*. In 1859 she sang Lady Macbeth and Zerlina, repeating both roles the following year, when she also appeared as Madelena in *Il trovatore*, Nance in *Marta*, and Orsini in *Lucrezia Borgia*, as well as Orfeo.
241   *IT*, 11 Feb. 1861. The previous year she had sung the role of Arturo in *Puritani*, with the *Freeman's Journal* (1 June 1860) commenting that she 'possesses all the qualities of a fine tenor, with the addition of a charmingly rounded *falsetto*.' The author of *Recollections of Dublin Castle* (p. 69) says 'it was often very amusing to watch the very natural and unfeigned astonishment of the newly-arrived stranger . . . as the lady . . . gave forth from her ample throat and chest those unexpected and charnel-house tones.'
242   Silvia Theodosia Hort (d. 1898) was the daughter of Sir William Hort (second baronet and papal count), MP for Kildare 1831–32, and sister of the third baronet (Sir Josiah) and fourth baronet (Sir William, general in the Crimean War).
243   *IT*, 11 Feb. 1861.
244   *IT*, 13 Feb. 1861.
245   *SNL*, 12 Feb. 1861.
246   *FJ*, 12 Feb. 1861.
247   *FJ* and *SNL*, 16 Apr. 1862.
248   Ibid.
249   *FJ*, 10 Apr. 1862.

250 *DEM*, undated report, 1863.
251 Secretary's day book, 8 June 1858 (NA 1120/7/1).
252 Ibid., 25 Oct. 1860.
253 Minutes of 22 Feb. 1856 (NA 1120/1/1).
254 Minutes of 7 Mar. 1856 (ibid.).
255 Minutes of 2 May 1856 (ibid.).
256 Minutes of 2 Dec. 1856 (ibid.).
257 Minutes of 9 Mar. 1858 (ibid.).
258 Minutes of 10 June 1856 (ibid.).
259 Minutes of 7 Apr. 1857 (ibid.).
260 Minutes of 14 Dec. 1858 (NA 1120/1/2).
261 Minutes of 18 June 1862 (NA 1120/1/3). The text on cornet method may have been by Arban, which was certainly in use in the Municipal School of Music some thirty years later. For Brod (1801–39) see *Grove III*, 476; for Devienne (1759–1803) see *NG*, vol. 5, 407–8; for Dauprat (1781–1868) see *NG*, vol. 5, 255; for Jancourt (1815–1901) see *NG*, vol. 9, 490.
262 Minutes of 2 Sep. 1856 (NA 1120/1/3).
263 Minutes of 27 Nov. 1861 (ibid.).
264 Minutes of 10 Sep. 1862 (ibid.).
265 See Ehrlich, *The Piano*, 39.
266 Advertisement by M. Marks, 18 Lower Gloucester Street (Seán MacDermott Street), in *FJ*, 24 Oct. 1855.
267 Minutes of 2 May 1856 (NA 1120/1/3).
268 Minutes of 21 Dec. 1858 and 21 June 1859 (NA 1120/1/1).
269 Turpin, *A School of Art*, 78.
270 Minutes of 3 Nov. 1857 (NA 1120/1/1).
271 Minutes of 8 June 1858 (NA 1120/1/2).
272 Secretary's day book, 26 May 1858 (NA 1120/7/1).
273 Ibid., 15 Jan., 1 Feb. and 11 Feb. 1859.
274 Minutes of 2 Sep. 1856 (NA 1120/7/1).
275 Minutes of 25 Nov. 1856 (NA 1120/1/2).
276 Rungeling on at least one occasion conducted the band of the Third Dragoon Guards (at a *conversazione* of the RHA) (*FJ*, 24 June 1856).
277 Minutes of 22 Sep. and 5 Oct. 1857 (NA 1120/7/1).
278 Minutes of 22 June 1858 (NA 1120/1/2).
279 Minutes of 26 Oct. and 8 Nov. 1858 (ibid.).
280 Minutes of 30 Sep. 1868 (NA 1120/1/4).
281 Minutes of 8 June 1858 (NA 1120/1/2).
282 Minutes of 15 June 1858 (ibid.).
283 Minutes of 21 May 1861 and 28 May 1862 (ibid.).
284 Minutes of 5 Feb. 1861 and 29 Jan. 1862 (ibid.).
285 Minutes of 5 Feb. 1862 (NA 1120/1/3).
286 Day book, 15 Nov. 1858 (NA 1120/7/1).
287 *FJ*, 15 Aug. 1857.
288 *FJ*, 26 Mar. 1856.
289 Minutes of 30 Sep. and 7 Oct. 1856 (NA 1120/1/1).
290 Minutes of 24 Feb. 1857 (NA 1120/1/1).
291 Secretary's day book, 10 and 17 Feb. 1859 (NA 1120/7/1).
292 *FJ*, 17 Oct. 1856.
293 *SNL*, 10 Apr. 1856. Aloys Fleischmann ('Music in nineteenth-century Ireland', 501) claims that Charles Hallé's recital of 1867 was the first.
294 *FJ*, 17 Oct. 1856.
295 He was 'elected' a scholar of the Academy at a Committee meeting on 26 March 1862.
296 Minutes of 25 Nov. 1863 (NA 1120/1/3).
297 In 1772 the RDS had ordained that 'no person shall be admitted as a scholar into the School for Drawing in Architecture who is not intended to follow some business

wherein a knowledge of Architecture is necessary' (Turpin, *A School of Art*, 51). In the twentieth century Seán Keating called the NCAD 'a sort of club for middle class girls' (ibid., 261).

298 Secretary's day book, Jan. 1863 (NA 1120/7/2).

299 Minutes of 17 Feb. 1857 (NA 1120/1/1).

300 *FJ*, 4 Jan. 1859.

301 Minutes of 24 Feb. 1857 (NA 1120/1/1); secretary's day book for 17 Nov. and 27 Nov. 1858 (NA 1120/7/1); letter no. 6734/58 of Commissioners of National Education; minutes of 30 Nov. 1858 (NA 1120/1/1).

302 1827–1914. A pupil of a Co. Cork hedge-school, he was employed by the Commissioners of National Education 1845–74; professor and subsequently principal of Commissioners' Training College 1874–93; member of council of RIA 1884–95; president, Royal Society of Antiquaries in Ireland 1906–08; author of (inter alia) *The Origin and History of Irish Names of Places* (1869–1913), *Ancient Irish Music* (1873), *Old Irish Music and Songs* (1909) and *English as We Speak it in Ireland* (1910), and a collector of folk-songs.

303 11 Apr. 1865 (NA 1120/7/2).

304 Minutes of 21 Sep. 1921. The Secretary of National Education notified the RIAM that the grant of £48 per year for violin tuition was to be discontinued from 28 February 1922.

305 Secretary's day book, 8 Dec. 1863 (NA 1120/7/2). It is unclear whether this child was the son of J. B. Logier's son (also Theodore) who advertised (*SNL*, 14 Jan. 1861) as a piano teacher at 15 Westland Row.

306 NA 1120/7/3.

307 Minutes of 25 May 1881 (NA 1120/1/8).

308 Minutes of 30 Nov. 1864 (NA 1120/1/4).

309 1826–1905. He succeeded his father as baronet in 1850 and the following year married the daughter of the third Lord Plunket, thus becoming related by marriage to the Greene family. He was also president of the early Dublin Photographic Society (*FJ*, 9 Apr. 1856) and took many photographs of Castletownshend and its environs, was a founder-member of the Society for Psychical Research and supposedly had the ability to levitate himself, was a keen yachtsman, and was great-grandfather of the Chaucerian scholar Sir Neville Coghill.

310 Marionette opera developed in seventeenth and eighteenth- century France and was brought to its height in Italy with the *fantoccini* troupes, which popularised the genre in London. It saw a resurgence of interest in the early and middle twentieth century on the part of composers such as Hindemith, Falla, Satie, Britten, Birtwistle, Copland, Honegger, and Chausson (J. M. Minniear, 'Puppet opera', *New Grove Opera*, 1177–79). It is possible that the genre lent itself to amateur operatic performance and several other opportunities for pretence, because the singers were concealed from view. Puppet opera continued in Ireland into the twentieth century: Brian Boydell in a letter to the editors recalls a performance by the Dublin Marionette Group (organised by Nelson Paine) at the Peacock Theatre in November 1944 of *Revelation at Low Tide* (a surrealist play by Boydell), Prokofiev's *Peter and the Wolf*, and Synge's *Riders to the Sea*, with improvised music on the oboe by Boydell for the first and third items. A later production of Ravel's *L'Enfant et les Sortilèges* also dates from this time. Joseph Groocock noted (*General Survey of Music in the Republic of Ireland*) the existence of the Puppet Opera Group, financially supported by the Shaw Trust, which visited fifty-five towns performing Verdi and Puccini operas in the nineteen-fifties.

311 *SNL, DEM, IT* and *FJ*, 16 Dec. 1862. Coghill was the author of many stage works, including another collaboration with Alan Close, the operetta *Schwarzerteufel* (1877), and *Fairstar* (1875), *Bric a Brac* (1888, from Ernest d'Hervilly), *Brinvilliers* (1888, with W. G. Wills), *Terrible Relations* (1889), *That Odious Phonograph* (1889), *Blue-Beard Up to Date* (1893), and a comic opera, *The Wolf's Crag* (1891). We are indebted to Sir Toby Coghill for this information.

312 *FJ*, 13 May 1865.

313 Unidentified newspaper report, 1867.

314 At the time, it was observed that 'one sees the same persons day by day walking up and down, apparently with a view to exhibiting themselves rather than with that of becoming acquainted with the objects around them' (quoted by Alun C. Davies in 'Ireland's Crystal Palace, 1853' in Goldstrom and Clarkson, *Irish Population, Economy and Society*, 267).

315 12 Oct. 1864 (NA 1120/1/4).

316 3 Feb. 1897 (NA 1120/1/15).

317 *FJ*, 19 Dec. 1865.

318 *FJ*, 20 Dec. 1865.

319 *IT*, 20 Dec. 1865.

320 Dom Raymund Thibaut, *Abbot Columba Marmion*, Sands 1932.

321 Minutes of 5 Sep. 1864 (NA 1120/7/2).

322 *FJ*, 7 Feb. 1868.

323 Ryan, 'Nationalism and Music in Ireland', 200.

324 See Jérôme Thébaux, 'Le Conservatoire de Musique: enjeux révolutionaires' in E. Hondré, *Le Conservatoire de Paris*', passim (our translation).

325 Ibid., 45.

326 Ibid., 46.

327 Ibid.

328 *First Report of the Educational Endowments (Ireland) Commission*, 133, para. 2724.

329 Thébaux, 50.

330 *NG*, vol. 11, 212.

331 Cazalet, *History of the Royal Academy of Music*, 272–5.

332 RAM minute book, 1849–54, 313, minute of 29 Apr. 1853. Corder (•••) states that Queen Victoria gave £100 annually.

333 Cazalet, *History of the Royal Academy of Music*, 275.

334 An academy was briefly founded in Belfast in 1854: the *News Letter* of 18 January carried an advertisement stating that an academy directed by W. Vipond Barry had been founded 'for the purpose of affording instruction in vocal and instrumental music to those individuals whose occupations during the day would prevent the possibility of such pursuits,' including singing, hymnody and psalmody, strings, wind, history of music, choral teaching, and a course for intending precentors. The academy ceased with Barr's serious illness five months later, which eventually caused him to emigrate to the West Indies. We are extremely grateful to Dr Roy Johnston for this information.

335 Farmer, *History of Music in Scotland*, 396.

336 Ibid.

337 Ibid., 397.

338 Patrick Stephenson ('The Antient Concert Rooms', 13) mistakenly states that Jozef Elsner played in Dublin in 1855, whereas it is certain that the Elsner in question was his namesake, the IAM professor.

339 C. R. H., 'Warsaw', *Grove III*, 187.

340 A. R., 'Helsingfors', *Grove III*, 233.

341 1804–78. QC 1840, counsel for O'Connell 1844 (but prosecuted William Smith O'Brien, Thomas Francis Meagher, Charles Gavan Duffy and John Mitchel in 1848), Solicitor-General for Ireland 1846, MP for Galway City and Attorney-General 1847, Chief Justice 1850, Commissioner of National Education 1861; returned for Galway City 1874.

342 He donated a grand piano and a double-bass, thought to be the work of the Klotz family of Mittenwald, which is very tall—almost as large as that of Dragonetti, preserved in the Victoria and Albert Museum. It was converted from a three-string to a four-string instrument by Heinrich Hoffmann in the early 1900s.

343 Minutes of directors' meeting, 24 May 1839; Council minutes 20 May 1864, 114 (RAM).

344 O'Loghlen had opposed secession from the Repeal Association, siding with James O'Hea and Francis Brady on O'Connell's part (Gavan Duffy, *Young Ireland*, 717, 722) and attempting strenuously to hold the two sides together (Gwynn, *Young Ireland and 1848*, 88, 162, 210, 221). Like Brady, he had been a member of the

Repeal Association's Parliamentary Committee, responsible for the publication of its research pamphlets.

345 *FJ*, 10 Dec. 1866.

346 Ibid.

347 Ibid.

348 Similarly—and almost simultaneously—the board of the RAM wrote in a memorial to Disraeli on 24 July 1867 that 'the Directors would be quite willing to place the Academy under the supervision of the Council of Education and would greatly desire to have a certain number of Directors nominated by the government associated with them'— adopted at a special meeting (directors' minute book (RAM), 19 July, 92–7).

349 *FJ*, 10 Dec. 1866.

350 Report to Committee by H. MacDonnell, 14 Nov. 1866.

351 *SNL*, 12 Feb. 1868.

352 Ibid.

353 letter of 22 Nov. 1867.

354 *FJ*, 10 Feb. 1868.

355 *FJ*, 12 Feb. 1868.

356 RIAM annual report, 21 Dec. 1870 (NA 1120/1/5).

357 *IT*, 10 Mar. 1869.

358 Letter of 14 Apr. 1868 (RAM).

359 The other members were Rev. C. W. Russell (president of St Patrick's College, Maynooth), Rev. Samuel Haughton (professor of geology at TCD), George Hamilton (formerly MP for the University of Dublin 1843–59), Prof. T. H. Huxley, Col. Robert Laffan, Prof. Wyville Thomson, and Capt. (later Sir) John Donnelly, who had worked with Cole on the reorganisation of the South Kensington system and had implemented the payment-by-results system in schools. For an account of the commission's work in relation to art schools see Turpin, *A School of Art*, 159 ff.

360 H. MacDonnell evidence, *Educational Endowments (Ireland) Commission, Minutes of Evidence, 1886*, para. 3728 and 3742.

361 Ibid., para. 3728 and 3748.

362 Ibid., para. 3732.

363 Ibid., para. 3737.

364 Ibid., para. 2065 ff.

365 He became a subscriber on 14 November (minutes of 27 Nov. 1866, NA 1120/1/4).

366 *Educational Endowments (Ireland) Commission, Minutes of Evidence, 1886*, 586–7.

367 Ibid., 835.

368 Ibid., 835.

369 Ibid., 841. Signs that he was contemplating a scheme to incorporate music education are contained in a letter from the directors of the RAM to the Prince of Wales of 26 June 1866 asking for support in moving to a site in South Kensington: 'The Directors are giving their full attention to the means by which the RAM may be enlarged and rendered equal to the best Continental Conservatoires' (RAM). At their meeting of 3 August a letter was received from the Royal Society of Arts (dated 20 July) referring to a report of its committee appointed 'to enquire and report on the state of musical education at home and abroad,' which had enumerated 'the steps which they submit should be adopted with the view to improve the organisation of the Institution and render it thoroughly efficient as a National Academy of Music' (RAM).

370 Unidentified newspaper, 10 Mar. 1869.

371 Minutes of 10 Mar. 1869 (NA 1120/1/5).

372 *SNL*, 10 Mar. 1869.

373 *IT*, 10 Mar. 1869.

374 Treasury letter no. 1318, 28 Mar. 1870 (NA 1120/1/5).

375 N. H. Gladstone to Sir C. O'Loghlen, 2 Apr. 1870 (NA 1120/1/5).

376 IAM to Gladstone, 27 Apr. 1870 (NA 1120/1/5).

377 The list included: 'Instrumentalists: F. Hughes (Leader at Melbourne), F. Walton (Drury Lane Orchestra), W. Levey (Composer & Director of Music at Drury Lane

Theatre), Richard Levey (Solo performer), N. Grandison (Philharmonic Orchestra & Organist of St Anne's), F. Gunn (Principal 2nd violin Theatre Royal Dublin), N. Woodward (Established in England), J. Byrne (Established in the U. States), M. Gunn (Philharmonic Orchestra & Monthly Pop Concerts), J. Clarke (Philharmonic Orchestra), J. Newland (Queen's Theatre Orchestra Dublin), J. Gunn (Philharmonic), J. Norman (Organist Rathgar & Philharmonic), F. Robinson (Belfast Teacher & Organist), — Hughes (Theatre Orchestra), — Collins (Theatre Orchestra), — Raymond, B. Dwyer, J. Klausman (Cornet American Theatre), J. Fitzsimon (Horn Theatre Royal Dublin); Church singers: Miss Cleary (Principal Soprano R. C. Chapel [presumably the Pro-Cathedral]), Miss Fulham (Contralto ditto), Miss Marmion (Soprano ditto also Concert Singer), Miss Cleary (Soprano R.C.C. Dublin), Miss Murray (Principal Contralto R.C.C. Dublin); Concert singers: Miss Basquerville (engaged at Theatre Royal Dublin), Miss Lally (Concert Singer), Miss Shea (at present singing under the name of Welma D'Alton with Mr. Woods Station Opera Company), Miss Henry (Chorus leader Station Opera Company), Miss Craig (Singing at Concerts), Miss Bessie Herbert (Principal Soprano all the Principal Concerts), Miss Henchy (Concert Singer), Miss Cruise (Soprano engaged at Covent Garden and Station Opera Concerts), Miss Fennell (Contralto All the principal concerts), Miss Maynes (Soprano concert singer established at Limerick); Teachers: Miss Ledwidge (Teacher of Pianoforte), Miss Chanler (Teacher of Singing at Liverpool), Miss Davis (Teacher of Pianoforte Dublin), Miss Macarteney (Teacher of Singing at Alexandra College Dublin), Miss O'Hea (Teacher of Pianoforte), Miss Bethel (Teacher of Pianoforte), Miss Harvey (ditto), Miss Gregg (ditto, Published some successful songs), Miss Barnwell (Teacher of singing), Miss McLaverty (Teacher of Singing, Composer of some successful songs), Miss Judge (Organist at Chapels of Dalkey and Ballybrack), Miss Hillsworth (Teacher of Pianoforte), Miss Reilly (Resident pianoforte teacher at first class school), Miss J. Herbert (Teacher of Singing and Harmonium at the National Model School Marlboro' Street), Miss Jackson (Playing pianoforte at Principal Concerts and Principal teacher in Masonic Orphans' School), Miss F. Judge (Teacher of Pianoforte), Miss Martin (Playing pianoforte at principal Concerts), Miss Thomas (Principal Soprano R.C.C. Dublin), Miss Wilkinson (Head Mistress Pianoforte at school), Miss Brooks (Teacher of Pianoforte), Miss Elsner (Pianoforte teacher and Concert player), Miss Boake (Pianoforte teacher).' The same boast had been made by the RAM in a memorial to Prince Albert in 1853: 'The Committee can refer with pride and satisfaction to the success which has attended most of those young persons in their subsequent progress in their profession—several of them are the most distinguished English vocalists; many of them fill the most important positions in the orchestras of the opera and Philharmonic Society, while others have honourably established themselves as teachers both in London and the various towns throughout the United Kingdom' (minutes of 29 Apr. 1853 (RAM)). Fourteen years later, in their memorial to the Chancellor of the Exchequer in 1867, they were able to repeat and extend the claim in referring to 'the prominent position taken in the profession and in some cases the European reputation achieved by those who have received their education in the Academy' (special meeting of 31 May 1867, minutes (RAM), 88.

378 IAM to Treasury, June 1870 (copy in minutes of 22 June 1870, NA 1120/1/5).
379 Treasury letter no. 11849, 27 June 1870 (NA 1120/1/5).
380 IAM to Treasury, 16 July 1870 (NA 1120/1/5).
381 *IT*, 12 July 1870.
382 Treasury letter no. 13780/70, 5 Aug. 1870 (NA 1120/1/5).
383 IAM to Treasury, 10 Aug. 1870 (NA 1120/1/5).
384 RIAM circular, Oct. 1870.
385 The great-great-great-uncle of the singer Chris de Burgh (né Davidson).
386 De Burgh to MacDonnell, 27 Nov. 1875 (NA 1120/1/7).
387 James Lauder, *The Glasgow Athenæum*, Glasgow; St Mungo Press 1897.
388 Information from Ministry of Culture, Warsaw.
389 White, *The Keeper's Recital*, 71.

390 Erkki Salmenhaara, 'Birth of a national and musical culture in Finland' in Aho, Jalkanen, Salmenhaara, and Virtamo, *Finnish Music*, 12–14.

391 C. V. Stanford, 'Some thoughts concerning folk-song and nationality', *Musical Quarterly*, 1, 1915.

392 Bartók *Essays*, 12.

393 J. S. W., 'Budapest' in *Grove III*, 997; Deszö Legány, 'Hungary', *NG*, vol. 8, 798–9; Frigyes, *Musical Education in Hungary*, 229–31.

394 Quoted by Ryan in 'Nationalism and Music in Ireland', 143.

Chapter 4 (p. 102–165)

1   2 Nov. 1870 (NA 1120/1/5). Many years later Brady was to receive a similar complaint from a neighbouring doctor. 'My house hours here when I see and examine patients are from 2.20 to 4.30. The piano practice heard through the back window of the RIAM looking out on my garden is so distracting that I am literally unable to work satisfactorily. Would it be possible for the authorities of the Academy to arrange that practice should not take place in that room at the hours specified?' Martin Dempsey to Brady, 3 Oct. 1900.

2   Minutes of 27 June 1876 (NA 1120/1/7).

3   1827–1892. Portraitist and cartoonist; art superintendent of Dublin International Exhibition 1865; director of NGI 1869–92; CB 1880, JP 1884. Brother of the artist Richard ('Dicky') Doyle and uncle of Sir Arthur Conan Doyle (Anon., *Richard Doyle and His Family*). On his death the *Times* (20 Feb. 1892) noted that Doyle was a Catholic (on the recommendation of Cardinal Wiseman he had been created a knight of the Order of Pius IX) and that 'he was popular in Dublin, though his politics were strongly Unionist.'

4   See Hutchinson, *The Dynamics of Cultural Nationalism*, 15–16.

5   12 May 1871 (NA 1120/1/5)

6   *FJ*, 10 May 1871.

7   19 Oct. 1865 (NA 1120/7/2).

8   *FJ*, 11 May 1871.

9   *FJ*, 12 May 1871.

10 *IT*, 25 Nov. 1871.

11 RIAM annual report, 1873.

12 *DEM*, 7 June 1872.

13 Letter from H. A. Bruce (Home Secretary) to Duke of Leinster, 13 Dec. 1872, quoted in *IT*, 20 Dec. 1872.

14 Stewart Blacker to Brady, 18 May 1876 (NA 1120/1/7).

15 Brady to Blacker, 23 May 1876, ibid.

16 Begley to Brady, 15 June 1876, ibid.

17 Begley to RIAM, 26 June 1876, ibid.

18 See *NG* vol. 11, 426–7. On her death in 1910 at the age of ninety-four, McGuckin's mother was described as 'the oldest musician in Ireland', having taught piano in Armagh 1854–73. She then returned to Dublin, where her husband became registrar of Mercer's Hospital (*IT*, 10 December 1910). McGuckin was the model for Bartell D'Arcy in Joyce's story 'The Dead'.

19 McGuckin to Brady, 3 May 1877 (NA 1120/1/7).

20 Brady to McGuckin, 22 Nov. 1877, ibid.

21 McGuckin to Brady, 30 Nov. 1877, ibid.

22 Brady to RIAM, 28 May 1877 (NA 1120/1/7).

23 Unidentified newspaper advertisement, 20 Nov. 1878.

24 Minutes of 24 May 1905 (NA 1120/1/23).

25 Minutes of 4 and 18 Dec. 1912, 18 June 1913 (NA 1120/1/23).

26 *FJ*, 13 Jan. 1913. Herbert K. Goodkind, *Violin Iconography of Antonio Stradivari, 1644–1737*, New York: privately printed 1972. The article in the *Freeman's Journal* went on to mention that 'there is only one other Stradivarius in Dublin, this being owned by Mr. Joshua Watson, of the Leinster School of Music . . . At one time in the city there

was a whole quartet of 'Strads', two violins, a viola and a cello . . . These were brought together by a Mr. Alan Dowell, a wine merchant, some ninety years ago . . . Mr. R. M. Levey often played on one in the lifetime of the owner. After the death of Mr. Dowell it came into his possession and he sold it in London for about £125 . . . The second violin went to Mr. Walter Sweetman who sold it afterwards in London. The viola, an extremely beautiful instrument, is in the hands of the Gore-Booth family . . . The cello . . . was sold to Signor Piatti.' This was the same instrument (cello) owned by Samuel Pigott (see above, p. 39). W. Beckett, 'Piatti's cello', *Dublin Historical Record*, vol. 32, no. 2 (Mar. 1979).

27   A manuscript note by Grove in the RCM archives lists potential staff, including for violin Joachim and Neruda, for piano Hallé and Pauer, for singing Madame Goldschmidt and Sims Reeves, and for harmony Sullivan and Stainer (RCM guardbooks, Jan. 1884–Mar. 1885, RCM).

28   Dublin Corporation minutes, 1883, item 98, re letter of Town Clerk of 20 Mar. 1883.

29   *Times*, 8 May 1883.

30   Letter from 'S. Grive' [*sic*] noted in DC minutes for 23 Apr. 1883.

31   At the RIAM Louie Kellett had enjoyed greater academic success than Edith Oldham, having won a Vandeleur scholarship for both piano and violin in December 1882.

32   See *NG*, vol. 20, 516.

33   See Young, *George Grove*, 189.

34   NA 1120/1/9.

35   Ibid.

36   *IT*, 12 July 1886.

37   George Grove to Edith Oldham, 4 Nov. 1888 (RCM).

38   Mrs Franklin Taylor to George Grove, 2 Aug. 1887 (RCM).

39   George Grove to Edith Oldham, 27 Mar. 1888 (RCM).

40   See *NG*, vol. 10, 571.

41   Details of the careers of those RCM teachers who are not included in *New Grove* can be found as follows: A. J. Caldicott (1842–1897): Brown and Stratton, *British Musical Biography; Musical Times*, 1897, 842; Richard Gompertz (1859–1921): *Grove II* (at the meting of the RCM Executive and Finance Committee of 18 May 1899 the then director, Parry, reported the resignation of Gompertz as 'another very severe disaster . . . His work was so valuable that I despair of ever being able to replace it'); Stephen Kemp (1849–1918): Saxe Wyndham and L'Epine, *Who's Who in Music*; *RCM Magazine*, 15, 1; Eliza Mazzucato (1858–?), also known as Eliza Young and Mrs Bicknell: Cohen, *International Encyclopaedia of Women Composers*; Gertrude Mayfield, *RCM Magazine*, 2, 3. We are deeply indebted to Celia Clarke of the RCM library for researching this information.

42   George Grove to DC, 16 Jan. 1886 (DC minutes of 19 Jan. 1886). In 1886 James Culwick would observe in his evidence to the Educational Endowments Commission that this commendation suggested that study in Dublin was 'not made sufficiently broad and intellectual' and that education in composition and musical 'grammar and anatomy' would broaden their scope (para. 8089, 7 June 1886).

43   Bridge to Brady, 15 Jan. 1887 (NA 1120/1/9).

44   Minutes of 3 Mar. 1869 (NA 1120/1/5).

45   Minutes of 15 and 22 Sep. 1869, ibid.

46   Vignoles, *Memoir of Sir Robert P. Stewart*, 209.

47   John O'Donovan, 'Big fish in a little pond', *IT*, 19 Dec. 1962.

48   Vignoles, *Memoir of Sir Robert P. Stewart*, 62.

49   Culwick, 'Sir Robert Stewart'.

50   Stewart to Brady, 11 Mar. 1878 (NA 1120/1/7). This letter also contains remarks on Stewart's attitude to teaching harmony, for which see chap. 8 (1) above.

51   Minutes of 13 Mar. 1878 (NA 1120/1/7).

52   Brady to Stewart, 14 Mar. 1878, ibid.

53   Minutes of 12 June 1884 (NA 1120/1/9).

54   George Grove to Edith Oldham, 21 Feb. 1892 (RCM).

55   Culwick, 'Sir Robert Stewart', 3, 5.
56   Greene and Stephens, *J. M. Synge*, 40 Others, however, had cause to regret his influence, among whom was George Lee (later styling himself Vandeleur Lee), whom Stewart had actively excluded from concert-giving in Dublin. See O'Donovan, *G. B. Shaw*, 24–5.
57   Patterson, for example, lectured on 'The Harp and Irish Music' at the Coffee Palace, Townsend Street, on 16 October 1895, and Culwick on 'The Distinctive Characteristics of Irish Music' for the National Literary Society on 15 February 1897. Culwick's remarks quoted here are taken from his published text on this subject, 4.
58   RAM to RIAM, 29 Mar. 1894 (NA 1120/1/31). When later that year a committee was soliciting subscriptions for a memorial to Stewart, the RAM declined to contribute, on the grounds that funds did not exist for such a purpose, adding, 'although as a body they thoroughly sympathised with the object in view' (RAM minutes, 14 June 1894).
59   Minutes of 16 and 23 May 1894 (NA 1120/1/31).
60   Culwick, 'Sir Robert Stewart', 10.
61   TCD ms. 4375.
62   Cf. *NG*, vol. 8, 758.
63   TCD ms. 4373.
64   *DE*, 23 Dec. 1889.
65   *Irish Builder*, 1 Apr. 1880.
66   See Daly, *Catholic Church Music in Ireland*, 31.
67   White, *The Keeper's Recital*, 100–1.
68   White, *The Keeper's Recital*, 101.
69   See *Irish Builder*, 1 Feb. 1873.
70   *FJ*, 1 Nov. 1851.
71   *FJ*, 4 Apr. 1854.
72   *FJ*, 9 Dec. 1854.
73   See Aloys Fleischmann, 'Music and Society, 1850-1921' in *New History of Ireland*, vol. 6, 500–22.
74   *FJ*, 17 May 1872.
75   *IT*, 17 May 1872.
76   *DEM*, 24 Oct. 1873.
77   Stanford, *Studies and Memories*, p. 126.
78   Andrew Marsh (John O'Donovan), 'Lovers and sons', *Irish Press*, 29 Sep. 1978.
79   Minutes of 25 Sep. 1907 (NA 1120/1/22).
80   NA 1120/1/7.
81   Brady to Joseph Robinson, 6 May 1875, ibid.
82   *IT*, 4 Oct. 1875.
83   See above, p. 256–7.
84   The costs of the choral class's three concerts had been: May 1874, £18; February 1875, £44; June 1875, £70.
85   Minutes of 10 Nov. 1875 (NA 1120/1/7).
86   Paolo Serrao to H. MacDonnell, 12 Jan. 1876, ibid.
87   Sir M. Costa to H. MacDonnell, 12 May 1876, ibid.
88   P. Viardot to H. MacDonnell, 20 and 29 May 1876, ibid.
89   Robinson to H. MacDonnell, 26 June 1876, ibid.
90   Robinson to Mayne, 17 Dec. 1880 (NA 1120/1/8).
91   Minutes of 13 Jan. 1878 (NA 1120/1/7).
92   Minutes of 6 Jan. 1878, ibid.
93   In 1873 the Academy also records Ethel and Emily Christian as piano students (NA 1120/7/3).
94   Minutes of 30 May 1879 (NA 1120/1/7).
95   Minutes of 4 June 1879, ibid.
96   Minutes of 10 Dec. 1879, (NA 1120/1/8).
97   Minutes of 22 Dec. 1880, ibid.
98   Minutes of 16 Feb. 1881, ibid.
99   Quarry to Brady, 5 Feb. 1882, ibid.

100 Minutes of 22 Feb. 1882, ibid.
101 Brady, memorandum for Council, 1 Mar. 1882, ibid.
102 Caracciolo to Brady, 3 May 1882, ibid.
103 Minutes of 11 Nov. 1884 (NA 1120/1/9).
104 Minutes of 18 and 15 Mar. 1885 (NA 1120/1/).
105 RAM minutes, 18 Oct. 1894 139 (RAM).
106 Minutes of 19 Sep. 1885 (NA 1120/1/9).
107 Minutes of 7 Oct. 1887, ibid.
108 Brasfort to Jozé, 18 Jan. 1890 (NA 1120/1/11).
109 Minutes of 22 Jan. 1890, ibid.
110 Brasfort to Jozé, 3 Feb. 1890, ibid.
111 Minutes of 20 Sep. 1884 (NA 1120/1/9).
112 RIAM annual report, 1884.
113 Minutes of 5 Mar. 1890 (NA 1120/1/11).
114 We are greatly indebted to Miss Annabel Stewart, niece of A. F. E. Stewart, for making available to us a copy of this unpublished history, 'The Elsners of Taunus: a Family Chronicle', from which much of the following information has been drawn.
115 Information from Annabel Stewart.
116 Elsner Stewart also tells us that a child who died in infancy was born in Great Brunswick Street; but as the birth occurred between those of William (1857) and Pauline (1865), after the Elsners had moved from there to St Stephen's Green and again from there to an unknown address, it is most unlikely that the place of burial is, as he put it, 'the nearby churchyard,' i.e. St Mark's.
117 Minutes of 27 Sep. 1865 (NA 1120/7/2).
118 Ibid.
119 *WIT*, 1 Dec. 1900.
120 *FJ*, 22 Feb. and 9 and 13 Mar. 1896, 17 Nov. 1897.
121 *WIT*, 13 Apr. 1901.
122 Related by T. R. G. Jozé to Annie Patterson (*WIT*, 21 July 1900).
123 Knowlson, *Damned to Fame: A Life of Samuel Beckett*, 25.
124 Ibid., 26.
125 *WIT*, 1 Dec. 1900.
126 George Grove to Edith Oldham, 17 May 1891 (RCM).
127 Ibid., 17 Jan. 1892.
128 Ibid., 23 Oct. 1892.
129 RIAM concert programme, 6 June 1872 (NA 1120/1/6).
130 *IT*, 19 Jan. 1873.
131 Sproule, the son of a surgeon, had been a pupil of Stewart and taught at the Academy and at Alexandra College until in 1879 ill-health caused him to take extended leave in the southern hemisphere, where he became an evangelical clergyman serving in Geelong, Caulfield, and eventually Elsternwick, near Melbourne, where he died in 1910.
132 Minutes of 5 Feb., 20 Aug. and 1 Nov. 1879 (NA 1120/1/7, 8).
133 Stewart to RIAM Governors, 10 June 1891 (NA 1120/1/11).
134 Minutes of 19 Apr. 1873 (NA 1120/1/7).
135 MacDonnell to the Directors of the Conservatoires of Paris, Brussels, Leipzig, Dresden, Vienna, Milan, Florence, and Naples; replies (extant in NA 1120/1/7) were received from Paris, Brussels, Florence, and the RAM.
136 Minutes of 30 Apr. 1873, ibid.
137 Minutes of 7 May 1873, ibid.
138 RAM to RIAM, 8 Apr. 1873, ibid.
139 RIM, Florence, to RIAM, 7 May 1873, ibid.
140 Thomas to RIAM, 28 May 1873, ibid.
141 Viardot to MacDonnell, 28 May 1873, ibid.
142 Lemmens to RIAM, 2 May 1873, ibid.
143 DC minutes, 1886, 591.
144 RAM to RIAM, 2 June 1874 (NA 1120/1/7).
145 Viardot to MacDonnell, n.d., ibid.

146 Viardot to MacDonnell, 23 Jan. 1875, ibid.
147 *IT*, 3 Feb. 1875.
148 A letter had been sent from the duke (at Clarence House) to the Treasury on 4 November, supported by a memo from Lord Frederick Cavendish from the Treasury on 9 Nov. 1880 (NA 1120/1/8).
149 Minutes of 5 May 1882, ibid.
150 Minutes of 10 Oct. 1883, ibid.
151 Brady to Robinson, 24 May 1893; Robinson to Brady, 26 May 1893, in minutes of 24 May 1893 (NA 1120/1/12).
152 Minutes of 14 Nov. 1883 (NA 1120/1/8).
153 18 Oct. 1877 (NA 1120/1/7) and secretary's letter book, May 1902 (RIAM).
154 When Mrs Crean retired in 1889 she received a retiring pension of £50 a year, and Miss Crean's salary as incoming lady superintendent was fixed at £100.
155 Evidence of land acquisition in Rathgar by Thomas Coulson of Harold's Cross in 1768–71 and 1778, and by Henry Coulson in 1804, is to be found in the Registry of Deeds, Dublin.
156 CCDB to Dublin Corporation, 14 Mar. 1884 (DC minutes, 7 April 1884, item 50).
157 NA 1120/12/1.
158 DC minutes, 1884, vol. 3, 584.
159 Educational Endowments (Ireland) Commission, 128.
160 PROI M4080, no. 2, in National Archives.
161 Educational Endowments (Ireland) Commission, 130.
162 Ibid., 133.
163 Turpin, *A School of Art in Dublin*, 87.
164 Educational Endowments (Ireland) Commission, 131.
165 Ibid., 131–2.
166 Ibid., 133.
167 Ibid.
168 Ibid.
169 Ibid., 135.
170 Ibid.
171 Ibid., 136.
172 PROI M4080, no. 4, in National Archives.
173 Educational Endowments (Ireland) Commission, 137.
174 Ibid.
175 Ibid., 139.
176 Ibid.
177 NA 1120/12/2.
178 Minutes of 16 Sep. 1942 (NA 1120/1/29).
179 Turpin, *A School of Art in Dublin*, 7.
180 Minutes of 29 June 1938 (NA 1120/1/29) and 24 June 1959 (RIAM).
181 1826–1894. Trained in Central Model School, Marlborough Street, Dublin, where he became headmaster in 1845 (succeeded by P. W. Joyce) and ultimately became Commissioner of National Education (in which his successor was W. J. M. Starkie). He was responsible for the introduction of the Intermediate Education Act (1878).
182 Cree, a barrister, was Clerk of Judgments, Records and Writs; he was also a major shareholder in Dublin Alliance and Consumers' Gas Company and the Midland and Great Western Railway, as well as a prominent member of the Feis Ceoil. He died in 1910.
183 Present were R. M. Levey in the chair, Elizabeth Scott-Fennell, Miss Kelly, Margaret O'Hea, Miss Bennett, Edith Oldham, Miss Wright, Sir Robert Stewart, Michele Esposito, Alexandre Billet, Herr Bluthner, J. C. van Maanen, Mr Connolly, J. F. Rudersdorff, Carl Lauer, Martin Roeder, and T. R. G. Jozé. Joseph Robinson was not present.
184 CCDB to RIAM, 26 Jan. 1889 (NA 1120/12/2).
185 RIAM to CCDB, 20 Nov. 1890 (NA 1120/1/11).

186 A further indication of the changing demography is the addresses (and occupations) of the inaugural Governors: of the twenty-four representative Governors, thirteen lived in the city centre, three in Rathmines or Terenure, four in Kingstown (Dún Laoghaire), and one each in Coolock, Stillorgan, Bray, and Dalkey. Occupationally there was little change: five were lawyers, four doctors, three merchants, two musicians, one an artist, one a priest, and two members of Parliament; six gave no occupation.

Intermezzo (p. 166–179)

1 NA 1120/7/3. The secretary's day book also records a Mrs James Oldham and a Wilton Oldham in the same class.

2 The company, trading as Samuel Oldham and Son, linen drapers, outfitters, silk mercers, shawl and mantle warehouse, had been in existence since at least 1849, when a sale was advertised in the *Freeman's Journal* on 16 July; another firm, George Oldham and Company, was operating a 'medical establishment' at 107 Grafton Street in 1851, with a branch at 64 Dame Street—'wholesale chemists and apothecaries'—by 1854 (*FJ*, 25 Apr. 1851, 14 Nov. 1854). Edith's elder sister Alice Oldham, among the first nine women graduates of the Royal University, became a mistress at Alexandra College, Dublin, in 1884, teaching botany, English, and logic, and was a leading figure in the Central Association of Irish Schoolmistresses: cf. O'Connor and Parkes. Her brother, Charles Hubert Oldham, was an economist who became principal of Rathmines School of Commerce in the nineteen-twenties and subsequently professor of economics at UCD. He was involved in setting up the *Dublin University Review* and the Contemporary Club, to which he read a paper on 'The Young Ireland Society' and where he became an associate of Kathleen Tynan, T. W. Rolleston, Michael Davitt, and John O'Leary (letter from N. Oldham to Edith Oldham, 30 Nov. 1885, RCM Archives, ms. 6863; Hubert Oldham to Edith Oldham, 21 Dec. 1885). The club continued in existence until at least 1935: cf. Mary Macken, 'W. B. Yeats, John O'Leary and the Contemporary Club', *Studies*, vol. 28 (1939), 136–42. His mother told Edith: 'I believe he fully thinks he is training the future legislators of Ireland in this club . . . they sit up nearly all Saturday night discussing the destiny of the nation' (N. Oldham to Edith Oldham, 29 Dec. 1885). In 1886 Hubert was asked by Parnell to stand for Parliament, which he declined (N. Oldham to Edith Oldham, 26 June 1886), but he toured England later that year lecturing on Home Rule. In April 1886 Mrs Oldham wrote to Edith: 'We are all in great excitement about Mr. Gladstone's home rule scheme . . . if his plan were carried out I think there would be no money left in Ireland or the possibility of making it. Hubert is very sanguine & excited about it.' At the end of 1886 Hubert was in discussions about the creation of a new paper, *North and South*, which intended, under his editorship, 'to unite all parties' (N. Oldham to Edith Oldham, 23 Dec. 1886). It was published for one year, from January to December 1887. He was described by Maud Gonne as 'a great believer in women and their duty as well as their right to take a share in public life' (*A Servant of the Queen*, 88).

3 She was offered teaching at the Dublin High School for Girls, then in Burlington Road, at the rate of £1 per month for three hours' teaching per week (N. Oldham to Edith Oldham, 2 Sep. and 4 Sep. 1882). (All letters quoted are in the RCM archives.)

4 Annie Oldham to Edith Oldham, 17 Sep. 1882.

5 Ernst Pauer (1826–1905) taught at the RAM 1859–64 and at the RCM 1876–96; he was the author of *The Art of Piano Playing* (1877); see *NG*, vol. 14, 305. He had played in Dublin at least four times. On 26 February 1853 he had played the Hummel Concerto in A minor (and a number of solo items) with the Philharmonic Society and was noted for his 'delicacy of touch and rotund brilliancy of tone' (*FJ*, 28 Feb. 1853); on 8 February 1861 he played the Beethoven Triple Concerto with Vieuxtemps and Piatti at the Philharmonic Society; on 20 December 1865 he played Beethoven's 'Emperor' Concerto, also with the Philharmonic Society; and on 7 February 1868 he was advertised in the *Freeman's Journal* as giving a recital (in the same series as Joachim) at a popular concert on 15 February.

6   Vignoles, *Memoir of Sir Robert P. Stewart*, 146.
7   N. Oldham to Edith Oldham, 12 June 1883.
8   N. Oldham to Edith Oldham, 26 June 1883.
9   George Grove to Edith Oldham, 23 Sep. 1884.
10   Lady Grove to Edith Oldham, 29 June 1900: 'Dear Miss Oldham, Thanks so much for your letter. I have been tearing up heaps of your letters which I felt you would not wish to be read by a publisher if such a person should appear.'
11   George Grove to Edith Oldham, 9 Apr. 1892.
12   George Grove to Edith Oldham, 4 Aug. 1890.
13   George Grove to Edith Oldham, 4 Nov. 1888.
14   George Grove to Edith Oldham, 9 Aug. 1890.
15   George Grove to Edith Oldham, 9 Aug. 1890.
16   George Grove to Edith Oldham, 1 Apr. 1888.
17   George Grove to Edith Oldham, 27 July 1892.
18   George Grove to Edith Oldham, 1 Aug. 1892.
19   George Grove to Edith Oldham, 25 Nov. 1889.
20   George Grove to Edith Oldham, 2 Mar. 1888.
21   George Grove to Edith Oldham, 27 Sep. 1891.
22   George Grove to Edith Oldham, 12 Feb. 1893. Edith had clearly written this, since Grove in another letter (15 Sep. 1887) had replied: 'It is a hard law of nature that one person should be such a tomb to another.'
23   George Grove to Edith Oldham, 26 Oct. 1884.
24   George Grove to Edith Oldham, 2 Mar. 1890.
25   George Grove to Edith Oldham, 30 Apr. 1892.
26   George Grove to Edith Oldham, 4 Nov. 1890.
27   George Grove to Edith Oldham, 29 Dec. 1889.
28   George Grove to Edith Oldham, 6 Oct. 1890.
29   George Grove to Edith Oldham, 27 Mar. 1892.
30   George Grove to Edith Oldham, 11 Aug. 1884.
31   N. Oldham to Edith Oldham, 20 Apr. 1883.
32   N. Oldham to Edith Oldham, 13 July 1883.
33   N. Oldham to Edith Oldham, 11 May 1883.
34   N. Oldham to Edith Oldham, 13 July 1883.
35   N. Oldham to Edith Oldham, 17 Nov. 1883.
36   N. Oldham to Edith Oldham, 16 June 1886.
37   George Grove to Edith Oldham, 29 Apr. 1886.
38   George Grove to Edith Oldham, 17 Oct. 1889.
39   N. Oldham to Edith Oldham, 23 Mar. 1886.
40   N. Oldham to Edith Oldham, 19 Mar. 1885.
41   George Grove to Edith Oldham, 2 Nov. 1887.
42   George Grove to Edith Oldham, 29 Dec. 1889.
43   N. Oldham to Edith Oldham, 23 Dec. 1885.
44   N. Oldham to Edith Oldham, 20 Nov. 1885.
45   N. Oldham to Edith Oldham, 10 Mar. 1886.
46   Alice Oldham to Edith Oldham, 28 July 1886.
47   N. Oldham to Edith Oldham, 17 Feb. 1887.
48   N. Oldham to Edith Oldham, 26 Jan. 1887. Quarry also taught at Alexandra College, where he was succeeded by Esposito.
49   Cf. Young, *George Grove*, 195 ff.
50   George Grove to Edith Oldham, 2 July 1887.
51   George Grove to Eldred Oldham, 2 July 1887.
52   N. Oldham to Edith Oldham, 23 July 1887.
53   N. Oldham to Edith Oldham, 4 July 1887.
54   George Grove to Edith Oldham, 30 Aug. 1888.
55   George Grove to Edith Oldham, 13 Apr. 1893.
56   George Grove to Edith Oldham, [?] Nov. 1891.

57   George Grove to Edith Oldham, 2 Feb. 1888.
58   George Grove to Edith Oldham, 23 Jan. 1889.
59   George Grove to Edith Oldham, 3 Mar. 1889.
60   George Grove to Edith Oldham, 14 Aug. 1890.
61   George Grove to Edith Oldham, 13 Nov. 1892.
62   George Grove to Edith Oldham, 18 Apr. [year uncertain].
63   George Grove to Edith Oldham, 31 July 1891.
64   George Grove to Edith Oldham, undated letter.
65   George Grove to Edith Oldham, 13 Nov. 1892. In Grove's case there is evidence that his own 'shock' occurred with the death of his daughter when he was forty-two years old.
66   George Grove to Edith Oldham, 25 Sep. 1887.
67   ibid.
68   George Grove to Edith Oldham, 17 Oct. 1889.
69   George Grove to Edith Oldham, 27 Jan. 1889.
70   George Grove to Edith Oldham, 17 Oct. 1889.
71   George Grove to Edith Oldham, 4 Nov. 1890.
72   George Grove to Edith Oldham, 6 Nov. 1892.
73   George Grove to Edith Oldham, 19 Feb. , 1888.
74   George Grove to Edith Oldham, 15 Sep. 1887.
75   A. J. Balfour to George Grove, 21 Dec. 1887.
76   George Grove to Edith Oldham, 7 May 1888.
77   George Grove to Edith Oldham, 18 Jan. 1888.
78   George Grove to Edith Oldham, 17 Oct. 1889.
79   George Grove to Edith Oldham, 21 Nov. 1897.
80   She was the founder-secretary of the Feis and the dedicatee of Esposito's cantata *Deirdre*.
81   Minutes of 28 May and 4 June 1902 (NA 1120/1/18).
82   Letter from McCann, White and Fitzgerald, Dublin, 11 Mar. 1960, to the bursar of the RCM.
83   Terence de Vere White to Celia Clarke, 6 May 1987 (RCM).

Chapter 5 (p. 180–285)

1   Died 1904. Lord Mayor of Dublin 1894–5, brother of John Blake Dillon (1816–66) and uncle of John Dillon (1851–1927).
2   Hone, 181.
3   Walter Starkie, 'What the Royal Dublin Society has done for music', 62.
4   See Hutchinson, *The Dynamics of Cultural Nationalism*, 115, 166, 224–5; Turpin, *A School of Art*, 184.
5   McCarthy, 'Music Education', 194.
6   Robinson: *Bryan Cooper*, 49, 110–11.
7   In 1910 Hill obtained subscriptions from his parents (the Marquess and Marchioness of Downshire), the Earl and Countess of Iveagh, Lord Rathmore, Sir Charles Cameron, the Earl and Countess of Bessborough, Lord and Lady O'Neill, the Earl of Rosse, Countess of Annesley, Duke of Leinster, Marchioness of Headfort, Marchioness of Waterford, Earl of Kilmorey, and Duke of Manchester.
8   Bruce Arnold, *Mainie Jellett*, 11.
9   H. Harty, *Early Memoirs*, 24.
10   P. Goodman, quoted by Ryan in 'Nationalism and Music in Ireland', 192.
11   Even here, a variety of motives and affiliations can be noted. Harty's decision to employ the title 'Irish' may be attributed more to the need to openly satisfy the Feis conditions than to any other reason; Esposito's, as a way of emphasising his assimilation into the Irish musical establishment; and Stanford's as a way of asserting his provincial roots from his London base. MacKenzie's 'Scottish Overture' might provide a parallel example.
12   See Micheál Ó Súilleabháin, 'All our central fire: music, mediation and the Irish psyche' in *Irish Journal of Psychology*, vol. 15 (1994), 331–53) and 'Around the house and mind the cosmos' in Pine, *Music in Ireland*.

13   Cf. McCarthy, *Music Education*, 257–60.
14   Letter of 1 Nov. 1907 to Alma Mahler, quoted by K. Aho in 'Music, Nationality and Society' 1995.
15   Ibid.
16   Yeats, *Autobiographies*, 170.
17   See Turpin, *A School of Art*, 206.
18   *Journal and Proceedings of the Arts and Crafts Society of Ireland*, 1901, quoted by Turpin in *A School of Art*, 206.
19   *Studio*, no. 26 (1902), 295, quoted by Turpin in *A School of Art*, 202.
20   Yeats, *Letters to the New Island*, 74.
21   Yeats, *Autobiographies*, 170.
22   O'Sullivan, 'The Legacy of Michele Esposito'.
23   The Greek *meta-phorein* has the equivalent meaning to the Latin *trans-ferre*—to carry across.
24   Samuel Beckett, *Trilogy*, 352.
25   Séamus Deane, 'An Example of Tradition', *Crane Bag*, vol. 3 (1979), 374.
26   Deane, *Strange Country*, 67.
27   A. Patterson, 'The interpretation of Irish music', *Journal of the Ivernian Society*, vol. 2 (1909), 31–42.
28   Ibid., 31.
29   Rogers, 'An Irish school of music'.
30   *Irish Musical Monthly*, vol. 1 (1902), 2.
31   DC minutes 14 Mar. 1904, item 127.
32   *FJ*, 5 Jan. 1898.
33   Kelly, 'The Political, Intellectual and Social Background to the Irish Literary Revival', Conclusion , vi.
34   *WIT*, 22 June 1901.
35   Ironically, Stanford's use of 'an old Irish lament in Petrie's MSS.' was attributed by Hans von Bülow to the influence of Brahms, whose simultaneously written Fourth Symphony contains the same phrase (Stanford, *Pages from an Unwritten Diary*, 262).
36   Yeats, *Uncollected Prose*, vol. 1, 255.
37   1837–1920. Castleknock; Irish College, Rome; curate 1861, PP 1882; DD, Bishop of Canea and auxiliary Bishop of Dublin 1883–; parish priest of St Mary's, Haddington Road, 1904–20; author of *History of Dublin Parishes* (Catholic Truth Society 1906) and translator of Haberl's *Magister Choralis* 1887; founder of Irish Society of St Cecilia 1878 and of *Lyra Ecclesiastica* 1879 (Daly, *Catholic Church Music*).
38   1837–1910. The son of one of the Academy's earliest supporters, Judge Richard Greene; dean of Christ Church Cathedral 1887–1907.
39   Born Belfast 1838, son of a Church of Ireland rector; died Dublin 1910; architect to dioceses of Down, Connor and Dromore 1865, subsequently consulting architect to Christ Church and St Patrick's Cathedrals, Dublin, St Patrick's (Protestant), Armagh, and St Columb's (Catholic), Derry; president RIAI, RSAI, and RIA; editor, *Irish Builder*; knighted 1900. His best-known work is Rathmines Town Hall (1897).
40   1859–1923; playwright, co-founder with W. B. Yeats and Lady Gregory of the Irish Literary Theatre, in 1906 of the Theatre of Ireland and in 1914 of the Irish Theatre (Hardwicke Street), president of Sinn Féin 1904–08, founder and benefactor of the Palestrina Choir and supporter of the Cecilian movement; expelled from (and reinstated by) the Kildare Street Club in 1903 for criticising the visit to Dublin of King Edward VII, having previously persuaded the club to purchase *Grove I*.
41   1857–1935; alderman, city of Dublin, 1900; chairman, Municipal Electricity Committee, 1900–06; chairman, Visiting Justices' Committee of the Dublin Prisons, 1900–09; chairman, National Relief Fund, 1914; knighted 1915.
42   1851–1948. Founder and editor of *Hibernia* 1882–83; director of National Museum 1907–16; vice-president of RIA 1908–09 and 1911–14; president, Society for Preservation of Irish Language and of Royal Society of Antiquaries of Ireland; Sinn Féin MP for North Roscommon 1917–27, Minister for Foreign Affairs 1919–21, Minister for Fine

Arts 1921–22; father of Joseph Mary Plunkett; papal count; author and editor of many antiquarian works, including Stokes's *Early Christian Art in Ireland* (1911–15).

43   1834–1912; medical doctor, inventor of the cystoscope and a pioneer in the use of hypnotism; president of RCPI 1884–86; crack shot with a rifle, especially when aiming at the necks of champagne bottles; an expert on the work of Thomas à Kempis, whose *Imitatio Christi* he translated; biographer of Sir Dominic Corrigan; member of Council of RIAM 1870, vice-president 1898; founder of Instrumental Club; amateur cellist, arranger and minor composer of music, and owner of a quartet of instruments by Perry, now in the National Museum; knighted 1896; Knight of St Gregory 1905; physician-in-ordinary to King Edward VII in Ireland 1901. Hutchinson (*The Dynamics of Cultural Nationalism*, 261) regards him as typical of the 'Catholic advance' in educational and social achievement of the time.

44   Daly, *Dublin*, 118.

45   Ibid., 207.

46   Ibid., 275.

47   Minutes of 30 Nov. 1892 and subsequently (NA 1120/1/12).

48   Baker to RIAM, 3 July 1891, ibid.

49   Minutes of 23 Jan. 1924 (NA 1120/1/26).

50   Daly, *Dublin*, 82.

51   Minutes of 19 Mar. 1890 (NA 1120/1/11).

52   City Treasurer to RIAM, 5 Dec. 1901 (NA 1120/1/18).

53   Minutes of 19 Oct. 1892 (NA 1120/1/12).

54   McGrath to Harvey, 20 Mar. 1902 (NA 1120/1/18).

55   Minutes of 10 June 1880 (NA 1120/1/8).

56   *DE*, 2 Mar. 1906.

57   *FJ*, 13 Mar. 1908.

58   *FJ*, 10 Feb. 1912.

59   *DE*, 28 Apr. 1913.

60   Minutes of 20 Jan. 1892 (NA 1120/1/12).

61   Minutes of 2 June 1897 (NA 1120/1/15).

62   Minutes of 23 Jan. 1901 (NA 1120/1/18).

63   *WIT*, 14 Apr. 1900.

64   J. Meenan, 'The Victorian doctors of Dublin', *Irish Journal of Medical Science*, July 1968, 318.

65   *DEM*, 7 June 1872.

66   *IT*, 7 June 1872.

67   Minutes of 29 Jan. and 12 Feb. 1890 (NA 1120/1/11).

68   *FJ*, 17 Dec. 1903.

69   Brady to Cree, 25 Oct. 1902 (NA 1120/3/3).

70   Ibid. Even before this, the Academy had approached the secretary of the City of Dublin Technical Schools in search of a grant, on the grounds that 'this Institution is fully worthy of being termed a Technical School in the strictest sense of the words, inasmuch as a very large proportion of those attending the classes study music with a view to adopting it as a means of livelyhood [*sic*].' Secretary's letter book, 25 June 1902 (RIAM).

71   *c.* 1835–1910. MRIA, secretary of National Board of Education under the presidency of Patrick Keenan and subsequently a Commissioner, and member of many charitable bodies.

72   Harty, *Early Memories*.

73   See Cécile Reynaud, 'Une vertu contestée: l'idéal de virtuosité dans la formation des élèves' in E. Hondré (ed.), *Le Conservatoire de Musique de Paris*, 109–21.

74   RIAM annual report, 1919, 9 (RIAM).

75   *Lyra Ecclesiastica*, vol. 1 (1879), 38.

76   See Daly, *Catholic Church Music*, 38, 68, 78, 91.

77   Aiello [Mario Esposito], *Al Musicista Michele Esposito*, 18. Although this publication is ostensibly edited by Giuseppe Lauro Aiello and is cited as such by recent scholars,

it was in fact mostly written by Mario Esposito, who inscribed copies *The author* (information by courtesy of Morgan Dockrell).

78   Esposito's addresses (in chronological order) were: Ardenza Terrace, Monkstown; 'Benburb', Leeson Park; 56 Lansdowne Road; 'St Andrew's', Serpentine Avenue; St James's Terrace, Clonskeagh; 'St Ronan's', Sandford Road, Ranelagh.

79   Silvestre, 'Mario Esposito'.

80   *The Letters of J. M. Synge*, 1, 88: 'In French it loses a good deal as she has put it into standard healthy style—but hasn't managed to give it any atmosphere or charm.'

81   As related by family legend. However, although Bianca and Vera Esposito attended the school, Alexandra College has no record of Nina having been a pupil. (Verbal communication from Anne O'Connor.)

82   J. Bowyer Bell, 'Waiting for Mario: the Espositos, Joyce and Beckett', *Éire-Ireland*, 1995, no. 2, 7–26.

83   Knowlson, *Damned to Fame*, 7, 73–4.

84   Knowlson, *Damned to Fame*, 72, and Ellmann, *James Joyce*, 160–1.

85   Hogan and Kilroy, *The Abbey Theatre*, vol. 3, 22.

86   Hogan and Kilroy, *The Abbey Theatre*, vol. 2, 129–30.

87   Ellmann, *Selected Letters of James Joyce*, 96.

88   Hogan and Kilroy, *The Abbey Theatre*, vol. 3, 27, 198; *Synge Letters*, vol. 1, 95–6.

89   Knowlson, *Damned to Fame*, 172.

90   J. Bowyer Bell, 'Waiting for Mario: the Espositos, Joyce and Beckett', *Éire-Ireland*, 1995, no. 2, 7–26.

91   Evidence in letter of Mario Esposito to Hubert Silvestre, 6 Feb. 1959, in Silvestre, 'Mario Esposito'.

92   Mario Esposito also (on his own admission) wrote 'a large number of ephemeral articles—war memoirs, musical and literary criticism and political commentary in various languages and under several pseudonyms' (letter of 24 Oct. 1958, ibid.).

93   [Mario Esposito], *Latin Learning in Mediaeval Ireland* (Michael Lapidge, ed.), London: Variorum Reprints 1988, vii.

94   Boylan, *All Cultured People*, 13.

95   1867–1945. Professor of early Irish history, UCD, 1908–45; founder and commander-in-chief of Irish Volunteers; Minister for Education 1922–25.

96   Evidence for this is drawn from the Art O'Brien Papers, NLI. J. Bowyer Bell, 'Waiting for Mario: the Espositos, Joyce and Beckett', *Éire-Ireland*, 1995, no. 2, 7–26.

97   He mentions the name of Cathal Brugha rather than Plunkett, but it was Plunkett who actually entrusted Mario Esposito with one part of his mission.

98   Brennan, *Allegiance*, 175–81. Brennan (1881–1964) was later a director of the *Irish Press*, minister to the United States 1938–47, and director of broadcasting, Radio Éireann, 1947–48.

99   O'Connor, Ulick, *Oliver St John Gogarty*, London: Cape 1964, 173.

100 Mario Esposito to Maurice Dockrell, 26 Feb. 1969 (by courtesy of Morgan Dockrell).

101 Harty, *Musical Times*, 1 Apr. 1920.

102 Enid Starkie, *A Lady's Child*.

103 This was suggested by one of his pupils, Clare Hand, to her pupil Terry de Valera (verbal communication by Terry de Valera to the editors). It was played on 2 June 1998 when FRIAMs were conferred on Terry de Valera and Richard Pine.

104 Kees van Hoek (in 'Michele Esposito: maestro of Dublin', *Irish Monthly*, vol. 71 (1943), 227) says that Esposito encountered considerable opposition to the idea of Sunday concerts but that this evaporated when the Catholic Archbishop, Walsh, took a season ticket; he also says that two conspicuous attenders were Arthur Griffith and James Montgomery, later the film censor.

105 *WIT*, 20 Apr. 1901.

106 Cf. F. S. L. Lyons, *Culture and Anarchy in Ireland*, 57–84.

107 Leerssen, *Remembrance and Imagination*, 159.

108 Discussed by Richard Pine in 'Music in the Irish Theatre', FM3, 7 Apr. 1995 (RTÉ Archives).

109 White, *The Keeper's Recital*, 113.

110 See Kelly, 'The Political, Intellectual and Social Background to the Irish Literary Revival', 33.
111 Ibid., 99; *United Ireland*, 23 May 1885.
112 *United Ireland*, 16 Mar. 1889.
113 *Time*, no. 4, Apr. 1890.
114 *United Ireland*, 30 Apr. 1892.
115 Ibid., 9 Apr. 1892.
116 Cf. Harry White (*The Keeper's Recital*, 110): 'Stanford's achievement was seminal in one respect. It raised the issue of an Irish art music especially in terms of examining the question of cultural discourse between two distinct traditions. It established the challenge of an Irish art music in the first place and it clarified the central difficulty which perforce it had to overcome. For those who remained in Ireland, it functioned as a means of exploration and perhaps as an exemplar which proved the urgency of cultural engagement if the concept of Irish art music was to survive into the twentieth century.'
117 White, *The Keeper's Recital*, 7.
118 Cf. Ryan, 'Nationalism and Music in Ireland', 44: 'For music to be indentured to [the cause of cultural nationalism] it was necessary for the composer to employ selective devices and to work within a limited range of forms . . . the creative artist had to be willing to forgo complete artistic freed in order to serve a particular end.'
119 *Synge Letters*, 1, 134.
120 *DEM*, 17 May 1910.
121 See C. V. Stanford, 'The case for a national opera' in *Studies and Memories*, 3–23.
122 *WIT*, 13 Oct. 1900.
123 *WIT*, 20 Oct. 1900.
124 *WIT*, 27 Oct. 1900.
125 *WIT*, 31 Aug. 1901.
126 *WIT*, 7 Sep. 1901.
127 *WIT*, 11 May 1901.
128 *FJ*, 19 Feb. 1906.
129 Greene and Stephens, *J. M. Synge*, 44.
130 On that occasion Charles Acton wrote of the andante movements for violin that 'they do not amount to anything more than all the other forgotten salon music of the period' (*IT*, 17 Apr. 1971).
131 The following details are extracted from Synge's notebook in TCD ms. 4414.
132 Werner had studied at the Amsterdam Conservatoire and in Berlin under Joachim and came to Dublin with references from Joachim, August Manns, and Arthur Chappell. After leaving the Academy because it would not accede to his demands for a much higher fee, he taught privately 'upon the same principle which is carried out at the Berlin, Paris and Vienna Conservatoires' (employing assistant teachers, who included Ernest May) and gave several annual series of recitals (*IT*, 28 Sep. 1891).
133 *FJ*, 18 Apr. 1893.
134 Minutes of 28 Sep. and 5 Oct. 1898 (NA 1120/1/16).
135 Carpenter, *My Uncle John*, 59.
136 Synge, *Collected Works II: Prose*, 14.
137 TCD ms. 4382, quoted by Carpenter in *My Uncle John*, 59.
138 Greene and Stephens, *J. M. Synge*.
139 Synge, *Collected Works II: Prose*, 3 (emphasis added).
140 Ibid., 234, 247.
141 A. Saddlemyer, 'Synge's Soundscape', *Irish University Review*, vol. 22 (1992), 55–68.
142 TCD ms. 4382.
143 Lyons, *Ireland since the Famine*, 227.
144 D. P. Moran, *The Philosophy of Irish Ireland*, 37.
145 Quoted by Robert Welch in *Changing States*, 187.
146 *United Irishman*, 31 Oct. 1903.
147 Rogers, 'An Irish school of music', 151.
148 McCarthy ('Music Education', 198–9) makes the point that at this time, 'in the opinion of classical-trained musicians, Irish traditional music needed to progress and become

modern. Such progress was conceived in terms of educating traditional musicians "in musical science," bringing the professional traditional musician into the market place by paying him for his performance, and developing the forms and repertoire of Irish music using models from European art music. The last of these avenues to progress was the one which most affected music education. If music of an Irish origin and character was to be introduced into the educational system, then certain modifications would need to be made. The major obstacles in transferring Irish traditional music from its indigenous settings into school settings at this time were: (1) the solo nature of performance which in a class setting would prove of limited use, (2) the unaccompanied, strictly melodic, and highly ornamental style of the vocal tradition when, in contrast, the contemporary musical mind was craving for concerted and harmonized works, (3) the inadequacy of traditional musical notation to reflect the nuances of the live performance, (4) the use of the Irish language which was wedded to traditional vocal music but was only being reintroduced into the schools, and (5) the lack of music educators who could stand inside both traditional and classical musical worlds, value each in its own context, respect and develop the uniqueness of each tradition in formal music education, and not merely graft the values and methods of the classical world onto the traditional.'

149   Hogan and Kilroy, *The Abbey Theatre*, vol. 2, 21.
150   Ibid., 10.
151   White, *The Keeper's Recital*, 114.
152   Ibid. Cf. also Ryan, 'Nationalism and Music in Ireland', 127: 'Other European nations have successfully blended their native stores of folksong with the universal tradition of art music, and have done so without the divisiveness which has characterized the Irish experience . . . Caught between two antipodal customs which effectively deprived him of a tradition, the Irish composer was forced to create outside of any supporting context. The creative artist searching for a tradition was faced with an unenviable choice: to espouse the indigenous tradition to a degree sufficient to satisfy its most ardent supporters necessitated turning one's back to a large measure on the great and consistent glories of Western art music . . . Any attempt at a synthesis would run the risk of alienating both camps and of compromising the integrity of the composer. Furthermore, to embrace either option would inevitably be regarded by some as a political statement.'
153   For a discussion of this event see Declan Kiberd, 'George Moore's Gaelic lawn party' in Welch, *The Way Back*, 13–27.
154   Mrs de Valera subsequently recalled that 'Esposito became very excited and in very broken English kept on saying 'singa—singa' (letter from Terry de Valera to Richard Pine, 27 June 1997).
155   Minutes, 11 Nov. 1896 (NA 1120/1/15).
156   Minutes, 25 Nov. 1896 (ibid.).
157   Minutes, 1 Nov. 1899 (NA 1120/1/17).
158   White, *The Keeper's Recital*, 44.
159   *Field Day Anthology of Irish Writing*, vol. 1, xxii.
160   *IT*, 13 Mar. 1912.
161   See McCarthy, 'Music Education', 197 ff.
162   RDS minutes, quoted by A. Hughes in 'The society and music', 265.
163   From 1893 to 1896 some recitals were held in Earslfort Terrace while the Leinster House concert room was rebuilt and an organ installed, which was inaugurated in 1899 by George Sinclair, then organist of Hereford Cathedral and a former pupil of Stewart at the RIAM (see Hughes, 'The society and music', 267).
164   RDS Council minutes, vol. 128. Admission for the general public was 2s and for members' guests 1s (today £4 and £2).
165   Minutes, 24 Nov. and 8 Dec. 1897, 23 Nov. and 23 Dec. 1898 (NA 1120/ 1/16).
166   Hughes, 'The society and music', 266.
167   *DE*, 21 Jan. 1908.
168   Walter Starkie, 'What the Royal Dublin Society has done for music, 62.
169   *FJ*, 19 Feb. 1895.

170 *FJ*, 31 Mar. 1896.
171 Undated.
172 *DE*, 20 Feb. 1912.
173 Knowlson, *Damned to Fame*, 52, 715.
174 George Grove to Edith Oldham, 31 July 1891 (RCM).
175 Walter Starkie, 'What the Royal Dublin Society has done for music', 61.
176 *FJ*, 5 Mar. 1895.
177 Hughes, 'The society and music', 267.
178 1873–1934. See *NG*, vol. 19, 629. Not Emile, as stated by Anthony Hughes.
179 Letter from Verbrugghen re the pier at Colwyn Bay, 22 May 1900: 'When I was asked at the end of December 1899 to undertake a senior violin class at the RIAM I had already engaged my professional services to the Colwyn Bay Victoria Pier Co. from April 12th until end of September. The Pavilion in which my services were required was scarcely begun at that time and it was evident in the mind of everyone that it would not be completed and for use until far in the summer. Moreover some of the important engagements were only commencing on June 30th so that in every probability the concerts at which I had to conduct would not start until that date. Under those circumstances I was so certain that it could be so, that I accepted to teach at the Academy until June 30th. but later on the Pier Directors took an energetic step and the contractors saw the advisability of doubling the working staff, in fact they did all in their power to have the building ready as soon as possible. It has now been decided to open on June 2nd and as my services cannot be spared owing to my peculiar position in the Company I beg the Governors to take my special case into consideration and allow me to owe my pupils their lessons which I will manage to give them after the holidays [*sic*]. No one can be more grieved than me as I have taken a real interest in my pupils—my conscience is also hurt but under the circumstances I hope the Governors will remember that I made great sacrifice of time and money to fulfil my duty at the Academy. I may say that I thought my connection would be longer and I have been rather disappointed at the number of pupils in my class—In fact I should not have thought that I should have been induced to come over for so little. However, the welcome I have received, both at the Academy and at my public appearances are a great gratification and were it not that the entire scheme here rests upon me I would certainly be able to manage but I feel certain that in future things will go on more smoothly.' As a result of this letter the Governors resolved that Verbrugghen's pupils could go to another teacher or receive a proportional refund. On 15 September 1900 it was decided that Verbrugghen was to have a three-year contract; but a week later (21 September 1900) Verbrugghen wrote: 'I have been engaged to play at some of the most important concerts in Great Britain next winter including Queens Hall, Hallé-Richter concerts, etc. and that I am not inclined to abandon such a fast spreading connection if the Governors cannot give me every possible help in view of making a good position for myself' (NA 1120/1/17). Although a committee consisting of Brady, Cruise, Tichborne, Beardwood, Dunn, Plunkett and Cree was set up to examine the options, no agreement could be reached, and Verbrugghen's connection with the RIAM came to an end. Verbrugghen subsequently joined the Scottish Orchestra in Glasgow, where he taught at the Athenæum.
180 *New Ireland Review*, no. 14 (Dec. 1900), 240.
181 Quoted ibid.
182 Esposito dedicated many works to close associates: *Deirdre* to Edith Oldham, the cello sonata to Bast, the Irish Suite (published by CE Editions) to Sir Stanley Cochrane, the five Irish Melodies for piano and violin to Victoria Delaney, another Irish air (op. 57 no. 1) to Patrick Delany and its companion (op. 57 no. 2) to Count Plunkett, the string quartet in D to W. P. Geoghegan, one violin sonata to Harty and another to Papini, and nocturnes (op. 36, nos. 1 and 2) to Albanesi and Archie Rosenthal, respectively. He even dedicated his Tarantella, op. 35, for piano duet to Sion Hill Convent, where he taught.
183 *FJ*, 26 Feb. 1895, 16 June 1896.

184 DC Minutes, 16 Dec. 1895.
185 Minutes of 16 June 1896 (NA 1120/1/15).
186 White, *The Keeper's Recital*, 113.
187 *United Ireland*, 14 Apr. 1894.
188 'The Eisteddfod and the Feis Ceoil', *New Ireland Review*, vol. 8 (Feb. 1898), 349.
189 *FJ*, 13 Mar. 1896.
190 Feis programme, 1897.
191 Minutes book of Feis Ceoil, 22 Oct. 1914.
192 George Grove to Edith Oldham (RCM).
193 Stanford was invited to be president of the Feis, but his inflexible insistence on the presence of a professional orchestra (the Hallé) and the inclusion in the programme of two concerts, one of Irish composers, the other to be 'international', caused his withdrawal—to the relief, it seems, of the Committee, who were alarmed at the likely costs (*FJ*, 29 Mar. 1895 and 16 June 1896).
194 *FJ*, 18 May 1897.
195 *FJ*, 29 Apr. 1897.
196 The 'analysis' of the concert programmes was published in *FJ*, 18 May 1897.
197 *FJ*, 28 Nov. 1896.
198 *FJ*, 9 May 1897.
199 The inclusion of Holmes, considered dubious by the Committee, is said to have been effected by strong representations on her behalf by W. B. Yeats (see Heneghan, *The Feis Ceoil*, 14).
200 *FJ*, 8 May 1897.
201 *All Ireland Journal*, 20 Jan. 1900.
202 Ryan, 'Nationalism and Music in Ireland', 293.
203 *FJ*, 28 Sep. 1895.
204 *FJ*, 30 Oct. 1895.
205 *FJ*, 20 Feb. 1895.
206 *FJ*, 21 Feb. 1895.
207 He had been receiving free tuition at the RIAM because of his talent and his inability to pay.
208 Edith Oldham had announced the formation of the choir as an effect of the interest in the Feis, in a letter to the Academy on 23 November 1897, which said that it had the support of Elizabeth Scott-Fennell and Gordon Cleather, and on 16 May 1898 Culwick himself wrote, asking for practice facilities, 'seeing that our object would be purely educational.'
209 *FJ*, 10 Dec. 1895.
210 Minutes of 9 May 1900 (NA 1120/1/17).
211 *FJ*, 12 Jan. 1897.
212 *FJ*, 2 Feb. 1897.
213 *FJ*, 17 May 1895.
214 *FJ*, 10 Sep. 1898.
215 *FJ*, 14 Sep. 1896.
216 *FJ*, 12 Nov. 1896.
217 *FJ*, 10 Nov. 1896.
218 *FJ*, 19 Nov. 1896.
219 *FJ*, 5 Jan. 1898.
220 Letter to Feis Ceoil committee, quoted in *FJ*, 29 Mar. 1895.
221 Mrs Page Thrower to RIAM secretary, 5 Dec. 1897 (NA 1120/1/16).
222 'Orchestral music' in Greer, *Hamilton Harty*, 90.
223 Esposito to Grove, 7 Dec. 1898 (RCM).
224 *IT*, 19 Nov. 1898.
225 *Musical Times*, 1 Feb. 99.
226 *FJ*, 1 Oct. 1898.
227 'General Rules of the Dublin Orchestral Society, 1899 (RIAM).
228 1876–1945. Brother of the Philip Levenston (1856–1913) who had taught for the Academy at the Model Schools for many years; he played in the Queen's and Gaiety

orchestras. The family also ran a dancing academy in 35 South Frederick Street, mentioned in *Ulysses* (Hyman, *The Jews of Ireland*, 145–6).

229   The original orchestra members of the DOS were: *first violins*: A. Wilhelmj, A. Benson, Patrick Delany, Victoria Delaney, Thomas Farrell, Richard Fleming, N. P. Healy, A. Leonard, P. M. Levenson, E. May, W. L. Richards, M. K. Roe; *second violins:* P. J. Griffith, J. A. Cluskey, G. W. Field, W. Harrison, J. V. Jones, Annie Powell, Mrs Rawlingson, B. Wilson, S. Wood, Miss Grogan; *violas:* Octave Grisard, Constance Bell, J. C. Evans, E. Knox, S. Levenston, D. P. McGowan, W. Mitchell, T. J. Mitchell; *cellos:* R. Johnston, Richard O'Reilly, A. E. Rawlingson, Miss Ronayne; *basses:* Oscar May, W. Duggan, T. M. Evans, W. Logan, A. O'Neill; flutes: C. Regazzoli, J. Holland; oboes: J. Buckley, G. Ellard; *clarinets:* James Conroy, J. L. Toole; *bassoons:* Mr Taylor, Mr Rowe; *horns:* W. Higgins, C. Morrissy, J. J. Finlay, J. Reynolds; *cornets:* J. Shelton, A. Holland; *trombones:* J. J. Gleeson, J. Rafferty, J. J. Tallon; *tuba:* J. Caffrey; *timpani:* Mr Tidswell.

230   *Musical Times*, 1 Feb. 1899.

231   *IT*, 2 Mar. 1899.

232   *WIT*, 10 Feb. 1900.

233   See Joseph Ryan, 'Music and the institutions', Thomas Davis Lecture, in Pine, *Music In Ireland*.

234   *IT* and *FJ*, 2 Mar. 1899.

235   *Musical Times*, 1 Apr. 1899.

236   *IT*, 14 Feb. 1901.

237   Minutes of DOS, 6 June 1902 (RIAM).

238   Ibid., 27 Nov. 1902.

239   Ibid., 12 Feb. and 2 Apr. 1903.

240   *WIT*, 23 Dec. 1899.

241   Annie Patterson, *WIT*, 3 Mar. 1900: see also *NG*, vol. 16, 622.

242   *IT*, 11 Apr. 1901.

243   Ibid.

244   DOS minutes, 18 Apr. 1900 (RIAM).

245   Ibid., 22 May 1900.

246   *WIT*, 20 Apr. 1901. The original support included donations of £25 each from Lords Iveagh, Ardilaun, and Ashbourne, Mrs Andrew Jameson, Archbishop Walsh, Count Plunkett, John (later Sir John) Nutting, Edward Martyn, and Louis Claude Purser, and annual subscriptions (guaranteed for six years) of £5 each from (among others) W. H. Beardwood, Frank Browning, J. C. Culwick, Sir Philip Smyly, Sir Charles Cameron, John Spencer Curwen, Sir Frederick Falkiner, Bishop Graves, A. P. Graves, P. W. Joyce, Thomas Lipton, Archbishop Plunkett, T. W. Rolleston, Messrs Bechstein, and Messrs Broadwood.

247   *FJ*, 11 Feb. 1906. 1857–1930; barrister 1881, KC 1899, bencher 1907, serjeant-at-law 1910; Solicitor-General 1911–12, Attorney-General 1912–13, Lord Chancellor 1913–18; baronet 1916, Baron Shandon 1918.

248   *WIT*, 20 Apr. 1901.

249   Harty, *Musical Times*, 1 Apr. 1920.

250   *Musical Times*, 1 July 1899.

251   *WIT*, 30 Dec. 1899.

252   *WIT*, 10 Feb. 1900.

253   *FJ*, 20 June 1906.

254   *WIT*, 5 Oct. 1901.

255   *WIT*, 30 Dec. 1899.

256   *DE*, 19 Jan. 1907.

257   A proposal for such a school, under the Dublin Libraries Act (1855), had first been mooted by N. Murphy, the Cork MP, in 1876 (NA 1120/1/7).

258   See Turpin, *A School of Art*, 147, 172.

259   The bands of the Working-Men's Club, York Street, St James's, Irish National Foresters, Bricklayers, Dundrum, Inchicore, St Kevin's (Bray), and St Mary's (Rathmines).

260   An article signed 'C.H.O.' (Charles Hubert Oldham) in the *Saturday Herald*, 15 July 1899, pointed out that these were brass and reed bands and that in addition there were numerous brass bands and fife and drum bands to be added to the complement in Dublin and its suburbs.

261   Dublin Corporation minutes, 10 Sep. 1888, item 267.

262   Dublin Corporation minutes, 3 Sep. 1888, item 252.

263   Ibid., item 267.

264   *Saturday Herald*, 15 July 1899.

265   Letter of 15 Oct. 1902 from Dublin Working-Men's Industrial Association (NA 1120/14/2).

266   Letter from Finance and Leases Committee, 28 Oct. 1890 (NA 1120/1/11).

267   DC to RIAM, 29 Mar. 1892 (NA 1120/1/12).

268   Report of Finance and Leases Committee, no. 66 (Dublin Corporation Reports, vol. 2, 447–8).

269   Dublin Corporation minutes, 11 Aug. 1890.

270   Minutes of 24 Sep. 1890 (NA 1120/1/11).

271   Ibid., 1 Oct. 1890.

272   *FJ*, 6 Oct. 1890.

273   Minutes of 13 Apr. 1892 and 30 Oct. 1901 (NA 1120/1/18).

274   In 1873 Murphy, as president of the Royal Cork Institution, had claimed a large part of the credit for obtaining the government grant for the RIAM and had announced his intention of attempting to found schools of music in Cork, Limerick and Belfast by public subscription and inducing the Corporation to make an annual subvention and thus 'to qualify persons with musical talent, taken from the humbler classes, to compete for the scholarships offered by the Irish Academy, and so enable them to proceed to Dublin, and avail of the higher opportunities of musical education available there' (unidentified newspaper article, 5 Nov. 1873).

275   Minutes of 25 Mar. 1891 (NA 1120/1/11).

276   RIAM annual report, 1891.

277   Minutes of 14 Mar. 1894 (NA 1120/1/13).

278   Ibid., 13 Apr. 1892 (NA 1120/1/12).

279   Letter of Finance and Leases Committee, 29 Mar. 1892 (ibid.).

280   *Saturday Herald*, 15 July 1899.

281   Minutes of 7 June 1899 (NA 1120/1/17).

282   *FJ*, 27 Jan. 1902. In 1905 Ireland's Own Band, the winners of the All-Ireland Championship, the Feis Ceoil Challenge Cup and the Grand Prize at the World's Fair in St Louis wrote to the Academy seeking engagements in the parks season. 'We claim to have more past and present pupils of the Municipal School than any band in the City, in fact we could justly call ourselves the Municipal School Band.' (The president, J. Handcock, vice-president, T. Malone, treasurer, J. Maher, and honorary secretary, James Brady, had all been cornet pupils in the eighteen-nineties.) Letter of 5 June 1905 (NA 1120/1/21).

283   Letter from Irwin to C. Grahame Harvey, 8 Nov. 1902 (NA 1120/1/19).

284   Letter from city treasurer to RIAM, 18 July 1902 (NA 1120/1/18).

285   Letter from city treasurer to L. Dix, 7 July 1902 (ibid.).

286   Conroy (d. 1912) was for many years bandmaster of the Dublin Metropolitan Police and formerly in the band of the Royal Welch Fusiliers.

287   Dublin Corporation Reports, 1897, vol. 3, 839, 1898, vol. 3, 923; RIAM Governors' minutes, 1 Dec. and 8 Dec. 1897 (NA 1120/1/16).

288   RIAM annual report, 1899.

289   Minutes of 16 Mar. 1904 (NA 1120/1/20).

290   Letter from RIAM to city treasurer, 6 Apr. 1904 (NA 1120/14/2).

291   Letter from city treasurer to RIAM, 20 Apr. 1904 (NA 1120/1/20).

292   Letter of 14 Apr. 1905 (ibid.).

293   The property of the MSM was listed as '1 Flute in F & case; 1 Concert flute & case; 1 oboe; 1 cornet, mouthpiece lost; 1 B Bombardon; 1 C Bombardon; 1 Valve trombone;

1 french horn & case; 1 B♭ clarinet & case; 2 fifes B♭; 3 side drums, 3 pairs of sticks, 3 slings & 2 cases; 1 cello & case; 13 band stands; 4 instruction cards; 1 Staff notation; 1 music board; 1 Brass music stand; 17 books—oboe scales & exercises, duets for flutes, flauto sinfonia Haydn, trios for flutes, No. 1 andantino con variazioni, the Nightingale, no. 2 nel pianoforte by H. Hill, grand trio by G. Gabrielsky, tutor for clarinet, 3 flute books, tutor for drum, tutor for bombardon, tutor for cornet, tutor for horn; Tenor Saxhorn; bass Baryton.'

294 Letter of 28 June 1905 (NA 1120/1/20).

295 Minutes of 4 Oct. 1905 (NA 1120/1/21).

296 Letters of 19 Oct., 1 Nov. and 11 Dec. 1905 (ibid.). The final ironic twist in the history of the RIAM's involvement with the MSM came in 1912 when, without prior warning, a letter was received from the Technical Education Committee asking if the Governors would 'undertake the conduct of the MSM.' A committee of the Board conferred with their opposite numbers in the Technical Committee, but no further steps were taken. In view of the fact that the Corporation records contain no indication of difficulties in relation to the running of the MSM, we cannot tell why this approach was made.

297 Minutes of 17 and 24 June 1891 (NA 1120/1/12).

298 Letter from Marchant to RIAM, 9 Feb. 1898 (NA 1120/1/16).

299 Nora Ahern, Star of the Sea, Sandymount; Eve Barnewell, St Paul's, Bray; Louisa Baine, Ballina; Charles Byrne, Holy Rosary, Midleton; Francis Breen, Wexford (RC); Maggie Cullen, Rathdrum (RC); May Daly, Cathedral, Tuam; Gerald Dowse, Straffan; Theodore Figgis, Presbyterian Church, Belfast; Katherine Fleming, Ballybrack (RC); Agnes Gillespie, Malahide; Margaret Greene, Howth; George Harrison, St George's, Dublin (see above, p. 497); Thomas Harrison, Rotunda Chapel; Lillie Hessler, Dolphin's Barn (RC); George Hillis, Methodist Church, Clontarf; Joseph Jackson, Greystones; Edith Lyons, Holy Family, Aughrim Street; Emily Manning, Ennis; Annie M'Gahy, St Brigid's Cathedral, Kildare; Annie McGough, St Mary's, Drogheda; Arthur McConnell, Presbyterian Church, Capetown; W. B. Nicholson, Stillorgan; Eve Newell, St Paul's, Glenageary; Arthur Oulton, Christ Church, Kingstown; Leonard Shanahan, Augustinian Church, Thomas Street; May Snow, Augustinian Church, Drogheda; Kathleen Tierney, Church of the Assumption, Dalkey; Judith Warren, St George's, Balbriggan; T. H. Weaving, Presbyterian Church, Rutland Square; Emily West, Rotunda Chapel.

300 Jozé and Marchant to Harvey, 20 Apr. 1905 (NA 1120/3/5).

301 D. Lee to the editors, 1997.

302 RIAM annual report, 1914.

303 *FJ*, 2 Mar. 1895.

304 letter of 11 Apr. 1900 (NA 1120/1/17).

305 Letter of 30 Dec. 1901, addressed from 14 Lansdowne Road, Dublin (NA 1120/1/18).

306 *IT*, 29 June 1899.

307 *IT*, 25 Aug. 1898.

308 The Starkie family in the Academy were the children of the Commissioner of National Education, W. J. M. Starkie—Muriel, Enid, and Walter—and their aunt Ida. Their cousins were the Hoeys, Ruth and Eustace. The Dowses were the children of Richard William Dowse (1849–1920) of 3 Harcourt Street, Dublin: Eleanor (piano), Amy (singing), Gerald (a reluctant organist, assistant at the Chapel Royal), Marie (violin), Bertha (violin), Lilian (cello), Hilda (viola), Nora (cello), Rosalind (violin, a member of the original 2RN orchestra), and Victor (piano), as well as five other sons who were not so musical. The three Alton sisters, Dora, Edith, and Emily, daughters of the provost of TCD, all became teachers at the Leinster School. The sons of Oscar May were Ernest, Oscar, and Albert Victor, the latter becoming the father of Cedric May, who carried on a music business for many years in St Stephen's Green, Dublin (Frederick was not a relation). The Lord family included Annie and her nieces Una and Nancie. The Jephson family included Cecile, Mollie, Dorothy, and Myrrha. The

Pottertons were Kathleen, Robert, and Maude. The Vances (daughters of the minister of the Unitarian Church in St Stephen's Green) were Sophie, Alice, Mary and Edith. For details of the Bloom sisters, see above, p. 532, note 27.

309   *DE*, 25 Nov. 1911.
310   *FJ*, 9 Mar. 1896.
311   Minutes of 11 Apr. 1890 (NA 1120/1/11).
312   *FJ*, 30 Nov. 1895.
313   *FJ*, 7 Jan. 1898.
314   *FJ*, 2 Jan. 1895.
315   *FJ*, 19 Apr. 1898.
316   Apropos his participation in a performance of the Preludes to *Lohengrin* and *Parsifal* (the latter receiving its premiere) before King Ludwig II, Bast told Annie Patterson: 'I had the advantage of being placed to face the famous composer, and could observe him during the whole performance. His personal influence when conducting had a magical effect upon the performers; he carried the whole orchestra with him . . . I do not think a more poetical performance than that of these two preludes could be realised' (*WIT*, 30 June 1900).
317   Ibid.
318   Minutes of 22 June, 19 July and 31 Aug. 1892 (NA 1120/1/12).
319   *Irish Statesman*, 4 Jan. 1930.
320   See Knowlson, *Damned to Fame*, 348–50.
321   *IT*, 1 Nov. 1912.
322   *WIT*, 8 Dec. 1900.
323   26 June 1901 (NA 1120/2/3).
324   *The Strad*, Nov. 1905.
325   Miss Crean to Governors, 25 Jan. 1896 (NA 1120/1/18). We believe that Miss Kohler, who was the daughter of a Belfast professor, may have been the mother of Walter Kohler Beckett, professor of composition at the Academy.
326   Minutes of 24 Nov. 1897 (NA 1120/1/15).
327   Minutes of 7 June 1899 (NA 1120/1/17).
328   *WIT*, 3 Nov. 1900.
329   *IT*, 1 Sep. 1911.
330   She was appointed in 1891, and a declamation class for male voice pupils began that year.
331   *WIT*, 24 Nov. 1900.
332   *Grove I*, 732, 744–5, records that he had published studies, nocturnes, rondos, fantasies, and other works.
333   Minutes of 11 Sep. 1875 (NA 1120/1/7).
334   Minutes of 12 Jan. 1876 (NA 1120/1/7).
335   Minutes of 27 June 1877 (ibid.).
336   Billet to RIAM, 1 July 1878 (NA 1120/1/ibid.).
337   Brady to Billet, 12 July 1878 (ibid.).
338   Billet to Brady, 17 July 1878 (ibid.).
339   Billet to RIAM, 27 Dec. 1888 (NA 1120/1/9).
340   RIAM to Billet, 2 Jan. 1889 (ibid.).
341   Minutes of 9 Oct. 1889 (NA 1120/1/10).
342   Minutes of 19 Oct. 1892 (NA 1120/1/12).
343   Minutes of 8 Jan. 1893 (ibid.).
344   RIAM to CCDB, 20 No. 1893 (NA 1120/1/13).
345   Minutes of 31 Jan. 1894 (ibid.).
346   Billet to Jozé, 9 Feb. 1894 (ibid.).
347   Applications had been received from Mme Marchesi, Signor Visetti, William Shakespeare, — Hearne, and Randal Woodhouse. Minutes of 12 Feb., 9 Apr. and 21 May, 1902 (NA 1120/1/18).
348   *FJ*, 7 Nov. 1902.
349   *Irish Society and Social Review*, 28 Apr. 1906.

350 Woodhouse to RIAM, 18 Nov. 1902. Board of Studies minutes, 25 Nov. 1902 (NA 1120/4/1).
351 Woodhouse to RIAM, 21 Apr. 1903. Board of Studies minutes, 1 May 1903 (NA 1120/4/2).
352 Ibid.
353 NA 1120/3/4.
354 *IT*, 23 Feb. 1911.
355 *IT*, 30 Dec. 1911.
356 Ibid., 4 June 1910.
357 *Irish Society*, 17 Feb. 1912.
358 Ibid., 24 Feb. 1912.
359 Ibid., 9 Mar. 1912.
360 *Evening Telegraph*, 14 May 1912.
361 Ibid., 15 May 1912.
362 Ibid., 16 May 1912.
363 Ibid.
364 *Irish Society*, 30 Sep. 1911.
365 Daly, *Catholic Church Music*, 143.
366 Appendix to sixtieth report, 1893, 331.
367 Thomas Mayne and Charles Dawson—the others being Bishop Donnelly, W. R. Molloy, George Cree, and Jozé.
368 T. Mayne to C. Grahame Harvey, 15 Dec. 1902 (NA 1120/1/19).
369 Minutes of 26 Oct. 1902 (ibid.).
370 Daly, *Catholic Church Music*, 146; although it would not be correct to state that 'Donnelly [was] perhaps unaware of Dublin Corporation's plans for a choral competition.'
371 See Noel Kelly, 'Music in Irish Primary Education, 1831–1922' in *Proceedings of Educational Studies Association Conference, Galway, 1979*.
372 Quoted by McCarthy in 'Music Education', 93.
373 Ibid., 162.
374 Minutes of 17 May 1893 (NA 1120/1/12).
375 Quoted by McCarthy in 'Music Education', 115.
376 Quoted ibid., 11.
377 Ibid., 108.
378 Ibid., 119.
379 *FJ*, 25 June 1902.
380 *FJ*, 3 July 1897.
381 *FJ*, 29 June 1898.
382 Donnelly to Harvey, 21 Dec. 1900 (NA 1120/1/18).
383 Minutes of 5 Oct. 1878 (NA 1120/1/8).
384 See McCarthy, 'Music Education', 151–5, 172–85.
385 Ibid., 158.
386 NA 1120/1/13, 27–35.
387 Minutes of 4 Mar. 1896 (NA 1120/1/14, 160).
388 McCarthy, 'Music Education', 176–7.
389 Ibid., 178.
390 *Irish Music Monthly*, 1 May 1902.
391 From 1890 the Associated Board had been actively promulgating its availability as an examining body and was regarded by H. C. Colles, the historian of the RCM, as 'spread[ing] its influence to the remotest parts of the British Empire' (Colles, *History of the Royal Academy of Music*, 21).
392 A. Fleischmann, 'The outlook of music in Ireland', *Studies*, vol. 24, Mar. 1935. Such protectionism was not limited to the examination system. In 1905 Alderman Cole had attempted to have all purchases of non-Irish manufacture prohibited from the Academy—a procedure that would have made it impossible for the Academy to purchase any pianos—which was diluted as follows: 'Any manufactured article

required by the Board after this date shall be of Irish make, unless in such specified cases as the board may decide to the contrary.' Minutes of 12 Apr. 1905 (NA 1120/1/21).

393   Minutes of 11 Jan. 1893 (NA 1120/1/12).
394   Minutes of 19 Feb. 1902 (NA 1120/1/18).
395   Commissioners of Intermediate Education to RIAM, 27 Mar. 1902 (ibid.).
396   RIAM to Intermediate Education Board, 4 Nov. 1902 (NA 1120/1/19).
397   Minutes of 15 May 1907 (NA 1120/1/21).
398   Brasfort to Board of Studies, 27 Nov. 1889. Board of Studies minutes, 27 Nov. 1889 (NA 1120/4/1).
399   *FJ*, 28 Jan. 1909.
400   *WIT*, 10 Feb. 1900.
401   Minority report, 12 Jan. 1909 (NA 1120/1/22).
402   Letter from Esposito to Harvey, 8 Feb. 1909, and minutes of 10 Feb. 1909 (ibid.).
403   Letter in minutes of 1 Feb. 1911 (ibid.).
404   *FJ*, 26 Jan. 1897.
405   Minutes of 22 Mar. 1911 (NA 1120/1/22).
406   Report by Esposito to Board of Studies, 1 Apr. 1911, in Governors' minutes (NA 1120/1/22).
407   In minutes of 7 Feb. 1911 (ibid.).
408   Minutes of 22 Mar. 1911 (ibid.).
409   Minutes of 29 Mar. 1911 (NA 1120/1/23).
410   Ibid.
411   Minutes of 26 Apr. 1911 (ibid.).
412   Minutes of 3 May 1911 (ibid.).
413   Letter of 9 May 1911 (ibid.).
414   Ibid.
415   Letter of 10 May 1911 (ibid.).
416   Minutes of 11 Nov. 1914 (NA 1120/1/24).
417   Minutes of 21 Feb. and 25 Apr. 1917 (ibid.).
418   Treasury to RIAM, 26 Nov. 1915, letter no. 27546/15 (in minutes of 24 Nov. 1915 (ibid.).
419   Minutes of 1 Dec. 1915.
420   Minutes of 1 Dec. 1915 (ibid.).
421   Letter from town clerk, 7 Dec. 1915 (ibid.).
422   Letter from Treasury, no. 30455/15, minutes of 21 Jan. 1916 (ibid.).
423   We are indebted to Marie O'Neill, 'Sarah Cecilia Harrison: artist and city councillor', *Dublin Historical Record*, vol. 40 (1989), no. 2, for this information.

Chapter 6 (p. 297–321)

I gratefully acknowledge the kind assistance of Theresa Doyle, Dorothy Shiel, Dorothy McAuley and Ciara Higgins in the preparation of this chapter.

1   Minutes of 26 Oct. 1892 (NA 1120/1/12, 102–3).
2   T. H. Weaving, 'Local centre and diploma examinations in music' in Aloys Fleischmann, *Music in Ireland*, 129.
3   Minutes of 31 May 1893 (NA 1120/1/12, 149).
4   Minutes of 8 June 1893 (ibid., 154).
5   Ibid., 161.
6   NA 1120/1/13, 28.
7   Ibid., 51.
8   Ibid., 62.
9   McCarthy, 'Music Education', 128–30. Because of the enclosed nature of some communities it was necessary on occasion to examine the nuns themselves in the convent. In 1931 the Prioress-General of the nuns in Eccles Street refused the offer of a private examination in the Academy in favour of paying a higher rate, of 7

guineas as opposed to 4, for the exam for a Certificate of Proficiency to take place in the convent (minutes of 11 Nov. 1931, NA 1120/1/28).

10 Minutes of 4 Mar. 1896 (NA 1120/1/13, 160).
11 Ibid., 204.
12 Ibid., 220.
13 Ibid., 230.
14 NA 1120/1/27.
15 NA 1120/1/19, 41.
16 NA 1120/1/21, 214.
17 NA 1120/1/22, 45.
18 Ibid., 139.
19 RIAM annual report, 1911.
20 NA 1120/1/22, 215.
21 NA 1120/1/23, 13.
22 RIAM annual report, 1914.
23 RIAM annual report, 1916.
24 Ibid.
25 NA 1120/1/25, 222.
26 RIAM annual report, 1921.
27 Minutes of 23 June 1922 (NA 1120/1/26, 40).
28 T. H. Weaving, 'The local centre examinations' in Dagg, *Centenary Souvenir*, 34.
29 Quoted by McCarthy in 'Music Education', 322.
30 Ibid.
31 RIAM annual report, 1933.
32 Minutes of 14 Jan. 1942 (NA 1120/1/29).
33 In *Music in Ireland*.
34 RIAM annual report, 1959.
35 Minutes of 10 Nov. 1971 (RIAM).
36 *Kilkenny People*, 21 Oct. 1994.
37 *Anglo-Celt*, 3 Nov. 1994.
38 *Tipperary Star*, 19 Nov. 1994.

Intermezzo (p. 322–336)

1 SMU minute book, 1963 (RIAM).
2 In 1913 she left the Academy (succeeded in the theory faculty by John F. Larchet) to join the Quinlan Opera Company. In 1974 the Academy received a bequest of over £1,200 from her estate, enabling it to establish the H. K. Edwards Bursary in her memory (minutes of 25 Sep. 1974, RIAM).
3 Nettie Edwards, 'Early days of the Students' Musical Union. 1905–1913' in Dagg, *Centenary Souvenir*, 38–9.
4 SMU Annual report, 1924 (RIAM).
5 SMU Annual report, 1923 (RIAM).
6 SMU Annual report, 1940 (RIAM).
7 For Joseph Rheinberger see *NG*, vol. 15, 791–2. Rheinberger's music continued to feature: his op. 191b was played on 8 November 1911.
8 For Jenö (Eugen) Hubay see *NG*, vol. 8, 752.
9 *Irish Society*, 15 June 1907.
10 Niels Gade (1817–90), Danish composer, conductor, violinist, educator, and administrator: *NG*, vol. 7, 73–5.
11 Frederick May, 'Memories of the Academy' in Dagg, *Centenary Souvenir*, 50.
12 *DE*, 8 Feb. 1907.
13 See *NG*, vol. 11, 746.
14 *Galway Express*, 4 June 1910.
15 *Irish Society*, June 1910.
16 See *NG*, vol. 1, 283.
17 *Wicklow Newsletter*, 2 Dec. 1911.

18   SMU annual report, 1950 (RIAM).
19   *FJ*, 9 Nov. 1911.
20   *IT*, 3 Mar. 1910.
21   Minutes of 21 Jan. 1912 (NA 1120/1/23).
22   *IT*, 20 Feb. 1913.
23   Dorothy Stokes was in error when, in her own reminiscence, 'Students' Musical Union, 1927–1942' in Dagg, *Centenary Souvenir*, 40, she gives 1927 as the first year for a Gilbert and Sullivan production.
24   Ibid.
25   Charles Osborne, 'Patter and parody', *BBC Music Magazine* (Proms Special), July 1997.
26   SMU annual report, 1936 (RIAM).
27   Minutes of 10 Feb. 1909 (NA 1120/1/22).
28   George Prescott MIIEE was a brother-in-law of Lily Simpson, with whom he had produced several G&S programmes for the SMU; it is therefore most unlikely that he would have had the intentions alleged in this incident.
29   Minutes of 12 and 26 Mar. 1930 (NA 1120/1/28).
30   SMU annual report 1934 (RIAM).
31   Published by CE Editions, 1923.
32   'Early English keyboard music played on a Dettmar square piano kindly lent by Mrs Egersdorff'.
33   Dorothy Stokes, 'Students' Musical Union, 1927–1942'. She was deceiving herself about the numbers taking part: the most numerous outing saw twenty hikers, but the average was probably between twelve and fifteen.
34   SMU scrapbook (RIAM). The participants on the inaugural hike were Joan White, Letty Keegan, May Connell, Francis Coleman, Una Kenny, Joan Lea, Nancie Lord, May Lord, Paddy Kirwan, Frank Kelly, Edith Ladley, Ethel Owens, Frances Drapes, and Dorothy Stokes.
35   3 November 1943, performed by the composer with Carmel Lang, Hazel de Courcey, Máire Larchet, and Betty Sullivan.
36   Charles Acton to SMU, 30 Jan. 1955 (RIAM).
37   Annie Keelan to SMU, 4 Feb. 1955 (RIAM).
38   SMU minutes, 8 Apr. 1954 (RIAM).
39   SMU annual report, 1934 (RIAM).
40   SMU annual report 1935 (RIAM).
41   SMU AGM minutes, 26 June 1935 (RIAM).
42   SMU annual report, 1939 (RIAM).
43   SMU annual report, 1945 (RIAM).
44   In his capacity as music critic of the *Irish Times*.
45   SMU annual report, 1966 (RIAM).
46   SMU annual report, 1945 (RIAM).
47   In fact a vote in favour of the proposal that the committee consist only of students was carried by 23 votes to 4, with many abstentions (SMU AGM minutes, 8 Jan. 1969, RIAM).
48   SMU minutes, 8 Jan. 1968 (RIAM).
49   SMU annual report, 1969 (RIAM).
50   SMU annual report, 1970 (RIAM).
51   *IT*, 29 Jan. 1968.
52   Minutes of 28 May 1975 (RIAM).
53   SMU minutes, 14 Jan. 1983 (RIAM).
54   SMU annual report, 1961 (RIAM).
55   The St Francis Xavier Hall, Upper Sherrard Street, Dublin, was the home of the RTÉSO from 1963 to 1981 and was the venue for twice-weekly 'invitation concerts' for most of that time.
56   SMU minutes, 8 Nov. 1969 (RIAM).

Chapter 7 (p. 337–390)

1   NA 1120/1/25.
2   NA 1120/1/26.
3   Buckland, *Irish Unionism*, 288.
4   Turpin, *A School of Art*, 233.
5   Hutchinson, *The Dynamics of Cultural Nationalism*, 197.
6   Edith Oldham, 'The Eisteddfod and the Feis Ceoil', *New Ireland Review*, 359–60.
7   Minutes of 22 Mar. 1922 (NA 1120/1/26).
8   23 June 1937 (NA 1120/1/29).
9   Lupton to Jeffares, 14 June 1933 (NA 1120/1/28).
10 Marie McCarthy in MEND, phase II, Interim Report, 61.
11 Viani, *Towards Music*.
12 Corder, *History of the Royal Academy of Music*, 95.
13 Starkie, *Recent Reforms in Irish Education*, Dublin: Blackie 1902, 31.
14 Kennedy, *Dreams and Responsibilities*, 22.
15 Cairns and Richards, *Writing Ireland*, 15.
16 Aloys Fleischmann, 'The outlook of music in Ireland', *Studies*, vol. 24 (1935), 821–30.
17 Aloys Fleischmann, 'Composition and the folk idiom', *Ireland Today*, 1 (Nov. 1936), 44.
18 Stanford, *Interludes*, 2–3.
19 Letter to Hubert Silvestre, 10 Apr. 1959, in Silvestre, 'Mario Esposito', 9–10 (our translation).
20 See Brown, *Ireland: A Social and Cultural History*, 250.
21 Éamonn Ó Gallchobhair, *Ireland Today*, 1 (Sep. 1936), 4.
22 The successful candidate was Timothy Walshe, at that time a members' Governor. A previous unsuccessful proposal to elect Bax a vice-president had been made on 9 April 1941, following the death of Sir Hamilton Harty, when Bax was proposed by Mrs W. J. M. Starkie, Bruce Flegg by Maud Aiken, Lady Harty by Edith French Boxwell, Walter Starkie by T. S. C. Dagg, and Denis McCullough (who was elected) by Liam Paul. Minutes of 13 June 1951 (NA 1120/1/29).
23 *Ireland Today*, 2 (Mar. 1937), 3.
24 Ibid.
25 Charles Acton, 'Towards an Irish music', *Envoy*, 3 (10 Sep. 1950), 76.
26 Denis Donoghue, 'The future of Irish music', *Studies*, 44 (1955), 113.
27 'The Irish musical fallacy', *Irish Statesman*, 2 (19 Apr. 1924), 175.
28 'Music and the nation', *Dublin Magazine*, vol. 6 (1935), 50–6.
29 Ibid.
30 Denis Donoghue, 'The future of Irish music', *Studies*, 1955.
31 Aaron Copland, *Music and Imagination*, Cambridge (Mass.): Harvard University Press 1952. Radio Éireann, from its earliest days, and especially during Fachtna Ó hAnnracháin's term as director of music (1948–61), gave significant support to Irish composers, by commissioning original works and arrangements for both the Symphony and Light Orchestras and for the Radio Éireann Singers.
32 Frederick May, 'Music and the nation'.
33 *Irish Press*, 23 Oct. 1934.
34 Rowsome to RIAM, 13 Oct. 1904 (NA 1120/14/2).
35 Turpin, *A School of Art*, 275.
36 Robinson, *Palette and Plough*, 136–7.
37 Ibid., 140.
38 Ibid., 112, 124. The Special Collections of the Academy library, and its establishment on a proper basis by means of the Monteagle donation, is described in chapter 10. The work of Dermod O'Brien—Monteagle's cousin—in putting the library in place needs to be recorded, however. It is not generally realised that the concerts by Jelly d'Aranyi in London and Dublin, and O'Brien's own fund-raising efforts among friends, succeeded in attracting only £500 of the £1,200 needed (a total of £24,000 today) and that he himself made up the balance.
39 See Arnold, *Mainie Jellett*, 187, 206.

40   Information to the editors from Noel Dagg.

41   He also performed an identical but larger function by building the Irish Hockey Union headquarters in Londonbridge Road, Dublin.

42   Minutes of 22 Sep. 1926: 'Letter received from Lucius O'Callaghan, Director, NGI, re collection of pictures of the late Sir Hugh Lane. On the motion of Dermod O'Brien . . . it was agreed that a similar resolution be sent to Lord Glenavy, Chairman of the Senate, and to Mr. William Cosgrave, President of the Dáil' (NA 1120/1/27).

43   Hutchinson, *The Dynamics of Cultural Nationalism*, 314.

44   Quoted by Kennedy in *Dreams and Responsibilities*, 128.

45   Ibid., 78.

46   Ibid., 104.

47   *IT*, 27 Jan. 1968.

48   25 Apr. 1928 (NA 1120/1/27).

49   25 May 1927 (ibid.). On 8 October 1930, George Prescott wrote to the Board as follows: 'During my last week as "visiting Governor" . . . the Secretary [Sealy Jeffares] reported to me that . . . certain papers and at least one book were gone, or at any rate were not in the Academy, also that he had been informed that on the morning after the dismissal of the late Secretary [Gladys Tuite], that lady came to the Academy at an early hour, before the arrival of others, and proceeded to burn a large quantity of papers, so large that . . . the debris spread half way across the room, and that further a large quantity was brought to the furnace outside and there burned.' This report was subsequently contradicted by Sir John Irwin (NA 1120/13/2).

50   Minutes of 8 Oct. 1930 (NA 1120/1/28).

51   Minutes of 28 June 1927 (NA 1120/1/27).

52   The minutes of 4 June 1902 record that 'as a special mark of our appreciation of Signor Esposito's service & in consequence of his long continued illness a cheque for £26.5.0 to be placed at Signor Esposito's disposal' (NA 1120/1/18).

53   Minutes of 5 Nov. 1924 (NA 1120/1/26).

54   Esposito to Harty, 2 Nov. 1924 (copy by courtesy of the Marshall family).

55   In addition to his colleagues, fellow-Governors and pupils it includes Harry Boland, James Cousins, A. P. Graves, R. C. Orpen RHA, Sarah Purser and Louis Claud Purser, Miss Bonaparte-Wyse, and the Clergy Daughters' School.

56   R. I. Best papers, NLI.

57   *IT*, 30 May 1928.

58   Visiting Governors' book, 15 Oct. 1929 (NA 1120/13/2).

59   *IT*, 19 Dec. 1929. Jean du Chastain returned to Dublin at least once, playing Liszt's First Concerto with the Philharmonic Orchestra in 1930.

60   Minutes of 8 Jan. 1930 (NA 1120/1/28).

61   M. Esposito to A. Yoakley (Chaloner).

62   Vera Esposito to Harty, 19 and 27 Nov. 1929 (copy by courtesy of the Marshall family).

63   In 1944 Esposito's remains were removed to the nearby cemetery of Santa Maria all' Antela to join those of his wife, who died that year. No trace can be found today of the inscription on his original grave. (Information by courtesy of Dr Angelo Barone.)

64   BMus 1915, MusD 1917, LRIAM 1923.

65   The minutes of 8 January 1930 record the Governors' inability to give financial assistance to one of Esposito's sisters after his death.

66   Ryan, 'Nationalism and Music in Ireland', 350.

67   In a letter to Harty, 2 Nov. 1924 (copy by courtesy of the Marshall family).

68   Máire Larchet won an Esposito Scholarship in 1932 and the Caroline Reilly Exhibition and the Coulson Exhibition and Coulson Academy Scholarship for violin in 1935 and 1936, respectively. Síle Larchet won the Esposito Scholarship in 1934 and the Coulson Exhibition and Coulson Academy Scholarship for cello in 1935 and 1936, respectively, and the Shandon Scholarship for piano in 1936. Gerald Larchet (later an amateur horn player and a structural engineer) won the Esposito Memorial Scholarship for piano in 1937.

69   J. F. Larchet, 'A plea for music' in W. Fitzgerald, *The Voice of Ireland*, 1923, 508.

70 J. F. Larchet, 'Dublin's contribution to music', *Dublin Civic Week Handbook* (1927).
71 Minutes of 2 Feb. 1921 (NA 1120/1/25).
72 Minutes of 15 Jan. 1930 (NA 1120/1/28).
73 See Cooke, *A Musical Journey*, 20.
74 Studied at the RAM, where she led the orchestra; winner of five gold medals at Feis Ceoil.
75 11 Feb. 1930 (NA 1120/1/28).
76 Draft Board of Studies minutes (NA 1120/4/9).
77 While this dispute was taking place, the Governors adopted a curriculum for the fellowship exam, against the advice of the Board of Studies, which pointed out that 'it is unusual to have two diplomas obtainable by examination as the higher depreciates the value of the lower' (Board of Governors' minutes, 21 May 1930, and Board of Studies minutes, 20 May 1930)—a state of affairs subsequently superseded by the dual diplomas of ARIAM and LRIAM, which were introduced by Larchet himself as a way of introducing an intermediate qualification between the then highest grade examination, grade VII, and the LRIAM. Minutes of 27 Oct. 1937 (NA 1120/1/27).
78 Minutes of 26 Mar. 1930 (NA 1120/1/28).
79 Minutes of 2 Dec. 1925 (NA 1120/1/27).
80 As recently as 1995 a proposal to limit the number of teaching staff who may be elected Governors was defeated after strenuous representations to the CCDB by three Governors—the present editors and the current director.
81 Board of Studies minutes, 6 July 1931 (NA 1120/4/4).
82 *Musical Times*, 1 Dec. 1900.
83 Quoted by Andrew Marsh [John O'Donovan] in 'If music be the food of promises', *Irish Press*, 16 Dec. 1970.
84 *DE*, 12 Feb. 1912.
85 *Evening Herald*, 21 Feb. 1912.
86 *IT*, 26 Mar. 1913.
87 Robinson, *Palette and Plough*, 124.
88 Minutes of 29 Mar. 1916 (NA 1120/1/24).
89 Minutes of 9 Oct. 1918 (NA 1120/1/25).
90 Minutes of 21 Feb. 1920 (ibid.).
91 Minutes of 7 Nov. 1923, 19 Mar. 1924, 1 Apr. 1925, 23 Feb. and 13 Apr. 1927, and 11 Nov. 1935 (NA 1120/1/26, 27, 29).
92 Minutes of 24 June 1942. By 20 September only £209 had been received in subscriptions (NA 1120/1/29).
93 Cf. Kennedy, *Dreams and Responsibilities*, 42, 58.
94 Minutes of 10 Nov. 1943 (NA 1120/1/29).
95 On 25 September 1940 it was decided to build an air-raid shelter in the basement of 37 Westland Row, at a cost of £112. Other wartime inconveniences included paper shortages and the need to black out the Academy windows.
96 Minutes of 14 Feb. 1945 (RIAM).
97 *IT*, 1 Dec. 1939.
98 *IT*, 7 Dec. 1944.
99 Minutes of 1 Sep. 1948 (RIAM).
100 Cooke, *A Musical Journey*, 68.
101 Minutes of 24 Jan. 1923 (NA 1120/1/26).
102 Minutes of 29 Sep. 1926 (NA 1120/1/27).
103 The original ICO was formed by János Fürst in 1962 and refounded as the New Irish Chamber Orchestra in 1970, with many of the original members. The present-day ICO is a wholly new foundation with a new basis of professional management and funding and is based in Limerick.
104 Minutes of 9 Jan. 1946 (RIAM).
105 Minutes of 25 June 1947 (RIAM).
106 Minutes of 26 Sep. 1951 (RIAM).
107 Verbal communication from Eimear Ó Broin.

108   Quoted by Kennedy in *Dreams and Responsibilities*, 41–3.
109   The programme for the opening night of 2RN included the No. 1 Army Band (conductor, Fritz Brase) in a selection 'Dedicated to Dr J. F. Larchet'; violin solos played by Arthur Darley; a harp solo by Annie Fagan; and piano solos by Dina Copeman. A typical evening schedule from a slightly later period (13 Mar. 1937) was: 5:30, Garda Síochána Band; 6:25, The Home Doctor (talk); 6:35, Sgáthán na nGaedheal; 6:45, News; 7:00, Aughrim Slopes Céilí Band; 8:00 Symphony Concert, conducted by George Hewson, with soloists Dorothy Stokes and Alice Bell: Overture, In der Natur (Dvořák), 'New World' Symphony (Dvořák), Concerto for Two Pianos, K365 (Mozart), Legend in C (Dvořák), Capriccio Italien (Tchaikovsky), Irish Melody 'The Maid of Mourne Shore', arranged by Hewson.
110   Irwin to RIAM, 17 Feb. 1926 (NA 1120/1/27).
111   Rooney to Jeffares, 15 Jan. 1934 (NA 1120/1/29).
112   Minutes of 24 Oct. 1945 (RIAM). This was not the first time in recent years that such a project had been envisaged. In 1936 a committee had been established, consisting of Larchet, Nora Sidford Fannin, M. W. O'Reilly, and M. Fitzpatrick, to discuss 'the advisability of increasing the Professorial staff . . . a new scheme for the administration of the Academy . . . [which] should include an arrangement for the linking up of the Municipal School of Music . . . and security of tenure and a pension scheme for staff.' Among the issues considered was whether the Academy's title should be changed to the National Music Academy of Ireland. The committee met from 9 July to 9 December 1936 but does not appear to have issued a report or made recommendations (manuscript minutes kept by Larchet, RIAM).
113   Minutes of 21 Dec. 1938 (NA 1120/1/29).
114   Minutes of 21 May 1947 (RIAM).
115   Minutes of 31 Jan. and 14 Feb. 1940 (NA 1120/1/29).
116   In 1939 President Hyde had been approached to see if he would consent to act as president of the Academy, but he felt that it was doubtful whether the Presidency of Ireland embraced the same powers as the Lord Lieutenant. The matter was referred to the Academy's solicitors and to the CCDB, without resolution (minutes of 29 Mar. 1939, NA 1120/1/29).
117   Miley and Miley to CCDB, n.d.
118   RIAM to CCDB, 11 Sep. 1948 (CCDB).
119   Letter of John O'Donovan, n.d.
120   Minutes of 27 Oct. and 10 Nov. 1948 (RIAM).
121   Minutes of 21 Feb. 1940 (NA 1120/1/29).
122   Minutes of 6 Mar. 1940 (ibid.).
123   In 1920 it had been proposed (unsuccessfully) that 'for the purpose of establishing closer relations between the Governors and the Professors, pupils and those interested in the welfare of the Academy, and stimulating their mutual interests, that each Governor shall attend in the Academy in continuous rotation for an hour each day for a week, to receive and report to the Governors complaints or suggestions on all matters relating to the welfare or progress of the Academy, and that the name of the attending Governor be posted in a prominent position in the Academy.' Minutes of 8 Dec. 1920 (NA 1120/1/25). Later, in 1929, Governors (other than professors) were arranged on an alphabetical rota to inspect the Academy during a two-week period. Minutes of 6 Mar. 1929 (NA 1120/1/25). This ceased in 1932 but was re-introduced intermittently as a way of reducing the amount of committee work.
124   Minutes of 9 June 1954 (RIAM).
125   Statement by Miss M. Furlong to meeting of 16 June 1954 (RIAM).
126   Minutes of 18 June 1954 (RIAM).
127   Minutes of 25 May 1955 (RIAM).
128   Minutes of 20 Feb. 1952 (RIAM).
129   Minutes of 30 Apr. 1952 (RIAM).
130   Verbal communication from Eimear Ó Broin, 21 Oct. 1997. Eimear Ó Broin also informed the editors that, in his recollection, his father had been engaged in

negotiations towards a merger of the two bodies before 1948 but that J. F. Larchet had been amenable to such a move only on condition that he became the director of the resulting conservatoire, a development that León Ó Broin was unwilling to countenance. See note 112 above.

131 Minutes of 10 Sep. and 19 Nov. 1952 (RIAM).
132 Letter to the editors, 12 Sep. 1996.
133 Minutes of 17 Sep. 1958 (RIAM).
134 Minutes of 9 July 1952 (RIAM).
135 Minutes of 8 Sep. and 10 Nov. 1954 (RIAM).
136 Minutes of 27 May and 9 Nov. 1955 (RIAM).
137 In a letter to the editors (22 May 1997) Jaroslav Vaneček writes: 'My wife and I . . . have no regrets, as we always believed that love and art don't stop at the border. You remember Joseph Plunkett's "I See His Blood upon the Rose"? We saw His blood in every note we have been teaching . . . I never look back in bitterness. All art is bridge-building.'
138 Minutes of 29 Feb. 1956 (RIAM).
139 Minutes of 27 Jan. 1960 (RIAM).
140 Minutes of 13 Oct. 1954 (RIAM).
141 D. McCullough to RIAM, 27 Oct. 1954 (RIAM).
142 1883–1968. Born in Belfast, son of a Fenian publican; worked with Bulmer Hobson and Seán Mac Diarmada in building the republican movement in the north. He eventually came to Dublin and founded a music business, which in 1970 merged with that of Pigott. In 1976 McCullough-Pigott Ltd established an entrance scholarship to the RIAM in his memory.
143 Minutes of 8 June 1955 (RIAM).
144 Cooke, *A Musical Journey*, 24.
145 Minutes of 22 Oct. 1935 (NA 1120/1/29).
146 The celebratory concert was performed by Audrey Chisholm, Renée Flynn and Violet Byrne, Gilbert Berg, Max Thöner, Anthony Hughes, Erich Eisenbrand and Rhona Marshall, André Prieur and Mercedes Bolger, Valerie Walker and Michele Incenzo, with the ubiquitous Dorothy Stokes as accompanist.
147 Minutes of 8 Jan. 1958 (RIAM).
148 Minutes of 12 Nov. 1958 (RIAM).
149 Meeting of 9 Feb. 1962 (RIAM).
150 *Dáil Debates*, 14 Mar. 1963, col. 1391.
151 Minutes of 14 Feb. 1962 (RIAM).
152 Minutes of 27 June 1962 (RIAM).
153 Minutes of 10 Oct. 1962 (RIAM).
154 Minutes of 14 Nov. 1962 (RIAM).
155 Minutes of 28 Nov. 1962 (RIAM).
156 Minutes of 30 Jan. 1963 (RIAM).
157 *Dáil Debates*, 19 Nov. 1975, col. 1530.
158 Of which there were two: NIHE, Limerick (now the University of Limerick), and NIHE, Dublin (the former Albert College, now Dublin City University).
159 'Report of meeting with the Minister for Education, 12 May 1976' (RIAM).
160 'Submission to the Department of An Taoiseach', n.d. (RIAM).
161 Despite sporadic attempts since the beginning of the twentieth century, the post of librarian had never been full-time or even continuous, a situation that prevailed until 1992 with the appointment of Philip Shields, whose assessment of the Academy's Special Collections constitutes chap. 10 of the present history. Unfortunately this neglect led to the disappearance of archival material from the Academy, which makes it at times difficult to document certain aspects of that history.
162 Minutes of 29 June 1977 (RIAM).
163 Minutes of 13 Jan. 1982 (RIAM).
164 Minutes of 20 Jan. 1982 (RIAM).
165 Although as far back as 1939 it was decided that each faculty should be regarded as a committee, under the chairmanship of its senior professor, to report on relevant matters to the Board of Studies.

166 RIAM to Department of Education, 1994.
167 RIAM to Arts Council, Feb. 1994.
168 This was envisaged in the Arts Council's report *The Place of the Arts in Irish Education* in 1979.
169 S. Heaney, 26 Feb. 1997 (RIAM).

Chapter 8 (p. 400–428)

1 After study in France under Pixis, Fétis, and Kalkbrenner, Osborne settled in London in 1843, where he became active with the Philharmonic Society and the Royal Academy of Music. O'Leary, who studied with Hauptmann, Plaidy and Rietz in Leipzig between 1847 and 1852, made his home in London thereafter, taking lessons with Cipriani Potter and Sterndale Bennett. He became a professor at the Royal Academy of Music in 1856 and at the National Training School on its inception in 1876.
2 Lamentable though this predicament might have been, the state of music in Ireland by mid-century was considerably better than it had been for many years. Although continuity was maintained in the Church of Ireland under Lord Mornington, the Roseingraves, Richard Woodward, and Sir John Stevenson, the professorship of music at Trinity College had become derelict on Lord Mornington's resignation in 1774 and was only taken up again by John Smith in 1845.
3 T. S. C. Dagg, 'The Academy, 1856–1956' in *Centenary Souvenir*, 5.
4 Stewart to Brady, 11 Mar. 1878; Brady to Stewart, 14 Mar. 1878 (NA 1120/1/7).
5 Ibid.
6 Vignoles, *Memoir of Sir Robert P. Stewart*; Culwick, *The Works of Sir Robert Stewart*.
7 See Stanford, *Pages from an Unwritten Diary*, 48–51.
8 Ibid., 50–1.
9 Diary of Sir Hubert Parry, 5 July 1892, Shulbrede Priory, Haslemere, Surrey.
10 Though Stewart attended the Schumann Festivals in Germany, according to Stanford he never appreciated Schumann's music or Brahms'. He did, however, become a fervent Wagnerite after the Bayreuth Festival in 1876 and again after hearing Angelo Neumann's production of *The Ring* in London in 1882 (Stanford, *Pages from an Unwritten Diary*, 50).
11 This is certainly evident from Stewart's two published organ works, the Concert Fantasia in D minor (pub. 1887) and the Introduction and Fugue of 1894.
12 See Stanford, *Pages from an Unwritten Diary*, 49.
13 See Vignoles, *Memoir of Sir Robert P. Stewart*, 204–5.
14 See Annie Patterson, 'Eminent Dublin musicians: Dr James Culwick', *WIT*, 4 Aug. 1900.
15 Parry's Piano Quartet (pub. Novello) dates from 1879. Stanford's Piano Quartet No. 1 in F, which was performed at least twice by the RIAM Ensemble (Griffith, Lauer, Rudersdorf, and Esposito) at the Royal Dublin Society and was therefore almost certainly known to Culwick, dates from the same year (pub. 1882). Mackenzie's Piano Quartet, also in E flat, was published by Kahnt of Leipzig in 1875.
16 Culwick's First Organ Sonata in D, op. 3, was dedicated to his friend Arthur H. Mann of King's College, Cambridge; the Second Organ Sonata in D minor, op. 19, was dedicated to Stewart.
17 Charles Wood won the Morley Open Scholarship in Composition in 1883. After leaving the RCM he went to Cambridge, first as an organ scholar at Selwyn College and then to Gonville and Caius, where he became the first musician to be made a fellow of the college. Wood's career thereafter concentrated principally on the university. Though much of his output consisted of music for the Anglican liturgy, he was also drawn to Irish traditional melody. His interest in native Irish music manifested itself in several collections of arrangements in collaboration with A. P. Graves, P. J. McCall and Pádraic Gregory, as well as in a number of instrumental works, namely *Patrick Sarsfield* (symphonic variations on an Irish air), the String Quartets Nos. 3 (1911–12) and 4 (1912), the Variations on an Irish Folk Song (*c.* 1917), and an unfinished opera *Pat in Fairyland*, to a libretto by J. Todhunter.

18   Stanford, *Pages from an Unwritten Diary*, 217–18.

19   Wood was appointed to teach harmony at the RCM in 1888.

20   Letter from Sir George Grove to Edith Oldham, 2 July 1891 (RCM).

21   Grove to Oldham, 21 Feb. 1892 (RCM).

22   See Dibble, *Hubert H. Parry*, 317.

23   Stanford drew his inspiration from the exploits of Carl Rosa, whose own opera company had promoted works in English. Moreover, his third opera, *The Canterbury Pilgrims* (1884), had formed part of an extraordinary series of indigenous operas (by Mackenzie, Goring Thomas and Corder) at Drury Lane in the eighteen-eighties, which Rosa undertook with varying degrees of financial success. His untimely death did not bring about the demise of the opera company, but it did severely temper the eagerness to commission native opera.

24   Stanford's surviving scrapbook collection (the so-called autograph book) of letters written to him by illustrious personages (RCM ms. 4253) provides abundant evidence of this personality trait.

25   It is no coincidence that in seeking material for his 'Irish' cantata, *Phaudrig Crohoore*, and *opéra comique, Shamus O'Brien*, he should have looked to one of the *Dublin University Magazine's* most illustrious editors (and owners), Sheridan Le Fanu.

26   See the letter from Moeran to Aloys Fleischmann, 10 Feb. 1937. Moeran became a pupil of Stanford's in 1913 and, with his own Irish roots, would undoubtedly have witnessed his teacher's support for Ulster.

27   British Library ms. 45850B, which contains 'Ulster' (f. 2), also contains two Ulster military marches (f. 3r and 3v), the first of which appears in the Fourth Rhapsody.

28   It is also undoubtedly significant that Stanford chose to withdraw *Shamus O'Brien* in 1914, when he thought the plot—the escape of the hero, Shamus, a rebel (during the aftermath of the Rebellion of 1798)—might be politically misconstrued by both nationalists and unionists. His death in March 1924 enabled the work to be revived in Dublin by Joseph O'Mara under the auspices of 'the new Aonach Tailteann' on 11 August 1924 at the Theatre Royal, Dublin.

29   See Geoffrey Bush's introduction to 'C. Villiers Stanford: Songs', *Musica Britannica*, 52 (London: Stainer and Bell 1986), xvi.

30   Letter from Stanford to F. J. H. Jenkinson, 1 Jan. 1892 (Cambridge University Library ms. 6463).

31   This case is made in Annie Patterson's article 'Native music and musicians in Ireland' in *The Music Student*, vol. 9 (1917), 219–21, in which Stanford and Graves are cited as prime movers in the setting up of the Feis. This is also confirmed in the correspondence between Stanford and Graves (see NLI ms. 17,797), in which the basic organisation of the Feis is discussed. Patterson also makes reference to Stanford's advisory role in her article 'The Feis Ceoil festival' (*WIT*, 1 May 1901, 3) and to his consent to act temporarily as president of the movement in the early stages. In fact Stanford held this temporary office for only a year, after which he retired after the Feis committee refused to endorse his suggestion of importing a professional orchestra (such as the Hallé) for the festival (see 'The Feis: local, or international?', *Musical News*, 18 July 1896, 57).

32   White, *The Keeper's Recital*, 109–10.

33   Joseph Ryan, 'Nationalism and Irish music' in *Irish Musical Studies, 3* (1995), 109.

34   An indication of this language-oriented policy of de-Anglicisation within the administrative infrastructure of music education is clear from Hardebeck's attack on the examinations organised by English bodies. 'Mr. Hardebeck announced that all professors [at the Cork Municipal School of Music] will have to learn the Irish language, as next year all lessons would have to be given in Irish, and "all those swindling hugger-mugger examinations of English bodies would be done away with." Those musical Englishmen had done more harm to them than anything else. They would make this school a board of Irish examinations for the whole Irish people.' (*Irish News*, 5 Sep. 1919).

35   White, *The Keeper's Recital*, 109–10.

36   For a full list of Esposito's compositions see Aiello [Mario Esposito], *Al Musicista Michele Esposito*, 71 ff.

37   Wills, 'Evaluation of the Influence of Michele Esposito'.

38   Esposito's Cello Sonata, op. 4, gained a prize from the ISM in 1899, the String Quartet No. 3, op. 60, was first in the Concorso Internazionale della Reale Accademia Filarmonica di Bologna in 1906, and his Cello Sonata, op. 46, won first prize in the Grande Concorso Internazionale della Società Musicale *Nouvelle di Parigi* in 1907.

39   This choice of repertoire was also reflected in an edition, *Early Italian Keyboard Music*, prepared by Esposito (1906) for Oliver Ditson's 'Musician's Library', which included pieces by Durante, Frescobaldi, Galuppi, Marcello, Martini, Paradies, and Alessandro Scarlatti.

40   According to the *Irish Times*, the inspiration for this idea stemmed from a recent performance in Dublin of Dvořák's 'New World' Symphony, which was, so the journalist believed, 'founded on negro melodies' (see Harty, *Early Memories*, n. 25, 29).

41   Harty also declared in his unfinished memoirs (*Early Memories*) that his relationship with Esposito quickly became one of friendship, which lasted until Esposito's death in 1929. Moreover, the links with his mentor continued by way of Esposito's company, CE Music Publishers, which published Harty's Violin Concerto, the Fantasy Scenes (from an Eastern Romance) and the Piano Concerto. Philip Hammond has also argued that Harty's predilection as a conductor for the works of Busoni, Pizzetti, Casella and Respighi originates from his friendship with Esposito (Philip Hammond, 'The Hallé years and after' in Greer, *Hamilton Harty*, 43).

42   Harty, *Early Memories*, 27–8. In 1896 Harty removed from Belfast to Dublin, where he spent four years before settling in London in 1900.

43   Harty won Feis prizes with the following compositions: Violin Sonata (1899); String Quartet in F (1900); Two Fantasiestücke for Piano Trio (1901); String Quartet in A (1902); Romance and Scherzo for Cello and Piano (1903); Irish Symphony (1904).

44   See *IT*, 19 May 1904, and *Musical Times*, 45 (1904), 396.

45   That Harty considered opportunity in Ireland at the turn of the century to be insufficient is evident from comments he made in an article for the *Musical Times*: 'The Irish musical student is greatly facile, and still more greatly indolent. He reaches a certain point and then drifts. Ireland offers him no scope; yet as a rule, he is reluctant to leave home' (see 'Hamilton Harty', *Musical Times*, 61 (1920), 228).

46   Before Harty's Whitman essays, Whitman's poetry had already enjoyed something of a vogue among British composers such as Stanford (Elegiac Ode and Songs of Faith), Charles Wood (Dirge for Two Veterans), Delius (Sea Drift), Holst (the Whitman Overture and The Mystic Trumpeter) and Vaughan Williams (Toward the Unknown Region and A Sea Symphony).

47   Harty's Dublin variations form part of a vital tradition in that genre, including Hurlstone's Variations on an Original Theme (1896), Parry's Symphonic Variations (1897), Stanford's Variations upon an English Theme 'Down among the Dead Men' (1898), Elgar's Enigma Variations (1899), Hurlstone's Variations on a Hungarian Air (1899) and Variations on a Swedish Air (1904), Coleridge-Taylor's Variations on an African Air (1906), and (perhaps significantly for Harty) Norman O'Neill's Theme and Variations on an Irish Air (1910).

48   See Arnold Bax, Foreword to Aloys Fleischmann, *Music in Ireland*, iv.

49   See Bax, *Farewell My Youth*, 41–8.

50   The Cloths of Heaven, composed in March 1916, was included in the first version of *The Curlew* in 1920. It was, however, excluded from the 1922 version and was subsequently reworked to Arthur Symons' poem 'The Sick Heart'.

51   Moeran's two most substantial song compositions were the Seven Poems of James Joyce (1929) and the Six Poems of Séamus O'Sullivan (1944), though he did produce a setting of Yeats's 'A Dream of Death' in 1925.

52   White, *The Keeper's Recital*, chap. 5.

53   See Ryan, 'Nationalism and Music', 109.

54   See J. Larchet, 'Music in the universities' in Aloys Fleischmann, *Music in Ireland*, 18.

55   See Arnold Bax, Foreword to Aloys Fleischmann, *Music in Ireland*, iv.

56   See W. H. Grattan Flood, 'Larchet, John F.' in *Grove III*, vol. 3, 90–1. For examples of Larchet's arrangements see Caoineadh na hÓige: Lament for Youth (two Irish melodies arr. for small orchestra) (1939), Two Characteristic Pieces (based on

traditional Irish airs) for string orchestra and xylophone (1952), and Máirseáil de Shórt Meidhréiseach: Marci Quazi [*sic*] Scherzo (1955).

57   An overview of this inter-war context can be gained from 'First performances of works by Irish composers, 1935–1941' in Aloys Fleischmann, *Music in Ireland*, 170–6.
58   Ibid., 169.
59   'Irish composers and foreign education: a study of influences' in Devine and White, *Irish Musical Studies, 4,* 271–84.
60   See the discussion in *Ireland To-day*, the *Bell* and other contemporary interdisciplinary journals from the mid-thirties to the early fifties, documented in my study *Die Musik Irlands im 20. Jahrhundert*, 55–63.
61   See the memorandum of the Department of Finance to the Department of the President, 21 May 1937, in Kennedy, *Dreams and Responsibilities*, 43.
62   A good introduction to Boydell's use of this technique is Gareth Cox, 'Octatonicism in the string quartets of Brian Boydell' in Devine and White, *Irish Musical Studies, 4*, 263–70.
63   Boydell's words, quoted by Michael Dungan in 'Everything except team games and horse-racing', *New Music News*, Feb. 1997.
64   'Ceathrar', a CD also containing Boydell's String Quartet No. 2 (1957), John Kinsella's Quartet No. 3 (1977), and Ian Wilson's Winter's Edge (1992) (Chandos, CHAN 9295, 1994).
65   In the 'Irish Composers Series' on the Marco Polo label.
66   Cf. Raymond Deane, 'Caterer and comforter?: the composer in modern Ireland', *Irish Review*, spring 1990, 1–4.

Chapter 9 (p. 435–469)

1   I am indebted to Hylda Beckett, Anna Brioscú, Annette Perry, Seán Lynch, Paul Deegan, James Cavanagh and the former lady superintendent of the RIAM, Margaret Furlong, for their help in preparing this chapter.
2   RIAM annual report, 1894.
3   RIAM annual report, 1913.
4   RIAM annual report, 1937.
5   Minutes of Board of Studies, 19 Mar. 1890 (NA 1120/4/1).
6   Ibid., 11 June 1890.
7   This tended to be an essay on the life and work of a composer.
8   Academy students were later obliged to obtain the permission of their teachers also, a regulation still in force today.
9   Notice of Diplomas and Certificates of Proficiency, 1899.
10   Ibid.
11   Board of Studies, 1 May 1903 (NA 1120/4/2).
12   Ibid., 17 Feb. 1905. Rather confusingly, L. Edward Steele reported in 1911 that the Governors had 'arranged a scheme of certificates whereby all who compete at the annual competitive examinations of the pupils of all grades in all subjects, receive, irrespective of any limits of age, certificates of proficiency. Those who secure 75 per cent. are granted a certificate for having "Passed with Honours", while those who obtain 65 per cent. are awarded a certificate for having "Passed the Examination." This wise regulation ought to act as a stimulus' (RIAM annual report, 1910, 17).
13   Board of Studies, 15 Dec. 1905 (NA 1120/4/2).
14   Ibid., 4 June 1915 (NA 1120/4/3).
15   Minutes of a special meeting of Routine Committee, 20 Jan. 1911 (NA 1120/3/8).
16   Board of Studies, 30 Nov. 1928 (NA 1120/4/4).
17   Board of Studies, 28 Feb. 1933 (NA 1120/4/5).
18   RIAM annual report, 1937.
19   RIAM annual report, 1943.
20   Notice of Rules and Regulations . . . 1899.
21   Board of Studies, 3 Dec. 1929 and amendment to Blue Scheme of 10 Apr. 1929 (NA 1120/4/4).

22   Board of Studies, 5 May 1975 (RIAM).
23   Ibid., 16 Dec. 1910 (NA 1120/4/2).
24   RIAM annual report, 1920.
25   RIAM annual report, 1929.
26   Board of Studies, 4 Feb. 1930 (NA 1120/4/5).
27   Ibid., 20 May 1930.
28   Ibid., 4 Dec. 1978, 10 Dec. 1979, 11 Feb. 1980 (RIAM).
29   TCD, in association with the RIAM and DIT College of Music, *Bachelor in Music Education Course Handbook*, 1996, 5.
30   In 1899, for example, it was recommended by the Routine Committee of the Academy that the age limits be revised so as to provide scholarships for female singers up to the age of 25, for male singers up to the age of 26, for cello students between the ages of 16 and 27, and for those students studying the double bass a Coulson scholarship for competition up to and including the age of 30 (minutes of the Routine Committee, 15 June 1899, NA 1120/3/2).
31   The Actors' Church Union at one time also provided a scholarship for singing, no longer awarded, and donated a cup for singers also, which was first awarded in 1973.
32   IAM Minutes, 26 Mar. 1862 (NA 1120/1/3).
33   Ibid. 12 Feb. and 17 Dec. 1862, 27 May 1863.
34   RIAM annual report, 1879.
35   RIAM annual report, 1878.
36   RIAM annual report, 1897. In this area, however, written accounts are slightly confusing. The minutes of the Examinations Committee of the period clearly regard many of the Vandeleur Scholarships as being of first-grade (i.e. senior grade) status, as in, for example, the minutes of 15 June 1899, when consideration is given to altering the age limits.
37   Dagg, *Centenary Souvenir*, 8; RIAM annual report, 1877.
38   RIAM annual report, 1878.
39   RIAM annual report, 1887.
40   All internal scholarships still require a pass in a set theoretical and aural examination held before the examinations, before candidates are allowed to proceed to the scholarship examination itself. For a brief period in the nineteen-eighties and early nineties, qualifying examinations in technical requirements were abolished, as they also formed part of the scholarship examination (Vandeleur Academy in all subjects, and Vandeleur for violin excepted); at the time of writing the scholarship system is once more under review.
41   Board of Studies, 27 Jan. 1931 (NA 1120/4/5).
42   RIAM annual report, 1882.
43   Board of Studies, 11 Oct. 1932 (NA 1120/4/5).
44   RIAM annual report, 1917. 'Ear training is the most important thing of all. From the very start, try hard to recognise notes and keys. Bells, the window-pane, the cuckoo: listen to the sounds they make . . . Make the effort to play easy pieces cleanly and beautifully; that's better than giving a second-rate performance of a difficult piece . . . You must get to the stage where you can understand music simply by looking at it . . . Showy passages fade as time passes; technique is only of value when it serves a higher purpose. Don't ever use your technique to show off. When playing a composition, try to create the effect the composer had in mind; that's all you need to do. Anything else is distortion . . . You must get to know all the great works by the great masters, through and through. Amongst your comrades, seek out the ones who know more than you do . . . Sing willingly in choirs, especially the middle parts. This will make you musical . . . What does being musical mean? You are musical if you have music not just in your fingers, but also in your head and heart . . . Listen assiduously to all folk-songs; they are a treasury of beautiful melodies. Become aware of the characteristics of the various nationalities . . . Be an industrious student of life, and also of other arts and sciences. The laws of morality are also those of art.' From *Album für die Jugend*. (Editors' note.)
45   RIAM annual report, 1930.

46   RIAM annual report, 1936.
47   This award commemorates one of the principal conductors of the Radio Éireann Orchestra (later RTÉSO) and is awarded to the senior student who achieves the highest mark at the annual scholarship examinations.
48   RIAM annual report, 1905.
49   RIAM annual report, 1916.
50   RIAM annual report, 1876.
51   RIAM annual report, 1887.
52   RIAM annual report, 1945.
53   RIAM annual report, 1963.
54   RIAM annual report, 1967.
55   Dagg, *Centenary Souvenir*, 42.
56   RIAM annual report, 1878.
57   RIAM annual report, 1881.
58   RIAM annual report, 1887.
59   RIAM annual report, 1891.
60   RIAM annual report, 1896.
61   RIAM annual report, 1897.
62   RIAM annual report, 1917.
63   RIAM annual report, 1946.
64   RIAM annual report, 1894; see also Grindle, *Irish Cathedral Music*.
65   RIAM annual report, 1925.
66   RIAM annual report, 1929.
67   Walter Beckett's relations include the playwright Samuel Beckett and the musicians John, Edward and Brian Beckett.
68   RIAM annual report, 1963.
69   Minutes of Routine Committee, 28 Nov. 1902 (NA 1120/4/3).
70   RIAM annual report, 1899.
71   RIAM annual report, 1888.
72   RIAM annual report, 1959.
73   Board of Studies, 21 June 1976 (RIAM).
74   McCarthy, 'Music Education', 162–3.
75   RIAM annual report, 1893.
76   RIAM annual report, 1890.
77   RIAM annual report, 1898.
78   RIAM annual report, 1900.
79   I am indebted to Deirdre Kelleher FRIAM for this information.
80   Feis Ceoil syllabus, 1997.

Chapter 10 (p. 476–488)

1   Typescript of address given by O'Brien, *c.* 1941 (RIAM).
2   Minutes of 9 May 1877 (NA 1120/1/7).
3   For more information on this see McCartney, 'The Guitar Collection of J. A. Hudleston'.
4   RIAM annual report, 1929, 15.
5   Typescript of address given by O'Brien, *c.* 1941 (RIAM).
6   RIAM annual report, 1934, 18.
7   Letter from O'Brien to the Minister for Industry and Commerce, 11 Oct. 1937 (RIAM). The concert, given on 17 December 1934, comprised works by Bach (Sonata in E minor), Brahms (Sonata in G, op. 78) and Beethoven (Sonata in F sharp, op. 78) and was reported in the *Times* two days later.
8   Maurice Headlam to O'Brien, 27 Nov. 1934 (RIAM).
9   Minutes of 17 June 1936 (NA 1120/1/29).
10   Minutes of 7 Oct. and 4 Nov. 1936 (NA 1120/2/25) and 23 June 1937 (NA 1120/2/26).
11   Minutes of 27 Sep. and 25 Oct. 1939 (NA 1120/2/26).

12   RIAM annual reports, 1939–51.
13   *IT*, 27 Feb. 1962, 8.
14   Hogan, *Anglo-Irish Music*, 80.
15   Stephenson, 'The Antient Concert Rooms'.
16   Minutes of 23 Oct. 1872 (NA 1120/1/6).
17   These stamps indicate a rather curious change in orthography around 1848, from *Ancient Concerts* to *Antient Concerts*, as if to underline the antiquarian nature of their interests. It is a matter of speculation how much the Antient Concerts Society was influenced by the London series of Concerts of Ancient (Antient) Music; certainly the Dublin society mixed classics such as Handel and Purcell with contemporary English oratorio music, and Mendelssohn was very popular in the repertoire.
18   *FJ*, 14 June 1849.
19   *FJ*, 18 Feb. 1848, 24 Feb. 1849, 25 Apr. 1851, 17 Feb. 1854.
20   *Grove III*, vol. 4, 408.
21   Stephenson, 'The Antient Concert Rooms', 5.
22   Walmisley's godfather and teacher was Thomas Atwood, a pupil of Mozart and the person who did most to popularise Mozart's music in England.
23   MacDonnell, *Book of Dates,* 13–14. The reliability of this source has been called into question.
24   Hogan, *Anglo-Irish Music*, 76.
25   Datable from a watermark on the flyleaf.
26   Hogan, *Anglo-Irish Music*, 220, 224.
27   Stanley Sadie, 'The wind music of J. C. Bach', *Music and Letters*, 37 (1956), 107–17.
28   The style of engraving is virtually identical to that of the J. C. Bach pieces, suggesting the same publisher.
29   *NG*, vol. 11, 132.
30   Humphries and Smith, *Music Publishing in the British Isles*, 50.
31   *Dublin Magazine*, Feb. 1820, 150. It should perhaps be pointed out that the reviewer was assessing these symphonies from the part-books alone, without the aid of a score.
32   Brian Boydell, 'Music, 1700–1850' in *New History of Ireland*, vol. 4, 601. Credit must go to Michael McCartney for his discovery of these works in the Anacreontic Society's Collection.
33   The address of Rhames indicates the period 1776–1806.
34   Erwin Doernberg, 'Adalbert Gyrowetz', *Music and Letters*, 44 (1963), 23.
35   It is of course possible that these belonged to the Anacreontic Society of Belfast, which performed glees.
36   Most probably Monteagle's grandfather, Thomas Spring Rice (1790–1866), first Baron Monteagle, who was Chancellor of the Exchequer 1835–39 and a leading Whig politician in the eighteen-thirties and forties.
37   Burney is credited with having been the first to recognise the 'Viennese School' by linking the names of Haydn, Beethoven, and Mozart. Compared with Hawkins, who produced a similarly monumental history in the same period (considered to be more scholarly and less opinionated), Burney was seen as a stylist of the first order, and contemporary critics were fulsome in their praise. Burney's reputation declined shortly after his death, and subsequent historians have drawn attention to his erratic opinions, such as his dismissal of J. S. Bach's work and his inattention to the works of Mozart in the *History*. For fuller discussion see Grant, *Dr Burney as Historian and Critic of Music*.
38   Minutes of 9 May 1877 (NA 1120/1/7).
39   McCartney, 'The Guitar Collection of J. A. Hudleston'.
40   Minutes of 29 May 1929 (NA 1120/2/22).
41   Watton, 'Michele Esposito'.
42   Aiello [Mario Esposito], *Al Musicista Michele Esposito*.
43   RIAM annual report, 1919.
44   A sketch for the final choral fugue in this work displays a highly academic approach to composition: all modulations, episodes and canons are labelled as such on the sketch.
45   Minutes of 16 May 1872 (NA 1120/1/6).

46   Stewart and Jozé, *Five Irish Melodies.*
47   Cruise and Papini, *Two Irish Airs.*
48   Walsh, *Opera in Dublin*, 241–4.
49   *Favourite Songs in the Opera 'Orfeo'.*
50   Walsh, *Opera in Dublin*, 131–3, 152–4.
51   See *New Grove Dictionary of Opera*, vol. 1, 1007.
52   Bunting, *General Collection of the Ancient Music of Ireland.*
53   Haydn, *Six Quatuors à Deux Violons.*
54   Donated by Emily Knox in 1946.
55   *FJ*, 7 Dec. 1854.
56   Bernarr Rainbow, 'Johann Bernhard Logier and the chiroplast controversy', *Musical Times*, vol. 131 (1990), 193–6.

Chapter 11 (p. 495–510)

This chapter owes its origins to an article for the programme of the first GPA Dublin International Piano Competition, held from 9 to 17 May 1988, and was subsequently republished in the *Irish Arts Review*, 1988. In preparing it I am deeply indebted to Joan Trimble FRIAM, a gold-mine of scholarly and historical knowledge, without whose kind personal contributions it could not have been written. I also owe much to the *Centenary Souvenir, 1856–1956,* published by the Academy, and to advice and gleanings from my colleague in the present endeavour, Richard Pine.

1   See above, p. 153–4.
2   See Paul Dekeyser's article on Kalkbrenner in *NG*, vol. 9, 777–9; also Pigott, *The Life and Music of John Field*, 100 et seq.
3   See Pigott, *The Life and Music of John Field.*
4   Nicholas Temperley, 'John Field', *NG*, vol. 6, 534–9.
5   For a fascinating discussion of Field's influence on Chopin's compositions see Branson, *John Field and Chopin.*
6   Quoted by Nicholas Temperley in 'John Field', *NG*, vol. 6, 534–9.
7   See Hogan, *Anglo-Irish Music*, 169 et seq.
8   Hogan, *Anglo-Irish Music*, 176 et seq.
9   *FJ*, 31 May 1848.
10   See *Grove III* and Jean Mongrédien, *NG*, vol. 14, 2.
11   Unidentified newspaper report, 1874.
12   RIAM minutes, 30 Oct. 1872; letter from Osborne to MacDonnell, 25 Oct. 1872 (NA 1120/1/6).
13   Letter from Brady to Yeo, 10 Mar. 1881 (NA 1120/1/8).
14   See *Grove III* and Nicholas Temperley, *NG*, vol. 20, 175–8; also Anon., *William Vincent Wallace.*
15   Stanford, *Pages from an Unwritten Diary*, 56.
16   Ibid., 58.
17   Ibid., 74.
18   Ibid.
19   *WIT*, 10 Nov. 1900.
20   Ibid.
21   The editors are indebted to Quarry's grandson, Prof. Jeffrey Switzer of Sidney Sussex College, Cambridge, for this information. Quarry's son Francis fought in the Boer War, then (aged 23) studied at Leipzig and became a concert pianist, but his career was permanently interrupted by the 1914–18 war. Quarry's daughter, Ruth, also studied privately in Leipzig with Teichmuller.
22   Stanford, *Pages from an Unwritten Diary*, 75.
23   Greene, *Charles Villiers Stanford*, xx.
24   Minutes of 1 Feb. 1882 (NA 1120/1/8).
25   *FJ*, 29 Oct. 1896.
26   *SNL*, 10 Apr. 1856.

27   *Grove III*; Hugh Macdonald, *NG*, vol. 8, 655–6; Davies, *César Franck and His Circle*.
28   *Grove V*, vol. 6, 186.
29   His brother Eugenio was the singularly uninspired conductor of Mamontov's Opera in St Petersburg, thanks to whom Rachmaninoff had a disastrous rehearsal of Glinka's *A Life for the Tsar* and a very successful performance conducting Chaliapin in *Boris Godunov* (Bertensson and Leyds, *Sergei Rachmaninov*, 77, 79, 82—but on p. 77 'Michele' should read 'Eugenio').
30   RIAM annual report, 1917.
31   See Watton, 'Michele Esposito', 42–52, 128–34.
32   George Grove to Edith Oldham, 1 July 1892 (RCM).
33   Ibid.
34   George Grove to Edith Oldham, 2 Mar. 1893.
35   *Grove III*; cf. Young, *George Grove*, 244–5.
36   See Greer, *Hamilton Harty*.
37   Between the world wars Kreisler was the author of a collection of 'Classical Manuscripts', pieces in eighteenth-century style allegedly by Pugnani, Scarlatti and other then forgotten baroque composers, such as the Praeludium and Allegro ('Pugnani-Kreisler'), which became staple encores of the violin repertoire, the correct authorship of which was detected and uncovered by Ernest Newman.
38   Áine Nic Thighearna FRIAM, *Sgálaí agus Cordaí Imdhealuighthe*, Dublin: Stationery Office 1936.
39   Scholes, *Oxford Companion to Music*, sub 'Rumba'.
40   See Harrison, *Catalogue of Contemporary Irish Music*.
41   T. S. C. Dagg, *Centenary Souvenir*, 28.
42   Ibid., 47; cf. also 44 et seq.
43   Enid Starkie, *A Lady's Child*, 237.
44   According to George Grove (letter to Edith Oldham, 22 July 1892), in 1883 or 1884 Margaret O'Hea and he had discussed the prospects of her working at the RCM.
45   See above, p. 179.
46   In 1926 she was the second student to broadcast on the infant Dublin Broadcasting Station (subsequently RÉ and RTÉ) (the first was Dina Copeman).
47   *IT*, unidentified report, 1910.
48   I have seen some of these programmes, thanks to the kindness of his daughter, Mrs Norah Morris.
49   Tilly Fleischmann, *Aspects of the Liszt Tradition*.
50   Ibid.
51   *IT*, 27 Sep. 1984. See also obituary by Charles Acton, *IT*, 17 Sep. 1984.
52   *Grove III*, vol. 1, 553.
53   On 12 Feb. 1937.
54   He also wrote very persuasively and perceptively on 'The concert pianist in Ireland' in Aloys Fleischmann, *Music in Ireland*.
55   In his capacity as president of the University Philosophical Society, TCD.
56   Wilson Lyle (in *A Dictionary of Pianists*) states that Lynch 'was reported having performed in a series of all Beethoven symphonies.' As the reader will see, the report was accurate.
57   *IT*, 23 Nov. 1976.
58   Harrison, *Music in Mediaeval Britain*; for his bibliography see *NG*, vol. 8, 254.

Chapter 12 (p. 513–516)

1   IAM minutes (NA 1120/1/1).
2   Report read at AGM, 10 Mar. 1869 (NA 1120/1/5).
3   Thackeray, *The Irish Sketch-Book, 1842*, London: Chapman and Hall 1843, 11.
4   Simpson Xavier Horwath Consulting, *A Strategic Vision for the Irish Music Industry*, Dublin 1994.
5   *Journal of the Ivernian Society*, vol. 2 (1909), 42.

Bibliography

Aho, K., Jalkanen, P., Salmenhaara, E., and Virtamo, K., *Finnish Music*, Helsinki: Otava 1996.

Aiello, Giuseppe Lauro [Mario Esposito], *Al Musicista Michele Esposito nel Primo Centenario della Nascita: Omaggio della Sua Città*, Castellammare di Stabia 1955.

Akenson, D. H., *The Irish Education Experiment*, London: Routledge and Kegan Paul 1970.

Akenson, D. H., *A Mirror to Kathleen's Face*, Montréal: McGill-Queen's University Press 1975.

Anon., *Recollections of Dublin Castle and of Dublin Society by a Native*, London: Chatto and Windus 1902.

Anon., *William Vincent Wallace, 1812–1865*, Dublin: Glasnevin Musical Society 1965.

Anon., *Richard Doyle and His Family*, London: Victoria and Albert Museum 1983.

Arnold, Bruce, *Mainie Jellett and the Modern Movement in Ireland*, New Haven (Conn.): Yale University Press 1991.

Barker, F., et al. (eds.), *1848: The Sociology of Literature*, Colchester: University of Essex 1978.

Barrett, W. A., *Balfe: His Life and Work*, London: Remington 1882.

Bartók Béla, *Essays*, London: Faber and Faber 1976.

Bax, Arnold, *Farewell My Youth*, London: Longmans Green 1943.

Beckett, J. C., *The Making of Modern Ireland, 1603–1923*, London: Faber and Faber 1966.

Benson, C., *The Place of the Arts in Irish Education*, Dublin: Arts Council 1979.

Bertensson, Sergei, and Leyds, Jan, *Sergei Rachmaninov*, London: Allen and Unwin 1965.

Boyce, D. G., *Nineteenth-Century Ireland: The Search for Stability*, Dublin: Gill and Macmillan 1990.

Boydell, Brian (ed.), *Four Centuries of Music in Ireland*, London: BBC 1979, 23.

Boydell, Brian, *A Dublin Musical Calendar, 1700–1760*, Dublin: Irish Academic Press 1988.

Boydell, Brian, *Rotunda Music in Eighteenth-Century Dublin*, Dublin: Irish Academic Press 1992.

Boylan, Patricia, *All Cultured People: A History of the United Arts Club, Dublin*, Gerrards Cross: Colin Smythe 1988.

Branson, David, *John Field and Chopin*, London: Barrie and Jenkins 1972.

Brennan, Robert, *Allegiance*, Dublin: Browne and Nolan 1950.

Brown, J., and Stratton, S., *British Musical Biography*, Birmingham 1897.

Brown, Terence, *Ireland: A Social and Cultural History, 1922–79*, London: Fontana 1981.

Buckland, Patrick, *Irish Unionism, 1: The Anglo-Irish and the New Ireland, 1886–1922*, Dublin: Gill and Macmillan 1973.

Bunting, Edward, *A General Collection of the Ancient Music of Ireland Arranged for the Pianoforte . . . To Which Is Prefixed a Historical and Critical Dissertation on the Egyptian, British and Irish Harp*, London: Clementi and Company [1809].

Cairns, D., and Richards, S., *Writing Ireland: Colonialism, Nationalism and Culture*, Manchester: Manchester University Press 1988.

Carlyle, Jane Welsh (ed. J. A. Froude), *Letters and Memorials of Jane Welsh Carlyle*, London 1883.

Carpenter, A. (ed.), *My Uncle John: Edward Stephens's Life of J. M. Synge*, London: Oxford University Press 1974.

Cazalet, W. W., *The History of the Royal Academy of Music*, London: T. Bosworth 1854.

Cohen, Ada, *International Encyclopaedia of Women Composers*, London: Books and Music 1987.

Colles, H. C., *History of the Royal Academy of Music*, London: Macmillan 1933.

Collins, Derek, 'Music in Dublin, 1792–1842', PhD thesis, QUB, forthcoming.

Coogan, Tim Pat (ed.), *Ireland and the Arts*, London: Quartet Books n.d.

Cooke, J., *A Musical Journey, 1890–1993*, Dublin: Dublin Institute of Technology 1994.

Cooke, Jim, *Ireland's Premier Coachbuilder: John Hutton and Sons, Dublin, 1779–1925*, privately printed, n.d.

Coolahan, John, *Irish Education: History and Structure*, Dublin: Institute of Public Administration 1981.

Corder, Frederick, *History of the Royal Academy of Music*, London: RAM 1922.

Croker, T. Crofton, *Researches in the South of Ireland*, London: John Murray 1824.

Culwick, James, *Distinctive Characteristics of Ancient Irish Melody*, Dublin: Ponsonby 1897.

Culwick, James, 'Sir Robert Stewart', text of a lecture delivered at Ripon, 21 July 1900, privately printed.

Culwick, James, *The Works of Sir Robert Stewart*, Dublin: Dublin University Press 1902.

Dagg, T. S. C. (ed.), *Centenary Souvenir*, Dublin: RIAM 1956.

Daly, Kieran, *Catholic Church Music in Ireland, 1878–1903: The Cecilian Reform Movement*, Dublin: Four Courts Press 1995.

Daly, Mary, *Dublin: The Deposed Capital: A Social and Economic History, 1860–1914*, Cork: Cork University Press 1985.

Davies, Laurence, *César Franck and His Circle*, London: Barrie and Jenkins 1970.

Davis, Thomas, *Prose Writings: Essays on Ireland* (ed. T. W. Rolleston), 1890.

Deane, Séamus, *Strange Country: Modernity and Nationhood in Irish Writing since 1790*, Oxford: Clarendon Press 1997.

de Courcy, Catherine, *The Foundation of the National Gallery of Ireland*, Dublin: National Gallery of Ireland, 1985.

Devine, P., and White, Harry (eds.), *Irish Musical Studies, 4*, Dublin: Four Courts Press 1996.

Dibble, Jeremy, *Hubert H. Parry: His Life and Music*, Oxford: Clarendon Press 1992.

Drudy, P. J. (ed.), *Ireland and Britain since 1922*, Cambridge: Cambridge University Press 1986.

Dunleavy, J. E., and Dunleavy, G. W., *Douglas Hyde, a Maker of Modern Ireland*, Berkeley: University of California Press 1991.

Ehrlich, C., *The Piano: A History* (revised ed.), Oxford: Clarendon Press 1990.

Ellmann, Richard (ed.), *Selected Letters of James Joyce*, London: Faber and Faber 1975.

Ellmann, Richard, *James Joyce*, New York: Oxford University Press 1982.

Farmer, H. G., *A History of Music in Scotland*, London: Hinrichsen 1947.

Fleischmann, Aloys (ed.), *Music in Ireland: A Symposium*, Cork: Cork University Press 1952.

Fleischmann, Tilly (edited by Michael O'Neill), *Aspects of the Liszt Tradition*, Cork: Adare Press 1986.

Flood, W. H. Grattan, *A History of Irish Music*, Dublin: Browne and Nolan 1905.

Flood, W. H. Grattan, *Introductory Sketch of Irish Musical History*, London: Reeves 1922.

Foster, R. F., *W. B. Yeats: A Life*, vol. 1, Oxford: Oxford University Press 1997.

Frigyes Sándor (ed.), *Musical Education in Hungary*, London: Boosey and Hawkes, 1969.

Gavan Duffy, Charles, *Young Ireland: A Fragment of Irish History, 1840–45*, London: Fisher Unwin 1896.

Gillen, Gerard, and White, Harry (eds.), *Irish Musical Studies, 1: Musicology in Ireland*, Dublin: Irish Academic Press 1990.

Gillen, Gerard, and White, Harry (eds.), *Irish Musical Studies, 3: Music and Irish Cultural History*, Dublin: Irish Academic Press 1995.

Glancy, Maria, *The Rise and Fall of the Dubedats of Dublin*, Dublin n.d.

Goldstrom, J. M., and Clarkson, L. A. (eds.), *Irish Population, Economy and Society*, Oxford: Clarendon Press 1981.

Grant, Kerry, *Dr Burney as Historian and Critic of Music*, Epping: Bowker 1983.

Graves, A. P., *To Return to All That*, London: Cape 1930.

Greene, David, and Stephens, Edward, *J. M. Synge, 1871–1909*, New York: Macmillan 1959.

Greene, Harry Plunket, *Charles Villiers Stanford*, London: Edward Arnold 1935.

Greer, David (ed.), *Hamilton Harty*, Belfast: Blackstaff Press 1979.

Grindle, W. Harry, *Irish Cathedral Music: A History of Music at the Cathedrals of the Church of Ireland*, Belfast: Institute of Irish Studies 1989.

Groocock, Joseph, *A General Survey of Music in the Republic of Ireland*, Dublin: Forás Éireann 1961.

Gwynn, Denis, *Young Ireland and 1848*, Cork: Cork University Press 1949.

Hardiman, James, *Irish Minstrelsy*, London: Robins 1831.

Harris, Bernard, and Freyer, Grattan, *The Achievement of Seán Ó Riada*, Ballina: Irish Humanities Centre 1981.

Harrison, Bernard (ed.), *Catalogue of Contemporary Irish Music*, Dublin: Irish Composers' Centre 1982.

Harrison, Frank Llewellyn, *Music in Mediaeval Britain*, London: Routledge and Kegan Paul 1958.

Harty, Hamilton, *Early Memories* (ed. D. Greer), Belfast: Queen's University 1979.

Heneghan, F., *The Feis Ceoil*, Dublin: City of Dublin VEC 1988.

Herron, D., *Deaf Ears?: A Report on the Provision of Music Education in Irish Schools*, Dublin: Arts Council 1985.

Hogan, Ita, *Anglo-Irish Music, 1780–1830*, Cork: Cork University Press 1966.

Hogan, Robert, and Kilroy, James, *The Abbey Theatre, vol. 2: Laying the Foundations, 1902–1904*, Dublin: Dolmen Press 1976.

Hogan, Robert, and Kilroy, James, *The Abbey Theatre, vol. 3: The Years of Synge, 1905– 1909*, Dublin: Dolmen Press 1976.

Hondre, E., *Le Conservatoire de Paris*, Paris: Conservatoire de Musique 1995.

Humphries, Charles, and Smith, William, *Music Publishing in the British Isles from the Beginning until the Middle of the Nineteenth Century*, New York: Barnes and Noble 1970.

Hutchinson, John, *The Dynamics of Cultural Nationalism: The Gaelic Revival and the Creation of the Irish Nation State*, London: Allen and Unwin 1987.

Hyman, Louis, *The Jews of Ireland: From Earliest Times to the Year 1910*, Shannon: Irish University Press 1972.

Inglis, Brian, *The Freedom of the Press in Ireland, 1784–1841*, London: Faber and Faber 1954.

Joyce, P. W., *A Social History of Ireland* (2nd ed.), Dublin: Gill 1913, vol. 1.

Kearney, Richard, *Postnationalist Ireland: Politics, Culture, Philosophy*, London: Routledge 1996.

Kelly, J. S., 'The Political, Intellectual and Social Background to the Irish Literary Revival to 1901', PhD thesis, University of Cambridge, 1971.

Kennedy, Brian, *Dreams and Responsibilities: The State and the Arts in Independent Ireland*, Dublin: Arts Council, n.d.

Kenny, Colum, *Tristram Kennedy and the Revival of Irish Legal Training, 1835–1885*, Dublin: Irish Academic Press, in association with the Irish Legal History Society, 1996.

Kiberd, Declan, *Inventing Ireland*, London: Cape 1995.

Klein, Axel, *Die Musik Irlands im 20. Jahrhundert*, Hildesheim: Georg Olms Verlag 1996.

Knowlson, James, *Damned to Fame: The Life of Samuel Beckett*, London: Bloomsbury 1996.

Lee, Joseph, *The Modernisation of Irish Society, 1848–1918*, Dublin: Gill and Macmillan 1973.

Leerssen, Joep, *Remembrance and Imagination: Patterns in the Historical and Literary Representation of Ireland in the Nineteenth Century*, Cork: Cork University Press, and Field Day 1996.

Levey, R. M., and O'Rorke, J., *Annals of the Theatre Royal, Dublin*, Dublin: Dollard 1880.

Litton, Frank (ed.), *Unequal Achievement: The Irish Experience, 1957–1982*, Dublin: Institute of Public Administration 1982.

Lyle, Wilson, *A Dictionary of Pianists*, London: Hale 1985.

Lyons, F. S. L., *Ireland since the Famine*, London: Fontana 1973.

Lyons, F. S. L., *Culture and Anarchy in Ireland, 1890–1939*, Oxford: Clarendon 1979.

Lyons, R. D., *Intellectual Resources of Ireland*, Dublin: 1873.

McCarthy, Dermot, *St Mary's Pro-Cathedral* (Irish Heritage series, 60), Dublin: Eason 1988.

McCarthy, Marie, 'Music Education and the Quest for Cultural Identity in Ireland, 1831–1989', PhD thesis, University of Michigan, 1990.

McCartney, Michael, 'The Guitar Collection of J. A. Hudleston', PhD Thesis, Queen's University, Belfast, forthcoming.

MacDonnell, H., et al., *The Story of the Strollers*, Dublin: privately printed 1997.

MacDonnell, Hercules, *A Book of Dates, Operatic, Dramatic and Musical*, Dublin: privately printed 1878.

McDowell, R. B., 'Ireland on the eve of the Famine' in R. Dudley Edwards and T. Desmond Williams (eds.), *The Great Famine: Studies in Irish History, 1845–52*, New York: New York University Press 1956, and Dublin: Lilliput Press 1994.

McElligott, T. J., *Education in Ireland*, Dublin: Institute of Public Administration 1966.

Mansergh, Nicholas, *The Irish Question*, London: Allen and Unwin 1975.

Mitchison, Rosalind (ed.), *The Roots of Nationalism: Studies in Northern Europe*, Edinburgh: John Donald 1980.

Molony, John, *A Soul Came Into Ireland: Thomas Davis, 1814–1845*, Dublin: Geography Publications 1995.

Murphy, John A., *The College: A History of Queen's/ University College, 1845–1995*, Cork: Cork University Press 1995.

Namier, Lewis, *1848: The Revolution of the Intellectuals*, London: Oxford University Press 1946.

Namier, Lewis, '1848: seed-plot of history' in *Avenues of History*, London: Hamish Hamilton 1952.

Namier, Lewis, *Personalities and Powers*, London: Hamish Hamilton 1955.

Nettel, J., *The Orchestra in England*, London: Cape 1946.

New Grove Dictionary of Opera, London: Macmillan 1992.

New History of Ireland, vol. 4, Oxford: Oxford University Press 1986.

New History of Ireland, vol. 6, Oxford: Oxford University Press 1996.

O'Connor, Anne, and Parkes, Susan, *Gladly Learn and Gladly Teach: A History of Alexandra College and School, Dublin, 1866–1966*, Dublin: Blackwater Press 1983.

O'Connor, Ulick, *Oliver St John Gogarty*, London: Cape 1964.

O'Donovan, John, *G. B. Shaw*, Dublin: Gill and Macmillan 1983.

O'Hegarty, P. S., *A History of Ireland under the Union, 1801 to 1922*, London: Methuen 1952.

O'Sullivan, Mary, 'The Legacy of Michele Esposito', MA thesis, St Patrick's College, Maynooth, 1991.

Petrie, George (ed. Charles Villiers Stanford), *The Complete Collection of Irish Music*, London: Boosey 1902–05.

The 'PIANO' Report: Report to the Minister for Arts, Culture and the Gaeltacht on the Provision and Institutional Arrangements Now for Orchestras and Ensembles, Dublin: Department of Arts, Culture and the Gaeltacht 1996.

Pigott, Patrick, *The Life and Music of John Field, 1782–1837*, London: Faber and Faber 1973.

Pine, Richard, *Music in Ireland, 1848–1998*, Dublin: Mercier Press 1998.

Rainbow, Bernarr, *The Land Without Music*, London: Novello 1967.

Reddy, L. G., *Count Plunkett: The Man and His Message*, Dublin n.d.

Richards, J. M., *Provision for the Arts: Report of an Enquiry Carried Out During 1974–75 throughout the Twenty-Six Counties of the Republic of Ireland*, Dublin: An Chomhairle Ealaíon 1976.

Robinson, Lennox, *Bryan Cooper*, London: Constable 1931.

Robinson, Lennox, *Palette and Plough: A Pen-and-Ink Drawing of Dermod O'Brien PRHA*, Dublin: Browne and Nolan 1948.

Rogers, B., 'An Irish school of music', *New Ireland Review*, 13 (Mar.–Aug. 1900).

Ryan, Joseph, 'Nationalism and Music in Ireland', PhD thesis, National University of Ireland, 1991.

Saxe Wyndham, H. (ed.), *Who's Who in Music*, 1915.

Scholes, Percy, *The Oxford Companion to Music*, London: Oxford University Press, many editions.

Shaw, Henry, *New City Pictorial Directory, 1850*, Dublin: Henry Shaw 1850 (facsimile reprint as *The Dublin Pictorial Guide and Directory of 1850*, Belfast: Friar's Bush Press 1988).

Sheehy, J., *The Rediscovery of Ireland's Past: The Celtic Revival, 1830–1930*, London: Thames and Hudson 1980.

Silvestre, Hubert, 'Mario Esposito: brève évocation de sa vie et de son œuvre', *Studi Medievali*, 1989, 7.

Smith, Cornelius, and Share, Bernard (eds.), *Whigs on the Green: The Stephen's Green Club, 1840–1990*, Dublin: Gill and Macmillan 1990.

Stanford, Charles Villiers, *Interludes*, London: Murray 1922.

Stanford, Charles Villiers, *Pages from an Unwritten Diary*, London: Edward Arnold 1914.

Stanford, Charles Villiers, *Studies and Memories*, London: Constable 1908.

Stanford, W. B., and McDowell, R. B., *Mahaffy*, London: Routledge and Kegan Paul 1971.

Starkie, Enid, *A Lady's Child*, London: Faber 1941.

Starkie, Walter, 'What the Royal Dublin Society has done for music', *RDS Bicentenary History*, 1931.

Stephenson, Patrick, 'The Antient Concert Rooms', *Dublin Historical Record*, vol. 5, no. 1 (Sep.–Nov. 1942).

Turner, W. J., *English Music*, London: Collins 1941.

Turpin, John, *A School of Art in Dublin since the Eighteenth Century: A History of the National College of Art and Design*, Dublin: Gill and Macmillan 1995.

Viani, A., *Towards Music*, Tralee: Kerryman 1945.

Vignoles, Olinthus J., *Memoir of Sir Robert P. Stewart*, Dublin: Hodges Figgis 1899.

Walker, Alan, *Franz Liszt: The Virtuoso Years, 1811–1847*, London: Faber and Faber 1983.

Walsh, T. J., *Opera in Dublin, 1707–1797: The Social Scene*, Dublin: Allen Figgis 1973.

Watton, Lorna, 'Michele Esposito: a Neapolitan Musician in Dublin, 1882–1928', MA thesis, Queen's University, Belfast, 1986.

Welch, Robert (ed.), *The Way Back: George Moore's 'The Untilled Field' and 'The Lake'*, Dublin: Wolfhound Press 1982.

Welch, Robert, *Changing States: Transformations in Modern Irish Writing*, London: Routledge 1993.

White, Harry, *The Keeper's Recital: Music and Cultural History in Ireland, 1770–1970*, Cork: Cork University Press 1998.

Wills, J., 'An Evaluation of the Influence of Michele Esposito in the History of Irish Piano Teaching, Performance and Composition, Including a Critical Study of Selected Piano Works', MMus thesis, RCM, 1991.

Woodham-Smith, Cecil, *The Great Hunger: Ireland, 1845–1849*, London: Hamish Hamilton 1962.

Wyse, Thomas, *Notes on Educational Reform . . .* Waterford: Redmond 1901.

Yeats, W. B., *Letters to the New Island*, New York: Macmillan 1989.

Yeats, W. B. (ed. J. Frayne, and C. Johnson), *Uncollected Prose*, London: Macmillan 1975.

Yeats, W. B., *Autobiographies*, London: Papermac 1987.

Young, Percy, *George Grove, 1820–1900: A Biography*, London: Macmillan 1980.

Index

To Miss Marie Doosa in kind remembrance of B. Palmieri

28/6/05